HARVARD ORIENTAL SERIES

Edited by MICHAEL WITZEL

VOLUME NINETY-SIX

# UTPALADEVA ON THE POWER OF ACTION

## A FIRST EDITION, ANNOTATED TRANSLATION AND STUDY OF *ĪŚVARAPRATYABHIJÑĀVIVṚTI*, CHAPTER 2.1

by

**Isabelle Ratié**

PUBLISHED BY THE DEPARTMENT OF SOUTH ASIAN STUDIES
HARVARD UNIVERSITY
DISTRIBUTED BY HARVARD UNIVERSITY PRESS,
CAMBRIDGE, MASSACHUSETTS
AND LONDON, ENGLAND

2021

For information write to Editor, Harvard Oriental Series, Department of South Asian Studies
1 Bow Street, Cambridge MA 02138, USA
617-495 3295; email: witzel@fas.harvard.edu

Library of Congress Cataloguing in Publication Data

Utpaladeva on the power of action. A first edition, annotated translation and study of Īśvarapratyabhijñāvivṛti, chapter 2.1

Harvard Oriental Series; v. 96 ISBN 9780674 270817

I. Ratié, I. 1976-
II. Title
III. Series: Harvard Oriental Series; 96
CIP

*Pour Alexis Sanderson et Raffaele Torella, en signe d'admiration*

# TABLE OF CONTENTS

# FOREWORD

The following pages contain the edition, translation and study of a hitherto unknown chapter of a Sanskrit text that has only come down to us in fragments, namely, the detailed commentary (*Vivṛti*) written by the Kashmirian Utpaladeva (c. 925–975 CE) so as to explain one of his own philosophical treatises, a major Śaiva nondualistic work entitled the *Recognition of the Lord* (*Īśvarapratyabhijñā*). Three chapters of this *Vivṛti* have recently come to light; the present book focuses on the first and shortest among them, chapter 2.1, which is devoted to the examination of the power of action (*kriyāśakti*) that the Śaivas ascribe to every conscious being. The chapter's main point is to show that even though the core of consciousness, i.e., its power to become aware of itself or to grasp itself, is the subtlest form of action, sequence (*krama*), whether temporal or spatial, only belongs to lower forms of action, so that Śiva—understood as an infinite, omniscient and omnipotent consciousness—has a dynamic essence without being in any way spatially or temporally limited. The text therefore discusses the nature of ordinary actions performed by transmigrating individuals as well as that of Śiva's cosmic creation, while engaging in debates on the nature of space and time. The first chapter of the book discusses the place of Utpaladeva's *Vivṛti* within the *Īśvarapratyabhijñā* corpus and relates how its known fragments were discovered. Chapter 2 describes the manuscript sources used for the edition. Chapter 3 provides a brief overview of Utpaladeva's system and of the philosophical context in which he wrote his treatise. Chapters 4 to 10 contain a detailed analysis of the text, the translation of which is given in chapter 11; the Sanskrit original is edited in chapter 12.

The recent discovery of parts of the detailed commentary that Utpaladeva composed to explain his own magnum opus has amply confirmed that his system is one of the most refined and original in the history of Indian philosophy; that he was the main innovator as far as Śaiva nondualistic philosophy is concerned; and that the *Vivṛti* was the most important textual layer of the *Īśvarapratyabhijñā* treatise. But the text edited here is not easy to understand. This is so for several reasons, not least of which are its polemical yet very elliptical character and the fact that despite years of painstaking (some might say: obsessive) efforts to gather fragments of this text from various annotations scribbled in the margins of manuscripts, I have failed to fill several remaining lacunae in the edition. Besides, we are fortunate enough to have at our disposal two brilliant commentaries on the *Īśvarapratyabhijñā* treatise by Abhinavagupta (c. 975–1025 CE), one of which is devoted to the *Vivṛti*; alas, however, Abhinavagupta does not comment on every aspect of Utpaladeva's text—far from that. For all these reasons, as well as, of course, my own shortcomings as a translator and historian, I still have numerous doubts about the translation and interpretations provided below, and I am painfully aware that they must still contain many errors. Hopefully these, once published, can be corrected by others more learned than me; and I will certainly have occasion for offering additional corrections in the forthcoming study of another, longer chapter of the *Vivṛti* that I am currently editing and translating.

This book is dedicated to two great masters of Śaiva studies, Alexis Sanderson and Raffaele Torella. Alexis Sanderson taught me to read Abhinavagupta's commentaries; and as explained below, without Raffaele Torella's pioneering studies on the Pratyabhijñā treatise, this book could not have been written, in this form or indeed any other. They know how hopelessly indebted I am to them; may they forgive the mistakes that they will undoubtedly spot in this work.

I also owe Harunaga Isaacson—whose astounding scholarship is only matched by his generosity—a debt of gratitude that I fear I can never repay in full, as he went with incredible swiftness and efficiency through more than two hundred pages of a previous version of this book, spotting mistakes of all kinds and significantly improving the manuscript in the process. Heartfelt thanks are also due to all the friends and colleagues with whom I read and discussed passages of this text in three workshops on Sanskrit works: *Chance and Contingency in Indian Philosophy*, organized by Phyllis Granoff (Yale University, New Haven, 2017); *Unpublished Editions of Kashmirian Sanskrit Texts*, organized by Jürgen Hanneder and myself (Sorbonne Nouvelle University, Paris, 2018); and the *Second Workshop in compared philosophy (India and the medieval West)*, organized by Hugo David, Vincent Eltschinger and Irène Rosier-Catach (EFEO Centre, Pondicherry,

2019). Special thanks are due to Phyllis Granoff, whose remarks on Abhinavagupta's explanation of a passage devoted to verse 2.1.4 were extremely helpful. Michael Witzel offered insightful remarks on the descriptions of manuscripts in chapter 2, and as explained below, I owe him and Makoto Fushimi the date proposed for D2. Johannes Bronkhorst spotted additional typos and shared a paper of his. Important passages in Abhinavagupta's *Tantrāloka* and Helārāja's *Prakīrṇaprakāśa* were respectively brought to my attention by Whitney Cox (who also carefully read the first five chapters and spotted various typos and infelicities) and Vincenzo Vergiani (who went through a couple of pages on technical grammatical issues and pointed out several inadequacies in them). Daniele Cuneo patiently listened to some of my far-fetched hypotheses on manuscript matters and read a couple of pages pertaining to a technical term of *alaṅkāraśāstra*. Emmanuel Francis and Giovanni Ciotti had a look at some of the manuscript scans at my disposal to confirm my hypotheses regarding some annotations in Southern scripts. Luther Obrock shared images of a Śāradā manuscript preserved at McGill University. I am also deeply grateful to the students who attended my graduate seminars on Indian philosophy at the Sorbonne Nouvelle in 2019–2020 and bravely suffered through a reading of the greater part of this *Vivṛti* chapter: Fabienne Bagnis, Beatrice Bonino, Clémentine Peroumal, Anaïs Dornier-Viavant, Sébastien Monassa, Lucas Pasquet and Hervé Pauly—it has been a great joy to read Utpaladeva and Abhinavagupta with them.

Thanks are also due to the libraries that have enabled me to study manuscripts of the Pratyabhijñā tradition. They are too numerous to be all mentioned here (see the bibliography below, part 1), but I am particularly grateful to the staff of the Shri Ragunatha Temple Manuscript Library (Jammu), the National Archives of India (Delhi) and the Library of the School of Oriental and African Studies (London). It should also be noted that in many cases, I gained access to the manuscripts consulted for this edition thanks to their digitization by the National Mission for Manuscripts. Last but not least, I am very grateful to Chetan Pandey, who has been photographing Kashmirian Sanskrit manuscripts in various institutions and private collections for years and has not spared efforts to make them easily accessible to all scholars (see https://egangotri.wordpress.com/). It is thanks to him in particular that I gained access to one of the most important manuscripts for the present work (J11).

# CHAPTER 1

# On the Discovery of the Fragments of Utpaladeva's *Īśvarapratyabhijñāvivṛti*

## 1. The Pratyabhijñā corpus

The treatise *On the Recognition of the Lord* (*Īśvarapratyabhijñā*) is made of several textual layers. Its author, Utpaladeva (c. 925–975), first wrote 190 stanzas (*Īśvarapratyabhijñā-kārikā*, hereafter ĪPK) in which he formulated his thought with great concision; but while he was composing these verses—often designated by himself and later authors as "aphorisms" (*sūtra*)—, he also provided a short explanation of their meaning in a brief prose commentary (*Īśvarapratyabhijñā-vṛtti*, hereafter *Vṛtti*).[1] He then added to these two texts a third one, the *Īśvarapratyabhijñā-vivṛti* or *-ṭīkā* (hereafter *Vivṛti*), a detailed prose commentary on the *Vṛtti*. While explaining these texts, Abhinavagupta often mentions "the author of the aphorisms," "the author of the *Vṛtti*" and "the author of the *Vivṛti*," thus giving the impression that he has three different persons in mind; yet he leaves no doubt whatsoever that Utpaladeva is the "author of the [whole] treatise"

[1] That the stanzas and *Vṛtti* were written at the same time is known from Abhinavagupta's testimony, as already noted in TORELLA 2002, p. xli. See ĪPVV, vol. I, p. 16: ***sphuraṇaprārambhaḥ sūtre sphuraṇanirvāhas tu vṛttāv*** *iti paramārthata aikyam anayor ekakālakṛtatvāt, vibhāgakalpanayā tu bheda iti darśitam.* "[Utpaladeva says in the *Vivṛti*] that '[its] manifestation was undertaken in the aphorism[s] and brought to completion in the *Vṛtti*'; [and] in reality, these two [texts] are one, because [they] were composed at the same time: it has been shown that [their] difference is [only] due to an artificial distinction."

(*śāstrakāra*, *granthakāra*) comprised of "the aphorism[s], the *Vṛtti* and the *Vivṛti*."[2]

Today the stanzas and *Vṛtti* are available in manuscript form and in the excellent edition and translation first published by Raffaele Torella in 1994.[3] Unfortunately, however, to date the *Vivṛti* is only known in the form of fragments. A few decades after the Pratyabhijñā treatise was written, the great Śaiva polymath Abhinavagupta (c. 975–1025), who was not Utpaladeva's direct disciple but had studied his work under a disciple of Utpaladeva's named Lakṣmaṇagupta,[4] composed two commentaries—both preserved in their entirety and published—on the treatise, viz. the *Īśvarapratyabhijñā-vimarśinī* (hereafter ĪPV), a synthetic explanation of the verses fully translated into English by K.C. Pandey;[5] and the *Īśvarapratyabhijñā-vivṛtivimarśinī* (hereafter ĪPVV), a particularly lengthy and detailed commentary on Utpaladeva's lost *Vivṛti*,[6] which still awaits a full translation. According to Bhāskarakaṇṭha, an eighteenth-century[7] author who composed a commentary on Abhinavagupta's ĪPV (the only one published to

[2] *sūtraṃ vṛttiṃ ṭīkāṃ ca* (ĪPVV, vol. I, p. 2). On the fact that according to Abhinavagupta, Utpaladeva himself insisted in his *Vivṛti* on the single authorship of the three works, see also for instance ĪPVV, vol. I, p. 3, quoted below, fn. 25, and ĪPVV, vol. I, p. 14, quoted below, fn. 26. On Abhinavagupta's assertion that Utpaladeva thus seems to take on different "roles" (*bhūmikā*) while remaining the single author of the treatise, see TORELLA 2002, p. xlii.

[3] It is referred to here as TORELLA 2002, that is to say, the revised edition of this remarkable work. The *kārikā*s and *Vṛtti* had already been edited in 1921 in the Kashmir Series of Text and Studies (see *Siddhitrayī*), but in a much less satisfactory form; the *Vṛtti* in particular is only given there up to ĪPK 3.2.9, whereas Raffaele Torella's edition includes the whole missing part (which he found in a manuscript in Malayalam script that is now preserved in Trivandrum).

[4] ĪPV, vol. I, p. 3 (v. 4); ĪPVV, vol. I, p. 1 (v. 2); vol. III, p. 406 (v. 3). On what we know about Lakṣmaṇagupta—or rather, on what we do not know about him (since the attribution of a work that has come down to us, the *Śāradātilaka*, seems to be spurious), see SANDERSON 2007b, pp. 230–232.

[5] See PANDEY 1954.

[6] In fact, Abhinavagupta's ĪPVV most often explains first the general meaning (*tātparyārtha/tātparya*) of a verse, then that of the *Vṛtti* thereon, before discussing the *Vivṛti* at length.

[7] See below, chapter 2, fn. 156.

date) known as the *Bhāskarī*, the ĪPV was written *after* the ĪPVV, because Abhinavagupta came to realize that his ĪPVV was too difficult to understand, and attempted to reach a wider audience:

> And the great master Abhinavagupta composed a very lengthy commentary called the *Long Pratyabhijñā* (*Bṛhat-pratyabhijñā*) on this [*Vivṛti*], for the benefit of all people; and having realized that people are incapable of studying it, the same [Abhinavagupta] composed [another] commentary that is well known as the *Vimarśinī* [and] consists in a summary of the aphorisms [constituted by] the *Pratyabhijñā-kārikā*.[8]

This opinion is repeatedly asserted in the *Bhāskarī*,[9] which portrays for instance an opponent who addresses Abhinavagupta as follows:

> But the author of the verses, [Utpaladeva,] first composed a short commentary (*vṛtti*) on the aphorisms, and then he himself wrote a detailed commentary (*ṭīkā*) on the [short commentary; and] you, [Abhinavagupta,] have composed a detailed commentary on this detailed commentary—so why

[8] *Bhāskarī*, vol. I, p. 3: *tatra ca sarvajanahitārthaṃ śrīmatābhinavaguptācāryeṇa bṛhatpratyabhijñākhyā bahuvistarā ṭīkā kṛtā. tadvicāraṇe ca janam aśakyaṃ jñātvā tenaiva pratyabhijñākārikāsūtreṣu saṃgrahamayī vimarśinīti prasiddhā ṭīkā kṛtā.*

[9] TORELLA 2002, p. xliii deems Bhāskarakaṇṭha's testimony contradictory since "he does not hesitate to invert the order" just described in *Bhāskarī*, vol. II, p. 316. The latter passage explains as follows the fact that the first of the verses at the end of the ĪPV describes the work as short: *laghvīty anena padena punar api svamukhena pratyabhijñāśāstraṃ prati bṛhatī kācid vimarśinī bhaviṣyatīti sūcitam.* "With the word 'short,' [Abhinavagupta] hints at the fact that [he] himself will again compose a certain *Vimarśinī*—a long one—on the Pratyabhijñā treatise." However, as pointed out in KAWAJIRI 2016b, fn. 10, p. 19, the passage in question does not belong to Bhāskarakaṇṭha's commentary, but to a South Indian *Īśvarapratyabhijñāvimarśinī-vyākhyā* that the editors used to fill several gaps in the *Bhāskarī*, including the final one (from vol. II, p. 312 onwards).

> was this effort undertaken again [with your second commentary], which is akin to grinding some [already] ground [flour]?[10]

According to Bhāskarakaṇṭha, the answer to this question is that Abhinavagupta wrote the ĪPV "while addressing those whose minds are incapable of understanding the meaning of the aphorisms with the [sole help of Utpaladeva's] short and detailed commentaries and [that of Abhinavagupta's] detailed commentary on the [latter]."[11]

K.C. Pandey had no doubt that this opinion was correct;[12] yet it seems that Bhāskarakaṇṭha—who is hardly reliable as regards the chronological order of his predecessors' works[13]—was wrong: as already noted by Raffaele Torella,[14] the ĪPVV must be posterior to the ĪPV since it explicitly mentions the latter.[15] In any case, the exegetical structure of this corpus can be conveniently represented in the following way:

---

[10] *Bhāskarī*, vol. I, p. 16: *nanv eteṣu sūtreṣu prathamaṃ sūtrakāreṇa vṛttiḥ kṛtā, tadanu ca tadupari svayam eva ṭīkā kṛtā, tasyāṣ ṭīkāyāś ca tvayā ṭīkā kṛteti kim ayaṃ piṣṭapeṣaṇasahodaraḥ punaḥ prayatna ārabdhaḥ...*

[11] Ibid.: *vṛttyā ṭīkayā taṭṭīkayā ca sūtrārthabodhe 'samarthabuddhīn uddiśya.*

[12] See PANDEY 1963, pp. 32 and 34–35.

[13] Thus he wrongly assumes that Utpaladeva wrote his commentary on Somānanda's ŚD before composing the Pratyabhijñā treatise. See *Bhāskarī*, vol. I, p. 2: *śrīmān utpaladevaḥ svagurunirmitaṃ śivadṛṣṭyākhyaṃ mahārahasyaśāstraṃ vyākhyāya tatpratibimbakalpaṃ kārikāmayam īśvarapratyabhijñākhyaṃ mahāśāstraṃ praṇīya...* "The venerable Utpaladeva, having [first] explained the great, esoteric treatise composed by his own master [and] called the *Śivadṛṣṭi*; having [then] composed in verses the great treatise called the *Īśvarapratyabhijñā*, which as it were a [mere] reflection of the [*Śivadṛṣṭi*]..." This cannot be correct, since Utpaladeva mentions his own treatise in several instances while commenting on his master's. See ŚDV, pp. 13–14, and ŚDV, p. 171, translated in RATIÉ 2014b, fn. 116, p. 163 and fn. 95, p. 154 (for a different translation of the former passage, see NEMEC 2011, pp. 117–118); see also ŚDV, p. 16 for an allusion to a *ṭīkā* that evidently refers to the *Vivṛti* on the Pratyabhijñā treatise. Bhāskarakaṇṭha's mistake was already noted in TORELLA 2002, fn. 71, p. xliii.

[14] TORELLA 2002, p. xliii.

[15] ĪPVV, vol. III, p. 230: *anenaivāśayenāsmābhiḥ sūtravimarśinyām ekarasatvenaivedaṃ sūtraṃ vyākhyātam, iha tu yāvadgati vicārayitum itthaṃ vibhāgenāpekṣā*

| UTPALADEVA | ABHINAVAGUPTA |
|---|---|
| *Kārikās* (ĪPK) | → *Vimarśinī* (ĪPV) |
| ↓ | |
| *Vṛtti* | |
| ↓ | |
| *Vivṛti* or *Ṭīkā* [fragments] | → *Vivṛtivimarśinī* (ĪPVV) |

It is unclear whether Georg Bühler fully understood this admittedly rather complex structure of the *śāstra* when, in 1877, he published his famous *Report* on Kashmirian Sanskrit manuscripts: he mentions Utpaladeva's

---

*vyākhyātā*... "And in the *Vimarśinī* on the aphorisms (*sūtravimarśinī*), I have explained this aphorism [2.4.15] while having this very intention in mind, [i.e., while explaining the notion of 'requirement' mentioned in the previous verse] in one way only; but here, this [notion of] requirement is explained in different ways so as to examine it as thoroughly as possible." According to GNOLI 1960, fn. 2, pp. xvi–xvii, such references to one's own works are "not probative" in determining the chronology of these works, because interpolations can be made "by the author himself," and R. Gnoli adduces as evidence of it two works by Abhinavagupta, namely, the ĪPVV and *Abhinavabhāratī* (henceforth ABh), which, according to him, "quote one another." The passages referred to are ĪPVV, vol. III, p. 138 and ABh, vol. II, p. 224. The former indeed mentions the ABh (*yad abhinavabhāratī*...; to this reference should be added ĪPVV, vol. II, p. 48: *yathoktam abhinavabhāratyām*..., and ibid., p. 179: *ayam artho 'bhinavabhāratyāṃ nāṭyavedavivṛtau vitatya vyutpādito 'smābhiḥ*, on which see RATIÉ 2011a, p. 513); but contrary to what one may surmise from R. Gnoli's footnote, the ABh, for its part, does not explicitly mention the ĪPVV—it only says that the topic at hand was explained "by the venerable master of my master, [Utpaladeva,] in the *Pratyabhijñā* and elsewhere; and by myself, in the explanation (*vivaraṇa*) of it, as well as in the *Bhedavādavidāraṇa* and [other works]" (*asmatparamagurupādaiḥ pratyabhijñādāv asmābhiś ca tadvivaraṇe bhedavādavidāraṇādau ca*; on the *Bhedavidāraṇa* see RATIÉ 2011a, p. 329). It is thus quite possible that the commentary on the Pratyabhijñā alluded to here was the ĪPV rather than the ĪPVV, and that the ABh was written between these two; so that R. Gnoli's assumption of an "interpolation" does not seem necessary.

"*Pratyabhijñā śāstra*"[16] without distinguishing the verses, *Vṛtti* and *Vivṛti*, and in the list of Utpaladeva's works, he only includes the aphorisms ("*Pratyabhijñāsūtra*").[17] As for Abhinavagupta's commentaries, at times he does distinguish them as the "*Vimarśinī* that is the long explanation" ("the *Vimarśinī, bṛhatī vṛtti*") and the one that is "the brief explanation" (*laghvī vṛtti*)[18]—a distinction that he most probably borrowed from the *Sarvadarśanasaṅgraha* (SDS), a late doxographical work that he mentions as his main source for the Pratyabhijñā tradition.[19] Yet only one "*Vimarśinī*" appears in his table of the works pertaining to the Pratyabhijñā corpus[20] (and in this connection, Georg Bühler refers the reader to manuscripts described p. xxx, one of which is an ĪPVV while the two others are certainly ĪPV manuscripts).

Marc Aurel Stein, on the other hand, was evidently aware of the structure of the Pratyabhijñā corpus when he wrote the Introduction to his 1894 catalogue of the manuscript collection preserved at the Raghunātha Temple Library in Jammu, and carefully distinguished the different works of which it is comprised:

> That Utpala[deva] composed not only the verses called the *Īśvarapratyabhijñāsūtra*s, as hitherto supposed, but also a *Vṛtti* and *Ṭīkā* of them is clearly indicated by Abhinavagupta in his *Īśvarapratyabhijñāsūtrārthavimarśinī* [...] and *Īśvarapratyabhijñāvivṛtivimarśinī* [...]; the first named work is a commentary on the *sūtra*s alone, the latter an exposition of Utpaladeva's own *Ṭīkā*.[21]

Despite these early clarifications, many confusions were subsequently made (and are still to be deplored) between the different texts that belong to this corpus, notably in catalogues of Indian and European libraries, which tend to confuse *Vṛtti* and *Vivṛti* and often present Abhinavagupta's

---

[16] BÜHLER 1877, pp. 81–82.

[17] Ibid., p. 82.

[18] Ibid., e.g. p. 80.

[19] Ibid., p. 79; on the depiction of the Pratyabhijñā treatise in the SDS see below, fn. 96.

[20] Ibid., p. 82.

[21] STEIN 1894, Introduction, p. xlii, fn. 2.

ĪPVV as a *Vivṛti*[22]—not to mention that on its English cover, the first volume of Abhinavagupta's ĪPV purports to be "*The Īśvarapratyabhijñāvimarśinī* of Utpaladeva with Commentary by Abhinavagupta"!

## 2. The justification for the treatise's different textual levels and the *Vivṛti*'s goal

According to Abhinavagupta, Utpaladeva's *Vṛtti* is merely concerned with giving the overall meaning of the stanzas without dwelling on any of their details; the *Vivṛti* provides a systematic explanation of the *Vṛtti*; his own ĪPV attempts to give a thorough explanation of the verses; and his ĪPVV explains the *Vivṛti*.[23] Thus he justifies as follows a lengthy explanation in his ĪPV:

> And the author of the *Vṛtti* has not taken the trouble of [getting into] such a [detailed] explanation [as the one just given here] because [he was only concerned with] explaining the [verses'] overall meaning; this is stated [by Utpaladeva himself in the *Vivṛti*, according to which the *Vṛtti*'s] "function is merely to explain the [aspect of] the verses' teaching that is concealed (*saṃvṛta*)." And this has not been touched upon by the author of the *Ṭīkā* either, [since in writing the *Ṭīkā*, Utpaladeva] intended to explain the *Vṛtti* alone; but since my goal [here] is exclusively to give an explanation of the verses, [I] have explained [this particular point] in detail, and this [holds good] in the case of all [the other verses of the treatise].[24]

But why did Utpaladeva choose to write three treatises in one as it were? Indian authors often compose works consisting of aphorisms and a short

---

[22] See (among numerous similar examples, some of which are mentioned in TORELLA 1988, p. 141) KAK & SHASTRI 1927, p. 3, which calls Abhinavagupta's ĪPVV the *Īśvarapratyabhijñāvivṛti* (spelled °*vivritti*).

[23] On the ĪPVV's goal see ibid., vol. I, p. 1: it is "an explanation that reflects upon the meaning of the *Ṭīkā*" (*ṭīkārthapravimarśinīm... vṛttim*, v. 2cd).

[24] ĪPV, vol. I, pp. 22–23: *iyati ca vyākhyāne vṛttikṛtā bharo na kṛtas tātparyavyākhyānāt, yad uktam* ***saṃvṛtasautranirdeśavivṛtimātravyāpārāyām*** *iti. ṭīkākāreṇāpi vṛttimātraṃ vyākhyātum udyatena nedaṃ spṛṣṭam. asmākaṃ tu sūtravyākhyāna eva udyama iti vibhajya vyākhyātam, evaṃ sarvatra.*

prose commentary (*vṛtti*), the *sūtra*s providing—in accordance with the literal meaning of the Sanskrit word—a "thread," that is, an easily remembered canvas for the whole work, while the auto-commentary clarifies whatever may be ambiguous in the aphorisms due to their brevity; one wonders, however, why Utpaladeva wrote not one but two commentaries on his own work.

This is something that he himself had felt the need to justify at the beginning of his *Vivṛti*, in a now lost passage that Abhinavagupta introduces as follows in the ĪPVV:

> In order to show the goal to be accomplished by the *Ṭīkā*, [but also] the single authorship of the aphorism[s], *Vṛtti* and *Ṭīkā*,[25] as well as the point of composing these different works even though their goals are [in fact those of] a single proponent, [Utpaladeva now] states [the sentence beginning with] "In the threefold Speech..."[26]

From the sequel of Abhinavagupta's lengthy commentary on the passage,[27] we know that in his *Vivṛti*, Utpaladeva had compared the three textual levels of his treatise to different stages in which the phonematic emanation of the universe occurs according to Bhartṛhari[28] and a number of Śaiva sources:[29]

---

[25] Cf. ĪPVV, vol. I, p. 3: *ekagranthakārakṛtatvaṃ tu svayam evākhyāsyati* ***trayyāṃ vācī****tyādinā*. "But [Utpaladeva] himself will explain that [all three textual layers] were composed by a single author in [the passage beginning with] 'In the threefold Speech...'."

[26] ĪPVV, vol. I, p. 14: *kariṣyamāṇaṭīkāprayojanaṃ sūtravṛttiṭīkānāṃ caikagranthakāranirmitatvam ekavaktṛprayojanatve* 'pi ca granthabhedanirmāṇasāphalyaṃ darśayitum āha* ***trayyāṃ vācīti***. [**ekavaktṛprayojanatve* S12; *ekavaktyaprayojanatva* J11; *ekavaktaprayojanatve* Ed.]

[27] ĪPVV, vol. I, p. 14–18; a brief summary of some of its parts is provided in TORELLA 2002, p. xlii.

[28] Utpaladeva's mention of the "threefold Speech" (*trayī vāc*) in this context is reminiscent of VP 1.134: *vaikharyā madhyamāyāś ca paśyantyāś caitad adbhutam* | *anekatīrthabhedāyās trayyā vācaḥ param padam* || "This is the supreme, wondrous abode of the threefold Speech with its numerous different paths—of the Gross, the Intermediary, and the Seeing One."

[29] On this famous theory of phonematic emanation see in particular PADOUX 1990. From ĪPVV, vol. I, p. 15, it appears that in this lost passage of the *Vivṛti*, Utpaladeva

the "Supreme Speech" (Parā Vāc/Paravāc)—that is, the highest form of reality, which is also the subtlest and most intense mode of consciousness's self-expression, described as an entirely nondual self-awareness occurring beyond any ordinary form of discourse—is said to progressively unfold at the three levels of Paśyantī, "the Seeing One" (where the awareness of duality begins to appear, but as a sheer potentiality), Madhyamā, "the Intermediary" (where duality and nonduality are both manifest without appearing as contradictory) and Vaikharī, "the Gross One" (the level of everyday language, where the manifestation of duality prevails in all respects).[30] Similarly, according to Abhinavagupta's commentary, the self-awareness of Utpaladeva (which is not distinct from Śiva, since Utpaladeva has fully recognized his identity with Him) manifests itself as more and more differentiated at the three textual levels of the treatise:

> Here is what [Utpaladeva] means: at the ontological level (*tattva*) that is Paravāc, the universe exists while being free of any separation; in Paśyantī, its differences are [only] faintly outlined; in Madhyamā, its differences develop; in Vaikharī, it is manifest with its differences made evident, since

also explicitly compared the three textual layers of his treatise to the way in which the Gāyatrī is said in some Brahmanical sources to be expressed by the three textual (Vedic) levels of the *Ṛc*, *Yajus* and *Sāman* (see e.g. BĀU 5.14.2 or ChU 3.12.1).

[30] ĪPVV, vol. I, pp. 14–15: *trayo 'vayavāḥ paśyantīmadhyamāvaikharīti yasyāḥ sā trayī parāmarśarūpā kroḍīkṛtābhinnasamastaparāmarśanīyarāśiḥ parā bhagavatī, vakti svarūpaṃ vimṛśatīti vāk. tasyāṃ c***aitad*** *iti paridṛśyamānaṃ vāṅmayaṃ pramitilakṣaṇaparāmarśarūpasaṃvedanānuviddhatayā śabdanaikaśarīraṃ viśvaṃ yathākrameṇa vikasitaṃ, paśyantyāṃ vikāsonmukhaṃ, madhyamāyāṃ vikasat, vaikharyāṃ pṛthaktayā parāmṛśyamānatvena labdhavikāsam.* "The 'threefold [Speech]' is the Supreme—[that is to say,] venerable—Speech. [It is threefold in that it] has three parts, namely Paśyantī, Madhyamā, Vaikharī; it consists in [self-]realization (*parāmarśa*), and it embraces the totality of whatever is an object of realization as being one [with itself]. [It is 'Speech'] because it expresses (*vac-*), [that is to say,] it realizes (*vimṛś-*) its own nature; and [Utpaladeva says in his *Vivṛti* that] in it, 'this,' [that is to say,] the universe [as we] perceive it, which consists in Speech—[in other words,] its substance is exclusively speech inasmuch as it is pervaded by consciousness in the form of a realization consisting in knowledge—progressively develops. In Paśyantī, it is about to develop; in Madhyamā, it is in the process of developing; in Vaikharī, it has fully developed, inasmuch as it is being realized as distinctly [differentiated]."

its form is realized as [fully] differentiated. In the same way, [the treatise] has a different efficacy for each [kind of] recipient [of the treatise's teachings] (*adhikārin*). Thus, at the ontological level of Paravāc, the ultimate reality is the awareness of the treatise's author, who is not distinct from Śiva; it exists in a state of [pure] identity, and it is designated by the word "heart" because it is the essence [of everything]. [It] is the [same reality that] exists in the aphorism[s] (*sūtra*) as a faint outlining (*āsūtraṇā*) of differentiation, [an outlining] consisting in a flashing forth characterized as being understandable by those people who are [already] capable of being led to understand the highest [truth].[31] In the *Vṛtti*, on the other hand, this same [reality] has unfolded; and in the *Vivṛti*, it is made fully evident by [stating] objections and refuting [them] (*ākṣepapratisamādhāna*),[32] [and] its differentiation is characterized as being understandable by all people. [This same reality is] thus [manifest in a different way] to each different [kind of] recipient [of the treatise's teaching]; for inasmuch as [the aphorisms, *Vṛtti* and *Vivṛti*] provide [them with] benefits of different kinds, those who are not under the influence of the imprints of differentiation that arise from the other systems achieve [both] superior and inferior successes[33] thanks to the sole aphorisms[s] and *Vṛtti*, [or even,] if they are [already] well versed [in the nondualistic doctrine,] by studying the sole meaning of the aphorisms, regardless of the *Vṛtti*. As for those in whom erroneous views have arisen due to their study of other religions (*tīrthāntara*), they also [end up] achieving these successes in the same way, [that is,] by [reaching a state where their] nature is not separated from the supreme heart that is the consciousness of the treatise's author; [but they only achieve it]

[31] This, at least, is how I tentatively understand *parapratipādyajanaviṣayatāpatti-yogyatālakṣaṇa°* in view of the next sentence (which, in contrast, has *sarvajana-pratipattiyogyatālakṣaṇa°*).

[32] The meaning of this compound is discussed below (on my reasons for reading it as a *dvandva*, see in particular fn. 39).

[33] That is to say, both liberation and the enjoyment of extraordinary powers (cf. e.g. ĪPV, vol. II, p. 273: ...*parāparasiddhilakṣaṇā jīvanmuktivibhūtiyogamayy artha-kriyā*...).

> once the *Ṭīkā*, which is a detailed explanation (*vivṛti*), removes the delusions that [they entertain due to other religions, so that] their heart comes to rest in the meaning of the aphorisms and *Vṛtti*, [and then] gradually comes to rest in the sole contemplation of the aphorisms' meaning.[34]

According to the Śaiva nondualists, ordinary language involves a fundamental duality, as there is no human discourse without the assumption of a separation (between the subject and object of a sentence, between them and the action expressed by its verb, etc.)—so that even the most accurate teachings about consciousness are inevitably inadequate in that they end up objectifying its pure subjectivity.[35] And the more explicit ordinary speech is, the more it presents reality as divided, because explaining means defining, delimiting, distinguishing—and therefore focusing on differences. In this respect, the *Vivṛti* is the lowest textual level of the treatise, because it is the most explicit one:[36] at the higher levels, differences are somehow present,

---

[34] ĪPVV, vol. I, p. 16: *etad uktaṃ bhavati: yathā paravāktattve vibhāgahānyā viśvaṃ sthitam, paśyantyām āsūtritabhedam, madhyamāyām unmīlitabhedam, vaikharyāṃ bhinnaparāmṛśyamānarūpatayā sphuṭībhūtabhedāvabhāsam, tathaiva bhinnānām adhikāriṇāṃ bhinnām arthakriyāṃ vidhatte. tathā paravāktattvasthāne śivābhinnaśāstrakārasaṃvedanaṃ tādātmyena yad vartamānaṃ paramārthatattvaṃ sāratvāc ca hṛdayaśabdavācyam, tat parapratipādyajanaviṣayatāpattiyogyatālakṣaṇasphuraṇātmakabhedāsūtraṇayā sthitaṃ sūtre; vṛttau tu tad eva unmīlitam, vivṛtau tv ākṣepapratisamādhānadiśā sphuṭībhūtaṃ sarvajanapratipattiyogyatālakṣaṇabhedaṃ bhavati. iti tasya tasyādhikāriṇaḥ, vividhaphaladāyitayā hy agṛhītadarśanāntarajanitabhedavāsanāgrahāḥ sūtramātrād vṛttisahitād abhivinītāḥ santo vṛttyanapekṣasūtrārthamātrapariśīlanadiśā parāparasiddhibhājo jāyante. tīrthāntarapariśīlanotthitamithyādṛṣṭayas tu vivṛtirūpayā ṭīkayāpasāritatathāvidhavimohāḥ sūtravṛttyarthaviśrāntahṛdayāḥ krameṇa sūtrārthabhāvanāviyogaviśrāntyā tathaiva śāstrakārasaṃvedanarūpaparahṛdayāvibhaktatattvatayā sidhyantīti.*

[35] See for instance ĪPV, vol. I, p. 33: *upadeśāvasare hi sarvātmanā tāvat sā prameyatāsya parihartum aśakyā.* "For when teaching, admittedly, it is impossible to entirely avoid objectifying this [conscious subject]." This does not mean that rational discourse would be deemed soteriologically useless by the Śaiva nondualists. On the contrary, it is the basis of the path taught in the Pratyabhijñā treatise; but it can only be helpful if it is used to make conscious individuals pay attention to their own, immediate (and therefore nondiscursive) experience by *eliminating* the erroneous theories constantly superimposed onto this experience.

[36] See for instance the quotations given below, fn. 46 and 53.

but in such a state that they remain entirely compatible with unity. In the case of Paśyantī and of the aphorisms equated with it, they only exist as a potentiality, just as a "faint outlining" (*āsūtraṇa/āsūtraṇā*, which Abhinavagupta links with the term *sūtra*) already contains *in nuce* the full picture that is to emerge from it, but only manifests its basic unity, without all the details liable to distract the viewer from it; and in the case of Madhyamā and the *Vṛtti* with which it is associated, differences become apparent, but without hindering the awareness of their underlying unity.

The *Vivṛti*, as opposed to the aphorisms and *Vṛtti*, is also permeated by the manifestation of difference inasmuch as its primary goal is to *critically examine other systems*—a point underscored by Abhinavagupta in the passage quoted above, which describes its method as specifically consisting in "[stating] objections and refuting [them]" (*ākṣepapratisamādhāna*). The compound brings to mind a mnemonic verse often quoted in secondary literature as a definition of the fivefold (or sixfold) function of Sanskrit commentaries, the last aspect of this definition being presented either as "the refutation of objections" or "the [statement of] objection[s], then [their] refutation."[37] Whatever the actual source of this verse may have been,[38] it is at least certain that in Utpaladeva and Abhinavagupta's time, stating the objections to which a text implicitly responded (*ākṣepa*) and explaining

[37] The verse is quoted in *Nyāyakośa*, s.v. *vyākhyānam*, p. 828: *padacchedaḥ padārthoktir vigraho vākyayojanā | ākṣepeṣu samādhānaṃ vyākhyānaṃ pañcalakṣaṇam* || "A commentary is characterized by these five [features]: the division of words, the statement of their meaning, the analysis of nominal compounds, the structure of sentences, the refutation of objections." The same work provides an alternative reading (*pāṭhāntaram*) for the verse's second half: *ākṣepo 'tha samādhānaṃ vyākhyānaṃ ṣaḍvidhaṃ matam* || "A commentary is considered to have six aspects: ....; the statement of objections, then [their] refutation." It is quoted e.g. in TUBB & BOOSE 2007, p. 3, and the verse's enumeration of these features is used there as a template for the structure of the entire manual. For other sources and variant readings, see in particular GRIMAL 2000, pp. 776–783 and GOODALL & ISAACSON 2003, pp. l–li (other studies that mention the verse include SEN 2003, pp. xlviii–xlix, GANERI 2010, p. 189, and FORMIGATTI 2011, pp. 73–74).

[38] The *Nyāyakośa*, to which most of the secondary sources mentioning this verse refer, was composed by Bhīmācārya Jhalakīkar and first published in 1874 CE; for the verse in question it gives as its source *Parāśarapurāṇa*, *adhyāya* 18 (= *Parāśaropapurāṇa*, 18.17ab–18cd), but somewhat similar lists are already mentioned by Buddhist and Jain authors such as Vasubandhu (fourth/fifth century) or Saṅghadāsa (sixth century): see below, fn. 40.

how the text succeeded in refuting them ([*prati*]*samādhāna*) was considered a major task of philosophical and religious commentaries[39]—and not only in Brahmanical circles.[40] It has also been emphasized that contrary to the other tasks that a commentary is expected to fullfill, stating the objections to which a text responds and showing how it refutes them goes beyond the formal explanation of the text's wording, and that an exegetical work

---

[39] Vācaspatimiśra's subcommentaries in particular often emphasize this aspect of the commentaries that they explain. See e.g. *Nyāyavārttikatātparyaṭīkā* (henceforth NVTṬ), p. 652, commenting on Uddyotakara's explanation of *Nyāyasūtra* (henceforth NS) 5.1.14: *sūtrārthaprayojanam ākṣepasamādhānābhyāṃ sphuṭīkaroti...* "[Uddyotakara] clarifies what the goal [pursued] with the meaning of the aphorism is by [stating] the objection [to which it responds] and the refutation [of it that the aphorism enables]..." This is also very common in his *Bhāmatī*; see, among many examples, p. 605, commenting on Śaṅkara's explanation of *Brahmasūtra* 2.3.19: ... *ākṣepasamādhānābhyām āha nanu ceti*, "He explains [this] with [the passage beginning with] 'But...,' by [stating] the objection [to which it responds] and the refutation [of it that it enables]." This, of course, is by no means peculiar to Vācaspatimiśra's works (see for instance the *ākṣepapratisamādhānaprakāra* in Jayanta's $NM_M$, vol. II, p. 620, etc.), and Abhinavagupta himself has recourse to the compound *ākṣepapratisamādhāna* (as a *dvandva*, hence the translation above) while explaining the *Vivṛti*. See e.g. ĪPVV, vol. II, p. 324: *etad eva sphuṭayaty ākṣepapratisamādhānābhyāṃ nanv ityādinā*. "This is precisely what [Utpaladeva] makes clear [in the *Vivṛti*] with [the passage] beginning with 'But...', by [stating] the objection [to which the *Vṛtti* responds] and the refutation [of it that it enables]." In light of such passages, which clearly point to the objections of opponents and the tools provided by the text to refute them, the translation of *ākṣepeṣu samādhānam* as "solving problems" in GANERI 2010, p. 189 (which might rest on SEN 2003, pp. xlviii–xlix) seems far too wide (cf. for instance *Bhāskarī*, vol. II, p. 6, where °*pūrvapakṣapratikṣepa*° is glossed *yaḥ pūrvapakṣas tasya pratikṣepaḥ pratisamādhānam*).

[40] Dharmakīrti for instance appears to use the word *pratisamādhāna* as a mere equivalent of *parihāra* in the "[statement of] objections and refutation [thereof]" (*codyaparihāra*), which is the last of the five features that a commentary on Buddhist *sūtra*s should display according to the *Vyākhyāyukti*: see ELTSCHINGER, KRASSER & TABER 2012, p. 70, fn. 143. On this list (wich bears some partial similarities with that recorded in the mnemonic stanza mentioned above, despite the distinct terminology), see CABEZÓN 1992, p. 238, SKILLING 2000, pp. 318-319, and VERHAGEN 2008; cf. the fivefold and sixfold lists provided by the Jain exegete Saṅghadāsa in *Bṛhatkalpabhāṣya* 302 and 309, on which see JYVÄSJÄRVI 2010, p. 148.

that addresses such issues becomes in the process "an argumentative treatise in its own right"—[41] and this is what the *Vivṛti* does according to Abhinavagupta. Utpaladeva's detailed commentary is openly polemical, in contrast with the verses and *Vṛtti* where debates most often remain implicit, and it is first and foremost meant to explain the *Vṛtti* by pointing out how it anticipates all kinds of implicit objections from various opponents; and precisely because it formulates these objections, as well as the arguments provided by the *Vṛtti* in response to them, it has the power of removing the wrong views fostered by other religious movements. It should be noted in this respect that the constant attention paid to other systems in the ĪPVV, which has sometimes been pointed out by modern scholars as a remarkable aspect of Abhinavagupta's approach,[42] is in fact, according to Abhinavagupta himself, the main defining feature of Utpaladeva's *Vivṛti*:

> The *Vivṛti* is the uncovering (*vivaraṇa*) of the treatise's meaning, which was [thus far] concealed (*saṃvṛta*), [that is to say,] veiled as it were. [This uncovering consists in] removing any obstruction [to the understanding of the treatise's meaning] by taking away the veils—heaps of dust as it were—that are the doctrines of [our] opponents [as long as they are] envisaged as acceptable hypotheses. Because the [*Vivṛti*] accomplishes this, it is [an integral part of] the work, just as well [as the aphorisms and *Vṛtti*].[43]

According to Abhinavagupta, the *Vivṛti*'s specific aim is thus to eliminate the wrong theories put forward by rivals of the Śaiva nondualistic movement. For all limited subjects, insofar as they are conscious subjects, constantly experience the ultimate reality in the form of an immediate self-awareness; yet the continual superimposition of wrong theories onto this bare experience of the absolute prevents ordinary individuals from realizing their true identity with Śiva. The *Vivṛti*, by exhibiting the inadequacies of such theories and thus eliminating them as possible obstacles to one's

[41] TUBB & BOOSE 2007, p. 5.

[42] See e.g. MCCREA 2016.

[43] ĪPVV, vol. I, p. 17: *śāstrārthasya saṃvṛtasyācchāditasyeva śaṅkyamānaparamatapāṃsurāśiprāyāvaraṇāpasāreṇāpagatāvaraṇatvaṃ vivaraṇam vivṛtiḥ, tatpratipādakatvād grantho 'pi.*

self-awareness, enables its readers to read the *sūtra*s and *Vṛtti* as an expression of their own experience as conscious beings. In the first of the concluding verses of the *Vivṛti*, which happens to be quoted by Abhinavagupta,[44] Utpaladeva himself points out this crucial cathartic role that provides ordinary readers with an opportunity to recover the full awareness of their own experience as conscious subjects:

> Having thus reduced to silence those who, denying their [own] self-awareness, hold this or that thesis, [I] have made obvious through clear reasonings the true nature of the subject [so far] soiled by them.[45]

This is the reason why, as emphasized by Abhinavagupta in his depiction of the respective *adhikārin*s of the aphorisms, *Vṛtti* and *Vivṛti*, the latter is addressed to "all people"[46] whereas the aphorisms and *Vṛtti*, by themselves, are only accessible to those already acquainted to some degree with non-dual Śaivism (or at least, to those whose minds are not polluted by other religious currents). The *Vivṛti* claims a universal readership, and in this respect it appears to be crucial in the accomplishment of Utpaladeva's goal as he defines it at the beginning of his *Vṛtti*—namely, enabling "all people" (*sarvam imam janam*)[47] to reach the Lord's recognition. Moreover, it is only in the *Vivṛti* that the polemical architecture of the Pratyabhijñā treatise becomes fully manifest, its very purpose being to critically examine the theses

[44] Abhinavagupta quotes it in full and ascribes it to Utpaladeva without further specifying its source while commenting on ĪPK 1.4.3 in his ĪPV (vol. I, p. 130). As shown in RATIÉ 2011a, p. 250 (see also RATIÉ 2016a, p. 225), it is nonetheless obvious from the end of the ĪPVV that it was the first of a series of verses concluding the *Vivṛti*. See ĪPVV, vol. III, p. 404: *vivṛtikāraḥ saṃkṣipya sarvam āh**ettham** ityādiślokaiḥ. anenāsmadukteneśvaratāprakāreṇa yā **svasaṃvittiḥ*** sthitā tām*. [****svasaṃvittiḥ*** corr.; *susaṃvittiḥ* Ed.]

[45] *itthaṃ svasaṃvittim apahnuvānair yat tad vadadbhiḥ kaluṣīkṛtaṃ yat | pramātṛtattvaṃ sphuṭayuktibhis tān mūkān vidhāya prakaṭīkṛtaṃ tat* ||

[46] Cf. ĪPVV, vol. I, p. 16: ... *sā sūtre sphuraddhṛdayā, vṛttau sphuritasārā, vivṛtau tu vyaktā sarvajanagocaratāṃ gatā*. "This [recognition of the Lord] flashes forth in its most condensed form (*hṛdaya*) in the aphorism[s]; its essence glimmers in the *Vṛtti*; but it is fully evident (*vyakta*) in the *Vivṛti*, [where it] becomes accessible to all people."

[47] *Vṛtti*, p. 1.

held by rival philosophico-religious currents; and as often emphasized by Abhinavagupta, Utpaladeva's whole Pratyabhijñā system as a "new [soteriological] path" (*navo mārgaḥ*)[48] is an attempt to force the individual subjects to pay attention to their own immediate experience of the absolute by subjecting their erroneous interpretations of it to a systematic rational inquiry—from this point of view, the *Vivṛti* appears again to constitute the most characteristic aspect of Utpaladeva's method. Thus in his ĪPV—supposedly devoted to the sole explanation of the aphorisms—, Abhinavagupta points out the crucial importance of this polemical dimension of the treatise:

> In the [soteriological path in which this treatise consists],[49] the nature of ultimate reality is made clear in the best [possible] way, inasmuch as [it is] thanks to the prior refutation of the opponents' theses [first] envisaged as acceptable hypotheses [that it] is explained.[50]

The *Vivṛti* was designed by its author as a systematic exposition of these refutations, and without it, the treatise's tight dialectical structure, which Utpaladeva obviously considered the most important aspect of the treatise from a soteriological point of view,[51] cannot be fully grasped. We should also be wary of considering the *Vivṛti* an unessential appendix to the "real" treatise defined as the aphorisms and *Vṛtti*: according to Abhinavagupta it is an integral part of it,[52] and he constantly draws from it in both of his commentaries. Abhinavagupta also underscores that because the *Vivṛti* is the most detailed exegetical level of the treatise, the "recognition of the Lord" that constitutes the very aim of the treatise as a whole is most evident there:

> In the same way, the recognition of the Lord, which [only] flashes forth in its most condensed form (*hṛdaya*) in the

---

[48] ĪPK 4.16; cf. *Vṛtti*, p. 80 (*abhinavo mārgaḥ*).

[49] *Bhāskarī*, vol. I, p. 82: *iha—asmiñ śāstramārge.*

[50] ĪPV, vol. I, p. 51: *iha yat paramārtharūpaṃ tad āśaṅkyamānapratipakṣapratikṣepeṇa nirūpayiṣyamāṇaṃ suṣṭhutamāṃ spaṣṭīkṛtaṃ bhavati.*

[51] On the importance of the polemical dimension of the treatise see also below, chapter 3, §1.

[52] See above, fn. 43.

> aphorism[s] and *Vṛtti*, reaches a state where it is fully evident (*vyakti*) in this *Vivṛti*.[53]

Yet, because it spells out what remains implicit in the verses and *Vṛtti* and purports to eliminate the errors propagated by other systems, it inevitably focuses on differences rather than unity, and to this extent, as repeatedly pointed out by Abhinavagupta, it constitutes the lowest level of exposition of a nondualistic system. This paradoxical status of the *Vivṛti*, presented *both* as the most important and lowest layer of the treatise, might have to do with the fact that with the Pratyabhijñā treatise, Utpaladeva endeavours to build an exoteric soteriological device capable of competing with what the Buddhist philosophical works can offer (hence its purely dialectical method and claim to address a universal audience), while still providing his fellow Śaiva nondualists with a soteriological fast lane as it were, a kind of privileged access to the absolute, since contrary to the other readers, they can gain the final insight of recognition merely by reading the aphorisms and (in the case of the less advanced at least) the *Vṛtti*. Abhinavagupta thus makes clear that Utpaladeva's path can be trodden at three different paces (corresponding to the three distinct textual layers of the treatise) depending on the *adhikārin*'s status.[54] And inasmuch as the treatise is seen as a new means designed for the liberation of all, the *Vivṛti* is its very core; but considered from an esoteric Śaiva viewpoint, it is the lowest way of formulating the doctrine.

In any case, it should not be concluded from Abhinavagupta's depiction of the different layers of the treatise that the *Vivṛti* was a simple text. Those who have tried to translate the *Vivṛti* have learnt to take with a pinch of salt Abhinavagupta's assertion that all is *vyakta* in this text: it is of course immensely helpful inasmuch as it greatly clarifies many points made in the aphorisms and *Vṛtti*, but it is also full of difficulties of its own, because it is highly polemical and therefore uses a technical terminology borrowed from a vast range of competing doctrines, but while doing so, it remains terse and elliptical—without Abhinavagupta's commentary on it, we would

---

[53] ĪPVV, vol. I, pp. 15–16: ... *tadvad īśvarapratyabhijñā sūtravṛttyoḥ sphuritahṛdayā yā, seha vivṛtau vyaktiṃ gatā.*

[54] See RATIÉ forthcoming c.

often be at a loss to understand it.[55] It also reveals at times a complexity in the meaning of the verses and their short explanation that we would not have suspected otherwise, as it often provides several interpretations (some of which might be deemed rather far-fetched were they not suggested by the author himself) where the *Vṛtti* only offers a straightforward one.[56] And its importance from a historical point of view can be seen from the fact that, besides expounding on the aphorisms and *Vṛtti*, it also discussed, sometimes at length, a number of philosophical topics that do not surface at all in the *kārikās* and *Vṛtti*.[57] A striking example (among numerous others) of Utpaladeva's tendency to include in the *Vivṛti* debates that are not found in the other layers of his treatise is the discussion on the issue of intersubjectivity in the Vijñānavāda,[58] which does not appear at all in ĪPK 1.5.5 and its *Vṛtti*, but is expounded in both of Abhinavagupta's commentaries because it was already a substantial part of the corresponding *Vivṛti*, as can be seen from recently discovered fragments of it.[59] And this, of course, makes its loss all the more regrettable.

### 3. The search for the *Vivṛti* and the discovery of the Delhi codex unicus

One of the first modern scholars to deplore the loss of Utpaladeva's *Vivṛti* was J.C. Chatterji, who, in his 1914 monograph on (nondualistic) Kashmir Śaivism, mentioned Utpaladeva's "*Ṭīkā* on his *Vṛtti*," which "must have been called *Vivṛti*," as "practically lost now," before adding:

---

[55] This, as suggested below, might have been one of the factors that led to the disappearance of this text while Abhinavagupta's less difficult commentaries were favoured.

[56] An example of this can be found in the *Vivṛti* fragment edited in RATIÉ forthcoming a, which gives no less than three interpretations of a single word (*tatra*, "there") in the corresponding verse. This propensity is already noted in TORELLA 2002, p. lxii: "In the *Ṭīkā*, which was composed later on, we already find multiple interpretations of the same verse, all considered equally possible but evidently being the outcome of further reflections."

[57] TORELLA 2002, p. xli, already notes that it "takes the *Kārikā* and *Vṛtti* as its starting point and often develops into far-reaching excursuses."

[58] See RATIÉ 2007.

[59] See RATIÉ 2016a.

> I have seen only a few leaves of a mutilated manuscript of the work. For the rest, we are left to infer what it must have been like from the *pratīka*s quoted in the *Pratyabhijñāvivṛti-vimarśinī* (or the *Bṛhatī Vṛtti* as it is also called) of Abhinava Gupta.[60]

Unfortunately, the author gives away no information as to where he has seen these "few leaves," what script or material was used, or which part of the work was covered (it seems likely, however, that these leaves later became known as the fragmentary codex unicus described below). In 1921, Madhusudan Kaul, in his Introduction to the second volume of Abhinavagupta's ĪPV in the Kashmir Series of Texts and Studies, asserts that Utpaladeva's *Ṭīkā* "is no more available now"[61] and betrays no awareness of the leaves alluded to by J.C. Chatterji. Seventeen years later, in his Preface to the first volume of Abhinavagupta's ĪPVV, Madhusudan Kaul explains that the pandits of the Srinagar Research Department postponed the edition of Abhinavagupta's ĪPVV for "many years" in the hope that they might find a manuscript of the work on which it commented, and eventually resolved to publish the commentary without Utpaladeva's text:

> Although the above material[62] was acquired and got prepared many years before now, yet it could not be utilized early in preparing the press copy of the work under edition because it was considered prudent to postpone it for some years and carry out in the meantime a vigorous search after the manuscript which could contain the complete gloss and commentary of Utpala Deva, both of which are in turn commented on exhaustively by Abhinava in the *Īśvarapratyabhijñāvivṛtivimarśinī*. In this direction I made every possible effort all the time I have been in association with the Research Department, but I could not succeed in coming across any manuscript which could satisfy my desire. Having thus no immediate prospect of success to obtain the required manuscript I took up the task in the belief that the posterity might succeed where I failed and might remove the defects which

[60] CHATTERJI 1914, p. 20, fn. 2.

[61] ĪPV, vol. II, Introduction, p. vii.

[62] Namely, the ĪPVV manuscripts described in the Preface.

> for want of the better material have been unavoidable in bringing about the present edition of Abhinava's detailed commentary.[63]

Should we surmise, from the assertion that he could come accross no manuscript "which could satisfy [his] desires," that the editor was aware of the existence of a fragmentary manuscript, but deemed it too damaged to be of any use (or worth any mention)? In any case, in the first, 1935 edition of his monograph on Abhinavagupta, K.C. Pandey feared that the *Vivṛti* might be forever lost:

> The readers will be pained to know that Utpalācārya's *Ṭīkā* [...] has not so far been found in spite of vigorous searches made by so many enthusiasts. Perhaps, unfortunately, it is irrecoverably lost.[64]

In his 1950 Introduction to the second volume of the *Bhāskarī* edition, the same author alludes again to Utpaladeva's *Vivṛti*, and there too makes no mention whatsoever of this fragment:

> Unfortunately, in spite of all search for it, no trace of the *Vivṛti* has so far been found.[65]

However, in the 1963 enlarged edition of his monograph on Abhinavagupta, K.C. Pandey makes a very exciting announcement:

> It was supposed to be irrecoverably lost. It is, however, a matter of very great satisfaction that the present writer, in the course of search for it in Kashmir, discovered a fragment of it. It contains all the three works of Utpalācārya, (i) the *Īśvarapratyabhijñākārikā*, (ii) the *Vṛtti* and (iii) the *Vivṛti*. It begins with the 6th *kārikā* of the *Jñānādhikāra,* Āhnika 3 [...]. It continues up to the 3rd *kārikā* of the Āhnika 5 [...]. In the latter portion there are many gaps; but the earlier is without them. We are trying to edit it and hope that if "He wills" it will be published in due course.[66]

---

63 ĪPVV, Preface, vol. I, pp. i–ii.

64 PANDEY 1935, p. 62.

65 *Bhāskarī*, vol. II, Introduction, p. viii.

66 PANDEY 1963, pp. 69–70.

The announced edition was never published. The fragment is mentioned again in R.C. Dwivedi's foreword to the 1986 reprint of the *Bhāskarī* as being "in the personal collection of Dr. K.C. Pandey" and still "unpublished,"[67] and Raffaele Torella has related in a 1988 article how, after K.C. Pandey's demise, he got in contact with his widow in the hope that the manuscript, or at least a transcript thereof, might still be among his papers. Mrs. Pandey let the Italian scholar examine a transcript of the fragment[68] and take a few photographs that enabled him to publish the edition and translation of the initial part of it in 1988.[69] In his next article on the *Vivṛti*, published 19 years later, Raffaele Torella further explained:

> My efforts in later years to secure the entire transcript were, despite the good offices of Professors N. Rastogi and J.P. Sinha, totally unsuccessful. By now, Pandey's transcript is to be considered definitively lost. The good fortune that sometimes helps scholars in their research, counteracting the obstacles set up by human unhelpfulness, took me in 1998 to the India National Archives in Delhi in search of the manuscripts used by the Pandits of the Srinagar Research Department for the editions of the Kashmir Series. I was interested in those manuscripts because of the important marginal notes that some of them contained, where I assumed to find quotations from lost Kashmiri works. When I chanced upon a Śāradā manuscript, entitled *Pratyabhijñāvivṛti* (Skt. ms. No. 30), belonging to a small fund of manuscripts that the Mahārāja of Jammu and Kashmir had transmitted to the National Archives in 1948, I began looking through it with the same skepticism with which I had in the past looked through manuscripts with the same title all over India (in all cases, the title had simply been the outcome of careless cataloguing). Very soon, however, I realized that what I had in front of me was precisely the original of Pandey's transcript [...]. Once

[67] See "General Editor's Note," *Bhāskarī* [1986], vol. I, pp. vii–viii.

[68] For a detailed description of the transcript see TORELLA 1988, p. 142.

[69] See TORELLA 1988.

> the transcript had become irretrievably lost to us, the original came to light again.[70]

The codex unicus that Raffaele Torella had just found (D), which covers 13 of the 190 verses of the treatise, was used as the basis of his edition and translation of this fragment, which remained for almost two decades the only known substantial part of Utpaladeva's magnum opus.[71]

## 4. The discovery of fragments in marginal annotations—and the lengthiest fragment known to date

As I was working on my PhD dissertation—a study of the notions of identity, difference and otherness in the Pratyabhijñā system, mainly based on Abhinavagupta's commentaries—,[72] I started gathering photographs of manuscripts belonging to the Pratyabhijñā corpus in the hope of completing some day a critical edition of Abhinavagupta's ĪPV. I collected digital images of several dozens of ĪPV manuscripts, about a third of which are richly annotated. Having avidly read Raffaele Torella's studies of the *Vivṛti* codex unicus, I was aware thanks to his remarks that some of the footnotes in the Kashmir Series of Text and Studies edition of the ĪPV—which in fact merely reproduced marginal and interlinear annotations in manuscripts—bear some short quotations of Utpaladeva's lost *Vivṛti*, so that I set out to study the marginal annotations in the manuscripts at my disposal.[73] These annotations, it turned out, were almost all quotations bearing on related topics and borrowed from various sources, Śaiva (particularly Utpaladeva's *Vṛtti* and most of all Abhinavagupta's ĪPVV, but also Somānanda's *Śivadṛṣṭi* and Utpaladeva's commentary thereon), Brahmanical (e.g. Bhartṛhari's *Vākyapadīya*[74] or Jayanta's *Nyāyamañjarī*)[75] and Buddhist (e.g.

[70] TORELLA 2007a, pp. 473–474.

[71] See TORELLA 2007a, 2007b, 2007c and 2007d.

[72] It was later published as RATIÉ 2011a.

[73] On marginal annotations in Kashmirian Sanskrit manuscripts, see FORMIGATTI 2011 and RATIÉ 2018b.

[74] Henceforth VP.

[75] Henceforth NM.

Dharmakīrti's *Pramāṇavārttika*[76] and *-svavṛtti* or his *Sambandhaparīkṣā*). By comparing the margins of these manuscripts with the *Vivṛti* fragment edited by Raffaele Torella, I established that some of these annotated manuscripts contained already known *Vivṛti* fragments, and I then set out to look for thus far unknown *Vivṛti* quotations by comparing these same margins with Abhinavagupta's commentary on Utpaladeva's lost work. By 2012 I had found several fragments that were much shorter than the one discovered by Raffaele Torella. None of them amounted to more than a few printed pages, but once put together, they significantly expanded our knowledge of the *Vivṛti*, as they gave us access to Utpaladeva's detailed commentary on seven additional verses (ĪPK 1.3.5 and 1.5.4–9); unfortunately, most of them were ridden with lacunae.[77] The edition, translation and study of several of these fragments (recovered from up to eight ĪPV annotated manuscripts) are now published.[78] In the meantime, Yohei Kawajiri, while studying one Nāgarī manuscript of Utpaladeva's *Vṛtti*, found shorter *Vivṛti* fragments, of which he has been publishing a diplomatic edition,[79] and I have also found another annotated *Vṛtti* manuscript (in Śāradā) that bears *Vivṛti* fragments.[80]

Yet what is by far the most interesting discovery regarding Utpaladeva's lost work was not made in the margins of any ĪPV or *Vṛtti* manuscript. In 2016, thanks to the efforts of Chetan Pandey, who has been taking photographs of numerous Kashmirian manuscripts and has made these documents available to the public, I was able to examine pictures of a Nāgarī-written ĪPVV manuscript preserved in Jammu (J11). My curiosity was aroused because, probably due to the unusual length of the work, complete ĪPVV manuscripts are much less common than ĪPV manuscripts;[81] but at

[76] Henceforth PV.

[77] See RATIÉ 2017a for a description of the extent of the treatise covered by these fragments.

[78] See RATIÉ 2016a, 2016b, 2007, and 2020.

[79] See KAWAJIRI 2016a, 2016b and forthcoming.

[80] For a description of these two *Vṛtti* manuscripts see below, chapter 2, §10.

[81] Cf. e.g. CHATTERJI 1914, p. 21: "Complete MSS. of this work are very rare in Kashmir. I have seen only one complete manuscript of the work and have heard of the existence of only one other."

first sight, this particular manuscript seemed to be of no relevance to the quest for *Vivṛti* fragments, since its margins are blank (apart from occasional corrections to the main text) for hundreds of folios. However, from folio 202a to folio 241b, things abruptly change: the margins are suddenly replete with annotations. These 79 annotated pages in fact bear a single fragment of the *Vivṛti* covering 25 additional verses of the treatise, and apart from a few minor lacunae, the text runs continuously from ĪPK 1.8.10 to ĪPK 2.3.8. A few months later, I came across a second ĪPVV manuscript (this one in Śāradā) that is now preserved in Srinagar (S12) and also bears the full text of Utpaladeva's *Vivṛti* from ĪPK 1.8.10 to ĪPK 2.3.8.[82] The newly discovered fragment is by far the lengthiest known to date, including the codex unicus preserved in Delhi (which covers 13 verses). The present book provides the edition, translation and study of chapter 2.1, one of the two chapters preserved in their entirety in this lengthy fragment.[83]

### 5. The marginalization of Utpaladeva's magnum opus

The discovery of these parts of Utpaladeva's *Vivṛti* sheds a new light on the respective roles played by Utpaladeva and Abhinavagupta in building the Pratyabhijñā system. For as already noted by Raffaele Torella in his first article devoted to the *Vivṛti*, Abhinavagupta's ĪPV has ended up "eclipsing all the other commentaries and becoming the standard one";[84] and as shown above, paradoxically, apart from the fragmentary codex unicus preserved in Delhi, all that is left today of Utpaladeva's most detailed explanation of his own treatise is to be found in the margins of Abhinavagupta's commentaries on that treatise. This marginalization (in all senses of the term) of Utpaladeva's magnum opus has led most modern scholars to regard Abhinavagupta as the most important writer in the Pratyabhijñā tradition. And Abhinavagupta, as a brilliant exegete of the Pratyabhijñā treatise, undoubtedly deserves much praise; but before the recently discovered fragments of

[82] On a smaller fragment found in both manuscripts and covering a part of the *Vivṛti* on ĪPK 1.7.10–11, see RATIÉ forthcoming a.

[83] Although the *Vivṛti* on chapter 2.3 preserved in these margins is much longer than the *Vivṛti* on chapters 2.1 and 2.2, the commentary on 2.3 is incomplete (it stops in the midst of the explanation of ĪPK 2.1.8; the last word of this passage quoted by Abhinavagupta, *sarva°*, occurs in ĪPVV, vol. III, p. 140).

[84] TORELLA 1988, p. 140.

the *Vivṛti* enabled us to compare all the texts within the Pratyabhijñā corpus, Abhinavagupta's importance in terms of conceptual innovation may have been overrated by modern scholars.

Thus in 1921, Madhusudan Kaul already insisted that Abhinavagupta's ĪPV is far more than a mere commentary on the Pratyabhijñā treatise and that the two of them are "inseparable."[85] Similarly, in 1938, K.A. Subramania Iyer and K.C. Pandey, at the outset of the Introduction to the first volume of their edition of the *Bhāskarī*, proclaimed that they "need offer no apology for publishing for the first time a commentary on the *Īśvarapratyabhijñāvimarśinī* of Abhinavagupta, the most important work on Kashmir Śaiva Philosophy," adding that its importance "cannot be overestimated."[86] In the 1935 version of his monograph on Abhinavagupta, K.C. Pandey had already stated about the ĪPK:

> This was the first work on the Pratyabhijñā system as such. In fact the system owes the name Pratyabhijñā to this book. Its importance, however, is due to two commentaries of Abhinavagupta, the *Vimarśinī* and the *Vivṛtivimarśinī*.[87]

In his 1950 Introduction to the second volume of the *Bhāskarī*'s edition, K.C. Pandey gives a more nuanced view of the relationship between Utpaladeva's treatise and Abhinavagupta's commentaries, pointing out that the success of Abhinavagupta's ĪPV probably arose from the fact that it gave a synthetic, clear yet precise explanation of the verses, whereas Utpaladeva's *Vṛtti* offers no detailed analysis of the verses and often reads like an independent work on which the *Vivṛti* primarily expounds.[88] Besides, K.C. Pandey emphasizes that Abhinavagupta's ĪPVV, much more

---

[85] ĪPV, vol. II, Introduction, p. vi: Abhinavagupta's commentary "is called *Vimarśinī* or the *Īśvarapratyabhijñāvimarśinī* by which it is widely known among the people of Kashmir. In fact, *Īśvarapratyabhijñā* and the *Vimarśinī* make the inseparable two. It can, in no way, be called a commentary or *Ṭīkā*."

[86] *Bhāskarī*, vol. I, Introduction, p. xi.

[87] PANDEY 1935, p. 99.

[88] *Bhāskarī*, vol. II, Introduction, p. vii: "Utpalācārya in his *Vṛtti* has not given any detailed explanation of the words employed in the *Kārikā*. His object was simply to state the substance of the *kārikā*s clearly [...]. Utpalācārya in his *Vṛtti*, never refers to any word of the *sūtra* for explaining its meaning. He seems to write an

detailed than the ĪPV, tends to dive into particularly arduous and technical discussions that can only be understood once the basic tenets of the system are mastered.[89] K.C. Pandey concludes:

> Thus we find that the only recognized text on the Pratyabhijñā system, that is available in full and in which the system is fairly well and accurately presented, is the *Vimarśinī* of Abhinavagupta. It is therefore the most important available work, which, though a commentary on the *Kārikā*, yet presents the system in such a way that one can get a fairly clear idea of the whole system, without having recourse to other texts, not excluding even the *Kārikā*.[90]

It is certainly true that among the "available" Pratyabhijñā works—that is, excluding the *Vivṛti*—, the ĪPV can be deemed "the most important" inasmuch as it gives a clear and synthetic view of the system that it expounds through a thorough analysis of Utpaladeva's verses. It is also undeniable that Abhinavagupta's brilliant exegetical skills (as opposed to Utpaladeva's terse formulations) must have been a significant factor in the process of marginalization of the *Vivṛti*. Yet this is by no means an acceptable justification for Pandey's repeated assertions that the Pratyabhijñā system owes its importance to Abhinavagupta's commentaries, unless the latter are merely meant to emphasize that Abhinavagupta played a crucial role in making Utpaladeva's ideas *popular*—but this, obviously, is not, or not

---

independent work, presenting summarily but clearly the fundamentals of his system. In his *Vivṛti* or *Ṭīkā*, he is not concerned with the explanation of the *sūtras* so much as with the elaboration of the ideas, presented in the *Vṛtti*. He has, therefore, not attempted a full exposition of the aphorisms anywhere. Abhinavagupta in his *Vimarśinī* tried to bring out the full import of the *sūtras* so as to show that all the details of the system are implied by the words of the *sūtras*. He was a very great grammarian. He, therefore, tried to bring out the implications of the words on the basis of the rules of grammar, to which there are frequent references in the work."

[89] Ibid., p. viii: "In his *Vivṛtivimarśinī* [...], Abhinavagupta enters into independent and lengthy discussions on various problems. But they can be understood only after the fundamentals of the system have been thoroughly grasped in detail."

[90] Ibid.

entirely,[91] what Pandey meant, since he openly considered Abhinavagupta's *philosophical* contribution to be decisive:

> If we take into consideration, for instance, three of his most important works, on which his reputation chiefly rests, we find that two of them, the *Īśvarapratyabhijñāvimarśinī* and the *Īśvarapratyabhijñāvivṛtivimarśinī*, are simply commentaries on Utpalācārya's *Īśvarapratyabhijñākārikā* and *Ṭīkā* respectively, and the third, the *Tantrāloka*, professedly follows the authority of the *Mālinīvijayatantra*. It is, therefore, not possible for us to attribute the authorship of any particular theory to Abhinava as we can do to Kant or Hegel. This, however, does not mean that he did not contribute anything to the "Realistic Idealism" of Kashmir. The fact, on the contrary, is that the philosophical system of Kashmir, with Abhinava's contribution to it left out of consideration, loses most of its importance. His contribution to the "Realistic Idealism" is of the same nature as that of the great Śaṅkara to the monistic Idealism of the Vedānta.[92]

Here Pandey seems to have in mind Abhinavagupta's undoubtedly major contribution to the doctrinal architecture of nondual Śaivism as a whole rather than to the sole Pratyabhijñā. Yet, while acknowledging that Abhinavagupta's ĪPV and ĪPVV are commentaries, he seems to suggest that they are of a philosophical import that is not to be found in the work of which they are supposedly mere explanations—and he does not specify what Abhinavagupta's innovations might be. This, it seems, has led to the kind of assessment by R.C. Dwivedi in his foreword to the reprint of the *Bhāskarī* to the effect that the ĪPV is "the most important work of the Pratyabhijñā school of Kashmir Śaivism"[93] for the following reasons:

---

[91] K.C. Pandey does emphasize this latter point at times; see e.g. PANDEY 1935, p. 168: "In fact the charm that this system had for his contemporaries and successors, the popularity that it enjoyed and the high esteem in which it is held even now by the Kashmir Pandits was and is due mostly to the labours of Abhinava both as a scholar and as a spiritualist (Yogin)."

[92] PANDEY 1935, p. 167.

[93] *Bhāskarī* [1986], vol. I, "General Editor's Note," p. v.

> Utpala's own commentaries are more in the nature of independent exposition of the Pratyabhijñā system than actual explanation of the text. Abhinavagupta's *Vimarśinī* offers explanation of the *kārikā*s and also reads like an independent work. It is available in full and it represents the systems comprehensively and correctly. Abhinavagupta's *Vimarśinī* is thus the most authentic commentary of the Pratyabhijñā system, which enjoys the reputation of an original work.[94]

Thus the ĪPV has come to be praised not only for being a comprehensive and clear description of Utpaladeva's system (which it definitely is), but also for constituting "the most authentic commentary" on it and "an original work"—and the latter assertions are far more problematic.

We should not believe, however, that this tendency of modern scholarship is at odds with the traditional understanding of the Pratyabhijñā corpus. That it is actually in line with a much older tradition can be seen from the fact that by the fourteenth century at least,[95] Abhinavagupta's commentaries had come to be regarded as integral parts of the treatise, along with the three original layers of Utpaladeva's work. Thus according to the SDS,

> The treatise of the Pratyabhijñā consists of the five explanations of the work [called *Śivadṛṣṭi*—namely,] the [*Īśvarapratyabhijñā*] aphorism[s], *Vṛtti*, *Vivṛti* and the two *Vimarśinī*s, [i.e.,] the short one and the long one.[96]

---

[94] Ibid., p. viii.

[95] According to the General Editor's Note by R.C. Dwivedi in *Bhāskarī*, vol. I, p. ix, and TORELLA 1988, p. 137, the verse from the SDS quoted below (fn. 96), which includes Abhinavagupta's commentaries within the Pratyabhijñā treatise, is already found in Madhurāja's unpublished *Śāstraparāmarśa* (v. 4; according to R.C. Dwivedi, the manuscript reads *pratyabhijñākhyaṃ* instead of *pratyabhijñāyāḥ*). It has been widely assumed since PANDEY 1963, which mentions (p. 20) a so-called "pen-picture" of Abhinavagupta by Madhurāja, that the latter was a direct disciple of Abhinavagupta; however, SANDERSON 2007a (p. 381, fn. 486) has pointed out that no evidence has been adduced so far to show that Madhurāja personally knew Abhinavagupta rather than just studying his works and that the description he offered of the great Śaiva master was anything more than an idealized portrait.

[96] SDS, p. 191: *sūtraṃ vṛttir vivṛtir laghvī bṛhatīty ubhe vimarśinyau | prakaraṇavivaraṇapañcakam iti śāstraṃ pratyabhijñāyāḥ ||*

Moreover, quotations from the ĪPVV found in the margins of ĪPV manuscripts have often undergone a subtle but telling metamorphosis: it is not rare to find there ĪPVV quotations in which all references to the fact that Abhinavagupta's ĪPVV is a commentary on Utpaladeva's *Vivṛti* have been obliterated. This can be seen for instance in the nineteenth-century SOAS manuscript, where, to give but one example, an ĪPVV quotation[97] is given, but stripped of the sentence *uktaṃ caitat kriyā ca paravāgvṛttyādiketyādipradeśeṣu*[98] ("and this has been said [by Utpaladeva] in places [of his *Vivṛti*] such as 'And the action that begins with the activity of the Supreme Speech'...").[99] In the same quotation, the words *iti sūtrārthaḥ, vṛttivivṛtī spaṣṭe* ("this was the meaning of [Utpaladeva's] verse; both [his] *Vṛtti* and *Vivṛti* [thereon] are [self-]evident")[100] are no longer to be found, and the quotation of the words *kālagrāsāt* from the *Vivṛti*[101] has also disappeared. In other words, Abhinavagupta's commentary on the *Vivṛti* as it is given in this margin of an ĪPV manuscript has been altered *so as to appear to be a commentary on Abhinavagupta's ĪPV*, and all traces of the *Vivṛti* as the *mūla*-text have been removed. And this is no isolated phenomenon: similar examples can be found in the margins of older ĪPV manuscripts, such as the seventeenth-century S3,[102] where ĪPVV quotations have also been edited so as to look like explanations of Abhinavagupta's shorter commentary.

---

[97] See SOAS, f. 198a (top margin), reproduced in Appendix 3 of RATIÉ 2018b (for a transcription of the marginal annotation mentioned here see ibid., p. 307, fn. 9).

[98] ĪPVV, vol. III, p. 3, ll. 15–17.

[99] This seems to be a quotation from Utpaladeva's *Vivṛti* on ĪPK 1.1.5 (not available to date except for Abhinavagupta's quotations of it); see ĪPVV, vol. I: 105: *ity āśaṅkyāha* ***paravāgvṛttyādike****ti*.

[100] Ibid.: ll. 18–19.

[101] Ibid., l. 19.

[102] See RATIÉ 2018b, p. 318, fn. 58.

## 6. The importance of the fragments for the assessment of Utpaladeva's and Abhinavagupta's philosophical contributions

Several factors might be invoked to explain this temptation, perceptible in the alterations undergone by these ĪPVV marginal quotations, to let Utpaladeva's most important work sink into oblivion. As pointed out by K.C. Pandey, Abhinavagupta's detailed, elegant and synthetic ĪPV might have been deemed clearer than Utpaladeva's highly inventive but elliptical work—in Terentianus' famous words, *pro captu lectoris habent sua fata libelli.* Besides, with the exception of Utpaladeva's devotional hymns, the latter's works are confined to the genre of philosophical treatises and commentaries, whereas Abhinavagupta has authored important works on various topics (the aesthetics of theatre, the aesthetics of poetry, the interpretation of Śaiva scriptures, the practice and meaning of Śaiva rituals...), so that his fame may have surpassed Utpaladeva's early on—and this may have greatly influenced the choices that were made as to which works should be copied preferably to others within the Pratyabhijñā corpus.

Whatever the reasons for these choices may have been, however, such decisions have profoundly affected our perception of the roles respectively played by Utpaladeva and Abhinavagupta in building the Pratyabhijñā system. Thus as pointed out above, before the publication of Raffaele Torella's pioneering studies on Utpaladeva's *Vivṛti*, historians of Indian philosophy had simply assumed that Abhinavagupta's commentaries were the most innovative works in this tradition, and they tended to ascribe to Abhinavagupta some ideas that they could find in the latter's works, but not in Utpaladeva's stanzas or *Vṛtti*. In his first article devoted to the *Vivṛti*, Raffaele Torella already questioned as follows Pandey's statement to the effect that the Pratyabhijñā system "owes" its "importance" to Abhinavagupta's commentaries:

> A close examination of the ĪPVV is already sufficient in itself to limit the validity of this statement. Despite the inevitable difficulty in reading a text like the ĪPVV, which is an extensive and diffuse commentary on a work that has not come down to us, it seems clear that the majority of the themes and subjects that Abhinavagupta touches on find their direct correspondence—or at least their starting point—in Utpaladeva's *ṭīkā*. In fact the ĪPV itself, which according to Abhinavagupta is intended to be a commentary on

> what the *kārikā*s are in themselves, accomplishes its task through a carefully gauged and considered systematization of a rich speculative material whose early origin is to be glimpsed in the *ṭīkā*. Only a direct reading of the *ṭīkā* would allow one to define the central role that Utpaladeva undoubtedly played in the elaboration of Pratyabhijñā philosophy.[103]

As more and more *Vivṛti* fragments are coming to light, we are now able to compare all the texts belonging to the Pratyabhijñā corpus; and is it is becoming ever more obvious that indeed, Abhinavagupta was a brilliant commentator, but also a very faithful one, and that Utpaladeva's *Vivṛti* was the truly innovative work.

An interesting example of such a distortion in our vision of the history of the Pratyabhijñā system is the issue of the famous "doctrine of reflections" (*pratibimbavāda*):[104] in many of his works, Abhinavagupta claims that the phenomena constituting the universe as we perceive it are similar to reflections in a mirror, because the variegated reflections that we may see in a mirror are perfectly real inasmuch as they really occur on the surface of the mirror, yet they are nothing over and above the surface of the mirror that makes them manifest by assuming their forms. In the same way, argues Abhinavagupta, all phenomena, which are perfectly real, are not to be discarded as mere illusions (contrary to what the representatives of Advaitavedānta contend), yet they are nothing over and above the unique, all-encompassing and all-powerful universal consciousness that makes them manifest by assuming their forms. So far this analogy was ascribed to Abhinavagupta, or at least most scholars credited him with being the first to make a full metaphysical use of it.[105] Utpaladeva himself, however, mentions in his commentary on another Śaiva work (Somānanda's *Śivadṛṣṭi*, hereafter ŚD) that he has explained at length in his detailed commentary

---

[103] TORELLA 1988, p. 140; see also TORELLA 2014.

[104] On this doctrine see LAWRENCE 2005 and RATIÉ 2017b.

[105] See for instance RASTOGI 1984, p. 28 and LAWRENCE 2005.

(*Ṭīkā*) on the Pratyabhijñā treatise how phenomena are similar to reflections,[106] and at the beginning of one of the recently edited *Vivṛti* fragments, he explicitly mentions the doctrine of reflections usually attributed to his commentator while summarizing the main theses established in the first part of his *Vivṛti*.[107] The ongoing edition and translation of several hitherto unknown *Vivṛti* chapters will certainly bring to light many more similar points, and should afford us an opportunity to reevaluate some of the assumptions that still prevail in secondary literature regarding Utpaladeva's and Abhinavagupta's respective ideas, but also their methods.

Thus modern scholars have pointed out that while Abhinavagupta seems to have been passionately engaged in quoting opponents, Utpaladeva apparently avoided giving direct quotations and favoured concise paraphrases and elliptical allusions.[108] This is certainly true if one only takes into consideration the verses and *Vṛtti*; but of course, these two genres, which favour extreme concision, are not usually conducive to providing numerous quotations of other works. What of the *Vivṛti* then? So far, from the fragment studied by Raffaele Torella, apart from the quotation of Śaiva sources that Abhinavagupta identifies as two (now lost) commentaries on the *Śivasūtras* by Bhaṭṭa Kallaṭa,[109] the only quotations known in the *Vivṛti* were

---

[106] *Śivadṛṣṭivṛtti* (hereafter ŚDV), pp. 14 and 16 (see RATIÉ 2017b, p. 232, n. 93; see also ibid., , p. 227, n. 64). There is also one brief allusion to this doctrine in Utpaladeva's short commentary on the Pratyabhijñā treatise (*Vṛtti*, p. 60). For Abhinavagupta's and Jayaratha's testimonies regarding the fact that Utpaladeva himself had expounded this theory see RATIÉ 2017b, pp. 226–228, n. 62 and nn. 66–67.

[107] See RATIÉ 2017a, p. 172.

[108] See e.g. TORELLA 2007d, p. 928, which presents Utpaladeva's citation of *Bhagavadgītā* (hereafter BhG) 7.12d in his *Vivṛti* on ĪPK 1.5.2 as "a rare exception to his usual dislike for quotations." See also MCCREA 2016, p. 265: "While it is obvious from his arguments that he was closely familiar with both older and more nearly contemporary Buddhist philosophical works, Utpala very rarely quotes or names his Buddhist interlocutors." The author contrasts "this nearly citation-free exposition of the various Buddhist positions in Utpala's works" with Abhinavagupta's "extraordinarily thorough and exacting effort to match up the positions Utpala ascribes to the Buddhist *vijñānavādin*s and *bāhyārthavādin*s with citations from actual Buddhist texts" in his commentaries.

[109] ĪPVV, vol. II, p. 30; see TORELLA 2007b, p. 561, fn. 112.

BhG 15.15,[110] BhG 7.12[111] and a brief passage from Dharmakīrti's *Pramāṇaviniścaya* (hereafter PVin).[112] The few fragments retrieved from ĪPV manuscripts that have been published to date contain one additional quotation from the PVin.[113] In the chapter studied below, there are two more quotations, both explicitly ascribed to their authors by Utpaladeva: one from Dharmakīrti's PVin (in the *Vivṛti* on ĪPK 2.1.4) and another from Bhartṛhari (in the *Vivṛti* on ĪPK 2.1.5). Of course, this handful of quotations cannot compare with the remarkable wealth of citations found in Abhinavagupta's ĪPVV; yet the number of known quotations by Utpaladeva has significantly increased in the past few years, which shows that here as in many other respects, caution is in order when it comes to assessing Utpaladeva's work, since the *Vivṛti* evidently (and quite naturally) contained more quotations than the verses and *Vṛtti*, and we cannot draw conclusions about their author's writing habits merely by taking into account the two latter texts: as long as we do not have a more substantial amount of the *Vivṛti* at our disposal, we should postpone passing any judgement on whether Utpaladeva disliked quoting from other works.

---

110 It is in fact quoted in the *Vṛtti* on ĪPK 1.3.7, but partially repeated in the *Vivṛti* ad loc.: see TORELLA 2007a, p. 480.

111 See TORELLA 2007d, p. 928.

112 See Ibid., p. 937.

113 PVin 1, pp. 24–25: see RATIÉ 2016b, p. 384. STERN 1991 had already spotted this quotation in ĪPV, vol. I, p. 101, fn. 17 and had already recognized the footnote as a fragment from Utpaladeva's *Vivṛti* (see STERN 1991, p. 158 and fn. 55).

# CHAPTER 2

# The Manuscript Sources Used for This Edition

## 1. Three distinct sets of annotations and a jigsaw puzzle

The sources used for this edition are all marginal (and in a few cases, interlinear) annotations found in Śāradā and Nāgarī manuscripts. Given the type of script used and the places (Srinagar and Jammu) where most of these manuscripts are preserved (or at least were acquired), it may be surmised that they were almost all made either in the valley of Kashmir or in Jammu, although this is confirmed by very few colophons.[114] In fact very few preserved colophons indicate at all where (or when) a manuscript was copied; it is noteworthy, however, that the scribe who copied S2 specifies that he did so not in Kashmir but in Ayodhyā, "after seeing various religions, countries, men of royal lineage, savants and *māntrika*s."[115] Besides, J11 contains many brief marginalia (mostly corrections) in Nāgarī and Śāradā, but also, more surprisingly, in two Southern scripts, namely, Grantha and Telugu[116]—and such marginal annotations in Southern scripts are not an isolated phenomenon in Kashmirian Sanskrit manuscripts: S7 for instance (an annotated ĪPV manuscript preserved in Srinagar that has been shown to

[114] The scribe who copied D2 specifies that he did so in Srinagar (see the description of D2 below, §9).

[115] See the description of S2 below, §9.

[116] See the description of J11 below, §8, and the remarks on the reading *bodhātmano* in the edition below (chapter 12, l. 94).

contain *Vivṛti* fragments,[117] although it does not have any from chapter 2.1) is written in Nāgarī, yet some of its marginal annotations are written in Śāradā, but also in Grantha.[118] In such cases one wonders whether the manuscript could have originally belonged to the South Indian pandit named Revatīramaṇa (Rīvatī Raman/Revatī Ramana) who came to Kashmir to acquire manuscripts of Śaiva works and ordered copies of a number of manuscripts but died in the valley, so that Mukund Rām Śāstrī eventually bought a part of his collection from one of these servants.[119] This, of course, is nothing more than a conjecture; it is also possible that manuscripts preserved in Jammu (such as J11) were annotated in Southern scripts because some of the pandits who were hired to work there on the *mahārāja*'s collection came from other areas of the subcontinent, including, it seems, Telugu-writing ones.[120] In any case, from such examples it is obvious that

---

[117] The published *Vivṛti* passages found in this manuscript pertain to ĪPK 1.3.5: see RATIÉ 2016b.

[118] See e.g. f. 41a, where the introduction to ĪPK 2.1.8, initially omitted, is provided in the bottom margin in Śāradā script, while the compound *deśakramo* is given in Grantha above *deśakramo 'pi* in the upper margin. Cf. e.g. f. 21b, where again, the faulty *aprakārūpam* is corrected with the marginal addition of °*śa*° (for *aprakāśarūpam*) in both Grantha and Nāgarī.

[119] TSā, Preface, p. i: "The second manuscript... belongs to the collection of books bearing on the Shaiva philosophy in general which one Rīvatī Raman of Southern India got copied during his visit to Kashmir for acquisition of rare manuscripts. On his death here in Kashmir these books fell into the hands of his servants, and from one of them I bought this manuscript copy of the *Tantrasāra* for my personal use." See also *Parātrīśikāvivaraṇa* (henceforth PTV), Preface, pp. 1–2: "The... most useful manuscript ... pertains to the collection of manuscripts which one Revatī Ramana of the Deccan got copied during his stay in Kashmir, it being not known exactly when. On his lamentable death which closed his scholarly career, these manuscripts fell into the hands of his servants, and it was from one of them that I bought this manuscript along with many others. It is generally correct and the many marginal notes in it solve many a mystery for the scholar."

[120] STEIN 1894, p. i, explains that when the *mahārāja* "provided rich endowments" for the founding and maintenance of the Jammu college and library, "competent teachers were drawn to the Raghunātha temple from different parts of India," and (p. iii) his "liberal patronage [...] attracted an increasing number of pandits to Jammu, where many found employ either at the court or in connection with various

the cultural environment in which these manuscripts were produced and annotated was not always exclusively Kashmirian.

The manuscript material used for this edition is comprised of three distinct sets: two ĪPVV annotated manuscripts (described below, §8); two annotated *Vṛtti* manuscripts (described below, §10), and ten annotated ĪPV manuscripts (described below, §9). The quantity of fragments preserved in their margins varies to a great extent within the ĪPV group in particular, but each of these groups has fragments that are not found in the two others—even though their quotations quite often overlap—and has distinctive features. Thus the ĪPVV manuscripts are the only ones to provide in full the text of several chapters, and the only ones to quote exclusively from Utpaladeva's *Vṛtti* and *Vivṛti*, whereas ĪPV and *Vṛtti* manuscripts bear in their margins annotations from many different sources pertaining to the genre of philosophical *śāstra*; besides, ĪPV and *Vṛtti* manuscripts quote passages from the fragment preserved in the Delhi codex unicus of the *Vivṛti*, whereas the ĪPVV manuscripts only quote fragments after that part of the text. It is also worthy of notice that those who annotated the *Vṛtti* manuscripts seem to have had a particular taste for the *Vivṛti's* introductions (*avataraṇikā*) to the verses, which they quote far more frequently than other manuscripts.

One of the difficulties encountered when looking for fragments of the *Vivṛti* in the margins of *Vṛtti* and ĪPV manuscripts is that their annotations quote from a whole range of works, but rarely mention by name the sources from which they borrow;[121] and even when they do so, they often offer titles that differ from the ones under which these texts are best known (thus Abhinavagupta's ĪPVV may be called the *Caturviṃsatisāhasrī*, and Utpaladeva's *Vivṛti*, the *Madhyamā*).[122] Although the advent of electronic texts has greatly simplified the task of identifying marginal citations, this has certainly not solved all problems, because the quotations bear numerous variants (which makes automatic searches somewhat unreliable), and most of all, because when, in a manuscript belonging to the Pratyabhijñā corpus,

scholastic and religious establishments." The Introduction to the catalogue specifically mentions pandits from Bengal, Rajasthan or Varanasi, but also (p. vii, fn. 1) a scholar whose name, Veṅkaṭa Śāstrī Tailaṅga, suggests a Southern origin.

[121] For examples of such explicit mentions see RATIÉ 2018d, p. 314, fn. 41.

[122] See RATIÉ 2017a, p. 168, fn. 17, and RATIÉ 2018b, p. 314, fn. 41.

we spot a marginal annotation that does not belong to any known Sanskrit philosophical work, we are still left with the necessity of proving that such comments are not a late gloss by some learned owner of the manuscript, but actually belong to Utpaladeva's magnum opus.

We must therefore determine first whether the margins of a given manuscript contain fragments of already known *Vivṛti* passages, which can be done by comparing them with the long *Vivṛti* fragment edited by Raffaele Torella on the basis of the Delhi codex unicus; if this is the case, and if we also encounter in these margins quotations from an unknown source that happen to correspond exactly to Abhinavagupta's explanations in his ĪPVV, while invariably containing, in the same order, all the words quoted by Abhinavagupta, the probability that we are indeed dealing with a *Vivṛti* fragment verges on absolute certainty.[123]

Now, a great deal of the quotations from Utpaladeva's *Vivṛti* preserved in these annotations are very short excerpts (many of them are no more than a sentence or even a mere segment of sentence). Given the number of witnesses used and the fact that the quotations are scattered in their margins along with quotations from various other works, the edition had to include a threefold apparatus, the highest level of which simply indicates in which manuscripts (and which margins within them) a given sentence (or segment thereof) appears; readers can get a glimpse of the complexity of the editing process just by having a look at the length of this first level of the apparatus, for instance with respect to passages of the *Vivṛti* on ĪPK 2.1.3, where most of the sources change with every few words.

## 2. Why we cannot dispense with annotations in ĪPV and *Vṛtti* manuscripts

Under such conditions, one might deem far simpler to consider only the two ĪPVV manuscripts for the edition of chapter 2.1, since they alone contain its full text, whereas the other manuscripts only provide sentences

[123] Unfortunately, if an annotation that is suspected of being a *Vivṛti* fragment does not contain any word quoted by Abhinavagupta, it becomes very difficult to prove that it is a genuine fragment (this rarely happens, but see e.g. fragment? no. 6 on ĪPK 1.5.8–9 in RATIÉ 2020). The passage given in KAWAJIRI 2016b, p. 24 as a "fragment" that "seems to be" from the *Vivṛti* on ĪPK 2.1.4, is in fact a quotation from Abhinavagupta's ĪPV (vol. II, p. 12, ll. 2–7).

(sometimes mere parts of them) dispersed in their margins and mixed with numerous irrelevant quotations. Nonetheless, however time-consuming the task of gathering these bits of sentence might be, it is worth the trouble, first of all because the two ĪPVV manuscripts, while providing us with the longest continuous fragment known to date, suffer from a number of lacunae, as is obvious at first sight from the fact that the scribes who copied them used dots or dashes to indicate whenever they could not read *akṣaras*. Unfortunately, the smaller fragments found in the margins of ĪPV and *Vṛtti* manuscripts do not always enable us to fill the gaps in ĪPVV manuscripts: conjectures had to be made in a number of cases, and the important lacuna that extends from the end of the commentary on ĪPK 2.1.6 to the beginning of that on ĪPK 2.1.8 could not be filled with any marginalia so far. Yet ĪPV and *Vṛtti* manuscripts are particularly precious when it comes to gaps in the ĪPVV manuscripts—to give but one example with respect to each group, in the *Vivṛti* on ĪPK 2.1.5 (l. 164), the compound *kālakrama*, which is missing in both S12 and J11, and without which the sentence remains unintelligible, was provided by two ĪPV manuscripts, D2 and SOAS; similarly, in the *Vivṛti* introducing ĪPK 2.1.6 (l. 184), the word *saṃsāriṇa*, missing in S12 and J11, could only be retrieved from the margins of the two *Vṛtti* manuscripts.

Besides, the quotations in ĪPV and *Vṛtti* manuscripts, however brief, sometimes contain better readings, with respect to both the text of the *Vṛtti*[124] and—more crucially for this study—that of the *Vivṛti*: for instance, in the *Vivṛti* on ĪPK 2.1.2, the words *sā kālāvaruddhasaṃvedyakulakavalīkaraṇena* (ll. 34–35), for which many variants are found in marginal annotations, are only transmitted correctly by ĪPV manuscripts D2 and SOAS, against ĪPVV manuscripts S12 and J11 (which give *sā kalā°*). In the *Vivṛti* on ĪPK 2.1.3 (ll. 47 and 49), the ĪPV manuscript S15 and the *Vṛtti* manuscript studied by Yohei Kawajiri give the correct reading *'vacchedakaś* (instead of *'vabodakaś* in both ĪPVV manuscripts) and *sā sā prasiddheti* (instead of

[124] See for instance the *Vṛtti* on ĪPK 2.1.5: the reading *kālakrama eva*, found in all the manuscripts consulted for the *Vṛtti* edition in TORELLA 2002, but also preserved in S15 and S19, is clearly better (as can be seen from the *Vivṛti*'s explanation of this passage) than the reading provided in S12 and J11 (*kālabheda eva*). See also e.g. the *Vṛtti* on ĪPK 2.1.6, where S15 and S19 provide the correct reading *abhyāvṛttigaṇanābhāvād ātmanīvārtheṣv api na* against the two ĪPVV manuscripts (and the *Vṛtti* edition).

*sā prasiddheti* in both ĪPVV manuscripts). In the *Vivṛti* on ĪPK 2.1.5, S12 and J11 share scribal errors (*paurvaparyam* for *paurvāparyam*, l. 159, or *vipariṇamater* for *vipariṇamate*, l. 161) of which the corresponding quotations in *Vṛtti* and ĪPV manuscripts are free; etc.

### 3. The obstacles to the determination of the annotations' genealogy

This means that we cannot afford not to take into account all three sets of annotations. Given the number of witnesses involved, however, can we not hope to simplify the editing task by eliminating manuscripts that can be shown to be mere copies of older witnesses? It is well known that the stemmatic method, which consists in tracing a genealogical "tree" of the surviving manuscripts, and which has been successfully applied in numerous cases of works transmitted by a manuscript tradition, greatly facilitates the editing work by determining which witnesses can be considered irrelevant, and has the advantage of showing at a glance which manuscripts are to be considered more important because they are closer to the Ur-text in the line of transmission. Can we hope to build, rather than a stemma codicum, a stemma marginaliorum? As seen above, each of the three sets of annotated manuscripts (ĪPVV, ĪPV and *Vṛtti*) shares fragments not found in the two others and has distinctive features, and it is tempting to draw from this the conclusion that these three distinct annotated traditions respectively go back to one single annotated antigraph of the ĪPVV, *Vṛtti* and ĪPV, and that the annotations in these three antigraphs were in turn made from either one or several manuscript(s) of Utpaladeva's *Vivṛti*. By applying the stemmatic method, that is, by assuming that the copy of a manuscript, or in this case, of a set of annotations, "will contain the same errors that were in the exemplar from which it was made, minus those that the scribe has seen and corrected, plus some additional ones,"[125] we should be able to establish the genealogy of each set of annotations.

It seems, however, that it is not reasonable to hope to build such a stemma in the foreseeable future, at least in the case of annotations found in *Vṛtti* and ĪPV manuscripts (the latter constituting the most numerous group), for the following reasons.

---

[125] This is the "axiom" defined as "the basis of stemmatic analysis" in WEST 1973, p. 32.

First of all, the transmission of annotations obviously differs from that of the main text in that a corpus of annotations is formed by accretion and may continue growing for centuries: new annotations may be added whenever a manuscript is copied, becomes the property of a new owner, or even is read anew by its current owner; so that we cannot simply imagine, for each annotated work (*Vṛtti*, ĪPV, ĪPVV), an original, single text constituted by a given set of annotations from which all others could be established to derive. This is why seventeenth-century S3, despite being in all probability the oldest witness in the group of annotated ĪPV manuscripts considered here,[126] lacks many *Vivṛti* fragments found in other, more recent ĪPV manuscripts such as S10, S15, D2 and SOAS. This is also why, even when we can establish from colophons that several manuscripts have a common ancestor (as is the case of D2, S1 and S5) or that one is probably an apograph of the other (as is the case of S15 and S2),[127] this is of little help with respect to the relationship of their annotations, whose genealogy is partly independent from that of the main text; thus S15, the main text of which is likely to have been copied from S2, contains in its margins numerous fragments of chapter 2.1, whereas the margins of S2 have only preserved one sentence from it.

It should be kept in mind, however, that in this respect the two ĪPVV manuscripts stand out in that contrary to the *Vṛtti* and ĪPV manuscripts, they do not seem to have been formed through a process of accretion of diverse quotations: in both of them, the annotations covering ĪPK 1.8.10 to ĪPK 2.3.8 can be regarded as being in fact *one single annotation*, not only because they were copied in a single hand in each case, but also, and more importantly,[128] because despite a few lacunae, those who wrote them down evidently strove to provide a continuous text; so we should not deal with the two ĪPVV witnesses as with the *Vṛtti* and ĪPV manuscripts. Setting aside for now this peculiar case of the ĪPVV manuscripts, what can we hope to know of the genealogy of the *Vṛtti* and ĪPV manuscripts?

---

[126] See below, §9.

[127] See below, §9.

[128] More importantly, because as emphasized below, the fact that annotations were copied in a single hand results in some cases from their being copied from an earlier manuscript where these annotations were originally written by different individuals.

In the case of annotations, we have no specific colophons, and the scant information that we may glean in the colophons of the manuscripts in which they were found can at best give us a terminus post quem for the time when the quotations were added in these margins; but of course, this does not give us any clue as to what their source was, and in the case of the *Vivṛti*, this does not tell us whether they were extracted directly from a *Vivṛti* manuscript or copied from annotations quoting the *Vivṛti* in the margins of some earlier manuscript of another text of the Pratyabhijñā corpus. Besides, it is not always easy to determine whether the annotations were copied—in part or in their entirety—by the very hand who copied the main text, and even when different hands can clearly be distinguished,[129] apart from extremely rare exceptions,[130] it is impossible to identify these hands due to the absence of colophons specifically devoted to the annotations. Moreover, even though in some of these manuscripts, we can tell from the different handwritings that several persons wrote down different annotations, it is also clear that in many cases, when an annotated manuscript got copied, its annotations were copied along with the main text by the scribe, so that the fact that these annotations were initially written down by different persons can no longer be ascertained in the new copy; and some further additions could be made in this new manuscript, which were then copied along with the other annotations in the next manuscript, etc. This means that it is often impossible to determine how many strata the marginalia of a given manuscript originally contained, because we cannot simply rely on differences in handwritings to do this. And although the difficulties just mentioned make the task of a stemma marginaliorum very complicated, they would

[129] One famous example is the main manuscript used by M.A. Stein for his edition of the *Rājataraṅgiṇī*, the marginal annotations of which can be traced back to at least four different hands according to the editor (see RT, Preface, pp. x–xii and STEIN 1900, pp. 47–48).

[130] M.A. Stein claims to have identified the annotator referred to as A2 in his RT edition (i.e., the author of the earliest annotations in what the editor calls the codex archetypus) as Bhaṭṭa Haraka, a contemporary of Ratnakaṇṭha's, on the basis of similarities in the handwriting of these annotations with that of the "deed of sale" of a *Mahābhārata* manuscript bearing marginal annotations in the same hand (see STEIN 1900, vol. I, p. 47).

not render it hopelessly difficult, were it not for the fact that marginal annotations in these manuscripts are affected by a massive phenomenon of contamination.[131]

The latter point is obvious from the fact that quite often, the very same annotation is found, sometimes with variant readings, yet very often written by the same hand, *at least twice in the same manuscript*. In the edition below, this happens regularly in three ĪPV manuscripts, namely D2, SOAS and S15. Thus as regards the *Vivṛti* on ĪPK 2.1.5, the same fragment (from *tathā cāsau jāyata iti...* to *bhāgāvabhāsaḥ*, ll. 161–163) is found in D2 both in the top margin of f. 213b and the bottom margin of f. 214b; it is also found twice in SOAS, in the top margin of f. 202a and in the bottom margin of f. 203a. Again, in D2, another fragment on the same verse is found twice (from *grāhakāvabhāsena...* to *bhaviṣyattā*, ll. 175–178), in the right margin of f. 213b and in the bottom margin of f. 215a; similarly, it appears twice in SOAS, in the left margin of f. 202a and in the bottom margin of f. 213b. In S15, the *Vṛtti* is often copied twice for each verse (often on the same folio, albeit in different margins), although in the latter case, contrary to what is seen in D2 and SOAS, the duplicated annotations are in different hands.

This also happens in *Vṛtti* manuscripts: Yohei Kawajiri has noticed with some surprise that some of the fragments found in the manuscript that he had been studying appear twice in its margins,[132] and according to him,

> This seems to suggest that a scribe wrote down these marginal notes on the basis of his teacher's oral instruction without reflecting on what his teacher intended to say, or that there were at least two scribes.[133]

---

[131] I.e., the scribe who copied a given manuscript used not one but several antigraphs to do so. This makes attempts at drawing a stemma particularly problematic, the stemmatic method being based on the assumption that a witness can be established to be the copy of a given antigraph if it shares its mistakes and adds some—a principle that loses its necessity in cases where contamination occurs.

[132] See KAWAJIRI 2016a, p. 95: "Strangely, this fragment gives the same *avataraṇikā* as the above"; KAWAJIRI forthcoming: "a scribe sometimes repeats some passages."

[133] KAWAJIRI forthcoming.

As for the hypothesis (which remains to be substantiated) that these annotations were exclusively written on the basis of an oral instruction,[134] given the length of the repeated quotations in ĪPV manuscripts, in any case it seems unlikely that they had as their sole source the teacher's memory (even if the latter dictated them to a pupil, he probably did so from some written source). It also seems improbable that a scribe might have repeated the same quotation (often with variant readings, and sometimes quite lengthy) in different margins out of sheer distraction, unless we assume that the teacher too was distracted enough to provide twice the same quotation in the course of his explanation of a given passage in the main text—but then we have to assume an awful lot of distraction on the part of all the protagonists. As for the alternative suggestion that "there were at least two scribes," I am not sure whether I correctly understand what Yohei Kawajiri has in mind here, but this could be much closer to my own understanding of the reason why some manuscripts bear such duplicated annotations. At any rate, the phenomenon far exceeds the case of the manuscript studied by Yohei Kawajiri, and is common even outside the Pratyabhijñā corpus; for example, Yasutaka Muroya's study shows that a fragment of the GBh appears twice in the margins of a NM manuscript.[135] Camillo Formigatti has also noticed and attempted to explain the fact that the same folio of a *Raghuvaṃśa* manuscript contains both the interlinear note *aruntudaṃ tu, marmaspṛk aruntudaṃ marmaspṛśaṃ*, and, in the bottom margin, the annotation *aruntudaṃ tu marmaspṛk i<ty a>mara<ḥ>*.[136] Camillo Formigatti's explanation runs as follows:

> The reason the quotation is repeated twice here is not evident. The scribe/commentator did not state the source of the quotation due to lack of space... In fact, the scribe/commentator felt compelled to report the source and therefore wrote the annotation once more in the bottom margin...The quota-

---

[134] For a discussion of the purposes of copying and annotating Kashmirian manuscripts see Ratié 2018b, pp. 320–325, which argues that both of these activities, while undoubtedly linked with teaching, were by no means limited to the context of an oral instruction.

[135] Muroya 2010, p. 232: Fragment 6, 18–19 occurs in G2, f. 13v, top margin, and is "repeated on 13v, right margin."

[136] Formigatti 2011, pp. 118 and 149.

> tion from Amara is repeated most probably because in annotation 160 it was difficult to read and incomplete, lacking the indication of the source. Still, the text of this annotation is wrong and incomplete.[137]

Although the hypothesis is ingenious, it seems to me that there is a much likelier cause for this very common phenomenon, namely: a scribe copying marginal annotations may have been relying on several annotated antigraphs, or he may have been relying on only one, but while merely adding annotations to an already existing set of marginalia in a given manuscript; and he refrained from copying twice the same annotation when it was found in the proximity of the same sentence(s) in the main text of several manuscripts, because he could immediately see, from the place occupied in the margins by the annotations in question, that they were one and the same; but if the same annotation was placed somewhat differently in one of the manuscripts, and/or contained too many variants, *it was not recognized as the same*, and it was therefore copied a second time at a slightly different place. This means that in all manuscripts containing duplicated annotations, we must assume that at least some of the annotations that appear only once were in fact available to the scribe from more than one source, and that he identified them as being one and the same quotation—which enabled him to choose variant readings for instance. And given the frequence of duplicated annotations, it is difficult not to suspect that this must have happened even in some manuscripts where we do not find duplicated annotations, because a skilled scribe could have successfully recognized the quotations that he copied from several annotated antigraphs at hand.

This phenomenon of contamination[138] is bound to make all assumptions regarding the history of the transmission of these fragments particularly fragile, and for now, the production of a complete stemma of the annotations that would not be purely speculative seems out of reach, all the more since the present edition uses manuscripts transmitting three different main texts,

---

[137] FORMIGATTI 2011, p. 149.

[138] It has of course already been noticed with respect to Kashmirian manuscripts in general (although not specifically with respect to annotations); on this issue see in particular HANNEDER 2017.

two of which—the ĪPV and ĪPVV—are very lengthy and remain themselves mostly unstudied as regards the history of their transmission (which, in the case of the ĪPV at least, is also complicated by the great number of surviving witnesses: so far I have been able to consult about 45 ĪPV manuscripts).

If it is unreasonable, in the present state of our knowledge, to try to build a complete stemma of the annotations, can we not at least set aside the Nāgarī manuscripts in order to concentrate our efforts on the study of the Śāradā ones? For it is well known that Nāgarī manuscripts (often presented as mere "transcripts" by the KSTS editors) only became common in the Kashmirian tradition from the second half of the 19th century,[139] and that they often abound in scribal errors because, as already pointed out by Georg Bühler in his 1877 report, most of them were not made by pandits (as had been the case until then), but by professional scribes who had no interest in the content of what they were copying.[140] And indeed, of the two ĪPVV manuscripts, J11, written in Nāgarī, has many more gross mistakes than its Śāradā counterpart, S12. We also have at our disposal two *Vṛtti* annotated manuscripts, one of which (S19) is in Śāradā while the other (L2, studied by Yohei Kawajiri) is in Nāgarī. So should we not dismiss the Nāgarī manuscripts as redundant witnesses, since they appear to be mere transcripts (and rather bad ones) of the Śāradā witnesses at our disposal?

## 4. The relationship between the *Vṛtti* annotated manuscripts

Let us first examine the relationship between the two *Vṛtti* manuscripts, S19 (in Śāradā) and L2 (in Nāgarī). Since L2 is obviously a late Nāgarī transcript of a Śāradā antigraph, one might naturally assume that it is but a copy of S19. And indeed, L2 as transcribed by Yohei Kawajiri[141] shares some mistakes with S19, and adds some; but it does not share all of S19's mistakes, far from that. To give just a few examples, l. 31 of this edition, L2

---

[139] Which is not to say that Nāgarī was never used in Kashmirian manuscripts before that time, or that the transmission of a text never went the other way around (see in particular WITZEL 1985 for a possible example of early transmission from Nāgarī to Śāradā; see also SLAJE 2005, p. 46, for the recent case of a "Śāradā transcript" of a Nāgarī edition).

[140] BÜHLER 1877, p. 33; for more references see also RATIÉ 2018b, pp. 331–335.

[141] See below, §10.

has the correct *nirvartyate* against *nivartye* in S19; again, ll. 32–33, L2 has the correct *sakramatvenopapādayiṣyamāṇarūpā* against S19's obviously wrong *samatveno°*; l. 33, L2 has the correct *punaḥ*, omitted in S19; etc. If we assume that L2 is nonetheless a copy of S19, in order to explain these better readings in L2 we must surmise that the scribe who copied L2 made numerous learned corrections, which is somewhat surprising given what we know of the production of many Nāgarī transcripts. Besides, S19 bears some fragments that L2 does not have; of course, this is not impossible at all if L2 is a copy of S19 (a scribe may omit parts of the text that is being copied). But more importantly, L2 also has quite a number of fragments that are not found at all in S19 (for instance ll. 21–22; 46–49; 53–54; 57–58; 60–62; etc.), so that it is at least certain that S19 could not have been the sole source of the annotations in L2.[142] Since Kashmirian Nāgarī manuscripts are most often mere copies of Śāradā exemplars, it is tempting to assume that it had a Śāradā antigraph that is not available to us for now and contains (or contained) all the annotations found in L2; but this is nothing more than a likely hypothesis for now. In any case, we cannot simply dismiss the testimony of L2, which is not a mere transcript of S19.

### 5. The relationship between the ĪPVV manuscripts

What of the relationship between S12 and J11? They have much in common, first and foremost the fact that contrary to ĪPV and *Vṛtti* manuscripts, they provide the longest known continuous fragment of the *Vivṛti*; and they share a great many readings, including obvious scribal errors and indications of lacunae with approximately the same number of missing characters.

There are many reasons to suspect that J11 is a transcript of S12. First, as far as I can see, J11 does not contain a single word of the *Vivṛti* that is not found in S12; and it shares the vast majority of S12's mistakes while adding many of its own. It also has some lacunae in passages where the text is found in full in S12; thus in the *Vivṛti* fragment bearing on ĪPK 1.7.10 that is preserved in both S12 and J11, the beginning of the fragment, preserved

[142] We can also rule out the much less likely hypothesis that the annotations in S19 might have been copied from those in L2, since as mentioned above, S19 has fragments that are not found in L2.

in S12 on f. 188b, is not found in J11, whereas the sequel of the fragment written in the margins of f. 189a in S12 is also copied in J11 (f. 189b),[143] and it seems natural to assume that this happened because J11's scribe simply failed to see the annotation on the first annotated folio in S12.

There are, however, a few elements that could be seen as going against the hypothesis that the annotations in J11 were copied from S12.

First of all, l. 135, S12 has a dittography (*pa paripūrṇam*) not found in J11, whose scribe does not seem to have been much of a corrector. It should be noted, however, that in S12 the first *pa* stands very close to the main text, and it is possible that the scribe who copied the annotation in J11 simply did not see that it belonged to the annotation. Besides, in the fragment pertaining to ĪPK 1.7.10–11, J11 has the correct reading *asyālokādivyatiriktasya*, whereas S12 has *asya lokādivyatiriktasya*: in this latter case, if we suppose that the annotation in J11 was copied from S12, we have no choice but to assume a rare correction on the part of J11's scribe.

It is also worthy of notice that the erroneous readings shared by S12 and J11 were sometimes corrected in S12 but not in J11; for example l. 235, the reading *ahantāvacchādita* was corrected into *ahantāvacchāditā* in S12, but not in J11; l. 21, the reading *viruddhām iva* was also corrected into *viruddham iva* in S12, but not in J11. On the other hand, some readings only found in corrections of S12 appear in J11 (for instance the reading *citrajñānasya*, l. 94). This could be taken to mean that both manuscripts were copied from a common unknown antigraph bearing these mistakes, and that some of these were corrected in only one of the manuscripts; but it could also be—and I take it to be the most likely hypothesis for now—that some of the corrections in S12 were made after J11 was copied from it.

More puzzling is the fact that the rather long passage missing in J11 under ĪPK 2.1.3–4 (ll. 66–93, corresponding to blank margins in ff. 205a and b in J11) is entirely readable in S12 (from f. 203b, bottom margin to 204b, top margin), and the lacuna in J11 starts in the midst of an annotation in S12 (in the bottom margin of f. 203b): if the annotations in J11 were indeed copied from S12, the person who did it stopped there, for no apparent reason, in the middle of a perfectly legible annotation—which is odd, although not impossible of course.

---

[143] See RATIÉ forthcoming a.

To sum up, on the basis of the evidence available so far, it seems very likely that J11 was copied from S12. Yet I have not proceeded to eliminate J11 from the edition as a mere apograph, first because this hypothesis can only be thoroughly tested once the text of the *Vivṛti* chapters 2.2 and 2.3 has been edited, and also because the margins of J11 bear some very interesting corrections (for instance that of *citrajñānasya* into *bodhātmano*, l. 94) that deserve to be included in the edition.

## 6. The relationship between the ĪPV manuscripts

As for the ĪPV manuscripts, as explained above it is particularly difficult to determine their relationships; it seems obvious, however, that some of the witnesses must be closely related. This is the case in particular of the annotations in D2, which have an evident link with those in SOAS as well as with the footnotes printed in the KSTS edition of the ĪPV. The latter is not surprising, as D2 is most probably one of the four manuscripts used by the KSTS editors (see below, §9), and many of the footnotes in the edition must have been taken from its margins—although not all of them, and unfortunately, the KSTS editors provide very little information as to the three other manuscripts beyond the identity of their owners (i.e. pandits of the Department and, in one case, the Library itself): Kha is not described at all, and only the number of pages and their being made of paper are specified as regards the others. Besides, we are informed that a "copy" of Ka was made in the office of the pandit who owned it in the Departement, but the script used to make the copy is not mentioned. So D2 can be considered one of the sources of the footnotes in the ĪPV edition, but at this point the other sources are unknown (the KSTS editors only tell us that "all these manuscripts... contain some marginal notes").[144]

The margins of D2 and SOAS also have a great deal in common: they provide the same fragments, and they usually introduce or conclude the quotations in the same way (for instance, as regards chapter 2.1 of the *Vivṛti*, the text edited below ll. 16–19 is preceded in both D2 and SOAS by *ayam arthaḥ* and followed by the same sentence from the ĪPVV; the passage ll. 30–35 appears in both manuscripts while being preceded by *madhyāyām*; for similar phenomena see also in the edition below ll. 43–44, 63–65, 65–

[144] ĪPV, vol. I, p. i.

66, 83-84, etc.). Besides, as mentioned above (§3), D2 and SOAS share duplicated annotations. They also share many erroneous readings, and SOAS adds some mistakes of its own,[145] including some that can be explained by comparing them with D2. Thus l. 106, the wrong reading *bhaved* found in SOAS may well have resulted from the fact that in D2, the long stroke of the character *tra* in the word *vicitra°* one line above could have been mistaken for an *e*. For all these reasons, it seems extremely likely that the annotations in SOAS were copied from D2,[146] and although in one instance SOAS is free of a scribal error found in D2 (l. 57), I assume that this is the result of a correction on the part of the scribe of the SOAS manuscript.

Unfortunately, however, the relationship between the other ĪPV manuscripts is much more complex than this apparently clear-cut case, and for the reasons mentioned above (§3), for now at least, little else can safely be said in this regard; hopefully the examination of the fragments that are yet to be edited can help us clarify this in the coming years.

A few additional words are nonetheless in order regarding S15, which stands apart in that it is the only ĪPV manuscript of my knowledge that gives in full the text of the chapter up to l. 66 (towards the end of the commentary on ĪPK 2.1.3). As suggested below (§9), its main text could have been copied from S2; but whereas the margins in S2 contain only one sentence from chapter 2.1 of the *Vivṛti*, those in S15 abound in fragments of it, including the lengthy quotation that provides the beginning of the chapter. One could therefore suspect that the beginning of the chapter was copied from one of the ĪPVV manuscripts, all the more since the margins of S15 bear many ĪPVV quotations, and its *Vivṛti* fragments share lacunae with both S12 and J11 and add mistakes not found in S12 and J11. Besides, since J11 has numerous mistakes of its own that are not found in S15, one might suspect that those who wrote down the annotations in S15 had S12 at their disposal among other sources and copied the beginning of chapter 2.1 from it. It should be noted, however, that in fact S15 does not share all the mistakes of S12 and J11: it rightly gives the reading *'vacchedakaś* where

[145] Besides the edition below, see RATIÉ 2016a, p. 224, fn. 8, on the added mistakes in SOAS with respect to the *Vivṛti* fragment already edited by R. Torella; see also, for similar cases in other fragments, RATIÉ 2020.

[146] Cf. RATIÉ 2018b, p. 309, fn. 16.

both S12 and J11 wrongly read *'vabodakaś* (l. 47), and l. 49, it rightly gives *sā sā prasiddheti* whereas both S12 and J11 omit the second *sā*. It could be surmised that the scribe who copied S15 rightly corrected S12, were it not for the fact that it also indicates in three instances some lacunae where the corresponding text in S12 is perfectly legible (ll. 2, 3 and 36). That a scribe may omit a part of the text to be copied is of course a common phenomenon; but it is much harder to explain how a scribe may have seen a lacuna when its antigraph is perfectly readable, let alone several of them. It therefore seems far more probable that the annotations in S15 were made from a source that is none of the annotated ĪPVV manuscripts and that is currently unknown to me.

**7. What can be said for now of the annotations' genealogy and date(s)**

To sum up, for now little can be said with certainty of the history of these annotations, particularly as regards the ĪPV group, and we can venture no more than the following:

> 1. Within the ĪPVV group, the annotations in S12 are likely to be the source of those in J11.
>
> 2. Within the ĪPV group, S3, despite being in all probability older than all the other ĪPV manuscripts considered here, is not the sole source of their annotations; the annotations in SOAS were most probably copied from those in D2; the margins of D2 were used to produce at least some of the footnotes in the KSTS edition of the ĪPV; and in the margins of S15, the continuous text of the *Vivṛti* on ĪPK 2.1.1 to 2.1.3 was not copied from any of the ĪPVV manuscripts used for this edition, but from another, unknown source.
>
> 3. Within the *Vṛtti* group, L2 cannot be considered an apograph of S19; and it was probably made from a Śāradā antigraph that is unavailable to date.

This, of course, is not much. One might further point out, however, that the ĪPV and *Vṛtti* groups, while preserving much shorter fragments than those found in the ĪPVV group, cover a far wider range of stanzas. Thus as mentioned above (§1), both the ĪPV and *Vṛtti* groups quote from the long fragment found in manuscript D (the *Vivṛti* codex unicus studied by Raffaele Torella), contrary to the ĪPVV group; besides, the *Vivṛti* fragments in the annotations of L2 studied by Yohei Kawajiri extend from ĪPK 1.1.2 to 3.1.6;[147] and I have not yet completed the exhaustive study of the margins of all the annotated ĪPV manuscripts of my knowledge that contain *Vivṛti* fragments, but it is already clear that they have preserved many fragments bearing on stanzas beyond those covered by the *Vivṛti* passages preserved in the margins of ĪPVV manuscripts (namely 1.7.10–11, 1.5.4–6, and 1.8.10–2.3.8). Moreover, in the ĪPV and *Vṛtti* groups, the *Vivṛti* fragments are found among quotations from many other texts (as is often seen in Kashmirian manuscripts), some of which at least—e.g. the very successful ĪPV, often quoted in the annotations of *Vṛtti* manuscripts—were certainly not in danger of disappearing when the annotations were made; whereas the margins of the ĪPVV group, which only quote from the *Vivṛti* and the *Vṛtti*, and preserve a very long continuous fragment and several shorter ones, give the distinct impression that someone realized that the *Vivṛti* was in immediate danger of disappearing altogether and strove to salvage whatever was left of it. It is therefore possible (although for now this is nothing but a hypothesis, which should be tested by further research in the coming years) that the *Vivṛti* codex unicus D had originally been part of the *Vivṛti* manuscript that is the source of the ĪPVV group of annotations, but had already been separated from that source at the time when the annotations preserved in ĪPVV manuscript S12 were made; that many of the quotations found in ĪPV and *Vṛtti* margins were made earlier, at a time when the source of the quotations (assuming that it was a single manuscript, the main text of which included the *Vivṛti*) covered a far greater part of the treatise,[148]

---

[147] See below, fn. 148.

[148] It seems rather likely, however, that its final part had already been lost. Yohei Kawajiri has noted, with respect to the *Vṛtti* manuscript that is the object of his studies (L2), that "marginal notes from the *Vivṛti* are not given for every *kārikā* and are not found after ĪPK 3.1.6," and concludes from this (KAWAJIRI 2016b, p. 18) that "it may safely be assumed that the text of the *Vivṛti* had already been lost to some extent and only fragments of the *Vivṛti* had been transmitted when the marginal notes were made." One might wonder whether this assumption is indeed safe given that Abhinavagupta's commentaries too are quoted only in part, and only for some *kārikās*, in all the ĪPV and *Vṛtti* manuscripts considered here, whereas both the ĪPV and ĪPVV have been transmitted to us in their entirety. Yet Yohei Kawajiri makes a very interesting and important point when noting that there are no *Vivṛti* quotations at all beyond ĪPK 3.1.6 in L2, and so far I have not found any *Vivṛti* fragment in ĪPV manuscripts either beyond ĪPK 3.1.6. This certainly gives some

including the one preserved in D; and that the ĪPV and *Vṛtti* annotations were written down by pandits who were not animated by the same feeling of urgency in rescuing the remains of the *Vivṛti* as that which seems to have governed the redaction of the annotations in the ĪPVV group.

One last point is worth examining here—namely, to what extent we can claim to determine the date of these annotations. Yohei Kawajiri has observed[149] that the manuscript studied by him "breaks off at the same point as other Northern manuscripts of the *Vṛtti* and contains the *Vṛtti* relative to ĪPK 1.1.1–3.2.8"; from this he concludes that we can determine "when these marginal notes were made."[150] In this connection he underscores the following points:

> The two facts that we can find some marginal notes after ĪPK 3.2.9, and that they are not comments on the *Vṛtti*, suggest that the marginal notes were made after the loss of the last portion of the *Vṛtti*. Given that the last portion of the *Vṛtti* was lost around the 13th or 14th century, it may safely be assumed that the marginal notes were made after that time. Still, we cannot exclude the possibility that there were at least two scribes, and that the second scribe made some notes after ĪPK 3.2.9.[151]

In itself, the hypothesis that the annotations were made after the 13th or 14th century is not unlikely at all; it should be pointed out, however, that for now it is hardly more than a guess, among other reasons because as far as I know, nothing enables us at the moment to determine that the last portion of the text ceased being available in Kashmir as early as in the 13th or 14th century—this loss may also have occurred later, and Yohei Kawajiri seems to take for granted what Raffaele Torella only presents in passing as a rather

---

weight to the hypothesis that the last part of the *Vivṛti* may have already been lost when the *Vṛtti* and ĪPV annotations were made.

149 KAWAJIRI 2016b, p. 18.

150 KAWAJIRI 2016b, p. 19.

151 KAWAJIRI 2016b, p. 19.

likely (but by no means established) hypothesis.[152] Moreover, as Yohei Kawajiri himself notes, it is not impossible (and it is in fact very likely) that the annotations in the margins of this manuscript were not written all at once by the very scribe who copied them in this particular Nāgarī manuscript: rather, many of them may have been copied (perhaps many times) from the margins of earlier manuscripts, and some of them may have originally been found in the margins of a complete *Vṛtti* manuscript, the last part of which could have been lost later.

Yohei Kawajiri further conjectures[153] that Bhāskarakaṇṭha did not have access to the ĪPVV (because he thinks that the ĪPVV was written prior to the ĪPV, whereas Abhinavagupta, as already noted by Raffaele Torella, makes a reference to the ĪPV in ĪPVV, vol. II, p. 230)[154] or to the *Vivṛti*, although he does not specify why he thinks this to have been the case. From this is drawn the following conclusion:

> We can say that the marginal notes of this manuscript were made after the 13th or 14th century and before the 17th or 18th century.[155]

Again, the hypothesis that the annotations were made at some point between the 13th and the 18th century is plausible; but a span of 500 years is hardly a date, so that it seems unwarranted to claim to know "when these marginal notes were made" from the previously mentioned points, which rather suggest that much research is still needed to determine when the annotations were made or when the *Vivṛti* ceased to be available in its complete form. Besides, the reasons adduced to establish this span are somewhat debatable. Thus the fact that Bhāskarakaṇṭha (who, as convincingly demonstrated by Stanislav Jager, must have been active circa 1725–

---

[152] TORELLA 2002, p. xlviii, mentions that from [a], i.e. the archetype for the Trivandrum manuscript, "at least another manuscript also derives, which was probably the only one that later survived Muslim invasion, although with the loss of the last portion." KAWAJIRI 2016b (ibid.) refers to this very sentence, obviously assuming that the loss of the last portion of this manuscript must have occured in the 13th or 14th century.

[153] KAWAJIRI 2016b, p. 19.

[154] TORELLA 2002, p. xliii; see also above, chapter 1, §1.

[155] KAWAJIRI 2016b, pp. 19–20.

1775)[156] is apparently unaware of one sentence in the ĪPVV (the printed edition of which is about 1200 pages long) does not seem to constitute much of a proof that he had no access at all to this work. As for the *Vivṛti*, I have pointed out elsewhere that Bhāskarakaṇṭha would not have misunderstood some difficult passages in the ĪPV had he taken into account parallel passages in the *Vivṛti*, which could indeed indicate that he had no access to those specific parts of the *Vivṛti* at least;[157] but this is by no means proof of it (other scholars have been known not to take into account some useful works available in their library), and it certainly does not allow us to establish that he knew no part of the *Vivṛti* at all. Besides, even if Bhāskarakaṇṭha had no access at all to the *Vivṛti*, this does not prove either that the annotations must have been made prior to his time. What could be seen as evidence of their predating the *Bhāskarī*, however, is that manuscript S3, demonstrably copied in the seventeenth century, bears many *Vivṛti* fragments in its margins, and these annotations must have been added soon after the manuscript's completion, since the margins' edges (now greatly worn on many folios) were obviously intact at the time. For now, we cannot say much more on the issue of the annotations' date(s).

That so little can be said at the moment regarding the genealogy and date(s) of these annotations may seem very disheartening; it should be kept in mind, however, that we are fortunate enough to have at our disposal both the text on which the *Vivṛti* was commenting and Abhinavagupta's detailed commentary on the *Vivṛti* itself (which regularly quotes from it and was written barely a few decades after its completion), plus another commentary by Abhinavagupta that highlights the gist of Utpaladeva's thought. Under such circumstances, although it is unreasonable for now to claim to fully understand the relationship between the manuscript witnesses at our disposal, I believe that it is certainly not so to endeavour a critical edition and translation of the text that they have preserved.

---

[156] On Bhāskarakaṇṭha's date and for further bibliographical references, see JAGER 2018, pp. 8–15; cf. below, fn. 203.

[157] RATIÉ 2017a, p. 167.

## 8. Description of the ĪPVV annotated manuscripts used for this edition

### S12

> Srinagar: Oriental Research Library, no. 2403; erroneously catalogued as an "*Īśvarapratyabhijñāvimarśinī*" (in both the library catalogue and the slip of the National Mission for Manuscripts). Paper, Śāradā script. 305 numbered folios[158] (with, on average, 32 lines per page and 30 characters per line). The written lines run parallel to the narrower side of the folios. Photographed by the National Mission for Manuscripts.

The text at the beginning of S12 before the first verse of the ĪPVV is almost identical with that found in a manuscript that was consulted for the ĪPVV edition in the Kashmir Series of Texts and Studies and is mentioned there as manuscript B (see ĪPVV, vol. I, Preface, p. i):

> *oṃ namaḥ śivāya oṃ śrīgaṇeśāya namaḥ oṃ śrīgurave*[159] *namaḥ oṃ śrīmacchrīvidyārūpāya gurave namaḥ* ‖ *oṃ śreyo* [']*stu*[160] ‖

The last words in S12 are also very close to those found in manuscript B, yet not identical with them (compare with ĪPVV, ibid.):

[158] The *Catalogue of Manuscripts* published in 2011 by the Department of Libraries and Research, Jammu & Kashmir, mentions 319 folios (p. 381); according to the slip from the National Mission for Manuscripts scans, there are 321. In the manuscript, Arabic numerals are given every 10 folios in the upper right corner (f. b); no. 10 is given on what is f. 9b according to the Śāradā number, etc. This goes on until no. 60 in Arabic numerals is given on what is f. 58b according to the count in Śāradā; no. 150 in Arabic numerals appears on f. 146b in Śāradā numerals, etc.

[159] *oṃ śrīgurave* S12; *śrīgurave* B.

[160] *oṃ śreyo* [']*stu* S12; *śreyo 'stu* B.

> *samāptā ceyam īśvarapratyabhijñāvivṛtivimarśinī* || *kṛtiḥ śrī-trinayanacaraṇacintanalabdhaprasiddher abhinavagupta-sya*[161] || *śubham astu sarvajagatāṃ parihitaniratā*[162] *bhavan-tu bhūtagaṇāḥ* || *doṣāḥ prayāntu śāntiṃ sarvatra sukhībha-vantu lokāḥ* ||

Even if we disregard the small divergences just noted, manuscript B cannot be identified with S12: the former is said to be comprised of 820 folios by the KSTS editors, whereas S12, which is complete, has 305 numbered folios, and manuscript B is probably none other than D4, which is currently preserved at the National Archives of India (Delhi) along with other manuscripts that originally belonged to the Oriental Research Department, Srinagar,[163] and which is said to consist of 821 leaves.[164] As for the relationship between S12 and D4, it could only be determined through a detailed examination of D4 which, unfortunately, remains a desideratum to date.[165]

S12 bears several sets of annotations quoting the *Vivṛti* and *Vṛtti*; they seem to be written in a different hand than that of the main text (the main text itself seems to have been written in different hands, the one that copied

---

[161] °*prasiddher abhinavaguptasya* S12; °*prasiddhīnām abhinavaguptasya pādānām* B.

[162] *parihitaniratā* S12 (evidently incorrect); *parahitaniratā* B.

[163] This is notably the case of two manuscripts of the *Śivadṛṣṭi* (hereafter ŚD) that were used by the Pandits of the Department for their KSTS edition of Somānanda's magnum opus and are in all probability none other than manuscripts D3 and D5 (see RATIÉ 2018a, p. 711, fn. 14). It is also the case of manuscript D2, which, as already noticed by Raffaele Torella, is certainly one of the four manuscripts used for the KSTS edition of Abhinavagupta's ĪPV (see below, §9, under D2).

[164] That is, according to the *Handlist of Manuscripts belonging to the archeology and research department, Jammu and Kashmir Government, Srinagar*, included in the *List of Gilgit Manuscripts and Sanskrit Manuscripts* at the National Archives of India.

[165] I did have a look at D4 during a research stay at the National Archives in India in 2008; at the time, however, I was not authorized to take pictures of this very bulky manuscript and did not have enough time to carry out a thorough examination of its hundreds of folios. As far as I remember, the manuscript does not bear any significant annotations, but it is quite possible that some of them escaped me if, as in the case of S12 and J11, they are only to be found on a few dozens of folios; and many of the leaves are illegible, the ink having blotted.

most of it being replaced by another one from f. 217b onwards).[166] The person who wrote down the annotations also made numerous corrections in the main text. The words of the *Vivṛti* that are quoted in Abhinavagupta's commentary are rubricated in the *Vivṛti* fragments as well as in the corresponding passages in the ĪPVV. The fragment that is by far the longest extends from f. 201a to f. 241a and covers ĪPK 1.8.10 to ĪPK 2.3.8 (the main text on f. 201a corresponds to ĪPVV, vol. III, p. 140). A relatively brief fragment is also found in S12 in the margins of ff. 119a–121b. It contains the text on ĪPK 1.5.4–5 already edited in RATIÉ 2016a,[167] then the one on ĪPK 1.5.6 already edited in RATIÉ 2020 as fragments 1 and 2. Another fragment, which covers a part of the explanation of ĪPK 1.7.10–11, appears in the margins of ff. 188b, 189a and b.[168]

### J11

> Jammu: Sri Ranbir Institute, Raghunath Mandir Library, no. 5077, "*Pratyabhijñāvṛttī īśvarapratyabhijñāvivṛti* [sic]." Paper, Nāgarī script. Besides the 9 first folios containing Utpaladeva's *Vṛtti*, 312 numbered folios (with, on average, 32 lines per page and 32 characters per line). The written lines run parallel to the narrower side of the folios. Photographed by Chetan Pandey's staff.

The first folios of J11 contain a Nāgarī transcript of a Śāradā manuscript of Utpaladeva's *Īśvarapratyabhijñāvṛtti*, the latter being in all probability S17, a manuscript now preserved at the Oriental Research Department (Srinagar) and described in TORELLA 2002, pp. lii–liii under siglum Jh. Thus J11 begins just as S17 does:

> *oṃ namo mahāmāyeśvaryai oṃ namaḥ śivāya saśivāya śivadāya namo namaḥ oṃ.*

---

[166] Compare for instance the way *tu* is written, with the curve of the *u* going far above the *t-* from 217b onwards, with the way the same syllable is written before that point, with the *-u* remaining entirely below the *t-*.

[167] Unfortunately, when I published this edition I was not yet aware of S12.

[168] For an edition, translation and study, see RATIÉ forthcoming a.

Utpaladeva's *Vṛtti* ends on folio 9b with the same colophon as S17's, a colophon that seems to indicate that Sundara Bhaṭṭāraka—the author of a hitherto unpublished commentary on the ĪPK only preserved, as far as I know, in S18—copied the *Vṛtti* manuscript[169] (i.e. presumably S17, of which the beginning of J11 is a Nāgarī transcript):

> *iti śrīmatsvandarabhaṭṭārekana*[170] *pratyabhijñāvṛttis sampūrṇīkṛteti śubham astu devādīnāṃ mānuṣyakīṭakānām.*[171]

Then, after a blank folio, the ĪPVV begins (and is numbered from 1 onwards) with the following words:

> *oṃ svasti śrīgaṇeśāya namaḥ oṃ namo praṇavārthāya śuddhajñānaikarūpiṇe nirmalāya prasannāya śrīdakṣiṇāmūrtaye namaḥ oṃ namaḥ śivāya oṃ srīgurave namaḥ oṃ śrīmacchrīvidyārūpāya gurave namaḥ oṃ śreyo* [']*stu oṃ namas tripurasvandaryai*[172] || *oṃ*

---

[169] TORELLA 2002, p. xliv, fn. 76, rather understands the final colophon in S17 as meaning that Sundara Bhaṭṭāraka "would have composed a commentary to take the place of the final part of the *Vṛtti* (missing in all the Kashmirian manuscripts)." It seems to me that this is not what is meant here, since in fact Sundara Bhaṭṭāraka's commentary as preserved in S18 (to which R. Torella did not have access when he wrote his book) does not just fill the final gap: it comments on the ĪPK from the beginning of the treatise (see ĪPK 1.1.1 on folio 1b, ĪPK 1.1.2 on folio 11a–b, ĪPK 1.1.3 on folio 15a, etc.). Besides, the sentence in question in S17 occurs in the colophon of a manuscript that does not contain Sundara Bhaṭṭāraka's commentary, even in part: the *Vṛtti* in S17 breaks at the usual place and, as noticed in TORELLA 2002, p. liii, "the remaining *kārikās* [are] without commentary." It therefore seems much more likely that the colophon in S17 simply states that "this *Pratyabhijāvṛtti* [manuscript] was completed by the master Sundara Bhaṭṭāraka—prosperity to [all] from gods to men and worms." Note also that S17 and S18 were obviously written by the same hand—probably that of Sundara Bhaṭṭāraka himself (see RATIÉ 2018b, p. 328).

[170] S17 has *śrīmatsundarabhaṭṭārakena*. The scribe of J11 often confuses *su-* and *sva-*; the peculiar Śāradā handwriting in S17 (Sundara Bhaṭṭāraka's?) may have made this confusion easier.

[171] According to TORELLA 2002, p. liii, the end of the colophon reads *mānuṣyakītānāṃ*; this must be a typo (both S17 and J11 read *mānuṣyakīṭakānām*, although one would rather expect *mānuṣyakīṭāntānām* or *mānuṣyakīṭakāntānām*).

[172] Again, for *tripurasundaryai* (see above, fn. 170).

The end of the manuscript, on folio 312b, says the following:

> *samāptā ceyam īśvarapratyabhijñāvivṛtivimarśinī* ‖ *kṛtiḥ śrī-tritayanacaraṇaciṃtanalabdhaprasiddher*[173] *abhinavaguptasya* ‖: – ‖: *śubham astu sarvajagatām* ‖: *oṃ* ‖:

J11 contains many corrections in different hands and even different scripts: Nāgarī, but also Śāradā and, quite unexpectedly, Grantha and Telugu.[174] It also bears annotations in Nāgarī (apparently by the same hand that copied the main text) quoting the *Vivṛti* and *Vṛtti*. The words of the *Vivṛti* quoted in Abhinavagupta's commentary are rubricated in the *Vivṛti* fragments given in the margins as well as in the corresponding passages in the ĪPVV. The lengthiest *Vivṛti* fragment, which covers ĪPK 1.8.10 to ĪPK 2.3.8, is found in the margins of the manuscript from f. 202a to f. 241b.[175] The main text on folio 241b corresponds to the commentary on ĪPK 2.3.8 found in ĪPVV, vol. III, p. 140; it ends at the same point as in S12 (with the last word *svātmani*, f. 214b, bottom margin, corresponding to the one in S12, f. 240a, top margin). J11 also has a part of the fragment on ĪPK 1.7.10–11 found in S12 (the annotations on ff. 189b and 190a in J11 correspond to the text found in ff. 189a and 189b in S12), but the text preserved in the first annotated folio in S12 (f. 188b) is lacking in J11. The fragment pertaining to the explanation of ĪPK 1.5.4–6 that is found in S12 does not appear either in the margins of J11.

---

[173] *śrītritayana°* is of course a mistake for *śrītrinayana°* (cf. the description of S12 above).

[174] See for instance f. 6b of the ĪPVV, where several marginal corrections in Grantha appear, the first of which inserts a °*pa*° to amend the erroneous reading *parokāram* into *paropakāram* (such corrections are very frequent throughout the manuscript and also appear in the initial part of it that provides the *Vṛtti*). For Telugu corrections see, among numerous examples, f. 11a, where °*ṇva*° is inserted in the right margin to correct the word *śṛṇvan* in Telugu characters (the correction was then made in Nāgarī in the text itself); below, in the same margin, is a Telugu *u*, also inserted in the text itself in Nāgarī. It looks like that in such cases, someone most familiar with Telugu corrected the text, and a scribe following these indications then inserted the corrections in Nāgarī (?).

[175] For the text found in ff. 202a, 202b and 203a, see RATIÉ 2017a.

## 9. Description of the ĪPV annotated manuscripts used for this edition

Many ĪPV manuscripts are annotated; the list below includes neither those that, while being annotated, do not contain any *Vivṛti* quotation in their margins, nor those that do contain some *Vivṛti* fragments but have none pertaining to chapter 2.1.[176]

### D2

> Delhi: National Archives of India (Manuscripts belonging to the Archeology and Research Department, Jammu and Kashmir Government, Srinagar, in "List of Gilgit Manuscripts and Sanskrit Mss"), no. 5, vol. II; "*Īśvarapratyabhijñāvimarśinī.*" Paper, Śāradā script. 390 numbered[177] folios (with, on average, 10 lines per page and 13 characters per line). The written lines run parallel to the narrower side of the folios. Dated 1831 CE? Black and white photocopies.

I briefly consulted the manuscript itself during a visit at the National Archives of India in 2008, but I did not have enough time to study it then, and I was not authorized to take photographs of it. I later got a set of photocopies of the entire manuscript; unfortunately, the photocopies are often bad and it is to be hoped that it can soon be photographed under better conditions in its entirety.

It immediately starts with the first introductory verse of the ĪPV after the following words:

> *oṃ svasti oṃ namaḥ śivāya* || *oṃ* || *oṃ*

At the end (f. 389a, l. 6), after the series of concluding verses edited in ĪPV, vol. II, p. 277, the manuscript reads:

> ⌊*ya*⌋*to likhitaḥ pūrvaṃ tatrāyaṃ ślokaḥ*

---

[176] $J_R$ for instance bears many fragments (see RATIÉ 2016b and RATIÉ 2020); unfortunately, in its present state it does not cover chapter 2.1.

[177] In Śāradā numerals, below the abbreviated title *pra bhi*, on the bottom left corner of some (but not all) of the folios.

> *śrīmatsomānandavaṃśo* [']*likhad drāg laghvīm etāṃ pratyabhijñāvivṛtim* | *bhogānando bālabhāve hṛdantassaṃvāsinyā devadevyā niyuktaḥ* ||
>
> *saṃvat 6 bhā va ti trayodaśyāṃ parataḥ caturdaśyāṃ cand° pre samāptam īśvarapratyabhijñāsūtravimarśinyākhyam* || || *idaṃ pustakaṃ likhitaṃ mayā kaularāmake*[*ṇa*] || || || || ||[178]

We thus learn that D2 was copied from an antigraph whose scribe was named Bhogānanda; this Bhogānanda had composed a verse at the end of the antigraph in which he claimed to belong to the genealogical line of a Somānanda and to have "swiftly" copied the ĪPV after this task was entrusted to him by the Goddess "while [he was still] a boy." As for the scribe of D2, after quoting the colophonic verse of the antigraph, he identifies himself as a Kaul Rāma(ka)/Rām Kaul[179] and specifies that he copied the manuscript in Pravarapura=Srinagar[180] in the year 6, in the month of Bhā[drapada] (August–September) on the 13th and 14th lunar days of the dark[181] fortnight. The year 6 of the Saptarṣi era could correspond to 1730–31 or 1830–31 CE;[182] in a previous version of this book I had only added in this respect: "perhaps others who are less ignorant than I am in calendrical matters can determine which year is the correct one from the other elements provided in the colophon." Upon reading this, Michael Witzel, noticing that the abbreviation *cand* must stand for Monday, further discussed the matter

[178] The sequel of the colophon is difficult to read from the photocopy at my disposal; in any case it seems that it merely contains the usual caveat that the scribe is not responsible for mistakes (it ends with the famous verse *yādṛśaṃ pustakaṃ dṛṣṭaṃ tādṛśaṃ likhitaṃ mayā* | *yadi śuddham aśuddhaṃ vā mama doṣo na vidyate* || "I have copied this book just as I saw it; whether it is correct or not is not my fault." The verse usually has *dīyate* rather than *vidyate*).

[179] Alexis Sanderson has pointed out to me (personal communication, 5/01/2019) that "the *-ka* of Rāmaka is expressive of courteous modesty, a common usage among Kashmirian scholars in later times when referring to themselves."

[180] On the abbreviation *pre* see WITZEL 1994, p. 13 (as pointed out to me by the author himself, p. 46, fn. 63, "(*Parihāsa*)*pure*=Srinagar" is a typo for "(*Pravara*-)*pure*=Srinagar").

[181] The abbreviation *va ti* stands for *vahulatithau* (see WITZEL 1994, p. 12).

[182] Following SIRCAR 1965, p. 320.

with Makoto Fushimi, and they offered as "the most plausible date" Monday, the 5th of September 1831 CE.

As already noted by Raffaele Torella, this manuscript was in all probability one of the four witnesses used by the editors of the KSTS in their ĪPV edition and is to be identified with the witness that they call Gha.[183] It is replete with annotations. Several fragments contained in its margins have already been published; they belong to parts of the text edited by Raffaele Torella,[184] but also to the *Vivṛti* on ĪPK 1.3.5[185], ĪPK 1.5.6 and 1.5.8–9.[186] The manuscript also bears many *Vivṛti* quotations pertaining to chapter 2.1.

### L

> Lucknow: Akhila Bhāratīya Saṃskṛta Pariṣad, no. 3366; "*Pratyabhijñāsūtravimarśinī laghvī.*" Paper, Śāradā script. 171 numbered folios (with, on average, 8 lines per page and 40 characters per line; the last folio is blank). The written lines run parallel to the wider side of the folios. Dated 1766 CE. Photographed by Mei Yang.

The verses are not rubricated; there are annotations in different hands, one of which seems to be that of the main text. The first page, before the initial verse of the ĪPV, reads as follows:

> *oṃ namo vighnahantre* || *oṃ namaḥ śivāya gurave* || *śrīrāmabhadrāya namaḥ oṃ*

At the end of the manuscript (f. 170b), after the final verses printed in the KSTS edition of the ĪPV, followed by *iti śivam*, one reads:

> *saṃvat 42 śrīvikramādityasaṃvat 1823 āṣāḍhaśuklatrayodaśyāṃ ravivāsare samāptam idaṃ śivaśāstraṃ śubhadaṃ śivam astu* || *śrīḥ* ||

---

[183] See TORELLA 2007b, p. 544, fn. 14; TORELLA 2007c, p. 479, fn. 8; TORELLA 2007d, p. 929, fn. 11.

[184] See RATIÉ 2016a, p. 223–224, fn. 5 and 7.

[185] See RATIÉ 2016b.

[186] See RATIÉ 2020.

The manuscript was thus completed on Sunday, the 13th of the bright fortnight of the month Āṣādha, [Saptarṣi]saṃvat 42/Vikramasaṃvat 1823—that is, according to Michio Yano's *pañcāṅga* program,[187] Sunday, the 20th of July 1766 CE.

No *Vivṛti* fragment has been edited from its margins so far; they only contain one sentence belonging to chapter 2.1.

### S1

> Srinagar: Oriental Research Library, no. 816; "*Īśvarapratyabhijñāvimarśinī.*" Paper, Śāradā script. 220 numbered folios (with, on average, 16 lines per page and 16 characters per line). The written lines run parallel to the narrower side of the folios. Photographed by the National Mission for Manuscripts.

The verses are rubricated; there are annotations in several hands, one of which seems to be responsible for the main text. On the first page, before the initial verse of the ĪPV, the manuscript reads as follows:

> *oṃ namo gurubhyaḥ parapadārohaṇaikapravīṇebhyaḥ oṃ oṃ*

At the end of the manuscript (ff. 220a–b), after the final verses that are printed in the KSTS edition of the ĪPV, followed by *iti śivam*, one reads

> *yato likhitā pūrvaṃ tatrāyaṃ ślokaḥ*

This is followed by the same verse that is quoted at the end of D2.[188] The colophon then reads:

> *tato likhitā yena tasyāyaṃ ślokaḥ*
>
> *saṃvicchaktyā jñātasadbindunādā nityaṃ śambho bhairavetyāptanādāḥ | antarvāsihṛtsarojāṅkapādāḥ śrīmadrāmānandapādāḥ jayanti || ||*

---

[187] http://www.cc.kyoto-su.ac.jp/~yanom/pancanga/index.html.

[188] See above; the only variant reading is *śrīmatsomānandavaṃśe* for *śrīmatsomānandavaṃśo*.

> *tato [']pi tato [']smābhir likhitā paṃ lambhodaraiḥ*[189] *pati-svāminakauśikaiḥ svātmopakārārtham.*
>
> *śubham astu sarvajagatām iti* || || *oṃ namo gurubhyaḥ para-padārohanaikapravīṇebhyaḥ* || || || *oṃ*

We thus learn that S1 and D2 are related: they have a common ancestor, copied by Bhogānanda,[190] whose colophonic verse is provided in both manuscripts. S1 adds another verse from a certain Rāmānanda, presented as having produced a copy of Bhogānanda's manuscript, after which S1's colophon specifies that the present manuscript was copied from Rāmānanda's by Pandit Lambhodara, of the Patisvāmina Kauśika *gotra*, for his own edification. No date is provided.

The manuscript, from which no *Vivṛti* fragment has been edited so far, only contains in its margins one sentence belonging to chapter 2.1 of the *Vivṛti* (contrary to D2, the annotations of which quote numerous *Vivṛti* fragments pertaining both to this chapter and others).

### S2

> Srinagar: Oriental Research Library, no. 1035; "*Īśvara-pratyabhijñāvimarśinī.*" Paper, Śāradā script. 79 numbered folios[191] (with, on average, 10 lines per page and 65 characters per line). The written lines run parallel to the wider side of the folios. Dated 1773 CE. Photographed by the National Mission for Manuscripts.

The paper is brownish; some of the edges are worn. On some of the folios (e.g. the first one), lines framing the main text and various annotations can be seen. The verses are rubricated. In the central part of the first page, the following is found before the initial verse of the ĪPV:

> *oṃ śrīdevī śaṅkaro jayatu oṃ namaḥ śivāya oṃ śrīgaṇeśaṃ guruṃ natvā śrīmacchaṅkarasvāminā īśvarapratyabhijñe-yaṃ kṛpālvarthaṃ vici[trya]*[?]*te.*

---

[189] Underlined with red ink.

[190] This is also the case of S5 (see below).

[191] The folios were numbered twice, with and without the abbreviation *ī pra.*

In the top margin, the following is written in smaller characters that could be from the same hand:

> *śrīmatsaṅgān deśadeśāntarāntaḥ svairaṃ svairaṃ sambhraman saṃbhraman vai svāmiśrīmacchaṅkaraiḥ likhyate* ['] *sau sadgūḍhārthā pratyabhijñā kṛpāloḥ saṃ 49 mārga śu ti 5 likhanaprārambhaḥ.*

At the end of the manuscript (f. 78b), after the final verses printed in the KSTS edition of the ĪPV (followed by *iti śivam*), one reads:

> *śrīmatsaṅgān*[192] *deśadeśāntarāntas svairaṃ svairaṃ sambhraman sambhraman vai*[193] *svāmiśrīmacchaṅkaraiś citriteyaṃ sadgūḍhārthā pratyabhijñā kṛpāloḥ* ‖ ‖ *nānā tīrthāni deśān nṛpanaravibudhān māntrikāṃś cāpi dṛṣṭvā prāpyāyodhyāṃ khavahnyaṣṭavidhuparimite vatsare pauṣaśukle bhaume* ['] *ṣṭamyāṃ kṛpālvābhidhatanayakaniṣṭhena*[194] *nunnena śīghraṃ vyālekhi pratyabhijñā naravaranutaśrīśaṅkarācāryanāmnā.*
>
> *śrīkṛpāloḥ śubhadā bhūyāt. saṃ 49 pau śu ti 8 bhaume. bhadraṃ paśyema pracarema bhadram. vikramāditya saṃ 1830.*

The scribe (who repeatedly calls the copied work "the Recognition," praising its true and secret meaning) is therefore a Master Śaṅkara (*śrīmacchaṅkarasvāmin*, *svāmiśrīmacchaṅkara*, *śaṅkarācārya*) who copied the manuscript in Ayodhyā at the request of his youngest son, named Kṛpālu,[195] after travelling through many different places and meeting various political and religious figures. In the initial colophon, the copy is said to have been undertaken "in [48]49 [Saptarṣi era = 1773 CE], on the fifth lunar day of the bright fortnight [in the month of] Mārga [=November–December]." The

---

[192] The manuscript seems to have *śrīsatsaṅgān*, but an *m* is written above the *s*, probably in an attempt to correct it, although the *s* has not been deleted.

[193] After the first *sambhraman*, about seven *akṣara*s were deleted, and *sambhraman vai* was written above them.

[194] The °*ta*° in °*tanaya*° is strangely shaped—perhaps because, as suggested to me by Harunaga Isaacson (personal communication, 16/08/2020), the scribe may have first written °*na*° before correcting it into °*ta*°.

[195] As noted by Alexis Sanderson (personal communication, 05/01/2019), "In its Kashmiri form Kripāl this is among the personal names given to Kashmirian brahmin men, at least in recent times."

final one says that the copy was "swiftly" made and completed "in the bright fortnight in the [month of] Pauṣa (December–January), in the year 1830 [of the Vikrama era = 1773 CE] (chronogram: *vidhu*= 1, *aṣṭa*= 8, *vahni*= 3, *kha*=0), on a Tuesday, the eighth [lunar day]," and repeats once more the date both in the Laukika and Vikrama eras. According to Michio Yano's *pañcāṅga* program,[196] the manuscript was thus undertaken on the 19th of November 1773 CE, and completed on the 22nd of December of the same year.

For known *Vivṛti* quotations in S2, see RATIÉ 2016b (on ĪPK 1.3.5). Most of the annotations in chapter 2.1 are quotations from the ĪPVV; I could only find in its margins one sentence from the *Vivṛti* chapter that is the object of this study.

### S3

> Srinagar: Oriental Research Library, no. 838, "*Īśvarapratyabhijñāvimarśinī*" (in the library catalogue; the slip of the National Mission for Manuscripts gives the title as "*Īśvarapratyabhijñākaumudi* [sic]"). Paper, Śāradā script. 142 numbered folios[197] (with, on average, 10 lines per page and 40 characters per line). The written lines run parallel to the wider side of the folios. 17th century CE. Photographed by the National Mission for Manuscripts.

The paper, brown, looks old and damaged; its edges are worn and the margins are at times entirely illegible. At the beginning, after a few entirely illegible characters, one can discern the following (immediately followed by Abhinavagupta's first introductory verse):

> [*oṃ nama*]*ḥ śivāya saśivāya* ||

---

[196] See above, fn. 187.

[197] In Śāradā numerals; Arabic numerals were added on the frame of the folios, but they often differ (in the following references are to the Śāradā numbering).

At the end, before quoting the fifth introductory verse of Abhinavagupta's ĪPVV (*pūrṇavyākaraṇāvagāhanaśuciḥ...*),[198] the copyist gives no date but provides his name in the following:

> *sampūrṇeyam pratyabhijñāsūtravimarśinī. iti śrīmadācāryābhinavaguptaviracitā pra[tyabhijñā]sūtravimarśinī hastākṣaracitriteyaṃ rājānakaśaṅkarakaṇṭheṇeti śivam.*

Since the scribe thus identifies himself as Rājānaka Śaṅkarakaṇṭha, the manuscript cannot be later than the end of the 17th century,[199] as this character was in all likelihood the author of a *Bhairavastotra*[200] and father of Rājānaka Ratnakaṇṭha,[201] a renowned Śaiva author who must have been active around 1680[202] and who presents himself in his works as the son of Rājānaka Śaṅkarakaṇṭha.[203]

---

[198] It is also found at the end of S15 (see below).

[199] Cf. the fairly recent, hand-written Sanskrit note in Nāgarī script attached to the beginning of the manuscript, which specifies that the person who copied it, namely Śaṅkarakaṇṭha, "lived in Kashmir during the reign of Shah Jahan" (*śāhajahānarājye kāśmīreṣu jīvitavān āsīt*), and adds that "there is no other manuscript older than this manuscript" (*prater asyā* [sic] *prācīnā nānyā kācana pratir vidyate*), by which is probably meant that the library contains no older manuscript of the ĪPV.

[200] See SANDERSON 2007a, p. 397, fn. 555.

[201] I thank Alexis Sanderson for first drawing my attention to the fact that a Rājānaka Śaṅkarakaṇṭha known to him "as the author of a *Bhairavastotra* transmitted in some manuscripts of the *Kalādīkṣāpaddhati* was the father of the well-known scholar Rājānaka Ratnakaṇṭha, who wrote his commentary on the *Stutikusumāñjali* of Jagaddhara according to its initial and final verses (which also tell us that Śaṅkarakaṇṭha was his father) from Śaka 1602 [AD 1680] to Vikrama 1738 [AD 1681] during the reign of Aurangzeb (*avaraṅgamahīpāle kṛtsnāṃ śāsati medinīm*). So the date proposed on the slip may well be right." (Personal written communication, 2008.) The "slip" referred to here is the hand-written note (see above, fn. 199) according to which Śaṅkarakaṇṭha lived during Shah Jahan's reign.

[202] On Ratnakaṇṭha, his dates and works, and the name of his father, see HANNEDER, JAGER & SANDERSON 2013, pp. 12–20.

[203] Ratnakaṇṭha, who was famous not only for composing works of his own, but also for his impressive abilities as a manuscript copyist, was until recently believed to have been the master of Bhāskarakaṇṭha, who has authored a commentary (the *Bhāskarī*) on Abhinavagupta's ĪPV (see e.g. HANNEDER, JAGER & SANDERSON 2013, p. 15). I no longer subscribe to this view, which I had accepted in previous

There are many annotations (often lengthy ones) in several hands. It appears that those containing most *Vivṛti* fragments (in small, rather cursive characters often slightly bent on the right) were not written by the scribe of the main text, but they must have been added quite early in the manuscript's life since they are often entirely illegible when the edges are worn. Several of the numerous *Vivṛti* fragments preserved in this manuscript's margins have already been published (they belong to the parts of the text edited by Raffaele Torella,[204] but also to those on ĪPK 1.3.5,[205] 1.5.4–5,[206] 1.5.6[207] and 1.5.8–9[208]). It also contains many fragments pertaining to chapter 2.1.

### S5

> Srinagar: Oriental Research Library, no. 1212.4, "*Īśvarapratyabhijñāvimarśinī*" (according to the library catalogue; the slip of the National Mission for Manuscripts identifies it as a "*Sāṃkhyatattvakaumudī* by Vācaspati Miśra"—Abhinavagupta's text is in fact copied after the latter). Paper, Śāradā script. 203 numbered folios for the ĪPV (with, on average, 12 lines per page and 18 characters per line). The written lines run parallel to the narrower side of the folios. A1 is a photocopy of it. Photographed by the National Mission for Manuscripts.

S5 is a composite manuscript made of texts copied by different hands; the ĪPV follows an incomplete *Sāṃkhyatattvakaumudī* (which does not seem to have been used by S.A. Srinivasan for his 1967 edition), a *Mundakopaniṣaddīpikā* and a *Vairāgyaśataka*. The ĪPV is on an off-white paper, with

---

publications (RATIÉ 2007a, p. 167, and RATIÉ 2018b, p. 327), since JAGER 2018, pp. 11–13, has shown that the Sanskrit text from which this information was taken had been thus far misinterpreted: in fact Ratnakaṇṭha was not Bhāskarakaṇṭha's teacher, but the teacher of his grandfather Vaiḍūryakaṇṭha and of his teacher Kaulanarottama.

[204] See RATIÉ 2016a, pp. 223–224.

[205] See RATIÉ 2016b.

[206] See RATIÉ 2016a, pp. 236 ff.

[207] See RATIÉ 2020.

[208] See Ibid.

verses highlighted in yellow. A1 (a "photo print" of Abhinavagupta's ĪPV wrongly described as an ĪPVV and preserved in Allahabad, Ganganatha Jha Kendriya Sanskrit Vidyapeetha, no. 1212) is but a photocopy of this manuscript preserved in Srinagar.

After the verses found at the end of the KSTS edition, there is a rather lengthy colophon (f. 203a), but the latter was evidently copied from a previous manuscript since the scribe indicates lacunae with dots in many instances. It shows that S5 is related with both D2 and S1, since it first includes (with several scribal mistakes and lacunae) the verse quoted in the final colophon of D2 and S1 and presented as belonging to a scribe named Bhogānanda who "first" copied the text:

> *yato likhi . . . pūrvaṃ tatrāyaṃ ślokaḥ* ‖ *śrīmatsomānanda-vaṃśo llikhad* [sic] *drāg laghvīm etāṃ pratyabhijñāvivṛttim* [sic] | *bhogānando bālabhāve hy anantaḥ* [sic] *saṃvādinyā* [sic] *devadevyāḥ* [sic] *niyuktaḥ* ‖

It then goes on with a text similar to that found in S1, i.e. by quoting a second verse by a certain Rāmānanda, presented as having copied the text from Bhogānanda's manuscript:

> *tato likhitā yena tasyāyaṃ ślokaḥ* ‖ *saṃvicchaktyā jñātasad-bindunādā nityaṃ śambho bhairavetyāptanādāḥ antarvāsi-hṛtsarojāṅkapādāḥ śrīmadrāmānandapādāḥ jayanti* ‖

It then adds (again, with many signs indicating lacunae):

> *. . . prati*[209] *śrīmacchaṅkarabhaṭṭārakasya śloko 'yam* ‖ *saṃ-vittattvānandabhūmau niṣaṇṇā nityaṃ śaive*[210] *tantrasāreṣu gītāḥ prādurbhū . . . vagaurīprasādāḥ śrīmadvīrāḥ śaṅkarā-khyāḥ jayantu* ‖ *śrīmacchrīmahāmaheśvarācāryavaryapu-ṇyapādāravindaśrīmacchrīvidyāpārijātanūtanasvāmī śrī-śaṅkarācāryavaryavicitritā vijñeyeśvarapratyabhijñety om* | *bhadraṃ bhavatu lekhakapāṭhakayoḥ* ‖

The colophon thus gives us a third verse by a certain Master Śaṅkara (*śrī-macchaṅkarabhaṭṭāraka*, *śrīśaṅkarācāryavarya*), who then proceeds to explicitly identify himself as the author of the new copy; and given the peculiar flourish adorning his name (he is said to be "a wish-granting tree? of

---

[209] Probably for *saṃprati*.

[210] Sic.

the venerable Śrīvidyā," *śrīmacchrīvidyāpārijāta*), it is very likely that he was the father of Bhaṭṭa Sundara/Sundarīdāsa/Bhaṭṭāraka Sundara, the author of a hitherto unpublished commentary (*Kaumudī*) on the ĪPK who uses the very same words to describe his father Śaṅkara (*śrīmacchrīvidyāpārijātaśrīmatśrīśaṅkarācāryavarya*).[211] It should be kept in mind, however, that S5 was certainly not copied by this Śaṅkara himself, since there are indications of lacunae in the verse ascribed to him as well as in its introduction: S5 had to be copied (directly or not) from the manuscript copied by Śaṅkara. The copyist of S2 (dated 1773 CE) also bears the name Śaṅkara,[212] but the colophon in S2 does not contain the verse quoted here, so that it cannot be assumed to be S5's antigraph.

The *Vivṛti* passages contained in the margins of this manuscript that have been published to date pertain to ĪPK 1.3.5;[213] I could only spot in it one *Vivṛti* sentence from chapter 2.1.

### S9

> Srinagar: Oriental Research Library, no. 1161, "*Īśvarapratyabhijñāvimarśinī.*" Paper, Śāradā script. 157 numbered folios (with, on average, 10 lines per page and 40 characters per line). The written lines run parallel to the wider side of the folios. Photographed by the National Mission for Manuscripts.

Some of this manuscript's annotations were studied in FORMIGATTI 2011 (Camillo Formigatti did not notice at the time that they contain some *Vivṛti* fragments). The general features of the manuscript are described ibid., pp. 40–41, under siglum Ś7. Camillo Formigatti remarks in particular that the manuscript was written "on two different types of paper" and in two different hands. Indeed, S9 appears to be made of two different manuscripts, the first of which is on darker paper and has the verses written in red ink

---

[211] See RATIÉ 2018b, p. 328.

[212] So does S15, but as explained below, it seems probable that the latter was copied from S2.

[213] See RATIÉ 2016b.

(whereas in the second they are merely rubricated); the second one starts on f. 15b and ends on f. 28a.

The beginning reads as follows before the ĪPV's initial verse:

*oṃ namaḥ śivāya saśivāya* || *oṃ gaṇādhipataye namaḥ* ||

At the end, after the verses printed at the end of the KSTS edition, Camillo Formigatti reads *iti śiv*[?] and assumes that one last folio might be lacking since there is no colophon and the last word seems incomplete.[214] It is doubtful, however, whether the last word is incomplete: the last sign, which Camillo Formigatti indicates with "[?]," looks like a small *m* above which is a long leftward loop; now, the same peculiar sign is also found in S2, at the end of the final word *bhadram* (f. 78b), and in the latter case it is quite clear that no folio is lacking beyond 78b. I therefore assume that this sign stands for a final *m*, and that S9 is in fact complete.

Regarding S9's margins, Camillo Formigatti further notes:

> There are at least two sets of marginal and interlinear annotations written in Śāradā in the form of long scholia on the margins and short glosses (mostly interlinear). The first set of annotations seems to have been written by the scribe, while the second one has been written by a second hand, after the reparation of the margins, since on some folios [...] the annotations have been written on the lamination used for the reparation. Moreover, some annotations written by the first hand have been covered by the lamination [...]. A very small number of glosses have been written with a violet ballpen and very few with blue crayon.[215]

The hitherto published *Vivṛti* passages found in this manuscript pertain to ĪPK 1.3.5.[216] I could only spot in it one *Vivṛti* sentence belonging to chapter 2.1, which is part of a relatively early set of annotations (it was partly covered by the lamination).

[214] See FORMIGATTI 2011, p. 41, fn. 77.

[215] FORMIGATTI 2011, p. 41.

[216] See RATIÉ 2016b.

**S10**

Srinagar: Oriental Research Library, no. 1477, "*Īśvarapratyabhijñāvimarśinī.*" Paper, Śāradā script. 173 numbered folios (with, on average, 8 lines per page and 36 characters per line). Folios 142 to 167 are missing; the manuscript was bound with the folio order inverted (it starts with the last folio and ends with the first). The written lines run parallel to the wider side of the folios. Photographed by the National Mission for Manuscripts.

The verses are rubricated in red. On the first folio, the ĪPV begins immediately after the following:

> *oṃ svasti oṃ śrīgaṇeśāya namaḥ oṃ namaḥ śivāya* || *oṃ namaḥ sarasvatyai* || *oṃ śrīdevyai namaḥ* || *śrīr astu oṃ*

On the last folio, after the final verses printed in the KSTS edition, one reads:

> *samāpteyaṃ pratyabhijñāyāṃ sūtrārthavimarśinīvṛttiḥ kṛtis trinayanacaraṇacintanalabdhaprasiddheḥ śrīmadācāryābhinavaguptasyeti śubham.*

There are many annotations in smaller characters, most of them in a handwriting similar to that of the main text; a few, however, display a very different handwriting (in black ink too). Besides, in the top margin of the first folio, the first ĪPK was copied in violet ink with a fairly recent Śāradā handwriting.

The annotations contain an important number of *Vivṛti* fragments, some of which (on ĪPK 1.7.10–11) have already been edited;[217] among these fragments are parts of the *Vivṛti* on the first four verses of chapter 2.1.

**S15**

Srinagar: Oriental Research Library, no. 787, "*Īśvarapratyabhijñāvimarśinī.*" Paper, Śāradā script. 166 numbered folios (with, on average, 16 lines per page and 20 characters per line). The written lines run parallel to the narrower side

[217] See RATIÉ forthcoming a.

of the folios. Photographed by the National Mission for Manuscripts.

There are several folios at the beginning that seem to have different origins. On the first, unnumbered one (right side) are pasted two images; the lower one is, quite unexpectedly, an image of the Puri Jagannātha; the one above it is the shape of an *oṃ*[218] within which several deities are depicted.[219] The next folio (right side) has a quotation of *Svacchandatantra* 4.238–239 in a rather awkward handwriting (the same hand is responsible for a few marginal annotations in the manuscript itself). On the second, unnumbered folio (left side) is a quotation from the AS replete with mistakes;[220] on the right page is a quotation from the *Tattvakaumudī* (henceforth TK).[221] On the third unnumbered folio (right side) are the words *oṃ śrīsarasvatyai namaḥ*, followed by a verse from Ānandavardhana's *Devīśataka*.[222] The next

[218] Cf. the somewhat similar image (used as the cover illustration for D'INTINO & POLLOCK eds. 2018) found in a 1793 *Bhāgavatapurāṇa* manuscript preserved at the Bibliothèque Nationale de France (Sanskrit No. 477), or the almost identical one in the 1795 *Mahābhārata* manuscript preserved in the Special Collections at the University of Edinburgh (No. Or 510):
https://commons.wikimedia.org/wiki/File:Brahma,_Vishnu,_and_Shiva_within_an_OM,_in_a_Mahabharata_manuscript_from_1795.jpg.
See also the description of a *Bhāgavatapurāṇa* at the British Library (No. 16624) in LOSTY 1982. I am also thankful to Luther Obrock for bringing to my attention, during a presentation in a workshop on Śāradā held in Hamburg (6–7/03/2020), a composite, richly illustrated Śāradā manuscript preserved at McGill University (Poleman No. 930) that contains a composition even more similar to the one in S15.

[219] Namely, from top to bottom (as far as can be seen from the scan at my disposal): a Śaiva form that could be an *ardhanārīśvara*, a reclining Śiva in ascetic garb, a reclining Brahmā, a sitting Viṣṇu, and a fifth, standing figure with a red complexion that seems to be another Śaiva form.

[220] *tvaṃ candrikā* śaśini* tigmarucau rucis tvaṃ tvaṃ cetanāsi puruṣe pavane balaṃ tvam* | tvaṃ svādutāsi* salile* śikhini tvam* ūṣmā niḥsāram eva nikhilaṃ tvadṛte* yadi syāt* || [**candrikā* AS; *candrakā* S15. **śaśini* AS; *śiṣini* S15. **balaṃ tvam* AS; *bhalatvam* S15. **svādutāsi* AS; *svādhitāsi* S15. **salile* AS; *salini* S15. **tvam* AS; *tam* S15. **tvadṛte* AS; *tadṛte* S15.]

[221] TK on *Sāṃkhyakārikā* (henceforth SK) 8, pp. 94–96 (from *tatra pūrvasmin...* to *udbhāvanīyam*).

[222] *Devīśataka* 50: *sara svatiprasādaṃ me sthitiṃ cittasarasvati | sarasvati kuru kṣetrakurukṣetrasarasvati* ||

unnumbered folio is blank. The following one is numbered 1 (with the abbreviation *śrī ī pra*) and heavily annotated. Both the main text and the marginal annotations are framed with red lines. The main text is the beginning of the ĪPV, preceded by *oṃ namah paramaśivāya*. The next folio (left side) is made on the same model but the text stops abruptly after ĪPK 1.1.1. The paper of the right page is different (of a much lighter shade), with no red frame, the characters are smaller (it seems to me, however, that they are in the same hand, but some of the annotations are certainly in a different hand). The text after *oṃ namaḥ śivāya* spreads on the next (left) page and appears to be the fragment of a commentary on the first verse of the ĪPV. The right page is blank, and then only (on the 17th page from the beginning) is the text of the ĪPV given in full from its first words. The long annotation in the margins of the latter page happens to be the same text of the commentary copied on the previous two pages; besides, some red frames recur here and there (for instance on f. 24b): it looks like the same person copied twice the beginning of the ĪPV (once with the red frame, once without).

On folio 1a (among numbered folios, starting from the second beginning), the first words of the manuscripts are the following:

> *oṃ namaḥ śivāya* || *oṃ śrīgaṇeśaṃ guruṃ natvā śrīmacchaṅkarasvāminā īśvarapratyabhijñeyaṃ*

After these, and before the ĪPV starts (preceded by *oṃ*), a few words were purposefully deleted, but one can still discern the following:

> *kṛpālvarthaṃ vicitryate.*

This is identical with the words found at the beginning of S2, and on the manuscript's data slip of the National Mission for Manuscripts, someone has written "18th Century Between Copyist." Since the same hand appears to have written in a red ballpen the indication "1773—AD Between" on the National Mission for Manuscripts data slip of S2, I assume that this person thought that S2 (dated 1773 CE thanks to its colophon, as mentioned above) and S15 had been written by the same scribe. It is striking, however, that the last words were deleted in S15; most of all, the two handwritings are very different. I therefore assume that S15 was copied from S2, the scribe of S15 having copied S2's initial colophon without realizing at first what it was (although I cannot explain why then the entire colophon was not deleted).

The manuscript ends on f. 177b. The page has two frames in red ink, the first one seemingly designed to separate the main text from marginal annotations, the second one to mark the limit of the latter. In the inner frame, after the final verses found in the KSTS edition, one reads:

> *sampūrṇeyaṃ pratyabhijñāsūtravimarśinī* ‖ ‖ *iti śrīmadācāryābhinavaguptaviracitā pratyabhijñāsūtravimarśinī samāptā* ‖ ‖

Then follows the fifth introductory verse of the ĪPVV (also found in S3 after the final colophon). In the outer frame (below and then vertically, on the right side), another verse by Abhinavagupta is quoted,[223] but there are no indications regarding the identity of the scribe or the circumstances in which the manuscript was copied.

The manuscript (which I had not consulted yet when I drew a list of annotated ĪPV manuscripts bearing *Vivṛti* fragments in RATIÉ 2016b) contains many important fragments. In particular, it is the only ĪPV manuscript of my knowledge that contains the whole beginning of the *Vivṛti*'s chapter 2.1 up to the middle of the commentary on 2.1.3. It also has the fragments on ĪPK 1.3.5 edited in RATIÉ 2016b (f. 28a), the fragment on ĪPK 1.5.4–5 edited in RATIÉ 2016a (f. 86b), the fragment on ĪPK 1.5.6 edited in RATIÉ 2020 (f. 87a), the fragments on ĪPK 1.5.8–9 edited ibid. (f. 50a), as well as (preceded by *oṃ*, ff. 86b–87a) the fragment on chapter 1.8 that was edited in

[223] This verse appears in ĪPVV, vol. II, p. 137 with a minor variant, and must belong to one of Abhinavagupta's *stotra*s (he introduces it, ibid., p. 136, with the words *yan mayā stutam*) but I do not know its source: *ātmany eva na māmi nāma visaradromāñcarekhāṅkurakrāntyā kiṃ ca davīyasīr* api diśo jānāmi rundhe haṭhāt* | *yan me bhairava bhairaveti raṭato hṛdgranthivisphoṭanatruṭyatpāṭavapāśapañjarabharaḥ kāyo 'pi mokṣāyate* ‖ [**kiṃ ca davīyasīr* S15; *kiṃcid aṇīyasīr* ĪPVV.] It is quoted and commented upon by the eighteenth-century author Śivopādhyāya/Śivasvāmin Upādhyāya (on his date see SANDERSON 2007a, pp. 422–423) in his *Vijñānabhairavavivṛti*, pp. 114–115. Śivopādhyāya gives the reading *kāyo 'py anantāyate*, but is aware of an alternative reading (ibid., p. 115: *kāyo 'pi mokṣāyata iti pāṭhāntaram*). It seems likely, however, that he only knows the verse from the ĪPVV, since it is the only work of Abhinavagupta's that he mentions in this respect (ibid.: *etat tu vivṛtivimarśinyām abhinavaguptapādair darśitam*), immediately after quoting the ĪPVV sentence (vol. II, p. 136, from *samastatādātmyabhāvanayā* on) that precedes the introduction of the verse.

RATIÉ 2017a. However, it does not appear to contain the fragment on 1.7.10 that is found in S12 and (to a lesser extent) J11.

### SOAS

> London: School of Oriental and African Studies Library, no. 207 in DOGRA 1978/no. 44255, "*Pratyabhijñā-sūtra* with *Sūtrārthavimarśinī*." Paper, Śāradā script. 377 numbered folios (with, on average, 11 lines per page and 13 characters per line). The written lines run parallel to the narrower side of the folios. Photographed (in black and white) by the Library of SOAS at my request.

The manuscript begins with the following words:

> *śrīgaṇeśāya namaḥ* ‖ *oṃ namaḥ śivāya* ‖

It then provides the text of the ĪPK alone until f. 13a, after which the foliation starts afresh, and this time the ĪPK are accompanied by Abhinavagupta's ĪPV, preceded by the following words:

> *oṃ namaḥ śivāya* ‖ *namo gaṇanāthāya oṃ*

At the end, on f. 376b, after the final verses edited in the KSTS edition, one reads:[224]

> *samāpteyaṃ pratyabhijñāyāṃ sūtrārthavimarśinīvṛttiḥ. kṛtis trinayanacaraṇacintanalabdhaprasiddheḥ śrīmadācāryābhinavaguptasyetiśivam* ‖ *lipir iyaṃ kuberagaṇeśasyeti.*

According to R.C. Dogra, the manuscript is from the "19th century;"[225] since there is no date in the colophon, but only a mention of what appears to be the scribe's name (Kuberagaṇeśa),[226] I assume that this is a mere guess

---

[224] On the next and final folio (377a) is a numbered list of the titles of chapters in the ĪPV preceded by the words *oṃ pratyabhijñāsūtravimarśinyām āhnikāni*.

[225] DOGRA 1978, p. 32.

[226] According to Alexis Sanderson (personal communication, 05/01/2019), "The Kubera element ought to be the *jāti* name (Kshm. *kram*). I guess that it is a sanskritized form of the Kram name Khobri that is among those of the priestly, Bācbaṭ, division of the Kashmirian brahmins listed in the Census of 1891, p. 139, number 7."

on the basis of the manuscript's general appearance. The only information that the library of SOAS could give me regarding this manuscript's inclusion in their South Asian collection is that it was donated in November 1942 by R.C. Reid as part as the D.D. Dickson collection.[227] The manuscript is replete with annotations and several fragments contained in its margins (which belong to parts of the text edited by Raffaele Torella,[228] but also to ĪPK 1.5.6 and 1.5.8–9[229]) have already been published; it bears many *Vivṛti* quotations pertaining to chapter 2.1.

## 10. Description of the *Vṛtti* annotated manuscripts used for this edition

### L2

> Diplomatic transcription by Yohei Kawajiri (KAWAJIRI 20016a, KAWAJIRI 2016b and KAWAJIRI forthcoming) of the following manuscript, to which I have not had direct access: Lucknow: Akhila Bharatiya Sanskrit Parishad, no. 4408. Paper, Nāgarī script.

Yohei Kawajiri's articles provide little information about the manuscript itself (they mention that it is written in Nāgarī and annotated). They offer a diplomatic transcription of some of the marginal annotations, without any translation or explanation their content. In KAWAJIRI 2016a, despite the article's title ("New Fragments of the *Īśvarapratyabhijñā-vivṛti*"), the annotations that may be identified as new fragments from the *Vivṛti* are scant (they are found, under the heading "New Fragments," pp. 93–99, but in fact a number of these very brief quotations are obviously not from the *Vivṛti*, as the author himself acknowledges). KAWAJIRI 2016b and KAWAJIRI forthcoming are both much richer in *Vivṛti* fragments; KAWAJIRI 2016b notably contains a number of fragments pertaining to chapter 2.1.

[227] Answer to my request via email, 25/01/2012, by Edward Hood, Archivist at the SOAS Library.

[228] See RATIÉ 2016a, p. 223–224, fn. 5 and 7.

[229] See RATIÉ 2020.

**S19**

> Srinagar: Oriental Research Library, no. 824 (according to the Library catalogue; the slip of the National Mission for Manuscripts erroneously gives 823 as the accession no.), "*Īśvarapratyabhijñākārikā*" (according to the Library catalogue; according to the slip of the National Mission for Manuscripts, it is "I. *Utpalastotrāvalī*; II. *Bhairavānukaraṇa-stotra*").[230] Paper, Śāradā script. 48 numbered folios (with, on average, 11 lines per page and 16 characters per line). The written lines run parallel to the narrower side of the folios. Photographed by the National Mission for Manuscripts.

S19 has already been described in TORELLA 2002, pp. l–li, under siglum Ṅ. The description specifies in particular that the manuscript, "measuring cm. 18,7x14,1," now lacks its first page, so that it starts with °*heśvare* | *ajaḍātmā*... (i.e. ĪPK 1.1.2), and that it ends as follows:

> *samāpteyaṃ pratyabhijñā. śubham astu sarvajagatām.*

Raffaele Torella also makes the following remarks:

> It has been profusely annotated by a different hand with single glosses or long passages (mostly drawn from the ĪPV) between the lines and often entirely covering the margins... Between ff. 35 and 40 there are a few pages without glosses. A passage based on the ĪPV is inserted in the text between f.2a, l. 8 and f.2b, l. 6.[231]

Indeed, many of the quotations are from Abhinavagupta's ĪPV; yet S19 also bears numerous *Vivṛti* fragments, including a number of quotations from chapter 2.1.

---

[230] The latter titles correspond to the content of manuscript 823, for which it was mistaken.

[231] TORELLA 2002, p. li.

# CHAPTER 3

# The Philosophical Context: Utpaladeva's Demonstration of the Self and His Absolute Idealism

Before examining the content of Utpaladeva's *Vivṛti*, chapter 2.1, it was thought convenient to provide here a few explanations regarding Utpaladeva's overall goal in writing the treatise to which this chapter belongs, and to briefly outline the two specific points alluded to in the introduction to that chapter (which opens the second part of the treatise) as having been established in the first part, namely: the thesis that the self exists; and the thesis that all objects are but internal forms taken on by consciousness.[232]

## 1. Utpaladeva's goal in the Pratyabhijñā treatise

Somānanda (fl. c. 900–950 CE) has often been presented as the founder of the Pratyabhijñā system. Bühler (probably following the SDS's doxographical account of it)[233] already saw in him its "first promulgator,"[234] and Madhusudhan Kaul, who once characterized Utpaladeva's Pratyabhijñā treatise as "a brief exposition of the *Śivadṛṣṭi*,"[235] seems to have considered that

---

[232] As a result, this chapter inevitably overlaps RATIÉ 2017c, which provides a brief overview of the Pratyabhijñā's main metaphysical tenets; I apologize for the repetitions. For a summary of the treatise's main innovations, one should also consult the important Introduction in TORELLA 2002.

[233] See above, chapter 1, fnn. 19 and 96.

[234] BÜHLER 1877, p. 81.

[235] *Siddhitrayī*, Introduction, p. 6.

Utpaladeva's contribution to Indian philosophy only consisted in "preaching and popularizing the teachings of his preceptor as given in the *Śivadṛṣṭi*."[236] Admittedly, Utpaladeva himself presents the "new path" expounded in his treatise as none other than Somānanda's[237] (he also claims that the truths explained in his treatise are already contained *in nuce* in the Śaiva nondualistic scriptures).[238] Abhinavagupta, for his part, describes Utpaladeva's work as a mere "reflection" (*pratibimbaka*)[239] of Somānanda's; and the ŚD, on which Utpaladeva has authored a commentary, undeniably had an immense impact on Utpaladeva's thought. However, not to mention that Somānanda's method is far less systematic than Utpaladeva's, a number of crucial concepts—among which the very notion of recognition that has given its name to the system—are not found in the ŚD,[240] and Somānanda is certainly more accurately described as Utpaladeva's most influential precursor than as the Pratyabhijñā system's founder.

Utpaladeva's undertaking arguably constitutes a small revolution within the Śaiva tradition insofar as he chooses to avoid all dogmatic, solely scripturally-based assertions; instead, he engages in a philosophical dialogue with all the other Indian currents of thought (whether Hindu or Buddhist) of any importance at the time.[241] This does not mean that Utpaladeva would cease to be a Śaiva or that he would question the authority of the Śaiva sacred texts: his main goal when entering the philosophical arena is to demonstrate the superiority of Śaiva nondualism over all its religious rivals. But his interlocutors reject the Śaiva scriptures while admitting the validity of other scriptural sources (the orthodox Hindus' Veda, the Buddhists' *sūtra*s,

---

[236] ĪPVV, Introduction, vol. I, p. iii.

[237] See ĪPK 4.16ab: *iti prakaṭito mayā sughaṭa eṣa mārgo navo mahāgurubhir ucyate sma śivadṛṣṭiśāstre yathā* | "I have thus shown this new, easy path as it was described by my great master in the treatise [entitled] *Śivadṛṣṭi*."

[238] See RATIÉ 2011a, p. 9, fn. 15 and RATIÉ 2013, p. 382, fn. 2.

[239] ĪPV, vol. I, p. 7.

[240] See TORELLA 2002, p. xx; RATIÉ 2011a, pp. 3–4, fn. 3.

[241] In this regard Utpaladeva is indebted not only to Somānanda but also to Sadyojyotis (c. 675–725 CE), who belongs to the Śaiva dualistic tradition of the Śaivasiddhānta. On this influence see RATIÉ 2016c. In both cases, however, Utpaladeva's endeavour appears far more systematic and encompassing than that of his predecessors.

etc.); discussing with them therefore requires having recourse to means of knowledge that, contrary to scripture, are universally acknowledged—that is, perception (or immediate experience) and inference. Utpaladeva thus describes his "new path" as a phenomenological and dialectical method capable *by itself* (i.e. without any recourse to scripture)[242] of making the reader realize his/her identity with the highest God, namely Śiva, understood as a single, all-powerful and all-encompassing consciousness that creates the world by merely imagining it. According to Utpaladeva, liberation from the beginningless cycle of rebirths (*saṃsāra*)—which is also the beginningless cycle of pain—is nothing but this blissful "recognition" (*pratyabhijñā*) of oneself as "the Lord" (*īśvara*), i.e. Śiva. This realization can be achieved by simply drawing attention to our most immediate experiences, that is, through a close examination of our various cognitive events and through the critical investigation of all the theories claiming to interpret these experiences. His method is therefore as deeply phenomenological as it is dialectical, and both aspects are equally vital to the system.[243]

Although Utpaladeva's ultimate goal is to defend the Śaiva nondualistic faith, his systematically polemical approach has a deep impact on the meaning of the metaphysical principles that he inherits from his religious tradition: in this constant dialogue with other schools of thought, he transforms the Śaiva nondualistic dogmas into concepts rationally justified and embedded in the complex structure of a philosophical system.

---

[242] Admittedly, one of the four parts of Utpaladeva's treatise, the "Part on Scriptures" (*Āgamādhikāra*), deals with notions found in Śaiva scriptural sources. However, this part only comes *after* the (much lengthier) sections of the treatise where Utpaladeva claims to establish the truth by relying solely on reason and experience: the *Āgamādhikāra* merely shows a posteriori that the results of Utpaladeva's demonstrations are compatible with the Śaiva scriptural teachings. See TORELLA 2002, p. xxx, and RATIÉ 2011a, p. 12. It has nonetheless been noted that even within the first two sections of the treatise, the "hermeneutical focus" is not "altogether invisible," particularly in ĪPK 1.5.12–14: see SANDERSON 2005, pp. 128–130. However, as pointed out in RATIÉ 2011a, p. 526, in this case too, Utpaladeva only mentions scriptural sources so as to show that what he has *already* established through other means also happens to be supported by the Śaiva scriptures.

[243] On these two aspects of Utpaladeva's method, see RATIÉ 2011a, pp. 7–10 and 727–728.

## 2. Utpaladeva's demonstration of the existence of the self (*ātman*)

As the introduction of the *Vivṛti* chapter on which the present work focuses reminds the reader, the first part (*adhikāra*) of the treatise is devoted to the power of knowledge (*jñānaśakti*). There, as this introduction further specifies, Utpaladeva endeavours to prove that this power, "the substratum and existence of which had [first] been questioned [by the Buddhist opponent], exists continuously in all knowing subjects" by showing that the manifesting entity (*prakāśa*) that is consciousness has a "unity" that exists "inside the self-awareness" (*svasaṃvedana*) of all cognitions. The "substratum" alluded to here is the self (*ātman*) understood as the enduring substance existing within every human being and guaranteeing his or her permanence; for in the first part of the treatise, Utpaladeva takes part in the controversy over its existence—a well-known pan-Indian debate that has already been raging for centuries by the time of the Pratyabhijñā treatise's composition.[244]

This notion of self is of great importance to Brahmanical schools, in particular because, as pointed out by the Mīmāṃsā, the injunctions to sacrifice found in the Veda are nonsensical if the agent of the sacrifice is not a lasting entity and as a consequence cannot enjoy later (i.e. mostly in some other life) the positive results that must ensue from the sacrifice.[245] Other Hindu schools, while not necessarily opposing this mainly[246] ritualistic point of view, rather seek liberation through gnosis: they consider that the cause of all pain lies in our mistaking the self for an entity such as the body, which, being subjected to change, is bound to perish, so that escaping from *saṃsāra* can only be the result of a knowledge discriminating between the self and what does not endure in us. Their Buddhists opponents, on the other hand, uphold the thesis of universal momentariness and contend that we are mistaken in believing that we, as individual subjects, have some kind of

[244] What follows is only a very cursory summary of Utpaladeva's position in this debate; for a detailed analysis see RATIÉ 2011a.

[245] See RATIÉ 2014a, pp. 14–22.

[246] Recent studies have shown that contrary to what is usually assumed, for the Mīmāṃsaka Kumārila Bhaṭṭa, knowing the self is not only useful in that it encourages to perform rites, and it may constitute an independent path towards liberation. On these little known "Vedāntic" aspects of Kumārila's work (and the difficulty of interpreting them) see e.g. MESQUITA 1994, TABER 2007 and YOSHIMIZU 2007.

continuous existence despite the inevitable changes affecting us. According to them, this erroneous conviction is the very root of existential pain, while understanding and cultivating the thought that there is no self (*nairātmya*) is the only "antidote" capable of counteracting the catastrophic effects of the belief in the self.

Utpaladeva sides with the Brahmanical schools in this controversy, defending the existence of the *ātman* against various Buddhists assaults. While claiming to do so, however, he also appropriates many an idea formulated in the first place by his Buddhist opponents.[247] And it is not only his relationship with the Buddhists that turns out to be more complex than it looks at first sight. The religious current to which he belongs systematically reverses the socio-religious values of purity and impurity that pervade the Brahmanical world, notably by presenting activities usually considered as utterly impure (the consumption of meat or alcohol, certain sexual practices, etc.) as a potential path towards liberation.[248] Utpaladeva adopts a similar strategy on the philosophical battlefield. On the one hand, he places at the very center of his system the notion of self-recognition—an explicit borrowing from the Mīmāṃsakas:[249] according to Śabara[250] and most of all Kumārila,[251] what proves the existence of the self is precisely the fact that we are able to *recognize* ourselves as the same person throughout time. On the other hand, in the very title of his work Utpaladeva places the term *īśvara*, "Lord," next to the word "recognition": according to him, recognizing oneself means *realizing that we are in fact the creator god himself*—and this is in glaring contradiction with Kumārila's fierce atheism.[252] Utpaladeva thus appropriates the conceptual core of Brahmanism (i.e., the

---

[247] See e.g. TORELLA 1992 and RATIÉ 2010a.

[248] See e.g. SANDERSON 1985 and SANDERSON 1995, pp. 78–87.

[249] See RATIÉ 2011, pp. 60–62 and 254–257, and RATIÉ 2014a, pp. 210–218.

[250] See BIARDEAU 1968.

[251] See BHATT 1989, chapter 12; TABER 1990; and RATIÉ 2014a.

[252] By atheism is only meant here the refusal to admit a creator god. On Kumārila's arguments in this respect see e.g. KRASSER 1999. Naiyāyika authors have elaborated various strategies to defend God's cosmic agency against Kumārila's critique: see e.g. CHEMPARATHY 1972 and KRASSER 2002. On Utpaladeva's response to Kumārila's arguments see TABER 1986 and RATIÉ 2016c.

doctrine of the self as what we recognize every time we say and think "I") but subverts it by completely transforming its metaphysical background:[253] the Mīmāṃsakas' belief in an objective world of multiple substances existing independently of consciousness, as well as their denial of the existence of a God creating or organizing the universe, are replaced with the thesis that all subjects and objects are ultimately nothing but God, that is, the universal consciousness.

What enables Utpaladeva to achieve this spectacular reversal of the Mīmāṃsakas' values is the metamorphosis to which he subjects the Brahmanical notion of self. Refusing to define it as a static substance capable of bearing transitory qualities, he rather presents it as a pure dynamism: according to the Śaiva, the self is nothing but the absolute freedom (*svātantrya*) that constitutes the essence of consciousness. The term *svātantrya* primarily designates the property of that which is autonomous, or exists and acts by itself, without requiring any external prompting or determination (contrary to what is heteronomous, *paratantra*). But translations such as "autonomy" or "independence" fail to grasp the entire range of meaning of the Sanskrit word in this context, because *svātantrya* designates, more than a mere absence of external influence, a positive power that nothing can hinder (the Śaivas often use it as an equivalent of terms such as *aiśvarya*, "sovereignty"), and also because—at least in Śaiva nondualistic literature—it has strong aesthetic connotations: *svātantrya* is the playfulness and aesthetic delight experienced in any artistic process, but also in any act of imagination.

In what way is this notion of *svātantrya* a satisfactory answer to the Buddhist denial of the self's existence? The Hindu upholders of the self belong to different traditions (Mīmāṃsā, Nyāya and Vaiśeṣika, but also currents that depart in a number of ways from Vedic orthodoxy: Sāṃkhya, Yoga and Vedānta). These traditions defend different theses as regards the nature of the *ātman*—for example, they disagree as to whether the self is conscious by nature (i.e. including in the liberated state) or not. They do agree, however, that the self is the substratum of the various ordinary conscious states, and must therefore be some kind of unchanging substance. And according

[253] This transformation also affects the very definition of self-recognition—on the divergences between Kumārila and Utpaladeva in this regard see RATIÉ 2011a, pp. 257–261.

to Utpaladeva, this is precisely why their defense of the self is doomed to succumb to the Buddhist attacks. For if the self cannot bear any change without becoming other, it cannot be a knower: as already pointed out by Dignāga, just as any agent, a knower must be somehow affected by the act of knowing that he or she performs—which is impossible in the case of a strictly unchanging entity; so the self can never be conscious.[254] Utpaladeva, while emphasizing that the various Brahmanical traditions cannot resist this Buddhist critique, sets out to show that the Buddhist argument only holds if the self's existence is understood in accordance with the way insentient things are. For objects only exist while conforming to a certain limited form that they have not chosen or produced and that characterizes them: a square ceases to be a square as soon as it no longer has four sides. But the very essence of consciousness lies in the fact that its existence is not determined by such a limited essence—or, according to a paradox highlighted by Abhinavagupta, the self (*ātman*) is characterized by the freedom not to remain merely oneself (*ātman*).[255] Thus we all know through immediate experience that in imagination, consciousness can take on countless forms at will. When we imagine something such as an elephant, our consciousness presents itself as a specific object distinct from consciousness, since we apprehend the imaginary object as an object, that is to say, an entity grasped as "this," whereas we apprehend consciousness itself as "I." But despite this distinction, we remain aware that the imagined elephant is *only imagined*—we know that in fact the elephant is only an aspect taken on by our consciousnes. Yet the imagining consciousness does not merely *become* the imagined elephant, nor does it *cease to exist* as a consciousness

---

[254] PS 1.44: *buddhijanmani puṃsaś ca vikṛtir yady anityatā* | *athāvikṛtir ātmāyaṃ pramāteti na yujyate* || "And if the person undergoes a modification when a cognition arises, he is impermanent; but if he does not undergo any modification, [stating] that the self is a knower is incorrect." On this argument see e.g. HATTORI 1968, pp. 69 and 171–172.

[255] See ĪPV, vol. I, 202, where the freedom (*svātantrya*) of consciousness is defined as "the fact of not just resting in [a state of] being merely oneself, contrary to insentient [objects]" (*ātmamātratāyām eva jaḍavad aviśrāntatvam*). See also ibid., p. 212, where freedom is said to be "the existence as the Great Lord" (*māheśvarya*) "because it differs from [the way in which] insentient [entities] exist while having a single, delimited nature" (*pariniṣṭhitaikarūpajaḍabhāvavailakṣaṇyāt*).

when taking on the elephant's form—it simply manifests itself as something distinct from itself. This infinite plasticity of consciousness, or this capacity to manifest itself in innumerable forms while remaining itself (even though it shows itself in the form of objects, i.e. *as what it is not*) is precisely what the Śaivas call "freedom," and according to them, this freedom transcends the pure momentariness upheld by the Buddhists: contrary to insentient objects, consciousness is capable of changing without perishing.

As pointed out by the Buddhists, however, our experience as conscious beings is not that of a single continuum of consciousness: if we pay attention to our cognitive activity, we must acknowledge that it occurs in the form of a series of heterogeneous, purely momentary cognitive events. But the Śaiva nondualists argue that even this constant experience of momentariness involves an awareness of the profound unity of consciousness. Utpaladeva shows this by appropriating and transforming the classic Naiyāyika and Mīmāṃsaka proofs of the self based on memory[256] and self-recognition.[257] These proofs rest on the assumption that memory could not occur without a permanent substratum of cognitions, and the Buddhist philosophers have developed a solid answer to such a line of argument: we can remember because every perception leaves a residual trace (*saṃskāra*) or an imprint (*vāsanā*) that remains latent in the cognitive series until a similar perception "awakes" the trace and triggers memory; yet the persistence of the latent trace does not require any enduring substratum because each cognition, while being momentary, causally determines the arising of the next cognition in such a way that the next cognition too bears a momentary latent trace.[258]

According to Utpaladeva, however, this explanation fails to account for the most characteristic feature of memory—namely, the fact that remembrance

---

[256] On the Naiyāyika proof of the self based on memory see e.g. OETKE 1988, pp. 254–260 and 345–360, and GANERI 1999. On Utpaladeva's use of the argument of memory see RATIÉ 2006 and TORELLA 2007b. For other proofs of the self adduced by Naiyāyikas (many of which appear in the Pratyabhijñā treatise) see e.g. CHAKRABARTI 1982 and 1992, PREISENDANZ 1994 and GANERI 2000.

[257] See above, fn. 250 and 251.

[258] On the Buddhist refutation of the memory argument see e.g. DUERLINGER 2003, pp. 96–98 and 238–251, and ELTSCHINGER & RATIÉ 2013, pp. 173–186.

is not just about a past object, but rather consists in the awareness of our *experiencing* an object in the past: remembrance is the *subjective* awareness of having perceived, and the Buddhists cannot explain it.[259]

To understand Utpaladeva's reasoning here, we must keep in mind that according to the Buddhist epistemologists, every cognition is aware of itself, or possesses *svasaṃvedana*, "self-awareness":[260] it is not known by becoming the object of a second cognition, but rather, through the most immediate kind of experience—every conscious activity involves the intuitive, prereflexive awareness of being conscious. Utpaladeva, who adopts this Buddhist notion of self-awareness[261] (and alludes to it from the very beginning of the *Vivṛti* chapter studied here), points out that as a consequence we must accept that consciousness *cannot be objectified*. A cognition can never be grasped as an object by another cognition, first of all because we are not aware of our own experiences (whether past or present) as we are aware of objects: we do not know that we are (or were) conscious as we know that there is a pot in front of us, because when aware of ourselves, we do not grasp ourselves as an entity distinct from consciousness (that is, as an apprehended "this" distinct from the apprehending "I").[262]

---

[259] See ĪPK 1.3.1: *satyaṃ kiṃtu smṛtijñānaṃ pūrvānubhavasaṃskṛteḥ | jātam apy ātmaniṣṭhaṃ tan nādyānubhavavedakam* || "[This might be] true; but even if[, as you Buddhists claim,] the memory cognition is produced by the residual trace [left by] the past experience, [since this memory cognition] is confined to itself, it cannot make [us] know the past experience." On Abhinavagupta's explanations see RATIÉ 2011a, pp. 63–65 and 110–112.

[260] On this famous Buddhist notion (interpreted in sometimes strikingly different ways by modern scholars) see e.g. WILLIAMS 1998, ARNOLD 2005, YAO 2005, ARNOLD 2010, KELLNER 2010 and KELLNER 2011b.

[261] See TORELLA 2007c and RATIÉ 2011a, pp. 112–124.

[262] See ĪPK 1.4.4: *naiva hy anubhavo bhāti smṛtau pūrvo 'rthavat pṛthak | prāg anvabhūvam aham ity ātmārohaṇabhāsanāt* || "For the past experience is not manifest in a memory in the same way as an object [is manifest, i.e.] separately [from the subject], since [when we remember, this experience] is manifest as resting on the self in the form '*I* once experienced.'" See also ĪPK 1.4.6, which explains that even when we talk about e.g. "our past experience," this does not qualify as a successful objectification of our past awareness, since it is nothing but another way (and according to Abhinavagupta, a rather convoluted one) of expressing the subjective

But the impossibility of objectifying any cognition also results from the fact that the very nature of an object is to be *passively* manifested (most Sanskrit words denoting the object of knowledge can also be translated as "that on which the action [of knowing] can be exerted"), while a cognition is what manifests the object in the very act of manifesting itself.[263] If we nonetheless try to apprehend the cognition as an object, we ipso facto fail to grasp its specificity, namely, its self-manifestation (*svaprakāśatva*)[264] or its capacity to *actively* manifest itself and the object—a capacity that, according to the Śaivas, is none other than the freedom of consciousnesss.

So when remembering, we are aware of ourselves as having cognized in the past, and the Buddhists cannot account for this phenomenon, since according to them nothing exists over and above momentary cognitions, yet their own theory of self-awareness entails that the present cognition cannot take as its object the past cognition. From the Buddhist perspective, every cognition must therefore be "confined to itself" (*ātmaniṣṭha*)[265] because while one cognition cannot take another as its object, there is no conscious entity beyond the momentary cognitions. As a consequence, the cognitive synthesis (*anusandhāna*) on which all our ordinary activities rest remains inexplicable.[266] The problem can only be solved by assuming that the self-

---

awareness that originally takes the form "I experienced": *smaryate yad dṛg āsīn me saivam ity api bhedataḥ | tad vyākaraṇam evāsyā mayā dṛṣṭam iti smṛteḥ ||* "Even that which is remembered [in the form] 'I had *this perception* in this way,'[i.e.] as [seemingly] distinct [from the subject], is a mere semantic analysis of [the fundamental expression of] memory [that takes the subjective form] '*I* perceived.'" For Abhinavagupta's explanations of these two verses see RATIÉ 2011a, pp. 222–229.

[263] See ĪPK 1.3.2a: *dṛk svābhāsaiva nānyena vedyā...* "A cognition cannot be known by another [cognition since it is] only self-manifest." For Abhinavagupta's explanation see RATIÉ 2011a, pp. 115–118.

[264] This is pointed out by Utpaladeva in the *Vivṛti*: see TORELLA 1988, p. 146.

[265] ĪPK 1.3.1 (see above, fn. 259). See also ĪPK 1.7.6: *bādhyabādhakabhāvo 'pi svātmaniṣṭhāvirodhinām | jñānānām udiyād ekapramātṛpariniṣṭhiteḥ ||* "Even the relation of contradiction between cognitions can [only] arise from [their] resting on a single knowing subject, since [by themselves cognitions], being self-confined, [can]not contradict each other."

[266] See ĪPK 1.3.6: *evam anyonyabhinnānām aparasparavedinām | jñānānām anusandhānajanmā naśyej janasthitiḥ ||* "If [things were] as [the Buddhists claim, then] everybody's [everyday] life, which results from [a constant activity of] synthesis

awareness of the present remembering cognition is none other than the self-awareness that belonged to the past experience—and this lasting self-awareness is precisely the self.[267]

## 3. Utpaladeva's demonstration of his nondualism (*Īśvarādvayavāda*)

Utpaladeva thus argues in the first part of his treatise that the only way to account for our most ordinary experiences and the synthesis that they involve is to admit that all momentary cognitions are various aspects of one single lasting consciousness. But he does not content himself with establishing that this consciousness is unitary: his goal is to show that it manifests itself in the form of the universe, that is, as insentient objects and as conscious beings that are limited in space and time. In other words, he wants to establish a kind of absolute idealism, and he shares with the Buddhist Vijñānavādins the conviction that perceived objects, which we ordinarily believe to be external to consciousness, are in fact mere aspects or appearances (*ākāra*) taken on by consciousness, just as the world of our dreams.[268] In his introduction to the beginning of chapter 2.1, Utpaladeva thus reminds his readers that in the first part of the treatise, he has shown not only how the unity of the manifesting consciousness exists within the self-awareness of any limited subject, but also "everywhere," and Abhinavagupta explains that this "everywhere" must be taken to mean "both outside and inside" the limited subject's self-awareness.[269] Indeed, in the first part of the treatise, Utpaladeva has demonstrated not only that any knowing subject, far from amounting to a mere series of momentary and

of [our various] cognitions, should perish[, because these cognitions would be] separated from each other [and] unable to know each other."

[267] See ĪPV, vol. I, pp. 288–289, translated in RATIÉ 2017c, p. 443. On the more complex inferential reasoning presented in chapter 1.3 of the Pratyabhijñā treatise, see RATIÉ 2011a, pp. 109–168; on the relationship between the two arguments, see ibid., 245–251.

[268] Recent studies have debated whether Indian Buddhist idealism is ontologically committed (i.e., actually denies the existence of any external world) or simply emphasizes the impossibility of ever gaining any epistemic access to such an external world. On this debate (and for further bibliographical references) see e.g. ARNOLD 2008, KELLNER & TABER 2014, RATIÉ 2014c and KELLNER 2017.

[269] See below, chapter 11, fn. 3.

heterogeneous cognitions, has a unitary consciousness, but also that the unity of consciousness is found as well in what we usually take to be insentient objects existing outside consciousness, because whatever appears to be external to consciousness is in fact still a form assumed by consciousness itself.[270]

Utpaladeva therefore sides with the Buddhist idealists in their dispute with the so-called Sautrāntikas,[271] another influential group of Buddhist thinkers according to whom although we can never have any direct access to the external world, we must infer the existence of a reality outside consciousness so as to account for the variety of our perceptions;[272] and Utpaladeva, as is repeatedly pointed out by Abhinavagupta, explicitly borrows a number of arguments from the Vijñānavādins in order to establish his own idealism.[273]

Yet Utpaladeva disagrees with them on one crucial point.[274] In the Vijñānavāda, since the cause of phenomenal variety cannot be the existence of various objects outside consciousness, it must be sought in the mechanism of residual traces also invoked to explain memory or the visions of our dreams. Our perceptions are thus said to occur as a result of latent traces left inside the cognitive series by previous experiences, and this causal chain of imprints producing perceptions that in turn cause imprints, etc., is beginningless, so that there is no point in looking for a first principle causing the manifested universe. The Śaiva nondualists, however, consider that the reason for the countless manifestations constituting the world is, rather than some impersonal mechanism of latent traces, the freedom (*svātantrya*) of the universal consciousness relishing its own creativity. In order to prove

---

[270] See in particular ĪPK 1.5.2–3, quoted below, chapter 10, §6, fn. 755.

[271] On the difficulty of determining the identity of these Sautrāntikas in medieval Indian philosophical literature, and for further bibliographical references, see RATIÉ 2011b, p. 481, fn. 5. In any case the theory commonly ascribed to these Sautrāntikas in and after Dharmakīrti's works seems to have been vigorously defended by the Kashmirian Buddhist philosopher Dharmottara (c. 740–800 CE), as shown by Abhinavagupta's testimony: see MCCREA & PATIL 2010, pp. 141–142, n. 71, and MCCREA 2016.

[272] On Utpaladeva's critique of the Sautrāntikas' position see RATIÉ 2011b.

[273] See RATIÉ 2010a and 2014c.

[274] See RATIÉ 2010a, pp. 460–464.

that the Vijñānavādins' explanation of phenomenal variety is unsound, Utpaladeva exploits a criticism of the imprint theory already levelled against the Vijñānavādins by the Sautrāntikas;[275] but he also endeavours to show that, although usually we do not pay attention to it, we are always somehow *experiencing* the creative will of consciousness: gathering and reworking a number of ideas and techniques found in the Śaiva tradition,[276] Utpaladeva builds a veritable phenomenology aimed at uncovering freedom at the heart of all experiences.

He thus invites his readers to focus on the banal yet wondrous ability that every conscious being has of imagining at will entities that nobody has ever perceived—such as (to give Abhinavagupta's example) "a five-trunked, four tusked elephant running in the sky."[277] In this regard the Śaivas strongly oppose the view of Brahmanical philosophers. The latter keep downplaying the power of imagination in order to show that the Buddhist idealists wrongly ascribe to consciousness the power to manifest the universe without relying on any external support (*ālambana*). Naiyāyikas and Mīmāṃsakas therefore explain that even the most extraordinary entities appearing in our dreams or imaginary constructions, far from being creations ex nihilo, are in fact made of various parts of objects perceived in the past that imagination merely assembles.[278] And indeed, we might suspect that we are capable of picturing up the fantastic elephant described by Abhinavagupta simply because we then put together elements previously perceived (tusks, trunks, the sky, a running elephant...). Utpaladeva nonetheless shows that imagination is a free creativity, first of all because even if it merely combines preexisting elements, as an activity of combination, it is perfectly free of any external determination. Moreover, the combined elements do not remain unaffected as they are integrated to the imaginary object: our imaginary creations are endowed with an organic unity, which would be impossible if the imagining consciousness did not profoundly transform the combined parts themselves into something new. When imagining, we are therefore experiencing the very power that constitutes the essence of God,

---

275 See RATIÉ 2010a, pp. 453–460.

276 See RATIÉ 2010a, pp. 467–468 and 472.

277 See RATIÉ 2010b, pp. 344 and 358.

278 See TABER 1994 and RATIÉ 2010b.

i.e. the ability of consciousness to create by freely manifesting itself as this or that object, and Utpaladeva insists that imagination is a path towards liberation, since in it we can recognize ourselves as the almighty universal consciousness.[279]

There is, however, an obvious objection to this reasoning: although we are capable of imagining, we are also aware of the vast difference between imagining and perceiving. And unlike imagination, perception involves the consciousness of a given that we do not choose: the perceived object imposes itself on us and we apprehend its presence and specific form whether we want it or not. Perception is first and foremost the experience of the passivity of consciousness confronted with what is other than it—and forced to take it into account. This is the major difficulty that the Śaiva nondualists need to overcome in order to demonstrate their idealism—and their way of solving this problem is perhaps the most extraordinary feature of their system.

Utpaladeva thus points out that the experience of perception is not a purely passive one: perceptual cognitions, far from merely reflecting their objects, involve at their very core an *act* of realization (*vimarśa*) that distinguishes consciousness from other entities such as mirrors.[280] Although the latter are endowed with the power to reflect, they remain inert, while consciousness, when perceiving objects, actively grasps itself as manifesting them. Thus when perceiving a patch of blue, consciousness grasps itself as perceiving

[279] On Utpaladeva's examination of the freedom of imagination (which was mainly conducted in lost parts of the *Vivṛti*, but the gist of which can be retrieved from Abhinavagupta's commentaries) see RATIÉ 2010b, pp. 353–361.

[280] See ĪPK 1.5.11: *svabhāvam avabhāsasya vimarśaṃ vidur anyathā | prakāśo 'rthoparakto 'pi sphaṭikādijaḍopamaḥ* || "[The wise] know that the nature of manifestation is a realization (*vimarśa*); otherwise the manifesting [consciousness] (*prakāśa*), while assuming the appearance of objects, would be similar to an insentient [entity] such as a piece of crystal." On this famous verse and its commentaries see e.g. ALPER 1987, pp. 176–241 and RATIÉ 2011a, pp. 495–508. Note that Harvey Alper's translation of *vimarśa* as "judgement" and his understanding of the notion as denoting first and foremost the consciousness of objects rather than self-awareness are problematic: *vimarśa* is the pre-conceptual and pre-reflexive act through which consciousness is always already grasping *itself* as having a specific form (whether objective or subjective), and it can only grasp itself in an objective form because all cognitive events ultimately rest on the subjective realization in which consciousness apprehends itself as a pure "I" (see RATIÉ 2011a, p. 160, fn. 115).

the blue, and it does so by *expressing* itself in various forms: "I," "this," "I see this," "this is a patch of blue," "I see this patch of blue," etc. For according to the Śaiva nondualists (who are much indebted in this respect to the grammarian-philosopher Bhartṛhari),[281] the Buddhist epistemologists wrongly draw a radical distinction between perception (considered as devoid of any linguistic aspect) and concept (understood as an essentially discursive thought).[282] The Śaivas insist that even what we usually consider to be the very first moment of a bare perception is in fact pervaded by language—or rather a kind of silent, proto-language which, as Abhinavagupta says, can be compared to expressive gestures such as nodding or pointing with a finger.[283] Utpaladeva thus argues that if perception were not already pervaded by some kind of verbal expression, we could not account for the many complex activities (running, reading, etc.) in which we engage without constantly telling ourselves "I am doing this": a runner pondering over each of his or her movements would not go very far, just as a reader focusing on the fact that (s)he is deciphering every single letter would keep losing track of the content of what (s)he is trying to read. Such activities are not *conceptualized*, either because we are too concentrated on what we are accomplishing to reflect on it while it is happening, or because we do it automatically as it were, while our mind is distracted. Yet these actions involve a kind of synthetic awareness: a runner would not run if (s)he did not grasp together, besides the environment in which (s)he is running, the movements that his or her body has just performed and those that (s)he is about to carry out. The running subject does not reflect on what (s)he is busy doing, yet (s)he links together various perceptual awarenesses, and

---

[281] On this crucial influence (and the divergence in this regard between Somānanda and Utpaladeva) see TORELLA 2002, pp. xxiii–xxviii, and TORELLA 2008.

[282] For a useful introduction to this famous dichotomy in the works of Dignāga and Dharmakīrti and its evolution among later Buddhist epistemologists, see MCCREA & PATIL 2010, pp. 9–34.

[283] See ĪPV, vol. I, pp. 205–206, where the subjective realization of consciousness as "I" is described as "an internal discourse" (*antarabhilāpa*) "independent of semantic convention" (*saṅketanirapekṣa*) and "similar to a nod turned inwards" (*antarmukhaśironirdeśaprakhya*). See also ibid., vol. II, pp. 260–261, where Abhinavagupta, while explaining that the expression inherent in realization is devoid of semantic convention, notes that this realization is "comparable to such [silent gestures] as pointing with a finger" (*aṅgulinirdeśādiprakhya*).

this is possible because his or her consciousness does not passively record sensory data but appropriates them through some kind of silent expression that can later be elaborated on when (s)he thinks back on what (s)he has done and explains it. This means that discursive thought is nothing but the development of a subtle, condensed expression already present in any act of perception.[284]

Admittedly, the fact that we are able to synthetically grasp the content of our perceptions does not entail that we actually *create* this content: showing that consciousness is not purely passive when confronted with the object does not amount to demonstrating that consciousness freely manifests itself in the form of the various things that we perceive—the Śaiva nondualists must therefore adduce further arguments to demonstrate that consciousness creates the perceived objects.

One of them regards the particular desire or will (*icchā*) that drives us when we decide to create something. When a potter for instance sets out to create a pot, his initial desire is restricted to a specific object, namely the pot—otherwise he would just as well create a cloth (and he would be a weaver!). But the object to which his desire must be restricted does not exist yet—so what is it that gives a specific aim to his creative urge? The natural answer to this question is that in such a case the potter simply imagines a pot before actually creating it, so that his desire is restricted by the imagined pot. But the imagined pot is also the product of a *creation*, albeit an imaginary one; so in order to picture up the pot, the potter must have first wished to create an imaginary pot—and how is this desire determined as the specific desire of an imaginary pot, if not thanks to the fact that the potter first imagines the imaginary pot before actually picturing it up? The only way to avoid an infinite regress is to admit that the objects of our creative desires are first

---

[284] See ĪPK 1.5.19: *sākṣātkārakṣaṇe'py asti vimarśaḥ katham anyathā* | *dhāvanādy upapadyeta pratisandhānavarjitam* || "Even at the [very] moment of immediate perception, there is a realization (*vimarśa*); otherwise how could such [activities] as running occur, [whereas without such a realization they would be] devoid of any synthesis?" For Abhinavagupta's explanations of this argument (that Utpaladeva had also put forward in a slightly different form in his lost *Vivṛti* on ĪPK 1.5.10, as can be gathered from ĪPVV, vol. II, pp. 169–170), see RATIÉ 2011a, pp. 163–167 and 491–493. Note that the example of running is reminiscent of Somānanda's ŚD, 1.9–11ab (the text is quoted by Abhinavagupta in this connection, see ĪPVV, vol. II, p. 170).

apprehended *as one with the subject*: creation is an apparent externalization through which the subject playfully projects him- or herself out of him- or herself as it were; and in the very first phase of this process, the object is still apprehended in its full unity with the subject, or as a manifestation by the subject of the subject.[285]

Of course Utpaladeva seems to be begging the question here, since showing that the objects of our creations are aspects of ourselves that we have playfully presented as distinct from us does not amount to demonstrating that such are the objects of our perceptions. His point, however, is that perceptions too involve *a desire to perceive*: as any act, perception presupposes a will to act in which the object of perception is experienced as one with consciousness, i.e. as an appearance that consciousness freely takes on. We all constantly go through this experience in which the object is grasped as still immersed in the subject, since it occurs at the very beginning of any perception; but we do not pay attention to it because we are almost instantly engrossed in the appearance of the object as a "this" separated from the "I" and seemingly independent from it (just as we are sometimes caught in our own game when day-dreaming and forget for a while that our imaginary world is nothing but our consciousness playing with itself). In ordinary circumstances we keep being distracted from this ever renewed experience of the objects' identity with consciousness, but it is sometimes brutally revealed to us when we are confronted with an unexpected or intensely emotional event: as Utpaladeva's master, Somānanda, had already explained, when experiencing extreme joy, terror, orgasm, or simply when we are suddenly struck by the realization that we have forgotten to perform some urgent task, the opposition between "I" and "this" dissolves, and what is left is an

[285] See ĪPK 1.5.10: *svāminaś cātmasaṃsthasya bhāvajātasya bhāsanam | asty eva na vinā tasmād icchāmarśaḥ pravartate ||* "Moreover, there is necessarily a manifestation of all objects [as] existing within the Lord's self; [for] without this [manifestation], the realization [consisting in] a will cannot occur." For Abhinavagupta's explanations see RATIÉ 2011a, pp. 481–493. This argument based on the necessity of avoiding an infinite regress in creative will appeared in a lost Śaiva work quoted by Abhinavagupta in this connection, the *Nareśvaraviveka* (see ĪPVV, vol. II, p. 167; RATIÉ 2011a, pp. 487–488). On the difficulty of determining its authorship and the hypothesis (which remains to be substantiated) that Utpaladeva might have composed it, see BANSAT-BOUDON & TRIPATHI 2011, p. 186, fn. 823, and TORELLA 2012, p. 296, fn. 61.

"effervescence of all powers"[286]—the pure dynamism of consciousness in its quivering desire to manifest the universe's infinite variety.

This does not mean, however, that our experience of the fundamental freedom of consciousness would be merely occasional. Thus one of Utpaladeva's proofs for idealism rests on an examination of what Western phenomenology has termed intentionality, that is to say, the fact that even in the most ordinary situations, consciousness is the consciousness *of* an object, or is object-oriented.[287] There is something paradoxical about his appeal to intentionality in order to establish the freedom of consciousness, because intentionality seems to be primarily the experience of the fact that consciousness is always confronting the otherness of an object obtruding on it. The Śaivas name *aunmukhya* this way that consciousness has of being *turned towards* or *directed upon* the object, and the Sanskrit word (an abstract substantive formed on the adjective *unmukha* that literally means "whose face is turned upwards") perfectly expresses this transcending presence of the object in intentionality: consciousness is intentional insofar as it is turned towards an object that stands above it or transcends it. Intentionality thus seems to betray the essential heteronomy of consciousness. Yet the Śaivas contend that intentionality, far from betraying the passivity

---

[286] *sarvaśaktivilolatā* (ŚD 1.11b). As noted in TORELLA 2002, p. xxv, fn. 34, and in NEMEC 2011, p. 115, fn. 115, Somānanda in turn derives this idea from Śaiva scriptural sources, in particular the *Vijñānabhairava.* Similarly, Utpaladeva inherits from earlier Śaiva sources (Somānanda's *Śivadṛṣṭi* and the Krama tradition) the idea that every perception involves at its very beginning an awareness of the identity between the object and the subject: see RATIÉ 2010a, p. 467, fn. 88 and 89.

[287] See ĪPK 1.5.15: *ātmānam ata evāyaṃ jñeyīkuryāt pṛthaksthiti | jñeyaṃ na tu tadaunmukhyāt khaṇḍyetāsya svatantratā* || "For this very reason, [consciousness] must make itself an object of knowledge; nonetheless, the object of knowledge has no separate existence—[otherwise] the freedom [of consciousness] would be ruined, because of the intentionality (*aunmukhya*) [of consciousness] regarding this [object]." For a translation and analysis of Abhinavagupta's commentaries thereon see RATIÉ 2010a, pp. 469–472.

of consciousness, reveals its creativity.[288] Thus according to Abhinavagupta,[289] Utpaladeva means that if the object were independent of consciousness, the very fact of intentionality would remain inexplicable, because being turned towards an object, or object-oriented, requires freedom. Were a consciousness not free, it would not be conscious at all because it would be incapable of any extroversion (real or apparent) towards any other entity: it would remain riveted to a self-contained identity, incapable of being anything besides itself, and therefore incapable of any relationship with anything—including the object. Intentionality entails the freedom not to remain confined to one's own nature, the freedom that consists in not "being merely oneself" (*ātmamātratā*),[290] contrary to insentient objects. And this freedom is conceivable only if consciousness is not really transcended by an object existing independently of it. In other words, intentionality occurs insofar as consciousness *chooses to manifest itself as intentional*, or to appear as if it were dependent on the object; and the intentional aim is possible only if consciousness takes the form of the object aimed at while aiming at it.

For all that, Utpaladeva's non-duality has very little to do with Advaita Vedānta's, which he criticizes as a fundamental misunderstanding of the very notion of non-duality:[291] according to him, the Vedāntins' Brahman is a concept arrived at by negating all differences, whereas genuine non-duality is such inasmuch as it embraces or encompasses everything, including all differences; and this is possible only if this non-duality is understood as the pure dynamism of consciousness rather than as a static, unchanging substance—which is why the Śaiva nondualists describe themselves not merely as proponents of non-duality, but as "proponents of the non-duality with/within the Lord" (*īśvarādvayavāda*).[292]

---

[288] In this respect their understanding of intentionality is certainly much closer to Husserl's than to Sartre's (see RATIÉ 2017c, p. 447).

[289] ĪPV, vol. I, p. 215. See RATIÉ 2017c, p. 447.

[290] See above, fn. 255.

[291] On this criticism see in particular RATIÉ 2011a, chapter 9.

[292] See e.g. ĪPVV, vol. II, p. 122 or ĪPVV, vol. II, p. 129.

# Chapter 4

# The Buddhist Objection Against Action and Its Refutation (ĪPK 2.1.1)

## 1. The Buddhist criticism of action

Utpaladeva's declared goal in the *Īśvarapratyabhijñā* treatise is to help his readers achieve liberation by pointing out that each of them in fact possesses unlimited powers of knowledge and action, which may trigger in them the recognition (*pratyabhijñā*) that they are the Lord (*īśvara*), i.e., Śiva, understood as an all-powerful, all-encompassing consciousness that playfully manifests itself in the form of the universe. The chapter edited and translated below is the first of the *Kriyādhikāra*, the part of the treatise devoted to the power of action (*kriyāśakti*), which follows the very lengthy *Jñānādhikāra* bearing on the power of knowledge (*jñānaśakti*).[293]

The first verse of chapter 2.1 reminds the reader that at the beginning of the treatise, Utpaladeva's Buddhist opponent has criticized our ordinary understanding of action as a unitary event occurring in successive phases; according to him, such a notion is absurd, because something that involves sequence (*krama*) can have no unity. Utpaladeva thus has this Buddhist interlocutor assert the following in the second chapter of the *Jñānādhikāra*:

> As for action, [in fact] it is the arising of an object—such as a body—in various places and [times]. It is nothing beyond [this, since we] do not perceive [anything over and above this

[293] For the sake of simplicity I have translated compounds such as *kriyāśakti* and *jñānaśakti* as "the power *of* action" or "the power *of* knowledge," by which I do not mean of course the power belonging to action/knowledge, but rather, the power that is action/knowledge (such Sanskrit compounds are analyzed as belonging to the *karmadhāraya* variety).

> multiplicity of momentary events]; nor can this [action] occur in sequence (*kramika*) [and] be one [or] belong to a unitary [entity].[294]

Utpaladeva's *Vṛtti* clarifies the Buddhist's position on action in the following way:

> As for action, it cannot be endowed with successive parts [and yet] be one [and] consist in the activity of [the various] factors of action (*kāraka*). [This is not possible,] because [something] occurring in sequence—[and therefore] connected with various moments—cannot have any unity in and of itself; nor can it have a substratum existing throughout (*vyāpin*) a temporal sequence [and yet] possessed of a unitary nature! Action only consists in going, changing, etc.; but this is nothing beyond the mere fact that [things] such as a body have a new existence occurring at various places and times that are different [from each other], since [we] perceive nothing else that would be distinct [from these momentary entities].[295]

When Devadatta goes from one village to another, we talk about "Devadatta's action" and therefore assume that Devadatta's action of going, somehow ontologically distinct and possessed of a certain unity, unfolds in various places and times; but sequence—whether spatial (*deśakrama*) or temporal (*kālakrama*)—entails a multiplicity that is contradictory both with the unity that we ascribe to action and with the conscious agent to whom the action supposedly belongs: how can action be one if it is spatially and temporally differentiated? And if Devadatta is a unitary consciousness who remains the same throughout the entire action, how can action, which involves so many spatial and temporal differences, belong to him?

The Buddhist portrayed by Abhinavagupta further explains that what we call action is in fact nothing but a series of heterogeneous momentary entities to which we mistakenly ascribe a unity through a process of recognition

[294] ĪPK 1.2.9: *kriyāpy arthasya kāyādes tattaddeśādijātatā | nānyādṛṣṭer na sāpy ekā kramikaikasya cocitā ||*

[295] *Vṛtti*, p. 9: *kriyāpi pūrvāparībhūtāvayavaikā kārakavyāpārarūpā na yuktā kramikasyānekakālaspṛśaḥ svātmaikyāyogāt, nāpi kālakramavyāpī caikasvabhāvaś ca tasyā āśrayo yuktaḥ. kevalaṃ gamanapariṇāmādirūpā sā kriyā, kāyādīnāṃ tu tattadbhinnadeśakālagatāpūrvasattāmātram etad atiriktasyānyasyānupalambhāt.*

(*pratyabhijñā*) based on a mere similarity that we confuse with a genuine identity:

> In this [world], to begin with, in that which consists in a motion and is the object of representations such as "he is going," "he is moving," "he is falling," only this much is [in fact] perceived: immediately after the nature of Devadatta occurring in a [specific] place that is a house, the nature of Devadatta located in a place outside [the house]; but we do not perceive any other action that would be distinct from these natures. As for the [thought]: "Devadatta is staying for a day," [in fact only the following] is manifest in it: the nature of Devadatta pervaded with the time of dawn, then the nature of [Devadatta] connected with [the first] watch of the day, etc. [Similarly,] in this [thought]: "the milk is undergoing a transformation," [this only is manifest]: the form of a sweet substance, [then] the form of a sour substance; a form that is liquid, [then] a form that is solid; etc. Thus, [whenever we think that we are experiencing an action, in fact] what is manifest is just a [momentary] entity (*bhāva*) [characterized] as having a specific place, time and aspect; and because of a [mere] similarity [between these various entities,] there occurs a recognition of these [entities as being one and the same] although [in fact they are] different, as in the case of the body, hair, nails and so on[296] [that we erroneously recognize as the same].[297]

[296] On the use of such examples by Buddhist authors to point out that recognition is in essence erroneous, see RATIÉ 2014a, pp. 48–50, fn. 136; p. 122, fn. 285; and pp. 201–202, fn. 553.

[297] ĪPV, vol. I, pp. 80–81: *iha parispandarūpaṃ tāvad gacchati calati patatītyādi yat pratibhāsagocaras tatra gṛhadeśagatadevadattasvarūpād anantaraṃ bāhyadeśavartidevadattasvarūpam ity etāvad upalabhyate, na tu tatsvarūpātiriktāṃ kāṃcid anyāṃ kriyāṃ pratīmaḥ. devadatto dinaṃ tiṣṭhatīty atra tu prabhātakālāviṣṭadevadattasvarūpaṃ tataḥ praharakālāliṅgitatatsvarūpam ityādi bhāti, dugdhaṃ pariṇamata ity atra madhuravasturūpam amlavasturūpaṃ dravarūpaṃ kaṭhinarūpam ityādi. evaṃ taddeśatayā tatkālatayā tadākāratayā ca bhāva eva bhāti, sādṛśyāc ca tatra pratyabhijñā bhinne 'pi kāyakeśanakhādāv iva.*

Action, understood as something distinct from purely momentary entities, is never perceived; it is a mere a conceptual construct, as the Buddhist Śāntarakṣita for instance points out:

> Action, [inasmuch as we] regard [it] as [something] perceptible [and not as a conceptual construct], is nothing over and above the real thing [itself], and no existence of this [action] that would be compatible with reason is [ever] perceived [in addition] to this [real thing]. Thus [actions] such as going cannot occur in [anything] whether impermanent or permanent, because no[thing] can be separated from the place [it] former[ly occupied] or reach another place. Rather, just as in the [case of] a lamp['s flame,] the illusion [that there is such a thing as an action] of going is due to the arising in a contiguous series of real things that are similar [yet] different, because [we] perceive [each of them] in different places.[298]

Śāntarakṣita's allusion to a lamp's flame is reminiscent of Vasubandhu's analysis of its apparent movement, which already presents action as nothing more than a figurative way of speaking:

> And how does a lamp['s flame] move? [We] talk about "the lamp['s flame]" in a figurative way, [when we actually mean] the series of [different, momentary] flames; [and we] say of the [new flame] arising [at every moment] in different places that it "moves" to this or that place.[299]

The Buddhist opponent portrayed by Abhinavagupta also insists that action is a mere conceptual construct—and an absurd one:

> When [we witness a so-called action,] there is a succession (*pūrvāpararūpatā*) of moments; but nothing is prior or posterior in itself, for [what is experienced] is nothing but the real thing [itself]. Therefore occurring in sequence, [that is,]

---

[298] $TS_Ś$ 704–706/$TS_K$ 705–707: *dṛśyatvābhimataṃ karma na vastuvyatireki ca | dṛśyate 'to 'pi* naivāsya sattā yuktyanupātinī || asthire vā sthire vaivaṃ gatyādīnām asambhavaḥ | prāktanāparadeśābhyāṃ vibhāgaprāptyayogataḥ || deśāntaropalabdhes tu nairantaryeṇa janmanaḥ | samānāparavastūnāṃ gatibhrāntiḥ pradīpavat ||* [**'to 'pi* $TS_Ś$; *so 'pi* $TS_K$.]

[299] AKBh 9, pp. 134–136: *kathaṃ ca pradīpo gacchati. pradīpa ity arciṣāṃ santāna upacaryate. sa deśāntareṣūtpadyamānas taṃ taṃ deśaṃ gacchatīty ucyate.*

succession, which is a characteristic of action, has as its essence a [mere] conceptual construct (*vikalpa*) and has nothing to do with any real thing; for these moments are not pervaded by each other's nature, [so that they cannot really be prior or posterior to each other]. So how could action be one? For sequence is pervaded by difference, since it is not found in [whatever] is free of differences, [and] unity is contradicted by difference; so how could [action both] occur in sequence and be one? If [our opponent were to reply that it is one] because it rests in a substratum (*āśraya*) that is one, even in that [case], no substratum whatsoever is experienced as being distinct from these moments, for only the moments occurring in a series are manifest. Besides, how could this substratum be one [whereas it must be] pervaded with moments of action that thus have different places, times and aspects? For this very reason, a recognition [of the type] "it is the same Devadatta who has reached the village," which occurs due to a [mere] similarity, does not have the power of making us grasp a real unity.[300]

## 2. Utpaladeva's claim that this criticism is already refuted

In the first stanza of the chapter devoted to the explanation of the power of action, Utpaladeva argues in a somewhat humorous response to his Buddhist interlocutor that although he is only starting now—with the beginning of the *Kriyādhikāra*—to examine action, no further effort is required on his part as regards the demonstration that action exists, because in fact his opponent's criticism of action is already refuted. In the *Jñānādhikāra*, Utpaladeva has shown that all conscious events pertain to a single, unitary consciousness; and this, according to him, renders ipso facto null and void the

300 ĪPV, vol. I, pp. 83–84: *tatra pūrvāpararūpatā kṣaṇānāṃ na tu svātmani kiṃcit pūrvam aparaṃ vā, vastumātraṃ hi tat. ato vikalpaprāṇitaṃ pūrvāparībhūtatvaṃ kramarūpatā kriyāyā lakṣaṇaṃ na vastu kiṃcit spṛśati, te hi kṣaṇā nānyonyasvarūpāviṣṭā iti katham ekā kriyā, kramo hi bhedena vyāpto 'bhinne tadabhāvāt, bhedasya viruddham aikyam iti kathaṃ kramikaikā ceti syāt. athaikatrāśraye 'vasthānād ekā, tatrāpi tatkṣaṇātirikto na kaścid āśrayo 'nubhūyate, kṣaṇā eva hi prabandhavṛttayo bhānti. kiṃ ca tathābhūtair bhinnadeśakālākāraiḥ kriyākṣaṇair āviṣṭa āśrayaḥ katham ekaḥ syāt. ata eva devadatto 'yaṃ sa eva grāmaṃ prāpta iti sādṛśyād bhavantī pratyabhijñā naikyaṃ vāstavaṃ gamayitum alam.*

criticism levelled by the Buddhist against action, so that no further demonstration is required to show that action can have a unitary agent and can itself be unitary. How can Utpaladeva make such a claim?

### 3. Action as the core of all conscious events: on *prakāśa* and *vimarśa* in Śaiva nondualism

In the *Vivṛti*'s introduction to ĪPK 2.1.1, Utpaladeva mentions that in the first part, he has already demonstrated "the unity of the manifesting [consciousness] (*prakāśa*) inside self-awareness (*svasaṃvedana*)." This is an allusion to the core of his demonstration that contrary to what the Buddhist contends, consciousness cannot be a mere series of purely momentary, irreducibly different cognitive events: in the course of his long and complex analysis of memory,[301] Utpaladeva has pointed out that according to his Buddhist opponent, each momentary cognition is possessed of a self-awareness (*svasaṃvedana*) through which it immediately and intuitively grasps itself; but in order to explain memory as the awareness of a previous subjective experience and not just as the grasping of a previously perceived object, the Buddhist must acknowledge that it is the *same* self-awareness that apprehended itself in the past as a present experience of a given object, and that apprehends itself now as the present memory of this past experience.

Utpaladeva has thus shown in the first part of his treatise that consciousness, as a manifesting entity (*prakāśa*), must have a profound continuity and cannot merely consist of a series of heterogeneous cognitive events. In the *Vivṛti*'s introduction to the first verse, he specifies that he has proven this unity not only "inside" self-awareness, but in fact "everywhere." This is the case because in chapter 1.5, Utpaladeva has not only shown that consciousness must be unitary, but also that all the objects of our ordinary experiences, which seem to exist outside consciousness, are in fact nothing but ways for a single, all-encompassing consciousness of manifesting itself, in a manner somewhat similar to that of a dreamer's consciousness taking on the form of a multiplicity of seemingly external objects and subjects.[302] And the crux of this demonstration of Utpaladeva's absolute idealism is his

---

[301] For a detailed account of this analysis see RATIÉ 2011a, chapters 1–4; for a brief summary, see RATIÉ 2016b, pp. 376–378.

[302] On what follows see RATIÉ 2011a, chapters 5–7, and RATIÉ 2010a.

contention that consciousness, understood as a manifesting entity (*prakāśa*) that makes all things appear by manifesting itself in their forms, has as its essence what he calls *vimarśa*.

The latter term, hopelessly untranslatable,[303] denotes consciousness's capacity not only to appear in this or that form but also to freely grasp itself *as being this and that*:[304] when I imagine an apple, my consciousness manifests itself in the form of an apple, but it is also capable of apprehending itself at will in various forms such as "I am imagining an apple"; "the apple"; "this, here, is an apple"; etc. This active grasping or realization may at will focus on the subject ("I am the one imagining the apple," "this apple is me") or the object ("it is an apple that I imagine," "this is an apple," etc.). And because it may entirely disregard (*anādara*[*ṇa*])[305] the subjective aspect of any conscious event while focusing on its objective aspect, it enables the absolute consciousness to manifest the universe as if it were distinct from it, whereas in fact the latter never loses its fundamental identity with consciousness: when we are day-dreaming, we sometimes become so engrossed in the imaginary world that we have built that we temporarily forget—or seem to forget—that this world is nothing but our own consciousness. This is possible because our consciousness can choose, out of its creative freedom (*svātantrya*), to grasp its own manifestation of itself in the form of external objects while disregarding the fact that these entities are nothing but internal forms of itself. This, according to the Śaiva nondualists, is consciousness's most extraordinary and paradoxical power, because consciousness, which is a pure *prakāśa*, must be transparent to itself, and we can never completely ignore what in fact we always know—namely,

[303] See RATIÉ 2011a, fn. 112, p. 159 for a non-exhaustive list of attempts to render it in a European language.

[304] See above, chapter 3, §3.

[305] On this ability of consciousness to neglect, or not to pay attention to, its own subjective aspect although it remains manifest, see e.g. RATIÉ 2011a, pp. 517 and 567–568.

that the objects imagined by us do not exist apart from us. Yet we can playfully choose to ignore this knowledge of ours[306] (which is why we are capable of enjoying fiction) and we can always grasp ourselves in this or that limited form. Such limited acts of grasping can be described as *idantāvimarśa* (literally, a "realization as this") inasmuch as they involve a realization of ourselves as being mere objects, things that may be apprehended as "this" (*idam*), i.e. as distinct from our own subjectivity expressed as "I" (*aham*); but they are possible only inasmuch as they ultimately rest on a full realization of ourselves as a subjective entity, *ahantāvimarśa* (literally, a "realization as I").

Now, in the course of the *Jñānādhikāra*, Utpaladeva has shown that this ability to grasp ourselves *as X*—which is deeply verbal, or rather, which constitutes the core of any verbal expression—happens to be nothing but what we call action (*kriyā*). More precisely, from the Śaiva nondualistic viewpoint, ordinary actions are nothing but externalized appearances of *vimarśa*: however trivial, our actions are nothing but the fundamental dynamism of *vimarśa* appearing as if it were external to consciousness, as if it were an objective reality rather than a purely subjective one.[307] Utpaladeva can thus claim in his *Vivṛti* on ĪPK 2.1.1 that "as soon as [we have shown

[306] This power to ignore what one knows is what the Śaiva nondualists call *māyāśakti*. See e.g. TĀ 4.11: *anāvṛte* svarūpe 'pi yad ātmācchādanaṃ vibhoḥ | saiva māyā yato bheda etāvān viśvavṛttikaḥ* || [**anāvṛte* corr.; *anāvṛtte* TĀ.] "Concealing oneself whereas one's own nature remains unveiled: this is precisely the Omnipresent Lord's *māyā* whence all this diversity occurring in the universe [arises]." Cf. ĪPV, vol. II, p. 128: *itaś ca kim atiduṣkaraṃ bhaviṣyati yat prakāśātmany akhaṇḍitatādrūpya eva prakāśamāne prakāśananiṣedhāvabhāsaḥ prakāśamānaḥ... saiṣā bhagavato māyāśaktir ucyate.* "And what could be [more] prodigiously difficult to accomplish than this: the appearance of a denial of [consciousness's] manifestation, [an appearance] that is manifest whereas the self, who is the manifesting [consciousness itself and] has in no way lost its nature, is being manifest? [...] This is precisely what [we] call the Lord's 'power of *māyā*.'"

[307] See e.g. ĪPV, vol. I, p. 338: *prakāśarūpatā jñānaṃ tatraiva svātantryātmā vimarśaḥ kriyā...* "Knowledge is the fact of consisting in the manifesting [consciousness], and within this very [knowledge], realization (*vimarśa*), which has freedom as its essence, is action (*kriyā*)..." Cf. ĪPV, vol. II, pp. 189–190: *jñānaṃ vimarśānuprāṇitaṃ vimarśa eva ca kriyā.* "Knowledge has realization as its essence, and action is nothing but realization."

this,] the unity of action and its belonging to an [entity] that is one are demonstrated by the same [token]": since action is nothing but *vimarśa*, which is the very nature (*svabhāva*) of consciousness,[308] and since the unity of consciousness has already been demonstrated at length, the Buddhist's objections regarding action are empty—the possessor of action (that is, the possessor of *vimarśa*) is nothing but consciousness, which has been demonstrated to be one, and "a nature belonging to [something that is] one must itself be one," so that action itself must be unitary.

### 4. The Vaiśeṣikas' contention that action has no unity of its own and the element of contradiction within all perceived actions

Admittedly, some of Utpaladeva's anti-Buddhist allies do not agree with the latter idea—namely, the Vaiśeṣikas, to whom the *Vivṛti* alludes at this point according to Abhinavagupta.[309] The Vaiśeṣikas do admit that action belongs to a unitary entity inasmuch as it inheres in a substance that is itself endowed with unity; thus according to Praśastapāda, "the five [sorts of action, i.e.,] throwing upwards, etc., all have one substance,"[310] and Vyomaśiva explains:

> [That they have one substance means that] one action occurs in a substance that [can] only be one, and also that only one [action can occur] in one [given substance].[311]

---

[308] See ĪPK 1.5.11 (quoted above, fn. 280), but this assertion that *vimarśa* is the very nature of consciousness is repeated throughout the treatise (see e.g. the *Vṛtti* on ĪPK 1.8.11, quoted below, fn. 328).

[309] See below, chapter 11, fn. 7.

[310] PDhS, p. 640: *utkṣepaṇādīnām pañcānām api... ekadravyavattvam...*

[311] *Vyomavatī*, vol. II, p. 244: *ekaṃ karmaikasminn eva dravye vartate, tathaikam evaikasminn iti*. Śrīdhara gives an almost identical explanation (NK, p. 640): *ekadaikasmin dravya ekam eva karma vartate, ekaṃ karmaikatraiva dravye vartata ity ekadravyavattvam*. "That [they] have one substance [means] that at one [given] time only one action occurs in one substance, [and that] one action occurs in a substance that [can] only [be] one."

Yet according to the Vaiśeṣikas, in fact action has no unity of its own, because numbers (and therefore unity) can only inhere in substances, not in qualities or actions, as specified in the VS:

> Because actions and qualities are devoid of number, unity does not exist everywhere.[312]

Nonetheless, according to the *Vivṛti*, "even" the Vaiśeṣikas, "who propound the thesis that there is [only] difference in action," must end up acknowledging that action is as good as (*-kalpa*) the nature of a unitary substance, and therefore have to concede that action itself is one, since as Utpaladeva has just argued, the nature of a unitary entity must itself be one. The reason why, according to him, the Vaiśeṣikas must admit that action is as it were the nature of the unitary substance in which it occurs is that action is invariably cognized as "not being separated" from the entity in which it inheres: we do not experience "walking" in itself, but Devadatta's walking, and action is always cognized as inhering in a given unitary substance. So according to Utpaladeva, even the Vaiśeṣikas, despite their denial of action's unity, must admit that action has some kind of unity (albeit a borrowed or indirect one) because they must admit that our cognitions of action involve the awareness of unity, be it only that of the substance in which it inheres. Utpaladeva takes this opportunity to point out by way of contrast that in his idealistic system, where what exists is what is manifest within consciousness, the unity of action itself—and not just its belonging to a unitary entity—cannot be doubted, precisely because whenever we witness the most ordinary actions and see Devadatta walking, going, etc., we are immediately aware of the profound unity of the agent, but also of his activity. Abhinavagupta comments as follows:

[312] VS 7.2.6: *niḥsaṃkhyatvāt karmaguṇānāṃ sarvaikatvaṃ na vidyate*. See also VS 7.2.5, *karmabhiḥ karmāṇi guṇair guṇāḥ* (which Candrānanda interprets as meaning "actions [are said to be devoid of unity and separateness] because of [the very nature of] actions, [and] qualities, because [of the very nature of] qualities") and VSV ad loc.: *tathaivāvayavaguṇaikārthasamavāyābhāvāt karmaguṇā naikatvapṛthaktvavantaḥ*. "In the same way, because there [can] be no inherence in a single entity that would [consist in] the parts [of action] or a quality, actions and qualities do not possess unity and separateness."

> "Whereas in [our system" means]: in [our] doctrine according to which things[313] have phenomena as their essence; for if existence has cognition (*pratīti*) as its essence, then how could [anyone] disregard cognition[, which presents action as unitary,] and establish [action] as having no unity, even by [hurling] imprecations [at this experienced unity of action]? This is what [Utpaladeva] is suggesting [here].[314]

The idea that things "have phenomena as their essence" (*ābhāsasāra*) is often found in the ĪPVV and was doubtless a leitmotiv of the *Vivṛti*.[315] It is closely linked with the epistemological principle that a given cognition is to be considered valid as long as it is not cancelled by a posterior one: since things boil down to their phenomena, they have no reality beyond their appearances, so that only experience can contradict experience, and phenomena must be accepted at face value unless they end up being contradicted by other phenomena. Thus when we mistake a glittering object seen from afar for a piece of silver and think "this is silver," what makes this cognition invalid is the subsequent cognition "this is mother-of-pearl" that arises when we get a closer look at the object. Similarly, what enables us to dis-

---

[313] Or real things/reality; as to the latter meaning see ĪPVV, vol. I, p. 288, quoted below, fn. 317, where *vastu* is replaced with *paramārtha*, but Abhinavagupta also explicitly uses *vastu* in the plural in this context (see e.g. ĪPV, vol. II, p. 241, quoted below, fn. 316, which has *vastūnām*) and sometimes uses instead *bhāva* ("[objective] entity") in the plural (see ĪPVV, vol. II, p. 343, quoted below, fn. 315).

[314] ĪPVV, vol. III, p. 2: ***iha tv*** *ity ābhāsasāravastuvāde. pratītisāro hi yadi bhāvaḥ, tat pratītim ullaṅghya bhedena kathaṃ śapathair api vyavasthāpyeteti ākūtam.*

[315] See ĪPVV, vol. II, p. 343: *ābhāsasāraṃ yāvadābhāsaṃ bhāvānāṃ tat tad rūpam iti hy uktam asakṛt.* "For [Utpaladeva] has explained many times that the various natures of [objective] entities 'have phenomena as their essence,'—[i.e.,] they boil down to phenomena." See also for instance ĪPVV, vol. I, p. 141, where Abhinavagupta quotes from the *Vivṛti* the words ***ābhāsasāratvena ceti***; vol. III, p. 36, where he quotes ***ābhāsasāratvād*** *iti*; ibid, where he quotes ***ābhāsasāratām*** *iti*, etc. Cf. here, at the end of the *Vivṛti* on 2.1.6, the compound *jñānāvabhāsasāratvena.*

tinguish a dream from the waking state is the fact that the phenomena experienced in a dream are contradicted or cancelled by those, incompatible with the previous ones, that arise when we wake up.[316]

Now, it is true that when witnessing an action, we do not merely cognize a unity, but also a seemingly contradictory multiplicity of elements: when Devadatta walks, we are aware that the same Devadatta goes from one point to the next, but we are also aware of things—his foot on the ground, his foot raised in the air, etc.—that are mutually incompatible, and incompatible with Devadatta's unity. Yet this, explains Abhinavagupta, is not a valid reason for the Buddhist to discard the reality of action, because while being aware of such incompatible aspects when we witness an action, *we are also aware that these contradictions do not actually cancel the unity of Devadatta or his action*: whereas the awareness "this is mother-of-pearl" instantly makes our previous cognition "this is silver" null and void, our awareness of action involves both unity and multiplicity, and yet the latter does not cancel the former. We do not consider that the individual Devadatta was a mere illusion just because we see him walk; we do not apprehend his action of walking as unreal because we grasp its different moments and places. The experience of action is paradoxical because it involves the awareness of a contradiction, and yet no cancellation of the validity of our

[316] Of course, the principle that "things have phenomena as its essence" also entails that the very status of the waking state is purely relative, and always in danger of being relegated to the status of a dream after being cancelled by an incompatible cognition. See ĪPV, vol. II, p. 241: *yāvac cānuvṛttisthairyaṃ niścayasya cakāsti tāvaj jāgaraḥ, tanmadhya eva ca niścayānuvṛttinirmūlanāt svapna ity avabhāsasāratvād vastūnāṃ svapne 'pi dīrghe yatra svapnāntaraṃ sa tadapekṣayā jāgrad eva; jāgradabhimatam api vā dīrghadīrghaṃ kālāntare niścayānuvṛttinirodhāj jāgradantarāpekṣayā svapna eveti mantavyam*. "And as long as the permanence—[that is,] the continuity—of [our] certainty [that our experience is genuine] is evident, this is the waking state; and if, in the very midst of this [state,] the continuity of this certainty is eradicated [by another, incompatible cognition], it is a dream. So because things have phenomena as their essence, even in a long dream in which another, [shorter] dream occurs is nothing but the waking state in relation to the [shorter dream]; and again, a [state of consciousness] that is even longer [than these two and] is considered the waking state [in relation to them] must [in turn] be considered to be nothing but a dream in relation to another waking state, because the continuity of [our] certainty gets interrupted at a later time." On this doctrine and its relationship with Kumārila's theory of intrinsic validity (*svataḥ prāmāṇya*), see RATIÉ 2011a, pp. 651–655.

perceptions. We must accept it because it has been established that "things have phenomena as its essence," and even the "imprecations" of the Buddhists who wish to deny the unity of action cannot change the fact that our immediate awareness of the unity in action is not subsequently cancelled; but how is it possible?

According to Abhinavagupta, it is so precisely because, as shown by Utpaladeva in the first part of the treatise, consciousness, as a manifesting dynamism, transcends all contradictions, and is in particular capable of embracing any given multiplicity without losing its unity, just as a single mirror can reflect countless different objects without being shattered by this reflected diversity. So if we admit that ordinary actions have as their substratum a consciousness that manifests itself in their manifold forms without ever losing its unity, the Buddhist's objection is no longer relevant:

> To explain, what was objected [by the Buddhist]—namely: "How could action be [both] one and successive? And if it belongs to a substratum, how could [this substratum] have a nature that is one? And how could relation be one [and yet] have a nature residing in two [relata]?"—boils down to this much: *How could there be something one* [*and yet*] *possessed of a multiple nature?* In this regard, [Utpaladeva has] said [in the first part of the treatise] that the difference between various phenomena [in consciousness], just as [that which] belongs to a mirror [reflecting a multiplicity of objects without losing its unity], does not cancel the unity [of the consciousness manifesting them], so that it does not lead to contradiction. As a consequence, it is indeed right [to say] that [something], the unity of which is well known through recognitions and perceptions that are not cancelled [by any subsequent cognition, and] which is a reality (*padārtha*) [since it] has phenomena as its essence,[317] is the substratum (*āśraya*)

[317] I.e., it must be admitted to be real, according to the principle that things have phenomena as their essence, precisely because it is known from cognitions that are not cancelled by any subsequent cognition. Cf. e.g. ĪPVV, vol. I, p. 288, where it is said that something must be admitted "by the proponent of the doctrine that reality has phenomena as its essence, because this phenomenon [appears] in a cognition that is not cancelled [by any subsequent cognition]" (*abādhitapratyayābhāsād ābhāsasāraparamārthavādinā*).

of action inasmuch as it assumes in its [unitary] self some aspects that are thus [various and] contradictory, [and] inasmuch as it manifests these different phenomena as occurring in sequence in this unitary self precisely because of [their] incompatibility[318].[319]

[318] On the meaning of *haṭha* as an equivalent of *virodha* here, see the parallel explanation in ĪPV, vol. II, p. 5, which specifies that the various phenomena are *virodhād eva karmarūpatayā nirbhāsamānāḥ*, "manifested in a sequential form precisely due to the contradiction [between them]."

[319] ĪPVV, vol. III, p. 2: *tathā hi yac coditam, ekā kramikā ca katham kriyā, āśrayasya ca tadyoge katham ekasvabhāvatā, sambandhaś ca dviṣṭhādirūpa ekaḥ katham iti tatreyān saṅkṣepaḥ: ekam anekasvabhāvaṃ kathaṃ syād iti. tatra darpaṇasyevānekābhāsabheda ekatām anapabādhamāno na virodham āvahatīty ukter nirbādhapratyabhijñāpratyakṣaprasādhitaikabhāvaḥ padārtha ābhāsasāras tathābhūtān eva viruddhān ākārān svātmany upagacchan haṭhād eva kramikāṃs tān ābhāsabhedān ātmany abhinne bhāsayan kriyāśraya iti yuktam eva.*

## CHAPTER 5

# The Crux of Chapter 2.1: The Problem of Sequence (ĪPK 2.1.2)

### 1. How can action belong to the ultimate consciousness if it involves sequence?

As seen above, Utpaladeva claims that the Buddhist objection against the reality of action is already refuted, and he does so on the basis of what he has already proven in the first part of his treatise—namely, that consciousness is a unitary, dynamic entity that transcends all contradictions. However, that action may belong to the highest reality (that is to say, the absolute consciousness playfully taking on the form of limited objects and subjects) is quite problematic, and in fact the whole chapter is meant to solve this problem. For action, it seems, necessarily entails some kind of sequence, it must spread across different moments; but the absolute consciousness is supposed to be beyond all limitations. So how could it be endowed with a power to act that necessarily involves sequence, and yet be free of any temporal restriction? According to Abhinavagupta, this is the objection to which the new verse must respond:

> "But the nature of action is precisely its occurring in sequence, and there is no sequence in the Lord, who consists in consciousness and is free of temporal division; so how could He possess this [action]?" Having anticipated this [objection, Utpaladeva] states [the following verse].[320]

---

[320] ĪPV, vol. II, p. 5: *nanu ca kramikatvam eva kriyāyāḥ svarūpam, kramaś ca kālakalanāhīne cinmaye bhagavati nāstīti katham asya sā bhaved ity āśaṅkyāha.* Cf.

The *Vivṛti*, for its part, merely states that the next verse is stated so as to examine "[action's property of] occurring in sequence, which seems contradictory"—i.e., as Abhinavagupta's introductions make clear, contradictory with the undivided, unlimited nature that the Śaivas ascribe to the ultimate consciousness.

### 2. The gist of Utpaladeva's response: sequence is not the essence of action

Utpaladeva's overall strategy to avoid this difficulty is summed up in ĪPK 2.1.2; it consists in showing that the contradiction is only apparent since actually, *sequence is not the very essence of action.*[321] This is no easy endeavour, because as underscored by Abhinavagupta in his commentaries, all systems are in agreement as to the fact that ordinary action occurs in sequence, although they disagree with respect to the means of knowledge (perception or inference) that enables us to be aware of this sequence:

> In [such an experience as] "[someone] is raising [and] putting down his hand," the anterior and posterior moments are endowed with sequence. In this regard, according to those—such as the Vaiśeṣikas—for whom action is nothing but these [various moments, action] is manifest [as] having a sequence through mere perception; whereas others consider that [action]'s succession can only be inferred, [action being according to them] a certain power residing in the hand, which is beyond the reach of the senses, which brings about the differences consisting in [the various moments] that are being thus directly perceived, which consists in the arising of activity, [and] which can always [only] be inferred. [In fact] action [so defined—that is to say,] ordinary [action]—can

ĪPVV, vol. III, p. 3: *nanu kramikatvam eva kriyāyāḥ prāṇitam, kramaś ca kālānavacchinne bhagavati kathaṃ syāt. etat samādhatte sūtreṇa.* "'But the essence of action is precisely its occurring in sequence; and how could there be any sequence in the Lord, who is undivided by time?' [It is] this view [that Utpaladeva] refutes with the [following] verse." On *īśvara* being *kālānavacchinna*, see e.g. YS 1.26: "Even the first [sages] have the [Lord] as their master, because [He] is undivided/uninterrupted by time" (*sa pūrveṣām api guruḥ kālenānavacchedāt*).

[321] Cf. e.g. the way in which Abhinavagupta formulates the gist of the chapter in ĪPVV, vol. III, p. 1 (quoted below, fn. 332).

> occur in sequence [as Utpaladeva's verse states]—i.e., this is possible—thanks to the particular power of the Highest Lord that is the power of time [and] consists in the capacity to manifest division within phenomena. However, the power of action that belongs to the Lord [and] is not distinct from [Him], being eternal, has nothing to do with time, [so that] one cannot even consider the possibility that it might occur in sequence.[322]

Indeed, the Vaiśeṣikas—from whom Abhinavagupta's example is obviously borrowed[323]—believe that the sequence pertaining to an action (i.e., the "anteriority and posteriority" of its elements) is directly perceived along with action itself,[324] whereas others—"that is to say," according to Bhāskarakaṇṭha, "Mīmāṃsakas and others,"[325] although here Abhinavagupta certainly also has in mind the tradition of the grammarians, first and foremost

---

[322] ĪPV, vol. II, pp. 6–7: *utkṣipaty avakṣipati* hastam iti ye pūrvottare kṣaṇās te kramavantaḥ. tatra yeṣāṃ ta eva kriyā kāṇādānām iva teṣāṃ sā sakramā pratyakṣeṇaiva bhāti, anye* tu manyante tathābhūtapratyakṣaparidṛśyamānarūpabhedasaṃpādikā* yāsau kācid atīndriyā hastagatā śaktir vyāpārodbodharūpā nityānumeyā tasyāḥ kevalaṃ pūrvāparībhūtatvam anumīyata iti. laukikyāḥ kriyāyāḥ sakramatvaṃ kālaśakter ābhāsavicchedanapradarśanasāmarthyarūpāt pārameśvarāc chaktiviśeṣād ghaṭata upapadyate. yā tu prabhoḥ saṃbandhinī tadavyatiriktā kriyāśaktiḥ śāśvatī kālenāspṛṣṭā tasyāḥ sakramatvam astīti saṃbhāvanāpi nāsti.* [**avakṣipati* S3, S1 (variant given above the word), cf. ĪPVV, vol. III, p. 3 and VS 1.1.6 (see below, fn. 324); *apakṣipati* J, L, SOAS, S1, S2, KSTS Ed., *Bhāskarī* Ed. **anye* conj. SANDERSON; *ye* S3, J, L, SOAS, S1, S2, KSTS Ed., *Bhāskarī* Ed. **tathābhūtapratyakṣaparidṛśyamānarūpabhedasaṃpādikā* S3, J, L, SOAS, *Bhāskarī* Ed.; *tathābhūtaparidṛśyamānabhedasaṃpādikā* S1, S2, KSTS Ed.]

[323] The Vaiśeṣika tradition equates action with movement; its enumeration of the five kinds of action begins with "raising" and "putting down" (*utkṣepaṇam avakṣepaṇam...*); and it analyzes in particular the movement of a hand (see e.g. VS 5.1.1: *ātmasaṃyogaprayatnābhyāṃ haste karma.* "The action in a hand [is produced] thanks to the contact with the self and [its] effort.")

[324] See VS 4.1.12: *saṃkhyāḥ parimāṇāni pṛthaktvaṃ saṃyogavibhāgau paratvāparatve karma ca rūpidravyasamavāyāc cākṣuṣāṇi.* "Numbers, magnitudes, separateness, conjunction and disjunction, anteriority and posteriority, as well as action, are visible if they inhere in a substance endowed with colour."

[325] *Bhāskarī*, vol. II, p. 10: *ye tu—mīmāṃsakādayas tv ity arthaḥ.* Bhāskarakaṇṭha probably has in mind the Prābhākaras: Śālikanāthamiśra, who quotes VS 4.1.12 (on

Bhartṛhari[326]—contend that action itself is not perceived (since all we perceive directly are different moments, whereas action per se, understood as their unity, remains imperceptible), but may nonetheless be inferred as the cause producing the differences characterizing these moments. Yet despite this divergence, Utpaladeva's philosophical interlocutors all admit that action is successive—and Utpaladeva does not deny it either, as long as the action considered is ordinary (*laukika*).

Thus according to him, actions are only affected by sequence in the realm of worldly existence, or existence within the cycle of rebirths (*saṃsāra*), which the power of *māyā*[327] brings about, as the *Vivṛti* specifies, "by manifesting the relation between the apprehending subject (*grāhaka*) and the apprehended subject (*grāhya*)." This relation, which plays a prominent part in Buddhist and Brahmanical epistemological discussions, entails both the opposition and mutual dependence of the subject and object, as is pointed out in another *Vivṛti* fragment that, while explaining the *Vṛtti* on ĪPK 1.8.11,[328] describes as follows the realm of transmigration:

---

which see above, fn. 324) in PraP, p. 79, criticizes the Vaiśeṣikas' contention that action is perceived and argues instead that it must be inferred "because with respect to a moving substance, one does not directly perceive any particular [entity] that would be distinct from disjunctions and conjunctions" (ibid.: *pratyakṣeṇa hi gacchati dravye vibhāgasaṃyogātiriktaviśeṣānupalabdheḥ*). As pointed out in JHA 1911, p. 91 and BHADURI 1947, p. 141, the Bhāṭṭa Mīmāṃsakas disagree: Pārthasārathimiśra argues that action is not in fact inferred but directly perceived (ŚDī, p. 71).

[326] On the importance of the idea that action is not directly perceptible and must be inferred (*anumeya*) in the grammatical tradition in general and in Bhartṛhari's VP more particularly, see OGAWA 1995; see also CARDONA 1991, pp. 453–455.

[327] On this power see above, fn. 306.

[328] *Vṛtti*, pp. 40–41: *sa paramātmā cidrūpo vimarśākhyenaiva mukhyasvabhāvenāvyabhicāriṇā maheśvaraḥ, cittattvasya viśvātmanaḥ śivasaṃjñasyāhaṃvimarśanam eva śuddhe jñānakriye, bhinnābhinnajñeyakāryagate tv īśvarasya śuddhāśuddhe, bhinnārthaviṣaye tu puṃsaḥ sattvarajovṛttirūpe prakāśapravṛttisaṃjñe tamasā saṃkucite 'śuddha eva.* "The Great Lord is this highest self consisting in consciousness with his invariable fundamental nature, which is precisely what [we] call 'realization.' Pure knowledge and action are nothing but the realization [in the form] 'I' of the reality of consciousness called Śiva that is the essence of the universe; where-

> On the contrary, when, due to the power of *māyā*, the existence of the same subjectivity pervades the aspects of [consciousness's] appearance [that consist of] the ontological principles, worlds and so on while being entirely concealed by a realization that takes an objective form, then one experiences the state of the transmigrating individual. This is what [the *Vṛtti*] says with "differentiated objects." And in that state, this I-realization [takes the form] "I, who am this [individual,] know this—e.g. this pot—and I act [upon it]." [It] consists in a [conscious] manifestation that is immersed in an aspect [of consciousness's appearance] that is nothing but a differentiated apprehending subject who is dependent on a differentiated apprehended object, [their differentiation and dependence being expressed] through the lack of syntactic agreement [of the words denoting them].[329]

In the realm of *saṃsāra*, consciousness apprehends itself as being split into two distinct entities, object and subject, that exist in contradistinction to each other and limit each other; and temporal sequence—i.e., the fact that actions cannot occur all at once—is only an aspect of the fundamental state of division that affects the phenomenal world. This aspect is brought about by what the *Vivṛti* calls the "power of time"—i.e., the power that consciousness has of appearing as it were temporally divided when it is not; but because the universal consciousness creates temporal divisions by manifesting itself in their form, it transcends them and remains unaffected by time. In it, action—an action that consists in a pure, full realization of one's own

---

as [the knowledge and action] that regard objects of knowledge and action [characterized as] both differentiated and undifferentiated, and that are both pure and impure, [are nothing but the I-realization] of Īśvara. As for [the knowledge and action] that regard [entirely] differentiated objects, consist in transformations of *sattva* and *rajas*, are called [conscious] manifestation and activity, are contracted by *tamas* and are only impure, [they are nothing but the I-realization] of the individual."

[329] The fragment is edited in RATIÉ 2017a, p. 176: ***saiva*** *punar ahantā māyāśaktivaśāt sarvam evedantāvimarśatirohitatattvabhuvanādyavabhāsabhāgavyāpyavasthānā yadā tadā saṃsāripuruṣadaśā, tad āha bhinnārtheti. tasyāṃ ca daśāyāṃ tad ahaṃvimarśanam* ***aham ayam*** *idaṃ ghaṭādi jānāmi* ***karomi ceti vaiyadhikaraṇyena*** *bhinnagrāhyāpekṣabhinnagrāhakamātrabhāgāvagāhiprakāśarūpaṃ...*

infinite subjectivity expressed as "I" (*ahamvimarśa*)—is perfectly free of sequence.

In his commentaries, Abhinavagupta insists, just as the verse does, that there can be no sequence for the ultimate consciousness's action, just as there can be no sequence for the ultimate consciousness itself;[330] and Utpaladeva's *Vṛtti* points out why this is the case by reminding the readers that the ultimate consciousness's action is its very nature (*svabhāva*)—namely *vimarśa*, as the *Vivṛti* specifies. It is telling that in his *Vṛtti*, Utpaladeva describes this nature as "without beginning or end" (*anādinidhana*)—a compound that is the very first word of Bhartṛhari's VP and serves there to qualify the Brahman.[331] The parallel is striking, as is the difference; for Utpaladeva, in order to underscore the essential dynamism of consciousness, uses Bhartṛhari's famous expression to describe the *action* pertaining to the ultimate reality, rather than ultimate reality itself.

The whole chapter, as an explanation of the power of action, is built as a justification of the distinction drawn in this *kārikā* between sequential ordinary action and the non-sequential action that constitutes the very essence of the Lord, as Abhinavagupta makes clear while summarizing the gist of chapter 2.1 in the ĪPVV:

> And in this [new part of the treatise devoted to action], in the eight verses [of the first chapter] beginning with "For the same reason, this [Buddhist] objection too..." and ending with "[Nonetheless,] the [very] fact that the difference in the [limited] knowing subjects and objects of knowledge is made manifest in this way...", [Utpaladeva] demonstrates that action has sequence [only] inasmuch as it is associated with the

---

330 ĪPV, vol. II, p. 7: *yathā prabhoḥ sakramatvam asaṃbhāvyaṃ tathā tasyā api.* "[And] just as one cannot [even] consider the possibility of occurring in sequence as far as the Lord is concerned, in the same way, [one cannot even consider this possibility] as regards this [eternal action] either."

331 VP 1.1: *anādinidhanaṃ brahma śabdatattvaṃ yad akṣaram | vivartate 'rthabhāvena prakriyā jagato yataḥ* || "This Brahman without beginning or end, which is the essence of Speech, which is verbal/imperishable (*akṣara*), which appears as the [various] objects, from which the production of the universe [arises]..."

> manifestation of sequence found in the bound subjects (*paśu-pramātṛ*), although in reality, in the Lord it is free of sequence.[332]

Abhinavagupta also underscores this crucial distinction in a passage of his TĀ that evidently draws upon ĪPK 2.1.2, as pointed out by Bhāskarakaṇṭha (who quotes it while explaining ĪPK 2.1.2)[333] as well as Jayaratha (who quotes ĪPK 2.1.2 while commenting on the TĀ verses):[334]

> Although consciousness is engaged in springing forth while taking the form of the knowing subject, object of knowledge and so on, because it is free of temporal sequence, it is full, being always arisen. An action such as cooking, however, is fit for sequence because it is divided by time: even if it is [only] devoid of the last moment intended [by its agent],[335] it fails to be [the action of] cooking![336]

Ordinary action is sequential: it is temporally divided, and all of its moments, up to the very last one, are required for it to reach completion. But this is not the case of the action that pertains to the pure levels of consciousness, since as Jayaratha makes clear, the absolute consciousness, although engaged in manifesting itself in temporally restricted forms, is itself free of temporal restrictions because it remains perfectly autonomous. It is therefore "always arisen" not in the sense of having performed the action of

---

[332] ĪPVV, vol. III, p. 1: *tatra ca ślokāṣṭakenāta eva yad apy uktam ityādinā tathā vijñātṛvijñeyabhedo yad avabhāsyata ityantena bhagavati vastuto 'kramāyā api kriyāyāḥ paśupramātṛgatakramāvabhāsanayogāt sakramatvam ity upapādyate.*

[333] *Bhāskarī*, vol. II, p. 11.

[334] TĀV, vol. II, p. 134.

[335] The word *api* is translated here according to what I take to be Jayaratha's gloss of it in TĀV, vol. II, p. 134: *anekakṣaṇapracayavattve 'pi*, "even if it includes the collection of numerous [other] moments..."

[336] TĀ 3.128cd–130ab: *ucchalanty api saṃvittiḥ kālakramavivarjanāt ‖ uditaiva satī pūrṇā mātṛmeyādirūpiṇī | pākādis tu kriyā kālaparicchedāt kramocitā ‖ matāntyakṣaṇavandhyāpi na pākatvaṃ prapadyate |*

arising (or parts of it) in the past, but rather, inasmuch as its action of arising is tenseless, being ever complete:[337]

> [It is] "always arisen," because it is not divided by time, since there is no interruption in its action of manifestation; that is to say, its nature never sets, [and this is] necessarily [so], because its consisting in pure consciousness never ceases to be. For this very reason, it is "full"; that is to say, it does not depend on anything else, because its [very] nature is to rest in nothing but itself.[338]

### 3. The "devouring of time" (*kālagrāsa*)

In the *Vivṛti*, Utpaladeva specifies that the reason why the ultimate consciousness thus remains unaffected by time is that it "devours" it:

> However, the [action] belonging to the Lord who consists in the manifesting [consciousness] is [precisely] His nature, which [we] call the I-realization (*ahaṃvimarśa*); [and it] is necessarily free of sequence because, due to [its] devouring all the objects that are constrained by time, it also devours time [itself].

This "devouring of time" (*kālagrāsa*) is evidently borrowed from the Krama tradition, according to which reality unfolds through consciousness's fivefold process (*krama*) of [initial] surge (*udyoga*), [objective] manifestation (*avabhāsa*), consuming [of objective entities] (*carvaṇa*), devouring of time (*kālagrāsa*) and [final] rest (*viśrānti*). The pentad is mentioned

---

[337] I am much indebted to Harunaga Isaacson for his very insightful remarks (personal communication, 17/08/2020) on the meaning of *uditaiva satī* here.

[338] TĀV, vol. II, p. 133: ... *avabhāsanakriyāvicchedābhāvāt kālānavacchedād uditaiva saṃvinmātrarūpatvāpracyāvān niyamenānastamitarūpety arthaḥ. ata eva pūrṇā svātmamātraviśrāntirūpatvād ananyāpekṣiṇīty arthaḥ.*

in many Krama sources,[339] and here is how Abhinavagupta explains this *kālagrāsa* in his commentary on this passage of the *Vivṛti*: [340]

> Why does [Utpaladeva] say here "because [...] it also devours time [itself]," whereas [the ultimate consciousness's] lack of sequentiality is ipso facto established due to the mere fact that it is undivided by time? [Here is the answer:] The Lord resides in the māyic knowing subject's realm too, [and not just in the pure realm,] while all the objects of knowledge are manifest. [But while being thus engaged in the māyic realm,] He "devours" all the objects—whether their form is external or internal—, [that is to say,] He brings [them] to rest in Himself, according to the principle stated [by Utpaladeva in the passages of his *Ajaḍapramātṛsiddhi*] beginning with *prakāśasyātmaviśrāntiḥ* [and] *idam ity asya vicchinnavimarśasya*;[341] [and] as soon as [He does that, it is not just these objects, but] also the sequence of manifestation that resides in them, that are immediately devoured. Therefore action is indeed devoid of sequence inasmuch as it is defined as the [subjective] realization (*vimarśa*), [in the form] "I," of the specific state that ends up in the resorption of the manifestation of all the [objective] entities pictured up by [freely] associating and [dissociating phenomena].[342]

The objective world is only a manifestation of the ultimate consciousness; and Utpaladeva will make clear in verses 4 and 5 that temporal sequence is the result of the ultimate consciousness's will to manifest the objective

---

339 It is found for instance in the Sanskrit commentary on Śitikaṇṭha's *Mahānayaprakāśa*, p. 42: *udayāvabhāsacarvaṇakālagrāsaviśrāntirūpabhāṣāṇāṃ pañcānāṃ...* See SANDERSON forthcoming for more references.

340 For other allusions to the Krama concept of *kālagrāsa* in Abhinavagupta's works, see SANDERSON 2007a, p. 370, fn. 452.

341 *Ajaḍapramātṛsiddhi* (henceforth APS) 15 and 22 (see below).

342 ĪPVV, vol. III, pp. 3–4: ***kālagrāsād apī****ti kālānavacchedāt tāvad akramatvaṃ sthitam eveti kim atrocyate. unmiṣite 'pi vedyagrāme māyāpramātṛpadam apy adhyāsīno bhagavān yāvad eva bāhyāntararūpaṃ vedyakulaṃ svātmani prakāśasyātmaviśrāntiḥ, idam ity asya vicchinnavimarśasyetyādinayena grasate viśramayati, tāvat tanniṣṭho 'vabhāsanakramo 'pi grasta eveti aham iti yā saṃyojanādicitritasamastabhāvaprakāśopasaṃhāraparyantadaśāviśeṣavimarśalakṣaṇā kriyā, sā niṣkramā eva.*

world in a specific way. Since the ultimate consciousness enters "the māyic subject's realm too" by taking the variegated forms of limited subjects and objects—instead of eternally abiding in an absolutely boundless and changeless state—, one might suspect that it ends up being affected by time. This is why, according to Abhinavagupta, the *Vivṛti* emphasizes here that the ultimate consciousness transcends the objective phenomena in whose forms it manifests itself: to use the Krama terminology, consciousness, while[343] manifesting the objective world as if it were external to itself, also "chews" or "consumes" this objective manifestation, i.e., it fully reintegrates it within its subjective nature by grasping it as internal to itself; and as soon as it does so, by the same token it "devours" time as well, because time is nothing but a way for consciousness of manifesting the objective world. Abhinavagupta thus presents the phases respectively depicted in the Krama as the "consuming" of the objective world and the "devouring of time" as mere aspects of the final phase—the "rest" or "quiescence" (*viśrānti*) in which consciousness brings back all objective manifestations to their true, purely subjective nature (and thus leads them to completion) by becoming aware of them in the pure form "I"—, as can be seen from the two quotations from Utpaladeva's APS that he gives in this connection:

> As far as the realization (*vimarśa*) separated [from the subject and taking the form] "this" is concerned, completion (*kṛtārthatā*), which [consists in] resting in one's own nature, is the realization "this is me."[344]
>
> For it is subjectivity that is celebrated as the manifestation's rest in its own nature.[345]

## 4. The identity of the Lord's action with that of individuals, and the ethical consequences of this principle

The last sentence of the *Vivṛti* on this verse specifies that "nonetheless, this [same action], which is full of pure freedom, [is also what] ends up being

[343] Or *after* manifesting it thus; but the sequence (*krama*) thus depicted is of course ontological rather than temporal, and its five elements are in fact beyond time.

[344] APS 15: *idam ity asya vicchinnavimarśasya kṛtārthatā | yā svasvarūpe viśrāntir vimarśaḥ so 'ham ity ayam ||*

[345] APS 22cd: *prakāśasyātmaviśrāntir ahaṃbhāvo hi kīrtitaḥ ||*

the artificial agency [of limited subjects]." The point is important, because so far the *Vivṛti* has been insisting on the *differences* between the Lord's action and the ordinary action that belongs to transmigrating individuals: the former is devoid of any temporal restriction and performed by virtue of an absolute freedom within a single, boundless consciousness; the latter, dependent on the division that splits consciousness into a limited subject and object, is sequential, rests on various external factors that transmigrating individuals do not control, and contributes to binding them ever more tightly to the *saṃsāra*, since the merit (*dharma*) or demerit (*adharma*) that accrues to each agent depending on the moral value of his or her acts requires a karmic retribution that must be experienced in subsequent existences. This distinction between the two kinds of action must be made here, because Utpaladeva has to show that the ultimate consciousness, although dynamic in essence, is free of temporal restrictions; yet it could be seen as threatening the nondualistic foundations of the system, by presenting too sharp a contrast between the divine sphere and the ordinary one. Utpaladeva therefore reminds his readers that ultimately, *this is one and the same action*, the action of ordinary individuals being nothing but divine action manifesting itself as if it were limited and sequential.

This brief remark has far-reaching consequences, if only because it strips the individual from all moral responsibility. For the treatise's goal is to make its readers notice the unlimited powers of knowledge and action that every individual intuitively experiences as his or hers while being constantly distracted from them, but these powers belong to the individual only inasmuch as the latter is in fact the ultimate consciousness: the potter, as an individual, is nothing but the inert object with which he identifies, so that only the ultimate consciousness can rightly be considered to be the agent of the actions and creations that we usually ascribe to transmigrating individuals—"and as a result, in the [operation leading to the production of a pot], the only potter is the Lord."[346] The transmigrating individual has no

[346] ĪPV, vol. II, p. 148: *ataś ca kumbhakṛd eva tatreśvaraḥ*.

real agency, or, as the *Vivṛti* says here, his or her agency is only "artificial."[347] Now, as pointed out by the interlocutor portrayed by Abhinavagupta, if this is the case, the very distinction between merit and demerit can no longer make any sense:

> But if it is so, since the potter has no agency, the distinction between merit and demerit must be reduced to naught![348]

Instead of attempting to avoid this consequence, Abhinavagupta welcomes it:

> If you trust both reason and scripture, [you must admit that] it is exactly so![349]

Once the nonduality of individuals with the ultimate consciousness is recognized, merit and demerit become utterly meaningless categories. According to Abhinavagupta, this is what Utpaladeva's reasonings demonstrate, and his demonstrations are in accordance with Śaiva nondualistic scriptures, which assert that individuals transmigrate only inasmuch as they erroneously see themselves as distinct agents and therefore believe in their moral responsibility: from the Śaiva nondualistic perspective, the very belief in the notions of merit and demerit becomes the "impurity" due to which consciousness binds itself to the transmigrating cycle.[350] This is not to say that karmic law would be altogether rejected: it is still valid, albeit only as long as individuals believe in their individual agency. Paradoxically, this position does not even amount to a sheer denial of the value of ethical behaviour beyond the mere preservation of social order in which the artificial *dharma/adharma* distinction results;[351] thus Utpaladeva argues in

---

347 See RATIÉ 2011a, pp. 572–573, for more references to this point in the Śaiva nondualistic corpus.

348 ĪPV, vol. II, p. 149: *nanv evaṃ kumbhakṛto nāsti kartṛtvam iti samutsīded dharmādharmavyavasthā.*

349 ĪPV, vol. II, p. 49: *yadi pratyeṣi yuktyāgamayos tad evam eva.*

350 See e.g. SANDERSON 1992, pp. 288–289. On "karmic impurity" in the *Pratyabhijñā* treatise see ĪPK III.2.5 and its commentaries, and RATIÉ 2011a, pp. 574–575, fn. 11.

351 See e.g. PTV, pp. 232–236 (too lengthy to be quoted here; see SANDERSON 2005, pp. 110–114, fn. 63; cf. GNOLI 1985b, pp. 149–150) where Abhinavagupta explains that the word *dharma* merely denotes one of the numerous forms—which vary

his treatise—obviously against his Buddhist rivals—that only his system provides a suitable frame for a genuinely altruistic attitude, because true concern for others can only stem from the blissful awareness of one's own fullness.[352]

Here, however, the *Vivṛti* does not even allude to the ethical consequences of the fact that all ordinary actions are ultimately nothing but aspects of the Lord's agency, evidently because its most urgent task is to justify the assertion, just made in ĪPK 2.1.2, that action is only sequential in the realm of *māyā*—and this is what Utpaladeva sets out to do in the next stanzas.

---

"with each tradition and region" (*pratiśāstraṃ pratideśam*) of the "inhibition" (*śaṅkā*) through which consciousness contracts itself—an inhibition that is artificial and was constructed (*kalpita*) so as to provide the "unenlightened" (*aprabuddha*) with a "stable [social] order" (*sthiti*).

[352] On Utpaladeva's contention that compassion and altruism only make sense in the Śaiva nondualistic system, see RATIÉ 2009.

# CHAPTER 6

# The Nature of Time (ĪPK 2.1.3)

Utpaladeva's next move is to discuss the nature of time. He has already mentioned it in ĪPK 2.1.2 when bringing up the "power of time" (*kālaśakti*) as that which is responsible for the appearance of sequence in ordinary action. All of this must be explained so as to justify the chapter's main point that sequence is not the essence of all actions and is only found in those pertaining to the realm of *māyā*. Utpaladeva therefore endeavours an examination of the way in which "another system" (*anyadarśana*)[353] defines time as what brings about such a division; and although he never names it, from his *Vivṛti* and Abhinavagupta's commentary on it, it is obvious that he primarily has the Vaiśeṣika in mind.

## 1. The first definition mentioned by Utpaladeva: time is nothing but actions

It is striking, however, that the first definition mentioned seems at first sight utterly incompatible with the understanding of time in classical Vaiśeṣika. According to this first definition, time is nothing but some well-known actions—such as the sun's movement in the sky—that we use to measure the duration of other, less well-known actions. A very similar thesis is summed up by Bhartṛhari in the chapter of the VP devoted to time:

> Others, who are specialists of time, know that time, which is the movement of the sun, planets and stars, is differentiated according to the varying number (*bheda*) of repetitions [of

[353] The expression is used in the *Vivṛti* as Utpaladeva makes clear that what he has explained so far only concerns a rival doctrine ("[But all of] this is merely a presentation of the established conclusions of another system, [and we Śaiva nondualists] have no fondness for this [view] in any [respect]...").

> these movements]. With respect to [any] action, the measurement of which is [already] known [and] which is used to measure other actions, [we] use the word "time."[354]

Helārāja, in his commentary, gives an explanation very close to that of Utpaladeva's summary of the thesis in his *Vivṛti*:

> The course of the sun and [other celestial bodies] is [what is] denoted by words such as "day," etc.; and a particular action such as the milking of cows is [also] given the name "time" because, given that its measurement has [already] been determined, it is the cause [that enables us] to measure a particular action such as staying [somewhere], which is different from the [first action], and the measure of which is not well known.[355]

The idea has been ascribed to astrologers/astronomers (*jyotirgaṇaka*)[356]—and with some reason, since mathematicians and astronomers measure time with actions (i.e. the movements of astral bodies, but also acts such as breathing or pronouncing syllables),[357] and the mathematician Bhāskara, while commenting on the *Āryabhaṭīya*, makes clear that for him and his peers, time boils down to the actions that we use to measure it:

> But what is time, or what is action? In this regard some say [that] time is distinct from action; others [say] that time is action. Let [us] admit that time is distinct from action—[still:] what is the point of [such an independent time]?

---

354 VP 3.9.76–77: *ādityagrahanakṣatraparispandam athāpare | bhinnam āvṛttibhedena kālaṃ kālavido viduḥ || kriyāntaraparicchedapravṛttā yā kriyāṃ prati | nirjñātaparimāṇā sā kāla ity abhidhīyate ||*

355 *Prakīrṇaprakāśa* (henceforth PP), vol. II, p. 70: *sūryādīnāṃ gatipracāro divasādiśabdavācyaḥ, godohādikriyāviśeṣaś ca paricchinnaparimāṇatvāt tadaparāprasiddhaparimāṇāsyādikriyāviśeṣaparicchedahetutvāt kālākhyām āsādayati.*

356 See NM$_M$, vol. I, pp. 366–367, quoted below, fn. 375; cf. SHARMA 1972, pp. 25–26, although the latter adduces no evidence from primary sources.

357 See e.g. the third chapter of the fifth-century *Āryabhaṭīya*, which is devoted to the measures of time. It is entitled *Kālakriyā*, "The Action of Time," and begins thus (3.1–2ab): *varṣaṃ dvādaśa māsās triṃśad divaso bhavet sa māsas tu | ṣaṣṭir nāḍyo divasaḥ ṣaṣṭiś ca vināḍikā nāḍī || gurvakṣarāṇi ṣaṣṭir vināḍikārkṣī ṣaḍ eva vā prāṇāḥ |* "A year is twelve months; a month is thirty days; a day is sixty *nāḍīs*; a *nāḍī* is sixty *vināḍikās*; a stellar *vināḍikā* is sixty long syllables or six respirations..."

> Whereas for us [mathematicians], the sun and moon's greatest movement away from each other [after a conjunction] is a fortnight; and their moving back towards each other is a month. Similarly, twelve months are a year, and so on—this is time![358]

This thesis is also defended by a major Sāṃkhya work, the *Yuktidīpikā*[359] (henceforth YD):

> As for what has been claimed, [viz.], that the world must arise due to time—it is not possible either. Why? Because this word ["time"] only refers to the movement of causes. For according to us, what is called "time" is not a [constitutive element of reality].[360] Rather, actions that are in the process of being performed—such as the movement of the sun, the milking of cows, the ringing of a bell and so forth—are the causes of the cognition that [something] similar [viz. another action] has a limited duration (*avadhi*) that is particularized (*viśiṣṭa*) [by them]; and nothing else (*eva*) [causes this cognition].[361]

The *Pātañjalayogaśāstravivaraṇa* (henceforth PYV) also explains:

---

358 *Āryabhaṭīyabhāṣya*, p. 172: *atha kaḥ kālaḥ, kā vā kriyā. atra kecid vadanti kriyāvyatiriktaḥ kālaḥ. apare kriyā kāla iti. kriyāvyatirikto 'stu kālaḥ, kim etena. asmākaṃ tu sūryācandramasoḥ paro viprakarṣaḥ so 'rdhamāsaḥ. yaś ca tayoḥ sannikarṣaḥ sa māsaḥ. evaṃ dvādaśa māsāḥ saṃvatsara ityādi kālaḥ.*

359 For an analysis of time in Sāṃkhya sources in general and in this work in particular, and for more bibliographical references, see RATIÉ forthcoming b.

360 Cf. YD, p. 247: *na kālo nāma kaścit padārtho 'sti, kiṃ tarhi kriyāsu kālasaṃjñā.* "What [we] call time is not a [constitutive element of] reality (*padārtha*). Rather, the word "time" [merely] refers to actions."

361 YD, p. 161: *yad apy uktaṃ kālāj jagadutpattir bhaviṣyatīti tad anupapannam. kasmāt. kāraṇaparispandasyaiva* tadabhidhānasanniveśāt. na hi naḥ kālo nāma kaścid asti. kiṃ tarhi kriyamāṇakriyāṇām evādityagatigodohaghaṇṭāstanitādīnāṃ viśiṣṭāvadhisarūpapratyayanimittatvam.* [**kāraṇaparispandasyaiva* mss. (see Ed., fn. 7); *karaṇaparispandasyaiva* em. Ed.]

> For what defines an action whose measure is not [yet] known is [simply] an action whose measure is [already] determined,[362] as [when we say] that [someone] sleeps until the milking of cows [is done], or that he studies until the cooking of rice [is completed]—and time is nothing but this.[363]

Abhinavagupta, in his commentary on the *Vivṛti*, also insists that time is nothing but our measuring one action with another, and that any action can be either that which we use to determine the duration of another one, or that whose duration we determine by comparing it with another action:

> But time is that through which one accomplishes the action [expressed by the verbal root] *kal-*, [that is to say,] that through which one breaks up and divides/measures; [so] how could an action, which is [rather] the *object* to be measured, be time [itself]? As a response to this, [Utpaladeva] says "[And another action] that is particularized [inasmuch as it is well known that it is to be accomplished in a specific sequence is in turn nothing but the time of the first action." This action is "particularized"] by the fact, which characterizes [it], that it is well known as having a specific duration (*iyattā*); [in other words, Utpaladeva] says that as regards the [action of the sun's movement] too, when [we] want to measure it [instead of using it as a measure], it is another action, such as the flow [of water called] *nālikā*, which is "time."[364]

According to the Vaiśeṣika, on the other hand, time is a distinct substance (*dravya*) that is one, eternal, timeless and conjoined with all composite substances; and it is distinct from action, as is clearly underscored by Helārāja

---

[362] Against the translation in RUKMANI 2001, vol. II, p. 115: "Action has a fixed measure as there is no knowledge of action as something that does not take notice of the measure."

[363] PYV, p. 310: *niyataparimāṇā hi kriyānavagataparimāṇāyāḥ kriyāyā lakṣaṇam, yathā—āgodohanaṃ svapiti, audanapākam adhīta iti. sa eva ca kālaḥ.*

[364] ĪPVV, vol. III, p. 5: *nanu yena kalati kṣipati paricchinatti sa kālaḥ, kriyā paricchedyā tat kathaṃ sā kālaḥ. atrāha* ***viśiṣṭeti*****, *iyattayā prasiddhatvam anena lakṣayatā tasyām api parimātum iṣṭāyāṃ nālikāsrutyādikriyāntaram eva* ***kāla*** *ityāha.* [****viśiṣṭeti*** corr.; *viśiṣṭa iti* Ed.]

for instance when he explains what he takes to be the gist of the Vaiśeṣikas' definition of time according to Bhartṛhari:[365]

> The Vaiśeṣikas profess that time, which has as its inferential marks cognitions such as [being temporally] close and distant,[366] is [all-]pervasive, one, [and] has no material shape; since for this reason it is not produced, it is eternal; it is distinct from action, and it is a measure (*paricchedaka*) of [objective] entities through actions such as birth, etc.[367]

Abhinavagupta too underscores that according to the Vaiśeṣikas, time, defined as a distinct substance, is something distinct (*anya*) from actions;[368] and in the sequel of the *Vivṛti* on ĪPK 2.1.3, Utpaladeva himself presents

---

[365] He is commenting on VP 3.9.1: *vyāpāravyatirekeṇa kālam eke pracakṣate | nityam ekaṃ vibhu dravyaṃ parimāṇaṃ kriyāvatām ||* "Some explain time as [being] distinct from activity, [as] an eternal, single, [all-]pervading substance that is the measure (*parimāṇa*) of [things] endowed with action."

[366] I.e., being close and distant while not being so in a spatial manner (see below, fn. 371).

[367] PP, vol. II, p. 41: *parāparādipratyayaliṅgo vyāpaka eko 'mūrto 'ta evākṛtakatvān nityaḥ kālaḥ kriyāvyatirikto janmādikriyādvāreṇa bhāvaparicchedako vaiśeṣikair āmnātaḥ.*

[368] See ĪPVV, vol. III, p. 5: ... *sūryasaṃcārādibhir yo 'nyo lakṣyate pravahaṇadharmā navapurāṇatādirūpaparatvāparatvatadvaicitryatadbāhulyād upakalpito* yaugapadyetaraciraśīghratādyasaṅkīrṇabhāvasvabhāvotthāpako vaiśeṣikāṇāṃ dravyarūpaḥ...* [**upakalpito* S12; *upakalpita°* J11, Ed.]. "According to the Vaiśeṣikas, [time] is marked by [actions] such as the sun's movement while being distinct [from them]; [it] possesses the property of flowing; [it] consists in a substance; [it] is assumed [to exist] due to the variety and multiplicity of the [properties] of being close and distant—which consist in being young, old, etc.—and [it] is responsible for the nature of the relation between [entities] that are distinct, such as being simultaneous or not, being slow[er] and quick[er], etc." This is a reference to the Vaiśeṣikas' contention that time must be inferred in order to account for the fact that the notions of proximity and distance are not merely spatial, and that things can be "far" from each other although in terms of location they happen to be close: see below, fn. 371. It might be deemed tempting to emend *°dharmā* into *°dharmī* in the passage above, but not to mention that S12 and J11 provide the same reading, the compound *pravahaṇadharman* occurs elsewhere in the ĪPVV (see e.g. vol. III, p. 7: *pravahaṇadharmaṇaḥ*, a reading also shared by S12 and J11); I take it to be a technical term whose source is unknown to me.

time in the Vaiśeṣika as a substance endowed with "an accomplished form" (*siddharūpa*)—an expression obviously used to distinguish it from actions.[369] However, Abhinavagupta's commentaries present the entire discussion under this verse as targeting the Vaiśeṣika; and according to them, with this beginning that equates time with actions, Utpaladeva wants to show that the defects in the Vaiśeṣikas' definition of time *unwittingly lead them to acknowledge the thesis that time is nothing but actions.*

Thus in the Vaiśeṣika, the definition of time is problematic inasmuch as time is supposed to be a single, permanent substance conjoined with all the substances endowed with a material shape, and yet it is first and foremost inferred as a measure (*paricchedaka, avacchedaka*)[370] enabling us to delimit things, i.e., as that which is responsible for our awareness of temporal *distinctions* between the simultaneous and the successive, the slow and the quick, etc.; such temporally determined cognitions are presented in the VS as the marks enabling us to infer the existence of an independent substance called "time."[371] Yet the Vaiśeṣikas acknowledge that, time being one and eternal, it cannot by itself account for the temporal distinctions that affect

---

[369] On this distinction see e.g. VP 3.7.79cd: *kriyāṇām eva sādhyatvāt siddharūpo 'bhidhīyate* || "[The object of action] is said to have an accomplished (*siddha*) form, since only actions are to be accomplished (*sādhya*)."

[370] The latter term is used several times in the *Vivṛti* on ĪPK 2.1.3, and in Abhinavagupta's commentary thereon; Helārāja uses the term *paricchedaka* while depicting the Vaiśeṣika's position on time (see above, fn. 367); so does the PYV (see below, fn. 376).

[371] VS 2.2.6: *aparasmin paraṃ yugapad ayugapac ciraṃ kṣipram iti kālaliṅgāni.* "[The cognitions that something is] distant with respect to something that [happens to be spatially] close, [that it is] simultaneous [or] not, slow [or] quick, are [inferential] marks of time." Cf. VSV, p. 17: *tatra pareṇa dikpradeśena saṃyukte yūni paratvajñāne jāte sthavire cāpareṇa dikpradeśena saṃyukte 'paratvajñānotpattau kṛṣṇakeśādivalīpalitādiparyālocanayā yena nimittena yūni aparatvajñānaṃ sthavire ca paratvajñānaṃ jāyate sa kālaḥ.* "Among these [marks of time, here is the first:] when the cognition of remoteness has arisen with respect to a young person who is conjoined with a place that is remote, and when the cognition of proximity arises with respect to an old person who is conjoined with a place that is close, [nonetheless,] through the observation of [the young person's] black hair, etc., and of [the old one's] wrinkles and grey hair, the cognition of proximity arises with respect to the young person, and the cognition of remoteness [arises] with respect to the old one; the cause thanks to which [these cognitions occur must] be time." See also below, fn. 385 and 386.

things. Praśastapāda thus argues that temporal divisions between past, present and future must rather result from adventitious properties (*upādhi*) that do not belong to the very nature of time, and these adventitious properties that account for time distinctions happen to be various actions:

> Although literally speaking, [time] is one since there is no [fundamental] distinction between the [various] inferential marks of time, [we] talk [about time] figuratively as if it were diverse due to the variety in adventitious properties (*upādhi*) [that are superimposed onto time and consist in] the undertaking of all effects, the performance of the actions [that produces them, their] persisting existence and destruction– just as, in the cases of a gem or a cook,[372] [we talk figuratively of a diversity whereas these entities are really one].[373]

Similarly, Jayanta for instance presents as follows the Vaiśeṣika view on this issue:

> But since according [to your demonstration], time is one, where does the distinction between present, [past and future] come from? Since [this distinction] is not found in [time], how can [you claim] that [your] inference [establishing the existence of time] has as its object the three times[, i.e. past,

[372] See the explanation in *Vyomavatī*, vol. I, p. 130: *atha kathaṃ nānātvam upacaryata ity āha maṇivat pācakavad veti. yathā maṇeḥ svarūpāparityāgenaivopādhibhedād upacaryate nānātvaṃ pīto rakta iti, tadvad ihāpi bhinnakriyopādhivaśād vartamānādibheda iti. yathā vā svarūpāparityāgenaiva puruṣasya nānākriyāvaśāt pācakādibhedas tadvad ihāpīti.* "But how is this diversity figuratively applied to [time]? [Praśastapāda] answers: 'just as in the cases of a gem or a cook.' [That is to say,] a [transparent] gem is said to be diverse figuratively [in such sentences as] 'it is yellow, it is red,' due to a variety of adventitious properties [superimposed onto it owing to the proximity of coloured objects], whereas the gem does not abandon its [unitary] nature at all; in the same way, in the [case of time] too, the difference between 'present,' ['past' and 'future'] is due to the adventitious properties that are the various actions; or again, for a man, the difference between such [a property] as being a cook [and the properties of being the agent of any other action] is [simply] due to [his] diverse actions, whereas he does not abandon [his unitary] nature at all; the same goes in the [case of time] too."

[373] PDhS, p. 170: *kālaliṅgāviśeṣād añjasaikatve 'pi sarvakāryāṇāṃ prārambhakriyābhinirvṛttisthitinirodhopādhibhedān maṇivat pācakavad vā nānātvopacāra iti.*

> present and future]? [– Answer:] the difference between present, etc. does not belong to the [very] nature of time; rather, although this [difference] is not real, it is assumed in order to establish our ordinary practices thanks to some adventitious property. [– Question:] But what is this adventitious property? [– Answer:] we say that it is an action.[374]

Now, if even the Vaiśeṣikas admit that temporal divisions result from actions rather than from time itself, one can argue that their concept of time as a permanent substance is useless, since such a permanent, inactive substance can play no part in bringing about temporal distinctions or measures; as a result, one may rather define time as being nothing but certain specific actions (such as those of celestial bodies) commonly used to measure other actions, in accordance with the thesis that Jayanta ascribes to "astrologers/astronomers"[375] and that is defended by the YD and PYV. Thus the latter argues:

> But for the [Vaiśeṣika,] who [considers that] time is distinct from actions, eternal [and] all-pervasive, even such [properties as] being slow or quick cannot be an inferential mark for the existence of time as a distinct [entity], because [these properties] boil down to nothing but action.[376]

---

[374] NM$_{M}$, vol. I, p. 369: *nanv evaṃ caikatvāt kālasya kuto vartamānādivibhāgaḥ. tadabhāvāt kathaṃ trikālaviṣayam anumānam ucyate? ucyate: na tāttvikaḥ kālasya bhedo vartamānādiḥ, kintv asann apy asau vyavahārasiddhaye kenacid upādhinā kalpyate. kaḥ punar asāv upādhiḥ. kriyeti brūmaḥ.*

[375] NM$_{M}$, vol. I, pp. 366–367/NM$_{V}$, vol. I, p. 201: *āha: na devadattādiparispandanibandhanāḥ kramākramādipratyayāḥ, kintu grahanakṣatrādiparispandanibandhanāḥ. sa eva ca grahatārādiparispandaḥ kāla ity ucyate... kālavidaś ca jyotirgaṇakās ta evainaṃ budhyante.* "[An objector] says: the cognitions of sequence, simultaneity and so on do not have as their basis the movements of Devadatta and [other individuals]; rather, they have as their basis the movements of planets, stars, etc.; and what [we] call time is [nothing but] the movements of planets, stars, etc. [...]. And it is astrologers/astronomers, who are specialists of time, who understand it [thus]." The compound *kālavid* is of course reminiscent of VP 3.9.76 (see above, fn. 354).

[376] PYV, p. 310: *yasya tu kriyāvyatiriktaḥ kālaḥ nityo vibhus tasya cirakṣipratvādy api kriyāmātre paryavasitatvāt pṛthakkālāstitve na liṅgaṃ ghaṭate.*

After stating that we only use well-known actions to measure other actions,[377] the PYV adds:

> For the eternal, [all-]pervasive, unchangeable [time postulated by the Vaiśeṣikas] cannot be the measure (*paricchedaka*) of something else—as for instance the [measure called] *prastha* [determines a weight or capacity]—, because it can have no relation [with anything else].[378]

If time is defined as an *avacchedaka*, we can dispense with the assumption of a distinct substance called time and we should consider that the word "time" simply refers to the various actions that enable us to measure temporal determinations. The argument is presented by Vācaspatimiśra as a defining feature of the Sāṃkhya philosophy:

> And [since] time [as it is] admitted by the Vaiśeṣikas is one, [it is] incapable of causing the diversity in [our] talking about [things as being past, present] and future; therefore let [us] admit that only the various [so-called] adventitious properties through which this [time allegedly] produces the variety [of temporal determinations] such as ["past," "present"] and "future" are [in fact] the [sole] causes of our talking about [things as being past, present] and future: regarding this [variety of temporal determinations,] what could be the point of [the Vaiśeṣika's] time, which is [as useless as] a humpback?[379]—This is what the masters of Sāṃkhya [declare].

---

[377] See above, fn. 363.

[378] PYV, p. 310: *na hi nityasya vibhos tasya kūṭasthasyāsambandhatvād vastvantaraparicchedakatvaṃ prasthādivad upapadyate.*

[379] On the compound *antargaḍu* (lit. an "internal growth"), often used to convey that the assumption of an imperceptible entity's existence is utterly useless, see e.g. the commentaries on Utpaladeva's ĪPK 1.2.5cd (*yady evam antargaḍunā ko'rthaḥ syāt sthāyinātmanā* || "If it is the case, [then] what could be the point of a permanent self [as useless as] a humpback?"). Abhinavagupta comments (ĪPV, vol. I, p. 64): *evaṃ tarhy antargaḍur yathāyāsāya param, tadvad ātmā sthiraḥ kalpanāyāsamātraphala iti kiṃ tena.* "If it is the case, just as a humpback only results in weariness, in the same way, a permanent self results in nothing but a weariness of the speculative faculty—so what is the point [of assuming its existence]?" The *Bhāskarī* further explains (vol. I, p. 98): *gaḍuḥ kubjapṛṣṭhastho māṃsapiṇḍaḥ, sa hi sphuṭam*

> Therefore [they] do not acknowledge an additional principle that would consist in time.[380]

It is precisely this criticism of the Vaiśeṣika understanding of time that is, according to Abhinavagupta, the main reason prompting Utpaladeva to formulate ĪPK 2.1.3 as an answer to it:

> But what is this time that is supposed to be a measure (*avacchedaka*) of [objective] entities? For how could this [time], which is acknowledged by some to consist in a particular permanent substance, be the cause of the [different] cognitions "slow," "quick," etc., with their various aspects, since it is one and has a particular conjunction [with all the substances endowed with a material shape]? If [it] is said to be thus [what measures things] because of adventitious properties (*upādhi*) [and not because of its own nature], [then] let [us admit that] only these adventitious properties exist, [and no distinct substance called time]; what is the point of this [time]?[381]

## 2. Utpaladeva's goal in ĪPK 2.1.3: showing that time is only the sequence involved in ordinary actions

So according to Abhinavagupta, although Utpaladeva's main interlocutors here are Vaiśeṣikas, in his *Vivṛti* on the beginning of this verse at least, he does not even consider the Vaiśeṣikas' definition of time as a permanent, unitary and static substance, because he adopts the criticism put forward by the Vaiśeṣikas' opponents, according to which such a substance is contradictory with the Vaiśeṣikas' fundamental acknowledgement that time is an *avacchedaka*, a measure that brings about delimitations in things. Utpaladeva's implicit contention is that if the Vaiśeṣikas maintain that time is such

---

*evāyāsakārī*. "*gaḍu* [designates] a mass of flesh on the back of [someone] whose back is humped; for obviously, this causes weariness!"

380 TK, p. 140: *kālaś ca vaiśeṣikābhimata eko nānāgatādivyavahārabhedaṃ vartayitum arhati. tasmād ayaṃ yair upādhibhedair anāgatādibhedam pratipadyate santu ta evopādhayo 'nāgatādivyavahārahetavaḥ, kṛtam atrāntargaḍunā kāleneti sāṃkhyācāryāḥ. tasmān na kālarūpatattvāntarābhyupagama iti.*

381 ĪPVV, vol. III, p. 4: *nanu ko'sau kālo yo bhāvānām avacchedaka ucyate. yo hi kaiścin nityadravyaviśeṣātmopagataḥ, sa ekatvāt saṃyogaviśeṣāc citrākāracirakṣiprādidhīhetuḥ katham. upādhibalāt tathābhidhāne ta evopādhayaḥ santu, kiṃ tena.*

an *avacchedaka*, as pointed out by their Sāṃkhya opponents, they must abandon the thesis of an eternal, unitary and unchanging substance called "time" and they must accept that time is nothing but certain actions used to measure other actions. Now, this equation of time with actions is unacceptable for Utpaladeva, whose main concern is *to dissociate time from action and to show that the former is not an intrinsic property of the latter*, so that action, in the form of *vimarśa*, can be the essence of the ultimate consciousness without necessarily entailing a temporal limitation in it.

Thus as Abhinavagupta makes clear while introducing ĪPK 2.1.3 in his ĪPVV, Utpaladeva wants to show that time is not actions, but the sequence (*krama*) found in certain actions (i.e., those pertaining to the realm of *māyā*), which is manifested by the Lord's power of time (*kālaśakti*):

> Having anticipated this [objection according to which time must be nothing but actions, Utpaladeva states] the [following] verse in order to explain that the power of time, which makes sequence manifest, is the power of the Lord Himself; and [as for] time, [it] is nothing but the sequence made manifest by this [power—a sequence] that is entirely dependent (*lagna*)[382] on the māyic knowing subject, since it exists while having [this subject as its] essence, [and] it resides in the [objective] entities that are liable to become the objects [perceived] by this [subject].[383]

Utpaladeva's own thesis is that time is nothing but sequence,[384] which in turn is nothing but the fact that certain phenomena cannot occur together

---

[382] Literally, it is "stuck" to this subject: the point is that sequence can only exist in connection with—and from the limited point of view of—the māyic subject, i.e., the transmigrating subject who is in fact the free universal consciousness but has forgotten his/her identity with it.

[383] ĪPVV, vol. III, p. 4: *ity āśaṅkya bhagavata eva śaktiḥ kramam avabhāsayantī kālaśaktiḥ, tadavabhāsyaś ca māyāpramātṛlagna eva pradhānatayā bhavann etadviṣayīkaraṇīyabhāvaniṣṭhaḥ krama eva kāla iti darśayituṃ sūtram.*

[384] In ĪPV, vol. II, p. 9, Abhinavagupta argues that the word *eva* in the verse must be understood both as meaning that time is *nothing but* sequence and that sequence is *nothing but* time: *sa eva ca sūryādīnāṃ svabhāvaviśeṣas tattvataḥ paramārthataḥ kramaḥ, nānyaḥ kaścit kramo nāma, krama eva ca kālo nānyo 'sau kaścid ity eva-*

with other phenomena; and according to him, this restriction in the way things appear is brought about by the ultimate consciousness's "power of time," that is to say, the Lord's ability to freely decide that certain phenomena can be manifested together while others cannot. In order to establish this, he is now going to show that time cannot be just actions, because what enables us to use any ordinary action as a measure of other actions is the fact that they all share a common, lasting (*sthira*) element—and this common element is not a relation with a single, distinct substance as the Vaiśeṣikas contend, but sequence.

### 3. Two understandings of time as a cause in the Vaiśeṣika

Yet in the *Vivṛti*, before showing this, Utpaladeva first points out that the Vaiśeṣikas' definition of time is ambiguous inasmuch as they ascribe two strikingly different functions to time.

Thus on the one hand, as already mentioned, they consider that time is what brings about delimitations or measures in the actions that we perceive—and in this regard, time is seen as a cause that acts on our cognitions (*pratīti*, *pratyaya*) rather than on things themselves: the Vaiśeṣikas define it as that which produces in us the *ideas* of this or that temporal distinction, such as

---

*kāro bhinnābhinnakramo yojyaḥ*. "And 'in reality,' [i.e.] in fact, sequence is nothing but this [time, which is in turn] the specific nature of [things] such as the sun; what is called 'sequence' is absolutely nothing over and above [time]. Moreover, time is nothing but sequence; it is nothing over and above [sequence]—so the particle *eva* must be taken both as being placed differently than it should [in the usual prose order, i.e. immediately after the word denoting time], and as being located in its rightful place, [i.e. immediately after the word denoting sequence]." As far as I can see, nothing in the *Vivṛti* supports this interpretation, the particle *eva* being more naturally read there as being located in its rightful place ("time is *nothing but* sequence"). The reason for this discrepancy might have to do with the fact that Abhinavagupta endeavours to show in his commentaries that the "marks of time" invoked by the Vaiśeṣikas to prove the existence of time can in fact be entirely accounted for on the mere basis of sequence (see below, fn. 393), so that we do not have to infer the existence of a distinct substance called "time" to explain them; and one of these "marks of time" happens to be the idea that something is "not simultaneous" (*ayugapad*), i.e., sequential—so Abhinavagupta might be forcing the interpretation of *eva* in the verse so as to have it suggest that sequence is not a mark of time *because it is nothing but time*.

simultaneity and sequence, slowness and speed, etc. Accordingly, while explaining VS 5.2.28, which claims that "Time [is explained] as a cause" (*kāraṇena kāla iti*), Candrānanda specifies:

> Just as space is explained as a cause, [i.e.] as being the cause of a difference in [our] cognitions (*pratyaya*), in the same way, time is explained [as] the efficient cause of the difference in [our] cognitions such as "[this] was done simultaneously."[385]

The same idea is expounded by Praśastapāda:

> Time has as its inferential marks the cognitions (*pratyaya*) of [being] mutually distant or close, of simultaneity and non-simultaneity, [and] of [being] slow and quick. Since these [cognitions] arise with respect to objects while being distinct from [all the other] cognitions already [described], they can have no other cause, so their cause must be time.[386]

On the other hand, the Vaiśeṣikas also consider that time is a cause in the sense that it exerts its influence on *things* themselves.[387] Thus Praśastapāda adds:

> And [time must also] be the cause of the arising, existence and destruction of all effects, because [they] are [all] described (*vyapadeśa*) in terms of [time].[388]

Vyomaśiva, while explaining this passage in Praśastapāda's PDhS, specifies that time is to be understood as an auxiliary cause (*sahakārin*) in the production of things:

---

385 VSV, p. 44: *yenaiva kāraṇena pratyayabhedahetutvena dig vyākhyātā tenaiva yugapat kṛtam ityādipratyayabhedasya kālo nimittakāraṇaṃ vyākhyātaḥ.*

386 PDhS, p. 164: *kālaḥ parāparavyatikarayaugapadyāyaugapadyacirakṣipraprapratyayaliṅgaḥ. teṣāṃ viṣayeṣu pūrvapratyayavilakṣaṇānām utpattāv anyanimittābhāvād yad atra nimittaṃ sa kālaḥ.* See also UI 1917, p. 134, on this idea in the surviving Chinese translation of Candramati's *Daśapadārthaśāstra.*

387 On this second aspect of the definition of time in Vaiśeṣika and its relationship with the first see e.g. KEITH 1921, p. 233; FRAUWALLNER 1956, vol. II, p. 111; PRASAD 1984, p. 235; HALBFASS 1992, pp. 212–213.

388 PDhS, p. 165: *sarvakāryāṇāṃ cotpattisthitivināśahetus tadvyapadeśāt.*

> Thus, the perception of an effect such as a flower [occurs] at a specific time and not at any other; therefore the fact that this [specific time] is a cause is known through invariable co-presence and co-absence. To explain: the arising of flowers such as [those of] the *pāṭala* [tree] only [occurs] in the season of spring, not at any other time, [so spring must be a cause of this arising; and this causality] can be inferred thus with respect to other effects as well. Similarly, the causality of time [is inferred] from the fact that [we] say [such things] as "[this] requires a time of maturation." To explain: since [what] the perception [of something] requires [is] an auxiliary cause (*sahakārin*), if time were not an auxiliary cause [of that thing], [we] could not [even] talk about [its] maturation.[389]

Now, according to Abhinavagupta, in his *Vivṛti* Utpaladeva explains the different options separated by the two particles "or" (*vā*) in the verse—viz. "Time is the movement of the sun, etc.; *or* this or that arising of flowers, etc.; *or* cold and heat...") by presenting the first two as roughly equivalent, since they both refer to the Vaiśeṣika's definition of time as a measure that affects cognitions, whereas the third alludes to the Vaiśeṣika contention that time plays a part in bringing about things themselves:

> The word "or" that occurs first [in the verse], while pointing out that two options—[viz. time is the movement of the sun, etc./time is the arising of flowers, etc.]—are being conceptually differentiated, [really] indicates that they amount to the same thing. And thus, while the first two options are posited with the intention [of conveying] that time contributes to the action of measuring (*pariccheda*), the third one [– i.e. time is cold and heat—is posited] with the intention [of conveying

[389] *Vyomavatī*, vol. I, p. 128: *tathā niyatakāle kusumādeḥ kāryasyopalambho na kālāntara ity anvayavyatirekābhyāṃ tasya kāraṇatvaṃ vijñāyate. tathā hi vasantasamaya eva pāṭalādikusumānām udgamo na kālāntara ity evaṃ kāryāntareṣv apy ūhyam. tathā prasavakālam apekṣata iti vyavahārāt kāraṇatvaṃ kālasya. tathā hi sahakāriṇam apekṣyopalabdheḥ kālasya sahakāritām antareṇa prasūtāv ayaṃ vyavahāro na syāt.*

> the idea found in VS 2.2.11, according to which] "the name 'time' applies to the cause."[390]

The *Vivṛti* emphasizes that it is only with this second aspect of the definition of time, which presents time as an auxiliary cause, that the Vaiśeṣikas can claim to establish time as something that has "an accomplished form" (*siddharūpa*)—i.e., as a distinct *thing*, as a substance rather than a mere action.[391] Yet Utpaladeva already seems to imply, while presenting this second aspect of the Vaiśeṣika's definition, that the thing in question can hardly be more than a collection of discrete elements that are in fact distinct from time itself, since the Vaiśeṣikas, when using the example of flowers growing in spring, must acknowledge that the time of spring only plays a causal role with respect to the growth of flowers inasmuch as it takes the form of "heat, etc." In any case the example to which he alludes in this connection—that of the specific temperatures of spring that are known to contribute to the production of various flowers—brings to mind Vyomaśiva's reasoning, although the idea is evidently much older than the *Vyomavatī*.[392]

[390] ĪPVV, vol. III, p. 6: *ādyo vāśabdo dvayoḥ pakṣayor vikalpyamānatām ācakṣāṇas tulyavṛttāntatām āha. tathā ca prathamau pakṣau paricchedakriyopayogī kāla ity anenāśayena sthitau, tṛtīyas tu kāraṇe kālākhyety anenāśayena.*

[391] See above, fn. 369 on the compound *siddharūpa*.

[392] It already appears for instance in the commentary on the Buddhist *Śataśāstra*, a fragment of which has survived in a Chinese translation executed in 404 CE. See the English translation of it in TUCCI 1929, p. 76, on time according to an "unbeliever": "Although when it is very subtle it cannot be seen, yet through the seasons, flowers, fruits and so on we know that time exists. And then, seeing the effect we know the cause." Cf. *Mahāprajñāpāramitāśāstra* (translated in Chinese in the same year); for a French translation see LAMOTTE 1949, pp. 76–77: "Mais comme le Dharma 'Temps' est subtil (*sūkṣma*), il est invisible (*adṛśya*) et inconnaissable (*ajñeya*). C'est par ses effets, fleurs (*puṣpa*), fruits (*phala*), etc., qu'on peut connaître son existence et voir ses caractères (*lakṣaṇa*) tels que: année passée ou année présente, autrefois ou récemment, lentement ou rapidement. Bien qu'on ne voie pas le Temps, il est possible de connaître son existence. Car c'est en voyant l'effet (*phala*) qu'on connaît l'existence de la cause (*hetu*). C'est pourquoi il existe un Dharma 'Temps.'"

## 4. Utpaladeva's criticism of the first understanding: why time cannot be certain actions used to measure others

In the *Vivṛti*, Utpaladeva then proceeds to dismiss both definitions of time. As pointed out above, he has already—and implicitly—reduced the first aspect of the Vaiśeṣika thesis (namely, that the substance called "time" must be inferred as the cause of our temporally determined cognitions) to the position held by Sāṃkhya opponents of the Vaiśeṣika system, according to which time, as the cause producing the awareness of temporal measures, can only be actions themselves; so Utpaladeva only has to refute the latter contention—a strategy that Abhinavagupta may have deemed somewhat insufficient, since for his part he endeavours to show that all the inferential marks adduced by the VS as proof of the existence of the substance called "time" can in fact be entirely accounted for on the mere basis of sequence.[393] As far as can be seen from the *Vivṛti*'s chapter 2.1, this line of argument was not borrowed from Utpaladeva himself, who had adopted the Sāṃkhya's more sweeping criticism of the Vaiśeṣika position, according to which the Vaiśeṣikas' definition of time can only lead to the acknowledgement that it is nothing but actions. And the *Vivṛti*, after presenting the Vaiśeṣika position, argues that time cannot thus be a measure (*avacchedaka*) constituted by certain specific actions, because such measures are a sheer matter of convention: any action can be used to assess the duration of other actions, and this is problematic, because if an action A is measured by an action B, action B in turn requires an action C in order to be measured, and so on ad infinitum.

[393] Compare the "marks of time" enumerated in VS 2.2.6—namely, the ideas that something spatially close is nonetheless distant, that it is simultaneous/sequential or slow/quick (see above, fn. 371)—with ĪPV, vol. II, pp. 9–10: *yaugapadyam apy ābhāsayor aparābhāsāpekṣayā krama eva. cirakṣiprādidhīr api vitatānyatvavaśād ābhāsabhede kramarūpa eva. paratvāparatvabuddhir api sphuṭatvādinā tatraiva.* "The fact that two phenomena are simultaneous is also nothing but sequence in relation to another, [third] phenomenon; the idea [that something is] slow, quick, etc. also [occurs] only with respect to a difference in phenomena that consists in nothing but sequence, depending on whether [this sequence] is extended or not; as for the awareness of proximity and distance, it also [occurs] only with respect to [sequence], depending on whether [it is apprehended] vividly or not, etc." On the mark of time that is sequence itself, see above, fn. 384. Cf. ĪPVV, vol. III, p. 7, ll. 22 ff. for a somewhat similar reasoning.

This is a well-known criticism, adduced for instance by Jayanta:

> In [experiences that we may describe as] "The sun has slowly set," "The moon has quickly arisen," "Mars and Venus seem to have arisen simultaneously," [we] perceive a [temporally determined] appearance, and [this appearance] cannot be explained as having as its cause the movement of some other planet, because there would follow an infinite regress; therefore time is not the movement of planets, etc., but something distinct that is responsible for [our] ordinary usage (*vyavahāra*) [of words denoting] succession, simultaneity, etc.[394]

The argument is certainly much older than the NM, since Bhartṛhari, while explaining the point of the "specialists of time" who believe that time is nothing more than actions, already underscores that the action used to measure another one "has a measurement that is [already] well known" (*nirjñātapariṇāma*),[395] and in the PYV, this point is explicitly used to show that the thesis according to which time is nothing but actions involves no infinite regress: this is so "because the action [used to measure a given time] is well known by all."[396] Abhinavagupta too emphasizes that those who reduce time to actions refute the accusation of infinite regress by arguing that the actions used as measure are the objects of a common knowledge (*prasiddhi*):

> Gold is measured for example by a weight[397] whose measure is [already] determined; and there is no infinite regress or

[394] NM$_M$, vol. I, pp. 366–367: *cireṇāstaṃgato bhānuḥ śītāṃśuḥ śīghram udgataḥ | uditāv iva dṛśyete yugapad bhaumabhārgavau || iti dṛśyate pratibhāsaḥ, na ca grahāntaraparispandakāraṇaka eṣa śakyate vaktum anavasthāprasaṅgāt; tasmān na grahādiparispandaḥ kālaḥ, kintu vastvantaraṃ yatkṛto 'yaṃ kramākramādivyavahāraḥ.*

[395] See above, fn. 354; cf. Helārāja's commentary, fn. 355.

[396] PYV, p. 310: ... *kriyāyāḥ sarvaprasiddhatvāt...* On the whole sentence and its interpretations, see RATIÉ forthcoming b.

[397] On the term *prativartaka*, see e.g. *Bhāskarī*, vol. II, p. 12: *prativartakaiḥ—guñjādirūpaiḥ pratimānakhaṇḍair ity arthaḥ.* "[The word] '*prativartaka*s' designates pieces that are weights (*pratimāna*) having the form of the *guñja* [berry] and so

> logical circle in that. In the same way, the movement of Caitra [is measured] by [another] action whose measure is well known (*prasiddha*), which consists in the rising and setting of the sun—this is what [we mean when we] say: "Caitra goes for the day." And the action of the sun too, if one wishes to measure it, is measured [in turn] by the [particular] flows [of water called] *nālikās*[398] that are well known, [as when we say:] "The sun is seen for thirty *nālikās*."[399]

At the beginning of the *Vivṛti* on ĪPK 2.1.3, Utpaladeva himself has repeatedly pointed out that those who reduce time to actions insist that a measuring action is a well-known (*prasiddha*) one, precisely because this is how they claim to dodge the acccusation of infinite regress. Now, however, the *Vivṛti* points out that this argument is only a way of pushing back the problem without solving it. Abhinavagupta sums up as follows Utpaladeva's exchange with his opponent on this issue:

> But even one's own will to create measures does not function [on its own,] without resting on common knowledge!—[This is] true; nonetheless, this common knowledge is not firm[ly established] (*ekaghana*)—[this is what Utpaladeva] says with "and [because] the common knowledge [on which this will is allegedly based is itself liable to an infinite regress].[400]

---

on." According to MONIER-WILLIAMS 1899, s.v., the berry of the *guñja* plant (Abrus precatorius), or the "artificial weight named after it," constitutes "the smallest of the jewellers' weights."

[398] See below, chapter 11, fn. 25.

[399] ĪPVV, vol. III, p. 4: *niyataparimāṇaṃ yat prativartakādi tena kanakaṃ mīyate; na cātrānavasthānyonyāśrayo vā. tadvat prasiddhaparimāṇayā kriyayārkodayāstamayamayyā caitragamanam. tad ucyate divasaṃ caitro gacchatīti. ādityakriyāpi yadā parimitsitā bhavati tadā prasiddhābhir nālikāsrutibhir mīyate, triṃśataṃ nālikāḥ sūryo dṛśyata iti...* Cf. e.g. ĪPVV, vol. III, p. 5: *anavasthādi ca kanakaprativartakavṛttāntena kṛtasamādhānam eva.* "And such [potential objections] as infinite regress are immediately refuted in the same manner [as they are in the case of] weights [used to measure] gold."

[400] ĪPVV, vol. III, p. 7: *nanu svecchāpi na prasiddhim* anavalambya vartate 'vacchedakakalpanāyai. satyam, prasiddhir api tu naikaghanety āha* ***prasiddheś ceti.*** [**na prasiddhim* S12, J11; *prasiddhim* Ed.]

As the opponent argues that although choosing a specific action to measure another one is a mere matter of convention, this convention is rooted in the "common knowledge" of the duration of a specific action, Utpaladeva replies that this common knowledge itself is problematic—where does it come from, if not from the measure of that action by another action? Quite amusingly, here Utpaladeva thus seems to be using a strategy in line with the Vaiśeṣika's, since he is emphasizing that in order to avoid infinite regress, we must assume that actions can only function as measures of time because there is something over and above them that constitutes time itself. Yet he is also going to show that this other entity cannot be the static substance imagined by the Vaiśeṣika, but only sequence.

### 5. Utpaladeva's refutation of the second understanding: why time cannot be this or that auxiliary cause

As pointed out by Abhinavagupta, Utpaladeva then turns to the second Vaiśeṣika contention, according to which time is an auxilary cause of such effects as the growth of plants:

> While correcting the thesis that time is cold, etc., with [the sentence beginning with] "[And from the fact that] cold, etc.," [Utpaladeva] comments on the point explained in [*Vaiśeṣika*]*sūtra* [2.2.11]: "The name 'time' applies to the cause."[401]

Utpaladeva argues in this respect that "from the fact that the cold, etc., contribute to the production of an effect, [what follows] is merely that [they] are a cause, [but] not [that they are] time": it is one thing to state that a specific temperature contributes to the production of the flower, and quite another to claim that this specific temperature happens to be time. When the Vaiśeṣikas say that the particular period of time that is spring is the cause of a flower's arising, they can only mean that the specific temperature found in spring contributes to the production of a specific effect, but this only shows that this temperature is a cause, rather than establishing time's

[401] ĪPVV, vol. III, p. 7: *śītādiḥ kāla ity amuṃ pakṣaṃ śodhayan kāraṇe kālākhyeti sūtrasyoktarūpam arthaṃ vyācaṣṭe* ***śītādīnām*** *iti*.

causality.[402] The Vaiśeṣika could reply that nonetheless, such a temperature only occurs at a certain time of the year, namely spring; but according to Utpaladeva, such a statement amounts to acknowledging that the action consisting in the occurrence of this particular temperature functions as a *measure* for other actions (i.e. as a mark letting us know, for instance, that the arising of flowers is about to take place)—but then Utpaladeva has already shown that such measures cannot be time itself, as this would imply an infinite regress. Abhinavagupta's commentary anticipates on the consequence that Utpaladeva is about to draw from this reasoning:

> And the cold, etc. can be time only due to their being measures [and not because they would be causes of a given effect]; and [their being measures] can only be due to [their] having [as their common characteristic] the fact that [they] consist in sequence, which has the property of flowing; therefore time is nothing but the sequence found in the [cold, etc.]—this is [what Utpaladeva] means [here].[403]

While commenting on the *Vivṛti*'s initial mention of this Vaiśeṣika definition of time as an auxiliary cause, Abhinavagupta had already expressed Utpaladeva's strategy in a nutshell:

> And [Utpaladeva will show] in this regard [that even] for that which happens to be a cause, being time can only be due to [its] being a measure [and not to its being a cause], and [that] only its consisting in sequence ensues if it is a measure.[404]

---

[402] Here Utpaladeva's criticism has a Buddhist ring to it and seems reminiscent of the way in which Prajñākaragupta for instance refutes the notion that time understood as an independent entity may be inferred as a cause (on the latter refutation see FRANCO 2011, p. 95).

[403] ĪPVV, vol. III, p. 7: *śītāder apy avacchedakataiva kālatāyām upayuktā, sā ca pravahaṇadharmakramarūpatvāveśenaiveti tadgataḥ krama eva kāla ity uktaṃ bhavati.*

[404] ĪPVV, vol. III, pp. 6–7: *tatra ca kāraṇasya sato'vacchedakatvam eva kālatāyām upayujyate, avacchedakatve ca kramarūpataivāgacchati...*

### 6. Why time is not a distinct substance: Utpaladeva's main divergence with the Vaiśeṣika

The *Vivṛti* finally turns to Utpaladeva's own definition of time. Since the Vaiśeṣikas themselves acknowledge that time must have a lasting, unitary nature, they must admit that it is the one and only element always found in all worldly actions, namely, sequence; whereas the various actions that we use as temporal measures are only "markers" (*upalakṣaṇa*), i.e., adventitious properties (*upādhi*) of things that can nonetheless serve to mark them, just as, to use a famous example, we may recognize Devadatta's house because we are told that it is the one on which a crow happens to be perched: the crow does not belong to the house's nature, nor does the word "crow" denote the house, yet we can use it to mark a specific house.[405] Similarly, actions are markers of time without being either time itself or the other actions that they thus help us measure, precisely because they all involve sequence without being sequence itself, since the latter, contrary to them, is a lasting, unitary reality—namely, the very fact that events occur in a stream or flow (*pravahaṇa*) rather than all at once or forever. According to the *Vivṛti*, this is why, although spring may be defined as a specific se-

---

405 On this example and the notion of *upalakṣaṇa* as an adventitious property enabling us to mark things, see OGAWA 2019, pp. 626-630. The example is found in MBh, vol. I, pp. 84–85, and used e.g. in VP 3.2.3: *adhruveṇa nimittena devadatta-gṛhaṃ yathā | gṛhītaṃ gṛhaśabdena śuddham evābhidhīyate ||* "Just as Devadatta's house is grasped through an impermanent mark [such as a crow perched on it, and yet] only the bare [house] is denoted by the word "house..." Helārāja, while explaining it, uses both the terms *upalakṣaṇa* and *upādhi*, his point being that an *upalakṣaṇa* enables us to mark something while not constituting an essential property of the thing in question. See PP, vol. I, p. 108: *ado devattasya gṛhaṃ yatrāsau kākaḥ prativasatīty atra niyatasvāmikagṛhopalakṣaṇāyopalakṣaṇabhūtasya* kākasyotpatite 'pi tasminn upalakṣaṇasya kṛtatvād adhruvatvam anityatvam iti...* [**atra niyata°* LI; *atrāniyata°* Ed.] "When [someone says :] 'Devadatta's house is the one where the crow is perched,' the crow, which is a marker (*upalakṣaṇa*) that enables [us] to mark the house of a specific owner, is 'impermanent,' [that is,] it lacks permanence, since one can [still] produce [another] marker [for the same house] even when the crow has flown away." (For a somewhat different interpretation see OGAWA 2019, p. 629 and LI 2018, p. 126). In the sequel of his explanation, Helārāja specifies that "in the same way" (*tathā*), "reality is marked by unreal, adventitious properties" (*asatyopādhyupalakṣitaṃ satyam*).

quence in the sun's movements, it can also constitute a marker for the sequence that is a flower's growth or Devadatta's birth—i.e., this is why we consider that different things share the same time without performing the same actions. Abhinavagupta explains:

> But [if] the time that is spring consists in the sequence of the sun, how [can] it [also] be the time of the mango tree's sprouting? Having anticipated this [question, Utpaladeva] says "this *same* [activity that is e.g. the movement of an objective entity such as the sun]..."; [and] with the word "same," he underscores the strength of his own thesis. [In other words,] just as it is the very nature belonging to gold that is called, [when] measured, a *māṣaka*—[i.e. it is designated by a word denoting a weight used to measure gold]—, yet this is only a marker for the [gold, a marker] that remains in the weight,[406] and nothing that would belong in one thing [i.e., the weight,] passes into something else, [i.e., the gold]; in the same way, for the phenomenon of the mango tree, what [constitutes] spring is [the mango tree's] own sequence of phenomena—which comprise a variety of flower buds, leaf buds and blossoms, etc., [and] which are manifested] as being [purely] internal [to the manifesting consciousness], as apprehended objects, and as [purely] external—, whereas the rise of the sun is only a marker for it. And one must make the same reasoning in all cases.[407]

Sequence is thus the lasting, unitary reality that, being a common feature of all actions, enables us to use any action as a temporal marker for others. Or, as Abhinavagupta puts it:

---

[406] On the term *prativartaka* see above, chapter 6, fn. 397.

[407] ĪPVV, vol. III, p. 8: *nanu sa vasantaḥ kālo 'rkasya kramarūpaḥ sahakārodbhedasya katham kāla ity āśaṅkya brūte* ***tenaiveti.*** ***eva****śabdenāsyaiva* pakṣasya dārḍhyaṃ dyotayati. yathā kanakasya svam eva rūpaṃ māṣaka iti paricchinnam ucyate, prativartakagataṃ tu tatropalakṣaṇamātram, na tv anyatratyam anyatra saṅkrāmati, tathaiva sahakārābhāsasyāntaratvagrāhyatvabāhyatvābhāsānāṃ korakamukulavikasvarādivaicitryabhājāṃ yo nijaḥ kramaḥ sa eva vasantaḥ, sa tv arkodayas tasyopalakṣaṇamātram. evaṃ sarvatra mantavyam.* [****eva****śabdenāsyaiva* conj.; *vāśabdenāsyaiva* S12, J11, Ed.]

> [According to the *Vivṛti*, time must be whatever] "has a lasting nature," [i.e., whatever is] well known as having a unitary nature by the agents of ordinary practice—and in all [circumstances], sequence, which has the property of flowing, is exactly so. Time [must be] precisely this [entity] that is one, "since there is no [fundamental] distinction between the [various] inferential marks of time."[408]

Here Abhinavagupta is quoting the Vaiśeṣika principle according to which time must be one "*kālaliṅgāviśeṣāt*,"[409] that is, because despite their differences, the marks of time all have a fundamental unity that leads to the single notion of time. And the fact that Abhinavagupta quotes it shows that he is aware that Utpaladeva's position can be seen as dangerously close to the Vaiśeṣikas': when the Śaiva nondualist claims that time is not actions themselves but a "lasting" element called *krama*, the presence of which enables us to use various actions as units of measure for other actions, how is his position really different from that of the Vaiśeṣika authors who claim that time cannot be actions themselves but rather, an eternal substance (*dravya*) distinct from them?

It is at this point of the *Vivṛti* that Utpaladeva spells out his major divergence with the Vaiśeṣika: according to him, time is not a *thing* that would have an existence of its own. Sequence is not a substance: Utpaladeva is about to define it (in ĪPK 2.1.4 and its commentaries) as the mere fact that some phenomena occur together while others do not. For now, he contents himself with emphasizing that it is our use of words that fools us into thinking of time not as this fluid way of occurring but as a substance: substantives like "spring," "past" or "future" carry a reified representation of time, just as the word "action" freezes as it were the dynamic reality that it is expected to convey by presenting it as a distinct, accomplished entity—to put it like Bhartṛhari, these words seem to denote things (*vastu*) whereas

408 ĪPVV, vol. III, p. 7: ***sthirarūpam*** *iti prasiddhaṃ vyavahartṝṇām ekarūpatvena, sarvatra ca kramasya tādṛśatvam eva pravahaṇadharmaṇaḥ kālaliṅgāviśeṣād ity ekaṃ yat tad eva kālaḥ.*

409 See PDhS, p. 170 (quoted above, fn. 373); VSV on VS 2.2.8, p. 17.

they really are about powers (*śakti*).[410] Utpaladeva adds that only conjugated verbs ("was," "is," "will be") somehow have the power of counteracting this reification by expressing the dynamism of action and time—an idea already found in Yāska's *Nirukta*[411] and developed in later grammatical works, including Patañjali's and Bhartṛhari's.[412] Abhinavagupta, for his part, makes clear that this is so because our very understanding of substantive forms such as "action" and "time" rests on the more immediate awareness of reality's fluidity or dynamism—an awareness brought about by the personal endings, and without which action could not be cognized at all. Thus while explaining ĪPK 1.5.17, according to which "an action is [directly] expressed only by a personal ending,"[413] Abhinavagupta explains:

> The powers that are e.g. action, the factors of action, conjunction and disjunction have as their ultimate reality a realization (*parāmarśa*) that may be respectively expressed through the use of such [linguistic elements] as personal end-

---

[410] See VP 3.6.1: *dik sādhanaṃ kriyā kāla iti vastvabhidhāyinaḥ | śaktirūpe padārthānām atyantam anavasthitāḥ ||* "If [the words] 'direction,' 'means of accomplishing [action],' 'action' and 'time' denoted things (*vastu*), they could not be established at all to [refer to] the nature of things' powers (*śakti*)." As noted in TORELLA 2002, p. 124, fn. 36, this verse is quoted in ĪPVV, vol. II, p. 215 while Abhinavagupta explains ĪPK 1.5.17 (on which see below, fn. 413).

[411] *Nirukta* 1.1: *pūrvāparībhūtaṃ bhāvam ākhyātenācaṣṭe vrajati pacatīti, upakramaprabhṛtyapavargaparyantaṃ mūrtaṃ sattvabhūtaṃ sattvanāmabhir vrajyā paktir iti.* "One expresses action endowed with succession by [using] a verb [in such sentences as] '[he] goes, [he] cooks,' [whereas one expresses action considered] as an entity (*sattva*), [and] frozen (*mūrta*) from its beginning—[i.e.] when one undertakes it—to its end—[i.e.] when it reaches completion—, by [using] nouns [expressive of] entities, [such as] 'a walk' [or] 'cooking.'" See SEYFORT RUEGG 1959, p. 24, JOSHI 1993, p. 11 and KAHRS 2013, pp. 4–5.

[412] See JOSHI 1993, pp. 24 and 36 and KAHRS 2013, p. 5.

[413] ĪPK 1.5.17: *nāhantādiparāmarśabhedād asyānyatātmanaḥ | ahaṃmṛśyatayaivāsya sṛṣṭes tiṅvācyakarmavat ||* "It is not the case that this self [of the various subjects in whose form the Lord manifests Himself] becomes other due to the variety of [ways that it has of] realizing (*parāmarśa*) [what its own nature is—i.e. by grasping this nature subjectively] as 'I,' but also [objectively, as 'the self', 'the Lord,'] etc. [It is not the case,] because [the Lord] creates this [self] as being precisely what may be grasped [subjectively] as 'I,' just as an action is [directly] expressed [only] by a personal ending."

> ings, the instrumental case, [the words] "and" and "or"; although, when expressed by such words as "cooking," "agent," "conjunction" and "disjunction," they receive a substantive form (*sattvabhāva*), they [all] rest on a fundamental realization (*mūlaparāmarśa*) that is [expressed] thus: "he cooks," "by Caitra," "and," "or"—otherwise, they would not be cognized at all. [And] in the case of [our awareness of the self] too, the same [distinction between two ways of expressing it] applies.[414]

Now, while commenting on the end of the *Vivṛti* on ĪPK 2.1.3, where Utpaladeva reminds his readers that the use of substantive words tends to reify action and time, Abhinavagupta alludes to ĪPK 1.5.17 as follows:

> With [the passage beginning with] "[Words] such as spring...", [Utpaladeva] is replying to the [following objection:] "But from words such as 'spring,' [what] comes to mind is a real thing that must be nonsequential, and whose form is accomplished—not sequence!" And [Utpaladeva] has [already] clarified this at length in [verse 1.5.17, which ends with the words] "just as an action is [directly] expressed [only] by a personal ending." For just as [we] cognize action only from a verb and from no other [word], similarly, time, which penetrates into the heart of action's nature, [is cognized] from the same [source, i.e., a verb].[415]

According to Abhinavagupta, while thus spelling out in the *Vivṛti* why the Vaiśeṣikas, deluded by ordinary practice and language, wrongly see time as a changeless substance, Utpaladeva also makes room for the Vaiśeṣika system as a view of the universe that, although inferior and transcended by the Śaiva view of ultimate reality, is valid—provided of course that it is

---

[414] ĪPV, vol. I, p. 220–221: *yathā kriyākārakasamuccayavikalpādiśaktayo yathāsvaṃ tiṅtṛtīyādicavādiprayogāvaseyaparāmarśaparamārthāḥ pākaḥ kartā samuccayo vikalpa ityādiśabdair abhidhīyamānāḥ sattvabhāvam āpāditā api pacati caitreṇa ca vety evaṃbhūte mūlaparāmarśe viśrāmyanti, anyathā tu tāḥ pratītā naiva bhaveyuḥ, tadvat tatrāpi.*

[415] ĪPVV, vol. III, p. 8: *nanu vasantādiśabdebhyo 'kramam eva siddharūpaṃ vastu pratipattipatham abhyeti, na kramaḥ. atrocyate* ***vasantādīti****, etac ca tiṅvācyakarmavad ity atra vitatyoktam. ākhyātapadād eva hi yathā kriyā pratīyate, nānyataḥ; tadvat tata eva kriyāsvarūpahṛdayapraviṣṭaḥ kālaḥ.*

integrated to the higher system of Śaiva nondualism—in the sphere of ordinary experience:

> And if [someone] talks about the permanence and unity [of time, as the Vaiśeṣikas do,] while only referring to [sequence in fact,] according to the reasoning [just] stated; and [if someone says] that [time] is a substance, [as the Vaiśeṣikas do], by superimposing autonomy [onto sequence]—then even the Vaiśeṣikas' doctrine incurs no harm, provided that one acknowledges that our [Śaiva nondualist] doctrine constitutes [its only] safe harbor! This is what [Utpaladeva] is hinting at [here].[416]

The Vaiśeṣikas are right in distinguishing time from actions; they are only mistaken in that they freeze the essential dynamism of sequence into a static substance—and as soon as they acknowledge that the nature of time is a flux (*pravahaṇa*) rather than an immutable substance (which is inevitable if they ascribe any causal role to time as regards the diversity of temporal determinations), they are simply conceding that, as Utpaladeva contends, time is nothing but sequence. As Abhinavagupta puts it:

> Even in the [Vaiśeṣika system, whose proponents] claim that "The name 'time' applies to the cause,"[417] with respect to [such temporally determined thoughts as] "he was born during the day" [or] "he was born at noon," [what is] established [to occur] is the cognition that only the sequence pertaining to the sun's movement is the cause [of these temporal determinations]—not [the cognition] that this cause would be] anything consisting in a permanent substance endowed with a nature that would be distinct [from this sequence]! If [our Vaiseṣika opponent replies]: "Although [time] is a substance, it is [able to] produce in these [cognitions] a variety in terms of [temporal] distance and proximity, consisting in [e.g.] being new and old, precisely because it possesses the property of flowing (*pravahaṇa*)," then, once again, it is the very fact that [time] is nothing but sequence that [he thus]

[416] ĪPVV, vol. III, p. 8: *tatraiva coktanītyā nityatvaikatve yadi vyavahriyete, dravyatvaṃ ca svātantryāropaṇena, tadā kāṇādamatasyāpi na kācit kṣatiḥ saty asmaddarśanaśaraṇabhāvopagamana ity ākūtam.*

[417] VS 2.2.11.

> establishes in accordance with experience, and not [the fact that it would be] a nature distinct [from sequence, as he wishes]! Therefore it is established that time is nothing but sequence, whose essence is an immersion in manifestation.[418]

In the *Vivṛti* on ĪPK 2.1.3, Utpaladeva says nothing more about the difference between the Vaiśeṣika view of time and his; Abhinavagupta's commentary, however, anticipates on the upcoming analysis of sequence by underscoring a crucial divergence between the Vaiśeṣika and Śaiva nondualistic views of time—namely the fact that sequence, contrary to the substance postulated by the Vaiśeṣika, has as its essence, in Abhinavagupta's words, "an immersion in manifestation"; that is, it only exists as a way for consciousness of manifesting itself, so that time has no objective reality. Or, as the ĪPVV puts it:

> In fact the [entity called time that is variously defined by our opponents] is nothing over and above sequence; therefore [we] only refer to sequence when [we] talk about time [as something existing] outside [conscious subjects]. And since [in fact] all the phenomena [manifested as external] to a conscious individual amount to a dream, an imaginary construct, a magic trick or an illusion [in that they are only internal], sequence [in them] is as [little] restricted to a specific duration (*iyattā*) as the sequence in the events that occurred during the night of Hariścandra. It is therefore the power of consciousness that manifests itself in these [temporal phenomena], because the variety of phenomena is created by this [very power], and because sequence is based on this [variety].[419]

---

[418] ĪPVV, vol. III, p. 5: *yatrāpi kāraṇe kālākhyety ucyate tatrāpi divase jāto madhyāhne jāta ity arkasaṃcārakramasyaiva kāraṇatāpratītiḥ siddhā, na tu nityadravyātmanaḥ pariniṣṭhitarūpasya kasyacit. dravyam api tatpravahaṇadharmakam eva navapurāṇatārūpaparatvāparatvatadvaicitryotthāpakam iti cet, tarhi punar api kramarūpataivāsyānubhavānusāreṇa vyavatiṣṭhate, na rūpāntaram iti krama evābhāsane 'nupraveśātmā kāla iti siddham.*

[419] ĪPVV, vol. III, p. 5: ... *so 'pi vastutaḥ kramarūpatāṃ nātikrāmatīti krama eva nāma bahiḥ kāla iti vyavahriyate. svapnasaṅkalpamāyendrajālaprāye ca cetanasyābhāsavarge* kramasyeyattāniyamo hariścandrarajanīvṛttāntakramasyeva. tad*

Whereas the Vaiśeṣikas see time as a substance existing outside consciousness and independent of it, the Śaiva nondualists consider it to be a mere modality of consciousness's manifestation. This is an important point. For the Śaiva nondualists reject the relativistic conception of time that is propounded in the YD or PYV and that equates time with actions: according to them, time cannot be reduced to a mere mental construct resulting from our comparing different actions, and they emphasize that time exists over and above actions, in the form of the sequence experienced in them. They also believe, however, that this reality to be distinguished from actions does not exist independently of consciousness and is but an aspect of its manifestation—which is why, according to them, *duration is only relative*: Abhinavagupta asserts here that all the temporal phenomena that we take to have an existence outside of us are comparable to dreams and imaginary constructs, in which what we perceive is acknowledged (even by the staunchest opponents of idealism) to have no external reality and to be an internal appearance of consciousness. He adds that in what we usually consider as an objective time existing outside consciousness, sequence is in fact as little restricted to a specific duration as the events pertaining to the night of Hariścandra—an allusion to the famous tale, found in various Indian sources, of king Hariścandra, who was once caught in a dream that seemed to last for twelve years, but woke up during the very night when the dream had begun.[420] This idea also features in chapter 6 of Abhinavagupta's TĀ, which teaches a practice whereby a yogin, focusing on the minimal measure of time that is a single breath, experiences ever larger periods of time within this single breath. Jayaratha, commenting on a verse according to which "Therefore the [cosmic] dissolutions and arisings are by nature nothing but the dynamic essence of consciousness; this is why it has been declared that in a [single] breath sixty years occur,"[421] explains:

---

*atra saṃvicchaktir eva pratapati tannirmitatvād ābhāsacitratāyās tadāśrayatvāc ca kramasya.* [**ca cetanasyābhāsavarge* conj.; *cetanasyābhāsavarge* S12, J11, Ed.; *ca tasyābhāsavarge* ms. Kha (Ed., fn. 1).]

[420] See in particular DONIGER O'FLAHERTY 1984, pp. 143–145.

[421] TĀ 6.181cd–182ab: *tena saṃvittvam evaitat spandamānaṃ svabhāvataḥ* || *layodayā iti prāṇe ṣaṣṭyabdodayakīrtanam* |

> Those dissolutions and arisings are said to be the essence of consciousness—[that is, they] are the freedom of consciousness; thus it must be admitted that all of this temporal diversity is entirely dependent on consciousness, and it is by no means some external nature that would be devoid of freedom.[422]

In this passage of the TĀ, Abhinavagupta, alluding to the definition of sequence that Utpaladeva is about to state here in the two following verses, further points out that time is no objective reality:

> The power of time, which [consists in] expressing the variety of actions, has [consciousness's] will (*icchā*) as its sole foundation: it does not have any restricted (*niyata*) form [that would exist] outside this [will]. In a dream within a dream,[423] just as in a dream, in deep sleep, in imagination, in absorption, when focusing on the sequence of the cosmic resorptions and emissions, a portion of time, although limited, appears as extended.[424]

Jayaratha, while explaining the passage, also alludes to the story of king Hariścandra:

> ... In the same way, in a dream, an experience, although temporally extended, may occur in a single moment, as Hariścandra's [did].[425]

Time is something more than actions, it cannot be reduced to the latter—in this respect the Śaiva nondualists are in agreement with the Vaiśeṣikas. Yet,

---

[422] TĀV, vol. IV, p. 152: *saṃvittvam iti ye nāma layodayās tat saṃvitsvātantryam ity evaṃ saṃvidadhīnam eva sarvam etat kālīyaṃ vaicitryaṃ, na punar asvādhīnaṃ kiṃcid rūpaṃ bahir astīty uktaṃ syāt.*

[423] On Abhinavagupta's analysis of this phenomenon see RATIÉ 2011a, pp. 650–655, and above, chapter 4, fn. 316.

[424] TĀ 6.182cd–184: *icchāmātrapratiṣṭheyaṃ kriyāvaicitryacarcanā || kālaśaktis tato bāhye naitasyā niyataṃ vapuḥ | svapnasvapne tathā svapne supte saṃkalpagocare || samādhau viśvasaṃhārasṛṣṭikramavivecane | mito'pi kila kālāṃśo vitatatvena bhāsate ||*

[425] TĀV, vol. IV, p. 154: *evaṃ svapne kṣaṇenaiva hariścandrasyevānekakāliko 'py anubhavo bhavet**. [**bhavet* conj.; *'bhavat* Ed.].

because sequence is a manifestation of consciousness, temporal limitations have no reality of their own, which is why dreamers and yogins may experience that which may seem impossible under ordinary conditions: the infinite elasticity of time.

# CHAPTER 7

# Sequence as the Result of the Ultimate Consciousness's Will (ĪPK 2.1.4)

## 1. The point of the verse: showing that sequence rests on the Lord's will

Having explained that time is nothing but sequence, Utpaladeva now proceeds to show—as he himself makes clear in the *Vivṛti*'s introduction to this new verse—that it must result from what he calls the power of time (*kālaśakti*), a power that he ascribes to "the Great Lord himself." Abhinavagupta's commentaries both point out that ĪPK 2.1.4 is meant to explain why temporal sequence cannot belong to the very nature of objective entities and must be the result of a power belonging to the ultimate consciousness. Thus the ĪPV introduces the new stanza in the following way:

> Having anticipated [the objection:] "But [if it is] so, [then] let [us admit] that what is called time is nothing but the nature of [objective] entities; what is this [so-called] power of time?", [Utpaladeva] states [the next verse].[426]

Similarly, the ĪPVV's introduction explains:

> In [the following] verse, here is [the objection] that Utpaladeva refutes: "But [if it is] so, let [us admit] that time is nothing but the nature of [objective] entities; and so what is this so-called 'power of time' [that is supposedly] other [than the nature of entities and] is [the reason] why [you] have stated in [verse 2.1.2]—beginning with 'And [for ordinary action,]

[426] ĪPV, vol. II, p. 10: *nanv evaṃ kālo nāma bhāvasvabhāvabhūta evāstu, kāsau kālaśaktir ity āśaṅkyāha...*

> occurring in sequence...'—[that occurring in sequence is possible] 'thanks to the power of time'?"[427]

From the very beginning of his *Vivṛti* on ĪPK 2.1.4, Utpaladeva clearly distinguishes this power of time—which he describes as a "power of dividing" (*kalanaśakti*)—[428] from time itself. The latter consists in sequence and is a property (albeit it an adventitious one) of objective entities, whereas the former is a power that, while producing the property of time in things, is not time itself (so that it is free of sequence) and consists in the ability to *manifest* time simply by manifesting the objective entities constituting the universe as being comprised of certain phenomena and not others. In his commentary on the *Vivṛti*, Abhinavagupta also insists on this distinction between time and its power:

> [The Lord's "agency in manifesting the pot, cloth, etc. as being varied"] is [His] action of manifesting the pot, cloth, etc. after making [them] "varied," [i.e.,] endowed with [certain] phenomena and not with [others]; this [action of manifesting] is precisely the dividing action of the Lord—who is [its] agent—, and this is precisely the power of manifesting time; [as for time itself, it is] an adventitious property of [objective] entities; it consists in sequence; [and it is] what is manifested [by this power].[429]

The reason why both the *Vivṛti* and ĪPVV insist on the difference between time and its power (whereas the distinction remains implicit in the verses and *Vṛtti*) is that it explains how the world that we experience can be temporally determined while the ultimate reality remains free of any temporal

---

[427] ĪPVV, vol. III, p. 9: *nanv evaṃ bhāvānāṃ svabhāva eva kāla ity astu; tataś ca kālaśaktir nāma kānyā, yenoktaṃ sakramatvaṃ cety atra kālaśaktita iti. etat samādhatte sūtreṇa.*

[428] Cf. TĀV, vol. IV (on TĀ 6.6): *tad yā nāma bhāvānām evam kalanā pariccchittiḥ sa eva kramākramātmā kāla iti.* "Thus what is called the *kalanā* of [objective entities, [i.e.,] the action of dividing [them] (*paricchitti*), is precisely time, which consists in sequence and simultaneity." On the technical term *kalana/kalanā*, often related to time in semantic analyses (*nirvacana*) of the word *kāla*, see HANNEDER 1998, p. 168 and BANSAT-BOUDON & TRIPATHI 2011, p. 279, fn. 1177.

[429] ĪPVV, vol. III, p. 10: ***vicitram*** *ity ābhāsānābhāsayuktaṃ kṛtvā yad ghaṭapaṭādyavabhāsakaraṇam iyam eva bhagavataḥ kartuḥ* ***kalanakriyā****, etad eva ca bhāvopādhibhūtasya kramātmanaḥ kālasyāviṣkriyamāṇasyāviṣkaraṇasāmarthyam.*

division. Thus when Jayaratha comments on a verse in Abhinavagupta's TĀ according to which time, in its highest form, is the ultimate power (*śakti*) of God called Kālī,[430] he formulates as follows the objection to which the verse responds:

> But all this world is manifest while being entirely dependent (*lagna*) upon consciousness, for otherwise, its very manifestation could not occur; and because consciousness is eternal, in it there can be no association with time. So how could this [time] even belong to all the [objective] entities that are entirely dependent on [this eternal consciousness]? Having anticipated this objection, [Abhinavagupta] states [the following verse].[431]

Jayaratha then explains how the distinction between time and its power justifies the assertion that consciousness remains in itself unaffected by time, just as fire, while having the power to burn, remains unburnt:

> That which is called the "association with time" of the ultimate manifesting consciousness is its *śakti*, [that is,] its power to divide (*kalana*) into various forms the world, which is made manifest by [consciousness's] own will, [and] which consists in [limited] knowing subjects, objects of knowledge, etc. But [consciousness has] no sequence or simultaneity in itself; for although fire is associated with the power of burning, there is no manifestation in itself of blisters and [other marks of being burnt]![432]

---

[430] TĀ 6.7: *kramākramātmā kālaś ca paraḥ saṃvidi vartate | kālī nāma parā śaktiḥ saiva devasya gīyate* || "And the ultimate [form of] time, which consists in sequence and simultaneity, resides within consciousness; it is celebrated as the ultimate power of God, named Kālī."

[431] TĀV, vol. IV, pp. 5–6: *nanu sarvam idaṃ jagat saṃvillagnam evāvabhāsate, anyathā hy asya bhānam eva na bhavet, saṃvidi ca nityatvāt kālayogo nāstīti katham asau tadanuṣaktasya bhāvajātasyāpi syād ity āśaṅkyāha...*

[432] TĀV, vol. IV, p. 7: *yan nāma parasya prakāśasya kālena yogaḥ sāsya śaktiḥ svecchāvabhāsitasya pramātṛprameyādyātmano jagatas tattadrūpatayā kalane sāmarthyam, na punaḥ svātmani kaścid akramaḥ kramo veti na hy agner dāhaśaktiyoge svātmani sphoṭādyāvirbhāvaḥ.*

### 2. Sequence, the incompatibility of phenomena, and consciousness's freedom

Utpaladeva's next move in the *Vivṛti* is to explain why the power of time—i.e., the power to manifest time in objective entities—is equated in the *Vṛtti* with the power to manifest a variety of objective entities that are distinct inasmuch as they are "devoid of each other's phenomena" (*anyonyābhāsa-śūnya*).

In his commentaries, Abhinavagupta spells out much of what remains implicit in Utpaladeva's elliptical *Vivṛti*—namely, that temporal sequence is not a mere difference in the nature of things (for things can differ from each other while existing *simultaneously*, for instance the fingers of a hand). Rather, time is the specific difference that results from the *incompatibility* of certain phenomena with others (the colour of the sun at its zenith cannot coexist with that of the sun about to set: one must be absent when the other is present).

Of course, one might object that such incompatibilities arise from the very nature of things and have nothing to do with consciousness; but in the *Jñānādhikāra*, Utpaladeva has already shown at length that what we ordinarily apprehend as objects existing outside consciousness are nothing but internal forms that consciousness takes on, just as, in dreams, we apprehend things and people that are nothing but our consciousness as if they were independent of it. And since Utpaladeva has already proven that there is no such thing as an external world and that all objective manifestations are ways for a unique consciousness of presenting itself in the form of objects, it is this universal consciousness that must freely choose which phenomena may occur along with others and which are incompatible, just as, when imagining, we can freely choose to combine or not to combine the various elementary phenomena out of which we build our imaginary world. The power of time is precisely this power of consciousness to manifest certain phenomena without others:

> In this [world], if time, whose essence is sequence, were merely a difference in the nature [of things], then, since four fingers [of the same hand] have different natures, [each of them] should exist at a different time! Therefore temporal sequence is [only] produced by the specific difference resulting from the presence and absence of [certain] phenomena, [for instance]: the presence of the phenomenon of the reddish

colour of dawn, and the absence of a multitude of bright rays. And [Utpaladeva] has [already] demonstrated at length that the presence and absence of phenomena are not produced by any external cause. Therefore these [presence and absence] are only due to the Lord, [that is to say,] the self whose nature is [nothing but] consciousness [and] who, in such [ordinary experiences] as dreams or imagination, is experienced through [mere] self awareness[433] to have power over the creation of variety in phenomena. For while manifesting in Himself the phenomena of the blue, etc., [the Lord] manifests [them] in infinitely varied ways. To explain: [He manifests] the phenomenon "red," the phenomenon "pot," the phenomenon "round" and the phenomenon "solid" as belonging to a single substratum (*sāmānādhikaraṇya*), [whereas He manifests] the phenomenon "pot" and the phenomenon "cloth" along with the manifestation of their separateness, [i.e.,] as not having each other's phenomena.[434] Yet [He also manifests each of them] as being in itself[435] a unitary (*ekarasa*) phenomenon, and in such a [manifestation,] there is no rise of sequence; but when He manifests both the phenomenon of autumn [as being] entirely devoid of the phenomenon of winter and the phenomenon of winter [as being entirely devoid] of the phenomenon of autumn, then temporal se-

[433] The point is that in dreams and imagination, all conscious beings—including those bound to saṃsāric existence—experience the power of consciousness to create phenomenal variety through self-awareness (*svasaṃvedana*), i.e. in the most immediate and irrefutable way.

[434] Literally "with an absence of phenomena in each other."

[435] Bhāskarakaṇṭha rather understands *svātmani* as meaning "in His own self [consisting in consciousness]" (*Bhāskarī*, vol. II, p. 16: *svātmani—cidrūpe svasmin*); in the corresponding passage of the ĪPVV (vol. III, p. 10), however, Abhinavagupta clearly contrasts this manifestation of each object as being unitary "in itself" with the lack of such a unitary manifestation "with respect to each other" (*svātmany ekarasenābhāsena, anyonyaṃ tv ekarasenānābhāsena*).

> quence arises. Therefore it is such a power of unfolding variety in phenomena that [we] call the Lord's "power of time."[436]

Abhinavagupta enumerates the various ways in which consciousness manifests phenomena and first specifies that they may occur as belonging to a single substratum, because Utpaladeva contends that any particular entity (*svalakṣaṇa*) considered to be a unitary substance—such as a pot or a cloth—is in fact made of a combination of various elementary phenomena that coalesce in order to form a single entity,[437] as explained in the *Vṛtti* on ĪPK 2.3.7:[438]

> The distinct rays of a lamp are manifest as an undifferentiated [mass of light]; so are the streams of rivers in [our] cognition of the ocean, and [so] are the various flavours in a beverage. In the same way, manifestations such as "whiteness," "great size" and "cloth," being capable of interpenetrating—contrary to the manifestations of the blue and yellow for instance—, can exist in immediate perception itself

---

[436] ĪPV, vol. II, pp. 11–13: *iha svabhāvabhedamātraṃ yadi kramātmā kālaḥ, tad aṅgulīcatuṣṭayaṃ bhinnasvabhāvam iti bhinnakālaṃ bhavet. tasmād aruṇābhāsasya sadbhāvaḥ sphuṭaprabhāpuñjasya cāsadbhāva ity evaṃbhūto yo bheda ābhāsasadbhāvāsadbhāvābhyām anuprāṇitas tatkṛtaḥ kramaḥ kālātmā. tau cābhāsānāṃ bhāvābhāvau na bāhyahetukṛtāv iti vistāryopapāditam. iti ya eva saṃvitsvabhāva ātmā svapnasaṃkalpādāv ābhāsavaicitryanirmāṇe prabhuḥ prabhaviṣṇur iti svasaṃviditas tata eva tau bhavataḥ. sa hy ātmani nīlādīn ābhāsān ābhāsayaṃś citratayāparimeyayā bhāsayati. tathā hi lohitābhāsaṃ ghaṭābhāsam unnatābhāsaṃ dṛḍhābhāsaṃ ca sāmānādhikaraṇyena, ghaṭābhāsaṃ paṭābhāsaṃ ca pṛthaktvāvabhāsenānyonyatrābhāsābhāvena, svātmani tv ekarasenābhāsena, iyati ca na kramasyodayaḥ. yadā tu śaradābhāsaṃ hemantābhāsena ca sarvathaiva śūnyam ābhāsayati hemantābhāsaṃ ca śaradābhāsena, tadā kālātmā krama uttiṣṭhatīti seyam itthaṃbhūtābhāsavaicitryaprathanaśaktir bhagavataḥ kālaśaktir ity ucyate.*

[437] On this doctrine and its relationship with Dharmakīrtian Buddhism, see the penetrating analysis in TORELLA 1992.

[438] ĪPK 2.3.7: *pṛthagdīpaprakāśānāṃ srotasāṃ sāgare yathā | aviruddhāvabhāsānām ekakāryā tathaikyadhīḥ ||* "Just as [our cognition of the unity] of the lights of different lamps, or [that of] waterstreams in the ocean, [our] cognition of the unity of phenomena that are not contradictory is produced by a unitary [entity].

> as the various phenomena of a unitary substance with a unitary effect[439]—this is what belonging to a single substratum is.[440]

As specified in ĪPK 2.3.7, however, only elementary phenomena that are not "contradictory" (*aviruddha*) may thus combine[441] (the phenomenon "pot," for instance, cannot combine with the phenomenon "cloth" in a single substratum, as one contradicts the other by making its presence impossible), and the ultimate consciousness's will is the only source of this difference between the phenomena that may combine and those that may not, since it freely decides[442] for instance that the phenomenon of visual form and that of the wind must be incompatible:

> Only the phenomena between which there is no contradiction [may] combine; for the phenomenon of visual form does not combine with that of the wind due to [their] contradiction; and this [contradiction] itself is made to arise by [the Lord's] power of necessity.[443]

The ultimate consciousness thus manifests phenomena in various ways since it manifests each of them in itself, but also in relation with the others, and such relations take numerous forms, since phenomena may either appear in countless combinations with other phenomena, or as separated from them. According to the *Vṛtti* on ĪPK 2.1.4, sequence arises when objects are

---

[439] On the meaning of *ekakārya°* here see TORELLA 2002, p. 167, fn. 15.

[440] *Vṛtti*, p. 51: *bhinnāḥ pradīpaprabhā avibhāgenāvabhāsante nadīpravāhāś ca sindhubuddhau pānake ca te te rasāḥ, tathā śauklyamahattvapaṭatvādyavabhāsāḥ parasparānupraveśakṣamāḥ, na tu nīlapītādyavabhāsāḥ, tattadekakāryaikadravyābhāsabhāvena kalpante pratyakṣa eva. tad etat sāmānādhikaraṇyam.* See TORELLA 1992, p. 336, and TORELLA 2002, p. 167.

[441] Cf. e.g. Abhinavagupta's remark to this effect in ĪPVV, vol. III, pp. 368–369 (quoted below, chapter 9, fn. 686).

[442] As Abhinavagupta makes clear elsewhere, this doctrine entails the paradoxical consequence that at the highlest levels of consciousness, where no combination of phenomena is restricted by the power of necessity, frogs can have matted hair and pots can have horns (see ĪPVV, vol. III, p. 369, quoted below, chapter 9, fn. 687).

[443] ĪPV, vol. II, pp. 97–98: *yeṣām avirodhas ta evābhāsā miśrībhavanti, na hi rūpābhāso mārutābhāsena miśrībhavati virodhāt, so 'pi ca niyatiśaktyutthāpitaḥ*. On the power of necessity (*niyatiśakti*) see RATIÉ 2011a, pp. 411–413.

manifested as being "devoid of each other's phenomena," and the *Vivṛti* on it specifies that "the mutual incompatibility of manifestations such as 'pot' and ['cloth'] is [precisely] the difference on which the cognition of sequence rests." In other words, although two particular objects such as a pot and a cloth may share some elementary phenomena (the colour "red" for instance), the dominant phenomena in them, "pot" and "cloth," are mutually exclusive, since wherever the phenomenon "pot" is present, it excludes the presence of the phenomenon "cloth"; and because the pot and cloth cannot share the same substratum, even when they are manifested together, they must at least exist in a spatial sequence, i.e., while being located in different places. Similarly, as Abhinavagupta's ĪPV makes clear, the realities that we call "autumn" and "winter" are mutually exclusive—and this is why they must appear in a temporal sequence—because the phenomena that make their specificity (e.g. the sun's movement in a particular sign of the zodiac) cannot occur in the same substratum.

### 3. Abhinavagupta's emphasis on Utpaladeva's debt to Bhartṛhari as regards time

The parallel passage in the ĪPVV is very close, but interestingly enough, it also quotes the VP in support of the idea that time is a power that belongs to the universal consciousness. Abhinavagupta thus rightly points out Utpaladeva's debt to Bhartṛhari (whom Utpaladeva himself quotes in the *Vivṛti* on the next verse) as regards the definition of time:

> If time were only a difference in the nature [of objective entities], the fingers [of a single hand] too would [necessarily] have a temporal difference! So temporal sequence does not have as its cause a mere difference [in the nature of objective entities], but rather, the specific difference that results from the manifestation [of certain phenomena] and its absence. And the presence and absence of phenomena occur in varied ways due to the Lord Himself, whose power to make sequence arise is seen [by all] in dreams, imagination and so on. This has been said by the master [Bhartṛhari]:
>
>> But that which is thus manifest is the power of
>> an [entity] that is necessarily one...[444]

---

[444] VP 2.22cd.

And similarly, elsewhere too [he has stated:]

> They say that [time] is the puppet-master (*sūtradhāra*) of the puppet that is the world (*lokayantra*);[445] it devides the universe with [its] exclusion (*pratibandha*) and assent (*abhyanujñā*).[446]

[And again:]

> If [time] did not exclude, and did not create through exclusion, the conditions [of things] would [all] be mixed up, being deprived of succession.[447]

For [Bhartṛhari,] by describing [time as a] freedom (*svātantrya*) to manifest and not to manifest [things], expresses the sovereignty (*aiśvarya*) [of the entity endowed with that power]; for it is the Lord who produces phenomena in varied ways.[448]

---

445 On the meaning of *yantra* here see PP, vol. II, p. 42: *yantrapuruṣaprakhyaṃ viśvaṃ sūtradhārapuruṣakalpakālapratibaddhaceṣṭam.* "The universe, described as a puppet (*yantrapuruṣa*), has its movements controlled by time, [the latter being] similar to a man who holds [its] threads." I take the word *yantrapuruṣa* to designate a puppet rather than the sort of automaton (*yantraputraka*) described e.g. by Bhoja (see ALI 2016, p. 3), since (not to mention that such automata seem to have become fashionable much later than Bhartṛhari) the main point here is that the device in question is entirely controlled by the "thread-holder" (*sūtradhāra*).

446 VP 3.9.4.

447 VP 3.9.5.

448 ĪPVV, vol. III, pp. 9–10: *svabhāvabhedamātraṃ cet kālaḥ, aṅgulīnām api kālabhedaḥ syāt. tasmād ābhāsanānābhāsanābhyāṃ yo bhedas tathābhūtabhedanimittakaḥ kālātmā kramo na bhedamātranimittakaḥ. ābhāsasadbhāvāsadbhāvau ca yau vaicitryeṇa tau svapnasaṅkalpanādau kramotthāpanadṛṣṭasāmarthyasya prabhaviṣṇor eva sakāśād bhavataḥ. yad uktaṃ tatrabhavatā: ekasyaiva tu sā śaktir yad evam avabhāsate* ‖ *iti, tathānyatrāpi: tam asya lokayantrasya sūtradhāraṃ pracakṣate* | *pratibandhābhyanujñābhyāṃ tena viśvaṃ vibhajyate* ‖ *yadi na pratibadhnīyāt pratibandhāc ca notsṛjet* | *avasthā vyatikīryeran paurvāparyavinākṛtāḥ** ‖ *iti. anena hi svātantryam ābhāsanānābhāsanayor vadataiśvaryam uktam, sa hi bhagavān citratayābhāsān karoti...* [**paurvāparyavinākṛtāḥ* corr.; *pauryāparyavinākṛtāḥ* Ed.]

According to Bhartṛhari, the power of time prevents certain phenomena from occurring while allowing others to appear, and it is this capacity of exclusion (*pratibandha*) and assent (*abhyanujñā*) that brings about sequence—an idea adopted by Utpaladeva, who considers that sequence is simply the fact that some phenomena are made not to appear while others are manifest. Abhinavagupta takes the opportunity to present Bhartṛhari as a Śaiva nondualist on the grounds that he uses the word "freedom"[449]—which in the Śaiva nondualistic system is synonymous with sovereignty (*aiśvarya*), i.e. literally, "the fact of being the Lord"—to describe the way in which time enables certain phenomena to occur together while preventing others from appearing: according to Abhinavagupta, here Utpaladeva is not integrating Bhartṛhari's doctrine of time to Śaiva nondualism—or rather, his integration of Bhartṛhari's doctrine of time is only possible because this doctrine is already in essence a Śaiva nondualistic one.

### 4. Utpaladeva's distinction between exclusive difference and variety

Utpaladeva, for his part, begins the *Vivṛti* on this verse by providing an interpretation of the *Vṛtti* that corresponds to the above-mentioned explanations in the ĪPV and ĪPVV. For the *Vṛtti* asserts that the cause of sequence is nothing but "the Lord's action of [bringing about] a variety of manifestations of [objective] entities that are different inasmuch as they are devoid of each other's phenomena"; and the *Vivṛti*'s first step is to explain that sequence arises from the "variety" of ways in which the ultimate consciousness manifests objective entities, since one of the ways in which it manifests them consists in making their phenomena appear as incompatible (such as "pot" and "cloth" that are mutually exclusive). Then, however, he seems to anticipate a distinction made in the next verse by offering a more complex (and far less natural) reading of the *Vṛtti* on ĪPK 2.1.4. According to this rather convoluted interpretation, the words "variety" and "different" in the *Vṛtti* suggest that in fact two distinct factors contribute to the production of sequence and respectively lead to its spatial and temporal kinds—namely, on the one hand, the already-explained difference (*bheda*) between entities

---

[449] See e.g. *Vākyapadīyavṛtti* (hereafter VPV) on VP 1.3, p. 18 (*kālākhyena svātantryeṇa...*); as already noticed in SUBRAMANIA IYER 1969, p. 22, Abhinavagupta has no doubt that the VPV was composed by Bhartṛhari himself.

whose phenomena entirely exclude each other, and on the other hand, variety (*citratva*, *vaicitrya*), understood as *a difference that is not contradictory with unity but rather rests on it.*

This distinction is essential to Utpaladeva's system, because the Śaiva nondualists are keen on emphasizing that their doctrine is not a nondualism in the sense that it would discard just any kind of difference. The Advaitavedānta constitutes in the Śaivas' eyes a very poor notion of nonduality inasmuch as it seeks to eliminate all differences from the nondual reality, and the unity that it presents as the heart of reality excludes (and must be excluded from) all differences, whereas according to the Śaiva nondualists, the ultimate nonduality *includes* or incompasses all differences.[450] They thus point out that insentient objects that are different from each other necessarily exclude each other (a blue patch cannot become yellow without ceasing to be a blue patch) whereas consciousness has the ability of immediately grasping a multiplicity while grounding it in its essential unity: when we get a glimpse of a variegated landscape, we grasp in a single perceptual cognition a multiplicity that is not contradictory with, or exclusive of, the unity of our cognition. So variety—defined as a difference grounded in unity—is not an illusion to be discarded, but rather, the heart of consciousness's reality; only exclusive or absolute difference (*ekarasabheda* or *atyantabheda*)[451] is erroneous in that it betrays an incomplete grasp of nonduality.

This idea is stated in several instances elsewhere in the treatise, but Utpaladeva brings it up at this point of the *Vivṛti* because in the next verse (ĪPK 2.1.5), he is going to distinguish two kinds of sequence, viz. the spatial (*deśakrama*) and the temporal (*kālakrama*).[452] And there he will explain that spatial difference arises from exclusive difference inasmuch as it is due to the manifestation of multiple material objects that present themselves as entirely distinct and incompatible (a pot and a cloth cannot exist in exactly the same locus because one cannot be precisely where the other is without

---

[450] On this essential distinction between Advaitavedānta and Īśvarādvayavāda, see RATIÉ 2011a, chapter 9.

[451] On these see e.g. ĪPV, vol. II, p. 268 and ĪPK 4.13; cf. RATIÉ 2011a, p. 710.

[452] See chapter 8 below.

becoming the other and thus ceasing to exist as what it used to be). Temporal sequence, on the other hand, involves the apprehension of a variety in the sense just defined: we experience it because we grasp a multiplicity that is admittedly contradictory in some respects (a child is not and cannot be an adult); and yet, while being aware of these contradictory aspects, we realize that they are grounded in a profound unity, as when we become aware that the adult standing in front of us *is* the child whom we knew years ago. Our awareness of time is fundamentally a recognition (*pratyabhijñā*), that is to say, the paradoxical realization that something *is not quite the same and yet must be the same*—and recognition is the cognition of a variety in the sense defined above. So time belongs in some ways to the sphere of error, because any temporally determined awareness involves a contradiction between aspects that are mutually incompatible, and thus entails a lack of awareness of reality's nonduality; yet it is less radically so than spatial sequence: our awareness of time is so to speak one step closer to the ultimate reality than our awareness of space, because there is no experience of time without a recognition, that is, the awareness of an underlying identity in a perceived multiplicity.

### 5. Utpaladeva's assertion that this distinction is accepted by the Buddhists and Bhartṛhari's followers

This idea that variety is to be distinguished from exclusive difference and can be considered to be the ultimate reality (understood as a unity encompassing all differences) plays an important role in Utpaladeva's definition of sequence; and while alluding to it at this point of the *Vivṛti*, he shows in passing that its value has been acknowledged by other currents of thought despite the seemingly irreconcilable differences that separate them. In this respect Utpaladeva quotes a verse by Dharmakīrti that also appears in Abhinavagupta's and Yogarāja's works.[453] The verse runs as follows:

> [A colour] such as the blue [that appears] in a variegated cognition [and] is a property (*upādhi*) of the cognition [itself] cannot be perceived [as] not mixed with anything else; for

[453] See e.g. Abhinavagupta's paraphrases of it in ĪPVV, vol. II, p. 85, but also vol. III, p. 212; see also PSV, p. 19, and, on the latter, BANSAT-BOUDON & TRIPATHI 2011, p. 91 (with the reservations expressed below, fn. 456, as to the translation and interpretation offered there).

> [someone] distinguishing it [from other colors] focuses on the object [itself, not on the cognition].[454]

Whatever Dharmakīrti's original intention may have been in composing it,[455] the Śaivas (including Yogarāja)[456] read it as meaning that in the perceptual cognition of a variegated patch of colour, the different colours belonging to the variegated patch cannot be apprehended separately unless

---

[454] PV, *Pratyakṣapariccheda* 220: *nīlādiś citravijñāne jñānopādhir ananyabhāk* | *aśakyadarśanas taṃ hi pataty arthe vivecayan* ||

[455] This remains debated: see e.g. DUNNE 2004, pp. 63 and 98 ff., INAMI 2011, pp. 182 ff., and KELLNER 2011, pp. 292–293.

[456] The translation and interpretation of the verse's quotation in Yogarāja's PSV that is provided in BANSAT-BOUDON & TRIPATHI 2011, p. 91, seems incompatible with the context and commentaries. Here the issue is not that the content of the cognition may be "always variable," but that a single perceptual cognition can present as its objective content a variegated colour (rather than a colour that is merely blue, or merely yellow, etc.). Besides, contrary to what is stated in this book (ibid.), Manorathanandin, just as Prajñākaragupta, understands *ananyabhāk* and *aśakyadarśanaḥ* as going together, so that if one follows Manorathanandin (which BANSAT-BOUDON & TRIPATHI 2011 claims to do), the passage cannot mean that the blue in the cognition "does not partake of anything else" such as "the colour yellow" and that it "cannot be perceived [differently, viz., as the colour yellow]"; it can only mean that the blue cannot be perceived apart from the other colours. See *Pramāṇavārttikavṛtti* (henceforth PVV), p. 184: *ananyabhāg ākārāntarāsahacaraḥ kevala ity arthaḥ, tādṛśo 'śakyadarśanaḥ sahaivākārāntaravedananiyamāt.* "It cannot be perceived (*aśakyadarśana*) as being such that (*tādṛśa*) it is not mixed with anything else (*ananyabhāk*), that is to say, alone, while not being accompanied by any other aspect, because it necessarily occurs (*niyama*) along with the awareness of other aspects, [and] only with [them]". The Śaivas adopt the same interpretation, as is clear from Abhinavagupta's paraphrase of the verse in ĪPVV, vol. II, p. 85: *citrarūpajñāne hi yo jñānasyopādhir jñānatādātmyena nirbhāsamāno nīlādiḥ, sa vijñānād yato bhedenāśakyadarśanaḥ, tato 'nanyabhāk san pītādiviviktaḥ sann aśakyadarśanaḥ...* "For [a colour] such as the blue that is manifest in a cognition whose form is variegated, [being] a property of the cognition—insofar as it consists in that cognition—, cannot be perceived as distinct from the cognition; therefore it cannot be perceived (*aśakyadarśana*) [as] not being mixed with anything else (*ananyabhāk*), [that is to say, as] being distinct from the yellow and [the other colors]." See also ĪPVV, vol. III, p. 11, where Abhinavagupta, explaining this passage in the *Vivṛti*, quotes the two compounds together (***anyonyāparityāgena paricchedād*** *ity anenānanyabhāk* | *aśakyadarśana ity...*).

one starts focusing on the external object itself (or on what one imagines to be such an object) rather than on what appears in the cognition, because the latter does not present as its object a mere collection of heterogeneous entities, but rather, a variety, i.e., a multiplicity grasped as endowed with a fundamental unity. According to Utpaladeva, this is proof that his Buddhist rivals too understand variety (that is, difference grounded in unity) as constituting the core of reality; and it is of course quite ironical that, as noted by Abhinavagupta, the *Vivṛti* thus invokes Dharmakīrti's authority to give more weight to this Śaiva idea:

> [In the passage beginning with] "And accordingly...," [Utpaladeva] gives weight to his [own] words by quoting the honourable [Dharmakīrti] on the contradiction [that may be considered to exist, on the one hand,] between unity and a variegated cognition, and, [on the other hand,] between unity and difference. For the first one[—viz. the contradiction that may be considered to exist between unity and a variegated cognition—] is described with the first three quarters of the verse, [where it is shown not be real since unity and a variegated cognition are experienced to be compatible]; whereas the other one, [—viz. the contradiction between unity and difference that is found in objects—is described] in the fourth [quarter of the verse].[457]

Utpaladeva also takes this opportunity to humorously remark that Dharmakīrti ends up sharing this idea with his fiercest opponents, since by accepting the distinction between exclusive difference and variety, he eventually acknowledges the variety "that belongs to the reality that is the Brahman"—that is, most probably, the variety that belongs to reality as defined by the followers of Bhartṛhari.[458] That the latter are alluded to here is not surprising, given that contrary to Advaitavedāntins such as Maṇḍanamiśra

---

[457] ĪPVV, vol. III, p. 11: ***tathā ce****ti citrabodhaikatvabhedaikatvayoś ca virodhe vāgbharam āryavacanena karoti. ādyaṃ hi pādatrayeṇātroktam, anyat tu turyeṇa.*

[458] Utpaladeva calls them elsewhere (ŚDV, p. 36) upholders of the *śabdaparabrahmādvayavāda*. Bhartṛhari is an omnipresent interlocutor in this chapter, he is explicitly mentioned and quoted by Utpaladeva himself in his *Vivṛti* on the next verse, and as seen above (fn. 444–447), Abhinavagupta quotes several verses from the VP while commenting on this verse in the ĪPVV; he obviously thinks that Utpaladeva has Bhartṛhari in mind here (see in particular below, fn. 461).

and Śaṅkara, Bhartṛhari concedes an ontological value to variety by admitting that the Brahman has a multiplicity of powers (*śakti*). Showing that the Buddhists and the (*śabda-*)*brahmavādin*s thus find themselves on the same metaphysical side when it comes to the ontological status of variety is of course an amusing idea, and Abhinavagupta evidently enjoys the joke. Thus he explains in the following way[459] Utpaladeva's use of the particle *eva* when the *Vivṛti* points out that "the *same* [Buddhist authors]" (*tair eva*) acknowledge with the followers of Bhartṛhari that variety belongs to the core of reality:

> The reality that is the Brahman is admitted to be varied in the same way by "the same"—[that is, by the same Buddhist authors] who contend that the blue [within a variegated patch] has the nature [just] stated [in Dharmakīrti's verse]—and by the Brahmavādins, whether they claim, [as the Buddhists,] that [this reality] is perishable/nonverbal (*anakṣara*)[460] or, [as the Brahmavādins,] that it is imperishable/verbal (*akṣara*).[461] Because the [Buddhists] admit that the consciousness of the omniscient [Buddha] is variegated with manifestations of entities and non-entities belonging to all times and places, and [because they admit that this consciousness] is itself unlimited by place and time insofar as it

---

[459] This passage brings to mind a famous sentence mentioning the Buddhist author Śaṅkaranandana in ĪPVV, vol. II, p. 199. This sentence was once taken as evidence of Śaṅkaranandana's conversion to Śaivism, but the comparison with both passages shows that in fact there Abhinavagupta was not alluding to Śaṅkaranandana's alleged leaning towards the Śaiva doctrine: just as in the sentence quoted below and referring to Dharmakīrti (who is not suspect of having converted to Śaivism), in ĪPVV, vol. II, p. 199, Abhinavagupta was just ironically remarking that even a Buddhist such as Śaṅkaranandana can see the light (provided, of course, that he is favoured by Śiva's grace): see RATIÉ 2020b.

[460] On the Buddhist contention that reality is nonverbal (*anakṣara/nirakṣara*), see e.g. OGAWA 2019, p. 614.

[461] The term *anakṣara* is an important clue that the *brahmavādin*s considered here are followers of Bhartṛhari: this is obviously an allusion to the famous definition of the Brahman in VP 1.1 (quoted above, fn. 331) as being *akṣara*, a word that means "imperishable" (the verse explains that the Brahman is "without beginning or end") but also denotes phonemes and speech (the verse also states that Brahman is "the essence of Speech").

> consists of consciousness, this [doctrine of ours,] which they seek to refute, flashes forth in them as soon as they recover a clear intuition [of reality] (*pratibhā*), which [may] arise thanks to the favour of the Great Lord [Śiva] (*maheśvara*) when He is kindly disposed [towards them] due to the maturation of [their past] meritorious acts and [their] realization of [the nature of] consciousness—this is [the meaning of] the particle *eva* here![462]

## 6. The objective entities in which sequence is found are mere manifestations of consciousness

Abhinavagupta introduces as follows Utpaladeva's last point in the *Vivṛti* on this verse:

> With "[As for these objective entities, they are in fact nothing but variegated manifestations produced by the power of] *māyā*," [Utpaladeva] answers [the following objection:] "But what are these so-called [objective] entities that are other [than the Lord, and] on account of which [you] say [in the *Vṛtti* that sequence occurs] 'in [objective] entities,' [thus]

[462] ĪPVV, vol. III, p. 11: ***tair eve****ty uktarūpanīlavādibhir* brahmavādibhir vaivaṃ tāvad vadadbhir anakṣaram akṣaram api brahmatattvaṃ citram aṅgīkṛtaṃ bhavati. sarvajñabodhasya sārvakālikasārvadeśikabhāvābhāvābhāsacitrasya svayaṃ ca bodharūpatayā deśakālānākalitasyāṅgīkaraṇād yair dūṣayitum abhīṣṭaṃ tat teṣām eva saṃvitparāmarśakuśalaparipākaprasannamaheśvaraprasādoditāvadātapratibhāpratilambhād eva sphuritam ity evakāraḥ.* [**uktarūpanīlavādibhir* conj.; *uktarūpair nīlādibhir* J11, S12, Ed.] Abhinavagupta's gloss has apprently crept in the only legible marginal annotation quoting this passage of the *Vivṛti*, and the annotation has the same reading as the ĪPVV edition (*uktarūpair nīlādibhir*). I do not see, however, how an alternative between "the blue, etc." and the *brahmavādin*s would make sense here. As indicated in ĪPVV, ibid., fn. 1, manuscript Ga consulted by the editors of the ĪPVV reads *brahmādibhiḥ* instead of *brahmavādibhiḥ*, but it is obvious from the context that the right reading is *brahmavādibhiḥ*. So I assume that in the ĪPVV too, the correct reading may have been *uktarūpanīlavādibhir* and that °*nīlavādibhir* got corrupted into *nīlādibhir* just as *brahmavādibhiḥ* got corrupted into *brahmādibhiḥ*.

> abandoning [the thesis that] they consist in [mere] manifestations?"[463]

Stating that sequence arises "in [objective] entities" as the *Vṛtti* does could mislead Utpaladeva's readers into thinking that sequence arises in things that exist independently of consciousness. The *Vivṛti* therefore makes clear that the definition of the Lord's creativity as the cause of sequence in objective entities is not to be taken a concession that things really have an autonomous existence. In his system the word *bhāva*, as he reminds his readers, designates consciousness itself insofar as it is erroneously taken to consist in distinct objective entities; it is these forms—in fact taken on by consciousness itself—that are affected by spatial and temporal sequence because they appear as limited, mutually exclusive realities. A cloth is not a pot, so that it cannot reside in the same locus; a cloth cannot be both brand new and worn, so that it must exist in these different states at different times—but in fact the pot, the brand new and the worn cloth are all ways for consciousness (which transcends their apparently contradictory forms) of manifesting itself in the form of objects.

[463] ĪPVV, vol. III, p. 11: *nanv avabhāsarūpatāṃ muktvā ke pare bhāvā nāma yenoktaṃ bhāveṣv iti. tatrāha* ***māyeti***.

# CHAPTER 8

# The Definition of Spatial and Temporal Sequence (ĪPK 2.1.5)

## 1. Space and time result from the variety of material shapes and actions

In the next stanza, Utpaladeva explains what constitutes the difference between the spatial and temporal kinds of sequence: the former arises from a variety of material shapes (*mūrti*);[464] the latter, from a variety of actions (*kriyā*).

Raffaele Torella has already noticed that this definition is reminiscent of Bhartṛhari's,[465] and this is confirmed by Utpaladeva's newly discovered *Vivṛti* on this verse, which explicitly mentions the grammarian-philosopher in this respect. For according to the VP,

---

[464] The term is difficult to render in English. NEMEC 2016 translates it as "material entity," and *mūrtatva*, as "materiality." One should bear in mind, however, that a material element such as ether (*ākāśa*) is considered *amūrta*, and is said to be so precisely because it has no definite shape; similarly, qualities such as colours or smells are considered *amūrta*. Besides, given Utpaladeva's own definition of the term in his *Vivṛti* as a mere form that is exclusive of any other form, and the original meaning of *mūrta* as "coagulated," "congealed," it is tempting to simply translate *mūrti* as "definite/fixed shape." However, the other definitions of *mūrti* alluded to by the Śaiva nondualists (see below, §4), which involve size and solidity, point to a slightly wider semantic spectrum. Finally, consciousness too can have specific forms or aspects (*ākāra*, etc.) that are not to be confused with *mūrti*s, i.e., shapes that, as noticed by Abhinavagupta, are understood by "ordinary people" as something that is "liable to be taken, accepted, given, etc." (see below, fn. 514)—hence the tentative (and certainly debatable) choice of translation here.

[465] TORELLA 2002, p. 154, fn. 5.

> Actions (*kriyā*) are divided due to time, [whereas] all material shapes (*mūrti*) [are divided] due to space; and all of this differentiation has as its basis nonduality.[466]

At first sight one might take Bhartṛhari's verse to mean that material shapes and actions are divided by spatial and temporal sequences—a point quite different from Utpaladeva's, since the Śaiva nondualist rather argues that spatial and temporal sequences result from the variety of material shapes and actions. However, Helārāja makes clear that in Bhartṛhari's stanza, space and time are not to be taken as spatial and temporal sequences, but as the *powers* of space and time.[467] In other words, Bhartṛhari does not mean that material shapes and actions are divided by spatial and temporal sequences, but rather, that spatial and temporal sequences—i.e., the division between material shapes and that between actions—are produced by the powers of space and time; and ĪPK 2.1.5 obviously echoes this idea.

Yet it is not this particular verse of the VP that Utpaladeva quotes in his *Vivṛti* on ĪPK 2.1.5, but the following sentence, which he explicitly ascribes to Bhartṛhari:

> For this is not successive; from the point of view of material shape as well as action, it is entirely full in every regard.

According to the *Vivṛti* itself, the quotation points out "that the spatial and temporal succession of [objective] entities is [respectively] produced by material shapes and actions," although it also emphasizes that a reality transcending material shapes and actions is free of both spatial and temporal determinations. Abhinavagupta quotes it without attribution in the ĪPV

---

[466] VP 3.7.153: *kālāt kriyā vibhajyanta ākāśāt sarvamūrtayaḥ | etāvāṃś caiva bhedo 'yam abhedopanibandhanaḥ ||*

[467] PP, vol. I, p. 351: *kālākāśayor api ca bhedaḥ śaktitvād atyantābhinnaparabrahmanimittaḥ.* "And the differentiation of both time and space has as its basis the Highest Brahman which is entirely nondual, because [space and time] are [the Brahman's] powers (*śakti*)."

while explaining another verse;[468] Helārāja also seems to allude to it.[469] Bhāskarakaṇṭha only describes it as the opinion of "an ancient" or "ancients" (*vṛddhasammati*, *vṛddhavākya*), without any reference to Bhartṛhari.[470] It might have been part of the VP's *Vṛtti* or the *Mahābhāṣyadīpikā* (which have both come down to us in an incomplete form); in any case, while commenting on Utpaladeva's statement that Bhartṛhari, by saying this, was "acknowledging" a definition of material shapes equivalent to that of the Śaiva nondualists, Abhinavagupta makes the following remark:

> And this is not just [Utpaladeva]'s personal opinion—this is [what] he says [with] "The master [Bhartṛhari too has said the following]." "[Thus] acknowledging..." means: [thus] accepting what is said by others as well, [i.e.] by Upaniṣadic sentences such as "The two appearances of material shapes and actions are nothing but the operation of the power of Nescience."[471]

The "Upaniṣadic sentence" alluded to here appears in VPV 1, p. 9, and while explaining it, the *Vākyapadīyapaddhati* (henceforth VPP) makes clear that "the two appearances of material shapes and actions" refer to spatial and temporal sequences:

> [The compound] "the two appearances of material shapes and actions" [means] the appearance of material shapes—

---

[468] ĪPV on ĪPK 2.1.7, vol. II, p. 21; there it is merely introduced with *tad uktam*, "This has been said...," and it reads *pūrṇam* instead of *paripūrṇam* (the same ĪPV passage as quoted in the top margin of S19, f. 28a, also has *paripūrṇam*).

[469] See PP on VP 3.6.19, vol. I, p. 225: *yady api apūrvāparaṃ hīdaṃ viśvaṃ mūrtitaḥ kriyātaś ca tathāpi...* "Even though 'For this universe is not successive, from the point of view of material shape as well as action,' nonetheless..." The absence of an *iti* particle could make one doubt that this is a quotation, were it not for the presence of *hi* at a place that would be most unnatural if these were all Helārāja's own words. I thank Vincenzo Vergiani (personal communication through email, 8/01/2017) for bringing this passage to my attention.

[470] *Bhāskarī*, vol. II, p. 23.

[471] ĪPVV, vol. III, p. 14: *na ceyaṃ svamanīṣikety āha* ***tatrabhavad*** *iti.* ***icchann*** *ity anyair api mūrtikriyāvivartāv avidyāśaktipravṛttimātram ityādibhiḥ śrutyantavākyair vyavahṛtam abhyupagacchann ity arthaḥ.*

> [i.e.,] existence in the form of a separation according to spatial differences—[and] the appearance of actions—[i.e.,] existence in a form associated with arising, perishing and so on.[472]

The VPV passage is often mentioned as evidence that Utpaladeva's reference to the couple *mūrti/kriyā* is grounded in Bhartṛhari's tradition;[473] in the VPV, however, it is explicitly given as a quotation,[474] and the VPP further points out that this is a scriptural statement[475]—a fact seldom taken into account in modern secondary sources, but that Abhinavagupta seems to be underscoring here while remarking that the idea is not just Bhartṛhari's[476] and is in fact rooted in the Upaniṣadic tradition.

Now, what is the definition of *mūrti* that Utpaladeva defends? From the outset of the *Vivṛti* on ĪPK 2.1.5, he points out that by the word *mūrti*, he simply means a form that is "manifest through the mutual[ly] exclusive difference of [multiple] objects"; according to him, a material shape is a form that is by nature incompatible with other such forms—and it is nothing else, because in his idealistic system, material shapes are just the universal consciousness manifesting itself as if it were a multiplicity of mutually exclusive entities; ultimately, space, understood as spatial sequence (i.e., as the *Vivṛti* defines it, "the fact that there are anterior and posterior places, and the [property of] extendedness") is consciousness manifesting itself as if it had a multiplicity of incompatible forms, i.e., as if it were objects.

As immediately made clear by the *Vivṛti*, this means that our cognitions, whether perceptual or not, have no material shape—and therefore no spatial sequence—because even though their objects may be plural (as in the case

---

[472] VPP, p. 9: *mūrtikriyāvivartāv iti deśabhedāvagraharūpeṇāvasthānaṃ mūrtivivartaḥ, utpādavināśādikriyopahitarūpāvasthānaṃ kriyāvivartaḥ.*

[473] See in particular TORELLA 2002, p. 154, fn. 5; NEMEC 2016, p. 363; on this famous passage see also (without reference to Utpaladeva) HACKER 1953, p. 20 and VERGIANI 2004, p. 5.

[474] VPV 1, p. 9: *uktaṃ ca... iti.* The source of the quotation is unknown to me.

[475] VPP, p. 9: *asmin vastuni pramāṇam āgamaṃ paṭhati mūrtikriyāvivartāv iti.* "Regarding this fact, [the author] cites scripture (*āgama*) as an authority [in the passage beginning with] 'The two appearances of material shapes and actions...'"

[476] As mentioned above (chapter 7, fn. 449), Abhinavagupta has no doubt that the VPV was written by Bhartṛhari himself.

of a variegated patch of colour), their manifestation is endowed with a unity provided by the cognition's self-awareness (*svasaṃvedana*), that is, its ability to grasp itself as being the unitary cognition of a variegated patch. This is not to say that we would be unable to cognize spatially determined things (we are most certainly capable of doing this), but that spatial sequence only affects the *objects* of our cognitions rather than the cognitions themselves. As Abhinavagupta puts it elsewhere:

> To a fool, the cognition of a mountain appears to be large, and the cognition of a jujube, small.[477]

Temporal sequence, on the other hand, arises from the variety of actions, and it is when witnessing *differences that we grasp as being grounded in a unity* that we become aware of an action, as well as of temporal sequence, as Abhinavagupta explains:

> The "variety" of the material shape (*mūrti*)—[that is to say,] the specific form of a [given] thing—[means its] being distinct (*vibheda*) [from others]; for instance, one specific form is "a house"; another is "a courtyard"; another is "a shop"; another is "a temple"; another is "a garden"; yet another is "a forest;" [and it is] from this variety, [when it is] being manifested, that the Lord manifests spatial sequence, which [consists in] being far and close, extended and not extended, etc. But when, [as in the case of a moving hand,] a material shape has no difference because, thanks to the manifestation of an intense recognition, one understands "this is the *same* specific form of a hand," and yet this [material shape] is manifest as having ever different forms, then this ever different form that is not compatible (*asahabhavat*) in a single nature because of the contradiction that this entails is [precisely] what [we] call "action." When [the Lord] manifests the "variety" of this [action]—[a variety] which consists in having a nature that is both limited and unlimited—through a unifying synthesis of this [variety] that [can be] mentally

[477] ĪPV, vol. I, p. 235: *...vimūḍhasya parvatasaṃvedanaṃ vitatam iva badarasaṃvedanaṃ ca sūkṣmam iva bhāti...*

> produced (*carcitena*) at will[478] because [one is aware of] the connection [of each different form involved in the action] with the accomplishment of the [action's] effect and [all the other intermediary forms, then] it is temporal sequence that He manifests.[479]

Abhinavagupta thus emphasizes a crucial point here—namely, the somewhat different ways in which the term "variety" (*vaicitrya*) in ĪPK 2.1.5 must be taken according to whether it is used to define space or time. For in the case of time, as the *Vivṛti* on ĪPK 2.1.4 has already made clear,[480] this "variety" is to be taken in the sense of a multiplicity that is grounded in unity—or, as explained here by Abhinavagupta, variety in this case designates the fact of having a nature that is both limited and unlimited (*parimitāparimitarūpatā*); whereas spatial variety was described in the *Vivṛti* on the previous verse as the fact that "[entities] such as the blue are posited [by consciousness] as existing separately, while being distinct from each other"—or, according to Abhinavagupta's commentary here, variety in this case simply means "being distinct" (*vibheda*) from others.

Yet even though Utpaladeva asserts in his *Vivṛti* on ĪPK 2.1.4 that "there is no unity" as far as spatial sequence is concerned, there must be some kind of minimal continuity within the variety that brings about space. Thus when Utpaladeva reminds his readers, in the *Vivṛti* on ĪPK 2.1.7, that the cause of spatial sequence is a "difference" (*bheda*)—i.e., says Abhinavagupta, an

---

[478] Following Bhāskarakaṇṭha's interpretation (*Bhāskarī*, vol. II, p. 18: *yathāruci: yathārucyanusāreṇa; carcitena: kalpitena*).

[479] ĪPV, vol. II, pp. 13–15: *padārthasya svaṃ rūpaṃ mūrtis tasyā yad vaicitryaṃ vibhedas tadyathā gṛham ity anyat svarūpaṃ prāṅgaṇam ity anyad vipaṇir ity anyad devakulam ity aparam udyānam ity anyad araṇyam iti taditarat. tasmād vaicitryād ābhāsyamānād deśarūpo dūrādūravitatatvāvitatatvādiḥ kramo bhavagatāvabhāsyate. yadā tu gāḍhapratyabhijñāprakāśabalāt tad evedaṃ hastasvarūpam iti pratipattau mūrter na* bhedaḥ, atha cānyānyarūpatvaṃ bhāti tadaikasmin svarūpe yad anyad anyad rūpaṃ tad virodhavaśād asahabhavat kriyety ucyate. tasyā yad vaicitryaṃ parimitāparimitarūpatātmakam tadekānusandhānena phalasiddhyādinibandhanavaśād yathāruci carcitena nirbhāsayan kālarūpaṃ kramam eva bhāsayati.* [**mūrter na* Ed. The reading *mūrtena* in RATIÉ 2011a, p. 202, fn. 67 (continued) is of course a typo and should be corrected along with the corresponding translation.]

[480] See above, chapter 7, §4.

"otherness" (*anyatva*)—between the presence and absence of a given phenomenon such as blue, Utpaladeva also explains that these presence and absence are brought about "simultaneously" (*yugapat*), and Abhinavagupta explains that this means "at the same time" (*samakāla*).[481] But in order to be aware that *there is a patch of blue here but not there* (that is, in order to be aware of a difference that is purely spatial and not temporal), we need to be able to grasp more than a mere absence of temporal sequence: this type of awareness is only possible provided that we grasp the place called "here" and the place called "there" *synthetically*—which means that in fact, the variety from which spatial sequence springs is not a sheer multiplicity.

The point, it seems, was acknowledged by the Śaiva nondualists. Thus while commenting on Utpaladeva's assertion that consciousness is "comparable to the surface of the even background of the painting (*citra*) that is the variety (*vaicitrya*) of the universe,"[482] Abhinavagupta remarks that we can only be aware of contemplating a painting if the various patches of colour that constitute it are apprehended as part of a totality:

> For if one became aware (*parāmṛś-*) of [the existence of various objects] such as blue or yellow only separately (*pṛthak*) [from each other], then, since these [various objects] would rest [only] in themselves, in the same way, [their perceptual] cognitions, being confined to their own respective object, would be as it were insentient, blind and deaf with respect to their mutual objects; and conceptual cognitions, which exist while conforming to the [perceptions that precede them,] would be exactly in the same case. So how could the understanding "this is a painting" (*citram idam*) [ever occur]?[483]

Even the cognition of spatiality involves the awareness of a minimal unity that binds together the entities existing in a spatial relationship—and this

---

481 See ĪPVV, vol. III, p. 23, quoted below, chapter 9, fn. 688.

482 ĪPK 2.3.15ab: *viśvavaicitryacitrasya samabhittitalopame* | On this important analogy and Abhinavagupta's explanation of it, see RATIÉ 2013.

483 ĪPV, vol. II, pp. 122–123: *yadi hi nīlapītādikaṃ pṛthag eva parāmṛśyate tadā svātmaviśrānteṣu teṣu tathaivānyonyaviṣaye*jaḍāndhabadhirakalpāni jñānāni svaviṣayamātraniṣṭhitāni, vikalpāś ca tadanusāreṇa bhavantas tathaiveti citram idam iti kathaṃkāraṃ pratipattiḥ.* [**tathaivānyonyaviṣaye* J, S1, SOAS, *Bhāskarī* Ed.; *tathā vānyonyaviṣaye* KSTS Ed.; *yathā vānyonyaviṣaye* L, S2.]

might be the reason why, in verse ĪPK 2.1.5, Utpaladeva uses the same word "variety" to describe both the source of time and that of space: *in both cases, what produces sequence is more than a pure multiplicity*,[484] even though this variety is not to be understood exactly in the same way, because time clearly involves a stronger kind of unity—namely, *identity*. Thus, as pointed out by Abhinavagupta in his ĪPV commentary on this verse, spatial sequence arises from the multiplicity of material shapes that, although bound together when we grasp them as being far from each other, close to each other, etc., *remain distinct* from each other (the house is *other* than the courtyard, shop, temple, garden, forest, etc.); whereas temporal sequence arises from the variety found in actions, because when we see a hand moving up and down, we *recognize* the hand as being *the same material shape* despite the multiple and incompatible forms that it then assumes.

## 2. The paradox of action

Admittedly, there is something highly paradoxical about this awareness of action. As Abhinavagupta points out in the passage just quoted, in it we are aware of forms that are contradictory (*viruddha*), that is, perfectly incompatible (such as Devadatta's foot on the ground and Devadatta's foot in the air); and yet the differences apprehended in any action do not have the power to cancel our awareness of the profound unity that binds these contradictory states, as Abhinavagupta further points out in the corresponding passage of the ĪPVV.[485] To be aware of an action is to grasp *both* the contradiction that affects a number of differentiated phenomena, and the fact that this contradiction is somehow transcended by the unity that flashes forth in the recognition (*pratyabhijñā*) that Devadatta, in all these contradictory states, is somehow *the same* walking person. And this extraordinary mixture of contradiction and absence thereof is not absurd, according to Abhinavagupta, because action is the manifestation of consciousness's essential dynamism, which transcends all contradictions since it is what makes contradiction possible by manifesting it:

---

[484] Abhinavagupta emphasizes in TĀ 15.194–196 (on which see below, §10, fn. 611) that this is a reason why spatiality can only make sense in an idealistic system.

[485] See ĪPVV, vol. III, p. 12, quoted below, fn. 576.

> And one cannot object: "How can a single nature have an ever different form?", since it is not just any [objective] entity that is thus conceptualized [when we become aware of an action]; for it is consciousness itself that is manifest in this way. And the fact that [it is able to] manifest [itself] in this way is precisely its sovereignty (*aiśvarya*), for no contradiction whatsoever can reign with respect to [its] manifestation; for [contradiction]—for instance [that] of pleasure and pain—is only produced *by* manifestation [itself],[486] since the essence of contradiction is simply the absence of such a [power][487] to manifest.[488]

Admittedly, in the sphere of ordinary practice, we ascribe action not just to conscious beings but also to insentient entities: we say that the chariot, and not just Devadatta, "moves." But as Utpaladeva emphasizes later in his *Vivṛti* on this verse, in doing so we take a mere metaphor for a literal statement, since in fact only sentient beings act;[489] and this projection of agency (which in fact solely belongs to consciousness) onto insentient entities results in our awareness that things are temporally determined—which, according to the *Vivṛti*, explains why we always apprehend the temporality of things with respect to our own.

---

[486] Cf. the marginal annotation in SOAS (also printed in ĪPV, vol. II, p. 15, fn. 37) according to which "[the contradiction of e.g. pleasure and pain] is the absence of manifestation of [things] such as pleasure along with the form that is pain; [and it is] 'produced by manifestation'—[the latter must be understood as] the agent [producing it]" (*sukhādīnāṃ duḥkharūpeṇābhāsanābhāvo bhāsanena kartrā kṛtaḥ*).

[487] See the same marginal annotation (ibid.), according to which "'such a [power' means] the presence of the power that is the act of manifesting" (*tatheti bhāsanakriyāsamarthanasattā*).

[488] ĪPV, vol. II, p. 15: *na caitad vācyam ekasvarūpasya katham anyad anyad rūpam iti yato nāsau kaścid bhāvo ya evaṃ vikalpyate, saṃvid eva hi tathā bhāti, tathābhāsanam eva cāsyā aiśvaryam, na hi bhāsane virodhaḥ kaścit prabhavati, sa hi sukhaduḥkhāder bhāsanakṛta eva, tathābhāsanābhāva eva hi virodhatattvam.*

[489] Cf. e.g. ĪPV, vol. II, p. 190: *na ca jñānaśaktivihīnasya kriyāyogaḥ.* "And [something] that is deprived of the power of knowledge cannot possess action."

### 3. Spatial sequence and the issue of sound (*śabda*)

In the *Vivṛti*, however, Utpaladeva does not immediately endeavour to explain temporal sequence and our paradoxical awareness of action: he first focuses on the explanation of spatial sequence and what is affected by it—that is, material shapes. After specifying in this connection that a cognition can have no material shape, he adds that sound (*śabda*), insofar as it is an "internal" form, has no material shape either, and Abhinavagupta explains that this subtle form of *śabda* is to be equated with the levels of speech known in the grammatical and tantric traditions as Paśyantī and Madhyamā.[490] In fact the Śaivas admit a fourth, ultimate level, Parā, but Utpaladeva does not mention it here, probably because this ultimate level—an absolute unity equated with the pure "I" realization—is precisely what takes the forms of the three other levels when it manifests differentiation.[491] In the *Vivṛti*, Utpaladeva specifies that Paśyantī consists in the apprehending subject (*grāhaka*) whereas Madhyamā takes the form of the act of apprehending (*grahaṇa*). He does so because at the Paśyantī level, the ultimate consciousness is said to apprehend itself as a pure will (*icchā*) to manifest the external world, and what prevails in that will is a purely subjective realization, since there the distinction between subject and object is still dim (*asphuṭa*), as consciousness grasps itself as desiring something that it is engaged in imagining, i.e., something that is a mere form of itself; whereas at the Madhyamā level, the distinction between signifier and signified, as well as that between subject and object, is becoming more vivid (although it remains merely "outlined," *āsūtrita*), so that at that stage, consciousness predominantly apprehends itself as the act of apprehending that both distinguishes and links the apprehending subject and apprehending object. As Jayaratha explains:

---

[490] On the levels of speech in Śaiva nondualism see in particular PADOUX 1990, chapter 4.

[491] See e.g. TĀ 3.236: *vibhāgābhāsane cāsya tridhā vapur udāhṛtam | paśyantī madhyamā sthūlā vaikharīty abhiśabditam ||* "And when [it] manifests differentiation, it is said to take a threefold form called Paśyantī, Madhyamā and Vaikharī, [that is,] the gross one." Cf. Jayaratha's explanation in TĀV, vol. II, p. 225: *asyeti parāvāgrūpasyāhamātmanaḥ parāmarśasya.* "'It' [means] the realization (*parāmarśa*), the essence of which is 'I,' [and which] consists in the [level of] Speech [called] Parā."

> For it is this Highest Sovereign [form of Speech, viz. the ultimate I-realization], who may be designated by the name Paśyantī, [i.e., "the Seeing One,"] when, by virtue of its own freedom, it wishes to appear in an external form; [it is thus called at that stage] because it takes the form of a perceiving subject, since [at that point] the sequence of the signified and signifier has not [yet] arisen, [and] since only the light of consciousness prevails because differentiation is [still] dim. Then [the ultimate realization] may be designated by the name Madhyamā, [i.e., "the Middle One,"] because it is intermediary between the perceiving subject and the perceived object insofar as [what] prevails [in it] is the act of perceiving, since although [in it] the differentiation [resulting in] the sequence of the signified and signifier is outlined, it only rests on the intellect and it is [therefore] both dim and vivid.[492]

Utpaladeva insists in the *Vivṛti* that at these levels, sound can have no material shape, because then it is still what it is at the highest stage—namely, *vimarśa*, the essential freedom or ability of consciousness to actively become aware of itself.[493] He links these two levels of sound with ether (*ākāśa*)—an element considered to be devoid of material shape even by dualists such as the Vaiśeṣikas—and distinguishes them from a third level that he describes as "related to air (*vāyu*), etc." and endowed with material shape, because it is affected by differences that appear to be incompatible with unity. Abhinavagupta explains that this third level, namely, the ontological and linguistic plane called Vaikharī ("the Solid one"),[494] includes all the words that we utter and hear in the sphere of ordinary practice, but also the various noises peculiar to air, fire, water and earth:

---

[492] TĀV, vol. II, p. 225: *saiva hi parameśvarī svasvātantryād bahīrūpatām ullilāsayiṣur vācyavācakakramānudayād vibhāgasyāsphuṭatvāc cijjyotiṣa eva prādhānyād draṣṭṛrūpatayā paśyantīśabdavyapadeśyā. tadanu vācyavācakakramasyāsūtritavibhāgatve 'pi sphuṭāsphuṭarūpatvena buddhimātraniṣṭhatayā darśanaprādhānyād draṣṭṛdṛśyayor antarālavartitvena madhyamāpadavācyā.*

[493] Cf. e.g. TĀV, vol. II, p. 225, quoted above, which specifies that the Parā level of speech is nothing but the I-realization; see also PADOUX 1990, pp. 175 ff.

[494] On the various semantic analyses of this term see PADOUX 1995, p. 216, fn. 115.

> [The *Vivṛti* sentence beginning with] "[Whereas] the sound that is related to air, etc." [means the following:] The sound related to air, which arises on the plane of Vaikharī as [the word] "pot" for instance, and as a [rustling sound] such as *śukaśuka*; the [crackling sound] related to fire, such as *dhagadhaga*; [the gargling sound] related to water, such as *chalacchala*; the [cracking sound] related to earth, such as *ṭakaṭaka*—[all of these sounds] definitely have a difference in terms of being distant [or close], etc., depending on whether [they] are of the same sort or of a different one.[495]

The idea that the Vaikharī level includes both ordinary human speech and the noises produced by inanimate objects is found e.g. in the VPV;[496] but the Nyāya and Vaiśeṣika traditions,[497] which also admit that *śabda* includes both speech and noise, assert that it is apprehended as spatially determined (when we hear a sound, we can tell that it comes from here or there, that it is distant or close, etc.).[498] This matters here, since Abhinavagupta wants to emphasize that ordinary sound (whether it is of a linguistic nature or not)

---

[495] ĪPVV, vol. III, p. 13: ***vāyavīyāder*** *iti ghaṭa ityāder vaikharīpadāpannasya śukaśukādeś ca vāyavīyasya, dhagadhagādes taijasasya, chalacchalādeḥ* sālilasya, ṭakaṭakādeḥ pārthivasya śabdasya dūrādibhedaḥ sajātīyavijātīyāpekṣayā bhavaty eva.* [**chalacchalādeḥ* corr.; *chalachalādeḥ* Ed.]

[496] See VPV on VP 1.142, pp. 133–134: *paraiḥ saṃvedyaṃ yasyāḥ śrotraviṣayatvena pratiniyataṃ śrutirūpaṃ sā vaikharī, śliṣṭā vyaktavarṇasamuccāraṇā prasiddhasādhubhāvā bhraṣṭasaṃskārā ca, tathā yākṣe yā dundubhau yā veṇau vīṇāyām ity aparimāṇabhedā.* "Vaikharī is [the speech] whose form is a sound that is fixed according to each [thing that it denotes and] that is cognized by others due to its being the object of the organ of hearing; [it may be] indistinct [or it may] involve a collection of distinct phonemes; [it may] have a well-established correctness and [it may] have lost its correctness; it has innumerable differences—for instance there is the one in the axle [of a cart], the one in a drum, the one in a flute [or] a *vīṇā*."

[497] See e.g. PDhS, p. 637: *sa dvividho varṇalakṣaṇo dhvanilakṣaṇaś ca. tatrākārādir varṇalakṣaṇaḥ, śaṅkhādinimitto dhvanilakṣaṇaś ca.* "[Sound] is of two sorts, [namely,] characterized by phonemes and characterized by [non-linguistic] sound. Among them, the one characterized by phonemes is the phoneme 'a', etc.; and the one characterized by [non-linguistic] sound is the one that has as its cause [blowing] in a conch for instance."

[498] On the explanation of this ability that we have to tell where a sound comes from (*digdeśavyapadeśa*), see e.g. Uddyotakara's discussion in *Nyāyavārttika* (henceforth NV), p. 278, too long to be quoted here.

is spatially determined. Yet the proponents of Nyāya and Vaiśeṣika also insist that *śabda* is a quality that exclusively belongs to the *ākāśa* element, and this is contradictory with Utpaladeva's thesis that spatiality arises from an incompatibility between different material shapes, since ether is supposed to be devoid of material shape (*amūrta*): the fact that sounds are heard as being spatially determined can no longer be explained in terms of differences between material shapes if, as the Vaiśeṣikas and Naiyāyikas contend, sounds exclusively belong to the shapeless *ākāśa*. This, however, is not an actual difficulty for Utpaladeva, because the Śaivas, contrary to the Vaiśeṣikas and Naiyāyikas, consider that ordinary sounds (including linguistic ones) are not qualities of ether but of the four other material elements—and this is the point that Abhinavagupta's commentary aims at emphasizing.

Thus the Naiyāyika Jayanta portrays in his NM an opponent of the thesis that *śabda* only belongs to ether; this unidentified opponent argues against it that if it were the case, sounds that are peculiar to the four other elements (and that are expressed in Jayanta's text with onomatopoeic forms of the kind[499] used by Abhinavagupta) could not be accounted for:

> [But] earth makes the [cracking] sound *paṭapaṭa*, water makes the [gargling] sound *calacala*, fire makes the [crackling] sound *dhagadhaga*, air makes the [rustling] sound *kathakatha*—so all [of these elements] must possess sound![500]

According to this interlocutor, such sounds are proof that *śabda* must reside in all five elements rather than just *ākāśa*. The latter thesis is of course

---

[499] Both $NM_M$ and $NM_V$ have *paṭapaṭa* instead of *ṭakaṭaka* (in the ĪPVV) for earth, *calacala* instead of *chalacchala* for water, and *kathakatha* for air; the $NM_V$ has *dhakadhaka* instead of *dhagadhaga* for fire. As can be seen below, the various sources mentioning such onomatopoeic forms contain many such variations.

[500] $NM_M$, vol. II, p. 384: *paṭapaṭāyate pṛthivī, calacalāyanta āpaḥ, dhagadhagāyate tejaḥ, kathakathāyate vāyur iti sarveṣāṃ śabdaḥ syāt.*

found in Sāṃkhya sources such as the YD[501] and TK,[502] which explicitly ascribe the quality of sound to the five *mahābhūtas*. But the reasoning that it must be so *because these elements make specific noises* is absent from these texts, whereas it is expressed in Śaiva (nondualist as well as Saiddhāntika) sources. Thus the *Mṛgendratantra* (henceforth MT) insists that *śabda* resides in all five elements[503] and asserts:

---

[501] YD, p. 225: *tatra śabdaguṇāc chabdatanmātrād ākāśam ekaguṇam, śabdasparśaguṇāt sparśatanmātrād dviguṇo vāyuḥ, śabdasparśarūpaguṇād rūpatanmātrāt triguṇaṃ tejaḥ, śabdasparśarūparasaguṇād rasatanmātrāc caturguṇā āpaḥ, śabdasparśarūparasagandhaguṇād gandhatanmātrāt pañcaguṇā pṛthivī.* "In this regard, from the subtle element 'sound,' which has sound as its quality, [arises] ether, which has [this] one quality; from the subtle element 'tactile sensation,' which has sound and tactile sensation as its qualities, [arises] air, which has [these] two qualities; from the subtle element 'visible form,' which has sound, tactile form and visible form as its qualities, [arises] fire, which has [these] three qualities; from the subtle element 'taste,' which has sound, tactile form, visible form and taste as its qualities, [arises] water, which has [these] four qualities; from the subtle element 'odour,' which has sound, tactile form, visible form, taste and odour as its qualities, [arises] earth, which has these [five] qualities." See BRONKHORST 1994, p. 311.

[502] TK on SK 22, p. 128: *pañcabhūtāny ākāśādīni, tatra śabdatanmātrād ākāśaṃ śabdaguṇam, śabdatanmātrasahitāt sparśatanmātrād vāyuḥ śabdasparśaguṇaḥ, śabdasparśatanmātrasahitād rūpatanmātrāt tejaḥ śabdasparśarūpaguṇam, śabdasparśarūpatanmātrasahitād rasatanmātrād āpaḥ śabdasparśarūparasaguṇāḥ, śabdasparśarūparasatanmātrasahitād gandhatanmātrāc chabdasparśarūparasagandhaguṇā pṛthivī jāyata iti.* "The 'five elements' are ether, [air, fire, water and earth]. Among them, ether, which has sound as its quality, arises from the subtle element of sound; air, which has sound and tactile form as its qualities, arises from the subtle element of tactile form with that of sound; fire, which has sound, tactile form and visible form as its qualities, arises from the subtle element of visible form with those of sound and tactile form; water, which has sound, tactile form, visible form and taste as its qualities, arises from the subtle element of taste with those of sound, tactile form and visible form; earth, which has sound, tactile form, visible form, taste and odour as its qualities, arises from the subtle element of odour with those of sound, tactile form, visible form and taste."

[503] MT 1.12.27c: *iti pañcasu śabdo 'yam...* "Therefore sound [resides] in the five [elements]."

> In air, [fire, water and earth,] the qualities that are sounds enable [us] to know that shaking, blazing, flowing, and solidity [occur in them]; in ether, [the qualities that are sounds] reside in echoes and possess phonemes.[504]

Nārāyaṇakaṇṭha's explanation spells out the argument also found in Abhinavagupta's ĪPVV and Jayanta's NM (again, with some variants in the onomatopoeic forms adduced):

> The qualities that are sounds in air, [fire, water and earth] make us know that shaking, blazing, etc. [occur in them], since a [rustling] sound such as *śakaśaka* makes us know that shaking [occurs] in wind; a [crackling] sound such as *dhakamadhakama* suggests blazing in fire; and similarly, a [gargling] sound such as *chalacchala* [suggests] flowing in water, and [the quality] consisting in a [cracking] sound such as *khaḍakhaḍa* expresses solidity in earth.[505]

Nārāyaṇakaṇṭha's commentary also invokes Sadyojyotis's authority, for the latter had already stated in his *Bhogakārikā* that *śabda* belongs to all five elements, while distinguishing the ethereal kind of sound from the others;[506] and Aghoraśiva's explanation of the latter specifies again that

[504] MT 1.12.20cd–21ab: *dhūnanajvalanaplāvakharatvāvedino guṇāḥ* ‖ *śabdā vāyvādiṣu vyomni savarṇapratiśabdagāḥ* ‖

[505] *Mṛgendratantravṛtti* (henceforth MTV) on MT 1.12.20–21, p. 258: *ye te vāyvādiṣu guṇāḥ śabdās te dhūnanajvalanādyāvedinaḥ, yataḥ śakaśakādiśabdo vāyau kampanāvedakaḥ, dhakamadhakamādiśabdo 'gnau jvalanaṃ sūcayati. evaṃ ca chalacchalādiśabdo* 'mbhasi vahanaṃ, khaḍakhaḍādiśabdātmakaś ca pṛthivyāṃ kharatvaṃ kathayati.* [**chalacchalādiśabdo* corr.; *chalachalādiśabdo* Ed.] Cf. MTV on MT 1.12.5, p. 247: *yathā pṛthivyāṃ khaṭakhaṭādirūpaḥ śabdaḥ...* "For example, in earth, sound takes the form *khaṭakhaṭa*, etc."

[506] *Bhogakārikā* 11: *śabdas taddravyajanitaḥ pṛthagbhūtacatuṣṭaye* | *pratiśabdakasaṃghāto nabhasy evodito budhaiḥ* ‖ "The sound produced by these substances [just mentioned, i.e., earth, air, water and fire, exists] in each of these four [elements; [but] all [sounds that are] echoes are said by the wise to belong exclusively to ether."

proof of this lies in the ability of earth, water, air and fire to produce specific sounds.[507]

On the nondualistic side, the TĀ explicitly rejects the Nyāya and Vaiśeṣika position that *śabda* exclusively belongs to ether while using exactly the same line of argument as the MT,[508] and Jayaratha explains Abhinavagupta's assertions that the sounds in earth, water, fire and air are "varied" by mentioning again the specific noises that they can produce[509]—an idea that is also stated by Abhinavagupta's disciple Kṣemarāja.[510]

---

[507] *Bhogakārikāvṛtti*, p. 206, mentions the following among several arguments against the Vaiśeṣika thesis that sound exclusively belongs to ether: *kiṃca, pṛthivyāṃ tāvat kaṭakaṭādikaḥ śabdo dṛśyate, jale cchalacchalādiḥ, agnau dhamadhamādiḥ, śakaśakādir vāyau, nabhasi ca pratiśabdātmaka iti.* "Moreover, to begin with, [we] perceive a [cracking] sound such as *kaṭakaṭa* in earth; in water, [a gargling sound] such as *chalacchala*; in fire, [a crackling sound] such as *dhamadhama*; in air, [a rustling sound] such as *śakaśaka*; and in ether, it consists in an echo." Cf. Aghoraśiva's *Tattvasaṅgrahaṭīkā* on Sadyojyotis's *Tattvasaṅgraha* 2, p. 116: *tathā hi pratyakṣeṇākāśe pratiśabdaḥ śrūyate, vāyau śakaśakādiḥ, agnau dhamadhamādiḥ, jale chalacchalādiḥ,* pṛthivyāṃ kaḍakaḍādiḥ.* [**chalacchalādiḥ* corr.; *chalachalādiḥ* Ed.] "To explain, [it is] thanks to direct perception [that we] hear echo in ether; [in the same way, we hear a rustling sound] such as *śakaśaka* in air; [a crackling] one such as *dhamadhama* in fire, [a gargling] one such as *chalacchala* in water, [a cracking] one such as *kaḍakaḍa* in earth."

[508] Compare the arguments put forward in TĀ 9.297–299 with MT 1.12.22–25.

[509] Jayaratha explains TĀ 9.294d–295b (*kṣitau* ‖ ... *śabdo vicitrakaḥ* | "In earth... sound is varied") by saying (TĀV, vol. VI, p. 237): *vicitraka iti khaṭakhaṭādirūpatvāt.* "[It is] 'varied' because it takes such a form as *khaṭakhaṭa*." He then comments on TĀ 9.295d (*citrāḥ śabdāś ca vāriṇi* ‖ "And in water sounds are varied"), TĀ 9.296b (*citrāḥ śabdāś ca pāvake* | "And in fire sounds are varied") and TĀ 9.296d (*dhvaniś citraś ca mārute* ‖ "And sound is varied in air") as follows (TĀV, vol. VI, p. 237): *citrā iti, chalacchalādirūpatvāt,* evam uttaratrāpi dhamadhamacaṭacaṭādirūpatayā vaicitryaṃ jñeyam.* [*chalacchalādi°* corr.; *chalachalādi°* Ed.] "[They are] varied because they take such forms as *chalacchala*; similarly, in the sequel too, the [variety] of [sounds in fire and air] is to be known from their having such forms as *dhamadhama* and *caṭacaṭa*."

[510] STU, on ST 12.7, vol. VI, pp. 4–5: ... *pṛthivyāḥ khaṭakhaṭarūpo* jalasya cchalacchalatā tejaso dhagadhagākṛtir vāyoḥ śukaśukasvabhāva* ākāśasya pratiśrutkākhyaḥ śabdaḥ.* [**khaṭakhaṭarūpo* corr..; *khaṭakhatārūpo* Ed. **śukaśukasvabhāva* corr.; *śukaśukāsvabhāva* Ed.] "[The sound] of earth takes the form *khaṭakhaṭa*; [the

So the Śaivas agree, against the Naiyāyikas and Vaiśeṣikas, that *śabda* may belong to the five elements; and here, Utpaladeva's main point is to distinguish these forms of *śabda* according to whether they are endowed with a material shape or not—and therefore spatially determined or not. For according to him, the higher levels of speech, which are associated with the shapeless ether, are nothing but an active awareness within cognitions, so that they have no spatial sequence; the inferior type of sound corresponding to the Vaikharī level, on the other hand, is associated with the four material elements that are endowed with a material shape, and as such is affected by spatial sequence—which is why the ordinary sounds that we hear are apprehended as being spatially determined.

### 4. A Vaiśeṣika objection: spatial sequence cannot result from a difference between material shapes

An objection is voiced at this point by an opponent who obviously belongs to the Vaiśeṣika tradition and questions the principle that spatial sequence results from differences between material shapes. For according to Praśastapāda and his followers, *śabda* is to be counted among "qualities of [a substance that] has no material shape" (*amūrtaguṇa*),[511] since it is a quality of ether, which is devoid of *mūrti*; and it cannot be a quality of the other elements. This opponent therefore points out that when Utpaladeva claims that sound may somehow be "related to air" (*vāyavīya*), he cannot mean that it *is* air itself, but merely that it has some kind of causal relationship with air, either as the effect of air (as the rustling sound that we consider to be the product of wind) or as its cause, if one considers with Sāṃkhya and Śaiva proponents that the gross element (*mahābhūta*) that is air arises from the subtle element (*tanmātra*) that is sound. But being the cause or the effect of something is not quite the same as being that very thing; and if sound could actually become one with air, it could no longer be also related to fire, etc., as Utpaladeva claims: the sound said to be related to air, being air itself, could have nothing to do with the sound said to be related to fire, etc.,

---

sound] of water [has] the form *chalacchala*; [the sound] of fire has the aspect *dhagadhaga*; [the sound] of air consists in *śukaśuka*; the sound of ether is called 'echo.'"

[511] PDhS, p. 241.

and as a result, the very notion of "sound" would be lost. So even if one admits with Utpaladeva, for the sake of argument, that *śabda* may somehow belong to the four elements endowed with material shape rather than just the shapeless ether, it must remain distinct from them, and as a consequence it must be devoid of material shape. Under such conditions, how could it have spatial sequence if the latter is, as Utpaladeva contends, the result of a difference *between material shapes*? If Utpaladeva's account of spatial sequence were correct, we could never hear sounds as being close or distant, etc.; yet we do apprehend them as being not just temporally but also spatially determined. As pointed out both in the *Vivṛti* and in Abhinavagupta's commentary thereon,[512] Utpaladeva's Vaiśeṣika opponent thus admits that sounds are apprehended as having a specific location; he only denies, against Utpaladeva, that *śabda* may have a material shape, and he draws from the shapelessness of sound the conclusion that Utpaladeva is wrong in thinking that spatial sequence arises from a variety in material shapes.

Utpaladeva answers by pointing out that in fact the disagreement hinges on a divergence as to what a material shape truly is: the opponent cannot understand why ordinary sound is in fact a material shape because he clings to his own, defective definition of *mūrti*. Abhinavagupta has already pointed out, earlier in his commentary on this verse, that Utpaladeva's definition of it is to be distinguished from two other definitions:

> [Utpaladeva's] intention [in this passage is to convey] that on the contrary, in this [system of ours], material shape is not the size of a substance that is not omnipresent (*asarvagatadravyaparimāṇa*); nor is it solidity (*kāṭhinya*).[513]

In his commentary on the passage at hand, he alludes again to these two theories:

> To this objection [stated] by [someone] who considers material shape [to be] the size of a substance that is not omnipresent, [Utpaladeva] replies: "It may be [said to be] so [elsewhere]." [That is to say:] It may be the case that among ordinary people or in another treatise, it is *said* that sound has

---

[512] See below, chapter 11, fn. 67.

[513] ĪPVV, vol. III, p. 13: *na tv asarvagatadravyaparimāṇam iha mūrtiḥ kāṭhinyaṃ vety āśayaḥ.*

> no material shape; for ordinary people believe that a [thing] endowed with a material shape is liable to be taken, accepted, given, etc., [whereas] sound is not; and it is in conformity with this [worldly belief] that [another treatise] claims that [a thing endowed with a material shape] is "not omnipresent." And in the [aphorism]: "[The word] 'compact mass' [is used] in the [sense of] a material shape," material shape is defined as solidity (*kāṭhinya*); but in this [treatise of ours], this is not the way [in which material shape is defined]—this [Utpaladeva] shows by suggesting the difference [between these beliefs and our definition] in [the passage beginning with] "but in this [treatise]..."[514]

The first doctrine mentioned is that of the Vaiśeṣikas, who contend that ether has no material shape because it is an omnipresent substance (whereas a material shape is by definition the limited size of a substance that is not omnipresent) and does not involve action, because action is only found in substances endowed with a material shape.[515] As for the other definition of

---

[514] ĪPVV, vol. III, pp. 13–14: *ity asarvagatadravyaparimāṇaṃ mūrtim upagacchatā codite pratyā**hāstv evam** iti. loke bhavatu amūrtavyavahāraḥ śabdasya śāstrāntare vā. loko hi saṅgrahaparigrahadānādiyogyaṃ mūrtaṃ manyate, na śabdam. tadanusāreṇaiva paribhāṣitam asarvagateti. mūrtau ghana ity atra ca kāṭhinyaṃ mūrtir uktā, sa ca neha prakāra iti darśayati viśeṣaṃ dyotayan **iha tv** iti.*

[515] See PDhS, p. 663: *ākāśakāladigātmanāṃ saty api dravyabhāve niṣkriyatvaṃ sāmānyādivad amūrtatvāt. mūrtir asarvagatadravyaparimāṇaṃ tadanuvidhāyinī ca kriyā. sā cākāśādiṣu nāsti, tasmān na teṣāṃ kriyāsambandho 'stīti.* "Although ether, time, space and the self are substances, they are not endowed with action, just as universals etc., because they do not have a material shape. Material shape is the size of a substance that is not omnipresent (*asarvagatadravyaparimāṇa*), and action conforms to this [material shape]; and this (*sā*) [material shape] does not exist in ether, etc. Therefore they have no relation with action." For a different interpretation see NEMEC 2016, p. 353. I do not think in particular that *sā* in the last sentence can be read as referring to action (as is assumed in that article), the thesis to be proven by the inference being precisely that ether, etc. can have no relation with action. The point is rather that since material shape and action are invariably concomitant, and since material shape (*sā=mūrtiḥ*) is not found in ether, etc., the latter cannot possess action. This is the commentators' understanding; see *Vyomavatī*, vol. II, p. 266, which specifies "and this, [viz.] material shape, does not exist in ether, etc." (*sā ca mūrtir ākāśādiṣu nāsti*), after pointing out (ibid., p. 265) the invariable concomitance on which the inference rests: *mūrtatvena hi kriyāvattvaṃ*

*mūrti* alluded to here, according to which material shape is solidity (*kāṭhinya*), it is explicitly linked by Abhinavagupta to Pāṇinian *sūtra* 3.3.77 (*mūrtau ghanaḥ*), and Abhinavagupta might have in mind the relevant gloss in the *Kāśikāvṛtti* (*mūrtiḥ kāṭhinyam*).[516] As long as one defines *mūrti* in such ways, ordinary sound may rightly be thought to be devoid of it; but this, according to Abhinavagupta, only reflects the naïve view of "the world," whereas Utpaladeva's definition of material shape is in accordance with reality.

Utpaladeva does not bother here to demonstrate the superiority of his definition and contents himself with invoking Bhartṛhari's authority on this point.[517] He does not spell out either why his own definition of material shape renders the Vaiśeṣika's objection null and void. He does hint, however, at a previous demonstration of his when mentioning that for him, *mūrti* is "nothing but the specific form of the thing" and is "devoid of action"; for he has already shown that contrary to what the Vaiśeṣikas hold, action must belong to sentient entities, because it involves both multiplicity and unity, whereas insentient objects only have one fixed form that is contradictory with any other given form, so that they cannot be appropriate substrata for any dynamic process. And this is precisely why in Utpaladeva's opinion, the Vaiśeṣika's objection that the sound related to air can have no material shape is pointless once one understands what a material shape really is. For consciousness (just as the higher levels of linguistic sound, which are nothing but consciousness's ability to actively become aware of itself)

---

*vyāptam*. "For being endowed with action is invariably concomitant with having a material shape." Cf. NK, p. 663: *kriyāvattvaṃ mūrtatvena vyāptaṃ mūrtatvaṃ cākāśādiṣu nāsti, ataḥ kriyāvattvam api na vidyata ity arthaḥ*. "Here is [what this] means: being endowed with action is invariably concomitant with having a material shape; and the [property of] having a material shape does not exist in ether, etc.; so the [property of] possessing action is not found [in them] either." The translation in JHA 1916, p. 646, also reflects this interpretation.

[516] Somānanda already alludes to the Vaiśeṣika definition in ŚD 2.76 (... *asarvagapramāṇaṃ hi mūrtiḥ...*) and Utpaladeva himself, in his commentary on the latter, mentions the two definitions that appear in this passage of the ĪPVV. See ŚDV, p. 87: ... *asarvagatadravyaparimāṇaṃ mūrtiḥ kāṭhinyaṃ vā...* See also NEMEC 2016, p. 353, although the latter tries to read *asarvagatadravyaparimāṇaṃ* and *kāṭhinyaṃ* as one and the same thesis rather than as belonging respectively to the Vaiśeṣikas and grammarians.

[517] See above, §1, on the quotation that Utpaladeva ascribes to Bhartṛhari.

can assume various forms without ceasing to be itself; whatever it is conscious of, it remains consciousness, because the essence of consciousness is its plasticity. In contrast, objects of knowledge—and such is the sound related to air—must conform to a specific form that they cannot abandon without becoming something else, and having a material shape is nothing but being thus strictly limited by this specific form.

Abhinavagupta points out, however, that this definition of material shape lays Utpaladeva open to an obvious objection: since consciousness and speech also have a specific nature (i.e. the very plasticity that Utpaladeva highlights as their distinguishing feature), they too must end up being spatially determined if spatial sequence arises from material shape, and if material shape is nothing but "the specific form of a thing." Abhinavagupta dodges the blow by arguing that Utpaladeva did not mean to equate having a material shape with having a specific nature, but rather, with having *the specific nature of an object of knowledge*[518]—a point that, according to the ĪPVV, is made by Utpaladeva himself when he reads the sentence that he has just ascribed to Bhartṛhari as distinguishing "knowledge and the sound related to ether" from objective entities:

> [– Objection:] But knowledge and realization too are not without a specific form (*svarūpa*); so there must be a spatial sequence in them too as a result of [this] material shape! [– Answer:] It is not the case, [for] material shape is not a mere specific form, but rather, [a specific form] that is manifested as being potentially on a par with [any] other object of knowledge; whereas knowledge and [linguistic] sound are not so, for they have to do with gnosis (*vidyā*), and they are not objects of knowledge (*vedya*). This [Utpaladeva] explains in [the passage] beginning with "whereas knowledge"..."[519]

---

[518] On Abhinavagupta's gloss of *vastu* as *vedya* here see below, chapter 11, fn. 75.

[519] ĪPVV, vol. III, p. 14: *nanu jñānavimarśāv api na niḥsvarūpāv iti tatrāpi syād deśakramo mūrtiprayuktaḥ. maivam, na svarūpamātraṃ mūrtir api tv ābhāsyamānaṃ vedyāntareṇa tulyakakṣyatāṃ sahamānam, na tv evaṃ jñānaśabdane, vidyoparakte hi te, na tu vedye. etad āha* ***jñāne****tyādinā.*

Whether Utpaladeva meant this or not, he does points out that even the Vaiśeṣika definition of material shape, however inadequate, does not undermine his definition of spatial sequence. As Abhinavagupta explains:

> [The passage beginning with] "Alternatively" [means the following]. Even if sound is devoid of material shape, it has substrata, [viz.] air and so on, which, for their part, have a material shape; and a quality has its substratum as a place. So the spatial difference in a substratum such as air, which is endowed with a material shape, seems to be in the [sound] as well, [and this is] due to the [fact that the quality is only perceived through what is called] inherence in what is connected (*saṃyuktasamavāya*),[520] [although] this [spatial difference] is not real [in sound itself]. So even if one acknowledges the [definition of] material shape [propounded] in other treatises, this is in no way a problem as regards [our thesis] that spatial sequence only belongs to [things] endowed with a material shape.[521]

If one does not acknowledge Utpaladeva's definition of material shape, and if the latter is understood in the Vaiśeṣika fashion as the size of a substance that is not omnipresent, then indeed, sound, which is not a substance, cannot have any *mūrti*; yet precisely because it is a quality (*guṇa*), it must reside in substrata (*guṇin*), and the latter, for their part, may be endowed with material shapes,[522] so that sound, although devoid of material shape, *appears* to have a spatial sequence, because according to the Vaiśeṣikas, a quality is only perceived indirectly, through the intermediary of the substratum in which it inheres. So even if *śabda* is believed to be a shapeless entity, it is also understood as not being in and of itself spatially determined, and spatial sequence must then be considered to affect only the material shapes of *śabda*'s substrata; in other words, Utpaladeva claims that even

---

[520] On this technical term see e.g. HALBFASS 1992, p. 101.

[521] ĪPVV, vol. III, p. 14: ***athave****ty amūrtasyāpi śabdasya mūrtās tāvat pavanādaya āśrayāḥ, guṇideśakaś ca guṇaḥ, tad guṇini vāyvādau mūrte yo deśabhedaḥ sa tatrāpi saṃyuktasamavāyāl lakṣyate, na pāramārthika iti mūrtānām eva deśakrama iti śāstrāntarīyamūrtyupagame 'pi na kiñcit khaṇḍitam.*

[522] Of course the argument is only valid provided that one accepts the Śaiva thesis that sound may exist not only in ether, but also in the four other elements (a concession that is in fact very unlikely as far as Vaiśeṣikas are concerned).

from the Vaiśeṣika's inferior viewpoint, his definition of spatial sequence still makes sense.

### 5. Temporal sequence only concerns conscious beings but is also projected onto insentient entities

Utpaladeva then turns to the definition of temporal sequence as the result of a variety of actions. He begins this explanation by reminding his readers that in the Śaiva nondualistic system, action can only belong to conscious beings, whereas insentient entities are incapable of agency because they are devoid of the autonomy or freedom (*svātantrya*) that characterizes all conscious subjects. Abhinavagupta sums up the same point as follows in a different context:

> To begin with, insentient [things] do not possess the power consisting in knowledge; as for [the power] consisting in action, the essence of which is freedom, there is not even a remote possibility [that they might be possessed of it], because [they] are devoid of freedom; and accordingly, some admit that [in a sentence] such as "The chariot moves," there is only a figurative expression (*upacāra*).[523]

In saying so, Abhinavagupta is only following Utpaladeva's lead; thus the latter specifies, in his *Vṛtti* on ĪPK 2.4.21:

> Thus action in the primary sense [of the term] (*mukhya*) is defined as a will to act [and] exclusively belongs to a single agent consisting in consciousness; there is no object involved in action (*karman*) without an agent (*kartṛ*), because [things] such as objects that are involved in action [are only ascribed agency] figuratively (*upacāra*), through the agent.[524]

And again, while explaing Utpaladeva's (currently unavailable) *Vivṛti* on ĪPK 2.4.21, Abhinavagupta explains:

---

[523] ĪPV, vol. I, pp. 38–39: *jaḍānāṃ tāvan na jñānātmikā śaktir asti, kriyātmikāpi svātantryaprāṇā svātantryavyapagamād asambhāvanābhūmir eva, tathā ca ratho gacchatītyādāv upacāraṃ kecana pratipannāḥ.*

[524] *Vṛtti*, p. 61: *evaṃ cidrūpasyaikasya kartur eva cikīrṣākhyā kriyā mukhyā, nākartṛkaṃ karmāsti karmādīnāṃ kartṛmukhenopacārataḥ.*

> With [the *Vivṛti* sentence beginning with] "But it is not...," [Utpaladeva says that] possessing action is not possible for an object involved in action, because it is devoid of will; therefore it is [only] ascribed [action] figuratively.[525]

In other words, the Śaiva nondualists interpret Pāṇinian rule 1.4.54, "the agent [in a sentence] is independent" (*svatantraḥ kartā*) in a very strong sense—that is to say, not as the mere statement that the agent is independent with respect to other factors involved in an action, but rather, as the assertion that the agent of any action must be endowed with free will. As a consequence, they accept that sentences such as "The chariot moves" can only be used figuratively (a position defended in particular by Naiyāyikas).[526] Since thus in truth action, whose essence is free will, only belongs to sentient beings, according to Abhinavagupta, even someone's inactivity is still a form of action inasmuch as one chooses not to act:

> For in the body and its limbs, action has as its very essence such a realization (*vimarśa*) as "I shall move" [or] "I shall move my head"; even an action that does not consist in a

---

[525] ĪPVV, vol. III, pp. 253–254: ***na tv*** *iti karmaṇaḥ kriyāveśo na saṃbhavatīcchāvirahitatvād ity upacaritaḥ saḥ.*

[526] Cf. *Bhāskarī*, vol. I, p. 60, which glosses "some" (*kecana*) in ĪPV, vol. I, p. 39 (quoted above, fn. 523) with *tārkikādayaḥ* (which certainly refers to Naiyāyikas and Vaiśeṣikas). On this "major point of disagreement between grammarians—Pāṇinīyas in particular—and Naiyāyikas," see e.g. CARDONA 1974, pp. 239 ff. The idea that an agent, as opposed to a mere insentient instrument, must be endowed with volition or conscious effort, is already found e.g. in Uddyotakara's NV, which endeavours to show, under NS 4.1.21, that the universe must have been created by an intelligent agent because insentient instruments cannot have any efficiency without such an agent; cf. Udayana's assertion that "action is nothing but [conscious] effort" (*Nyāyakusumāñjali* 5.8c: *yatna eva kṛtiḥ*), in response to an objector arguing (ibid., p. 55) that most verbal suffixes merely indicate an activity (*vyāpāra*) but not a "cognition that is an effort" (*yatnajñāna*), "as for instance when [we say] 'The chariot moves'" (*ratho gacchatīty ādau*). See also Gaṅgeśa's clear statement of the point in *Tattvacintāmaṇi*, p. 819 (and the analysis of it in WADA 2007): *ākhyātasya yatnavācakatvād acetane ratho gacchatītyādāv ākhyāte vyāpāralakṣaṇā.* "Because a verbal suffix expresses a [conscious] effort (*yatna*), with respect to an insentient [entity], for instance [in a sentence such as] 'The chariot moves,' in the verbal suffix, activity is [only] expressed figuratively." On the Mīmāṃsakas' diverging views on this topic (and on the fact that some of them, such as Someśvara, agree at least in part with this Naiyāyika theory), see JOSHI 1993, pp. 33–36.

> movement, [and takes] such [a form] as "I shall stay put," is ultimately nothing but a realization [occurring] sequentially in the agent.[527]

On the other hand, even the mere action of existing cannot be said to belong to insentient objects, as Utpaladeva points out in his *Vṛtti* on ĪPK 2.4.20:

> Even as regards an insentient [entity]'s action of existing, which [we express as] "It is,'" "It exists," there is no agency [on the insentient entity's part], because [an insentient entity] has no freedom, [whereas the action of existing] involves a will to exist.[528] So the ultimate truth in this respect is that it is the knowing subject who makes the [insentient entity] exist; or [it is] the [knowing subject who] exists in various forms, such as the Himālaya.[529] [530]

This means that, if Utpaladeva is right in following Bhartṛhari when he defines temporal sequence as the result of actions' diversity, *time does not concern insentient objects*, which, as entities endowed with a material shape, can only be affected by spatial sequence. Yet in the course of our everyday experiences, we do ascribe a temporal sequence to things as well as to other subjects, and Utpaladeva allows for an explanation of this phenomenon by specifying that we ascribe agency to things in a figurative way (*upacāra*), but we tend to be oblivious of this figurative aspect and we end up taking at face value such expressions as "The chariot moves," thus wrongly attributing the power to act to insentient beings. This is why, when we consider insentient things from the limited point of view of everyday

---

527 See ĪPVV, vol. I, p. 105: *calāmi śiraś cālayāmīty evaṃbhūtavimarśasāraiva hi śarīre tadavayave ca kriyā. aparispandarūpāpi tiṣṭhāmītyādikā kriyā kartari kramikatāparāmarśaparamārthaiva.*

528 On the possible interpretations of *bubhūṣāyogena* see ĪPVV, vol. III, p. 252, discussed in RATIÉ 2011a, p. 684, fn. 91.

529 The mention of the Himālaya is an allusion to the first verse of Kālidāsa's *Kumārasambhava*, as is made clear by Abhinavagupta in ĪPVV, vol. III, p. 248 (see RATIÉ 2011a, p. 685).

530 *Vṛtti*, p. 61: *jaḍasyāpy asti bhavatīty asyām api sattākriyāyāṃ bubhūṣāyogena svātantryābhāvād akartṛtvam, tena pramātaiva taṃ bhāvayati tena tena vā himācalādinā rūpeṇa sa bhavatīty atra paramārthaḥ.*

life, we think of them as spatially *and* temporally determined; yet, as Abhinavagupta's commentary points out, we must keep in mind that Utpaladeva's *Vivṛti* clearly distinguishes two levels—one absolute, the other relative—in this regard:

> Having thus explained the metaphorical status [of action ascribed to insentient things] from the [perspective of] existence in the ultimate sense, [Utpaladeva] now says, in conformity with the common understanding (*prasiddhi*), "On the other hand, inasmuch as, according to the [common] understanding, [we take action to] literal[ly belong to insentient things]..." "[We may consider that there is] a temporal difference too" [means the following]: it is not just spatial difference that belongs to what is plural, but also this [temporal difference]; the [word] "too" suggests this plurality. [Yet Utpaladeva] will specify in the sequel that [in reality] temporal sequence [exclusively] belongs to what is one, in [the passage] beginning with "However, [something that is apprehended as] one...."[531]

The *Vivṛti* next endeavours to describe how the subject thus projects temporality onto objects and to define the categories of past, present and future. Unfortunately, the explanation of this important issue has come down to us in a somewhat lacunary form, but from the text as it is preserved and Abhinavagupta's commentary, it is clear that the main point was to highlight that we always grasp insentient objects as being past, present or future according to the specific *actions* that we ascribe to things. And Utpaladeva's position in this respect is both very close to that of the Naiyāyikas, and quite different from it.

It is very close in that the Naiyāyikas too emphasize that our awareness of past, future and present has to do with our awareness of action; thus while commenting on Pakṣilasvāmin's assertion that time "is revealed by action,

---

[531] ĪPVV, vol. III, p. 15: *evaṃ paramārthasthityā gauṇatvaṃ nirūpya prasiddhyanusāreṇāha* ***yathāpratīti mukhyāṃ veti. kālabhedo 'pīty*** *anekasya na paraṃ deśabhedaḥ, yāvad ayam apīty* ***apir*** *anekatām ākṣipati. ekasya kālakramo 'gre vakṣyata* ***ekasya punar*** *ityādinā.*

[as when we think: 'the fruit] is falling'"[532] (rather than thinking that it has fallen or that it will fall), Uddyotakara explains:

> When a substance is perceived [as being] connected with an action, it is the time particularized by this connection that we call "present"; and due to its being beyond the connection with this action, [we call it] "past." But when the causes of this action are ready [to act and] their powers are not impeded, then [we call] that time "future," [thinking] that the action will occur.[533]

In the *Vivṛti*, Utpaladeva also argues that an object is apprehended as being present inasmuch as we grasp its existence (*sattā*)—that is, inasmuch as we take it to be the agent of the action of existing (an action that, as seen above, is in fact performed by consciousness manifesting itself in the form of an existing object, but that deluded subjects wrongly ascribe to insentient beings); and we think of the object as belonging to the present if we grasp this action as simultaneous with ourselves. The point seems reminiscent of the Nyāya's view that our awareness of the present results from our awareness of an action being performed; and the Naiyāyikas too explicitly acknowledge that this action may be not only a complex one (such as falling, cooking and so on), but also the mere action of existing. Thus according to Pakṣilasvāmin,

> And the present time is grasped in two ways: sometimes, it is revealed by the [mere action of] existing of a thing,[534] for instance [when we think] "this substance exists"; [and]

[532] *Nyāyasūtrabhāṣya* (henceforth NBh) on NS 2.1.40, p. 81: *kriyāvyaṅgyaḥ patatīti.*

[533] NV, p. 240: *yadā dravyaṃ kriyāsaṃbaddham upalabhate so 'yaṃ saṃbandhaviśiṣṭaḥ kālo vartamāna ity ucyate. kriyāsaṃbandhātikramāc cātītaḥ. yadā tu kriyākāraṇāny ābhimukhyenāvasthitāny apratibaddhaśaktikāni, tadā bhaviṣyati kriyety anāgataḥ kāla iti.*

[534] According to NV, p. 242: *kvacit kriyāmātravyaṅgyaḥ kvacit kriyāsantānavyaṅgyaḥ, kriyāmātravyaṅgyo vidyate dravyam iti, kriyāsantānavyaṅgyaḥ pacati cchinattīti.* "Sometimes it is revealed by a mere action; sometimes it is revealed by a series of actions. It is revealed by a mere action [when we think] 'this substance exists'; it is revealed by a series of actions [when we think] 'he cooks' [or] 'he cuts.'"

> sometimes it is revealed by a series of actions, for instance [when we think] "he cooks" [or] "he cuts."[535]

As for our awareness that something is past or future, Utpaladeva again seems to follow the Naiyāyikas in highlighting that it always occurs in relation to our awareness of the present;[536] for he describes our understanding that something is past or future as involving both the awareness of the present and that of an element that is contradictory with it. Thus according to the *Vivṛti*, our awareness of the past results from our apprehending not one but two different actions: when we see a sprout emerging from the ground, we conceptually construct the object "seed" as a past one because on the one hand, our awareness of the growing sprout includes the phenomenon of the necessary existence of a cause such as the seed for the present sprout. On the other hand, however, the concept of this cause grasped as necessarily existing—i.e., as performing the action of existing—is accompanied by the phenomenon of the cause's action of perishing (*vināśa*), since we are also aware that the cause, which we do not perceive, has disappeared—and our understanding that an object is past arises from these contradictory phenomena.

Regarding the future, the *Vivṛti* tersely remarks that the situation of a present subject thinking about a future object is the same as that of a past subject thinking about a present object. According to Abhinavagupta, Utpaladeva offers this analogy, rather than providing an example of something apprehended as future in Utpaladeva's own time, because of the incertainty that anything apprehended as future involves for ordinary limited subjects:[537]

> [Utpaladeva] has given no illustration in the case of [objects] that are past and present because they are well known; but in the case of the [object] that is future, according to the principle "For there is no means of knowledge with respect to

[535] NBh, p. 83: *ubhayathā ca vartamānaḥ kālo gṛhyate, kvacid arthasadbhāvavyaṅgyo yathāsti dravyam iti, kvacit kriyāsantānavyaṅgyo yathā pacati cchinattīti.*

[536] Cf. e.g. NS 2.1.40: *tayor apy abhāvo vartamānābhāve tadapekṣatvāt.* "If the present did not exist, the [past and future] too would be nonexistent, because [they] are relative to the [present]."

[537] Abhinavagupta specifies later in his commentary that for omniscient beings this is not an issue; see ĪPVV, vol. III, p. 20, quoted below, chapter 9, fn. 642.

> what is to come,"[538] [Utpaladeva] has doubts about stories such as that of Viṣṇu Kalkin as an illustration of [things allegedly occuring] in the future; [so] he gives another illustration by saying [that an object is future for a present subject] "just as [the manifestation that is present now was future for that subject at the time of the past manifestation]." [That is to say: the future object is for the present knowing subject] just as [a servant's] task today is for a master whose will is not impeded and who imagined yesterday the task [to be performed by his servant] today.[539]

Utpaladeva's remark on the future seems no less reminiscent of the Nyāya's position as his definitions of our awareness of past and present; thus as seen above, according to Uddyotakara, we think of something as being future when the "causes" of an action "are ready [to act and] their powers are not impeded"—a definition that Abhinavagupta could have had in mind when providing his example of a master planning a task for his servant and "whose will is not impeded."

So Utpaladeva's insistence on the fact that temporal divisions are ascribed to things in relation to the two actions of existing and perishing is clearly reminiscent of the Naiyāyikas' position on the topic; but Utpaladeva does not contend himself with agreeing with his dualist opponents, whose position he obviously equates with the "common understanding" rather than the ultimate truth. While highlighting that our sense of things' temporal determinations arises from our awareness of their actions, Utpaladeva thus repeatedly emphasizes that in fact, literally speaking, action only belongs to consciousness—which is why the temporal determinations seemingly affecting things are always relative to the subject grasping these things: insentient objects can be past, present or future, but *only in relation to a given subject*, and insasmuch as this subject superimposes onto objects an agency

[538] Abhinavagupta also invokes it in his ABh, vol. I, p. 27 and vol. II, p. 209.

[539] ĪPVV, vol. II, p. 15: *bhūtavartamānayoḥ prasiddhatvān nodāharaṇam uktam, bhāvini tu bhaviṣyati pramāṇābhāvād iti nyāyena kalkiviṣṇvādivṛttānte* bhaviṣyad-udāharaṇe vicikitsur udāharaṇāntaram āha* ***yatheti****. adyatanadinakaraṇīyam iva hyodinasaṅkalpitādyatanakartavyasyāpratihatecchasya svāminaḥ.* [**kalki*° corr.; *karki*° Ed.]

that in truth belongs solely to consciousness; so the objects' temporal sequence cannot be considered an objective reality or, as the Naiyāyikas contend, the result of an objective, mind-independent substance called "time." Abhinavagupta notices that from this point of view, there is a striking difference between the *Vṛtti* and the *Vivṛti* on verse 2.1.5:

> [An objector might ask:] "Why is it explained in the *Vivṛti* that [the object, whether apprehended as present, past or future,] "is manifest," and [is so] for a knowing subject," [whereas] this [point] was not touched upon in the *Vṛtti*? [For] the *Vṛtti* merely [states that there is also temporal sequence for things that are plural] "through action." [Utpaladeva] answers this [in the passage beginning with] "[Even though this action that consists in existence or perishing is commonly understood as belonging to insentient things in such a way that the primary meaning of the word "action"] is not impeded...."[540]

The *Vṛtti* only mentions that objects may have temporal determinations thanks to action, so that it can be read as defending a view of past, present and future that is broadly compatible with that of Nyāya; but the *Vivṛti* spells out the crucial difference between Utpaladeva's understanding of time and that of the Naiyāyikas—namely, the fact that past, present and future are grounded in subjectivity, since only consciousness can ultimately be responsible for the actions of existing and perishing that we ascribe to insentient entities and that are the causes of our considering them temporally. According to Abhinavagupta, Utpaladeva justifies this discrepancy between the *Vṛtti* and the *Vivṛti* by pointing out again the distinction between the ordinary or common understanding (*pratīti*) of action—with which the *Vṛtti*'s definition remains fully compatible—and the ultimate truth in this respect. For the *Vivṛti* highlights that the action ascribed to insentient things "is [commonly] understood (*pratīta*)... [in such a way that the primary meaning of the word "action"] is not impeded (*askhalita*)." This is an allusion to the definition—whose basic principle is accepted in most Indian philosophical traditions—of the mechanism through which figurative speech is produced and recognized. In his commentary on Ānandavardhana's *Dhvanyāloka* (henceforth DhĀ), Abhinavagupta describes this

[540] ĪPVV, vol. III, p. 15: ... *kimartham* ***pramātur*** *iti* ***bhātīti*** *ca vivṛtau darśitam, yad vṛttau na spṛṣṭam; kriyāmukhenetīyatī vṛttiḥ. etat pariharaty* ***askhalite****ti.*

mechanism as follows while commenting on Ānandavardhana's mention—probably borrowed from Dharmakīrti[541]—of a word that has no "stumbling (*skhalat*) course":[542]

> Secondary expression (*lakṣaṇā*) is the operation of a word that is such that this [word] has a "stumbling course"; [that is to say,] its power of making [us] understand [something] is being impeded by the operation of [something] that contradicts [it].[543]

According to a famous example,[544] when we hear about "a village on the Gaṅgā" (*gaṅgāyāṃ ghoṣaḥ*), the primary meaning of these words is impeded by the obvious fact that no village can actually be "on" water; the primary meaning being obstructed by this contradiction, our mind moves to a secondary meaning, and we understand that the phrase is in fact about a village on a *bank* of the Gaṅgā. Utpaladeva himself seems to have made use of this example to explain how we come to talk about things' agency, as can be seen from Abhinavagupta's commentary on the *Vivṛti* (which is unfortunately unavailable for now) on ĪPK 2.4.20:

---

[541] See McCREA 2008, p. 192, n. 42, which mentions PV, *Pratyakṣapariccheda* 37 (where the compound *skhaladgati* is used to define figurative speech) and adds "I can find no other use of the term in this sense prior to Ānandavardhana." Note that later poeticians seem to have been aware of this probable source, since Bhoja for instance quotes Dharmakīrti's verse while discussing the figurative use of words in the *Śṛṅgāraprakāśa* (see HONDA 2011).

[542] DhĀ 1.17d.

[543] *Dhvanyālokalocana* (henceforth DhĀL), p. 149: ... *skhalantī bādhakavyāpāreṇa vidhurīkriyamāṇā gatir avabodhanaśaktir yasya śabdasya tadīyo vyāpāro lakṣaṇā*. See INGALLS, MASSON & PATWARDHAN 1990, p. 186. In RATIÉ 2014a, p. 60, fn. 159, the rendering of *skhaladvṛtti* as "pas toujours vraie" in the translation of TSPŚ, vol. I, p. 116, which discusses the use of the word *ātman* (i.e. whether it is literal or figurative) should be corrected, as it fails to convey the technical meaning of this compound. A similar defect is found for instance in KAJIYAMA 1966, p. 120 on a similar topic mentioned by Mokṣākaragupta (*skhaladvṛtti* is translated as "false identification") or in MIMAKI 1976, e.g. p. 153, where the compound used by Ratnakīrti in his debate with a Naiyāyika opponent on nonbeing (*abhāva*) is translated as "une connaissance faussée," whereas the discussion revolves around the role of figurative speech in the awareness of nonbeing.

[544] See e.g. KUNJUNNI RAJA 1969, pp. 232 ff.

> [– Objection:] But [if] thus [action only belongs to conscious beings], how [is it that we say that] "The Himālaya exists"?[545] [Utpaladeva] answers with [the sentence beginning with] "However, the figurative use of [the word] agency..." [He] means that the basis for this superimposition [of agency onto insentient beings] is the fact that [insentient beings] exist within [consciousness];[546] that is to say, [they] are dependent on [consciousness]. [And so] there is a superimposition of the freedom [of consciousness—this freedom] being conveyed [by the word "agency"]—onto the [insentient entity that depends on it]. With [the sentence] beginning with "The riverbank...," [Utpaladeva] illustrates with an analogy this superimposition of the freedom that is expressed [when we talk about agency] onto this object.[547]

However, in the *Vivṛti* on ĪPK 2.1.5, rather than highlighting the proximity between the expression "a village on the Gaṅgā" and the numerous phrases in which we ascribe agency to unconscious beings, Utpaladeva points out a crucial difference between them. For in the case of our ascribing action to insentient beings, as when we say that "The chariot moves," we do not usually experience a "stumbling course" in the meaning of words that would make us realize that we are not using literally a word denoting action. Utpaladeva emphasizes that we are not usually aware that action is only metaphorically ascribed to unconscious entities. Yet he warns his readers that he will explain in the sequel of the treatise how, despite the fact that we are ordinarily blind to the figurative status of things' agency, our talking about the action of an insentient thing must be figurative in that it

---

[545] Again, the example given here is an allusion to the first verse in Kālidāsa's *Kumārasambhava* (see above, fn. 529).

[546] On "existing within [something]" (*tātsthya*) as a basis for figurative expression (i.e., for designating something with the name of the place where it resides), see e.g. RENOU 1957, p. 157; cf. KUNJUNNI RAJA 1969, p. 240.

[547] ĪPVV, vol. III, p. 252: *nanv evaṃ himavān astīti katham. āha* ***kartṛtopacāras tv*** *ity āropaṇe nimittaṃ tatpāratantryātmakaṃ tātsthyaṃ nāmety arthaḥ. svātantryasya gamyamānasyātrāropaṇam ity atrārthe 'bhidhīyamānasvātantryāropaṃ dṛṣṭāntīkaroti* ***kūlam*** *ityādinā.*

"can only result from [their] relation with consciousness," because this action can only occur "due to a will for such [an action to occur]." Abhinavagupta identifies as follows the passage in question:

> "[And we] will state..." [is an allusion to the following:] in chapter [2.4] on the realization of the true nature of cause and effect, the fact that what is plural and possesses a variety of material shapes has a temporal variety due to the variety of actions [that ultimately belong to consciousness] is explained both in the *Vṛtti* and *Vivṛti* with respect to [the second part of] verse [2.4.19] beginning with "[But it is possible in the case of what consists in consciousness and is] unitary, because [its] phenomena [may] be differentiated."[548]

The verse thus identified by Abhinavagupta runs as follows:

> And for an insentient [thing, being] thus [an agent] is impossible owing to the contradiction between difference and unity; but it is possible in the case of what consists in consciousness [and] is unitary, because [its] phenomena [may] be differentiated.[549]

Action, which consists both in unity and difference, cannot belong to an insentient reality but only to a conscious one, because only a conscious entity can take different forms without losing its fundamental unity, as the *Vṛtti* on this verse points out:

> The [differentiation of a unitary entity that characterizes action] is not possible for an insentient [thing], whose nature is not differentiated, because of the contradiction between its existence [as one fixed nature] and the difference [involved in action; but] it is possible in the case of what is limpid [as the surface of a mirror], consists in consciousness [and] is unitary, because in the same way [as in the case of a limpid

---

[548] ĪPVV, vol. III, p. 15: ***vakṣyata*** *iti kāryakāraṇatattvavimarśaprakaraṇa ābhāsabhedād ekatretyādau sūtre mūrtivaicitryavato 'nekasya kriyāvaicitryāt kālavaicitryaṃ vartitaṃ vivṛtaṃ ca.*

[549] ĪPK 2.1.19: *na ca yuktaṃ jaḍasyaivaṃ bhedābhedavirodhataḥ | ābhāsabhedād ekatra cidātmani tu yujyate ||*

> mirror,] there is no contradiction [between consciousness's unity] and its bearing many reflections.[550]

Action involves both differentiated forms and an underlying unity, whereas insentient things are incapable of assuming a variety of forms: if a pot takes on the shape of a plate, it ceases to be a pot and becomes a plate, because things have one definite form that they cannot leave without ceasing to be what they are, and this inability of things to take on more than one exclusive form is precisely what Utpaladeva calls *mūrti*. In contrast, consciousness, just as the surface of a mirror endowed with manifold reflections, is capable of taking on a variety of forms without losing its unity. Unfortunately, the *Vivṛti* on this verse has not been discovered so far; at any rate, here is how Abhinavagupta explains the gist of the verse in his ĪPV:

> For what [we] call "insentient" has a nature that is circumscribed; it has fallen into the state of an object of knowledge. And [if it is an agent,] it must be considered to be differentiated, because of the difference in forms [that action involves], as in [a multiplicity] such as blue [versus] yellow, etc.; and [yet,] since [action also involves] having a unitary nature, it [must also] be undifferentiated, as in [a unity] such as "blue." But the same nature cannot be both differentiated and undifferentiated [in the case of an object], because of the contradiction between an assertion and [its] negation [when they are stated] at the same time in the same respect. In contrast, having a form involving both difference and unity is experienced in that which is "limpid," [i.e., in that] which has not fallen into the condition of the object of knowledge, and which, on the contrary, has as its true nature the manifesting [consciousness] (*prakāśa*) due to its consisting in consciousness; [in other words, it] has a unitary nature that is consciousness. For [we know] through mere [direct] experience [that] the appearance of a limpid [entity] such as a mirror may be differentiated into countless forms—such as a mountain, an elephant and so on—without having its nature

[550] *Vṛtti* on ĪPK 2.1.19, p. 60: *jaḍasyābhinnātmano bhedenāvasthiter virodhād ayuktam, svacche cidātmany ekasminn evam anekapratibimbadhāraṇenāvirodhād yujyate.* See TORELLA 2002, p. 186.

> broken at all [...].[551] Therefore this is what the sovereign power [of consciousness described here as its] limpidity is, namely: both the differentiation into innumerable manifestations, and unity. And for someone perched on the summit of a mountain, it is in a single cognition that the countless things found in a city are manifest; so agency can only belong to what consists in consciousness, because [only that] can possess the power of action, since [only that] is capable of possessing differences without being differentiated.[552]

The existence of insentient things is governed by the principle of noncontradiction: they must conform to a single specific form or disappear. Consciousness, however, can assume an infinity of forms without losing its unity. This is why the *Vivṛti* on verse 2.1.5 emphasizes that objects, which are plural—i.e., whose forms are incompatible—have spatial sequence and may also be considered to have a temporal sequence, but only through actions that, in fact, only pertain to the conscious subjects who are aware of them. Strictly speaking, temporal sequence, which entails unity, only affects conscious individuals; yet conscious individuals also project it onto insentient entities.

### 6. An object regarded as one has no spatial sequence

Utpaladeva then goes on to explain that only plural entities can be grasped as having a spatial existence: as long as we consider something to be fundamentally one, we are not aware of it as being spatially determined. Thus

---

[551] For a French translation and analysis of the ĪPV's entire commentary on this verse (too long to be quoted here) see RATIÉ 2011a, pp. 281–286.

[552] ĪPV, vol. II, pp. 176–178 (as edited in RATIÉ 2011a, pp. 282 ff.): *jaḍo hi nāma pariniṣṭhitasvabhāvaḥ prameyapadapatitaḥ. sa ca rūpabhedād bhinno vyavasthāpanīyo nīlapītādivat, ekasvabhāvatvāc cābhinno nīlavat. na tu sa eva svabhāvo bhinnaś cābhinnaś ca bhavitum arhati vidhiniṣedhayor ekatraikadā virodhāt. yat tu prameyadaśāpatitaṃ na bhavati kiṃ tu cidrūpatayā prakāśaparamārtharūpaṃ cidekasvabhāvaṃ svacchaṃ tatra bhedābhedarūpatopalabhyate. anubhavād eva hi svacchasyādarśāder akhaṇḍitasvasvabhāvasyaiva parvatamataṅgajādirūpasahasrasaṃbhinnaṃ vapur upapadyate... tasmān nirmalatāmāhātmyam etad yad anantāvabhāsasaṃbhedaś caikatā ca. giriśikharoparivartinaś caikatraiva bodhe nagaragatapadārthasahasrābhāsa iti cidrūpasyaiva kartṛtvam upapannam, abhinnasya bhedāveśasahiṣṇutvena kriyāśaktyāveśasaṃbhavāt.*

we are conscious of the spatial relationship entertained by various objects—such as, to use Utpaladeva's examples, a house, a palace and a courtyard—only if we grasp these various objects together, as a collection of distinct entities; but when we think of a given individual such as Caitra, we do not think of him as a spatially determined entity. This is not to say that we cannot apprehend Caitra as being in the house, sitting outside the palace, or entering the courtyard; but we only think of him in such a way when we grasp him as being part of a larger set of things, i.e., as belonging to a collection of plural entities (Caitra and the house, etc.).

One could of course object that even when we only consider a single object, we are capable of apprehending it with its spatial determinations: we can think of a house as being spatially extended, even if our cognition of it excludes the distant palace or the adjacent courtyard. But according to the Śaiva nondualists, this is only possible as long as we apprehend this single object *as being composed of a multiplicity of parts*: the house that we have in mind is only spatially determined inasmuch as we think of it as divided into storeys, rooms, etc.

Utpaladeva's position here is once again reminiscent of Bhartṛhari's. According to the latter, objects are in and of themselves devoid of any spatial determination:

> [Objective] entities are devoid of places, parts, sequence, and adjacent things [that may influence them] (*upāśraya*);[553] but

[553] The term *upāśraya* usually designates the substrate on which something rests, but here it rather refers to something that, while being alien to a given entity, produces a change in it. This is made clear by Helārāja's gloss (PP, vol. I, p. 222): *tathāvidyamāna upāśraya upādhiḥ svabhāvānyathātvāpādako yeṣāṃ te nirupāśrayāḥ.* "Similarly, these [objective entities] are devoid of *upāśraya* inasmuch as no *upāśraya*, [i.e.,] no adventitious property (*upādhi*) that would bring about an alteration in their nature, is found in them." The VP and VPV use the term several times while mentioning the idea that a crystal, although colourless, may be perceived as endowed with colour due to its proximity with coloured objects located behind or underneath it, these objects being called *upāśraya*s (see e.g. VP 3.3.40 and its analysis in HOUBEN 1995, pp. 257–262; cf. VPV 1, p. 147).

> because [their] form[s] get associated (*saṃsargirūpa*) [in different ways],[554] the difference in [their] powers is possible.[555]

Any perceptible object such as a pot can be apprehended as being spatially determined;[556] but this is only the case because we then apprehend it as a collection of parts (the pot as such being partless,[557] and therefore free of spatial sequence), and we can do so because we then grasp the pot not as what it is per se, but in relation to other entities. Helārāja concludes "Thus in and of themselves, things have no parts,"[558] and adds shortly thereafter:

> And since there is no difference into parts, neither can sequence [belong to things] in the primary sense (*mukhya*), because sequence rests on difference.[559]

We may divide the pot into the handle in contact with the hand that holds it, the roundish basis in contact with the water held in the pot, etc. Such distinctions, however, remain alien to the pot's essence, because they only

---

554 Cf. PP, vol. I, p. 222: ... *saṃsargibhedāt...*

555 VP 3.6.14: *adeśāś cāpy abhāgāś ca niṣkramā nirupāśrayāḥ | bhāvāḥ saṃsargirūpāt tu śaktibhedaḥ prakalpate ||*

556 See Helārāja's introduction to VP 3.6.15 (PP, vol. I, p. 222): *nanu deśabhedabhinnaḥ pratīyamānāvayavo mahāparimāṇo ghaṭādir avayavī dṛśyata iti kathaṃ tatrādeśatādy upapadyata ity āśaṅkyāha...* "[– Objection:] 'But [we] see that a whole such as a pot, which is of a macroscopic size, [and] whose parts are being cognized, is differentiated by a spatial difference! So in this [case] how could [the objective entity] be devoid of places, etc.?' Having anticipated [this objection, Bhartṛhari] replies..."

557 VP 3.6.15: *nirbhāgātmakatā tulyā paramāṇor ghaṭasya ca | bhāgaḥ śaktyantaraṃ tatra parimāṇaṃ ca yat tayoḥ ||* "The essence of a pot is as undivided as that of an atom; the division in them is [only] another power; so is their size."

558 PP, vol. I, p. 222: *evaṃ svataḥ padārthānām avayavā na santi...*

559 PP, vol. I, p. 222: *avayavabhedābhāvāc ca kramo 'py amukhyaḥ, bhedādhiṣṭhānatvāt kramasya.*

exist in connection with other things, so that they are only ascribed to the pot in a secondary or figurative way.[560]

In his commentary on Utpaladeva's *Vivṛti*, Abhinavagupta points out the paradox involved in this thesis that a thing taken by itself has no spatial sequence: it means that when we consider the parts of an object, which are plural, these parts have a spatial order; yet the same object considered as a whole (and independently of other objects) has none. Or, as Abhinavagupta puts it:

> Although the [property of] extendedness exists in the house, this [extendedness] does not produce a spatial difference for the house [itself], but [only] for the parts of the house![561]

How can the same thing be at once spatially determined and devoid of spatial determinations? Abhinavagupta's way of solving the problem consists in reminding his readers that according to the Śaiva nondualists, the parts and whole are not objective realities that would exist on their own, independently of a knowing subject apprehending them. Rather, they are different ways for the subject of becoming aware of reality: when we think of a cloth as a single entity rather than as a collection of threads, the content of our awareness is devoid of any spatial determination, whereas we do grasp it as an object endowed with a spatial existence when we consider it either in connection with other objects (as the cloth that is spread on the sofa), or as made of a multiplicity of parts (as the cloth made of a particular kind of threads). Because such thoughts can remain perfectly distinct from each other, the parts and the whole should not be confused, and the fact that they may have different properties is not contradictory:

> But the threads, [as opposed to the cloth of which they are parts, must] be plural; [and so] they have [the property of]

---

[560] Thus according to Helārāja (PP, vol. I, p. 223), things such as a pot have no parts for the following reason: *svato bhāgavattva ekatvāyogāt. arthāntarasaṃbandhanimittā ca bhāgavattā na mukhyā, paramāṇor api prasaṅgāt.* "[This is the case] because if [things] had parts in and of themselves, their unity would be impossible; but [if their] having parts is caused by a relation with something else, [this property of having parts] does not [belong to the thing] in the primary sense; [otherwise] as a consequence, an atom too should possess [this property, which is absurd]."

[561] ĪPVV, vol. III, p. 16: *gṛhe 'pi yad vaitatyaṃ tan na gṛhasya deśabhedaṃ karoti, api tu gṛhāvayavānām.*

> extendedness, which is nothing but spatial sequence. And in the cognition of the threads, the cloth does not flash forth, nor do the threads [flash forth] in the cognition of the cloth. And a thing[562] has manifestation as its essence; for in [any] given phenomenon, a given knowing subject manifests himself. Therefore the parts and the whole are not mixed up—enough with this![563]

This idea that something endowed with unity is necessarily devoid of spatial determinations (or necessarily *apprehended* as being devoid of them, which amounts to the same in the Śaiva nondualists' idealistic system) is alloted a relatively brief exposition in the long *Vivṛti* on ĪPK 2.1.5. This, however, is not to be taken as a sign that Utpaladeva deemed it unimportant; on the contrary, the *Vivṛti*'s brevity on this topic might be due to the fact that, as emphasized by Abhinavagupta, it is already sufficiently highlighted in the *Vṛtti*, of which it is the main point:

> [As for] the gist of the *Vṛtti* [on this verse, it] is [as follows]: in something that is plural, spatial sequence is for instance a house and a courtyard, [and] temporal sequence is for instance a mango blossom, a jasmine blossom and so on; but in [something] that is one, there is no spatial sequence because there is no distance, [proximity], etc.—[and] even extendedness [only] belongs to the parts [that are plural]. Therefore in [something] that is one, there is only temporal sequence, as the mango fruit becoming ripe.[564]

---

562 See above, fn. 313.

563 ĪPVV, vol. III, p. 16: *anekatvaṃ tu tantūnām, teṣāṃ deśakrama eva vaitatyam; tantubuddhau ca na paṭaḥ parisphurati, paṭadhiyi ca na tantavaḥ. ābhāsanasāraṃ ca vastu, kaścit pramātā hi kvacid ābhāse pratapati, tato 'saṅkareṇaivāvayavā avayavī cety āstāṃ tāvat.*

564 ĪPVV, vol. III, p. 12: *anekasmin vastuni deśakramo gṛhāṅganavat kālakramaḥ sahakāramallikādivat. ekasmiṃs tu na deśakramo dūratāder abhāvāt, vaitatyam apy aṃśānām. tad ekatra kālakrama eva pacyamānāmraphalavad iti vṛttitātparyam.*

### 7. Action, the six modifications in the process of becoming (*bhāvavikāra*), and temporal sequence

Utpaladeva then endeavours to explain what makes us think of a person as a temporally determined entity, so that we may entertain about him or her such thoughts as "this [individual], who was a child, will be an old man." According to him, we see someone and think that (s)he is the *same* person whom we once knew as young and who is now older, because this person, while being apprehended as one, is also understood to be the substratum of the "modifications in [the process of] becoming" (*bhāvavikāra*).[565] The latter term designates the actions expressed by the verbs meaning "to be born/arise" (*jan-*), "to exist" (*as-*), "to change" (*vipariṇam-*), "to grow" (*vivṛdh-*), "to decay" (*apakṣi-*), "to perish" (*vinaś-*). These *bhāvavikāras*, which play an important role in Bhartṛhari's explanation of temporal sequence,[566] are already referred to by Yāska and Patañjali, who both ascribe their definition to Vārṣyāyaṇi,[567] and Utpaladeva's description of them in his *Vivṛti* on ĪPK 2.1.5 is almost identical to that found in the *Nirukta*:

---

[565] The compound is difficult to translate due to the ambiguity of the term *bhāva*. Although several scholars have chosen to render it as "transformations of Being" (e.g. SUBRAMANIA IYER 1969, p. 126; HOUBEN 1995, p. 267, FILLIOZAT 2009, p. 218) or "transformation of existence" (HOUBEN 1995, p. 267), Yāska is known to use *bhāva* in the sense of the "action" or "process" that verbs express (see JOSHI 1993, p. 21). The translation offered in SEYFORT RUEGG 1959, p. 24, "modifications du devenir" (cf. for instance RENOU 1977, p. 12), is perhaps more accurate than renderings involving the terms "being" or even "existence."

[566] See VP 1.3cd, quoted by Abhinavagupta in this connection (see below, fn. 569), and the long passage in VP 3.1 on the *bhāvavikāras*, particularly VP 3.1.36: *saiva bhāvavikāreṣu ṣaḍ avasthāḥ prapadyate | krameṇa śaktibhiḥ svābhir evaṃ pratyavabhāsate* || "It is this [Being] that assumes the six conditions in the modifications in [the process of] becoming; thanks to its own powers, it thus appears sequentially."

[567] See HOUBEN 1995, p. 267.

> Vārṣyāyaṇi [has said] that there are six modifications in [the process of] becoming: "It is born," "it exists," "it changes," "it grows," "it decays," "it perishes."[568]

In his *Vivṛti* on ĪPK 2.1.3, Utpaladeva had already explained that time is nothing over and above the sequence of these *bhāvavikāras* by specifying that it "has as its essence nothing but the sequence of birth, existence, transformation, etc."; and in his explanation of the latter passage, Abhinavagupta, while quoting Bhartṛhari, had explicitly equated time with the sequence of these six basic modifications:

> Time is ultimately nothing but the sequence of the six modifications in [the process of] becoming; for no action is anything over and above these modifications in [the process of] becoming. As the master Bhartṛhari has said: "The modifications that are birth, etc., are the sources (*yoni*) of the difference between the six [ways of] becoming."[569]

The *Vivṛti* on ĪPK 2.1.5 comes back to this point. It first emphasizes in this respect that anything that is regarded as an effect is affected by succession, because although we grasp this entity as one, the actions that are the *bhāvavikāras*—actions of which this entity is the substratum—are "differentiated," or, as Utpaladeva further explains in the same *Vivṛti* passage, their difference involves a "mutual exclusion": they are manifested by the absolutely free universal consciousness in such a way that they cannot occur together, and the entity's temporality varies according to which of them is present.

---

[568] *Nirukta* 1.2: *ṣaḍ bhāvavikārā bhavantīti vārṣyāyaṇiḥ. jāyate 'sti vipariṇamate vardhate 'pakṣīyate vinaśyatīti.* Cf. MBh, vol. I, p. 258: *ṣaḍ bhāvavikārā iti ha smāha bhagavān vārṣyāyaṇiḥ, jāyate 'sti vipariṇamate vardhate 'pakṣīyate vinaśyatīti.* "Indeed, the venerable Vārṣyāyaṇi has enumerated the six modifications in [the process of] becoming: 'it is born,' 'it exists,' it changes,' 'it grows,' 'it decays,' 'it perishes.'" See also e.g. VP 1.3, quoted by Abhinavagupta (see below, fn. 569); Helārāja mentions "the author of the *Nirukta*" (*niruktakāra*, PP, vol. I, p. 43) while explaining the *bhāvavikāras* in VP 3.1.36 (quoted above, fn. 566).

[569] ĪPVV, vol. III, p. 9: *bhāvavikāraṣaṭkakramaparamārtha eva kālaḥ. na hi bhāvavikārādhikā kācit kriyāsti. yathāha tatrabhavān: janmādayo vikārāḥ ṣaḍ bhāvabhedasya yonaya iti.* The quotation is borrowed from VP 1.3cd.

Utpaladeva presents this series of modifications as the source of temporality, since it is the difference between these six elements that brings about sequence in their unitary substratum; yet he also insists that temporal sequence does not merely concern the series of these modifications, but also every single element in it, since "there is a manifestation of [different] parts even in the nature of each of these [modifications in the process of becoming] that are birth, existence, transformation and so on." That is to say, each action within this chain is itself made of distinct parts (birth for instance is itself a process, for which one may discern a beginning, an end, and intermediary events), so that it too is sequential. Utpaladeva does not explain whether the parts of each *bhāvavikāra* are in turn made of smaller parts, and when this process of division is supposed to end, but Abhinavagupta comments:

> [The *Vivṛti* says:] "Besides, [there is a manifestation of different parts even in the nature of each] of these [modifications in the process of becoming"; i.e., they themselves are] sequential. [In other words,] there is sequence in them too, down to the single moment (*kṣaṇa*); and this [moment] is ordinarily experienced (*vyavahārya*) as occurring between a prior [moment] and a posterior [one], rather than [as] pure [of any relation with other moments]—so even in that [single moment], there must still be sequence.[570]

Even a single moment—which is supposedly the smallest time unit—is ordinarily apprehended in relation with the moments that precede and follow it; inasmuch as it is grasped as part of a plurality of elements and as being connected with them by some sort of unity, *it is itself affected by sequence*. The reasoning used to explain this paradox is somewhat similar to the one just invoked so as to explain how a pot can be both with and without spatial determinations: as long as we consider the pot while disregarding its parts or its belonging to a plurality of elements, it cannot have any spatial sequence, yet it is spatially determined as soon as we become aware of it as a whole made of parts or as a part within a larger whole. In the same way, a moment is temporally determined only inasmuch as it is apprehended as part of a series of other moments: taken in itself, however—that is, as a

---

[570] ĪPVV, vol. III, pp. 16–17: ***teṣām eva ce****ti kramavatām, tatrāpi kramo yāvad ekaḥ kṣaṇaḥ. sa ca pūrvāparamadhyapātī vyavahāryo, na tu śuddha iti tatrāpi kramavattaiva.*

partless reality that is not integral to any whole—, the pure (*śuddha*) moment, being free of sequence, must be alien to temporality. As a consequence, properly speaking it cannot even be said to be present, as pointed out elsewhere by Abhinavagupta:

> What could be the present as long as both [past] and [future] are not distinguished [from it]? For the [present only] becomes a distinct [reality] through the natures of past and future.[571]

The *Vivṛti*, however, does not dwell on this paradox. Utpaladeva, having first pointed out that temporal sequence occurs due to the difference resulting from the six fundamental modifications, adds that this difference from which temporal determinations arise is also due to the fact that these modifications "pervade all [other] actions." The exact relationship between the *bhāvavikāra*s and all other actions is not defined as explicitly as one might wish, but Utpaladeva does seem to understand the former as the basic forms of which all possible actions are but varieties. Thus he specifies that in a series of actions such as "having bathed and eaten, X goes," temporal sequence arises in the unitary individual performing them due to the difference between the actions of bathing, eating and going, but these in turn amount to *bhāvavikāra*s "such as transformation"—and they too are sequential not only as a multiplicity of distinct actions, but also because "even in itself, [each action of] bathing, eating and so on involves a difference in the phenomena of its own parts," so that each of them is also affected by temporal sequence.

### 8. Action, time and recognition

At this point the *Vivṛti* provides what is probably the most synthetic and clear definition of ordinary action in the Pratyabhijñā system:

> For what is called action is nothing but a particular form that is manifest as having parts that are [mutually] contradictory, [and] that [nonetheless] has something unitary as its substratum; for it is due to this contradiction that [action, by] arising

---

[571] MŚV 1.151cd–152ab: *avibhāgas tayor yāvat tāvat kā vartamānatā* ‖ *bhūtabhāvisvabhāvābhyāṃ sā hi yāti vibhāgitām* ‖ See HANNEDER 1998, p. 83.

> in a unitary [substratum] although it cannot occur in [the form of] a fully unfolded manifestation, manifests sequence.

Action is profoundly one, and there is no awareness of action without an awareness of this unity; yet action as we experience it in our everyday lives is also the manifestation of a multiplicity of contradictory elements, and temporal sequence arises because this contradiction, which lacks the power to eliminate our awareness of unity, nonetheless prevents us from grasping these elements as existing together. Again, Utpaladeva's debt to Bhartṛhari is obvious here, and Abhinavagupta's commentary unsurprisingly quotes VP 3.8.11:

> This is what the master [Bhartṛhari has said in]: "Thus this [reality], although one, is expressed by verbs [i.e. becomes an action] inasmuch as its sequence is brought about by moments that [occur] one after the other, through the superimposition (*adhyāsa*) of the [totality in the parts]."[572] [573]

A few verses before this one, Bharthạri had already explained that action is a totality of parts brought together and unified by consciousness:

> [What is] called "action" is a totality of [momentary elements] that arise in a sequence; the unity [of this totality] with the parts is superimposed by consciousness, which subordinates [these parts to the totality].[574]

Yet a striking difference between these quotations from the VP and Utpaladeva's descriptions of action is that the latter systematically emphasize the remarkable role of contradiction (*virodha*, *viruddhatva*) in any action. Thus

---

[572] My understanding of *tadadhyāsāt* rests on PP, p. 12 (*avayaveṣu tu samudāyādhyāsāt...*). K.A. Subramania Iyer's edition of the PP gives the reading *asadadhyāsāt* in the verse, as does W. Rau's edition of the VP; whatever the original reading, it seems probable that both Helārāja and Abhinavagupta read *tadadhyāsāt* (the editorial choices below, fn. 573, regard Abhinavagupta's quotation, not what the verse may originally have been).

[573] ĪPVV, vol. III, p. 17: *yat tatrabhavān pūrvottarais tathā kṣaṇaiḥ* samavasthāpitakramaḥ | ekaḥ so 'pi tadadhyāsād* ākhyātair abhidhīyate ||* [**tathā kṣaṇaiḥ* S12, J11, ĪPVV Ed; *tathā bhāgaiḥ* VP (Rau); *tadā bhāgaiḥ* VP 3. **so 'pi tadadhyāsād* S12, J11, ĪPVV Ed; *so 'py asadadhyāsād* VP (Rau), VP 3.] Cf. above, fn. 572.

[574] VP 3.8.4: *guṇabhūtair avayavaiḥ samūhaḥ kramajanmanām | buddhyā prakalpitābhedaḥ kriyeti vyapadiśyate ||*

as seen above,[575] Utpaladeva describes the awareness of time as twofold: it occurs when we grasp a plurality of contradictory elements that, due to their incompatibility, limit and cancel each other—and in this respect it belongs to the fragmented world of *māyā*; yet it also entails the awareness of a unity that is capable of embracing and transcending all of these contradictions. This is why the awareness of time paradoxically affords us a glimpse of the absolute, which, because it is pure consciousness, is capable of including all differences without being limited by them, and of overcoming all contradictions, while manifesting them. According to Utpaladeva, this glimpse takes place whenever we are aware that something or someone is undergoing changes. In such a case, despite the incompatibility of the various states thus undergone, the fact that the thing or person affected by these modifications has a fundamental unity never ceases to be manifest; it "remains unconcealed thanks to the unity of the [recognitive] realization (*vimarśa*) [that grasps it as being the same]." This is a crucial point, and it is no coincidence that while summing up the gist of ĪPK 2.1.5, Abhinavagupta, who is acutely aware of the importance of this idea, chooses to quote this specific passage:

> The variety of material shapes—[the latter being objective] entities that are nothing but objects of knowledge—is differentiated into such [things] as a house, courtyard, shop, temple, garden, forest, etc. The Lord manifests spatial sequence—which consists in being extended and not being extended—"from" [this variety, i.e.,] thanks to it, [simply by] manifesting this variety. But [something] such as a hand [remains] one, as far as its nature is concerned, through the force of [our] recognition [that it is] one [despite its various movements; Utpaladeva] will explain this [in the *Vivṛti* when stating that this thing] "has as its essence a unitary substance that remains unconcealed thanks to the unity of the [recognitive] realization [that grasps it as being the same]." The variety of actions belonging to this [unitary entity] takes such forms as "Caitra is walking" [or] "the fruit is becoming ripe"; [and it consists in] having ever different places [and/or] ever different properties, [but] without cancelling

[575] Chapter 7, §4.

> the unity of [this thing's] nature. [It is] thanks to the manifestation of this [variety of actions] that the Lord manifests temporal sequence for [something that remains] one, although [in fact temporal sequence] is not appropriate [for this unitary thing] inasmuch as it involves contradictory forms; [and He manifests this temporal sequence simply by] manifesting, by virtue of [His] freedom, [both] contradiction and the absence thereof—this is the [general] meaning of the verse.[576]

Again, while explaining Utpaladeva's statement that temporal sequence "is distinguished from spatial sequence by the fact that it rests on a unitary substratum," Abhinavagupta once more specifies that temporal sequence entails a unitary apprehension that is a recognition:

> "By the fact that it rests on a unitary substratum" [means the following]: Because it occurs in [something] unitary, since it is established to be one by a realization [consisting in] a recognition (*pratyabhijñā*), it is distinguished from spatial sequence, which only occurs in [something] plural—the implied meaning is that in this [unitary entity], one cannot [even] imagine a spatial sequence.[577]

The Pratyabhijñā system thus ascribes to time a somewhat ambivalent role in bondage and liberation. On the one hand, time, as Utpaladeva is about to point out in the next couple of verses, only belongs to the sphere of limited

---

[576] ĪPVV, vol. III, p. 12: *mūrtīnāṃ saṃvedyarūpāṇāṃ bhāvānāṃ yad vaicitryaṃ gṛhaprāṅgaṇavipaṇidevakulārāmāraṇyādibhedena, tato hetos tad vaicitryam ābhāsayan parameśvaro deśakramaṃ vaitatyāvaitatyātmakam avabhāsayati. ekapratyabhijñābalāt tu yat svarūpeṇābhinnaṃ hastādi, yad vakṣyati* ***vimarśaikyenātirohitābhinnadravyātmana*** *iti, tasya yad anyānyadeśatvam anyānyadharmatvaṃ svarūpaikatām abādhamānaṃ gacchati caitraḥ pacyate phalam ityevaṃbhūtaṃ kriyāvaicitryam. tasya nirbhāsanād dhetor īśvaro virodham avirodhaṃ ca svātantryān nirbhāsayan kālākhyaṃ kramam ekasya viruddharūpatayānucitam apy avabhāsayatīti sūtrārthaḥ.*

[577] ĪPVV, vol. III, p. 17: ***ekāśrayatvene****ty ekasminn api pratyabhijñāpratyavamarśaikyena siddher yato bhavati tato deśakramād anekatraiva vartamānād bhidyate, nātra deśakramaḥ saṃbhāvanīya iti yāvat.*

individuals; and as one of the five "sheaths" (*kañcuka*)[578] constricting the self of transmigrating individuals, it is a binding force that contributes to their enslavement in *saṃsāra*. While explaining ĪPK 3.1.9, according to which the conscious individual, who is in fact nothing but an "object of knowledge," is covered by the five sheaths of "time, etc.",[579] Abhinavagupta thus specifies that the essence of objectivity is nothing but limitation, i.e., the fact of being constricted by the *kañcuka*s, the first of which is the limiting factor of time:

> For being limited is the essence of objectivity (*prameyatva*) and of the distinction from the [pure] knowing subject; and this [limitation] is [precisely] the state of being covered by the five sheaths of time, etc.[580]

And again:

> And for the subjectivity [consisting in an erroneous self-identification with] the void, etc., being limited is nothing but the five [sheaths of] time, etc.[581]

On the other hand, as noted above,[582] the experience of time is so to speak closer to that of ultimate reality than that of space. This is so because, as repeatedly emphasized by Utpaladeva, there is no experience of time without the awareness of a unity—or, as Abhinavagupta keeps pointing out, the experience of time is necessarily that of a recognition, i.e., the realization

---

578 Namely *kāla*, *kalā*, *vidyā*, *rāga* and *niyati* (at least this is the most common list, accepted by Utpaladeva). On this Śaiva notion of *kañcuka*s, which is shared by Saiddhāntikas and *īśvarādvayavādin*s, see TORELLA 1998.

579 ĪPK 3.1.9: *yaś ca pramātā śūnyādiḥ prameye vyatirekiṇi | mātā sa meyaḥ san kālādikapañcakaveṣṭitaḥ* || "And the knowing subject who [wrongly identifies with] the void, [intellect, vital breath and body, and] who knows an object of knowledge distinct [from himself], is covered by the five [sheaths of] time, etc., being [himself nothing but] an object of knowledge."

580 ĪPVV, vol. III, p. 285: *pārimityaṃ hy atra prameyatve mātur vyatireke ca prāṇas tad eva ca kālādipañcakakañcukanicitatvam.*

581 ĪPV, vol. II, p. 207: *parimitatvaṃ ca śūnyāder ahaṃbhāvasya yat tad eva kālādipañcakam.*

582 In chapter 7, §4.

(*vimarśa*, *pratyavamarśa*, etc.) of the profound unity of a reality that manifests itself as plural. In the Pratyabhijñā system, temporality not only has as its condition the very nonduality that it hides by seemingly constricting it; it also involves at its core the manifestation of this nonduality in the form of the recognition without which there can be no awareness of succession. Admittedly, the nondual reality that keeps flashing forth at the heart of every instant is accompanied by a fragmented and contradictory appearance of reality without which there is no awareness of time either—and this is why, in chapter 1.6, Utpaladeva insists that when we recognize someone (including ourselves) or something, the synthesis through which we realize the unity of past and present phenomena belonging to that person or thing[583] is in fact a mere conceptual construct rather than a genuine intuition of reality:

> In the case of that whose manifestation occurs at a specific time [rather than always], the synthesis (*yojanā*) with a phenomenon that is past, etc., [which is] due to a residual trace, is also considered a conceptual construct (*kalpanā*) [since it] regards [something] that has separated manifestations.[584]

Abhinavagupta explains:

> In the case of that which consists in a particular [entity] such as a body, whose manifestation "occurs at a specific time"—[i.e., it only] occurs sometimes [since it] has a specific place, time and aspect—, [there can be a] *yojanā*, [i.e.,] a synthesis. [This synthesis occurs] with a past phenomenon—[viz.] the manifestation of a child's body for instance—[and takes such a form] as: "I, who [was] a child, am now an adult"; and given that [Utpaladeva] uses [the word] "etc.," [one must understand that] this synthesis [can also occur] with a posterior, future manifestation [and take such a form] as "I will be an

[583] Abhinavagupta specifies that this is true not only of the syntheses that regard persons but also of those concerning objects (ĪPV, vol. I, p. 257): *evaṃ sa evāyaṃ ghaṭo iti ghaṭādyanusaṃdhāne 'pi vikalpatvaṃ mantavyam.* "In the same way, in the case of a synthesis regarding [something] such as a pot as well—[for instance, the one that takes the form] 'this is the same pot [seen before]'—, one must consider that [it is] a conceptual construct."

[584] ĪPK 1.6.6: *kādācitkāvabhāse yā pūrvābhāsādiyojanā | saṃskārāt kalpanā proktā sāpi bhinnāvabhāsini ||*

> old man." Any such synthesis is nothing but a *kalpanā*, [that is,] a conceptual construct.[585]

The various phenomena that we then synthesize in fact remain "separated," that is, mutually exclusive or contradictory, and the unity of which we are aware does not succeed in thoroughly dissolving this contradiction, as Abhinavagupta makes clear:

> [The reason] why [this synthesis is a mere conceptual construct] is that even now, [when the synthesis is occurring,] the body, etc. [with which an individual identifies] keep having separated manifestations. For if [the subject] produced the synthesis "I am this" while seeing the absolute fullness of the [objects that are] the body, etc.—[that is, while seeing] that they are free of any separation—, then this would be [the pure level of consciousness called] the Sadāśiva level! [And] who would [dare] describe [this level] as the domain of conceptual construct, whereas [at such a level] the synthesis only concerns what is not separated?[586]

Nonetheless, as explained by Abhinavagupta, even in a synthesis tainted by the subject's erroneous identification with objective entities, the pure power of knowledge ([*śuddha*]*vidyāśakti*)—that is to say, the power through which the bound individuals (*paśu*) may become aware of their true identity with the absolutely free consciousness[587]—does flash forth, albeit fleetingly:

---

[585] ĪPV, vol. I, p. 256: *kādācitkaḥ kadācidbhavo niyatadeśakālākāro 'vabhāso yasya dehādeḥ svalakṣaṇarūpasya, tatra yā pūrvābhāsena bālādiśarīrāvabhāsena yojanā yo 'haṃ bālaḥ sa evādya yuvety anusaṃdhānam, ādigrahaṇād uttareṇa bhāvinābhāsena saha yojanā sthaviro bhavitāsmīti, sā yojanā sarvā kalpanā vikalpa eva.*

[586] ĪPV, vol. I, pp. 256–257 (on ĪPK 1.6.6, quoted above, fn. 584): ... *yato bhinnāvabhāsitvam eva dehādes tadānīm apy avicchinnam, yadi hi tasya dehādeḥ sarvataḥ pūrṇatvam avacchedahīnatvaṃ paśyann anusaṃdhānam aham idam iti vidadhyāt tad iyaṃ sadāśivabhūḥ, kena vikalpāspadatvena bhaṇyate yāvatāvicchinne eva so 'nusaṃdhiḥ.*

[587] See ĪPK 3.1.7ac: *tasyaiśvaryasvabhāvasya paśubhāve prakāśikā | vidyāśaktis...* "The power of [pure] knowledge is what reveals this [true] nature of being the Lord in the state of the bound individual (*paśu*)..." Cf. *Vṛtti* ad loc., p. 63: *saṃsāriṇām aiśvaryasya svātmanaḥ pratyabhijñānaṃ vidyayā.* "For the transmigrating subjects,

> Nonetheless, since at these [impure] levels of synthesis, the power of [pure] knowledge flashes forth powerfully, as a lightning bolt, the masters have admitted that they are a [soteriological] means (*abhyupāya*) that must be resorted to first so as to [achieve] a constant contact with the highest level [of reality].[588]

In chapter 2.1 and its commentaries, neither Utpaladeva nor Abhinavagupta spells this out; but by emphasizing in several instances that time, contrary to space, primarily belongs to consciousness and is first and foremost a recognition, both authors seem to hint that the experience of time may be both a binding factor and an opportunity to achieve liberation.

### 9. The limited subject and the awareness of present, past and future

Abhinavagupta introduces as follows the *Vivṛti*'s next point:

> [– Objection:] "Fine, let [us admit] that time thus consists in sequence; yet how [can we explain] its taking present, [past and future] forms [if it is] so?" Utpaladeva answers [this question] with [the passage] beginning with "[And as soon as the existence of phenomena such as] bathing...".[589]

How it is that our awareness of time is not just that of sequence, but that of a sequence that is specifically determined as involving past, present and future? As pointed out in the *Vivṛti* itself, Utpaladeva's answer rests on a "principle that is going to be stated," and Abhinavagupta specifies that it will be so "in the next verse"; for ĪPK 2.1.6 explains that time, whether it affects the manifestations of things or persons, only exists in relation to the

---

the recognition of oneself as being the Lord [occurs] thanks to the [power of pure] knowledge." See also ĪPK 3.2.2: *eṣa pramātā māyāndhaḥ saṃsārī karmabandhanaḥ | vidyābhijñāpitaiśvaryaś cidghano mukta ucyate ||* "This knowing subject, blinded by *māyā*, transmigrating, bound by *karman*, is said to be liberated [when,] having been made to recognize (*abhijñāpita*) that he is the Lord by [pure] knowledge (*vidyā*), he is nothing but [pure] consciousness."

588 ĪPV, vol. I, pp. 257–258: *kiṃtv etāsv anusaṃdhānabhūmiṣu vidyāśaktir ādhikyenāciradyutivad uddīpyata iti tāsāṃ parapadapariśīlanaprathamakalpābhyupāyatvam abhyupāgaman guravaḥ.*

589 ĪPVV, vol. III, p. 17: *nanu bhavatv evaṃ kramarūpatā kālasya, vartamānādirūpatā tu katham ittham ity āha* ***snāne****tyādinā.*

knowing subject apprehending these phenomena. It has no independent existence in the objects apprehended by the subject; rather, it is projected by the subject onto things, and Utpaladeva's concern here is to show that what we consider as present is simply any object that is manifested as something that only occurs with the limited subject:

> According to the principle that is going to be stated in the next verse, a phenomenon is called present if it has a form that is vivid and [new]; and what is such a [phenomenon]? It is one whose unfolding only occurs together with the phenomenon of the apprehending subject who belongs to the sphere of *māyā*, [i.e.,] the body and [other objects with which limited individuals wrongly identify].[590]

What is present is anything that occurs together with the phenomenon of the subject who has lost the full awareness of his/her absolutely free subjectivity and wrongly thinks that (s)he is a particular object of the world. In chapter 1.6, Utpaladeva has explained that this object with which transmigrating individuals confuse their own essence may be of four kinds, namely the body (*deha*, *śarīra*), vital breath (*prāṇa*), intellect (*buddhi*) and void (*śūnya*).[591] Since this enumeration is going to be alluded to by Utpaladeva himself in the next verse, a few words of explanation regarding this typology might not be out of place here.[592]

---

[590] ĪPVV, vol. III, p. 17: *uttarasūtravakṣyamāṇena nyāyena vartamānaḥ sa ābhāsa ucyate yasya sphuṭādirūpatā. tādṛśaś ca kaḥ. yasya grāhakābhāsena śarīrādinā māyīyena sahaiva prathanam.*

[591] See ĪPK 1.6.4–5: *cittattvaṃ māyayā hitvā bhinna evāvabhāti yaḥ | dehe buddhāv atha prāṇe kalpite nabhasīva vā || pramātṛtvenāham iti vimarśo 'nyavyapohanāt | vikalpa eva sa parapratiyogyavabhāsajaḥ ||* "The realization 'I' [of consciousness] as being a knowing subject, which, having [seemingly] abandoned the true nature of consciousness due to *māyā*, is manifest with respect to [something] that is separated—[namely] the body, intellect, vital breath or the [void], which is imagined as [a kind of] ether—, is a mere conceptual construct, because [it entails] an exclusion from what [the 'I'] is not; [and this construct] arises from the manifestation of [something] that is the counterpart (*pratiyogin*) [of the I and] other [than it]."

[592] For a more detailed analysis of the typology of limited subjects in the Pratyabhijñā system see RATIÉ 2011a, pp. 204–208.

In his commentaries on ĪPK 1.6.4–5, Abhinavagupta explains that the different elements in the list of objects with which limited subjects confuse their own self correspond to doctrines that may be seen as various levels of understanding—or rather, of misunderstanding—of the self's nature,[593] starting with that of the Cārvākas (the materialists who consider that a person is nothing but his/her body).[594] Above them are some Vedāntins (*śrutyantavid*) who believe that vital breath is the true nature of the self,[595] which brings to mind the *Taittirīyopaniṣad*'s ascending scale of *ātmans*.[596] Then come "the followers of Kaṇāda, etc." (that is, Vaiśeṣikas and Naiyāyikas), who, according to Abhinavagupta, believe that the self must be the

[593] Kṣemarāja gives a somewhat different description of these misinterpretations of the self's nature in his auto-commentary on PH 8.

[594] ĪPV, vol. I, pp. 249–251: *tathā ca dehābhimānabhūmikāyāṃ sthitāś cārvākāś caitanyaviśiṣṭaḥ kāyaḥ puruṣa iti kāyam eva prādhānyenāhuḥ.* "And thus the Cārvākas stay at the level of the [wrong] self-identification with the body; they assert that it is the body that is the essence [of the self when stating that] 'the person is the body particularized by consciousness.'" The oft-quoted sentence is listed as fragment A10 of the *Bārhaspatyasūtras* in NAMAI 1976.

[595] ĪPV, vol. I, p. 251: *strībālamūrkhāṇāṃ tathābhimānāt tato'pi vivekavantaḥ pākajotpattipariṇāmādibalād asthiraṃ śarīraṃ manvānāḥ prāṇaśaktisamadhiṣṭhānena ca vinā vikāraśatāveśaṃ śarīrasya paśyanto bubhukṣāpipāsāyogayogyaṃ prāṇam evātmānaṃ kecana śrutyantavido manyante.* "Some Vedāntins, being more discerning than the [Cārvākas]—because such a self-identification [as the one defended by the Cārvākas] belongs to women, children and imbeciles—, considering that the body does not last, because of the transformation that is the arising [of new properties in it] due to the heat [of digestion], etc., [and] seeing that when the body is no [longer] controlled by the power of vital breath, it undergoes countless modifications, consider that it is vital breath—which may be associated with hunger and thirst—that is the self."

[596] Abhinavagupta's hierarchy of self-identifications seems to echo in part *Taittirīyopaniṣad* 2.1–5; this is noticed by Bhāskarakaṇṭha, who quotes it several times in his commentary on this passage (see *Bhāskarī*, vol. I, pp. 318 ff.). According to the Upaniṣad, there is, beyond a material *ātman* "made of the essence of food" (*annarasamaya*), a series of different selves, each of which is more internal than the previous one: a self "made of vital breath" (*prāṇamaya*), one "made of mind" (*manomaya*), one "made of consciousness" (*vijñānamaya*), and finally, one "made of bliss" (*ānandamaya*).

*buddhi* understood as the substratum of cognitions.[597] The enumeration comes to an end with some Vedāntins described as "proponents of the empty Brahman" as well as "the Sāṃkhyas, etc.," who identify the self with the void;[598] the Śaiva nondualists criticize in this respect those who, while rightly considering that the self is none of the objects of knowledge because it transcends objectivity, end up hypostasizing this apophatic approach and identifying the self's nature with this sheer negation, thus failing to grasp its reality.

Utpaladeva contends that limited subjects who thus confuse their own essence with one of these four objects apprehend any other object as "present" if the latter is immediately apprehended as occurring together with the object with which they wrongly identify, and if, due to this immediate con-

---

597 ĪPV, vol. I, pp. 251–252: *tato 'pi samadhikavivekabhājaḥ prāṇasyāpy anityatvād anusaṃdhānayogyatām apaśyanto jñānasukhādyāśrayabhūtāṃ buddhim eva kāṇādaprabhṛtaya ātmānam āhuḥ*. "The followers of Kaṇāda, etc., being more discerning than these [Vedāntins,] claim that the self is nothing but the intellect, which is the substratum of cognitions, pleasure and so on, because they do not see how [vital breath] could be capable of the [cognitive] synthesis [made possible by the self,] since vital breath too is impermanent." This depiction of the Vaiśeṣika and Nyāya's position regarding the nature of the self (which Naiyāyikas and Vaiśeṣikas would certainly deem unfair) is an allusion to some of the arguments in favour of the self's existence in the NBh under NS 1.1.10 and 3.1.1: according to Pakṣilasvāmin, there could be no cognitive synthesis (*anusaṃdhi*, *anusaṃdhāna*, *pratisaṃdhi*) without the existence of the self understood as a permanent substratum of cognitions—a point much exploited by the Śaiva nondualists (see RATIÉ 2011a, pp. 66–69 and 265–270).

598 ĪPV, vol. I, p. 252 (as edited in RATIÉ 2010c, p. 464, fn. 107): *apare tu tasyā api yogidaśāyāṃ vedyabhāvād aparatvaṃ manyamānā asaṃvedyaparvarūpaṃ yan na kiṃcid rūpaṃ sakalavedyarāśivinirmuktaṃ śūnyatvān nabhastulyaṃ na tu mahābhūtākāśasvabhāvaṃ pramātṛtattvam śūnyabrahmavādisāṃkhyaprabhṛtaya āhuḥ*. "Others, however—[i.e.] those who uphold the thesis of an empty *brahman*, the Sāṃkhyas, etc.—, considering that the [intellect] too is different [from the self,] because in the condition [experienced by] yogins, [the intellect also] has the status of an object of knowledge, claim that the true nature of the knowing subject is [precisely] the part [of reality] that is not an object of knowledge, which is no form whatsoever, which is devoid of all objects of knowledge without exception, [and] which is similar to ether because it is void; yet it is not the nature of ether, [as the latter is] a material element."

nection, the object is grasped as "vivid" and "new." In the *Vivṛti*, Utpaladeva specifies that this awareness of the coexistence of the two entities is due to the fact that then there is "no indirect relationship"[599] between them "internally," i.e., no connection between the subject and the object that would be entirely mediated by the object's status as a residual trace, because this indirect relationship between the subject and object only occurs when the respective manifestations of the object and subject are accompanied by the phenomenon of their mutual incompatibility. Abhinavagupta explains that one may thus define the property of existing in the present as the mere "fact of existing together," but only if this simultaneous existence is understood as resulting from the *absence* of a certain phenomenon (i.e., that of the mutual incompatibility between the subject and object's manifestations) rather than the presence of something positive:

> If [someone answers that what we call "present" is the mere fact of] existing together (*sahabhāva*), [Utpaladeva] states [as a reply] the passage beginning with "[because there is no indirect relationship of this manifestation with that of the apprehended object] internally, [an indirect relationship that would be due to the phenomenon of a mutual incompatibility," which means the following]. [It is present because] there is no indirect relationship, which would be due to the phenomenon of mutual incompatibility that has already been described [above] as the presence of certain phenomena [and] that would take this form: "when the phenomenon of the apprehending subject [occurs], there is no manifestation of this apprehended object; and when the phenomenon of this apprehended object occurs, there is no manifestation of the apprehending subject." It is with respect to this [absence of the phenomenon of mutual incompatibility] that [we] talk about

[599] The term *vyavadhāna* is difficult to translate. Although it may refer to an entity that conceals something else (or even the very act of this concealment), it often designates the "interposition" or "mediation" of something between two elements that it both separates and connects, hence the tentative rendering here.

> "[manifestations that] unfold together"—the so-called "existing together" is nothing but that.[600]

The present time as limited subjects experience it is not the pure, positive apprehension of nonsequential coexistence (which only belongs to the pure levels of consciousness, where the awareness of consciousness's essential fullness and nonduality remain intact); it is, rather, the apprehension of a given object while the additional phenomenon of its incompatibility with the limited subject is *lacking*. In other words, even what we usually take to be the ontologically fullest aspect of time, the present, is in fact wanting, precisely because it is thoroughly dependent upon the limited subject's perspective.

Utpaladeva thus shows how his thesis is in accordance with our everyday understanding of time[601] by distinguishing the three temporal aspects of past, present and future according to this relationship between the limited subject and the object considered by him/her: for this object, belonging to the present time is nothing but the existence of a vivid phenomenon (i.e., a phenomenon grasped as occurring together with the subject, because no incompatibility between them is manifest), whereas past and future entities are those that are not apprehended as such. One could of course object that this does not account for our awareness of the difference separating the past from the future, and according to Abhinavagupta, Utpaladeva anticipates this criticism[602] by explaining that if the present is the existence of a vivid

[600] ĪPVV, vol. III, pp. 17–18: *sa sahabhāva iti ced āh**āntar** iti. yadā sa grāhakābhāsas tadā tasya grāhyasyābhāsanaṃ na; yadā ca sa grāhyābhāsas tadā tasya grāhakasyābhāsanaṃ netyevaṃbhūto yo 'nyonyam abhāvasyābhāsa ābhāsasattvam ityevaṃ pūrvam uktas tena yo vyavadhānābhāvaḥ, tam avalambya sā sahaprathety ucyate, ayam asau sahabhāvo nāma.*

[601] Cf. ĪPVV, vol. III, p. 18: *etal lokena saṃvādayati **sphuṭa** iti.* "This he shows to be in conformity with ordinary people['s experience] in '[Thus being present is nothing but the existence of a] vivid [phenomenon]...'."

[602] ĪPVV, vol. III, p. 18: *nanv evam abhāvavyavadhāne sati vartamānatvābhāve tulye kathaṃ bhāvibhūtatvabheda ity āśaṅkya tam upapādayaty **asattvam** iti.*"'But [if it is] so, since [in the cases of the past and future] there is an indirect relationship [between the manifestations of the apprehending subject and apprehended object] due to [the phenomenon of mutual] incompatibility [between them], given that in both [cases] there is no present time, how can there be a difference between being

phenomenon grasped as unfolding simulteanously with the subject, the past is both the existence and nonexistence of this phenomenon, whereas the future is its utter nonexistence. Abhinavagupta explains that the vivid phenomenon of a past object can be said to be both existent and nonexistent because, although it no longer exists externally (i.e., as an object grasped by the subject as existing outside his or her consciousness), the object's experience endures internally in the form of a residual trace that is latent but may, when stimulated, produce a memory of the object;[603] whereas the vivid phenomenon of the future object, as pointed out by Utpaladeva, has no existence at all in the sense that this object is only apprehended in the form of a conceptual construct (*vikalpa*), which has none of the vividness characterizing immediate experience.

This explanation could sound somewhat unsatisfactory insofar as Utpaladeva and Abhinavagupta concede that memory too (and not just the conceptual construct of an imaginary object) lacks the vividness of immediate experience: contrary to direct perception, it is supposedly *asphuṭa*. While commenting on chapter 1.6, however, Abhinavagupta has already made clear that the residual trace (*saṃskāra*) accepted by all Indian philosophical traditions so as to account for the phenomenon of memory is in fact nothing but the continuous existence, albeit in an internal form, of the immediate experience that we once had of the remembered object—and in this respect, a memory is certainly more vivid than a mere conceptual construct, because the former includes the immediate awareness *of having had the direct (and therefore vivid) perception of the past object*. Yet the present cognition that is memory has no object of its own, it has to borrow it from the past experience while this object no longer exists now (at least not in the form in which it existed in the past), which is why a memory is less vivid than a perception:

---

future and being past?' Having anticipated this [question, Utpaladeva] shows how [this difference] is possible with [the passage beginning with 'whereas being future is just its] nonexistence.'"

603 See ĪPVV, vol. III, p. 18: ***bhavanadharmāpī****ty evaṃ sphuritasya bāhyarūpasyaiva bālyasyādhunāpi saṃskāratayāntar aparikṣataṃ bhavanam ity arthaḥ.* "'Although [it] has the property of existing' means [the following]: For the childhood that thus [once] flashed forth in an *external* form, even now, existence remains intact internally due to its [being present] as a residual trace (*saṃskāra*)."

In that [regard], what [we] call "residual trace" is [nothing but] the continuous existence (*anuvartamānatā*) of the [past] experience at another, [later] time too; therefore, since this experience that exists continuously is differentiated by the phenomenon of [a specific object] such as blue, [cognitions] such as memory too are manifest in this way, [i.e., as having this or that specific object,] because they receive their nature from that [experience].[604] This is precisely why the [objective] phenomenon [that constitutes the object of memory, since it] cannot occur at the time of memory [itself because it really belongs to the previous experience,] is only delimited by the past time of that experience—therefore it is proclaimed that in and of themselves, memory and so on have no object and that they grasp [something] that is [already] grasped. [And] this [fact that memory has no object of its own] is precisely its lack of vividness; so the difference between phenomena in experience, memory and so on is [now] established: the external manifestation of all internal phenomena without any indirect relationship (*vyavadhāna*)[605] is vividness, whereas [the same manifestation] through the indirect relationship [resulting from a residual trace][606] is a lack of vividness due to the fact that [this manifestation does] not belong to the [present] time.[607]

---

[604] It seems to me that Bhāskarakaṇṭha is wrong in identifying the *tat* with the object rather than with the experience in which the residual trace consists (*Bhāskarī*, vol. I, p. 337: *tattādātmyāpannam—tan nīlam iti nīlatādātmyayuktam*).

[605] Bhāskarakaṇṭha has the reading *anyāvyavadhānena*, "without the indirect relationship with/due to [something] else," which he glosses (*Bhāskarī*, vol. I, p. 337) with the words *saṃskāravyavadhānarahitatvena*, "while being free of the indirect relationship with/due to a residual trace."

[606] According to *Bhāskarī*, vol. I, p. 337: *vyavadhānena, saṃskārakṛtenety arthaḥ.*

[607] ĪPV, vol. I, p. 268: *tatra saṃskāro nāmānubhavasya kālāntare 'py anuvartamānatā, ato 'sāv anuvartamāno 'nubhavo yato nīlādyābhāsasaṃbhinnas tatas tattādātmyāpannaṃ smaraṇādy api tathā nirbhāsate. tata eva smaraṇakālāsaṃbhavy ābhāsas tadanubhavapūrvakālakalita eveti svayaṃ smaraṇāder nirviṣayatvaṃ gṛhītagrāhitvaṃ codghoṣyate. etad evāsphuṭatvam iti siddho 'nubhavasmaraṇādāv ābhāsabhedaḥ, antarābhāsavargasya bahirābhāsanam avyavadhānena sphuṭatā, vyavadhānena tu tātkālikatvābhāvād asphuṭateti.*

### 10. Time and space only make sense in an idealistic system

The end of the *Vivṛti* on ĪPK 2.1.5 as it is preserved in the marginal annotations at my disposal is unfortunately far too lacunary to be understood on its own; yet its gist can be retrieved from Abhinavagupta's commentary.

According to the latter, Utpaladeva first endeavoured to point out that temporal sequence as described so far cannot be accounted for in a dualistic doctrine and only makes sense within the metaphysical frame of Śaiva nondualism:

> Now, this temporal sequence, which cannot be denied since it is established for all people, and through [mere] self-awareness, cannot be rationally accounted for in a doctrine [according to which there are] exernal objects, [i.e.] in a dualism. Therefore, since it must be accounted for, the only way out [of this difficulty is] this doctrine [of ours] according to which reality is phenomena—not the externalist doctrine. While showing this, [Utpaladeva] points out how the explanation of time contributes to [bringing about] the Lord's recognition [in the passage beginning with] "For this reason..."[608]

Time cannot be satisfactorily accounted for in a system that presents the universe as existing independently of consciousness; it only makes sense from the Śaiva nondualists' idealistic standpoint, so that the rational explanation of time provided in the treatise can help induce the recognition of oneself as the Lord in its readers. Why is that?

As seen above, Utpaladeva's and Abhinavagupta's strategies when it comes to pointing out how space and time cannot be objective realities existing outside consciousness seem to be slightly different (although of course we have to be very cautious in trying to evaluate this difference as long as we do not have Utpaladeva's entire *Vivṛti* at our disposal). Thus Abhinavagupta, following a line of argument found in Sāṃkhya sources, and formulating it in terms that are strikingly similar to Vācaspatimiśra's summary

---

[608] ĪPVV, vol. III, p. 18: *idānīm etasya kālakramasya sakalalokasiddhatvena svasaṃvedanasiddhatvena cānapahnavanīyasya bāhyārthanaye bhedadṛśi samarthanā na kathaṃcid yujyate. tad avaśyasamarthanīye 'sminn ābhāsavastuvāda eva śaraṇaṃ na bāhyavāda iti darśayann īśvarapratyabhijñopayogam asya kālaprakaraṇasya darśayaty* ***ata eveti.***

of it in particular, argues that a unitary substance existing outside consciousness, such as time as it is defined in the Vaiśeṣika, cannot account for temporal diversity, precisely because it is supposedly one, so that the Vaiśeṣikas themselves must admit that this diversity is rather caused by adventitious properties—and this acknowledgement amounts to conceding that the inference of the substance "time" is gratuitous, since the Vaiśeṣikas claim that the substance called "time" must be inferred as the cause of this diversity.[609] In his TĀ, Abhinavagupta applies the same criticism to the Vaiśeṣika's inference of space as a mind-independent substance:

> Even if a certain [objectively existing thing that you] call "space" exists, no cognition such as "east," "west," etc. may result from this [space, which is supposedly] one, if there is no superimposition of an adventitious property [on it].[610] If [the Vaiśeṣika opponent retorts] that [indeed, in his system it is] an adventitious property that is taught [to be] the property of being east, then space [as the Vaiśeṣika claims to infer it] is useless! But if it is only adventitious properties [that explain spatial differences], how could [these adventitious properties] thus result in variety? Therefore it is the manifesting power of consciousness (*saṃvitprakāśa*) that, intoxicated with picturing up the variety defined as the distinction between east and so on, [creates spatial sequence] by dividing the manifestations of material shapes.[611]

---

[609] See above, chapter 6, §1 (particularly fn. 380 and 381).

[610] Cf. TĀV, vol. IX, p. 96: *nanūktam eva hi kāṇādaiḥ kevalavṛkṣādipratyayavilakṣaṇapūrvādipratyayānumeyā dig astīti. sā caikā sarvatra tatpratyayāviśeṣāt. nanu yady evaṃ tat katham anupāhitarūpāyā ekasyās tasyāḥ pūrvāparādiko bhedo bhaved ity āha pūrvety ādi.* "[– Objection:] But it has been said by Kaṇāda's followers that space is to be inferred from the cognitions of [a tree for instance being] east, etc., which are distinct from cognitions such as that of the tree devoid [of any spatial determination]; and this [space] is one, because in all cases there is no difference in [our] cognitions of it. [– Answer:] But if it is so, then how could the difference between 'east,' 'west' and so on result from this unitary [space, if] no adventitious property has been superimposed onto its nature?—This is what [Abhinavagupta] says with 'no [cognition such as] east,' etc."

[611] TĀ 15.194–6 (I thank Whitney Cox for sharing with me COX forthcoming, which brought this passage to my attention, even though my understanding of it is quite

If only adventitious properties account for the diversity of spatial determinations, the objective substance "space" posited by the Vaiśeṣika is useless, and what causes spatial determinations must be material shapes; but since material shapes can have no relationship with each other by themselves, as they remain irreducibly contradictory with each other, only consciousness grasping them as an ensemble can playfully create the variety—i.e., the difference grounded in unity—in which space consists.

This argument against the Vaiśeṣika view of space is of course very similar to the argument against the Vaiśeṣika view of time. As seen above,[612] according to Abhinavagupta, in fact Utpaladeva's *Vivṛti* on this chapter implicitly presupposes this line of argument, at least as far as time is concerned; and although Abhinavagupta may have projected the reasoning summed up in Vācaspatimiśra's TK onto Utpaladeva's *Vivṛti*, it is possible that Utpaladeva himself had it in mind, but did not formulate it here, perhaps because he had already made this point in the first part of the treatise. In any case, in the *Vivṛti* on ĪPK 2.1.5, Utpaladeva is also very much concerned with showing that time and space cannot be explained away in a dualistic system; but rather than directly attacking the Vaiśeṣika's inferences of time and space as unitary mind-independent substances supposedly producing the various temporal and spatial determinations, as seen above, he repeatedly points out some features of space and time that could not be explained if they indeed belonged to objective entities: the fact that temporal sequence only appears in entities apprehended as being endowed with action, and that even insentient things can only seem to be affected by temporal sequence inasmuch as a conscious subject ascribes to them actions such as existing and perishing; the fact that spatial sequence only affects a given entity as long as a conscious subject considers it as part of a larger whole, or as a whole made of part, whereas an entity envisaged as a unity is not grasped as being spatially determined; or again, the fact (about to be

---

different): *yady apy asti nu* diṅ nāma kācit pūrvāparādikaḥ* | pratyayo hi na tasyāḥ syād ekasyā anupāhiteḥ || upādhiḥ pūrvatādiṣṭa iti cet tat kṛtaṃ diśā | upādhimātraṃ tu tathā vaicitryāya kathaṃ bhavet || tasmāt saṃvitprakāśo 'yaṃ mūrtyābhāsanabhāgataḥ | pūrvādidigvibhāgākhyavaicitryollekhadurmadaḥ ||* [**nu* corr. GNOLI 1999, p. 353; *na* Ed. **pūrvāparādikaḥ* corr. GNOLI 1999, p. 353; *pūrvāparādikā* Ed.]

612 Chapter 6, §1.

examined in more detail in ĪPK 2.1.6) that time—just as space—is subjectively organized in that things are present, past or future *in relation to a given conscious subject* (just as they are remote or close in relation to that subject). In what is preserved of this passage, Utpaladeva seems to have emphasized in particular that temporal determinations remain hopelessly contradictory (*viruddha*) from a dualistic point of view (since temporal sequence has as its core the contradiction between unity and multiplicity, while the past for instance is defined as both existing and nonexistent, etc.), whereas "inasmuch as [things] have as their essence manifestation, which is consciousness," these contradictions cease being irreducible, because they are transcended by the absolute consciousness that manifests them without having its nature affected by them.

### 11. The Buddhist reduction of time and its criticism: Utpaladeva's use of the *satkāryavāda* controversy

The lacunary end of the *Vivṛti* on ĪPK 2.1.5 also dealt with an objection—in all probability voiced by a Buddhist opponent—to the effect that something one can have no temporal sequence whatsoever, but rather, exists (for a single moment?) after being nonexistent, or ceases to exist (immediately?) after existing.[613] According to this opponent, there is no such thing as time, whether we conceive it as a substance or as a property inherent in objects, and even Utpaladeva's definition of it is still a way of hypostasizing a reality that is nothing beyond the particulars that come to exist and disappear:

> The [following] could be [objected]: "There is no temporal sequence whatsoever for something that is one. Rather, the [entity] that existed [in the past] no [longer] exists; and [the entity] that did not exist [previously] now exists. And what

[613] Cf. Jayaratha's remark immediately after explaining the refutation of the Vaiśeṣika view on space in TĀ 15 (TĀV, vol. IX, p. 97): *nanu tarhi bhāvasvabhāvādhikadikkālāpahnavavādibhiḥ saugatair eva jitam ity āha...* "But then the Buddhists win, [as they] deny that space and time are anything beyond the nature of [objective] entities! This is why [Abhinavagupta] adds [the following]..."

> [we] ordinarily refer to with the concepts of 'past,' 'future' and 'present' is ultimately nothing but this."[614]

The point made here brings to mind Prajñākaragupta's assertion that "what [we] call time is nothing,"[615] because temporal assertions such as "this has been done slowly" refer to nothing but the entities themselves.[616] It is also very similar to the position defended by Śāntarakṣita and Kamalaśīla while criticizing the Vaiśeṣika inference of time—namely, that time is nothing but the entities (*bhāva*) themselves. Thus Śāntarakṣita argues as follows:

> The cognition [that something is] "distant," "close" and so on is based on a mental apprehension that arises from specific conventions—it is not due to time or space: since their nature is partless and one, [they] cannot produce [the cognition] that [something] is close, distant and so on. If [you reply that they arise] due to the diversity [of entities] that are in relation with [them], then surely these two are useless![617]

Kamalaśīla's commentary makes clear that entities (*bhāva*) are enough to account for all spatial and temporal determinations, since a partless, unitary substance cannot be the cause of the differences between "close," "distant" and so on, and since it is vain to argue in response that these differences result from the entities in relation with space and time:

> For if one thus imagines [that the properties of being close, distant and so on are due to the diversity of entities that are in relation with space and time], these two, [i.e.] space and

614 ĪPVV, vol. III, p. 18: *syād etat: naikasya kaścit kālakramaḥ, api tu sa eva bhūtvā na bhavaty abhūtvā ca bhavati. ayam eva ca paramārtho bhūtabhāvivartamānavikalpair vyavahriyate.*

615 *Pramāṇavārttikālaṅkāra* (henceforth PVA), p. 112: *na kālo nāma kaścit.* For a summary of Prajñākaragupta's refutation of time as a substance see FRANCO 2011, pp. 94–96.

616 PVA, p. 112: *ciraṃ kṛtam ityādau ghaṭādikam evāvabhāsate, na tu tatrāparaḥ kālaḥ.* "In such [experiences as]: 'This has been done slowly,' [what is] manifest is nothing but [an entity] such as a pot, and in [such experiences] there is no 'time' that would be other [than this entity]."

617 $TS_Ś$ 628–629/$TS_K$ 629–630: *viśiṣṭasamayodbhūtamanaskāranibandhanam | parāparādivijñānaṃ na kālān na diśaś ca tat || niraṃśaikasvabhāvatvāt paurvāparyādyasambhavaḥ || tayoḥ sambandhibhedāc ced evaṃ tau niṣphalau nanu ||*

> time, must be useless, because the effect supposedly brought about by them is accomplished solely by the [entities] that are [allegedly] in relation with them. To explain: [you] consider that time is the cause that produces the cognitions "anterior," "posterior," [or the cognitions of the time units called] *kṣaṇa, lava, nimeṣa, kāṣṭhā, kalā, muhūrta*, day and night, fortnight and so on; and [you consider that] space is the cause of states such as "eastern," "northern," etc. Now, this whole diversity is not found in the very nature of [space and time]; on the contrary, it exists in the differentiated [entities that are supposedly in relation with them]—so the assumption of [space and time's existence] is entirely vain.[618]

Here is how Abhinavagupta sums up Utpaladeva's response:

> With [the passage beginning with] "of [something already] existing (*sataḥ*)...," [Utpaladeva] answers that this is not the case. And here one must assume that [just as the nonexistence of what exists], "the arising of what is nonexistent" [is impossible]; and this will be explained [later in the treatise,] in [verse 2.4.3 beginning with] "That which is nonexistent is nonexistent." But if there is no [independent] object whatsoever in reality, then what could be blamed for involving a contradiction? And what blame could there be for it, since its reality consists of consciousness and is free?[619]

Thus according to Abhinavagupta's testimony, Utpaladeva replied to the Buddhist reduction of time to entities by having recourse to arguments traditionally used in defence of the Sāṃkhya doctrine known as the "thesis

---

618 TSP$_{Ś}$, vol. I, pp. 259–260/TSP$_{K}$, vol. I, p. 209: *evaṃ hi kalpyamāne tau dikkālau niṣphalau syātām, tatsādhyābhimatasya kāryasya tair eva sambandhibhir niṣpāditatvāt. tathā hi kālaḥ pūrvāparakṣaṇalavanimeṣakāṣṭhākalāmuhūrtāhorātrārdhamāsādipratyayaprasavahetuḥ, dik ca pūrvottarādivyavasthāhetur iṣyate. ayaṃ ca bhedaḥ sakalas tayor na svātmani vidyate. bhedeṣu punar astīti vyarthaiva tatparikalpanā.*

619 ĪPVV, vol. III, p. 18: *naivam ity āha* ***sata*** *iti. asataś cotpattir iti mantavyam iha. etac ca yad asat tad asad ity atra vakṣyate. yadā tu na kaścid artho nāma paramārthatas tadā tu kasya virodhaparyanuyogaḥ, yat kilāsya tattvaṃ tat cidrūpaṃ svatantraṃ ceti tasyāpi kaḥ paryanuyogaḥ.*

that the effect exists [before the operation of its cause]" (*satkāryavāda*),[620] and in this connection Abhinavagupta specifically mentions ĪPK 2.4.3. The latter deserves a brief examination here, as the lacunose passage in the *Vivṛti* on 2.1.5 made a very similar point:

> That which is nonexistent is nonexistent: having an existing nature is not rationally possible for [something] nonexistent. Then again, for an [already] existing [entity], there is no point in acquiring existence. And yet, [in the world we] talk [about the relation of cause and effect].[621]

The first part of the verse, which states that something nonexistent cannot come to existence, is reminiscent of the thesis held by the followers of Vārṣagaṇya (/Vṛṣagaṇa), who is believed to have written an important Sāṃkhya treatise—the now lost *Ṣaṣṭitantra*—and to whom the *Yogācārabhūmi* ascribes the authorship of the *satkāryavāda*;[622] it also brings to mind the first reason adduced in SK 9 in favour of the *satkāryavāda*, namely, "because there is no production of the nonexistent" (*asadakaraṇāt*).[623] In the second part of the verse, Utpaladeva points out (and here he is relying on an argument put forward in many Buddhist and Naiyāyika sources)[624] that on the other hand, postulating that the effect already exists before the operation of its cause is absurd since something that already exists no longer needs to acquire existence, so that if such a thesis is adopted, the relation

---

[620] On this doctrine, its criticisms and Utpaladeva's original interpretation of it, see RATIÉ 2014b.

[621] ĪPK 2.4.3: *yad asat tad asad yuktā nāsataḥ satsvarūpatā | sato 'pi na punaḥ sattālābhenārtho 'tha cocyate ||* According to the commentaries it is to be read together with ĪPK 2.4.4a (*kāryakāraṇatā loke...*); it has been translated here accordingly.

[622] See RATIÉ 2014b, pp. 130–134, for Sanskrit quotations and bibliographical references.

[623] SK 9: *asadakaraṇād upādānagrahaṇāt sarvasambhavābhāvāt | śaktasya śakyakaraṇāt kāraṇabhāvāc ca sat kāryam ||* "Because there is no production of the nonexistent; because one grasps a material cause [adapted to the effect one wishes to produce]; because [a particular thing] cannot arise from everything; because [a cause] capable [of producing a particular effect] produces [only] what it can [produce]; and because [the effect] has the cause as its nature, the effect exists [before the operation of its cause]." Abhinavagupta quotes the beginning of the verse in a different context; see ĪPVV, vol. I, p. 171.

[624] See RATIÉ 2014b, pp. 134–136 for Sanskrit quotations and references.

of cause and effect can no longer make sense,[625] whereas we constantly make use of this relation in our daily experiences and must therefore account for it. Abhinavagupta explains that the only way to solve the problem is to suppose that the cause and its effect are in fact nothing but the same consciousness appearing at will in their forms—in which case the contradiction vanishes.

The point is important, because the Sāṃkhyas themselves have given a solution (which apparently dates back at least to Vārṣagaṇya) to this same dilemma.[626] According to them, the effect is not made to exist by the cause—since it already exists in the cause in a latent form or as a potentiality (*śakti*)—, but the cause does produce something, namely, the effect's manifestation (*abhivyakti*, *vyakti*). This *abhivyakti* theory thus claims to answer the objection that a cause is useless if the effect already exists, since the cause is required for the manifestation of the effect—and yet it does not affect in any way the very existence of the effect.

In ĪPK 2.4.3 and its *Vṛtti*, no mention is made of this Sāṃkhya notion of *abhivyakti*; in fact, however, there are many clues (including marginal annotations)[627] showing that Utpaladeva's *Vivṛti* on that verse criticized it, and that it did so by pointing out that this manifestation itself can be understood as a causal operation that is in turn problematic as regards the ontological status of its effect: if the cause merely brings about the manifestation of the effect, was this manifestation already present in a latent form before the cause's operation, or was it not? In the latter case, the *satkāryavādin* is contradicting his own position; in the former case, he is caught in an infinite

[625] ĪPV, vol. II, p. 139: *atha sann eva ghaṭas tarhi kim anyad upayācyate daṇḍacakrasūtrāt.* "If, on the other hand, the pot does exist [before the operation of its cause], then what else could [still] be asked from the [potter's] stick, wheel and thread [that are supposed to cause the pot's existence]?" Cf ĪPVV, vol. III, p. 187: *athāsya sattātmakaṃ rūpaṃ tad ayaṃ kim upayācatāṃ daṇḍādibhyaḥ.* "If, on the other hand, the nature of the [pot] is to exist, then what could it [still] ask from the [potter's] stick and so on?"

[626] See RATIÉ 2014b, pp. 136–138, for Sanskrit quotations (notably from the YD and TK) and further bibliographical references.

[627] See RATIÉ 2014b, pp. 142–143. It is of course possible that at least some of these notes are not mere glosses but quotations from the lost *Vivṛti* on chapter 2.4; to date, however, I have found no proof of this.

regress.[628] The criticism was commonplace in Naiyāyika and Buddhist sources,[629] and it is also found in Somānanda's ŚV and Utpaladeva's commentary thereon;[630] in this respect it is a pity that Utpaladeva's *Vivṛti* on chapter 2.4 is not available to date, because it must have formulated this criticism, and it also probably included an explanation of the reason why the *abhivyakti* theory is no longer problematic in the Śaiva nondualists' system. At any rate it is clear from Abhinavagupta's commentaries that the main goal of the nondualist Śaivas in appropriating the Sāṃkhya *satkāryavāda* was to show that the relationship between the Sāṃkhya notions of potentiality (*śakti*) and manifestation (*vyakti/abhivyakti*) can only make sense if they are interpreted along Śaiva nondualistic lines; thus while explaining ĪPK 1.6.6, Abhinavagupta specifies:

> Therefore it is only in the doctrine of the nonduality [of everything with] consciousness, [i.e.,] if one acknowledges that all [objective] entities consist in reflections in the mirror of consciousness, that the distinction between potentiality (*śakti*) and manifestation (*vyakti*) becomes possible, [since this distinction is then understood as] having as its real nature the acts of folding (*nimeṣaṇa*) and unfolding (*unmeṣaṇa*)

[628] See e.g. the marginal annotation in S8, f. 160b, right margin: *yat tūcyate, ghaṭaḥ sann eva kāraṇavyāpāreṇābhivyajyata iti nanu sābhivyaktiḥ saty asatī vā. satī ced vyarthaḥ kāraṇavyāpāraḥ. asatī ced asataḥ sattāpādanam aśakyaṃ śaśaviṣāṇasyeva...* "As for what [the Sāṃkhyas] say, [namely:] 'The pot, which does exist [before the operation of its cause,] is manifested through the operation of the cause,' [one must object to it:] 'But this manifestation [itself], does it exist or is it nonexistent? If it exists, the operation of the cause is useless; [but] if it is nonexistent, [the cause] cannot bring about the existence of a nonexistent [thing], just as [no cause can bring about the existence] of a hare's horn..."

[629] See RATIÉ 2014b, pp. 143–146.

[630] See ŚD 4.35–37ab and ŚDV, pp. 161–162, quoted and translated in RATIÉ 2014b, pp. 146–147.

> [through which consciousness conceals and manifests its nature[631] and] which take [infinitely] variegated [appearances] thanks to the power of consciousness—and not otherwise.[632]

The Sāṃkhya notion of *śakti* eventually boils down to the idea that *things can exist apart from their manifestation*, since for the Sāṃkhyas, it designates the unmanifested state in which the effect exists before the cause reveals it, or the state in which the effect *could be* manifested but is not; and this distinction is problematic, because the manifestation of the effect can be regarded as a reality distinct from the effect itself and therefore subjected to the alternative of existence or nonexistence, so that if the advocate of the *satkāryavāda* chooses to say that this manifestation already exists before the operation of the cause in order to save the *satkāryavāda*, he must either contradict his own principle that the effect only exists in some *unmanifest* state before the operation of the cause, or admit that the *manifestation* of the pot is already present in the clay and is nonetheless *manifest for nobody*. The problem vanishes in the idealistic system of the Pratyabhijñā, because the pot can be ever manifest as an internal form grasped by the absolute consciousness and yet remain unperceived as an external form for the various limited individuals, and because even when the pot becomes perceptible as an external form for the limited individuals, this manifestation is nothing new, but only amounts to the individuals' limited awareness of the ever manifest internal form of the pot.

It is unclear whether the missing passage of the *Vivṛti* on ĪPK 2.1.5 explicitly mentioned the Sāṃkhyas' *abhivyakti* theory or the Śaiva nondualists' reformulation of it. From Abhinavagupta's commentary, however, it is certain that Utpaladeva used this whole controversy against his Buddhist opponents so as to show that time cannot merely be defined as the fact that things come to existence and vanish: he must have pointed out there that this very fact can only makes sense in a Śaiva nondualistic metaphysical

---

[631] *nimeṣa/nimeṣaṇa* and *unmeṣa/unmeṣaṇa* are two untranslatable terms usually denoting the movement through which eyes (or flowers) close and open, and more generally, the folding or concealment of that which has the power to appear, and the disclosure or unfolding of that which has the power to hide.

[632] ĪPVV, vol. II, p. 312: *tasmāc cidadvayavāda eva saṃviddarpaṇapratibimbarūpe bhāvakalāpe 'bhyupagamyamāne śaktivyaktivibhāgaḥ saṃvicchakticitritanimeṣaṇonmeṣaṇaparamārtha upapadyate, nānyathā.*

frame, provided that a single consciousness playfully appears and disappears in these various forms, and he must have explained that if, in Abhinavagupta's words, "there is no [independent] object whatsoever in reality", the contradiction between existence and nonexistence vanishes, and temporal sequence can be accounted for as resulting from the ultimate consciousness's will to manifest certain phenomena as incompatible with each other while belonging to a single substratum.

## 12. The issue of the yogic perception of past and future events

In the missing passage, Utpaladeva then proceeded to examine the objection that yogins are often ascribed the power of directly perceiving past or future things.[633] For if they have a vivid (*sphuṭa*) apprehension of such objects, according to Utpaladeva's own definition of the three times (which specifies that what is present is simply what is vividly perceived), these vividly manifested objects should be present rather than past or future,[634] which is absurd:

> Having thus stated as a side consequence that things have manifestation as their essence, [Utpaladeva still] has to explain the subject at hand, [namely, the definition of past, present and future]; so he expounds [this] in [the passage beginning with] "But for yogins..." The word "But" suggests the [following] objection: "If being present is nothing but being vividly manifest, then, in the cognition of a yogin that immediately perceives past and future things, surely, the past and future [things] have vividness, for what could immediate

[633] On this widely—yet by no means unanimously—shared belief in classical India, and the philosophical discussions thereon, see in particular TABER 2005, pp. 54–57 and n. 23, pp. 179–181.

[634] Buddhists philosophers had to face a similar predicament. See e.g. FRANCO 2011, pp. 94–96, for a summary of the way in which Prajñākaragupta deals with this issue: according to him, a yogin sees past and future objects as present; he only determines them as being past or future upon coming out of his state of absorption, and ultimately, the status of entities as past or future only depends on the fact that ordinary people do not perceive them immediately.

> perception be otherwise? And so it follows that these [past and future things] must be present!"[635]

According to Abhinavagupta, Utpaladeva's answer consisted in saying that such a power does not belong to true yogins who have fully realized non-dualism, since for them, there can no longer be any distinction between past, present and future; as for those who claim to perceive past or future objects in some immediate way, they must still apprehend things as past or future, even though this difference may remain in them only in the shape of residual traces. They must therefore be inferior yogins who have failed to get rid of this distinction because the objects that they grasp are still associated with the yogin's body:

> [Utpaladeva now states] the grounds for rejecting this [objection] in [the passage beginning with] *anyonya-*. Here is what [it] means: What on earth could be the difference between past, [present and future] for [someone] who has completely abandoned the plane of the māyic subject, even though he is a yogin? Whereas this [difference between past, present and future] may subsist as a residual trace only for [someone] who has not abandoned the [plane of the māyic subject]. And due to the fact that [this yogin] has not completely abandoned the [plane of the māyic subject], since, as [already] explained, [for such a yogin], the phenomenon of a [past] object may exist together with the phenomenon of [the yogin's] body that is future [in that it will only occur later,] at the time of [yogic] absorption, in this case too] there can be both a phenomenon and its absence; so how could the phenomenon of that object be present [in the temporal sense] (*vartamāna*)? For [Utpaladeva] has [already] said [above] that this, [i.e. being present in the temporal sense,] is not just vividness, [but rather,] the *presence* [in the existential sense] (*sattva*) [of a vivid phenomenon]; [and] because of [his] use

[635] ĪPVV, vol. III, p. 19: *evaṃ prasaṅgād ābhāsasāratvaṃ vastūnām abhidhāya prakṛtam eva nirūpaṇīyam iti darśayati* ***yogināṃ tv*** *iti.* ***tu****śabda āśaṅkām imāṃ sūcayati: yadi sphuṭābhāsamānataiva vartamānatā tarhi yogino yad atītānāgatavastusākṣātkāri jñānaṃ tatra tayor atītānāgatayoḥ sphuṭatvaṃ tāvat. sākṣātkriyā hy anyathā kā. tataś ca tayor vartamānatāprasaṅga iti.*

> of [the word] "past" [here], [something] future too is implied.[636]

So the lost *Vivṛti* on this passage, while not questioning the alleged capacity of certain yogins to perceive past or future objects, must have explained that only inferior yogins can claim to possess such a power, which still presupposes temporal distinctions. It also argued that in such cases, even though a past object for instance may be immediately perceived by a yogin in a state of yogic absorption, he must still apprehend this object as past, however vivid his perception of it may be. The reason invoked to justify this position is not entirely clear (to me at least) from Abhinavagupta's sole commentary; the point seems to have been, however, that while perceiving a past object, a yogin must apprehend it in relation to his own body as it exists at the time of yogic absorption, and the latter is only future, i.e., nonexistent, in relation to the vividly perceived object. The yogin, while grasping the *presence* of the past object, must therefore apprehend along with it the *absence* of the manifestation of his body (at least as it will exist at the time of yogic absorption); and Utpaladeva has already distinguished the awareness of the past from that of the present by explaining that the latter only involves a presence, whereas that of the past involves both presence and absence,[637] as is the case here.

---

[636] ĪPVV, vol. III, p. 19: *atra nirākaraṇahetur* ***anyonye****ti. etad uktaṃ bhavati: yogino 'pi sarvadā parityaktamāyāpramātṛpadasya ko nāmātītādibhedaḥ. tat tv aparityajata eva saṃskāraśeṣatayā* bhavet saḥ. tadaparityāge ca dehābhāsena samādhānakālabhāvinā saha tasya grāhyābhāsasyoktasthityā saṃbhavata evābhāsānābhāsāv iti kathaṃ vartamānatā. na hi sphuṭatvam eva sā sattvam ity uktam. atītagrahaṇaṃ bhāvino 'py upalakṣaṇam.* [**saṃskāraśeṣatayā* corr.; *saṃskāra śeṣatayā* Ed.]

[637] See above, §9.

# CHAPTER 9

# The Limited Realm of Temporal and Spatial Sequence (ĪPK 2.1.6–7)

## 1. Why there is temporal sequence for limited subjects

As the *Vivṛti*'s introduction to the next verse makes clear, the point of ĪPK 2.1.6 is to highlight that temporal sequence is only manifest for the limited subject, not for the ultimate consciousness. The *Vivṛti* then underscores once more that time is not an unchanging property that would exist in things; and it points out how it cannot be admitted to be so even from the inferior, dualistic viewpoint. For the Śaiva nondualists do not believe that a property such as "being blue" can have any existence independently of a conscious subject grasping it, and Utpaladeva has already demonstrated this point at length in chapter 1.5. Abhinavagupta sums up as follows his position on this issue:

> If the fact that an object such as the blue is manifest were nothing but the fact that it has [something] such as the blue as its form, instead of being some other [kind of] identity with the [conscious] manifestation that transcends the object's form, then [we] can surmise that the blue would [exist] for all, or for no one, or that in fact [the blue] would be blue only in itself; for [if the object and its conscious manifestation were two radically distinct entities,] it would be impossible for one to rest on the other; or [rather, the blue] would be neither blue nor not blue in itself, because it could not be made to exist [as blue or not blue] without the help of the conscious manifestation! Similarly, the very fact that this [object] is manifest would [exist] for all, or for no one, or

> only in itself; or rather, it would not even exist in itself—so the [whole] world would be blind.[638]

Being blue is not an objective property that would exist independently of consciousness's activity of manifestation; it can only be one of consciousness's countless ways of manifesting itself. At the beginning of the *Vivṛti* on verse 2.1.6, however, Utpaladeva admits the dualists' point of view for the sake of argument, in order to show that even if one accepts that such properties as "being blue" or "being yellow" truly belong to objects and exist independently of the conscious entities being aware of them, time cannot be counted among them. For these properties are said to be independent from the subject because, whatever change the subject apprehending them may undergo, we usually believe (rightly or not) that they remain the same—that the patch of blue or yellow is unchanging (*avicala*) in that it keeps existing whether we see it or not, so that it could be seen by any other subject in its vicinity. But such are not the temporal properties of objects understood as "past," "present" or "future" (i.e., their A-properties, in McTaggart's terminology, which Utpaladeva's position sometimes brings to mind):[639]

> That which belongs to an object while being unchanging (*avicala*) does not depend on anything else, as [the property of] being blue; but the [temporal property of objects] is not unchanging.[640]

---

[638] ĪPV, vol. I, pp. 154–155: *artho nīlādis tasya nīlādirūpataiva yadi prakāśamānatā na punar aparā kācid arthaśarīrottīrṇā prakāśātmatā, tarhi yathā sarvān prati nīlam eva tatsambhāvanayā bhaṇyate, na kaṃcid vā prati, vastuto vā svātmany eva tan nīlaṃ parasya paraniṣṭhatānupapatteḥ, svātmani vā na nīlaṃ nānīlaṃ prakāśānugraheṇa vinā vyavasthānāyogāt. tathā prakāśamānatāpy asya sarvān prati na kaṃcid vā prati, api tu svātmany eva, svātmany api vā na syād ity andhatā jagataḥ.*

[639] MCTAGGART 1908 famously argues for the "unreality of time" on the grounds that while the properties of the B-series (in which events are ordered as "earlier than" and "later than") are unchanging, those of the A-series (in which they are ordered as being "past", "present" or "future") keep changing, so that any temporally determined object has to be past, present *and* future, whereas those properties are incompatible.

[640] ĪPVV, vol. III, p. 20: *yad avicalaṃ bhāvasya tan nānyāpekṣaṃ nīlatvam iva, na cāvicalam etat.*

This is so, as highlighted by the *Vivṛti*, because the same object that a subject existing now apprehends as *present* is *future* for the past subject who thought about it yesterday, and it is *past* for a future subject remembering it tomorrow: the time of the object is unsteady (*vicala*), it keeps changing according to the subject's perspective on it, so that it cannot be considered independent of that subject.

One could suspect that the argument is not consistent with the Śaiva nondualistic idealism inasmuch as a given present object may not be cognized at all by past or future subjects: in Utpaladeva's idealistic system, which claims to equate reality and manifestation, how could a present object be said to be future for past subjects and past for future subjects if all these subjects have no awareness of it? Abhinavagupta seems to anticipate this objection and explains that here, Utpaladeva has in mind omniscient subjects:

> [Utpaladeva mentions knowing subjects who are] "past" [and] "future"; for [gods] such as Brahmā and Viṣṇu, who are omniscient, and the Mantreśvaras, etc.,[641] talk and act (*vyavahṛ-*) [about that object] in this way [i.e., as past and future. For] the practical experience (*vyavahāra*) of this current cosmic age may flash forth as being future for [an omniscient subject who appeared in the past] such as Rāma; and [it may flash forth] as being past for those [who will appear in the future] such as Viṣṇu Kalkin.[642]

The *Vivṛti* then explains that since thus the time of an object is only established in relation to the subject's own time, it is this subject—understood

[641] Mantreśvaras are one category of experients among seven (Śiva, Mantramaheśvara, Mantreśvara, Mantra, Vijñānākala, Pralayākala and Sakala) that are often distinguished in Śaiva sources—both Saiddhāntika and nondualistic—according to the ontological level of emanation to which they belong. On this distinction, and the many variations in its details, see in particular the footnotes in TORELLA 2002, pp. 199–202, and VASUDEVA 2004, pp. 151–178. The subjects alluded to here exist on pure ontological levels (for Mantreśvaras, the *īśvaratattva*: see e.g. ĪPVV, vol. III, p. 264, quoted below, fn. 679), so that, just as gods, they are aware of all objects.

[642] ĪPVV, vol. III, p. 20: ***atītānām āgāminām*** *ity evaṃ hi sarvajñabrahmaviṣṇvādayo mantreśvarādayaś ca vyavaharanti. aidaṃyugīno vyavahāro rāmāder āgāmitayā parisphuraṇayogyaḥ kalkiviṣṇupramukhānāṃ* ca bhūtatayā...* [**kalki°* corr.; *karki°* Ed.]

as a transmigrating individual who, because (s)he misunderstands the nature of his/her own self, is temporally limited—who "must [be what] produces a temporal distinction in the various objects [of which he is aware." Time only exists in things because we project it onto them. While commenting on ĪPK 3.1.9, which explains that the limited subject is covered by the "sheaths" of "time, etc.",[643] Abhinavagupta describes as follows how time spreads from the limited subject to the objects:

> To explain: time, drawing an outline (*āsūtrayan*) of sequence in the knowing subject [and then] expanding[644] [from that subject], also flows as a consequence of this into the object of knowledge. [That is, by] becoming aware (*parāmṛśan*) of the self, [wrongly] identified with the body, as if it were endowed with sequence, in [such a form] as "I, who was thin, am becoming fat and will become fatter," [the knowing subject] also manifests the sequence consisting in past, [present and future] in the object of knowledge that [appears] in connection with this [self].[645]

Similarly, while commenting on ĪPK 2.1.6 in the ĪPV, Abhinavagupta describes this projection of temporality onto objects in the following way:

> And because, for the very reason that his immersion in subjectivity is incomplete, this knowing subject possesses temporal sequence in superabundance, he manifests temporal sequence in [objective] entities as well, [in such forms as:] "I am the [same person] who was a child, and the phenomenon of a pot too existed at the same time as that [child]."[646]

In the margins of the manuscripts at my disposal, the text of the *Vivṛti* breaks in the midst of the commentary on ĪPK 2.1.6, and the lacuna (by far

---

[643] See above, chapter 8, fn. 579.

[644] Literally, "yawning" or "gaping" in it.

[645] ĪPV, vol. II, p. 207: *tathā hi kālaḥ kramam āsūtrayan pramātari vijṛmbhamāṇas tadanusāreṇa prameye 'pi prasarati, yo 'haṃ kṛśo 'bhavaṃ sa sthūlo varte bhaviṣyāmi sthūlatara ity evam ātmānaṃ deharūpaṃ kramavantam iva parāmṛśaṃs tatsahacāriṇi prameye 'pi bhūtādirūpaṃ kramaṃ prakāśayati.*

[646] ĪPV, vol. II, pp. 19–20: *sa ca yataḥ pramātāhaṃbhāvasamāveśanād aparipūrṇād ata evodriktakālakramatvād bhāveṣv api kālakramam ābhāsayati, yo 'haṃ bālo 'bhavaṃ tatsahabhāvī ghaṭābhāso 'py abhavad iti.*

the most important in chapter 2.1) extends to the rest of the commentary on this verse as well as the next verse. Abhinavagupta's explanation is mostly too elliptical to be translated without the text on which it comments, but from the words that he quotes and some of his glosses, it seems that in the lost passage, Utpaladeva had endeavoured to explain how the limited subject projects temporality onto the objects of which (s)he is aware (for instance by ascribing a past time to objects whose manifestation only occurs in memory and is closely associated with a past manifestation of the limited subject),[647] but also why time exists for the limited subject and not for the ultimate consciousness: according to the verse, the reason for this is that the limited subject's manifestation "undergoes interruptions," and the *Vivṛti* seems to have pointed out that it is so because there can be "an absence of the phenomena of the body, etc."—that is, the very things that the limited subjects confuse with their self are not always manifest.[648] Since Utpaladeva's *Vivṛti* on this point remains unavailable for now, Abhinavagupta's very clear and synthetic ĪPV on ĪPK 2.1.6 is particularly helpful:

> ["In every object," i.e.,] in all the things whose nature is [both] one and plural, the difference resulting from the presence and absence of a phenomenon is defined as the "source" of temporal sequence—[i.e.,] the cause of its arising—for the knowing subject [who wrongly identifies with] the vital breath, intellect, body and void. [This] is possible because this [knowing subject who wrongly identifies with] the void, etc., has a manifestation that "undergoes interruptions." For manifestation is not his own nature, since [this nature, inasmuch as he confuses it with an object,] is insentient, just as the blue for instance; rather, his manifestation is a flashing forth that [actually] belongs to consciousness. So when this [knowing subject] does not have [this borrowed flashing forth]—as for instance, when [the knowing subject who identifies with] the body is asleep, or when the [knowing subject who identifies with] the void, vital breath or [the intel-

---

[647] See e.g. ĪPVV, vol. III, p. 21: ***śūnyadehādyābhāsaprākkāla*** *iti bahuvrīhiḥ.* ***smṛtim*** *iti smṛtau kevalaṃ bhāsate ity arthaḥ.* ***aviśeṣeṇeti*** *pramātṛbhāgo vārthabhāgo vā nātroddiṣṭa ity arthaḥ...*

[648] See e.g. ĪPVV, vol. III, p. 21: *ābhāsābhāvaṃ dehāder dṛḍhīkaroti* ***śarīrāder*** *iti...*

> lect] falls back [from a yogic meditative state] into the ordinary course of the saṃsāric world—, his manifestation is interrupted (*vicchidyate*). Thus [for this limited knowing subject,] there is a temporal sequence resulting from the presence and absence of [certain] phenomena, as when [we think:] "I used to consist in the phenomenon of the body of a child, [and] I now consist in the phenomenon of an adult's body."[649]

In the limited subject, manifestation is not constant but only occasional, because it is not some unchanging property that would belong to the very nature of the transmigrating individual. The latter, by identifying with an object appearing to be distinct from consciousness and devoid of its essential spontaneity, has taken on this objective nature and is therefore in itself as inert as any insentient object. Manifestation can only occur in that subject due to a flashing forth of something distinct from this insentient reality, i.e., consciousness, and in the bound soul, this flashing forth, being extrinsic, is only intermittent: when the subject who wrongly identifies with his body is asleep, or when the subjects who wrongly identify with higher realities accessible through yogic exercise, such as the intellect, vital breath and void, are no longer absorbed in their meditation, the very locus that they usually ascribe to their own subjectivity disappears, and as a result they are no longer manifest (at least in the form that they see as their very nature). And as pointed out by Abhinavagupta in the ĪPVV, that whose manifestation is nonexistent is, as already explained by Utpaladeva, either past or future—that is, subject to time:

> For manifestation is not this [knowing subject]'s own nature, since [this nature, inasmuch as he confuses it with an object,]

[649] ĪPV, vol. II, pp. 18–19: *sarveṣu vastuṣv ekānekarūpeṣu yaḥ kālātmā kramas tasya ya ākara utpattinibandhanam iti vyākhyāta ābhāsasya bhāvābhāvakṛto bhedaḥ sa śūnyaprāṇabuddhidehasya mātur* bhavatīti saṃbhāvyate yataḥ sa śūnyādir vicchinnabhāḥ. na hi tasya bhāsanaṃ svarūpaṃ nīlādivaj jaḍatvāt; api tu saṃvitsphuraṇam asya bhāsanam. tad yadāsya nāsti, yathā supte dehasya saṃsārayātrāpatitatve śūnyasya prāṇāder tadāsya bhāsanaṃ vicchidyata ity ābhāsasadbhāvāsadbhāvakṛtaḥ kālakramo ' sty atīto 'haṃ bāladehābhāsarūpo bhavāmi yuvadehābhāsarūpa iti.* [*°*dehasya mātur* conj.; ° *dehāder* P, J, L, S1, S2, SOAS, KSTS Ed., *Bhāskarī* Ed. ; cf. the verse's phrasing, and the parallel passage in ĪPVV, vol. III, p. 20: *śūnyadhīprāṇadehalakṣaṇasya pramātrīkṛtasya*.]

> is insentient, just as the blue for instance; for his manifestation is nothing but a flashing forth [actually] belonging to consciousness. For when consciousness does not flash forth as consisting in that [nature that this knowing subject believes to be his], he has no manifestation, as when [he is] in a state of stupor. Therefore, because this [knowing subject] is [then] associated with a non-manifestation, he takes a form that is past or [future]; and [this past or future form] also accrues to objective entities in relation to him.[650]

## 2. Why there is no temporal sequence for the ultimate consciousness: the lost passage on the meaning of *sakṛt*

On the other hand, according to Utpaladeva's verse, in the ultimate consciousness, manifestation is not intermittent but occurs in a way described as *sakṛt*—an important word, the meaning of which is discussed in all the commentaries on ĪPK 2.1.6. In his commentary on ĪPK 2.1.7, Abhinavagupta quotes a sentence that he takes to be Utpaladeva's source for this word and specifies that Utpaladeva alludes to this particular text in both verses with the intention of showing that he is not just stating a personal opinion of his, but a scriptural tenet:

> And thus is made clear that this is a scriptural statement, and not [just Utpaladeva's] personal opinion...[651]

The word *sakṛt* may have been originally borrowed from the *Chāndogyopaniṣad* (henceforth ChU), for the latter proclaims the following:

> For indeed, this world of *brahman* is manifest once and forever (*sakṛt*).[652]

---

[650] ĪPVV, vol. III, p. 20: *tasya hi bhāsanaṃ na svarūpaṃ nīlādivad eva jaḍatvāt, saṃvitsphuraṇam eva hy asyāpi bhāsanam, yadā hi na saṃvit tadātmatayā sphurati, tadā nāsya bhāsanaṃ mūrcchāyām iva. tatas tasyānābhāsanayogād asti bhūtādirūpatā, tadapekṣayā ca bhāvānām api.*

[651] ĪPVV, vol. III, p. 23: ... *ity āgamo 'yaṃ na svamanīṣiketi ca prathitaṃ bhavati...*

[652] ChU 8.4.2: ... *sakṛtvibhāto hy evaiṣa brahmalokaḥ.*

However, as already pointed out by Raffaele Torella,[653] Utpaladeva's use of this term probably echoes another text (that in turn may have borrowed the word from the ChU), since the sentence quoted by Abhinavagupta is not the ChU's. It runs as follows:

> This self is manifest once and forever; for this [self] that is full, in no [circumstance] can there be any absence of manifestation.[654]

Abhinavagupta's reason for quoting this is not just the word *sakṛt* that appears in ĪPK 2.1.6 and its *Vṛtti*, but also the *Vṛtti* on ĪPK 2.1.7, which paraphrases the scriptural sentence in question with "given that [for Him], in no [circumstance] can there be any absence of manifestation."[655] The origin of the sentence is unclear to me; Abhinavagupta ascribes it to a work called *Sārasvatasaṅgraha* (?),[656] and a few pages earlier, he mentions the expression *sakṛdvibhāta* as "the phrase [used] by those who know the Brahman",[657] which seems to point to a Vedāntic source[658] rather than a Śaiva

[653] TORELLA 2002, fn. 8, p. 155.

[654] ĪPVV, vol. III, p. 23: *sakṛdvibhāto 'yam ātmā pūrṇasyāsya na kvāpy aprakāśanasaṃbhava iti.*

[655] *...na kvāpy aprakāśasambhavāt...*

[656] The quotation is followed (ĪPVV, vol. III, p. 23) by the words *iti sārasvatasaṅgrahasūtraikadeśārtho...* I do not know what this *Sārasvatasaṅgraha*(*sūtra*) is. It is assumed to be "a Śaiva text" in TORELLA 2002 (ibid.) and BANSAT-BOUDON & TRIPATHI 2011 (p. 110, fn. 455). TORELLA 1999, fn. 69, pp. 40–41, wonders if this is not an alternative title for the *Śivasūtra*s (because of Kṣemarāja's testimony, on which see below, fn. 659).

[657] ĪPVV, vol. III, p. 20: ... *sakṛdvibhāta ity anayā brahmavidvācoyuktyā satatam avicchinnaprakāśaikasvabhāvaḥ paramārthapramātā nirūpitaḥ...* "With this phrase [used] by those who know the Brahman, [namely,] 'manifest once and forever,' is explained the knowing subject in the ultimate sense, whose nature is nothing but an uninterrupted manifestation..."

[658] As already noted in TORELLA 2002, fn. 8, p. 155, the compound *sakṛdvibhāta* is found not only in the ChU but also in Gauḍapāda's *Āgamaśāstra* 3.36–37 and 4.81. It is also found in works ascribed to Śaṅkara; see e.g. *Upadeśasāhasrī* 10.1ab: *dṛśirūpaṃ gaganopamaṃ paraṃ sakṛdvibhātaṃ tv ajam ekam akṣaram* | "Consisting in the act of vision, similar to the sky, supreme, manifest one and for ever, unborn, one, imperishable..." RASTOGI 1979, p. 251, mentions *sakṛdvibhāto 'yam ātmā* among "Vedic passages" without providing any reference.

one—but his disciple Kṣemarāja presents the same sentence as a *Śivasūtra* (whereas it is not found in the *Śivasūtras* as they have come down to us and as they are commented upon by Kṣemarāja himself).[659] Jayaratha, who is particularly fond of the quotation, often mentions it as a "principle" (*nyāya*) without providing any detail as to its origin.[660] In any case, from Abhinavagupta's commentary on ĪPK 2.1.6–7, it is obvious that in the lost *Vivṛti* passage, Utpaladeva discussed in detail the meaning of the word *sakṛt* (borrowed from this scriptural source, and used both in the verse and *Vṛtti*), and that this occupied much of the commentary on ĪPK 2.1.6.

Depending on the context, the term may be rendered as "once only," "together/simultaneously," or "always/eternally"; and the *Vṛtti* on ĪPK 2.1.6 already makes clear that at least the first and third senses are intended, since it specifies that there can be no temporal difference in the free subject (described in the verse as the one who is "manifested once and forever," *bhātasya... sakṛt*), "because there is no interruption (*aviccheda*) in his action of manifesting, since it is impossible to count any repetition [in this action]." According to the *Vṛtti*, the word is thus to be read as meaning "eternally" or "always" (because the ultimate consciousness is absolutely always manifest)—an understanding that is already found in Vedāntic sources such as

---

[659] *Spandasandoha*, p. 25: *asti ca śivasūtram sakṛdvibhāto 'yam ātmā pūrṇo 'sya na kvāpy aprakāśasambhava iti*. The ĪPVV quotation reads *pūrṇasyāsya* instead of *pūrṇo 'sya* and *aprakāśana°* instead of *aprakāśa°* (see below, fn. 654). Note that in the same passage, Kṣemarāja quotes another aphorism, "The universe is replete with consciousness, full of the self" (*cidghanam ātmapūrṇaṃ viśvam*), which is also quoted by Abhinavagupta immediately after commenting on the first one in his commentary on the *Vivṛti* (ĪPVV, vol. III, p. 23).

[660] See e.g. TĀV, vol. IV, pp. 397–398: *sakṛdvibhāto 'yam ātmeti nyāyenāvabhāsanakriyāvicchedābhāvāt...*, "Because, according to the principle 'This self is manifest once and forever,' there is no interruption in [his] action of manifesting...". See also ibid., vol. II, p. 133, commenting on TĀ 3.128cd–129ab (quoted above, chapter 5, fn. 336): *mātṛmeyādirūpatvena bahir ullasanty api saṃvittiḥ sakṛdvibhāto 'yam ātmeti nyāyenāvabhāsanakriyāvicchedābhāvāt kālānavacchedād uditaiva...* "Although consciousness is engaged in springing forth externally, in the form of the knowing subject, object and knowledge and so on, it is 'always arisen,' because it is not divided by time, since there is no interruption in its action of manifestation, according to the principle 'This self is manifest once and forever'..."

Śaṅkara's commentary on the ChU,[661] or the commentary on Gauḍapāda's *Āgamaśāstra* ascribed to the same author;[662] but Utpaladeva's point is that it should *also* be read as meaning "only once," since the ultimate consciousness's manifestation is devoid of anything that could be described as a repetition, i.e., as a discontinuous series of events (hence the translation "once and forever" here, which is borrowed from Raffaele Torella's translation of the *Vṛtti*).

According to Raffaele Torella, the explanation of *sakṛt* found in the ĪPVV on the missing part of the *Vivṛti* on ĪPK 2.1.6[663] is to be understood in the following way:

> Consciousness shines "once only" (this is the primary meaning of *sakṛt*), but as this shining is never interrupted the expression may also be taken in its secondary meaning of "constantly, always, once and forever...[664]

It is true that according to Abhinavagupta, the passage in question has to do with a secondary meaning or figurative use (*upacāra*) of the term.[665] Besides, as further pointed out by Raffaele Torella,[666] much earlier in the ĪPVV, Abhinavagupta clearly states that *sakṛt* may not only mean "once" but also "always":

> But by [using] the word *sakṛt*, which means "only once" or may be a synonym of "always," [Utpaladeva] has prevented

[661] See ChUBh, p. 456: *sakṛdvibhātaḥ sadā vibhātaḥ*... "[The compound] *sakṛdvibhāta* [means] 'always manifest...'"

[662] See *Āgamaśāstravivaraṇa*, p. 480: *kiṃca sakṛdvibhātaṃ sadaiva vibhātaṃ sadā bhārupam*... "Moreover, [the Brahman] is *sakṛdvibhāta*, [i.e.,] it is absolutely always manifest, it always has a manifesting nature..."

[663] ĪPVV, vol. III, pp. 21–22.

[664] TORELLA 2002, fn. 8, p. 155.

[665] See e.g. ĪPVV, vol. III, p. 21: ***tene**ty uktena nyāyenaupacārikavṛttyā sakṛcchabdārtha iti*... "[The passage beginning with] *tena* [means]: 'since the meaning of the word *sakṛt* is figurative, according to the reasoning [just] explained..."

[666] Ibid.

> [his readers] from [wrongly] supposing that [in this case there might be] any interruption.[667]

Nonetheless, the issue of the figurative use of the term, which was taken up in the missing part of the *Vivṛti*, seems to have been slightly more complex than it appears at first sight, and connected with the interpretation of a Pāṇinian rule. Thus in his *Vṛtti*, Utpaladeva insists that in the case of the consciousness whose manifestation is *sakṛt*, there is no temporal differentiation "since it is impossible to count any repetition" (*abhyāvṛttigaṇanābhāvāt*), which is a direct allusion to the following Pāṇinian aphorism:

> The *-kṛtvas* suffix [is used] for a number when one counts the repetition of an action (*kriyābhyāvṛttigaṇana*).[668]

The suffix in question ("X times") indicates how many times an action occurs (*pañcakṛtvas* = five times, etc.) when one "counts the repetition of an action." Yet Pāṇini immediately goes on to specify cases where another suffix must be used:

> The *-s* suffix [is used] after *dvi*, *tri* and *catur* [for "twice," etc.];[669] and *sakṛt* [i.e. "once" is used as a substitute] for *eka*.[670]

In the *Vivṛti*, Utpaladeva seems to have considered the objection of someone who supposes that this means that the suffix *-s* and *sakṛt* must both be used, as Pāṇini says, "when one counts the repetition of an action." This poses no problem in the case of words meaning "twice," "three times" or "four times," since the situation then clearly involves a repetition; but if both suffixes are to be used when an action is repeated, *sakṛt* cannot be properly employed to describe an action that is one (*eka*)—and therefore free of repetition. According to Abhinavagupta, the lost *Vivṛti* passage addressed this issue:

---

[667] ĪPVV, vol. II, p. 262: *sakṛcchabdena tv ekavāravācinā sadārthaparyāyena vā vicchedaśaṅkā nivāritā.*

[668] A 5.4.17: *saṃkhyāyāḥ kriyābhyāvṛttigaṇane kṛtvasuc.*

[669] A 5.4.18: *dvitricaturbhyaḥ suc.*

[670] A 5.4.19: *ekasya sakṛc ca.*

> [– Objection:] "But with respect to [something] that is one, how could repetition (*āvartana*) be intended? So how can one use a suffix that has the meaning of *kṛtvas* [i.e. that is used when counting a repetition] after the word 'one'?" [Utpaladeva] refutes this objection with [the passage] beginning with "For an [action?] that is one..." [And his answer consists in saying that in such a case] it is merely existence (*sthiti*) [and not a repetition] that is meant figuratively (*upacar-*) by [using a suffix that denotes] *āvṛtti*.[671]

Utpaladeva apparently answered the objection by explaining that indeed, according to Pāṇini, *sakṛt* is used when counting an action's *abhyāvṛtti*, a word glossed here with the terms *āvartana* or *āvṛtti*, which normally mean "repetition"; but according to him, here [*abhy*]*āvṛtti* must have a figurative sense (since, as already pointed out in Patañjali's MBh or the KV, in the case of *sakṛt* the very notion of a "repetition" mentioned in A 5.4.17 must be set aside),[672] and it can really mean nothing but "existence" (*sthiti*). According to the sequel of Abhinavagupta's rather lengthy explanation of the lost passage (at least as far as I understand it, and it remains partly obscure to me), the reason why we are thus entitled to understand *āvṛtti* in such a way is that for an action that is truly uninterrupted, *āvṛtti* can only mean the fact of "taking place all at once" (*sāhacarya*) rather than "repetition," because any attempt to distinguish various occurrences of the same act is doomed to fail, and these occurrences end up presenting themselves together—that is, as one:

---

671 ĪPVV, vol. III, p. 21: *nanv ekatve ka āvartanārtha ity ekaśabdāt kathaṃ kṛtvorthapratyayaprayoga ityāśaṅkāṃ nivārayaty* ***ekasyā*** *ityādinā. sthitir evāvṛttitvenopacaryate.*

672 See e.g. the beginning of the commentary in MBh, vol. II, p. 432: *sakṛdādeśe 'bhyāvṛttigrahaṇaṃ nivartyam. kiṃ prayojanam. punaḥ punar āvṛttir abhyāvṛttir na caikasya punaḥ punar āvṛttir bhavati.* "When one uses [the word] *sakṛt* as a substitute [for one], the understanding of [the term] *abhyāvṛtti* [mentioned in 5.4.17] must be set aside. Why? [The word] *abhyāvṛtti* [means] a repetition (*āvṛtti*) [taking place] again and again, and there can be no repetition again and again for [something that is] one." Cf. KV on A 5.4.17, vol. II, p. 561: *ekasya sakṛc cety atra kriyaiva gaṇyate, nābhyāvṛttir asambhavāt.* "In the [case described in the *sūtra*] 'And *sakṛt* [is used as a substitute] for one,' it is only action that is counted, and not repetition, because [in that case repetition] is not possible."

> And the basis for this [figurative use] is that if [one considers] an existence that is second, third, etc., for the action resting in the unity of this [existence], consisting in an *āvṛtti* is [in fact] what is called "taking place all at once" (*sāhacarya*); for as soon as one wishes to express the first existence [as a distinct occurrence] so as to negate the existence that is second, etc., the first existence flashes forth together with the second existence, etc., that one wished to negate.[673]

### 3. Why even the ultimate consciousness's objects have no temporal sequence: objectivity at the levels of Sadāśiva and Īśvara

According to the *Vṛtti* on ĪPK 2.1.6, for the subject who is thus manifest "once and forever," there is no temporal difference "either in himself or even in objects" (*ātmanīvārtheṣv api*). Abhinavagupta's commentary provides a small clue that the very end of the lost *Vivṛti* passage on this verse must have explained why even objects, inasmuch as they are objects for that consciousness, must be free of any temporal determinations. For his commentary on this verse ends thus:

> [In the sentence beginning with] "If indeed...", [Utpaladeva means]: in the state of the venerable Sadāśiva and Īśa.[674]

The ontological levels (*tattva*) called Sadāśiva and Īśvara(/Īśa) in the Śaiva tradition belong to the "pure" (*śuddha*) part of emanation (as opposed to the one, from the level of *māyā* down to that of the earth, where consciousness no longer grasps its fullness). Given that in them consciousness is aware of all the *objects* of the universe, these levels can be considered an inferior (*apara*) kind of self-realization (in contrast with the level called Śivatattva); yet they also belong to the superior (*para*) aspect of reality inasmuch as in them, consciousness apprehends all objects as being nothing

---

673 ĪPVV, vol. III, p. 21: *nimittaṃ cātra dvitīyatṛtīyādau sthitau tadekabhāvaviśrāntakriyāyā yad āvṛttirūpatvam asti tat sāhacaryaṃ nāma. dvitīyādikāṃ hi sthitiṃ niṣeddhuṃ yāvat tām ādyāṃ sthitiṃ vivakṣati* tāvat sā prathamā sthitir dvitīyādisthitibhir niṣiṣitsitābhiḥ saha sphurati.* [**vivakṣati* corr.; *vivakṣyati* Ed.]

674 ĪPVV, vol. III, p. 22: ***yadi nāme****ti śrīsadāśiveśadaśāyām.*

but subjective aspects of itself.[675] In the recently recovered *Vivṛti* on the end of chapter 1.8, Utpaladeva describes as follows this level of reality:

> When this same subjectivity,[676] being full of the manifestation of ontological levels and worlds that are separated [from it insofar as they appear] in an objective form, unfolds [in the form] "I am this," then [there is purity], because the nature [of consciousness] remains unconcealed as before, since even though this [state] involves the manifestation of an alteration [of reality] due to the separation of objectivity [that appears at that stage], it is [still] full of the unity of subjectivity, freedom, will and so on, which have not disappeared. [Yet] even though it is pure, even in this state of Īśvara there is impurity inasmuch as, by preparing objects for the confusion of *māyā* that is full of duality,[677] it is the cause of impurity [...]. But [this state] is not impure in itself (*svayam*); for [it is] not [possible] to ascribe to one [and the same entity] the properties of purity and impurity, which are contradictory.[678]

The two levels of Sadāśiva and Īśvara are only distinguished insofar as in Sadāśiva, the process through which consciousness manifests itself in the form of objects has barely begun and is more pronounced in Īśvaratattva,

---

675 See ĪPK 3.1.5: *atrāparatvaṃ bhāvānām anātmatvena bhāsanāt* | *paratāhantayācchādāt parāparadaśā hi sā* || "Here there is an inferior state, because [objective] entities are manifested as not being the self; [and yet] it is a superior state since [these objective entities] are encompassed by subjectivity—for this is the state that is both superior and inferior." According to ĪPV, vol. II, p. 199 and ĪPVV, vol. III, p. 274, the word "here" (*atra*) in the verse refers to the "two ontological levels" (*tattvadvaya*) of Sadāśiva and Īśvara (cf. *Bhāskarī*, vol. II, p. 227: *tattvadvaya iti sadāśivarūpa īśvararūpe cety arthaḥ*).

676 That is to say, the subjectivity that is already found at the level of Śivatattva.

677 Rather than "by drawing an outline of objects through the confusion of *māyā* that is full of duality," as initially translated in RATIÉ 2017a, p. 183.

678 *Vivṛti* on ĪPK 1.8.11 (edited in RATIÉ 2017a, p. 176): ***saivā****hantā yadedantāvacchinnatattvabhuvanāvabhāsamayy aham idam iti* prathate tadedantāvicchedavikārāvabhāse 'py atrābhraṣṭāhantāsvātantryecchādinaikyamayatvāt pūrvavat svabhāvātirodhānāc* ***chuddhatve'pi*** *dvaitamayamāyāvimohaviṣayoparacanād* ***aśuddhihetutvād*** *īśvaradaśāyām apy aśuddhis... na tu svayam aśuddhatā, na hy ekatra viruddhāśuddhiśuddhidharmādhyāsaḥ*. [**iti* conj. ; om. S12, J11, RATIÉ 2017a.]

the differentiation between subject and object (and between the various objects) being fainter in Sadāśiva. Thus while explaining ĪPK 3.1.2,[679] which he takes to be a depiction of the Sadāśiva and Īśvara levels, Abhinavagupta specifies:

> Among these [two levels, here is what defines the Sadāśiva one]. For the category of pure conscious beings called Mantramaheśvaras,[680] the totality of [objective] entities is similar to that of the [objective] entities that may be grasped by the internal organs of [ordinary subjects] such as ourselves at the [time] of [their] first emission [out of subjectivity, when we start imagining them]; it is comparable to a barely sketched picture, [it is still] dim so to speak. [It is] also [similar to the totality of objective entities that may be grasped by our internal organs] at the time of [their] resorption [into subjectivity; i.e.,] just as [the imaginary objects that we grasp when they are] about to be disappear [within subjectivity,] it is manifest as a [mere] reflection [appearing on the mirror of consciousness, and not as an ontologically independent entity]. The ontological level of Sadāśiva—[i.e.], the ontological realm of the specific [level of] consciousness [called Sadāśiva—occurs] when this totality of [objective] entities has its manifestation unfolded thus for this category of conscious beings.[681] In contrast, the ontological level of Īśvara is the state [of consciousness corresponding to the objective entities'] maintenance; [it occurs] when [the totality of objective entities is manifest] for [the category of conscious beings] consisting in the Mantreśvaras and so on[682]—[i.e., when the

[679] ĪPK 3.1.2: *kiṃtv āntaradeśodrekāt sādākhyaṃ tattvam āditaḥ | bahirbhāvaparatve tu parataḥ pārameśvaram* || "Nonetheless, at the beginning, due to the preeminence of internality, the ontological level of Sadākhya [occurs]; but then, when there is a preeminence of externality, the [ontological level] of Parameśvara [occurs]."

[680] See above, fn. 641.

[681] Cf. the parallel passage in ĪPV, vol. II, pp. 192–193 (quoted in RATIÉ 2011a, p. 699, fn. 140) and the end of the *Vivṛti* on ĪPK 2.1.8 (see below), which describes objectivity in Sadāśiva'state as a "mere reflection" (*chāyāmātra*).

[682] See above, fn. 641.

> totality of objective entities] is similar to [the one] grasped by the external organs [and] comparable to a fully [drawn] picture.[683]

That Utpaladeva mentioned these two levels in the lost portion of the *Vivṛti* on ĪPK 2.1.6 is not surprising, because it is at these levels that objectivity (including the most familiar objects of everyday experience) is grasped by the ultimate consciousness as being one with it. And according to Abhinavagupta's explanation of ĪPK 2.1.6, here is the reason why objects of knowledge are devoid of temporal determinations when apprehended in such a way:

> But there is no temporal sequence in the self of the knowing subject who consists in [pure] consciousness [and] whose manifestation is uninterrupted, in accordance with the phrase "manifest once and forever" [used in the verse]; nor is there [any temporal sequence] in all the [objective] entities that are objects of knowledge in relation to this [pure consciousness]—for the [totality of objects] is manifest in it in an undifferentiated state (*abhedena*).[684]

What is this "undifferentiated state"? It cannot be a pure absence of difference, otherwise there could not even be any awareness of objectivity (which presupposes the distinction between subject and object). Nor does it mean, it seems, that the differences that enable different objects to be distinguished from each other are not found in this state; for according to Abhinavagupta, at the levels of Sadāśiva and Īśvara, *all the objects of the universe are already present*, even though there, the restrictions (*niyama*) created by Śiva's "power of necessity" (*niyatiśakti*)—according to which a given object has a specific set of properties and is incompatible with speci-

[683] ĪPVV, vol. III, p. 264: *tatra śuddhacaitanyavargasya mantramaheśvarākhyasya yad bhāvacakram asmadādyantaḥkaraṇavedyabhāvarāśisadṛśaṃ dhyāmalaprāyam unmīlitamātracitrakalpaṃ prathamasṛṣṭau, saṃhāre ca dhvaṃsonmukham iva pratibimbatayā bhāti, tatra bhāvacakre tasya caitanyavargasya tathāprathane nāma yac cidviśeṣasāmānyaṃ tat sadāśivatattvam. mantreśvarādirūpasya tu bahiṣkaraṇavedyasadṛśi pūrṇacitrapratime sthityavastheśvaratattvam.*

[684] ĪPV, vol. II, p. 20: *na tu yaḥ sakṛd vibhāta ity anayā vācoyuktyāvicchinnabhāsanaḥ pramātā saṃvidrūpas tasya svātmani kālakramo nāpi tadapekṣayā vedye bhāvajāte, tad dhi tatrābhedena bhātīti.*

fic phenomena—do not apply. Thus in the ĪPVV, an objector argues as follows that since there can be no restriction whatsoever within the Lord, the objects cannot be present at the pure levels of consciousness:

> But in aphorism [2.3.7,[685] which begins with] *pṛthagdīpa-*, [Utpaladeva] has demonstrated that [there can be] a combination [of phenomena forming a particular entity only in the case] of phenomena that are not contradictory. And contradiction as well as the lack thereof [only exist] for knowing subjects who are bound (*paśupramātṛ*), in relation to the power of necessity; but in the Lord, there [can] be no restriction whatsoever according to contradiction and the lack thereof, and therefore, given that there is no [such] restriction [in the Lord, in Him] why would the phenomenon "having horns" not combine with the phenomenon "having as [one's] aspect a large basis and a hollow" [that usually belongs to a pot]? And so these [particular entities] are fit for us [transmigrating subjects, but] how could there be any manifestation of these particular [entities] in the Lord?[686]

In response to this objection, Abhinavagupta makes clear that in fact all particular objects must be manifest in the absolute consciousness, even though there they are grasped as being free of the restrictions that apply in the world of transmigrating subjects:

> In the Lord, [the combination of phenomena constituting this or that particular object] is not restricted [by the power of necessity], and this is why in relation to the Lord, even a pot has horns, even a frog is resplendent with a mass of matted hair! [And each of them] is manifest as having a form that is

---

[685] See below, chapter 7, fn. 438.

[686] In ĪPVV, vol. III, pp. 368–369: *nanu pṛthagdīpasūtre 'viruddhābhāsānāṃ melanam upapāditam. virodhāvirodhau ca niyatiśaktyapekṣayā paśupramātṝn prati, na tu bhagavati ko 'pi virodhāvirodhaniyamaḥ; tataś ca niyamābhāve viṣāṇitvābhāsasya pṛtubudhnodarākārābhāsenāpi kiṃ na miśratā? tataś cāsmaducitā ete kathaṃ bhagavati svalakṣaṇābhāsaḥ.* See RATIÉ 2011a, p. 703, fn. 146.

> immediately apprehended [rather than conceptually constructed].[687]

The pot as we encounter it in our everyday lives appears at these levels, but not according to the "exclusion from the other" (*anyāpoha*[*na*]) that usually determines the existence of objects in the *vyavahāra*: in Sadāśiva and Īśvara, the pot and the non-pot are not incompatible because their differences can all exist together—and if there is no such incompatibility, there can be no sequence, either spatial or temporal.

### 4. Spatial sequence too only exists for limited subjects (ĪPK 2.1.7)

From Abhinavagupta's commentaries, it seems that the lost *Vivṛti* on the next verse was brief and that a part of it simply reminded the reader of the definition of spatial sequence already given in ĪPK 2.1.4–5:

> So what is the cause of this spatial sequence? [Utpaladeva] answers that it has as its cause the "difference"—[viz., here,] the otherness—brought about by the presence and absence of a phenomenon such as the blue. [These presence and absence, which take the forms]: "the blue is manifest" and "[the blue] is not manifest," are brought about "simultaneously"—[i.e.,] at the same time—by the power of consciousness, the nature of which has [already] been described [and] which is characterized by its agency [in producing] variegated phenomena.[688]

While doing this, the *Vivṛti* must also have made clear that just as temporal sequence, spatial sequence exists only for the limited subject, who apprehends him-/herself as spatially determined, and who also projects this determination onto the objects of which (s)he is aware:

> In the same way, spatial sequence too is manifest for the [knowing subject] "whose self is limited" [according to the verse, i.e.,] for the [subject] whose nature is circumscribed

---

[687] ĪPVV, vol. III, p. 369: *bhagavati na niyataṃ tata eveśvarāpekṣayā ghaṭo 'pi viṣāṇī, maṇḍūko 'pi jaṭābhārabbhāsvaraḥ sākṣātkārarūpa evāvabhāti...*

[688] ĪPVV, vol. III, p. 23: *sa tarhi digdeśakramaḥ kiṃnimittakaḥ. āha citrābhāsakāritvalakṣaṇayoktarūpayā saṃvicchaktyā* ***yugapat*** *samakālam upapāditau yāv ābhāsasya nīlādeḥ sadbhāvāsadbhāvau nīlaṃ bhāti na bhāti ceti, tābhyām ānīto yo* ***bhedo*** *'nyatvam, tannimitāko 'sau.*

> [and] who [identifies with the objects] beginning with the void and ending with the body. [It appears to this subject] in himself, [i.e.,] in [such] a form [as] "I stand here," but also in [objective] entities, in relation to [him]self, in [such] a form [as]: "this, which is to a limited extent in contact with me, is close; and that which is not is far."[689]

Utpaladeva must also have pointed out there, as Abhinavagupta does in his commentaries, that the ultimate consciousness remains for its part unaffected by spatial differences, and that further, in it objective entities too are free of all spatial sequence, because they are apprehended subjectively, as forms of the unlimited, absolutely full consciousness:

> Since for the unlimited knowing subject, [objective] entities are manifest as being himself, [as being] full, [i.e.,] as having as their nature nothing but the conscious manifestation, it is as being equivalent to his own self, [i.e.] as being unlimited, as being devoid of any spatial sequence, that they are manifest in himself.[690] So in relation to His pure self, the Lord has no spatial sequence; nor do the [objective] entities [have any spatial sequence] in relation to the Lord. A place (*deśa*) is [simply] the specific form of a [limited] thing such as a pot, and the same [goes] for the body, vital breath, void and [intellect with which limited subjects wrongly identify]; therefore spatial location (*avasthāna*) is [merely] due to the mutual exclusion of places [thus defined], [and] so the knowing subject who [identifies with] the body, etc., sees all things—

---

[689] ĪPV, vol. I, p. 20: *evaṃ deśakramo 'pi mitātmanaḥ paricchinnasvarūpasya śūnyāder dehāntasya svātmani bhātīha tiṣṭhāmīti, svāpekṣayā ca bhāveṣv api yan mama saṃyogapārimityena vartate tad antikam itarad dūram iti.*

[690] This can also be read as saying that objective entities are manifested "as being full of his own self" (*svātmanā pūrṇāḥ*), but cf. the gloss in ĪPV, vol. I, pp. 20–21: *amitasya svarūpeyattāśūnyasya tu saṃvittattvasya bhāvāḥ svātmanāhaṃbhāvena yato bhānti tataḥ pūrṇā aparicchinnasvarūpeyattākāḥ.* "But for the true nature of consciousness that is 'unlimited' [according to the verse—i.e.,] that is free of limitations in its nature—, since [objective] entities are manifest as being itself, [i.e.] subjectively, [they] are full, [i.e.,] they are such that their nature is not circumscribed."

i.e. the pot, etc.—as having different places with respect to himself, and [also] in relation to each other.[691]

[691] ĪPVV, vol. III, p. 22: *svātmanā pūrṇā yataḥ prakāśamātrasvabhāvā aparimitasya pramātur bhāvā bhānti, tataḥ svātmatulyā eva, amitā eva, deśakramavihīnā eva bhānty ātmanīti śuddhasvātmāpekṣayā neśvarasya deśakramo, nāpīśvarāpekṣayā bhāvānām. ghaṭādeḥ padārthasya svaṃ rūpaṃ deśaḥ, śarīraprāṇaśūnyāder evam; tataḥ parasparadeśaparihāreṇāvasthānam iti sa śarīrādiḥ pramātā ghaṭādiṃ padārthavargaṃ svataḥ parasparataś ca bhinnadeśaṃ paśyati.*

# CHAPTER 10

## Space, Time and the Ultimate Consciousness's Creative Power (ĪPK 2.1.8)

Utpaladeva has shown, in verses 6 and 7, that spatial and temporal sequences only occur in the realm of limited subjects and objects; but by doing so, hasn't he eliminated the very possibility for the ultimate consciousness of being active? According to Abhinavagupta, it is this objection that the last verse of the chapter is meant to address:

> But [if it is] so, as a consequence there can be no action at all in the Lord, since [in the Lord] there is no association with temporal sequence, [and the latter] pervades the nature of action![692]

The last verse argues that this is not the case, because sequence in the limited realm is in fact nothing but a manifestation of the Lord's own nonsequential action:

> In the [next] verse, while putting to rest this objection, and while showing that both [the spatial and temporal] forms of sequence are unfoldings of the very power of action, [Utpaladeva] also points out the usefulness of this explanation of time as regards the Lord's recognition.[693]

---

[692] ĪPVV, vol. III, p. 24: *nanv evaṃ bhagavati nāsty eva kriyety āyātaṃ kriyāsvarūpavyāpakakālakramayogābhāvāt.*

[693] ĪPVV, vol. III, p. 24: *ity āśaṅkāṃ śamayann ubhayam api idaṃ kramarūpaṃ kriyāśakter eva vijṛmbhitam iti ca darśayann asya kālaprakaraṇasya īśvarapratyabhijñopayogam api darśayati sūtreṇa.*

According to Abhinavagupta, Utpaladeva thus underscores how this whole analysis of temporal sequence is useful in bringing about the Lord's recognition, as already claimed earlier in the *Vivṛti*:[694] with this final verse, the author of the Pratyabhijñā treatise reminds his readers that time can only be explained as the ultimate consciousness's will. And true to his nondualistic dialectic, he endeavours to show that the two domains of sequentiality and nonsequentiality, which he has so far carefully distinguished, are ultimately grounded in the same unitary reality, as Abhinavagupta points out at the end of his summary of chapter 2.1:

> Then with two verses [i.e. 2.1.6 and 2.1.7, Utpaladeva] distinguishes the realms of sequentiality and non-sequentiality; and in the [last] verse, he explains that although this distinction exists, in reality both rest on one single [reality].[695]

### 1. Equating sequential manifestation with the nonsequential action of consciousness

Unfortunately, the lacuna that deprives us of the end of the *Vivṛti* on ĪPK 2.1.6 and the entire *Vivṛti* on ĪPK 2.1.7 extends to the beginning of the *Vivṛti* on ĪPK 2.1.8. The gist of this beginning, however, is fairly obvious from Abhinavagupta's explanations. At the outset of his commentary on ĪPK 2.1.8 in the ĪPVV, Abhinavagupta thus remarks that the last verse spells out a point that had not been made yet (or had been left implicit) in the rest of the chapter:

> The true nature of spatial and temporal sequence is not entirely [covered by] what [has been said] thus far; rather, something else remains to be said in this respect. This is what is conveyed [in the verse with the expression] "in this way" [when it says "the very fact that the difference in the limited knowing subjects and objects of knowledge is made manifest in this way..." That is to say,] all the knowing subjects and objects are manifested [as] endowed with spatial and temporal sequence, [and] therefore [as being] differentiated;

[694] See below, chapter 11, the *Vivṛti*'s introduction to ĪPK 2.1.3 and fn. 20.

[695] ĪPV, vol. II, p. 2: *tataḥ ślokadvayena sakramatvākramatvayor viṣayavibhāgaḥ; viṣayavibhāge ca sati vastuta ekatraiva tayor viṣrāntir iti ślokena nirūpyate.*

> [and] it is the very fact of this manifestation that *is* the Lord's power of creation, which consists in His power of action.[696]

In the sequel of his explanation, Abhinavagupta tells us that the *Vivṛti* itself introduced the last verse with this point:

> It is with this intention in mind that [Utpaladeva] introduces [the verse] with [the sentence beginning with the words] "Therefore in this regard." [That is to say], in this regard, something more is added [with this verse] to what has [already] been explained; by [pointing this out, Utpaladeva] explains [the meaning of the word] "nonetheless" [in the verse].[697]

Apart from the "nonetheless" with which it begins, ĪPK 2.1.8 rings like a concluding statement, and by thus pointing out that the idea put forward here is a novelty in the chapter, Utpaladeva and Abhinavagupta both certainly intended to show that the verse does not incur the reproach of redundancy (*paunaruktya*) because it is not a mere summary of what has been established thus far. One might doubt whether it is really the case inasmuch as in ĪPK 2.1.4 and its *Vivṛti*, Utpaladeva has already shown that sequence must be due to the Lord's "power of time," and the latter is already defined there and in the following verse as the Lord's action (*kriyā*) of manifesting things as being varied. Besides, Utpaladeva has already pointed out, in ĪPK 2.1.6–7, that sequence only belongs to the limited realm, and that in the ultimate consciousness, even things that are spatially and temporally determined are apprehended as free of any sequence. The new verse can nonetheless be seen as going one step further inasmuch as it claims that the manifestation of the sequential world is not just the *result* of the ultimate consciousness's nonsequential action, but *is* this action itself: Utpaladeva is now equating the spatial and temporal unfolding of the universe with the nonsequential action of the ultimate consciousness—and according to

---

[696] ĪPVV, vol. III, p. 24: *naitāvad deśakālakramatattvam, api tv anyad apy atra vaktavyam asti. tad ucyate tatheti deśakālakramavāṃs tata eva bhinnaḥ pramātṛprameyavargo 'vabhāsyate, etat yad avabhāsanam, tad bhagavata eva nirmāṇasāmarthyaṃ kriyāśaktirūpam.*

[697] ĪPVV, vol. III, p. 25: *anenāśayenāvatārayati* ***tad atre****ty atroktaṃ tad adhikam ucyata iti kintv iti vyākhyātam.*

Abhinavagupta's commentaries on ĪPK 2.1.8, what enables Utpaladeva to do this is his definition of will (*icchā*) as the core of action.[698]

## 2. The allusion to aesthetic wonder in the lost beginning of the *Vivṛti* on ĪPK 2.1.8

In the missing part of the *Vivṛti*, Utpaladeva must have then proceeded to explain the words *evaṃ viduṣaḥ* in the verse, apparently by specifying that the ultimate consciousness "knows thus" in the sense already made clear in the previous verse, which states that for the unlimited subject, all objects are manifested "as full" (*pūrṇa*), i.e., as being as unlimited as itself—an idea that the *Vṛtti* on ĪPK 2.1.8 explicitly echoes by saying that the Lord "is manifest thus as being full." The *Vivṛti* on ĪPK 2.1.8 must have in turn specified that this fullness is inseparable of a sense of aesthetic wonder (*camatkāra/camatkṛti*) without which it would remain a mere word:

> [Utpaladeva] explains [the verse's phrase "the Lord, even though He] knows [everything] thus" [with the *Vivṛti* passage] ending with [the words] *sthitaiva*; for the condition beginning with the venerable Sadāśiva consists in the power of knowledge.[699] "But in that" [means]: in that [state of] fullness—the implicit meaning is that otherwise, this fullness would have a purely nominal existence. This [very] fact of "being the Highest Lord" *is* "the power" [of creation] of [Him] who possesses wonder (*camatkṛti*) due to [His] being

[698] See below, §3. Since the very beginning of the *Vivṛti* is lacking, it is impossible to determine whether this idea, so important in both of Abhinavagupta's commentaries, was already explicitly stated in Utpaladeva's detailed explanation; at any rate the word *icchā* does not appear at all in the verse, *Vṛtti* and remaining *Vivṛti*.

[699] On the Sadāśiva level see above, chapter 9, §3.

> full:[700] in this [*Vivṛti*] sentence is [thus provided] the [correct] way of construing the [initial] part of the *Vṛtti* [on this verse].[701]

This notion of aesthetic wonder plays a central part in the Pratyabhijñā system: Utpaladeva—who, as already pointed out by Raniero Gnoli, is probably the first Indian philosopher to use the terms *camatkāra/camatkṛti* in a technical sense[702]—describes this rapturous awareness as the heart of all sentiency when he explains, in his *Vṛtti* on the famous verse 1.5.11 defining *vimarśa*,[703] that without the latter, the conscious manifestation (*prakāśa*) would be devoid of the aesthetic wonder that constitutes its core:

> Realization (*pratyavamarśa*) is the fundamental essence of conscious manifestation: without it, this [manifestation], although endowed with the differentiated aspects of [this or that] object, would only have the limpidity [of a mirror], but not sentiency, because [it] would be devoid of aesthetic wonder.[704]

---

[700] As far as I can see, the *Vivṛti* as it is preserved starts in the midst of this sentence, and I am not sure whether the words *nirbharatayā camatkṛtimato yā* constitute an actual quotation of its missing part, or (as seems most probable) a series of words selectively quoted from it so as to emphasize its overall structure (as is the case of the immediately following words in the commentary, which can be found scattered in the preserved part of Utpaladeva's sentence), or even a mere paraphrase.

[701] ĪPVV, vol. III, p. 25: *evaṃ viduṣa iti vyācaṣṭe* ***sthitaive****tyantena. jñānaśaktirūpā hi śrīsadāśivādidaśā.* ***tatra tv*** *iti pūrṇatāyām, anyathā hi nāmamātreṇa pūrṇatā sā bhaved iti bhāvaḥ. nirbharatayā camatkṛtimato yā* ***parameśvarataiṣā śaktir*** *iti vākyamadhye vṛttikhaṇḍayojanā.*

[702] See GNOLI 1985, pp. xlv–xlvi, which mentions ŚDV on ŚD 1.8 and ŚSĀ (Chowkhamba Ed.), p. 41 (= 5.15). To these references, CUNEO 2016 (pp. 31–32, fn. 7) adds the *Vṛtti* on ĪPK 1.5.11, 4.1 and 4.6; ŚSĀ 13.14; and ŚDV on ŚD 1.38. One should keep in mind, however, that this list cannot be exhaustive (as is hoped in CUNEO 2016, ibid.), and is probably far from being so even if one adds this lost *Vivṛti* passage, because obviously Utpaladeva dealt at length with the notion elsewhere in his *Vivṛti*; in this regard, the *Vivṛti* on ĪPK 1.5.11, which remains unavailable to date, must have been particularly important.

[703] See above, chapter 3, fn. 280.

[704] *Vṛtti*, p. 22: *prakāśasya mukhya ātmā pratyavamarśaḥ, taṃ vinārthabheditākārasyāpy asya svacchatāmātraṃ na tv ajāḍyaṃ camatkṛter abhāvāt.*

This idea recurs here, at the end of chapter 2.1, because, as Abhinavagupta makes clear while commenting upon Utpaladeva's lost *Vivṛti* on ĪPK 1.5.11, this amazed awareness of beauty is nothing but consciousness's delighted apprehension of its own fullness:

> But why does the *Vṛtti*, instead of saying "[the conscious manifestation] would be insentient, because [it] would be devoid of realization," [says that it would be insentient] "because [it] would be devoid of aesthetic wonder"? For aesthetic wonder, which is the action of [someone] who is in the process of enjoying, is [what is] called "bliss," which consists in obtaining enjoyment. Having anticipated this [question, Utpaladeva] says "And this [bliss] is precisely..." [That is to say: this bliss is precisely the realization] that has [just] been said to be the [very] life of conscious manifestation. This is what [Utpaladeva] means [here]: what is called "bliss" is nothing but the manifestation of "one's own nature"—[that is to say,] one's own self, one's own nature that is entirely full (*paripūrṇa*)—, inasmuch as it is becoming fully realized.[705]

In his *Vivṛti* on verse 2.1.8, after making clear that "thus" in "[the Lord] knows thus" means that He grasps everything—including entities spatially and temporally determined—as His own full nature, Utpaladeva must therefore have pointed out that in the Lord, the awareness of sequential manifestation must be bliss—the aesthetic relish of one's absolutely full nature.

### 3. The gist of the verse according to Abhinavagupta: will (*icchā*) as the core of action

How can Utpaladeva thus claim that the manifestation of sequence is not simply the result of the Lord's nonsequential power of action, but this power itself? Abhinavagupta, in both of his commentaries, explains that it is so

[705] ĪPVV, vol. II, p. 177: *nanu vimarśābhāvāj jaḍatā syād iti vaktavye camatkṛter abhāvād iti kathaṃ vṛttiḥ. camatkṛtir hi bhuñjānasya yā kriyā bhogasamāpattimaya ānandaḥ sa ucyata ity āśaṅkyāha* ***sa eva ce****ti yaḥ prakāśasya prāṇatvenoktaḥ. etad uktam bhavati: svarūpasya svātmanaḥ paripūrṇanijasvabhāvasya*prakāśanam eva parāmarśamayatāṃ dadhad ānanda ity ucyate.* [**paripūrṇanijasvabhāvasya* conj.; *paripūrṇanijasvabhāva°* Ed.]

because the essence of action is will (*icchā*)—and will, the nature of which is fundamentally undivided,[706] is the nonsequential source from which all sequential actions unfold. The word *icchā* appears neither in the verse, nor in the *Vṛtti* and *Vivṛti* thereon (at least in the current form of the latter, the first sentences of which are still lacking to date); yet Abhinavagupta explains in both of his commentaries that this is an anticipation of Utpaladeva's equation of action and will at the very end of the *Kriyādhikāra*, where Utpaladeva concludes:

> Thus causality, agency, action are nothing but such a will (*icchā*) belonging to whom wishes to exist (*tiṣṭhāsu*) in this way in the form of the world, as the phenomena of the pot, cloth and so on.[707]

The *Vṛtti* on that verse explicitly equates the power of action with this free will:

> It is the will to exist in the form of a universe—[a will] belonging to that which consists in consciousness [and] is free—that *is* causality with respect to the universe; [i.e., it is this will that is] the power of action that consists in agency.[708]

Abhinavagupta believes that this idea is the very basis of Utpaladeva's reasoning in ĪPK 2.1.8, which he presents as follows in the ĪPV:

> In [the system taught in] this [treatise],[709] action is actually nothing but the Highest Lord's will, the nature of which is an unimpeded freedom, which is full of an uninterrupted

---

[706] On the unity experienced in will and the Śaiva nondualists' contention that in any creative urge, objects are experienced as merged in subjectivity, i.e., as one with it, see above, chapter 3, §3 (particularly fn. 285, which quotes ĪPK 1.5.10).

[707] ĪPK 2.4.21: *itthaṃ tathā ghaṭaphaṭādyābhāsajagadātmanā | tiṣṭhāso evam icchaiva hetutā kartṛtā kriyā ||*

[708] *Vṛtti*, p. 61: *cidvapuṣaḥ svatantrasya viśvātmanā sthātum icchaiva jagat prati kāraṇatā kartṛtārūpā saiva kriyāśaktiḥ.*

[709] Cf. *Bhāskarī*, vol. II, p. 24: *iha—asmin pratyabhijñāśāstre.*

self-realization, [and] which consists in a perfect independence.[710] This will be summed up at the end of this [second] part [of the treatise devoted to action, with verse 2.4.21, which states] "Thus causality, agency, action are nothing but such a will..." And for [limited subjects] too, such as Caitra or Maitra, it is this same inner will—[which takes in their case such a form as] "I am going to cook"—that is [their] action; and [since] thus [their action is this single will taking the form] "I am going to cook," it is not interrupted for this [limited subject[711] either], despite the relationship with numerous [different] movements such as placing [a pot] on the fire, etc. Rather, it is precisely that which consists in will [and takes the form] "I am going to cook" that is manifest in the form of such [various] movements; yet in fact, there is no sequence whatsoever in this [inner will]. In the same way, for the Lord too, in the realization consisting in will—the true nature of which is nothing but "I," and which takes such forms as "I am going to exert my power," "I am going to be manifest," "I am going to flash forth," "I am going to pulsate" [or] "I am going to realize"—, there is no sequence whatsoever. And it is precisely this [realization] that is expressed in the sentence "let sequence arise within the diversity of [limited] knowing subjects and objects of knowledge"; so in that [will] too, there is no sequence whatsoever.[712]

---

[710] Lit., it consists in "not being turned towards any other"/"not expecting [anything] from anyone else" (*ananyonmukhatā*); on this perfect autonomy of consciousness (which also entails its being fundamentally free of intentionality in the phenomenological sense of the term—or rather, which means that any intentional act of consciousness is grounded in a non-intentional awareness), see RATIÉ 2011a, pp. 503–504, and 529–543.

[711] Cf *Bhāskarī*, vol. II, p. 25: *asya—caitramaitrādeḥ.*

[712] ĪPV, vol. II, pp. 22–23: *iha tattvataḥ parameśvarasyāpratihatasvātantryarūpāvicchinnasvātmavimarśamayy ananyonmukhatārūpecchaiva kriyety upasaṃhariṣyata adhikārānte, evam icchaiva hetutā kartṛtā kriyeti. caitramaitrāder api pacāmīti yaivāntar icchā saiva kriyā, tathā cādhiśrayaṇādibahutaraspandanasaṃbandhe 'pi pacāmīti nāsya vicchidyate. yat tu pacāmītīcchārūpaṃ tad eva tathāspandanātmatayā bhāti, tatra tu na kaścit kramas tattvataḥ. evam īśvarasyāpi, īśe bhāse sphurāmi ghūrṇe pratyavamṛśāmīty evaṃrūpaṃ yad icchātmakaṃ vimarśanam*

Similarly, in the ĪPVV, Abhinavagupta sums up the gist of ĪPK 2.1.8 as follows:

> Here is what [Utpaladeva] means: in this [system,] action is nothing but the Lord's will—this will be summed up in [verse 2.4.21, which states] "Thus causality, agency, action are nothing but such a will..." Even the will of [an ordinary individual such as] Caitra, [which takes such a form as] "I am going to cook," is precisely that which, being continuous even though [there are] countless [different] movements—[viz.] putting [the pot] on the fire, etc.—, manifests itself as bearing[713] the [various] phenomena of [objective] entities that have a sequential form, although in itself it is devoid of sequence. Exactly in the same way, the will of the Highest Lord too, which, in Him, [takes the form] "let sequence arise in knowing subjects and objects of knowledge," and which has as its ultimate reality [a realization expressed] as "I am going to exert my power," "I am going to flash forth," "I am going to realize," "I am going to pulsate," is manifest as being sequential although it is in itself free of sequence, because it assumes the appearance (*uparāga*) of the differences pertaining to knowing subjects and objects of knowledge—just as the surface of a mirror, although free of sequence, assumes the appearance [of] being sequential due to the sequence of a constantly flowing, large river [that is reflected in it], and due to the innumerable [reflected] forms of lightning that keep arising and disappearing [during a thunderstorm]. Therefore in all cases without exception, action is in itself absolutely free of sequence, [yet it] acquires sequence as an assumed appearance—so it does not have a sequential form that would be genuine (*śuddha*) [and] that would pervade it, as a result of which [action] would have to be denied in the Lord on the grounds that [we] do not apprehend [in

*aham ity etāvanmātratattvaṃ na tatra kaścit kramaḥ. etad eva cocyate pramātṛprameyavaicitryakrama ullasatv ity* amunā vākyena, tad atrāpi na kaścit kramaḥ.* [**ullasatv ity* J, P, S2 (p.c.), S3, S10, S15, SOAS, *Bhāskarī* Ed.; *ullasatv* L, S1 (p.c.), S5, S9 (p.c.), D2, KSTS Ed.]

[713] Literally, as being "strewn" or "spangled" (*rūṣita*) with these phenomena.

> Him the sequence allegedly] pervading [action]. This was the general meaning of the verse.[714]

What gives its unity to any ordinary action is the undivided, nonsequential will of its agent, and ordinary action is nothing but the sequential unfolding of this nonsequential creative urge. According to Abhinavagupta, verse 2.1.8 argues that in the same way, the whole cosmic creation is nothing but the sequential unfolding of the ultimate consciousness's nonsequential desire. And this sequential manifestation of a nonsequential reality, although paradoxical, is not contradictory, because we can see on a daily basis that that which possesses the power to manifest also has the power to present itself as what it is not: at this point Abhinavagupta has recourse to his favoured analogy of the unitary surface of a mirror, which, although in itself devoid of sequence (because it is free of multiplicity), may manifest sequence without losing its nonsequential nature.[715] In the ĪPV, Abhinavagupta points out that as a result, the Lord's power of action may be understood both as the power to create a sequential universe within which all actions are sequential, and as the power to be seemingly affected by sequence:

---

[714] ĪPVV, vol. III, pp. 24–25: *etad uktaṃ bhavati: ihecchaiva bhagavataḥ kriyā, yad upasaṃhariṣyata evam icchaiva hetutā kartṛtā kriyeti. caitrasyāpi pacāmīti yaivecchā saivādhiśrayaṇādispandasahasre 'py anapāyinī svātmanākramāpi kramarūpabhāvābhāsarūṣitā bhāti; tathaiva parameśvarasyāpi jñātṛjñeyakrama ullasatv iti yā svātmanīcchā, īśe sphurāmi pratyavamṛśāmi ghūrṇa ityādiparamārthā, sā svayam akramāpi pramātṛprameyabhedoparāgāt sakramā bhāti, makuramaṇḍalam ivākramam api nityapravahadvitatasaritkrameṇodayamānavyayamānataḍitsahasrarūpeṇa coparaktaṃ sakramam. tataḥ sarvatraiveyaṃ kriyā svayam akramaivoparāgāt kramaṃ pratipadyata iti nāsyāḥ śuddham eva kramarūpaṃ vyāpakaṃ yena vyāpakānupalabdhyā bhagavati sā niṣidhyeteti sūtrārthaḥ.*

[715] The same analogy appears in the ĪPV, vol. II, pp. 23–24: ... *bhagavadicchā pramātṛprameyabhedaparyavasitā tatkramopaśliṣṭā bhāti darpaṇatalam iva vitatapravahannadīpravāhakramasamāśliṣṭam, atra ca kevalaṃ darpaṇasya tathecchā nāsti, parameśvarasya tu sāsti.* "... The Lord's will, which ends up in the differentiation between the [limited] subjects and objects, is manifest as being closely associated with the sequence that belongs to them, just as the surface of a mirror [seems to be] closely associated with the sequence that belongs to the current of a large, flowing river; only in the [latter case], there is no such will on the mirror's part, whereas the Highest Lord has it."

> Therefore [in this verse,] the [Lord]'s power of action is [to be understood] in two [senses]: it is both [His] power to create actions that have a sequential form, and [His] assuming the appearance (*uparāga*) of actions that have a sequential form.[716]

Because sequence is thus an adventitious property of action rather than its very nature, and because the creative activity of consciousness consists in making its own action appear as if it were sequential, the view that action cannot belong to the ultimate reality due to its being sequential stands refuted:

> Therefore even though from a naïve point of view, one may object that action cannot belong to the [Lord] on the grounds that there is no sequence [in Him] since there is no interruption in [His] manifestation, nonetheless, in this way, His power of action is shown to be logically sound—this is the [verse's] connection [with what precedes].[717]

### 4. The power of action as the (great) universal of Being

In the *Vivṛti* as it has come down to us, Utpaladeva begins by reminding his readers that the power of creation mentioned in the verse has already been said to be "the [very fact of] being the Highest Lord" (*parameśvaratā*) and consists in a "universal" (*sāmānya*). Abhinavagupta does not comment on this, but it seems probable that what Utpaladeva has in mind here are the statements, in chapter 1.5, that *vimarśa* is consciousness's very sovereignty (*aiśvarya*—literally, its "being the Lord"),[718] as well as "the great being" (*mahāsattā*):

---

[716] ĪPV, vol. II, p. 24: *ity ubhayathāsya kriyāśaktiḥ kramarūpakriyānirmāṇasāmarthyaṃ kramarūpakriyoparāgayogaś ceti.*

[717] ĪPV, vol. II, pp. 24–25: *ato bhāsanavicchedābhāvāt kramābhāve sthūladṛṣṭyā yady apy asya bhavet kriyānupapattiśaṅkā, kiṃ tv evam asya kriyāśaktir upapanneti saṃgatiḥ.*

[718] ĪPK 1.5.13: *citiḥ pratyavamarśātmā parā vāk svarasoditā | svātantryam etan mukhyaṃ tad aiśvaryaṃ paramātmanaḥ ||* "The act of consciousness (*citi*), which has realization as its essence, is the supreme Speech that arises freely; it is freedom in the primary sense—it is the sovereignty (*aiśvarya*) of the supreme self."

> It is the flashing forth, the great being that is not determined by space and time; it is this [power of action of consciousness] that is called the heart of the Highest Lord because it is His essence.[719]

This great being is so all-pervading that it permeates even nonbeing,[720] as the *Vṛtti* on this verse emphasizes:

> The fact of having a flashing forth nature, the agency in flashing forth, being, existing, [i.e.] the agency in existing, which is not the contrary of nonbeing [since it] pervades [even] nonbeing, [and] which is eternal since it is not affected at all by space and time—[this] is the power of action [understood as] a conscious act (*citikriyāśakti*), which has as its essence realization.[721]

It thus constitutes the universal (*sāmānya*) par excellence as Bhartṛhari understands it, i.e. the all-pervading being,[722] or what his commentator Helārāja calls the "great universal" (*mahāsāmānya*).[723] The *Vivṛti* on 2.1.8, which reminds Utpaladeva's readers that the power of creation is the very fact of "being the Highest Lord" and "consists in a universal," is very likely to be an allusion to this equation in ĪPK 1.5.14 of consciousness's power of action with the great being. This equation is again clearly stated by Abhinavagupta towards the end of the treatise, while he is commenting on ĪPK

---

[719] ĪPK 1.5.14: *sā sphurattā mahāsattā deśakālāviśeṣinī | saiṣā sāratayā proktā hṛdayaṃ parameṣṭhinaḥ ||*

[720] Cf. ĪPV, vol. I, pp. 209–210: *sattā ca bhavanakartṛtā sarvakriyāsu svātantryam. sā ca khapuṣpādikam api vyāpnotīti mahatī.* "And being is the agency in existing, the freedom in all actions; and it is [said to be] 'Great' because it pervades even the flower in the sky and [any other nonbeing]."

[721] *Vṛtti* on ĪPK 1.5.14, p. 23: *sphuradrūpatā sphuraṇakartṛtābhāvāpratiyoginy abhāvavyāpinī sattā bhavattā bhavanakartṛtā nityā deśakālāsparśāt saiva pratyamarśātmā citikriyāśaktiḥ...*

[722] See TORELLA 2002, p. 121, fn. 29, which mentions in this respect the notion of *mahāsāmānya* in Bhartṛhari's tradition.

[723] This is how he glosses the word *sattā* (PP, vol. I, p. 41). For Abhinavagupta's use of the term *mahāsāmānya* see e.g. ĪPVV, vol. II, p. 202 (*sattātmakaṃ mahāsāmānyam...*). Cf. also for instance Kṣemarāja's NTU, vol. II, p. 286: *astitvamātraṃ prakāśātmamahāsattārūpam...* "The universal of existence (*astitvamātra*), which consists in the great being, whose essence is the manifesting consciousness..."

4.6a, according to which "being, bliss, action belong to the Lord" (*sattānandaḥ kriyā patyuḥ*):

> This universal Lord possesses "being," [that is to say,] the agency in being, which consists in the act of flashing forth that has already been described in [verse 1.5.14, beginning with] "It is the flashing forth, the great being..." Because [it] is nothing over and above the realization of conscious manifestation, this [being] is precisely what [we] call the "power of action," inasmuch as it consists in the aesthetic wonder that is realization; and this same [being] is bliss, because its nature is to rest in oneself, since [it is] perfectly independent.[724] Therefore the Lord consists precisely in this [being that is also bliss and action], for the very reason that it has consciousness as its essence.[725]

The ultimate consciousness's power of creation is nothing but its *vimarśa*, because its creative activity is simply consciousness manifesting itself—and becoming aware of this manifestation—in the countless forms of the universe: the being that pervades everything, far from being a static property belonging to objective entities, is this pure dynamism.[726] That Utpaladeva reminds us at the end of chapter 2.1 of this point made much earlier in the treatise is probably no coincidence, because in ĪPK 1.5.14, he had already specified that this great being is "not determined by space or time" (*deśakālāviśeṣin*). He had obviously explained this idea at length in his *Vivṛti* thereon,[727] while commenting on the *Vṛtti*'s further statement that the

[724] On this notion see above, fn. 710.

[725] ĪPV, vol. II, p. 257: *tasya viśvapater yā sattā bhavanakartṛtā sphurattārūpā pūrvaṃ vyākhyātā sā sphurattā mahāsattety atra, saiva prakāśasya vimarśāvyatirekād vimarśātmakacamatkārarūpā satī kriyāśaktir ucyate, paraunmukhyatyāgena svātmaviśrāntirūpatvāc ca saivānandaḥ, tad evaṃ bhagavataś cidātmatayaiveyadrūpatā.*

[726] On this dynamic ontology see RATIÉ 2011a, pp. 683–694.

[727] See ĪPVV, vol. II, from the bottom of p. 201 onwards. The passage is too long to be quoted here, but see in particular ĪPVV, vol. II, pp. 202–203: *nanv evaṃ prameyasya deśakālayoga idaṃ tad iti yat sattātmakaṃ mahāsāmānyaṃ bhāti, yac ca gotvādikam aparaṃ tasya vyāpitvanityatve na syātām iti codyaṃ pariharatī**dam** ityādinā. ākārasaṃkoco 'nyonyābhāvalakṣaṇo nātra saṃkocakaḥ, sarveṇa hi rūpeṇa*

great being is "not affected at all by space and time,"[728] and here is how Abhinavagupta sums up Utpaladeva's explanation in the ĪPV:

> Because it is this [great being] that creates space and time—just as [it creates objects] such as the blue—, it cannot be determined by them; indeed, [only] that which is manifest as being on a par with [something else] is a determining attribute (*viśeṣaṇa*) for that [other entity]—for instance, Caitra's bracelet[, which is a determining attribute for Caitra as it makes him a bracelet-bearer]; and space and time are not manifest [as being] on a par with realization, since the manifestation of [space and time] takes an objective form, whereas that of [realization] takes a subjective one, so that it is impossible [for them] to be on a par! Thus [the great being] is omnipresent and eternal due to the fact that it is not affected at all by space and time; and yet all places and times are affected [by it], because of their association [with it inasmuch as] it creates [them]; this is also why [the great being] is omnipresent and eternal.[729]

The spatially and temporally determined manifestation is nothing but a way for the great being of manifesting itself; yet the creative dynamism of consciousness escapes all spatial and temporal determinations, as the latter, which belong to the realm of objectivity, can only constitute a determining

*saṃvidvimarśo bhavati...* "[– Objection:] 'But [if] thus an object of knowledge is associated with space and time, [then] the great universal consisting in being, which is manifest [objectively, in the form] 'this is that,' as well as [any] lower [universal] such as cowness, can be neither omnipresent nor eternal!' [Utpaladeva] refutes this objection with [the sentence] beginning with 'This,' [which means the following.] The contraction in the appearance [of consciousness], which is characterized as a mutual incompatibility [of certain phenomena resulting in the manifestation of spatial and temporal sequence], does not contract the [nature of realization itself]; for the realization of the [pure] consciousness exists in every form..."

[728] See above, fn. 721.

[729] ĪPV, vol. I, pp. 210–211: *deśakālau nīlādivat saiva sṛjatīti tābhyāṃ viśeṣaṇīyā na bhavati, yat kila yena tulyakakṣyatayā bhāti tat tasya viśeṣaṇaṃ kaṭaka iva caitrasya. na ca deśakālau vimarśena tulyakakṣyau bhātaḥ, tayor idantayā tasya cāhantayā prakāśe tulyakakṣyatvānupapatteḥ. evaṃ deśakālāsparśāt vibhutvaṃ nityatvaṃ ca, sakaladeśakālasparśo 'pi tannirmāṇayogād iti tato 'pi vyāpakatvanityatve.*

attribute for objects.[730] Besides, consciousness's power of action is omnipresent and eternal not only because it thus escapes all spatial and temporal determinations, but also because all spatial and temporal determinations are pervaded by it, inasmuch as the great being is what makes them exist by taking their forms. The point is important, because it explains how, according to verse 2.1.8, the sequential manifestation *is* the non-sequential power of action: the latter transcends the former inasmuch as it is not truly limited but only appears to be so; yet the former is nothing but the latter, as all spatial and temporal determinations are simply consciousness's creative power to manifest itself in their countless forms.

### 5. The power of great creation (*mahāsṛṣṭiśakti*) and the cosmic functions of Rudra, Brahmā and Viṣṇu

The *Vivṛti*'s next step consists in defining the ultimate consciousness's dynamism not only as the (great) universal, but also as "the power of great creation" (*mahāsṛṣṭiśakti*). The "great creation" is described by Śaiva authors as the "original pattern"[731] of all cosmic creations, which contains in itself all creations and resorptions and from which they all unfold. In Abhinavagupta's words, "what consists in the great creation contains in nuce

---

[730] The idea was obviously expressed in the *Vivṛti* on ĪPK 1.5.14. See ĪPVV, vol. II, p. 202: *anena cedam uktam: yat khaṇḍitaprathākaṃ* tad eva kvacit kadācic ca bhavad deśakālābhyāṃ kāraṇabhūtābhyām āviśyeteti kṛtakasyaiva tau viśeṣaṇaṃ nākṛtakasya. saṃvedanasya prameyakakṣyāpatitasyaiva ca pramātṛsaṃyojyamānābhāsāntarābhidhānadharmayojanasahiṣṇos tau viśeṣaṇam, na prameyatottīrṇasya pramātrekarūpasya saṃvedanasya.* [**khaṇḍitaprathākam* corr.; *khaṇḍitapṛthākam* Ed.] "And here is what [Utpaladeva] means with this [passage]: only [an entity] whose manifestation undergoes interruptions may be pervaded by space and time as causes [contributing to its specificity], inasmuch as [this entity] only exists in certain places and times. Therefore these two, [space and time,] are a determining attribute only for what is created, but not for what is uncreated; and they are a determining attribute for consciousness only inasmuch as [this consciousness] has fallen into a state that is equivalent to [that of] an object of knowledge, [and] is [therefore] liable to be associated with names and properties of other [objective] phenomena that are combined with this [limited] knowing subject; but [they cannot be a determining attribute] for the consciousness that transcends objectivity [and] only consists in a knowing subject."

[731] PADOUX 1990, p. 306.

hundreds of crores of infinite creations and [resorptions]";[732] Kṣemarāja, for his part, mentions that this "power of great creation contains in nuce the manifold display of all the creations and resorptions of the universe."[733] As pointed out by Abhinavagupta, this paradigmatic creation is not to be understood as the *first* cosmic emanation, since it is free of any temporal or spatial determination:

> In this [power of action] resides the Highest Lord's great creation, which is full, [and] in which all the [cosmic] resorptions and creations are included [as its] parts. And it is absolutely impossible to say that it is the first creation; for in a reality that is without space and time, how would such [sequential determinations] as "the first" [even] be possible?[734]

This great creation is primordial in an ontological, rather than temporal sense, inasmuch as all cosmic emanations partake of it. The *Vivṛti*, by alluding to both the "great being" and the "great creation" while explaining the final verse of the chapter, thus underscores that the power of action is both the fundamental dynamic urge at the basis of all existence, and what contains in itself the infinite variety of cosmic emissions and dissolutions.

The *Vivṛti* immediately specifies that this power of great creation includes "even resorption." The paradox is underscored by Abhinavagupta, who portrays an opponent considering that this is a sheer absurdity:

> "But what is this nonsense: "Dissolution is included in creation"? For [this] is a contradiction!" [In the sentence beginning with] "For even in resorption...," [Utpaladeva] explains that this is not [in fact] a contradiction.[735]

Indeed, the *Vivṛti* proceeds to justify this point by announcing that the sequel of the treatise will show how creation and resorption only differ inasmuch as in the latter, things must have an internal existence, whereas they

---

[732] PTV, p. 83: *mahāsṛṣṭirūpo garbhīkṛtānantasṛṣṭyādikoṭiśataḥ...*

[733] NTU, vol. II, p. 286: *garbhīkṛtāśeṣaviśvasṛṣṭisaṃhāraprapañcamahāsṛṣṭiśakti°.*

[734] MŚV 1.366cd–367: *pūrṇeyaṃ parameśasya mahāsṛṣṭir iha sthitā ‖ yasyāṃ saṃhārasṛṣṭyaṃśā viśve te madhyavartinaḥ | sā cādyā sṛṣṭir ity eva naiva vaktuṃ bhavet kṣamam ‖ adeśakāle tattve hi katham ādyādisaṃbhavaḥ |*

[735] ĪPVV, vol. III, p. 25: *nanu saṃhāraḥ sṛṣṭau praviṣṭa iti kā bhāṣā virodhāt. na virodho 'yam ity āha* ***saṃhāre 'pi hī****ti.*

exist both internally and externally in the former. In fact, Utpaladeva has already explained at the end of the *Jñānādhikāra* that things always exist at least in an internal form, so that their ceasing to exist externally does not amount to their anihilation:

> [We] consider that existing externally is an adventitious property (*upādhi*) of the manifestations that include being and nonbeing, and not their [very] essence; therefore these [manifestations] always exist [at least] insofar as they are internal.[736]

The *Kriyādhikāra*—and particularly its fourth chapter, which Utpaladeva probably has in mind here—then shows that action consists in the gradual externalization of an internal reality, any effect being the mere externalization of a reality that exists within the subject:

> An entity [A] that is [first] internal in relation to an [entity B] is, [once] external to that very [entity B], its effect; and [we] talk about this double existence, external and internal, in relation to the knowing subject.[737]

The cosmic creation or emanation (*sṛṣṭi*) amounts to the manifestation of an internal reality *as if it were external*, i.e., it is its apparent projection outside consciousness; and cosmic resorption or dissolution (*saṃhāra*) is the reverse process through which the world is merged back into consciousness. This internalization, however, does not lead to the elimination of all objectivity: in cosmic resorption, the universe's objectivity subsists, but only, as the *Vivṛti* points out, in the form of seeds (*bīja*)—that is, as specified by Abhinavagupta, as residual traces (*saṃskāra*),[738] just as, in the consciousness of a sleeper who is no longer aware of sensory objects, objectivity must remain in some latent form.

The *Vivṛti* then explains that it is this power of great creation that is divided into the powers of creation, maintenance and resorption usually attributed

---

736 ĪPK 1.8.5: *bhāvābhāvāvabhāsānāṃ bāhyatopādhir iṣyate | nātmā sattā tatas teṣām āntarāṇāṃ satāṃ sadā ||*

737 ĪPK 2.4.6: *bahis tasyaiva tatkāryaṃ yad antar yadapekṣayā | pramātrapekṣayā coktā dvayī bāhyāntarasthitiḥ ||*

738 See below, chapter 11, fn. 128.

to Brahmā, Viṣṇu and Rudra. The Pratyabhijñā system concedes the existence of this triad: Rudra is the deity presiding over the state of resorption, where subjectivity is limited but free of objects (although they remain as residual traces); Brahmā presides over creation, defined as the state of limited subjectivity where objects of knowledge appear; Viṣṇu presides over maintenance as it insures the continued existence of these objects. Yet the three deities are nothing but limited aspects of the ultimate consciousness. Utpaladeva defines them as follows in the third part of the treatise, devoted to āgamic doctrines:

> Since this [is so],[739] Rudra is the deity presiding over the state in which there is nothing but this [limited] subjectivity; Brahmā and Viṣṇu reside in the flow of differentiated objects of knowledge.[740]

Abhinavagupta explains Rudra's status in the following way while commenting on this verse:

> The Lord Rudra—who is [in fact] nothing but the venerable Lord (*īśvara*)—possesses this form of [limited] subjectivity, [i.e., the subjectivity that is] restricted by the five [sheaths] of time, etc.;[741] [this form] is the status of the deity presiding over the state called resorption (*saṃhāra*), in which the entire mass of the objects of knowledge has been resorbed. [He has this status] because he brings about that state and because he brings about the urge towards himself in people who are his worshippers and who manage to remain absorbed in the meditation on this state.[742]

---

[739] On the meaning of *tatra* here, see ĪPV, vol. II, p. 216: *tatrety evambhūte 'sminn āgamasiddhe yuktyanugate ca tattvasvarūpe sati...* "[The word] *tatra* [means]: 'since the nature of the [various] ontological levels is established by scripture to be as [described in the previous chapter], and is [also] in accordance with reason..."

[740] ĪPK 3.2.1: *tatraitanmātṛtāmātrasthitau rudro 'dhidaivatam | bhinnaprameyaprasare brahmaviṣṇū vyavasthitau ||*

[741] On these sheaths see above, chapter 8, fn. 578.

[742] ĪPV, vol. II, pp. 216–217: ... *yad etat kālādipañcakaveṣṭitaṃ pramātṛtārūpaṃ tad eva yasyāṃ śuddham upasaṃhṛtaprameyajātaṃ bhavati daśāyāṃ saṃhārākhyāyāṃ tasyām adhiṣṭhātṛdevatātvaṃ taddaśāsaṃpādanena svopāsakalokasya*

As for Brahmā and Viṣṇu, they are described as follows by Abhinavagupta:

> As for Brahmā, he possesses the status of the deity who presides over [what the verse calls] "the flow," [i.e., in his case,] the emission of the differentiated object[s] of knowledge; [and] Viṣṇu is the deity presiding over "the flow," which, [in his case,] consists in carrying this stream of [objects] once the differentiated object[s] of knowledge [are] produced.[743]

In the *Vivṛti*, while acknowledging this distinction between the three gods' cosmic functions, Utpaladeva also insists that it is ultimately unreal since it is "produced by the power of *māyā*" (that is, the power through which the absolute consciousness chooses to ignore its own nature and to manifest itself as if it were limited).[744] Abhinavagupta spells this out as follows:

> The differentiation of "this"—[i.e.] this great power of creation—into the forms of Brahmā, [Viṣṇu and Rudra], which is variously expressed [when we make distinctions such as] "this is the power of creation," "this is the power of maintenance," "this is the power of resorption," is produced by the power of *māyā*. [This differentiation occurs] even though the [various entities] that are diversely created, [i.e.] the knowing subjects who consist in qualities (*guṇa*)[745]—beginning

---

*taddaśādhyānāveśasamāpannasya svābhimukhyasaṃpādanena ca bhajamāno bhaṭṭāraka īśvara eva rudro bhagavān...*

[743] ĪPV, vol. II, p. 217: *bhinnasya tu prameyasya prasare saṃpādane 'dhiṣṭhātṛdevatātvaṃ bhajan brahmā, prasṛte bhinne prameye tatsantānapravahaṇalakṣaṇe prasare 'dhiṣṭhātṛdevatā viṣṇuḥ.*

[744] See above, chapter 4, fn. 306.

[745] The three *guṇa*s or qualities (viz. *sattva*, *rajas* and *tamas*) that constitute the inanimate world according to the Sāṃkhya are said to pervade the limited subjects in the Pratyabhijñā system, and they are described in the latter as respectively corresponding, within the limited subjects, to the ultimate consciousness's powers of knowledge, action and *māyā*. See e.g. Utpaladeva's *Vṛtti* on ĪPK 4.4, p. 74: *īśvarasya jñānakriye te māyayā sahite paśoḥ sattvarajastamāṃsi.* "The Lord's knowledge and action as well as [His] *māyā* are, for the bound individual (*paśu*), the [qualities of] *sattva*, *rajas* and *tamas*." Utpaladeva nonetheless insists that in the bound individuals these qualities are no longer powers, since they appear in them as distinct

> with Prajāpati and ending with immovable [sentient] entities—and the objects of knowledge such as a pot, pleasure,[746] and so on, which [also] consist in qualities, [all result] from a creation that is absolutely one (*ekaghana*).[747]

And again:

> [The *Vivṛti* sentence] "For in that [realm of *māyā*, it is due to the Lord who has taken on the forms of Brahmā, Viṣṇu and Rudra that the separation between all knowing subjects and objects is determined" means the following:] in [that] realm of *māyā*, it is the Lord Himself who exists in the forms of Brahmā and so on. By [saying] this, [Utpaladeva has] shown that even as regards the agency of the great creation, since it is the Highest Lord who performs creation, maintenance and resorption, [His] universal agency is absolutely full.[748]

Utpaladeva and Abhinavagupta thus ascribe all cosmic functions to Śiva himself. Although he performs these functions while taking the forms of Brahmā, Viṣṇu and Rudra, he is the single dynamic reality that unfolds from the purest *vimarśa* down to the sphere of *māyā*, where these aspects of his creativity become differentiated into lower divinities that appear to be rulers[749] whereas their power is in fact nothing but that of the universal

---

from the subject, i.e. as objective entities. See e.g. the *Vṛtti* on ĪPK 4.5, p. 75: *sattvarajastamasāṃ ca bhedenāvabhāsanān na śaktivyapadeśaḥ śaktiśaktimator abhedāt.* "Since *sattva*, *rajas* and *tamas* are manifested as distinct [from the limited subject], they can]not be called [his] powers, because a power and its posessor are not distinct."

[746] The pot and pleasure are respectively paradigmatic of objects experienced as external and internal to the limited knowing subjects.

[747] ĪPVV, vol. III, p. 25: ***asyā*** *iti mahatyāḥ sṛṣṭiśakter yo brahmādirūpatayā viśeṣo jñātṝṇāṃ prajāpatyādisthāvarāntānāṃ guṇamayānāṃ prameyānāṃ ca ghaṭasukhādīnāṃ guṇamayānāṃ tathā tathā sṛjyamānānām ekaghanasṛṣṭitāyām apīyaṃ sṛṣṭiśaktir iyaṃ sthitiśaktir iyaṃ saṃhāraśaktir iti samuccīyamānaḥ sa māyāśaktyā kṛtaḥ.*

[748] ĪPVV, vol. III, pp. 25–26: ***tatra hīti*** *māyāpada īśvara eva brahmādirūpeṇa sthitaḥ. anena mahāsṛṣṭikartṛtve 'pi parameśvarasya sṛṣṭisthitisaṃhārakāritvena pūrṇam eva sarvakartṛtvam upapāditam.*

[749] See e.g. ĪPV, vol. I, p. 207: "Viṣṇu, Viriñca [i.e. Brahmā], Indra and so on, who are only appointed [to rule] in the realm of *māyā*..." ( *māyāgarbhādhikṛtānām eva*

consciousness. In the *Vivṛti*'s words, the latter is only mentally constructed (*kalpita*) as having the three forms of Brahmā, Viṣṇu and Rudra, when it is really one.

Utpaladeva then emphasizes that although the distinction between subjects and objects vanishes at least in its external form for Rudra, in whose realm objectivity only remains in the latent form of residual traces, for Brahmā and Viṣṇu (presented as the two distinctly dualistic deities), objects are vividly distinct from subjects. Abhinavagupta explains as follows this paradox according to which the three gods, who are eternal and supposedly apprehend the same universe, thus grasp contradictory realities:

> "But [if it is] so, since the three deities are ever present, given that the resorption appropriate for the Lord Rudra is incompatible with both [creation and maintenance], creation and maintenance should never be seen!" As a response to this, [Utpaladeva] states [the sentence beginning with] "And among these...", [i.e.,] among these three deities. This is what [Utpaladeva] means [here]: In [our] system [according to which] things have phenomena as their ultimate reality, [things] are just as they are for [any given] knowing subject who, in the course of his ordinary experiences, says/thinks (*vyavahāra*) "These [things] appear to me thus." However, [we] have [already] explained how, thanks to the Lord's will, the [various subjects may] become one (*melana*) with respect to one specific aspect of phenomena. And therefore at first, from the points of view of the knowing subjects who are the Lord Rudra, [but also] yogins having attained the level of deep sleep and firmly established in the highest cessation [of mental operations], Pralayākalas and Vijñānākalas,[750] and from the points of view of the [ordinary] living beings that have reached a state of deep sleep, it is only the [latent] existence of [objective] entities in the form of seeds that is manifest—for these [subjects] have become one [thanks to the Lord's will] with respect to that phenomenon. [But] from the points of view of the Lords Brahmā and Viṣṇu, and of

*viṣṇuviriñcendrādīnām*). Cf. TSā, p. 64: *māyāgarbhādhikāriṇaṃ viṣṇubrahmādikaṃ...*

[750] On these Śaiva categories of knowing subjects see above, fn. 641.

> the transmigrating knowing subjects living in the waking and dreaming states, [it is] the fact that [objective entities] are new and have a continuous existence that is manifest, because these [subjects] have become one with respect to that [phenomenon].[751]

Abhinavagupta thus provides an excellent synthesis of the idealistic principles that constitute the core of Utpaladeva's metaphysics and are only alluded to in the *Vivṛti* on this last verse: (1) things only exist insofar as they are apprehended by a subject—and they exist *in the way in which they are thus apprehended.* (2) Yet, precisely because things do not have any reality independently of the subjects who are aware of them, different subjects may apprehend them differently (the universe is not quite the same for Rudra, Brahmā and Viṣṇu), and in fact this difference in the way in which subjects grasp things is precisely what makes them distinct subjects. (3) Because these different subjects are in fact nothing but the ultimate consciousness playfully manifesting itself in the form of various limited perspectives on itself, the ultimate consciousness is free to merge these distinct knowers back into a single subjectivity, and it can do so *even while some differences between them remain manifest*, by making them share only one specific aspect of the objective world. Abhinavagupta himself notes here that this point has been dealt with at length earlier in the treatise; this was probably done in Utpaladeva's currently unavailable *Vivṛti* on ĪPK 1.5.10, but the gist of the reasoning can be retrieved from the ĪPV on that verse. There Abhinavagupta explains as follows how the universal consciousness can choose to unify different subjects with respect to one single aspect of the phenomenal universe:

> Even within this [manifestation of differentiated knowing subjects and objects of knowledge, consciousness] unifies

---

[751] ĪPVV, vol. III, p. 26: *nanv evaṃ devatātritayasya sadā saṃnihitatve rudrabhaṭṭārakoditaḥ saṃhāra ubhayavipakṣa iti na sṛṣṭisthitī dṛśyeyātām. atrocyate* ***tatra ce****ti devatātrayamadhye. etad uktaṃ bhavati: ābhāsaparamārthavastuvāde yasya pramātur yeṣu yathā mamaivam amī bhāsanta iti vyavahāras tasya te tathā. kvacit tv ābhāsāṃśe bhagavadicchāta eṣāṃ melanam ity uktam. tataś cādyatve bhagavadrudrapramātrapekṣayā paranirodhasamavasthitasuṣuptibhūmikārūḍhayogipramātrapekṣayā pralayākalavijñānākalapramātrapekṣayā gāḍhasuṣuptāpannajīvadapekṣayā ca bījabhāva eva bhāvānāṃ bhāti. te hi tatrābhāse militāḥ. brahmaviṣṇubhaṭṭārakāpekṣayā jāgratsvapnapadacārisaṃsāripramātrapekṣayā ca nūtanatānuvartamānatā ca bhāti ta atrānyonyaṃ militā yataḥ.*

> the subjects with respect to a specific phenomenon, just as spectators [become one] with respect to the dance of a beautifully-hipped [woman]. For they become one only with respect to that phenomenon; yet with respect to the aspect of phenomena constituted by the body, vital breath and intellect [with which they identify, or] such [internal objects] as pleasure, because differences do not [entirely] vanish, there is no complete unity [between them].[752]

Just as spectators engrossed in a show become one as far as the object of their fascination is concerned,[753] the various subjects of the universe may become one with Rudra, Brahmā or Viṣṇu inasmuch as they share the awareness of a specific aspect of objective phenomena, without entirely losing their individuality because they remain distinct as far as other phenomena are concerned. Similarly, Rudra, Brahmā and Viṣṇu themselves can share the awareness of the objective universe (at least in its internal form) while remaining distinct in other respects—and this is why, according to the Śaiva nondualists, absolute idealism is not contradictory with intersubjectivity and the notion of a common world. But whether cosmic activity is grasped as being that of Brahmā, Viṣṇu or Rudra, or whether it is envisaged as the "great creation" encompassing the various aspects attributed to the three deities, the very essence of this creation, as underscored by the *Vivṛti*, is the subject-object differentiation (of which the various cosmic "phases" usually ascribed to Brahmā, Viṣṇu and Rudra are only different states): *it is this differentiation that makes a world possible*. The power of cosmic creation is ultimately nothing but this ability to separate subject and object, and the *Vivṛti* insists that "in all cases, even [when it occurs] in the form of the three [deities] that are Brahmā, [Viṣṇu and Rudra,] creation is [thus] nothing but the [already] described determination of a separation (*vibhāga*) between the [knowing subjects and objects of knowledge] that exist inside the Highest Lord," Brahmā's emission being nothing but the

[752] ĪPV, vol. I, pp. 194–195 (as edited in RATIÉ 2011a, p. 584): *tatrāpi kvacid ābhāse pramātṝn ekīkaroti nitambinīnṛtta iva prekṣakān. tāvati hi teṣām ābhāsa aikyam. śarīraprāṇabuddhisukhādyābhāsāṃśe tu bhedasyāvigalanān na sarvathaikyam.*

[753] Cf. for instance ĪPV, vol. II, pp. 209–210: *kadācit tu naṭamallaprekṣādāv īśvarecchayaikībhaveyur api.* "Sometimes, however, these [powers belonging to distinct individuals] may also be merged into one [single power] thanks to the Lord's will, for example with respect to a show [performed] by actors or wrestlers."

external appearance of this separation, Viṣṇu's maintenance, the continuation of its external existence, and Rudra's resorption, its internal existence as residual traces. Abhinavagupta explains:

> "In all cases," [i.e., whether it occurs] in the forms of Brahmā, Viṣṇu, Rudra or Īśvara, what [we] call "creation" can be expressed [differently] with the words "creation," "maintenance" and "resorption" simply because it varies according to whether it is a new [creation, one] that exists continuously, or [one] that subsists in the form of [something] left as a seed; [and] because of [Utpaladeva's use of] the word "even," it can also be expressed by the words "great creation" [inasmuch as it occurs] in its pure form. [This creation, whichever form it may take,] has as its sole essence the manifestation of the aforementioned separation between subjects of knowledge and objects of knowledge.[754]

## 6. The cosmic creation does not conceal the true nature of the ultimate consciousness

As pointed out both by Utpaladeva and Abhinavagupta, however, this definition of the power of cosmic creation as the ability to distinguish subjects and objects might be considered problematic, because Utpaladeva has shown in chapter 1.5 that *prakāśa*, the manifesting consciousness—or the conscious manifestation, *prakāśa* meaning both—is fundamentally one. chapter 1.5, which claims to establish the Śaiva nondualists' idealism on rational grounds, thus explains that the knowing subject and object of knowledge must be one single reality, namely, *prakāśa*, for the awareness of any object to be possible; for if the entities of which we are aware were not forms taken on by consciousness, subject and object would remain forever alien to each other, and their very relationship would be inexplicable. The point is summed up at the beginning of chapter 1.5:

[754] ĪPVV, vol. III, p. 26: *sarvadā brahmarūpeṇa viṣṇurūpeṇa rudrarūpeṇeśvararūpeṇa ca navatayānuvartamānatayā bījāvaśeṣitāgamanena cāvāntaravaicitryamātrāt sṛṣṭisthitisaṃhāraśabdavācyā,* ***apiśabdāc*** *ca śuddharūpeṇa mahāsṛṣṭiśabdavācyā sṛṣṭir nāma yocyate soktasya jñātṛjñeyavibhāgasya yad avabhāsanaṃ tadātmikaiva.*

> If [the object] did not have as its essence the conscious manifestation, it would remain devoid of conscious manifestation [after being cognized] just as before; and conscious manifestation cannot be separated: being the conscious manifestation is the object's [very] essence. If the conscious manifestation were [indeed] separated [from the object] while being free of [any internal] separation, the confusion of [everything that is] an object would ensue; so any object that is liable to be made manifest has as its essence the conscious manifestation, and no [entity] that is not the conscious manifestation can be established.[755]

Now, if the power of cosmic creation boils down to the separation (*vibhāga*) of subjects and objects, isn't this fundamental split a denial of consciousness's nonduality? If this distinction itself is manifest, how could it not affect the very nature of *prakāśa*? And how could even objects be manifest if the very nature of the conscious manifestation is thus divided? The ĪPVV highlights the problem as follows:

> But due to this determination [of subjects and objects] as being separated, this very separation must be manifest, [and] the conscious manifestation's lack of separation is hereby shattered; so [objective] entities should not [even] be manifest! Having anticipated this [objection], with [the sentence beginning with] "However, although the Great Lord...", [Utpaladeva] explains [in the *Vivṛti*] the [part of the] *Vṛtti* that begins with "and [the enduring existence of His full nature] is not [concealed...]."[756]

Indeed, the *Vṛtti* asserts that "the enduring existence" of the Highest Lord's full nature "is not concealed" by the determination of knowing subjects and objects of knowledge as being separated from him and from each other; and the *Vivṛti* specifies that this point is made at the end of the *Vṛtti* so as to

---

[755] ĪPK 1.5.2–3: *prāg ivārtho 'prakāśaḥ syāt prakāśātmatayā vinā | na ca prakāśo bhinnaḥ syād ātmārthasya prakāśatā || bhinne prakāśe cābhinne saṃkaro viṣayasya tat | prakāśātmā prakāśyo 'rtho nāprakāśaś ca sidhyati ||*

[756] ĪPVV, vol. III, pp. 26–27: *nanv anena vibhāgāvasāyena vibhāgasyaivāvabhāsanāt prakāśāvibhāgo vicchedita iti prakāśamānatvaṃ na syād bhāvānām ity āśaṅkya yā vṛttir na cetyādikā, tāṃ vivṛṇoti* ***maheśvarasya tv*** *iti.*

show that in fact, the separation of the subjects and objects and the fundamental unity of *prakāśa* are not contradictory. According to the *Vivṛti*, this latter clarification is necessary, because in the first part of the *Vṛtti*, the manifestation of this separation is said to belong to the Highest Lord, "*even though* He is manifest thus as being full"—a concession that could be read as the acknowledgement of a contradiction. Utpaladeva clarifies in the *Vivṛti* that the reason why there is no such contradiction is that from the Great Lord's standpoint, although limited subjects and objects "are expressed in an objective form, they are manifest while being covered with subjectivity, thanks to the predominance of His agency."

The *Vivṛti* thus defines what the *Vṛtti* calls the "determination" (*avasāya*) of subjects and objects' separation as the fact that things are "expressed" (*nirdiṣṭa*, which may mean "designated," "stated," "defined") "in an objective way" (*idantā*, i.e. again, literally, "as being this"): it is really nothing but consciousness choosing to depict itself *as being this*, i.e., as being an object distinct from the "I." And because *vimarśa*, the ability to actively grasp oneself *as...*, is also the power of expression (*nirdeśa*)[757] that constitutes the core of all language,[758] the absolute consciousness's power of creation is its ability to assert itself as being countless distinct subjects and objects. The separation involved in the cosmogonic process does not actually split the nature of consciousness, because it is the essence of consciousness to thus be capable of appearing to be separated while remaining one: when we choose to imagine an object that we do not currently perceive, in order to picture up the object, our consciousness splits itself into the imagined object (expressed as "the elephant") and imagining subject (expressed as "I"); yet there is no real rupture within consciousness, no actual separation—and in fact, it is the fundamental unity of the imagined object and imagining subject that enables the very act of imagination.

Admittedly, one obvious difference between any ordinary act of imagination and the cosmogonic process as it is understood in the Pratyabhijñā tradition is the fact that in the latter case, the awareness of unity is somehow

---

[757] Abhinavagupta uses the substantive while explaining the verbal adjective *nirdiṣṭa* (see ĪPVV, vol. III, p. 27, quoted below, fn. 762).

[758] On *vimarśa* as an inward, silent or proto-linguistic expression, and for more uses of the term *nirdeśa* in this respect, see e.g. above, fn. 283.

lost or forgotten—hence the very need for a "recognition," and the soteriological endeavour to rescue the bound souls that have lost their freedom in the *saṃsāra*. But an ordinary individual too may sometimes become so engrossed in day-dreaming that (s)he seems to lose for a while all awareness of reality; and according to the Śaiva nondualists, such a temporary lapse is only possible because the day-dreamer somehow remains aware that it is but a fantasy, i.e., that the imagined world is nothing but appearances taken on by the imagining consciousness; and similarly, at the highest level, the universal consciousness must remain aware that the separation is only apparent, and entirely grounded in unity. Thus according to the *Vivṛti* here, from the highest point of view, the creative expression through which consciousness presents itself as a multiplicity of distinct subjects and objects does not conceal its true, nondual nature, because for the Highest Lord, the limited subjects and objects are manifest "while being covered with subjectivity" (*ahantā*—literally, with the "being I"), a choice of words that echoes the last sentence of the *Vṛtti*, according to which the full nature of consciousness is not "concealed" (*tirodhīyate*) by the determination of the separation that results in a world of objects. From the ultimate point of view, it is not subjectivity that is covered (and therefore concealed) by objectivity; rather, objectivity is covered with (i.e., grasped as being entirely inherent in, or encompassed by) subjectivity. In his commentary on this passage, Abhinavagupta explains that this is so because at the pure levels where consciousness remains aware of its absolute plenitude, limited subjects and objects are still grasped as being in a relation of "coreference" or "sharing a single substratum" (*sāmānādhikaraṇya*). The latter word is used by Indian grammarians to designate the fact that several words are in syntactic agreement, and as seen above (chapter 7, §2), Utpaladeva also employs it when describing how a specific collection of elementary phenomena (e.g. "round," "red," "solid," "pot") combines to form a single particular entity (the pot that I see on the ground). Here, the point is that these subjects and objects are all grasped as being but limited expressions of a single reality, namely the full "I" (*aham*):

> [It is the great Lord, who is] full of the five ontological levels (*tattva*) beginning with [Śuddha]vidyā and ending with Śiva, [who] is engaged in producing this separation in the form of Brahmā, etc.; so for [Him, since He] is of this nature, [these

> entities], although they can be expressed as being differentiated, are manifest in Himself [as being] "covered with subjectivity," [that is to say,] as sharing a single substratum (*sāmānādhikaraṇya*) [with the "I"], which culminates in [their] forming one single subtle vibration (*ekalolībhāvagamana*);[759] [and they are] also [manifest thus] for those who partake of the states [of consciousness called] the fourth (*turya*) and the one beyond the [fourth] (*tadatīta*), which consist in such an immersion (*samāpatti*)[760] [in subjectivity. This is so] "due to the predominance of His agency," which will be explained in the [verse][761] beginning with "[And on the contrary, for the self who is nothing but consciousness,] agency [and consciousness] are predominant."[762]

At the pure levels of the universal consciousness, objects are apprehended as one with the "I": consciousness, while externalizing itself by playfully presenting itself in the forms of distinct subjects and objects, also grasps them as one with itself and with its very ability to manifest oneself as if one were outside oneself. And this, as the ĪPVV specifies, is an experience shared by any individual having reached the states of consciousness called the "fourth" and "the one beyond" the fourth. This is an allusion to a well-

[759] Literally, something like "reaching a unitary state of vibrating"; cf. the compound *sarvaśaktivilolatā* in ŚD 1.11b, rendered in TORELLA 2002, p. XXV, as "the effervescence of all powers" and in NEMEC 2011, p. 115, as "all the powers are active." Utpaladeva's gloss on the latter highlights the idea that all powers merge into a dynamic unity (ŚDV, p. 12: *sarvaśaktīnāṃ vilolatā miśrībhāvaḥ*, "the state of vibrating of all powers, [i.e. their] merging together").

[760] The term denotes a kind of yogic absorption that culminates in an identification (*tādātmya*) with the reality that is being contemplated; see e.g. VASUDEVA 2004, pp. 221–222.

[761] ĪPK 3.2.12 (see below, fn. 766).

[762] ĪPVV, vol. III, p. 27: *vidyādiśivāntakatattvapañcakamayasya brahmādirūpatayā vibhāgaṃ kurvatas tadrūpasya sato bhedanirdeśayogyā api svātmany ahantayā sāmānādhikaraṇyenaikalolībhāvagamanaparyantenāvacchāditāḥ, tathāvidhasamāpattilakṣaṇaturyatadatītapadabhājāṃ ca bhāsante kartṛtāyā udrekān mukhyatvaṃ kartṛtāyā ity atra vakṣyamāṇāt.*

known Śaiva division of states of consciousness[763] that contrasts the three ordinary states belonging to the *saṃsāric* sphere of experience—namely, the waking state (*jāgrat*), dream (*svapna*), and deep sleep (*suṣupti*), where subjectivity is subordinated to objectivity and therefore seemingly deprived of its dynamism[764]—with two deeper, underlying states in which it is subjectivity that dominates objectivity.[765]

In order to explain the term "predominance" (*udreka*) used in the *Vivṛti*, the ĪPVV explicitly mentions the passage in the *Āgamādhikāra* where Utpala-

---

[763] On *turya* and *turyātīta* in particular see e.g. VASUDEVA 2004, pp. 229–232, TORELLA 2002, fn. 35, p. 209, and GOODALL & RASTELLI (2013, eds.), s.v. *turya* and *turyātīta*.

[764] See e.g. ĪPV, vol. II, p. 230 (commenting on ĪPK 3.2.11–12, quoted below, fn. 766): ... *yat... caitanyaṃ... tad guṇatvenāpradhānatvena sthitaṃ yato mitam idantāpannadehādiśūnyāntaprameyabhāganimagnatvāt prameyaṃ. yo gauro yaḥ sukhī yas tṛṣito yaḥ sarvarūparahitaḥ so 'ham iti hīndantaivāntarlīnāhaṃbhāvā saṃsāriṇāṃ parisphurati, seyaṃ jāgratsvapnasuṣuptarūpā saṃsārāvasthā.* "[For the transmigrating individual,] consciousness 'exists in a subordinate way,' [i.e.,] as not being predominant, because it is 'limited,' [i.e.,] it is a [mere] object of knowledge insofar as it has sunked into the aspect [of consciousness's appearance constituted by] objects of knowledge, from the body to the void, which have come to exist as 'this.' For it is an objectivity into which subjectivity has sunk that flashes forth for transmigrating subjects [when they think about themselves:] 'I have a fair complexion; I am happy; I am thirsty; I am devoid of any [specific] form'—[and] this is precisely the saṃsāric condition, which consists of the waking state, dreaming state, and deep sleep." The four examples of thoughts mentioned here respectively correspond to the body, intellect, vital air and void with which transmigrating subjects are said to confuse their self.

[765] See e.g. ĪPV, vol. II, p. 243: ... *kartṛtāprādhānyonmeṣāt turyarūpāt prabhṛti tatsthairyātmakaturyātītadaśāntam upādeyam...* "One must strive to attain [the states] beginning with the disclosure of agency's predominance [over objectivity], i.e. the fourth [state], and ending with the one beyond the fourth, which consists in [achieving] steadfastness in this [fourth state]." Cf. *Bhāskarī*, vol. II, p. 270, which glosses *kartṛtāprādhānyonmeṣāt* with *parāhantāprādhānyaprādurbhāvāt*, "the disclosure of the highest subjectivity's predominance." Abhinavagupta's most interesting remarks regarding *turya* and *turyātīta* are to be found in his commentaries on ĪPK 3.2.11–12, but the latter passages are too long to be examined here; besides, the texts recorded by the editions seem problematic in several regards, and amending them would require an inquiry that is beyond the scope of this study.

deva specifies that in the transmigrating individual, the true nature of consciousness, i.e. its agency, is limited and only exists "in a subordinate way," because the passivity and insentiency of the object (body, etc.) with which the individual identifies is grasped by him as the dominant feature of his own nature; whereas in the pure self, consciousness and its agency are predominant—i.e., they are apprehended in their full nature, and as prevailing over every other aspect:

> And for the [transmigrating individual] who does not consist in [pure] consciousness [and wrongly identifies with] the void and [other insentient entities], this true nature of consciousness, i.e. agency, is limited; [it is only] animated by the limited power of action (*kalā*), and [it only] exists in a subordinate way. In contrast (*ca*), for the self who is [nothing but] consciousness, agency and consciousness are predominant, the void and [other insentient entities] being subordinated to these, [and this self's] knowledge consists in an immersion in them.[766]

Finally, the *Vivṛti* on verse 2.1.8 adds that it is not just in the realm of *māyā* that the great creation includes resorption. Thus the level of Sadāśiva belongs to the pure part of emanation; yet Sadāśiva can be said to possess the equivalent of the māyic cosmic phase called resorption inasmuch as it involves the merging of objects into subjectivity. Abhinavagupta explains:

> But in relation to the Lord [defined as consciousness] from [the ontological level of] Śiva down to [that of Śuddha]vidyā, why should the manifestation of [objective] entities that is designated by the word[s] "great creation" not [include] resorption as well? [Utpaladeva] responds: [very well,] let [us] admit [that it includes] resorption; for just as the [objects'] reduction to the status of seeds—[i.e. residual traces]—is resorption [in the realm of *māyā*], so is [their] being immersed within subjectivity [in the pure realm]. At

[766] ĪPK 3.2.11–12 (Abhinavagupta quotes the beginning of ĪPK 3.2.12 while explaining "due to the predominance of His agency" at the end of the *Vivṛti* on ĪPK 2.1.8): *kalodbalitam etac ca cittattvaṃ kartṛtāmayam | acidrūpasya śūnyāder mitaṃ guṇatayā sthitam || mukhyatvaṃ kartṛtāyāś ca bodhasya ca cidātmanaḥ | śūnyādau tadguṇe jñānaṃ tatsamāveśalakṣaṇam ||*

> the level of Śiva, however, one cannot even talk about [objective] entities,[767] so that there [can] be neither creation nor resorption; it is precisely for this reason that [Utpaladeva] specifies "Sadāśiva." [The *Vivṛti* adds that] "[One may use] the expression ['resorption' as well as that of 'creation'"; i.e.,] at this [Sadāśiva level,] the two expressions "creation" and "resorption" refer to a single reality.[768]

In Sadāśiva, all the subjects and objects constituting the universe are present; but they are only so in the form of what the *Vivṛti* calls a "mere reflection" (*chāyāmātra*) and is described elsewhere as a faint outline similar to the first sketch of a painting,[769] because at that stage consciousness apprehends them while being fully aware of their identity with the infinite subject. As a result, objectivity, although present, is somehow cancelled by the awareness of its identity with the fundamental "I," from which things are both "separated and not separated" according to the *Vivṛti*. Yet Utpaladeva also emphasizes the fundamental difference between the great creation (i.e., the eternal pulsation through which the universe keeps being created and dissolved) in the realm of *māyā*, and its counterpart at the pure levels of

---

[767] On Śivatattva in the Pratyabhijñā system see in particular TORELLA 2002, fn. 2, pp. 189–190. In RATIÉ 2017a, p. 182, the passage describing the emergence of objectivity at the pure levels is clumsily rendered in that the translation does not make clear that this is no longer the Śivatattva level per se (even though the latter is also understood to pervade all the other levels), but the Sadāśiva level. The translation should therefore read "And then, [i.e. at the Sadāśiva level]" rather than "And then [i.e. when consciousness is in the state of Śiva]." In the translation of ĪPVV, vol. II, p. 437, provided ibid. (fn. 78), the addition in brackets "in the state of Śiva" should also be replaced with "at the pure levels."

[768] ĪPVV, vol. III, p. 27: *nanu bhagavantaṃ śivādividyāntam apekṣya yad bhāvābhāsanaṃ mahāsṛṣṭiśabdenoktaṃ tat saṃhāro 'pi na kasmāt. āha, bhavatv asau saṃhāraḥ; yathā hi bījatopagamanaṃ saṃhāraḥ, tathāhantāntarmagnatāpi. śivatve tu bhāvānāṃ nāmāpi nāstīti na* sṛṣṭir na saṃhāraḥ.* tadartham evoktaṃ* ***sadāśive-ti. uktir*** *iti vastv ekam eva sṛṣṭisaṃhāravācoyuktyor atra.* [**na* conj.; *na tu* Ed. **yathā hi... saṃhāraḥ* om. S12, J11 (cf. ms. Kha according to Ed.)]

[769] See in particular ĪPVV, vol. III, p. 264, which compares the ontological level of Sadāśiva with a painting (*citra*) that is barely sketched (*unmīlitamātra*) and dim (*dhyāmala*), as opposed to the "full picture" (*pūrṇacitra*) of objectivity that emerges at the level of Īśvara (see RATIÉ 2011a, fn. 140, pp. 699–700 for a translation of the passage and the parallel explanation in ĪPV, vol. II, pp. 192–193).

emanation: since there is no time in the latter, there can be no temporal separation between the creation of the universe and its dissolution, so that both are, as Abhinavagupta says, "a single reality." The ĪPVV further emphasizes the paradox:

> But [surely, the Lord's cosmic activity] takes the form of creation in a state [that occurs] first, [and then it] takes the form of resorption in [another] state [that occurs] later; so how could the reality of [each of] these [two activities] not be distinct? [Utpaladeva] answers this [question] with "but [in it] there is no [temporal separation]." For in it, in reality there is no succession whatsoever. And grace is the unfolding manifestation of such a [nonsequential] form; whereas concealment is nothing but the lower, [māyic forms] (*avāntara*)[770] of maintenance and creation. Thus the Lord has as its essence the power of manifoldly displaying this fivefold [cosmic] activity (*kṛtyapañcaka*)—this is the gist [of this passage].[771]

The creation and destruction of the universe only appear to be sequential inasmuch as they are manifested in the temporally restricted realm of *māyā*; in fact, however, they are mere aspects of a single, nonsequential action, so that the periodic resorption of the universe at the māyic level is only the sequential image of the nonsequential immersion of objectivity within sub-

---

770 On this meaning of *avāntara* (literally "intermediary"), as opposed to the great creation, see e.g. TĀ 14.2cd–4ab: *niyatiṃ karmaphalayor āśrityaiṣa maheśvaraḥ || sṛṣṭisaṃsthitisaṃhārān vidhatte 'vāntarasthitīn | mahāsarge punaḥ sṛṣṭisaṃhārānantyaśālini || ekaḥ sa devo viśvātmā niyatityāgataḥ prabhuḥ |* "The Great Lord performs [cosmic] creations, maintenances and resorptions that have a lower (*avāntara*) status when He relies on the necessity of the act and its result; whereas in the great creation, which is replete with an infinity of creations and resorptions, the Lord, who is the universe's essence, exerts His power alone, independently of necessity."

771 ĪPVV, vol. III, p. 27: *nanu pūrvāvasthāyāṃ sṛṣṭirūpatā, uttarāvasthāyāṃ saṃhārarūpatā, tat kathaṃ vastv atra na bhidyata iti. atrāha* ***na tv*** *iti. na hy atra paurvāparyaṃ* kiṃcit paramārthataḥ.* evaṃrūpaprathā cānugrahaḥ, sthitisṛṣṭyavāntararūpa eva ca vilaya iti kṛtyapañcakaprapañcanaśaktisāro bhagavān iti tātparyārthaḥ.* [**paurvāparyaṃ* corr.; *paurvāparye* S12, J11, Ed. **paramārthataḥ* corr.; *paramārthaḥ* S12, J11; *paramārthatā* Ed.]

jectivity that eternally occurs at the Sadāśiva level. The five cosmic activities (*kṛtyapañcaka*) traditionally ascribed to Śiva—namely creation (*sṛṣṭi*), maintenance (*sthiti*), resorption (*saṃhāra*), concealment (*vilaya/tirodhāna*), and grace (*anugraha*)—are thus interpreted in the Pratyabhijñā system as aspects of a single, nonsequential dynamism rather than as a temporally determined cycle of distinct events, grace being defined as the full unfolding of the nonsequential unity of creation and resorption within Sadāśiva, while concealment—i.e., the obscuration of the unity and plenitude of consciousness's nature—is understood as the sequential creation and maintenance, in the saṃsāric world, of separated subjects and objects. And because in fact consciousness's creativity transcends all temporal boundaries, it occurs eternally, *even at the māyic levels*: in chapter 1.6 (which Abhinavagupta certainly has in mind when making the comments just cited), Utpaladeva already emphasizes that the Lord's creative activity does not only occur with the inceptive creation of the universe (*ādisarga*), but always, including in all circumstances of worldly existence, because the sequential manifestation that constitutes all wordly existence is his doing. The *Vṛtti* on verse 1.6.7[772] thus specifies:

> Whether in the inceptive creation [of the universe] (*ādisarga*) or in worldly activities (*vyavahāra*), the Great Lord, while positing the body, etc.[773] as being the self thanks to

[772] ĪPK 1.6.7 runs as follows: *tad evaṃ vyavahāre 'pi prabhur dehādim āviśan | bhāntam evāntar arthaugham icchayā bhāsayed bahiḥ* || "Thus even in worldly activities, it is the Lord who, by entering the body, etc., must manifest externally, out of [His mere] will, all the objects that [remain] internally manifested."

[773] The verb *abhiniviś-* used here may have different meanings, among which "to enter," but also "to be attached to/fond of" something (the *Vivṛti* on ĪPK 2.1.3 uses the corresponding substantive *abhiniveśa* in this sense), and "to regard/posit/identify X as being Y" (the phenomenological use of the French word "visée" is certainly an apt translation of the substantive *abhiniveśa*, for which I can find no satisfactory equivalent in English). In the *Vṛtti*, the use of the compound *ātmatvena* ("as being the self") in connection with it clearly points to the latter sense, which could be seen as a relatively rare Vedāntic echo in Utpaladeva's writings; cf. e.g. Śaṅkara's *Brahmasūtrabhāṣya*, p. 172: *dṛśyate cātmana eva sato dehādisaṃghāte 'nātmany ātmatvābhiniveśo...* "And [we] see that one regards (*abhiniveśa*) what is not the Self—[i.e.] an aggregate such as the body—as being the Self, whereas only the Self exists... (The *Bhāmatī*, ibid., explains *abhiniveśaḥ* here as *mithyābhimānaḥ*,

> [His] power of *māyā*, [and] while [thus] creating a [limited] knowing subject, sequentially manifests the various objects as being external—[although they also] remain internally manifest—thanks to [His] creative power.[774]

Abhinavagupta explains in this connection that the the five cosmic activities occur "absolutely always" (*sadaiva, satatam eva*): they are not only exerted during exceedingly rare cosmic events, but constantly, because at the pure level they are mere aspects of a single, eternal dynamism, and in the realm of *māyā*, if not eternal (since they become temporally affected), at least they occur at every single moment—including in the midst of the transmigrating individuals' most ordinary experiences:

> It is not only at the well-known[775] times of [cosmic] creation, maintenance, resorption, concealment and grace, but also at the time of countless worldly activities between [different

"an erroneous belief/identification"). It should be noted, however, that the compound *ātmābhiniveśa* is also commonly used in Buddhist philosophical literature with the meaning of "attachment to/belief in the Self" (see ELTSCHINGER & RATIÉ 2013, pp. 7, 11, 13, etc.), and *abhiniviś-* is also used to convey that one sees something (i.e. the *skandhas*) *as* the self (see e.g. ibid., p. 16). Yet this does not mean that the first sense of the term ("to enter, to penetrate") should be entirely excluded as regards this passage of the *Vṛtti*, all the more since it explains ĪPK 1.6.7, where it is the verb *āviś-* ("to enter," "to take possession of") that is used, and without any equivalent of *ātmatvena* (see above, fn. 772). In ĪPVV, vol. II, p. 315, Abhinavagupta comments on the overall meaning of the verse by saying *āviśati—pramātṛtayā svīkaroti*, "it enters [them, i.e.,] it appropriates them as being knowing subjects"—which seems to be an attempt (based on the currently unavailable *Vivṛti* ad loc.?) to conciliate both meanings. For instances where *abhiniviś-* clearly has the phenomenological meaning of "regarding/positing something as...," see e.g. ĪPV, vol. II, p. 206: ... *aham iti saṃvidrūpatābhiniveśasthānaṃ saṃpāditam...* "[The void, etc., although they are objects,] have come to be posited as consisting in consciousness." Cf. the parallel passage in ĪPVV, vol. III, p. 280; see also e.g. *Bhāskarī*, vol. II, p. 233: *abhiniviśyate, pramātrātmasthāne sthāpyate*. "[The intellect] '*abhiniviśyate*,' [i.e.] it is posited (*sthāpyate*) by the knowing subject as being himself"; etc.

[774] *Vṛtti*, p. 29: *ādisarge vā vyavahāre 'pi vā maheśvaro māyāśaktyā dehādim ātmatvenābhiniviśya pramātāraṃ kurvann antaḥsthitaṃ vibhāntam eva taṃ tam arthaṃ krameṇa bahīrūpaṃ kartṛśaktyā bhāsayati.*

[775] In the sense that they are traditionally mentioned in Purāṇas, scriptures and so on.

> transmigrating individuals]—such as selling and buying, debating, teaching, watching a show, etc.—that the Lord, [who acts] "out of [His mere] will," [i.e.,] who is free, manifests "externally" all the objects [that remain] "internally manifested"—[i.e.,] that have not abandoned [their identity with] the manifesting consciousness (*prakāśa*). [He manifests them thus] by "entering" the bodies, vital breaths and so on that are differentiated as [being] Caitra, Maitra, etc.; [i.e.,] by *creating* them as a unitary entity with respect to this limited aspect [of their experience that is the common activity in which they are engaged];[776] by manifesting the *continuity* of this very [creation of their unity]; by *resorbing* [their] unity with [other] subjects [encountered] previously; by performing *concealment* inasmuch as [He] hides His own nature that is absolutely one with them; and by manifesting the power of *grace* with the aspect [of their experience that is their] immersion in unity—He, who is absolutely always engaged in performing the five [cosmic] activities.[777]

The idea recurs in Kṣemarāja's PH:

> Even though [consciousness, due to the contraction of its powers, has become the transmigrating subject covered by impurities,] it performs the five [cosmic] activities just as well.[778]

---

[776] On this idea that the universal consciousness merges different subjects into one with respect to certain shared objects only, see above, §5, particularly fn. 752.

[777] ĪPVV, vol. II, p. 316: *na kevalaṃ prasiddheṣu sṛṣṭisthitisaṃhāratirodhānānugrahakāleṣu yāvad asminn anyonyakrayavikrayavivādopadeśaprekṣāprabhṛtyanantavyavahārakāle 'pi, dehaprāṇādīṃś caitramaitrādibhinnān āviśann aikyena tāvaty aṃśe nirmimāṇas tatraiva sthitiṃ bhāsayan pūrvapramātraikyaṃ saṃharan, tadekaghananijarūpanimīlanād vilayam upadarśayann aikyāveśāṃsenānugrahakalāṃ nirbhāsayann antar* bhāntam evātyaktaprakāśam* eva santam artharāśim icchayā prabhuḥ svatantraḥ kṛtyapañcakasampādane sadaivodyukto bahir ekābhāsatayā bhāsayati.* [**nirbhāsayann antar* conj.; *nirbhāsayan* Ed. **evātyaktaprakāśam* conj.; *evātyantaprakāśam* ĪPVV.] See also ĪPV, vol. I, pp. 261–262 (translated in RATIÉ 2011a, pp. 577–578).

[778] PH 10: *tathāpi tadvat pañcakṛtyāni karoti.*

The auto-commentary quotes ĪPK 1.6.7[779] and proceeds to explains how the cosmic functions are performed within the saṃsāric world. Kṣemarāja's perspective differs from Abhinavagupta's (and can thus be seen to complete it) in that it focuses on the object rather than the subject of wordly experience:

> According to the view on this point that is expressed in the *Pratyabhijñākārikā*, when the Great Lord who consists in consciousness, entering the realm of the body, vital breath and so on while [manifesting itself as if it were] turned outwards, manifests an object such as the blue as endowed with a specific place, time and [form], then He is the one who *creates* with respect to this aspect that is a phenomenon endowed with a specific place, time and [form]; with respect to the aspect that is a phenomenon endowed with another specific place, time and [form], He is the one who *resorbs*; with respect to the aspect of the phenomenon such as blue, He is the one who *maintains*; with respect to the aspect of the phenomenon as being separated [from the subject and other objects], He is the one who *conceals*; and as far as [He] manifests [the objective phenomenon's] unity with the manifesting consciousness, He is the one who *bestows grace*.[780]

In the Pratyabhijñā system, the five cosmic activities attributed to Śiva are not separated by eons and utterly incompatible with each other: they pervade every moment of worldly existence, and even in the temporally divided realm of *māyā*, where every activity is affected by sequence, they occur simultaneously, because they are nothing but aspects of the eternal dynamism of consciousness.

---

[779] PH, p. 23.

[780] PH, pp. 23–24: *iti pratyabhijñākārikoktārthadṛṣṭyā dehaprāṇādipadam āviśaṃś cidrūpo maheśvaro bahirmukhībhāvāvasare nīlādikam arthaṃ niyatadeśakāladitayā yadābhāsayati, tadā niyatadeśakālādyābhāsāṃśe 'sya sraṣṭṛtā; anyadeśakālādyābhāsāṃśe 'sya saṃhartṛtā; nīlādyābhāsāṃśe sthāpakatā; bhedenābhāsāṃśe vilayakāritā; prakāśaikyena prakāśane 'nugrahītṛtā.*

# CHAPTER 11

## *Īśvarapratyabhijñāvivṛti*, Chapter 2.1: Translation

### VIVṚTI

Thus so far,[1] in order to examine the main topic [of the treatise, we] have established that the power of knowledge—the substratum and existence of which had [first] been questioned [by the Buddhist opponent]—exists continuously in all knowing subjects; [and we have achieved this] by demonstrating the unity of the manifesting [consciousness] (*prakāśa*) inside self-awareness (*svasaṃvedana*)[2]—[and indeed,] everywhere, [i.e., outside it as well].[3] Now [the next verse, beginning with] "For the same reason...", is stated in order to establish the power of action:

### ĪPK 2.1.1

For the same reason, this [Buddhist] objection too—[namely:] "Action, which occurs in sequence (*sakrama*), can neither belong to [an entity that is] one [nor be] one," etc.—is refuted by the demonstration [of the true nature] of [consciousness, which is] one.

---

[1] For a summary of the theses that were established in the first part of the treatise and that are briefly alluded to in this introduction to its second part, see above, chapter 3.

[2] On this demonstration see above, chapter 3, §2.

[3] According to Abhinavagupta's commentary, ĪPVV, vol. III, p. 2: ***sarvatre****ti bahir antaś ca*. "Everywhere [means] both outside and inside [self-awareness]." In other words, the first part of the treatise has established the unity of consciousness both within any self-aware entity and (thanks to chapter 1.5) in what appears to be external to consciousness, i.e., in objects that are seemingly independent of it. On the latter demonstration see above, chapter 3, §3.

## VṚTTI

Because [we] have demonstrated the true nature of consciousness, which is one, the activity belonging to [this consciousness] that is one must [itself] be one; so [our opponent's] refutation of action too is [now] disproved.

## VIVṚTI

[The Buddhist] claims that action, which occurs in sequence, cannot have unity or belong to [an entity] that is one.[4] [Here is what we reply] to this: in the course of demonstrating [the existence of the power of] knowledge, [we] have said that the activity characterized as manifesting (*prakāśa*) that belongs to the self—[the latter, which the Buddhist] calls "self-awareness,"[5] having as its essence the manifesting [consciousness itself] (*prakāśa*)—is the [very] nature [of the self, a nature for which] the term "realization" (*vimarśa*) is a [mere] synonym.[6] [And] as soon as [we have shown this,] the unity of action and its belonging to [an entity] that is one are demonstrated by the same [token]! This is what [the *Vṛtti*] says with [the words] "[because we have demonstrated] the true nature of consciousness, which

---

[4] On this contention see above, chapter 4, §1.

[5] While refusing to acknowledge the existence of an enduring self, the Buddhists who belong to Dignāga and Dharmakīrti's tradition consider that each cognition is endowed with an immediate awareness of itself. According to Utpaladeva, however, they are deluded into seeing this self-awareness as the purely momentary property of irreducibly distinct cognitions, whereas it is none other than the enduring self that they seek to deny; and in fact, the Buddhist principle that each cognition is self-aware, if taken to its ultimate consequences, must inevitably lead to the demonstration of a permanent *ātman* (see above, chapter 3, §2).

[6] That is to say, the first part of the treatise has established not only that consciousness is one (as the introduction to this chapter reminds us), but also that it has a dynamic nature (see above, chapter 3, §2). Thus consciousness is primarily defined as *prakāśa*, a term that means both "a manifesting [entity/agent]" (in non-technical contexts it can designate light) and the activity of manifestation (also termed *prakāśana*) or even the resulting manifested appearance: consciousness is what manifests things while manifesting itself. Yet its manifesting power does not consist in passively reflecting a given (as mirrors do), but in actively becoming aware of itself, in grasping or realizing (*vimarśa*) its own dynamic essence (see above, chapter 4, §3). Action (in its subtlest form of a purely conscious act of self-apprehension) is therefore the very nature (*svabhāva*) of the self; and since Utpaladeva has proven the latter's unity by demonstrating its permanence, action itself must be one.

is one." For a nature belonging to [an entity that is] one must itself be one, and even those who propound the thesis that there is [only] difference in action (*kriyābhedavādin*)[7] admit that action, although it consists in activity, is as good as the nature (*svabhāva*) [of an entity that is one,] inasmuch as it is cognized as not being separated [from a substance possessed of unity], due to [its] inherence (*samavāya*) [in that substance];[8] whereas in [our idealistic system, where things have phenomena as their essence],[9] because one cognizes [action itself] as being unitary, the fact that action belongs to [an entity] that is one—which is nothing but its being tightly conjoined (*upaśleṣa*) with that [entity] that is one—is possible precisely because [action] itself has a unity[10]—this is what [the *Vṛtti*] says with "[our opponent's] refutation of action too [is now disproved]."

Now, in order to examine [action's property of] occurring in sequence (*sakramatva*), which seems to be contradictory [with the Lord's nature],[11] is

---

[7] Abhinavagupta specifies that they are "the followers of Kaṇāda, etc.," i.e., the Vaiśeṣikas and (most probably) Naiyāyikas, in ĪPVV, vol. III, p. 2 (***icchantīti** kāṇādādyāḥ*).

[8] See above, chapter 4, §4: the Vaiśeṣikas consider that action has no unity of its own since numbers can only exist in substances; they do admit, however, that an action can only exist in a substance that is endowed with unity. Utpaladeva therefore argues here that they must concede that action too (and not just the substance in which it occurs) has some kind of unity, because what constitutes the nature of a unitary entity must itself be one, and action, inasmuch as it is always apprehended along with the unitary substance in which it inheres, must be considered to be "as good as" the nature of that unitary substance.

[9] According to ĪPVV, vol. III, p. 2, quoted above, chapter 4, fn. 314.

[10] That is to say, in Utpaladeva's system, action does not merely have a unity by proxy so to speak, as the indirect result of the fact that the substance in which it inheres happens to be one. According to him, action too is one, and is apprehended as such; but the entity to which action belongs (i.e. the agent) and action itself are not in fact two distinct realities, action being nothing but the dynamic nature of the agent—which is why he can claim here that action can belong to an agent that is one precisely because it is itself one.

[11] This is what should be understood here according to both of Abhinavagupta's commentaries; see above, chapter 5, §1.

stated [the following verse, beginning with] "[And for ordinary action,] occurring in sequence...":

### ĪPK 2.1.2

And for ordinary (*laukika*) action, occurring in sequence is possible thanks to the power of time; but there can be no [occurring in sequence] for the eternal [action] that belongs to the Lord, just as [there can be no occurring in sequence] for the Lord [Himself].

### VṚTTI

The action of [entities] that have [entirely][12] differentiated manifestations[13] due to the power of *māyā* occurs in sequence thanks to the power of time; but not [the action] that consists in self-realization (*ātmavimarśa*), is without beginning or end,[14] [and] is the [very] nature of the Lord.

### VIVṚTI

In this [world], the power of *māyā* brings about the existence pertaining to the cycle of rebirths (*saṃsāra*) in the aspect [of consciousness's appearance that is constituted by] objects of knowledge, the manifestations of which are entirely[15] differentiated; [and it brings about this existence precisely] by manifesting the relation between the apprehending subject (*grāhaka*) and the apprehended object (*grāhya*).[16] According to a principle that will

---

[12] Cf. the particle *eva* in the *Vivṛti* ad loc.; this is to be understood in contrast with the manifestations occurring at the pure levels of consciousness, which are either fully undifferentiated or both differentiated and undifferentiated (see in particular Utpaladeva's *Vṛtti* on ĪPK 1.8.11, quoted above, chapter 5, fn. 328; the full text of the *Vivṛti* on it is edited and translated in RATIÉ 2017a).

[13] The translation of the compound *bhinnāvabhāsānām* as a *bahuvrīhi* follows the *Vivṛti*'s explanation.

[14] This expression (*anādinidhana*) is of course reminiscent of VP 1.1, although Bhartṛhari uses to qualify the Brahman whereas it is the ultimate reality's *action* that Utpaladeva describes thus (see above, chapter 5, §2).

[15] On the meaning of *eva* here see above, fn. 12.

[16] On this relation, in which the limited subject and object are both dependent on and opposed to each other, see above, chapter 5, §2.

be explained [later in the chapter], in that aspect [of consciousness's appearance that is constituted by] objects of knowledge, due to the measure/division (*avaccheda*)[17] [brought about] by the power of time, action must be temporally measured/divided (*kālāvacchinna*), [and] its form will be shown to occur in sequence—this is what [the *Vṛtti*] says with "[The action of entities that have entirely differentiated manifestations] due to the power of *māyā*." However, the [action] belonging to the Lord who consists in the manifesting [consciousness] is [precisely] His nature, which [we] call the "I-realization" (*ahaṃvimarśa*); [and it] is necessarily free of sequence because, due to [its] devouring all the objects that are constrained (*avaruddha*) by time, it also devours time [itself].[18] This is what [the *Vṛtti*] says with "but not [the action that consists in] self-realization..." Nonetheless, this [same action], which is full of pure freedom, [is also what] ends up being the artificial agency [of limited subjects].[19]

As a consequence of this examination of action's [property of] occurring in sequence, and also because, as will be explained [later, this] contributes to [bringing about] the Lord's recognition,[20] [the following verse] is now stated in order to explain the nature of time:

---

[17] The term *avaccheda* means both measuring something (i.e. ascertaining its limits, or delimiting it from a purely cognitive point of view, as the *Vivṛti* on ĪPK 2.1.3 explains) and actually dividing something; while translating I sometimes had to choose one translation over the other according to the context, but in some cases both meanings could be intended.

[18] The "devouring of time" (*kālagrāsa*) is a technical term borrowed from the Krama tradition: see above, chapter 5, §3. The point is that consciousness, while manifesting itself in the form of an objective universe distinct from itself, also merges all objects back into subjectivity by apprehending them as "I"; and by the same token, as explained by Abhinavagupta (ĪPVV, vol. III, pp. 3–4, quoted above, fn. 342), it also "devours" time itself, since temporal sequence, which is confined to the objective realm, is immersed in the unity of subjective realization along with the "devoured" objects.

[19] On this last point, only made in passing here, that the Lord's action is what manifests itself as the ordinary action of transmigrating individuals, see above, chapter 5, §4.

[20] According to Abhinavagupta, this is an allusion to verses 2.1.4 ff.; see ĪPVV, vol. III, p. 5: ***vakṣyamāṇād*** *iti kramo bhedetyādisūtreṣu*. That is to say, explaining the

## ĪPK 2.1.3

Time is the movement of the sun, etc.; or this or that arising of flowers, etc.; or cold and heat—but in reality, [time] is nothing but sequence (*krama*) marked (*lakṣya*) by these.

## VṚTTI

Time is this or that well-known action,[21] or cold, etc.; [but in fact], it is nothing but the sequence marked (*upalakṣita*) by these, [a sequence] which is an adventitious property (*upādhi*) of [objective] entities that are manifested as being entirely differentiated—[and time is nothing but this sequence,] because only this [sequence can] contribute [to the measurement of temporal differences].

## VIVṚTI

[22]The thing denoted (*padārtha*) [by the word] "time" is acknowledged [to exist as] the cause of [our] delimiting (*pariccheda*) things' particular na-

nature of time helps bring about the recognition of the Lord because, as argued in ĪPK 2.1.4, temporal sequence is the result of an incompatibility between certain phenomena that can only be explained as the Lord's will to prevent certain phenomena from occurring together.

[21] This first definition of time in the *Vṛtti* actually covers the first two options mentioned in the verse. Abhinavagupta thus points out (ĪPVV, vol. III, pp. 6–7, see above, chapter 6, fn. 390) that the first "or" (*vā*), which, in the verse, could be taken to separate the definition of time as "the movement of the sun, etc." from that of time as "this or that arising of flowers, etc.", actually indicates that these two "amount to the same thing"—namely, the thesis that time is nothing but actions.

[22] In what follows Utpaladeva explains the first definition of time put forward in the verse, viz. the thesis that because time is what enables us to measure, it must be none other than actions such as the movement of the sun, which, being regular and well known, can be used as points of reference to measure other actions. This is not Utpaladeva's own position (according to him, time is rather the sequence marked by such actions); and although the definition of time as an *avacchedaka* belongs to the Vaiśeṣika, the equation of time with well-known actions is in fact defended by opponents of the Vaiśeṣika (notably Sāṃkhyas) who do not accept its view of time

tures for the sake of [our] ordinary practices (*vyavahāra*); and it is undoubtedly well known [as] a measure (*avacchedaka*)[23] [of things]. It is therefore taught to be the [very] thing that [constitutes] a [temporal] marker (*upalakṣaṇa*),[24] [namely,] a well-known action [that enables us to measure other actions]: it is a particular movement of [something] such as the sun—[a movement] that [in turn] may be described in terms of *nālikā*s and [other units of measure made of other actions];[25] [and] it is well known [insofar it] has [already] enabled [us] to obtain numerous [things] that [we] wanted to obtain [by measuring them with it]—this is what [the *Vṛtti*] says with [the words] "[Time is] this or that well-known [action]." [And] another [action] that is particularized inasmuch as it is well known that it is to be accomplished in a [specific] sequence is [in turn] nothing but the time of the

---

as a distinct *padārtha* consisting in a permanent substance. Yet Abhinavagupta explains that for now, Utpaladeva only examines this equation of time with actions, because he considers that the Vaiśeṣikas' contradictory definition of time as what makes temporal distinctions possible must lead them to unwittingly admit it: see above, chapter 6, §1. The Vaiśeṣikas' view of time as a permanent substance is nonetheless mentioned and criticized later in the *Vivṛti* on this verse.

23 Utpaladeva's implicit reasoning here (which is explicitly stated in Sāṃkhya and Yoga sources in particular: see above, chapter 6, §1) is that the Vaiśeṣikas, by presenting time as an *avacchedaka*, i.e. as something that enables us to delimit or measure, effectively end up negating their own view that time is a unitary and unchanging substance, because the latter could not be the cause of the differences in which temporal delimitations consist, and because only actions can be used as measures for other actions.

24 An *upalakṣaṇa* is a feature that serves to distinguish a given entity from others although it does not belong to the very nature of that entity (as already specified in the *Vṛtti*, and as repeated in the *Vivṛti*, it is a mere adventitious property, *upādhi*): see above, chapter 6, §6, fn. 405.

25 A *nālikā* is a period of twenty-four minutes. As to the way in which its measure is obtained, see e.g. *Arthaśāstra* 2.20.35 (translation KANGLE 1963, p. 139): *suvarṇamāṣakāś catvāraś caturaṅgulāyāmāḥ kumbhacchidram āḍhakam ambhaso vā nālikā.* "Or a hole in a jar [with a dimension] of four *māṣaka*s of gold made four *aṅgula*s in length, [with] an *āḍhaka* of water [running through it,] measures one *nālikā*." In other words, the measure called *nālikā* is in fact the action of water running through a specific device, which can be used as a marker to determine the duration of other actions.

[first action].[26] Therefore [in the verse], there is an [implicit] inclusion of such [other well-known actions] as the milking of cows,[27] [as indicated by the word "movement" (*saṃcāra*); and] because of the use of [the word] "etc." in "the [movement] of the sun, *etc.*", one should consider that] other celestial bodies [such as the moon] are included.[28] [As for] the arising of flowers, etc., it is [mentioned in the verse as a definition of time because this arising] is well known among farmers, [whereas] they do not know about the movement of [celestal bodies] such as the sun;[29] [so] they use this [arising of flowers] as a marker (*tena... upalakṣayanti*) for the movement of [something] such as the sun that is also called e.g. "spring." Again, because of the use of [the word] "etc." in ["this or that arising of flowers, *etc.*",] the arising of [something else] such as rice, which is well known by farmers, is included; and again, for those who might not be acquainted [with

[26] According to ĪPVV, vol. III, p. 5 (quoted above, chapter 6, fn. 364). The reasoning and wording here are close to those in YD, p. 161 (quoted above, chapter 6, fn. 361) and PYV, p. 310 (quoted ibid., fn. 363).

[27] This example is mentioned in the YD, PYV and PP (see above, chapter 6, fn. 355, 361, 363, 376). Cf. e.g. MONIER-WILLIAMS 1899 (s.v.), according to which *godoha/godohana* can denote both the milking of cows and the time that it takes to accomplish this action.

[28] Cf. ĪPVV, vol. III, p. 6: *nanu yadi saṃcāreṇa* ***godohādir*** *lakṣyate, na tv ādigrahaṇena svīkriyate, tarhi sūtre kimartham tat. ucyate* ***'nyagraha*** *iti candrāder anyasya grahasya parigrahaḥ. yuktaṃ caitat, godohādisaṃgrahāya ced ādipadaṃ syāt, saṃcārādir iti brūyāt.* "But if[, as the *Vivṛti* contends, other actions] such as the milking of cows are indicated [in the verse] with the [mere word] 'movement,' whereas they are not included by the use of the word 'etc.', then why is this [word 'etc.'] employed [at all] in the verse? [Utpaladeva] answers [this question with the words] 'other celestial bodies...' [That is to say,] other celestial bodies such as the moon are included [in 'the movement of the sun, *etc.*'] And this is right: if the word 'etc.' were meant to convey the milking of cows and [other actions, Utpaladeva] would have said 'the [sun's] *movement, etc.* ([*sūrya*]*saṃcārādi*), [rather than 'the movement *of the sun, etc.* (*sūryādisaṃcāra*)]."

[29] As noted in MONIER-WILLIAMS 1899 (s.v.), the movement (*saṃcāra*) of the sun does not merely designate the sun's apparent daily motion from East to West but also its entrance into a new sign. Cf. ĪPVV, vol. III, p. 8: *mīnameṣarāśisaṃcaraṇanimittārkasyodayādikriyā vartamānā vasanta ity anubhūyate.* "[What we call] 'spring' [is what we] experience [as] the action of arising, etc. of the sun, [an action occurring in the] present [and that] is characterized as the [sun's] movement towards the zodiac signs [known as] 'pisces' and 'aries.'"

this], thanks to the repetition [in the verse] of [the word] *tat* [in "*this* or *that* arising of flowers, etc.," one should understand that any other well-known action] such as the arrival of a particular [species] of birds is included; and this is [in turn] a marker (*upalakṣaṇa*) for [some other action] that is not well known by farmers. All of this is made clear [in the *Vṛtti*] with the repetition of [the word] *sā* [in "*this or that* well-known action"].

[30]Not only does time contribute to measuring (*avaccheda*) [i.e. distinguishing our various] cognitions (*pratīti*): [insofar as it] has an accomplished form [rather than being an action,[31] that is, inasmuch as it is] heat, etc., it is also well known to contribute [to the production of things themselves] as [their] auxiliary cause for instance;[32] this is what [the *Vṛtti*] says with "cold,

[30] From here on Utpaladeva explains that the Vaiśeṣika definition of time does not present it only as an *avacchedaka*, i.e., as what enables us to measure other actions that we perceive (so that it only affects our *cognitions* of these actions), but also as an auxiliary cause that contributes to the production of effects independently of the way in which we perceive them (since the specific temperatures that only occur in spring for instance help flowers grow). On this second aspect of the Vaiśeṣika view see above, chapter 6, §3.

[31] In the ĪPVV edition (vol. III, p. 7) as in manuscripts S12 and J11, Abhinavagupta's gloss is given as ***siddharūpaḥ*** *kriyātmā*, "[it] has an accomplished form, [i.e., it] consists in an action." It seems to me that it should be emended into ***siddharūpo*** *'kriyātmā*, "[it] has an accomplished form, [i.e., it] consists in [something] that is not an action," since as pointed out further in Abhinavagupta's commentary, the Vaiśeṣikas, whose doctrine is targeted here, believe that time "has an accomplished form" (*siddharūpa*, see ĪPVV, vol. III, p. 8, quoted above, chapter 6, fn. 415) inasmuch as it is *not* an action but a distinct, permanent substance. On the distinction between actions as what is to be accomplished (*sādhya*) and things (i.e. substances) as that whose form is accomplished (*siddha*), see e.g. VP 3.7.79cd, quoted above, chapter 6, fn. 369.

[32] See above, chapter 6, §3: one of the arguments adduced by Vaiśeṣika authors to prove the existence of an entity called "time" consists in pointing out that the temperatures that specifically occur at the time of spring are auxiliary causes in the growth of flowers. According to ĪPVV, vol. III, p. 7, the "etc." here means that the material cause of a particular entity is also included (***ādi****padāt svalakṣaṇasyopādānakāraṇam api*).

etc." [But all of] this[33] is merely a presentation of the established conclusions of another system, [and we Śaiva nondualists] have no fondness for this [view] in any [respect], because measures (*avacchedaka*) are created by virtue of one's mere will, and because the common knowledge (*prasiddhi*) [on which this will is allegedly based] is [itself] liable to an infinite regress (*anavasthita*).[34] And from the fact that the cold, etc., contribute to the production of an effect, [what follows] is merely that [they] are a cause, [but] not [that they are] time! As for their being time, it [could] only [follow] from their being measures; but [their being measures][35] has [already] been said to be liable to an infinite regress (*anavasthita*)![36]

Therefore time must be whatever is marked by all these [actions mentioned in the verse],[37] has a lasting (*sthira*) nature and contributes to measuring [i.e. distinguishing our] cognitions of things;[38] and if [we] examine [our] cognitions, [we will find that time thus defined] can only be sequence itself—this is what [the *Vṛtti*] says with "[time is nothing but the sequence] marked by these." To explain: the experience of "spring" for instance is

---

[33] See ĪPVV, vol. III, p. 7: ***etad*** *iti sarvam*; i.e., "this" includes both of the options considered (that time may be this or that particular action providing a measure for other actions; or that it may be the cause of this or that particular effect).

[34] On this argument see above, chapter 6, §4: those who define time as actions that enable us to measure other actions claim to avoid infinite regress on the grounds that the actions thus used as measures are already "well known"; but this knowledge itself must be established by measuring the action that is taken as a point of reference, etc., so that the threat of infinite regress is not actually averted.

[35] According to ĪPVV, vol. III, p. 7: ***etac cety*** *avacchedakatvam*.

[36] On this argument see above, chapter 6, §5: the point is that such things as the specific temperatures occurring in spring can only be called "time" inasmuch as they can constitute temporal measures, but what enables us to use them as temporal measures is not their specific nature (as can be seen from the fact that temporal measures are established as a matter of mere convention), but only the sequence that they involve, which must be time itself.

[37] According to ĪPVV, vol. III, p. 7: *etena sarveṇa sūtroktenopalakṣyamāṇaṃ yat kiñcit kalpitam avacchedakam.* "[It must be] 'whatever' is conceived as a measure while being marked by all the [actions] mentioned in the verse."

[38] See ĪPVV, vol. III, p. 7: *sa ca padārthānāṃ prameyāṇāṃ pratītim avacchinatti.* "And it measures/distinguishes the cognition[s] of things [understood as] objects of knowledge."

simply [the experience] of that which consists in a [certain] sequence of arisings of [an objective entity] such as the sun, and which is an adventitious property of [this objective entity] such as the sun; [yet], because it may be a marker for the [coming to] existence of [other] objective entities that did not exist [until then], this same [activity] that is e.g. the movement of [an objective entity] such as the sun [also] marks the very sequence belonging to [these other objective entities, so that] a sequential object such as a flower or even [a conscious individual] such as Devadatta [can] be manifested with this same adventitious property[39]—this is what [the *Vṛtti*] says with "[a sequence which is an adventitious property of objective entities] that are manifest as being [entirely] differentiated."

[40]Words such as "spring," and words such as "past" or "future," do not express the nature of time directly, just as the word "action" [does not express] action [directly], but only through a reference to something that is nonsequential (*yugapad*), posited as [something] distinct (*vyavasthita*), and accomplished (*siddha*); whereas such words as "was," "is", "will be" counteract (*pratikārin*) [this inadequate characterization] as appropriate [expressions] of the experience of time. Therefore the thing that is being

[39] See chapter 6, §6: the action of a given entity can constitute a temporal marker that is conventionally applied to measure the actions of other entities, and it is the common, lasting element in all actions, namely sequence, that enables us to thus use actions as temporal markers, sequence being what is variously marked by them while remaining the same, just as (to use Abhinavagupta's analogy), when different weights are used to measure gold, the nature of gold itself remains unaffected.

[40] From here on, as noted by Abhinavagupta (see ĪPVV, vol. III, p. 8, quoted above, chapter 6, fn. 415), Utpaladeva reminds his readers of a point that he has already made under ĪPK 1.5.17 (quoted above, chapter 6, fn. 413) following several grammatical sources (see above, fn. 410–412)—namely, that contrary to our use of inflected verbs, that of substantive words such as "action" tends to reify (or, quite literally, substantivize) the dynamic reality that such terms are supposed to convey. See above, chapter 6, §6: Utpaladeva thus emphasizes here what he considers to be the most important difference between his view of time and the Vaiśeṣikas', since just as them, he sees time as an element that is common to all ordinary actions and "has a lasting nature," but contrary to them, he identifies it with sequence, the essence of which is a flux or flow (*pravahaṇa*), rather than a static entity, and he considers that the Vaiśeṣikas are fooled into believing that time is a distinct substance by the substantive power that language has of presenting dynamic processes as things.

posited as [something] distinct [when we] characterize [it] with [the word] "time" must be examined in the same way, [i.e., as being inadequately posited as a distinct substance by this substantive word] whereas it has as its essence nothing but the sequence of birth, existence, transformation, etc.;[41] this is what [the *Vṛtti*] says with [the words] "because only this [sequence can] contribute [to the measurement of temporal differences]." For it is only sequence, inasmuch as [we] use it to measure such differences, that [we thus] determine [as being a distinct reality called "time"]—this is the meaning [of the end of the *Vṛtti*,] which explains [the words] "in reality, [time is nothing but sequence" in the verse].

As a result of this examination of the nature of sequence, [we must] assume that it is the Great Lord Himself who possesses the power of time[, since He is the one] who produces the manifestation of [sequence]—this is what the [next verse beginning with] *krama* explains.[42]

### ĪPK 2.1.4

Sequence is based on a difference; this difference in turn [arises] from the presence and absence of [certain] phenomena. As for the presence and absence of [certain] phenomena, they [come] from the Lord, who produces phenomena [as being] varied.

### VṚTTI

The cause of sequence in [objective] entities is nothing but the Lord's action of [bringing about] a variety of manifestations of [objective] entities that are different inasmuch as they are devoid of each other's phenomena (*anyonyābhāsaśūnya*).

---

[41] As Abhinavagupta makes clear (see ĪPVV, vol. III, p. 9, quoted above, chapter 8, fn. 569), this is an allusion to the six "modifications in [the process of] becoming" enumerated by Yāska and Patañjali; Utpaladeva comes back to this list in the *Vivṛti* on 2.1.5. For more on these *bhāvavikāra*s, see above, chapter 8, §7.

[42] Cf. ĪPVV, vol. III, p. 10: ***paryālocanaye****ty anyathānupapattyā kramasyeti ākūtam*. "With [the sentence beginning with] 'As a result of this examination...,' [Utpaladeva] hints at the [following: we must assume that it is the Great Lord Himself who possesses the power of time,] because of the impossibility of sequence otherwise."

### VIVṚTI

The Lord's action of dividing (*kalanakriyā*)[43] is nothing but [His] agency in manifesting the pot, cloth, etc., [as being] varied. [It is this agency] that is the power of manifesting time; [as for time itself,[44] it] consists in sequence and it is an adventitious property of [objective] entities.[45] In [the *Vṛtti* compound] beginning with *anyonyābhāsa-*, this is what [the words] "nothing but the Lord's action of [bringing about] a variety of manifestations" convey;[46] for due to this variety, there is a mutual incompatibility of phenomena such as "pot" and ["cloth"].[47] This [latter point] is mentioned

[43] On this term see above, chapter 7, fn. 428.

[44] On this distinction between time and the power of time (i.e. the power to manifest time, which, as Abhinavagupta makes clear, is nothing but the power to manifest objective entities as being endowed with certain phenomena and devoid of others), see above, chapter 7, §1.

[45] The translation follows ĪPVV, vol. III, p. 10, quoted above, chapter 7, fn. 429.

[46] According to ĪPVV, vol. III, p. 10: ***ityādāv*** *ity asmin vākye yad* ***avabhāse****tyādi śakalakaṃ tat kartṛ,* ***tad*** *iti vivṛtiprārambhe yad uktaṃ tat karmabhūtam* ***āhe****ti saṅgatiḥ*. "'In the [*Vivṛti*] sentence [beginning with the words 'In the *Vṛtti* compound] beginning with...', the [grammatical] subject [of the verb 'convey'] is the bit [of compound] beginning with *avabhāsa-*, [i.e., the subject of the verb 'convey' is 'the words 'nothing but the Lord's action of [bringing about] a variety of manifestations';] as for [the word] 'this' [in 'this is what...'], which designates [everything] that was said at the beginning of the *Vivṛti* [on this verse], it is the [grammatical] object [of the verb] 'convey'—such is the [grammatical] structure [of the *Vivṛti* sentence]."

[47] Literally, "there is a mutual absence of phenomena such as 'pot,' etc."—i.e., the phenomenon "pot" must be absent wherever the phenomenon "cloth" is present, and conversely. See above, chapter 7, §2: Abhinavagupta explains that this is said to be due to the Lord's "variety of manifestations" in the *Vṛtti* because it results from the fact that the ultimate consciousness manifests each elementary phenomenon in "various" ways, i.e., as being capable of combining in a single substratum (as when the elementary phenomena "pot," "solid,"round," "red," etc., coalesce to form the single particular substance that we apprehend as a specific pot), but also—among other possible modes of manifestation—as being separated, i.e., as being incapable of sharing the same substratum (as "pot" and "cloth" are). Sequence, whether spatial or temporal, arises from such an incompatibility between elementary phenomena.

[in the verse] with "as for the presence and absence of [certain] phenomena"; [and] the explanation of this [part of the verse][48] is [provided in the *Vṛtti* when it says that the Lord manifests] "[entities that are different inasmuch as they are devoid of] each other's phenomena." Because [a given] phenomenon cannot be both present and absent in the same substratum,[49] and because [the presence and absence of phenomena] is mentioned [in the verse][50] as the cause of the difference [that makes sequence appear], one understands the meaning of the expression "each other" (*anyonya*) [here, namely, that these objects have mutually incompatible phenomena];[51] and the mutual incompatibility[52] of manifestations such as "pot" and ["cloth"] is [precisely] the difference on which the cognition of sequence rests—this is what [the *Vṛtti*] conveys [with the words] "different inasmuch they are devoid [of each other's phenomena]."

---

[48] Following ĪPVV, vol. III, p. 10: ***asyeti*** *sautrasya.*

[49] Cf. ĪPVV, vol..., p. 10: *anyathā ghaṭo nābhāsetābhāseta ca...* "Otherwise [the pot would not be manifest and [yet] would be manifest [in the same substratum]."

[50] According to ĪPVV, vol. III, p. 10: ***upādānād*** *iti sūtre.*

[51] See above, chapter 7, §2: spatial sequence arises because the universal consciousness manifests phenomena such as "pot" and "cloth" as not being able to share the same substratum (so that although particular substances such as a pot and a cloth may share a number of elementary phenomena, e.g. a specific colour, they must exist in different places, because each of them has a phenomenon, i.e. "pot"/"cloth," excluding the other). In his commentaries, Abhinavagupta also specifies that temporal sequence arises because the realities that we call "autumn" and "winter" for instance are "devoid" of each other's main phenomena, even though the case of temporal sequence is somewhat different from that of spatial sequence, as the *Vivṛti* is about to make clear.

[52] Literally, "the mutual absence" (see above, fn. 47).

[53][So far we have only] mentioned [as a cause of sequence][54] the fact that [objective] entities are different due to their being devoid of each other's phenomena. For this very reason,[55] the variety of [their] manifestations *and* the difference [caused by their being devoid of each other's phenomena] are mentioned as [two] different [factors contributing to the production of sequence when the *Vṛtti* says "the Lord's action of bringing about the *variety* of the manifestations of objective entities that are *different* inasmuch as they are devoid of each other's phenomena."[56] And these two factors must be distinguished because] what consists in consciousness [can] have variety even though it has a unity, whereas [mere] difference is contradicted

---

[53] See above, chapter 7, §4: from here on the *Vivṛti* offers a more complex interpretation of the *Vṛtti*, where "the Lord's action of bringing about the variety of the manifestations of objective entities that are different inasmuch as they are devoid of each other's phenomena" is no longer understood as simply meaning that the Lord produces objective entities as having incompatible phenomena due to the variety of ways in which He manifests them. The same passage is now going to be read as distinguishing two factors of sequence—viz., on the one hand, the exclusive difference that prevents a cloth from being a pot (which leads to spatial sequence), expressed by the words "different inasmuch as they are devoid of each other's phenomena"; and on the other hand, the variety—understood as a difference grounded in unity—that enables the same object to be manifold without ceasing to be one (which leads to temporal sequence), expressed by "the variety of the manifestations." This anticipates the distinction between spatial and temporal sequences that will be dealt with in the next verse.

[54] Cf. ĪPVV, vol. III, p. 10: ***bhinnatvam*** *iti kramaṃ praty upayogīti bhāvaḥ*. "The implied meaning in [the words] 'the fact that [objective entities] are different' is that [this fact] contributes to the production of sequence."

[55] Cf. ĪPVV, vol. III, pp. 10–11: ***ata eveti*** *yato 'smin prakṛte krame dvayam upayogi*. "'For this very reason,' [i.e.,] because [in fact] two [factors] contribute to the production of the subject at hand, [namely] sequence..."

[56] According to ĪPVV, vol. III, p. 11: ***upātta*** *iti vṛttau bhinnāvabhāsavaicitryaśabdābhyāṃ napuṃsakaikaśeṣo 'tra dvayasyopayogitāṃ darśayati*. "[They] are 'mentioned' in the *Vṛtti* with the words 'different' [on the one hand] and 'variety of the manifestations' [on the other hand]. In the [*Vivṛti* sentence,] the use of the [dual] neutre [in *upātte*] for both [*avabhāsacitratvam*, which is neutre, and *bhedaḥ*, which is masculine,] makes clear that both of them contribute to the production [of sequence]."

by unity due to [their] mutual exclusion. And accordingly, the honourable Dharmakīrti [has said]:

> [A colour] such as the blue [that appears] in a variegated cognition [and] is a property (*upādhi*) of the cognition [itself] cannot be perceived [as] not mixed with anything else; for [someone] distinguishing it [from other colors] focuses on the object [itself, not on the cognition].[57]

For when [entities] such as the blue are posited [by consciousness] as existing separately, while being distinct (*bhinna*) from each other, [and] in the form of objects, there is a spatial sequence, and there is no unity; whereas since, due to [its] unity insofar as it consists in consciousness, [a cognition can be] divided [into a multiplicity] while [each element thus divided] retains [the ability to appear] along with the others, the same [Buddhist authors] admit that variety belongs to the reality that is the Brahman (*brahmatattva*)![58]

Therefore [it is] the Highest Lord's existence as the [objective] entities constituting the variegated universe [that is] is the cause (*bīja*)[59] of the unfolding manifestation (*prathā*) of time; this is what [the *Vṛtti*] says with "the

---

[57] On this famous verse by Dharmakīrti and the Śaiva nondualists' understanding of it see above, chapter 7, §5. Utpaladeva quotes it here so as to show that his Buddhist rivals acknowledge the distinction between the exclusive difference found in objects (which is contradictory with unity) and variety (defined as a difference that, instead of being incompatible with unity, is grounded in the latter); so that even they admit that variety thus defined belongs to consciousness and is the essence of reality.

[58] On Abhinavagupta's explanation of this remark see above, chapter 7, fn. 462: Utpaladeva is humourously noting that the Buddhists unwittingly end up sharing the idea that variety is the essence of reality with their Brahmanical opponents, namely, the followers of Bhartṛhari (who also acknowledge variety as Utpaladeva defines it inasmuch as they admit the Brahman's multiplicity of powers).

[59] According to ĪPVV, vol. III, p. 11: *citraṃ kṛtvā yā viśvātmabhāvena bhagavataḥ sthitir idam eva kālaprathane nimittam*. "It is the Lord's existence as the [objective] entity constituting the universe after [He] has made [it] varied that is precisely the cause of the unfolding manifestation of time." On the meaning of "after [He] has made [it] varied" here, see ĪPVV, vol. III, p. 10, quoted above, chapter 7, fn. 429: making objectivity varied means manifesting objects as distinct from each other because they are "endowed with [certain] phenomena and not with [others]," i.e., because they have mutually incompatible phenomena.

cause of sequence in [objective] entities [is nothing but the Lord's action..." [60]As for these objective entities, they are in fact] nothing but variegated manifestations [produced] by the power of *māyā*; due to their mutual exclusion, [which itself occurs] because [they] are [erroneously] believed (*abhimāna*) to consist in distinct [objective] entities, they exist as manifestations involving a sequence in both forms, [viz.] space and time.

So variety, insofar as it belongs to material shapes and actions, produces a sequence of both sorts; [i.e., it] respectively [produces] [sequence] as space and time. This is what is explained [in the next verse, beginning with] "[The Lord manifests spatial sequence from a variety of] material shapes."

### ĪPK 2.1.5

The Lord manifests spatial sequence from a variety[61] of material shapes (*mūrti*); He also [manifests] temporal sequence from the manifestation of a variety of actions.

### VṚTTI

For [something] plural there is a spatial sequence due to the phenomenon of a mutual[ly exclusive] (*anyonya*) difference; and there is also a temporal sequence through action. But for an [objective] entity (*bhāva*)[62] that is one, there is only a temporal sequence, [which is] due to the difference in the various actions of birth, existence, transformation, etc.

---

[60] Utpaladeva is about to make clear that the *Vṛtti*'s definition of sequence as occurring "in [objective] entities" does not amount to acknowledging that it actually occurs outside consciousness: see above, chapter 7, §6.

[61] On the different shades of meaning of this term depending on whether it is used with respect to space or time see above, chapter 8, §1: as clarified by the *Vṛtti* (and as already stated in the *Vivṛti* on the previous verse), in the case of space, variety is in fact a mutually exclusive difference, whereas in the case of time, it is a difference grounded in unity.

[62] Cf. the gloss with *artha* in the *Vivṛti* below; note, however, that as is made clear in the *Vivṛti*, in fact here Utpaladeva primarily has in mind the limited subject, who belongs to the realm of objects inasmuch as (s)he identifies with an insentient entity such as his/her body, even though his/her conscious status also provides him/her with a unity of which purely insentient objects are devoid.

## VIVṚTI

Material shape (*mūrti*) is nothing but the specific form (*svarūpa*) that is manifest through the mutual[ly exclusive] difference of [multiple] objects. A cognition consisting in memory, experience, etc., has no material shape, because there is no manifestation of difference [in it] thanks to the unity of [its] self-awareness. Sound (*śabda*) has no material shape [either] insofar as it is [the kind of sound] that consists in a signifier [while being] an internal, [subtle form] related to ether (*ākāśa*), whether it has as its essence the apprehending subject or whether it consists in the act of apprehending;[63] [just as cognition, this kind of sound has no material shape] because it has no difference [either], given that it has the same unity [as cognition] thanks to the self-awareness [that it also involves]. However, the [sound] that is related to air, etc.[64] [and occurs at the ordinary level of speech] has [a material shape] due to the unfolding of difference [in it].[65]

Spatial sequence occurs due to the presence of material shapes—this is what [the *Vṛtti*] says with [the sentence:] "For [something] plural [there is a spatial sequence due to the phenomenon of] a mutual[ly exclusive difference." By saying] "for [something] plural," [the *Vṛtti*] explains [the verse's mention of] material shape, because [spatial sequence—i.e.,] the fact that there are anterior and posterior places, and [the property of] extendedness—appear due to the phenomenon of a mutual[ly exclusive] difference

---

[63] That is, whether it corresponds to the ontological and linguistic planes called Paśyantī or Madhyamā, subtle sound has no material shape; on Abhinavagupta's explanation see above, chapter 8, §3.

[64] That is to say, the type of *śabda* that is related to air, fire, water and earth. Contrary to the Vaiśeṣikas and Naiyāyikas, who consider that sound resides exclusively in ether and that the latter is devoid of material shape, the Śaivas (Saiddhāntikas and nondualists alike) believe that it is found in all five elements (including air, fire, water and earth, which, unlike ether, are said to be all endowed with material shapes), and that only the subtler forms of *śabda* called Paśyantī and Madhyamā are related to ether. On this important divergence see above, chapter 8, §3.

[65] In other words, according to Utpaladeva, the only level of *śabda* that is endowed with a material shape is the lowest one, called Vaikharī—see above, chapter 8, §3.

that pertains to things endowed with a material shape—[i.e.,] due to the plurality [of these things endowed with a material shape].[66]

[– Objection:][67] But even the sound [that you claim to be] related to air, if it belongs to air, [can] only [be its] effect or [its] cause;[68] but it does not penetrate the [very] nature? of air [and so it has no material shape]![69] Or even if it does penetrate [it], for all that it cannot become one with it, because of the contradiction [that would ensue otherwise] between this [type of] sound and another one [such as the sound related to fire], since [they]

---

[66] That is to say, although the word *mūrti* is absent in the *Vṛtti*, the term "plural" (literally "not one", *aneka*) suffices to make clear that spatial sequence only concerns material shapes, because contrary to conscious entities, material shapes have no unity insasmuch as they are defined by their mutually incompatible differences (a pot is not and cannot be a cloth without ceasing to be itself), whereas the unity of consciousness enables it to encompass and transcend the differences that it manifests.

[67] On its gist see ĪPVV, vol. III, p. 13: *atra kaścic chabdasya mūrtatvam asahamāno deśakramaṃ ca mṛṣyamāno* na mūrtatā deśakramopayojiketi pūrvapakṣayati* ***nanv*** *iti.* [**mṛṣyamāno* corr.; *mṛśyamāno* ĪPVV.] "Someone who cannot stand [the idea of] sound having a material shape [but] accepts [its] spatial sequence [now] objects to the [thesis just expounded by Utpaladeva] that having a material shape does not contribute to [bringing about] spatial sequence [in the sentence beginning with] 'But...'." The opponent voicing this objection belongs to the Vaiśeṣika, according to which *śabda* is an *amūrtaguṇa*; see above, Chapter 8, §4.

[68] See ĪPVV, vol. III, p. 13: ***kārya*** *iti śukaśukādi,* ***kāraṇam*** *iti śabdatanmātram api hi vāyoḥ kāraṇam, śabdasparśajo hi vāyuḥ.* "[It can only be its] 'effect,' [i.e., a rustling sound] such as *śukaśuka*, [or its] 'cause'; for [according to you], the subtle element (*tanmātra*) 'sound' is also the cause of [the gross element] 'air'; for air arises from sound and tactile form." On the thesis, held by some Sāṃkhya sources and adopted by the Śaivas, that the gross elements (*mahābhūta*), including air, arise from the subtle elements (*tanmātra*), including sound, and that air in particular arises from sound and tactile form (and has these two as its qualities), see above, chapter 8, §4.

[69] There is a brief lacuna here, as indicated by the scribes in S12 and J11, so that the edition and translation are conjectural. Nonetheless, the gist of the passage seems clear from ĪPVV, vol. III, p. 13: ***āviśatīti*** *na vāyur evāsau yena mūrtaḥ syād ity arthaḥ.* "'[It does not] penetrate...' means that it is not air itself; [and] it could have a material shape due to [its being air itself, but it is not the case]!"

would [then] be entirely different;[70] and [so] this sound, even if it is the quality of another element [rather than ether],[71] can only be devoid of material shape! So how could it have spatial sequence while not having a material shape, [whereas according to you, spatial sequence] is caused by a variety in material shapes? And yet sounds [occurring] exactly at the same time do appear [to us as] belonging to different places;[72] so spatial differentiation cannot pertain exclusively to [things] possessed of a material shape!

[– Answer:] It may be [said to be] so [elsewhere];[73] but in this [treatise] material shape is taught to be nothing but the specific form of the thing, which is devoid of action; and this [material shape] is not defined [here] as [it is] in other treatises![74] This is why in the *Vṛtti*, material shape is explained as being merely the specific form of a thing [by simply saying] "for

---

[70] Again, there is a short lacuna here, followed by what I take to be a corruption, so that the translation is merely tentative. It rests on the context and on ĪPVV, vol. III, p. 13: ***tasye**ti vāyavīyasya, **anyasye**ti taijasādeḥ.* "[It cannot become one with it, because of the contradiction that would ensue otherwise] 'between this' [type of sound, i.e.] the one related to air, [and] 'another one,' [i.e. a sound] such as the sound related to fire]."

[71] Namely, air, which, unlike ether, has a material shape.

[72] The Vaiśeṣika objector is emphasizing that the sequence apprehended in sounds is not just temporal (since it may occur in sounds that happen to be simultaneous) but also spatial; and according to him, Utpaladeva cannot explain this if he clings to the thesis that spatial sequence has as its cause a difference in material shapes. See ĪPVV, vol. III, p. 13: *yadi ca mūrtir nibandhanaṃ deśakrame śabdasya tarhi sa na syāt, asti so 'syeti darśayati **yugapad eva ce**ti.* "And if material shape were the cause of spatial sequence, then sound should not have any [spatial sequence]; yet it does! This [is what the Vaiśeṣika objector] shows in [the passage beginning with] 'And yet sounds [occurring] exactly at the same time...'

[73] That is, according to ĪPVV, vol. III, pp. 13–14 (quoted above, chapter 8, fn. 514), "among ordinary people," but also in learned traditions such as the Vaiśeṣika and grammatical treatises.

[74] According to Abhinavagupta (see above, chapter 8, §4), the rival definitions of material shape that Utpaladeva is discarding here include the Vaiśeṣikas' and Pāṇini's; according to the first (which is certainly the main target here), *mūrti* is the size of a substance that is not omnipresent, and action can only occur in a substance endowed with it; according to the second, it is solidity.

[something] plural."[75] The master Bhartṛhari too has stated [the following, thus] acknowledging that material shape is nothing but the mere specific form of a thing:

> For this is not successive; from the point of view of material shape as well as action, it is entirely full in every regard.[76]

For by saying this, [Bhartṛhari] has taught that the spatial and temporal succession of [objective] entities is [respectively] produced by material shapes and actions, whereas knowledge and the sound related to ether do not have [what] results in spatial differentiation, which is [precisely the property of] being endowed with material shape; so [by saying this he] has [also] stated that [they] have no material shape.

Alternatively, [even if one accepts the Vaiśeṣika's definition of material shape rather than ours,][77] it is the substratum of qualities [such as sound] that is [their] place; and this very [substratum] is particularized by these [qualities], but a material shape does not exist on its own, independently of a substratum such as air, and [it is] this [substratum possessed of a material shape] that may be differentiated for instance by [spatial] succession, due

---

[75] See above, fn. 66, and ĪPVV, vol. III, p. 14: ***anekasyeti*** *padenānena mūrtir vivṛtā vedyavasturūpatvena*. "[The *Vivṛti* quotes] 'for something plural' [because in the *Vṛtti*,] with this [single] word, material shape is explained as being the form of a thing that is a [mere] object of knowledge (*vedya*)." Utpaladeva considers that action only belongs to sentient entities, not to things that have a material shape (see above, chapter 8, §5), which is why, according to Abhinavagupta, when stating that material shape is nothing but the specific form of a "thing" (*vastu*), Utpaladeva is using the latter word in the sense of an object of knowledge (cf. ĪPVV, ibid.: *vedyasvarūpaṃ tu yat tad eva mūrtiḥ...*).

[76] On this quotation (which I could not trace), other occurrences of it, and Abhinavagupta's comments, see above, chapter 8, §1.

[77] According to ĪPVV, vol. III, p. 14 (quoted above, chapter 8, §4, fn. 521): Utpaladeva wants to show in what follows that his explanation of spatial sequence as the result of a variety of material shapes still holds even if one accepts the Vaiśeṣikas' definition of material shape as the size of a substance that is not omnipresent.

to the variety with respect to other substrata [endowed with other material shapes].[78]

[79]Action exclusively belongs to what consists in consciousness, because [only what consists in consciousness can be] an agent and can constitute a single substratum [for action in the form of] the agent; [it] is also metaphorical[ly ascribed] to [insentient[80] things] that are possessed of a material shape, because [in their case we] talk about agency figuratively. On the other hand (*vā*), inasmuch as, according to the [common] understanding, [we] take action to literal[ly belong to insentient things, we] may [consider that] there is a temporal difference too [for plural, insentient things] owing to the variety of [the actions that we ascribe to them].[81]

---

[78] That is to say (according to ĪPVV, vol. III, p. 14, quoted above, chapter 8, §4, fn. 521): although if one clings to the Vaiśeṣika's definition of *mūrti*, sound can have no material shape since it is a quality and not a substance, even from that standpoint, it is still legitimate to say that we apprehend sound as being spatially determined owing to a variety of material shapes, because one can then consider that sound, despite being shapeless in itself, *appears* to be spatially determined inasmuch as we only apprehend it (as well as any other quality) as inhering in a substance such as air, which, for its part, possesses a material shape.

[79] According to Abhinavagupta, from here on the *Vivṛti* explains the second half of ĪPK 2.1.5, that is, the definition of the temporal type of sequence, as opposed to the spatial one. See ĪPVV, vol. III, p. 14: *prathamaṃ ślokārdhaṃ vyākhyāyāparaṃ tu vyākhyātum upakramate* ***saṃvedanātmana eva*** *ityādinā*. "Having explained the first half of the verse, [Utpaladeva] now proceeds to explain the other [half in the passage] beginning with '[Action] exclusively belongs to what consists in consciousness...'" For an analysis of this passage see above, chapter 8, §5: Utpaladeva explains that action, which supposes an underlying unity lacking in insentient objects, can only be said to belong to them figuratively; we believe that things can act because we are oblivious of this fact and end up superimposing temporality onto them. According to Utpaladeva, this is why the temporal determinations of things (in particular their being past, present or future) are always relative to the subject considering them.

[80] According to ĪPVV, vol. III, p. 15: ***mūrtimatām apīti*** *vedyatvenāsaṃvedanātmanām apīty arthaḥ*. "[It is] 'also' [metaphorically ascribed] to [things] that are possessed of a material shape'—that is to say, [it is] also [metaphorically ascribed] to [things] that do not consist in consciousness since they are [mere] objects of knowledge."

[81] According to ĪPVV, vol. III, p. 15, quoted above, chapter 8, fn. 531.

And thus an [object] is manifest [as being] present for a knowing subject if the existence of this [object] is manifest for this [subject] in his own time.[82] But [...] [an object is manifest for a knowing subject as being] past if, when [...] an action is manifest, a conceptual construct of the [object] that is not present arises [in the knowing subject] through the manifestation of [its] existence (*sattā*) as a cause [for this action; this conceptual construct consists in imagining this cause] as having a present manifestation, [but] it is accompanied by the phenomenon of the perishing of the manifestation of the object that is e.g. the cause of [...] [the action?] occurring in front of [the subject].[83] [And] the [object] is future for a knowing subject, just as the manifestation that is present [now] was future [for that subject] at the time of a past manifestation.[84] Therefore it is only in relation to these two actions

---

[82] The translation follows Abhinavagupta's glosses in ĪPVV, vol. III, p. 15: ***yasyeti** pramātuḥ, **yasyety** arthasya, **tasyeti** pramātuḥ, **sa** ity arthaḥ, **vartamāno bhātīti** sambandhaḥ.*

[83] This sentence suffers from several lacunae and the translation is conjectural. It rests on ĪPVV, vol. III, p. 15: *pramātur arthasya yasyānābhāsamānasya kāraṇa-sattāvabhāsanena vartamānāvabhāsatvaṃ kalpyate kāraṇāvabhāsasya vartamāna-sya pratyakṣasya vināśābhāsena saha, so 'rthaḥ pramātur bhātīti saṅgatiḥ.* "An object is manifest [as past] for a knowing subject if it is not being [perceptually] manifest for that knowing subject, [and yet] its being manifest as present is conceptually constructed through the manifestation of [its] existence as a cause; [this manifestation is nonetheless] accompanied by the phenomenon of the perishing of the directly perceived, present manifestation of this cause—this is the structure [of this sentence]." In other words, when we think "The sprout is growing," the awareness of this action entails the awareness that the cause "seed" must exist; yet our awareness of the seed's necessary existence is inextricably linked with the awareness of its perishing, since we do not have any direct perception of it—and we thus consider "past" anything to which we thus ascribe both the action of existing and that of perishing.

[84] Abhinavagupta illustrates the analogy by giving the example of a master who decided yesterday what task his servant should perform today; see above, chapter 8, fn. 539. On the proximity of these definitions of past, present and future with those given in the Nyāya tradition (and on what makes Utpaladeva's position different from the Nyāya's in this respect) see above, chapter 8, §5.

of existing and perishing [of phenomena that are manifest to a given subject][85] that [insentient things] having a material shape are also temporally divided [into past, present and future] in relation to each other;[86] this [is what the *Vṛtti*] says with "[and there is also a temporal sequence] through action." And [we] will explain [in the sequel][87] that even though this action [that consists in] existence or [perishing] is [commonly] understood to belong to insentient [things in such a way that the primary meaning of the word "action"] is not impeded (*askhalita*),[88] [in fact this action of insentient

---

[85] Cf. ĪPVV, vol. III, p. 15: *sattāvināśau dvāv iti bhāvavikārau dvābhyām evāvabhāsabhāvābhāvābhyāṃ saṃgṛhītāv iti darśayati.* "[The compounded words *sattāvināśadvi-* mean] the two [actions that are] existence and perishing; [here Utpaladeva] is making clear that these two modifications in [the process of] becoming are [to be] understood [as being] nothing but the presence and absence of [certain] manifestations."

[86] This is how I tentatively understand the compound *anyonyāpekṣayā* (on which Abhinavagupta does not comment)—i.e., as meaning that insentient things endowed with a material shape not only have spatial determinations, but are also temporally determined as past, present and future in relation to each other (an object X can be thought of as older than an object Y, etc.), although ultimately, such temporal distinctions in things are all grounded in the subject who is aware of them (if I apprehend a pot as past in relation to a present cloth, it is because I apprehend both the pot and the cloth as respectively past and present in relation to my own temporality, as Utpaladeva has just pointed out).

[87] According to Abhinavagupta (see ĪPVV, vol. III, p. 14, quoted above, chapter 8, fn. 548), Utpaladeva is alluding here to his lengthy justification of the thesis that action exclusively belongs to consciousness because it presupposes a will (*icchā*) to act in ĪPV 2.4.19, its *Vṛtti* and (currently unavailable) *Vivṛti*; see above, chapter 8, §5 on these.

[88] This technical term is used to describe the mechanism of metaphorical usage. The point is that we are immediately aware, upon hearing such a phrase as "a village on the Gaṅgā," that the village cannot be literally "on" the Gaṅgā but only on its bank, the function of the primary meaning being halted or impeded (*skhalita*) by the awareness that villages cannot actually be "on" a river—and this is how we understand that such an expression is merely figurative. On the other hand, in everyday circumstances, speakers are not aware, when uttering or hearing such a sentence as "The chariot moves," that the primary meaning of the verb is impeded by the impossibility for an insentient being of possessing a conscious will to act; i.e., they take it literally. On this point and Abhinavagupta's comment see above, chapter 8, §5.

beings] can only result from [their] relation with consciousness, because [it only] occurs due to a will for such [an action to occur].

[89]However, something[90] that is [apprehended as] one, such as [the individual called] Caitra, has no spatial sequence—even though [he] has different phenomena [according to whether he is] in the house, the palace, the courtyard ans so on—because there is no difference in [his] nature [inasmuch as he is considered] all at once, [and not as made of different parts or in connection with other things], given that [then there is] no manifestation of extendedness [in him], since he does not acquire a spatial existence by his [sole] nature.[91]

[92]But when, because [this entity apprehended as one is] the substratum of birth, existence, transformation and so on, action is the only [aspect of it that is] differentiated—[as when we think:] "This [individual], who was a child, will be an old man"—, then, since there is a difference between the presence and absence of these various actions' manifestations, there is a succession [that occurs] only with respect to time and nothing else.[93] [This

---

[89] For an analysis of the following paragraph—according to which an object has no spatial sequence as long as it is regarded as one—see above, chapter 8, §6.

[90] See above, fn. 62.

[91] That is to say, one entity taken by itself (and as a unity rather than as a collection of parts) has no spatial sequence, because existing spatially, or having extendedness (*vaitatya*), means being connected with several places, and this involves a difference incompatible with the unity of the entity in question. See ĪPVV, vol. III, p. 16: *vaitatyaṃ hi bhūyodeśasaṃyogaḥ, deśasya bhūyastvaṃ bhedāt.* "For extendedness is the connection with several places, and the fact that there are several places comes from a difference." In his commentary, Abhinavagupta points out the paradox of this assertion: it means that if we consider the parts of an object, which are plural, these parts have a spatial order, whereas the object considered as a whole (and independently of other objects) has none. On this paradox and the way the Śaiva nondualists claim to solve it, see below, chapter 8, §6.

[92] For an analysis of the following depiction of the manner in which temporal determinations arise from actions in individual subjects, see above, chapter 8, §§7–8.

[93] According to Abhinavagupta, the apparently redundant presence of *eva* after the compound ending in *-mātra* is meant to emphasize the exclusion of both spatial sequence and any kind of difference in the entity's nature (ĪPVV, vol. III, p. 16): ***mātra****padena deśakramam,* ***eva****kāreṇa svarūpabhedaṃ nirasyati.* "With the word

succession] belongs to [something] whose essence is a unitary substance that remains unconcealed thanks to the unity of the [recognitive] realization [that grasps it as being the same];[94] this is what [the *Vṛtti*] says in [the passage beginning with] "But for an [objective entity] that is one..."

[To explain:] first of all, the sequence of the six modifications in [the process of] becoming (*bhāvavikāra*)[95] is established to belong to every [unitary] reality [inasmuch as it] consists in an effect, [as does a limited individual]. Thus a manifestation of the action of birth [occurs with respect to a given individual in the form] "X is born"; in the same way, a manifestation of the actions of existing, etc., [occurs with respect to that individual in the forms] "[X] exists," "changes," "grows", "decays," "perishes." Besides, there is a manifestation of [different] parts even in the nature of each of these [modifications in the process of becoming] that are birth, existence, transformation and so on;[96] [97]therefore [each of them too has] this temporal sequence, which [occurs] due to the mutual exclusion of the phenomena of [their] contradictory parts while resting on the action of an [entity] that is one. [And] in a substratum that is one, but whose manifestation does not fully unfold simultaneously (*sahāprathana*), this same temporal sequence occurs due to a difference [that results] from the six modifications in [the

---

*mātra* [meaning 'only,' Utpaladeva] excludes spatial sequence; with the particle *eva* [i.e. 'and nothing else,' he excludes] a difference in [the thing's very] nature."

[94] For Abhinavagupta's explanation of this passage in his summary of the verse and *Vṛtti* in ĪPVV, vol. III, p. 12, see above, chapter 8, §8, fn. 576.

[95] On these six *bhāvavikāras* (birth, existence, change, growth, decay and perishing), already referred to by Yāska and Patañjali, see above, chapter 8, §7.

[96] That is to say: not only does the life of a given individual have temporal sequence due to its being divided into distinct parts by the different actions of birth, existence and so on, but temporal sequence also pervades each of these actions, since each of them can be divided into further parts. Abhinavagupta explains that this division goes down to the minimal temporal part that is the moment (*kṣaṇa*), and that in fact even the latter, which is supposedly devoid of duration, still has sequence insofar as it is ordinarily apprehended in relation with other moments that precede and follow it. See ĪPVV, vol. III, pp. 16–17, quoted above, chapter 8, fn. 570.

[97] The passage that follows (up to the sentence beginning with "Similarly...") is difficult, in part because it is not easy to determine where sentences begin and end, and also because Abhinavagupta's commentary remains silent on it, so that the translation offered here is merely tentative.

process of] becoming, but also (*ca*) from the fact that these [six modifications] pervade all [other] actions. [Thus] even in [a series of actions such as]: "Having bathed and eaten, X goes," temporal sequence [occurs] in [a substratum that is] one [and yet] involves a difference between the [respective] phenomena of the specific actions that are bathing, [eating and going, which amount to modifications in the process of becoming] such as transformation; and even in itself, [each action of] bathing, eating and so on involves a difference in the phenomena of its own parts, [so that each of them is also sequential]. Similarly,[98] in the fruit of a pomegranate [tree] for instance, [although the fruit is apprehended as one,] there is a difference between the phenomena "being dark," "being red," etc., which is nothing but the difference between the phenomena pertaining to the action of transformation, [viz. ripening].[99] For what is called action is nothing but a particular form that is manifest as having parts that are [mutually] contradictory, [and] that [nonetheless] has something unitary as its substratum; for it is due to this contradiction that [action, by] arising in a unitary [substratum] although it cannot occur in [the form of] a fully unfolded manifestation (*prathā*), manifests sequence; and this [temporal sequence] is distinguished from spatial sequence by the fact that it rests on a unitary substratum.[100]

[101]And as soon as the existence of phenomena such as bathing, eating and so on [thus] becomes sequential in a unitary [substratum], according to the

[98] I tentatively construe this *tathā* as the correlative of *yathā* in *yathā bhedena sa eva kālakramo bhavati* (cf. ĪPVV, vol. III, p. 17: *acetanagatam api pariṇāmaṃ bhedena vyācaṣṭe* ***dāḍimādiphala*** *iti*. "With '[Similarly,] in the fruit of a pomegranate tree for instance...', Utpaladeva] explains that even the transformation [that occurs] in unconscious entities is due to a difference."). I therefore suppose that *snātvā bhuktvā* etc., up to *svāvayavābhāsabhedaḥ*, is an interpolated clause in this long correlative sentence; but this understanding of the overall structure of the passage might be wrong.

[99] According to ĪPVV, vol. III, p. 17: *pākākhyo 'yaṃ* ***pariṇāma*** *ity arthaḥ*. "That is to say, this transformation is what is called ripening."

[100] According to Abhinavagupta, this means that the awareness of temporal sequence entails a recognition (*pratyabhijñā*), which is not the case of spatial sequence (see ĪPVV, vol. III, p. 17, quoted above, chapter 8, fn. 577).

[101] For an analysis of the following depiction of the individual subject's apprehension of the past, present and future see above, chapter 8, §9.

principle that is going to be stated [in the next verse], [we] call "present" a manifestation whose unfolding (*prathā*) [occurs] together with the manifestation of the apprehending subject, because there is no indirect relationship (*vyavadhāna*)[102] [of this manifestation with that of the apprehending subject] internally,[103] [an indirect relationship] that would be due to the phenomenon of a mutual incompatibility [preventing the object and the subject from appearing together;[104] and] accordingly, this [manifestation] is [apprehended as] vivid [and] new. [Thus] being present is nothing but the existence of a vivid phenomenon; being past is both the existence and nonexistence [of this vivid phenomenon], whereas being future is just [its] nonexistence; for in [the thought] "X was a child," the manifestation of childhood, although it has the property of existing (*bhavanadharman*) [in the form of a residual trace],[105] does not exist externally [now], whereas in [the thought] "X will be an old man," the manifestation [in an external form][106] has no existence at all: it is only the object of a mere conceptual construct.

For this reason, in reality [...] just as the [past's] existence and nonexistence are contradicted, so is temporal sequence,[107] [and] similarly the [...] perishing must be contradicted. But inasmuch as [things] have as their essence manifestation, which is consciousness, [...].[108]

---

102 On this term and its tentative translation here see above, chapter 8, §9, fn. 599.

103 That is, in the form of a residual trace: see above, chapter 8, §9, particularly fn. 607.

104 That is to say: limited subjects deem "present" whatever object they immediately apprehend as existing together with the particular object (such as their body) with which they wrongly identify; and this apprehension is due to the fact that the phenomenon of these two entities' mutual incompatibility is lacking. On this definition of the present time see ĪPVV, vol. III, p. 18, quoted above, chapter 8, §9, fn. 600.

105 According to ĪPVV, vol. III, p. 18 (quoted above, chapter 8, §9, fn. 603).

106 According to ĪPVV, vol. III, p. 18: ***avabhāsasyeti*** *bāhyatārūpasya*.

107 According to ĪPVV, vol. III, p. 18: ***tathe****ti viruddhaḥ*. "'So [is temporal sequence' means that it too is] contradicted."

108 This passage is unfortunately too lacunary in S12 and J11 to be translated, but its gist can be retrieved from Abhinavagupta's commentary: see above, chapter 8,

Moreover,[109] [temporal] sequence, which is due to the presence and absence of phenomena [and appears] in [objective] entities, is only manifest for the knowing subject who transmigrates, in relation to his own time; but [it is] not [manifest] for the Lord—this is [what the next verse, beginning with] "[Moreover,] in every [object]," explains.

## ĪPK 2.1.6

Moreover,[110] in every [object], the difference in phenomena may be the source of temporal sequence for the knowing subject who is the void and so on,[111] whose manifestation undergoes interruptions (*vicchinna*); but not for [the knowing subject] who is manifest once and forever (*sakṛt*).[112]

---

§§10–12. Apparently the damaged part of the text pointed out that temporal sequence as defined above cannot be accounted for in a dualistic doctrine but only in the metaphysical frame of Śaiva nondualism. It also rejected the Buddhist objection that time is a mental construct based on nothing but the fact that things arise and vanish. Finally, it examined the issue of *yogin*s who are credited with the power to directly perceive past or future things, and it answered an objection to the effect that if they have a vivid apprehension of such objects, and if Utpaladeva's definition of past, present and future is correct, these vividly manifested objects should be present rather than past or future, which is absurd.

[109] I assume that here the particle *api* has the same meaning ascribed by Abhinavagupta to the one in the verse that this sentence introduces (see below, fn. 110).

[110] This is how I understand *api* in light of its gloss in ĪPVV, vol. III, p. 20 (*apiśabdaḥ prameyaṃ samuccinoti*. "[Here] the word *api* adds a topic.").

[111] That is to say, for the transmigrating individual who, as explained in ĪPK 1.6.4–5 and their commentaries, wrongly identifies with the body, vital breath, intellect or void (on these see above, chapter 8, §9), so that (s)he ends up being hardly more than the insentient object with which (s)he confuses his/her subjectivity. See also ĪPVV, vol. III, p. 20, which explains *śūnyāder mātuḥ* in the verse as *śūnyadhīprāṇadehalakṣaṇasya pramātrīkṛtasya*, "[that which] has been made into a knowing subject [but only] consists in [the objective entities that are] the void, intellect, vital breath and body."

[112] On the meaning of *sakṛt* here see above, chapter 9, §2.

## VṚTTI

In every object, [it is] a variegated manifestation [that] is the cause of the phenomenon of temporal sequence for the knowing subject who is nothing but the void, body and so on; for with the exception of memory, the past time is not manifest now as [it used to], and [it is] in relation to his own present that the [limited knowing subject] talks and acts (*vyavaharati*) about the past and future. However, for [the subject] who is manifest once and forever, there is no temporal difference either in himself or even in objects, because there is no interruption in [his] action of manifesting, since it is impossible to count any repetition [in this action].[113]

## VIVṚTI

[114][What we] call time rests on conscious subjects, [and] it is not a property of objects of knowledge that [may be considered] independent from anything else [inasmuch as it] is endowed with an unchanging nature, as [the property of] being blue or yellow for instance.[115] To explain: the same ob-

---

[113] This is an allusion to Pāṇini (A 5.4.17, see above, chapter 9, §2).

[114] For an analysis of what follows see above, chapter 9, §1: Utpaladeva argues that time is not a property inherent in the objects' nature. He has already dealt in part with this issue in the *Vivṛti* on ĪPK 2.1.5, while examining the role played by action (which, strictly speaking, only belongs to conscious entities) in the arising of temporal sequence (see above, chapter 8, §5), and while showing how our awareness that things are temporally determined is structured by that of our own temporality, since past, future and present are defined in relation to the subject's "own time" (see above, chapter 8, §9). Now he further points out that time cannot be an objective property of things (and must therefore be projected onto them by conscious subjects), because the *same* object has different times (past, present or future) depending on the temporality of the subjects apprehending it.

[115] According to ĪPVV, vol. III, p. 20 (quoted above, chapter 9, fn. 640). Utpaladeva does not actually believe that the properties of being blue or yellow exist independently of any subject, but here he places himself in the dualistic perspective so as to make clear that even from that standpoint (which he deems inferior), time cannot be understood as an objective property, because it is devoid of the stability ascribed to objective properties, since the same object becomes past, present or future depending on the subject's own time. According to Abhinavagupta, it is this variation in the temporality of a given object that the next sentence shows (see ibid.: *vicalatvam upapādayati **tathā hīti***).

ject is present for a present knowing subject because its existence is manifest at the time of this [subject's] own existence, but [it] is future for past knowing subjects, [and it is] past for future [knowing subjects]. Since thus the time of an object is only established in relation to the specific time of a conscious subject, the conscious subject, who is [himself] affected by temporal succession in the manner [already] explained—[that is,] through the presence and absence of the phenomena of his own actions—, [and] who is nothing but a transmigrating individual—[that is,] a knowing subject who is [reduced to] one of the [objects] that are the void, the vital breath, the intellect or the body [and] has fallen into the realm of practical existence—must [be what] produces a temporal distinction in the various objects [of which he is aware], in accordance with the phenomena of the actions of perishing, etc. [that he ascribes to them]; this is [what the *Vṛtti*] says with "In every object...". And when this conscious subject who is a transmigrating individual determines some objects of knowledge as separated from himself, then with respect to them [...].[116]

## ĪPK 2.1.7

Spatial sequence too is manifest in [objective] entities for the knowing subject whose self is limited; but for the unlimited [knowing subject, objective]

[116] From here on starts the most important lacuna in the chapter. On the gist of the missing part of the *Vivṛti*'s explanation of this verse as it can be retrieved from Abhinavagupta's commentary, see above, chapter 9, §§1–3: Utpaladeva clarified why temporality only concerns limited subjects and not the pure consciousness (namely, because the formers' manifestation "undergoes interruptions," an expression that he seems to have explained by saying that the locus to which the limited subjects wrongly ascribe their subjectivity, which is an insentient object such as the body, only appears intermittently, since manifestation is not its very nature but a feature borrowed from another entity, i.e. consciousness). The *Vivṛti* also emphasized that in contrast, manifestation is the very essence of absolute consciousness, so that in the latter it occurs once and forever (*sakṛt*), i.e., without any discontinuity; while doing so, it provided a detailed analysis of the word *sakṛt* and its figurative use in this context (on which see above, chapter 9, §2). It also explained why even objects, inasmuch as they are apprehended by the unlimited consciousness (i.e., at the ontological levels that the Śaivas call Sadāśiva and Īśvara), must be free of temporal determinations (see above, chapter 9, §3).

entities are manifest as being himself, [as being] full[117]—just as his own self.

### VṚTTI

[It is] with respect to the limited knowing subject that [objective] entities are differentiated from this [subject] and among themselves, and that they can be talked about as being "far," etc.; but for the Lord, who is replete with manifestation (*prakāśaghana*), nothing is manifest [as being] differentiated or far from Himself or from each other, given that [for Him], in no [circumstance] can there be any absence of manifestation,[118] even in an atom, since His [very] nature is only manifestation.

### VIVṚTI

[...][119]

### ĪPK 2.1.8

Nonetheless, the [very] fact that (*yat*) the difference in the [limited] knowing subjects and objects of knowledge is made manifest in this way—[i.e.

---

[117] Or they are manifest "as being full of his own self"; the translation given here follows Abhinavagupta's gloss of *svātmanā pūrṇāḥ* in ĪPV, vol. I, pp. 20–21, quoted above, chapter 9, fn. 690.

[118] According to Abhinavagupta, this is a reference to a scriptural source (the same from which the word *sakṛt*, "once and forever," is borrowed in ĪPK 2.1.6 and its *Vṛtti*); on the quotation and its source see above, chapter 9, §2.

[119] The *Vivṛti* on this verse is not preserved in the manuscript sources consulted for this edition. For its gist as far as can be gathered from Abhinavagupta's commentary see above, chapter 9, §4.

sequentially][120]—is the power of creation that belongs to the Lord, even though[121] He knows [everything] thus, [as being full].

## VṚTTI

The fact that [objective] entities consisting in [limited] knowing subjects and objects of knowledge are determined as being separated from Himself and from each other is precisely the power of creation of the Highest Lord, even though He is manifest thus as being full; and the enduring existence (*sthiti*) of His [full] nature is not concealed by such a determination.

---

[120] See ĪPVV, vol. III, p. 24 (quoted above, chapter 10, fn. 696), where Abhinavagupta reads "in this way" as meaning "[as] endowed with spatial and temporal sequence" (*tatheti deśakālakramavān*). Cf. ĪPV, vol. II, p. 24, according to which the manifested difference is "characterized 'in this way,' [i.e.,], as a difference in forms that produces spatial sequence and as a difference in actions that produces temporal sequence" (*tatheti svarūpabhedena deśakramakāriṇā kriyābhedena ca kālakramasampādakenopalakṣitaḥ*).

[121] The translation follows the *Vṛtti*, the opening words of which (*evaṃ pūrṇatayā prakāśamānasyāpi parameśvarasya*) suggest that *api* in the verse is not in its natural place and should be read along with *evaṃ viduṣaḥ*; cf. ĪPVV, vol. III, p. 27 (quoted below, fn. 141), where Abhinavagupta explicitly reads the beginning of the *Vṛtti* as an explanation of *api* in the verse. Note, however, that the ĪPV provides a different interpretation, for which I can find no basis in the *Vivṛti* as it has come down to us, and according to which *api* should rather be read along with *īśituḥ*. See ĪPV, vol. II, p. 24: *yat tad avabhāsanaṃ seśitur api nirmāṇaśaktiḥ kriyāśaktiḥ, na tu kevalaṃ śūnyāder eva kriyā*. "The fact of this manifestation *is* the power of creation—[i.e.] the power of action—of the Lord *too* (*api*); [i.e.], it is not the case that action only belongs to [limited subjects] such as [those identifying with] the void."

VIVṚTI

[...][122] This, which has [already] been described as the [very fact of] being the Highest Lord (*parameśvaratā*), [and] which consists in a universal (*sāmānya*),[123] is[124] the power of [great] creation;[125] [i.e., it is] so great that[126] it includes even[127] resorption. For even in resorption, [objective] entities still have objectivity (*idantā*) insofar as they [continue to] exist in the form of the seeds [constituted by residual traces];[128] only [we] will explain [in the

---

[122] The lacuna that starts in the midst of the *Vivṛti* on ĪPK 2.1.6 extends to the first sentence(s) of the commentary on this verse. For the gist of the missing passage as it can be retrieved from Abhinavagupta's commentaries, see above, chapter 10, §§1–2. The introduction must have emphasized that this concluding verse does not merely sum up the previous demonstrations of the chapter but adds a new point by equating the spatial and temporal unfolding of the universe with the Lord's nonsequential action, the former being a mere aspect of the latter. The first preserved sentence is probably incomplete; from ĪPVV, vol. III, p. 25 (quoted above, chapter 10, fn. 701), it seems that its first words were "But there" (*tatra tu*) and that it specified that the "power of great creation" belongs to the Highest Lord who possesses a sense of aesthetic wonder (*camatkṛti*) due to his fullness.

[123] I take this to be an allusion to Utpaladeva's assertion in ĪPK 1.5.13–14 that the pure *vimarśa*, i.e., the power of action, is consciousness's very sovereignty (*aiśvarya*, i.e. literally, the very "fact of being the Lord") as well as the "great being" (*mahāsattā*) that Abhinavagupta calls "the great universal" (*mahāsāmānya*) and that Utpaladeva describes as escaping all spatial and temporal determinations while pervading them; see above, chapter 10, §4.

[124] According to ĪPVV, vol. III, p. 25 (*yā parameśvarataiṣā śaktiḥ...*).

[125] On this power, the definition of which occupies much of the *Vivṛti* on this final verse, see above, chapter 10, §5.

[126] Cf. ĪPVV, vol. III, p. 25: ***mahac**chabdaṃ vyācaṣṭe **yatreti***. "[Utpaladeva] explains the word 'great' with 'that it includes...'."

[127] Cf. ĪPVV, vol. III, p. 25, ***api**śabdād anye koṭiśaḥ sṛṣṭisaṃhārāḥ*. "Because of the word 'even' (*api*), [one must understand that] other countless creations and resorptions [are included as well]."

[128] Cf. ĪPVV, vol. III, p. 25: ***bījātmane**ti saṃskāraśeṣataucityena*. "'In the form of seeds—[that is,] in the appropriate state [for things] that remain as residual traces." In other words, even in the cosmic state of resorption, things are still present, albeit in a latent form. One might wonder what difference remains then between cosmic creation or maintenance and cosmic resorption, and answering this question is, according to Abhinavagupta, the purpose of Utpaladeva's next assertion. See ibid.:

sequel] that creation and resorption are differentiated [from each other] according to whether [things] exist externally or [just] internally.[129] And this differentiation of the [power of great creation]—viz. the creation, while assuming the [different] forms of Brahmā, Viṣṇu and Rudra,[130] of knowing subjects and objects of knowledge endowed with countless differences, [all of them being] qualities (*guṇa*)[131]—is produced by the power of *māyā*.[132] For in that [realm of *māyā*],[133] it is due to the Lord who has taken on the forms of Brahmā, [Viṣṇu and Rudra] that the separation of all knowing subjects and objects of knowledge is determined; this is what [the *Vṛtti* says with] "the fact that [objective entities consisting in limited] knowing subjects and objects of knowledge [are determined as being separated...] is precisely the power of creation [of the Highest Lord]." In all cases, even [when it occurs] while taking the form of the three [deities] that are Brahmā, [Viṣṇu and Rudra],[134] creation is [thus] nothing but the Highest Lord's determination of the [already] described separation of [the knowing subjects and

---

*nanv evaṃ kaḥ saṃhārārthaḥ. āha* ***kevalam*** *iti.* "[Utpaladeva answers the question:] 'But [if it is] so, what could 'resorption' mean?' [with the passage beginning with] 'only.'"

[129] On this distinction see above, chapter 10, §5.

[130] On Brahmā, Viṣṇu and Rudra understood as limited subjective forms of the ultimate consciousness, see above, chapter 10, §5.

[131] In the Pratyabhijñā system, limited subjects (and not only objects of knowledge) are described as made of the three qualities (*guṇa*) of the Sāṃkhya (see above, chapter 10, fn. 745), and Abhinavagupta's commentary makes clear that here *guṇānām* is to be understood in apposition with both *jñātṝṇām* and *jñeyānām* (see ibid., fn. 747).

[132] This follows Abhinavagupta's interpretation in ĪPVV, vol. III, p. 25 (quoted above, chapter 10, fn. 747).

[133] According to ĪPVV, vol. III, p. 25: ***tatra hī****ti māyāpade.*

[134] According to Abhinavagupta, by saying "in all cases" and by using the word "even," Utpaladeva indicates that, while defining creation as the separation of subjects and objects, he does not only have in mind the process of cosmic emission ascribed to Brahmā as well as the cosmic operations of maintenance and resorption attributed to Viṣṇu and Rudra (i.e. the entire range of great creation in its māyic aspects), but also the great creation in its "pure" (*śuddha*) form, beyond the māyic realm (see ĪPVV, vol. III, p. 26, quoted above, chapter 10, fn. 754), even though,

objects of knowledge] that exist inside [Him]. And maintenance is the continuous existence for some time of these [knowing subjects and objects of knowledge] that are thus [made manifest as separated].[135] Again, resorption is the existence of these knowing subjects and [objects of knowledge] in the aforementioned separated [form, but] as merely consisting of seeds. [And all of] this is nothing but the great creation of the Lord, which is [only] mentally constructed (*kalpita*) thus as having three [different] forms [but is really one]. And among these [three deities],[136] although for the Lord Rudra, the separation [of subjects and objects] disappears in its external [form] because he performs resorption, to Brahmā and Viṣṇu, [objective] entities do appear as separated.[137]

[138]However, although the Great Lord creates [these entities] thus [as separated,] to Him, even though they are expressed in an objective form, they are manifest while being covered with subjectivity,[139] thanks to the predominance (*udreka*) of His agency—this is what [the *Vṛtti*] says with "[and the

---

as Utpaladeva is about to specify in the *Vivṛti*, the separation that characterizes creation is apprehended as being "covered with subjectivity" in the pure realm.

[135] According to ĪPVV, vol. III, p. 26: ***tādṛśāṃ** ceti vibhāgenāvabhāsitānām.*

[136] Following ĪPVV, vol. III, p. 26: ***tatra** ceti devatātrayamadhye.*

[137] The same universe is thus manifest in seemingly contradictory forms for these three eternal deities; on Abhinavagupta's justification of this paradox see ĪPVV, vol. III, p. 26, quoted above, chapter 10, fn. 751.

[138] From here on the *Vivṛti* turns to the explanation of the *Vṛtti*'s last point, namely, that the determination of knowing subjects and objects of knowledge as being separated from the ultimate consciousness and from each other does not make the awareness of the real nature of consciousness disappear, at least not from its highest forms. For an analysis of the following passage see above, chapter 10, §6.

[139] The word *avacchādita* could even be taken as meaning "veiled," "concealed," "hidden," were it not for the fact that these entities are said to be "manifest" in the same sentence. The point is that they are manifest, *but as being entirely subordinated*, ontologically speaking, to the reality of which they are but limited aspects, i.e., subjectivity. In other words, seen from the pure levels of consciousness, it is not the subjective, unitary reality that is "concealed" (*tirodhīyate*) by the appearance of objectivity, as the last part of the *Vṛtti* insists; rather, it is objectivity that is "covered with" or "encompassed by" subjectivity.

enduring existence of His full nature is not concealed] by such a determination." This [last part of the *Vṛtti* on verse 2.1.8][140] eliminates a contradiction that was hinted at as a potential objection (*āśaṅkita*) with the word [meaning] "even though" (*api*) in [the *Vṛtti*'s opening words,] "even though He is manifest thus as being full";[141] [namely, the contradiction] that [one might suppose to exist] between, [on the one hand,] the determination of the separation of the knowing subjects and objects of knowledge, and, [on the other hand], the absolute unity of the manifesting [consciousness]. [And] one may also use the expression "resorption" as well [as that of "creation"] as regards this great creation [when talking] about the state of Sadāśiva,[142] [given that it] consists in the unfolding manifestation of [objective] entities as mere reflections (*chāyāmātra*),[143] [i.e.,] as being both

---

[140] Following ĪPVV, vol. III, p. 27: ***eteneti*** *na cetyādinā vṛttigranthena virodhaḥ parihṛtaḥ*. "'This,' namely the text of the *Vṛtti*, from 'and [the enduring existence of His full nature] is not...', eliminates the contradiction."

[141] Following ĪPVV, vol. III, p. 27: *ko 'sau. yaḥ pūrvake vṛttigranthe sautrasyāpi-śabdasya vivaraṇe 'piśabdenāśaṅkitaḥ sambhāvyamānatvenoktaḥ*. "What is this [contradiction]? [It is the one] that was *āśaṅkita*, [i.e.,] suggested as a possibility with the word *api* [that was used] in the *Vṛtti*'s previous [passage] while explaining the word *api* in the verse."

[142] See ĪPVV, vol. III, p. 27, quoted above, chapter 10, fn. 768: the point here is that the great creation can be said to include both cosmic creation and resorption not just in the realm of *māyā*, but also at the pure levels of consciousness (or rather at the Sadāśiva level, as it is impossible to even talk about objects at the Śiva level), because in Sadāśiva, objects are both created (in that they are manifest as somehow distinct from the I) and resorbed into the I.

[143] The word *chāyā* means "shadow," and *chāyāmātreṇa* can of course be read here as meaning "as mere shadows," the point being that objective phenomena are immediately grasped in Sadāśiva as having no reality of their own. Yet the word can also designate a reflection (in which case it is an equivalent of *pratibimba*), and it often does in the Pratyabhijñā corpus (see e.g. ĪPV, vol. I, p. 197: *pratibimbarūpā cchāyā*). Now, Abhinavagupta explains in ĪPVV, vol. III, p. 264 (quoted above, chapter 9, fn. 683) that in Sadāśiva, the totality of objects is apprehended "as a [mere] reflection" (*pratibimbatayā*); i.e., phenomena are grasped as having no independent status whatsoever, as mere forms taken on by consciousness, just as reflections are apprehended as mere aspects of a mirror (on this "doctrine of reflections," and the fact that although usually ascribed to Abhinavagupta, it was probably already fully developed in Utpaladeva's treatise, see above, chapter 1, §6, and

separated and not separated from the I; but in it there is no temporal separation [between creation and resorption].[144]

RATIÉ 2017b). See also ĪPV, vol. I, p. 247, which mentions the pure I-realization occurring "in the limpid self glittering with reflections" (*chāyācchuritasvacchātmani*); Bhāskarakaṇṭha identifies it as belonging to the level "beginning with Sadāśiva" (*sadāśivādīnām*, *Bhāskarī*, vol. I, p. 313), while explaining that here *chāyā* means "reflection" (ibid.: *chāyā—pratibimbaḥ*). In short, the translation of *chāyā* as "reflection" is probably more satisfactory than "shadow," both because the word designates a particular (and playful or aesthetically pleasing) manifestation of *light* (rather than the lack thereof), and because Utpaladeva's main intention is apparently not to convey that in Sadāśiva, objects are grasped as being as utterly unsubstantial as shadows, but rather, that at this level, they are both present in all their diversity *and* fully recognized as forms that the unitary subjectivity playfully takes on.

144 I.e., although one may talk about the great creation as including resorption both at the *māyic* levels and in the state of Sadāśiva, the significant difference between both realms is that in Sadāśivatattva, since there is no temporality, there can be no temporal separation between creation and resorption, and both terms must refer to "a single reality," as Abhinavagupta specifies in ĪPVV, vol. III, p. 27 (quoted above, chapter 10, fn. 768), before he endeavours to define the five cosmic functions (*kṛtyapañcaka*) traditionally ascribed to Śiva in light of the *Vivṛti*'s remarks on this final verse (see above, chapter 10, §6).

# CHAPTER 12

# *Īśvarapratyabhijñāvivṛti*, Chapter 2.1: Edition

## Preliminary remarks

In the following edition, the words in bold are those quoted by Abhinavagupta in the ĪPVV. Since the *Vivṛti* is a detailed explanation of the *Vṛtti*, which in turn explains the stanzas, and since the marginal annotations used to edit the *Vivṛti* often provide important variant readings for the *Vṛtti* as well, I have systematically included both the stanzas and *Vṛtti* in the following edition, although with a few exceptions that are not indicated below, the stanzas (for which no variant reading is to be found as far as the sources consulted here are concerned) do not appear in the margins but only in the main text of the manuscripts that were consulted; the *Vṛtti*, however, is almost always quoted along with the *Vivṛti* in marginal annotations.

The spelling of Sanskrit words has been standardized. Such corrections concern in particular dental consonants (*cittra* → *citra*, *satva* → *sattva*, etc.), nasals (*svātaṃtryam* → *svātantryam*, etc.) and the use of *v* for *b* (*vījam* → *bījam*). The application of *sandhi* rules has also been standardized, particularly regarding sibilants (*bhedas syāt* → *bhedaḥ syāt*, etc.; *avabhāsas śūnya°* → *avabhāsaḥ śūnya°*, etc.; *vastunaṣ ṣaṇṇāṃ* → *vastunaḥ ṣaṇṇām*, etc.) and vowels (*arthe iti* → *artha iti*, etc.). The same has been done throughout this book with quotations from the ĪPV and ĪPVV editions (which both apply the *sandhi* rules arbitrarily). No special mark has been used to distinguish *upadhmānīya*s and *jihvāmūlīya*s (which systematically occur e.g. in S12), while the elisions of *a* through *sandhi* are marked with *avagraha*s (mostly absent in the manuscript sources that were consulted).

The first apparatus below the text indicates the marginal sources for a specific sentence or segment thereof. The second apparatus is critical. The notes below the second apparatus explain some of the editorial choices, discuss the ĪPVV readings or add details regarding the manuscripts and their marginalia. For a detailed description of the manuscripts used, see above, chapter 2.

### Abbreviations

| | |
|---|---|
| a.c. | ante correctionem |
| b.m. | bottom margin |
| conj. | conjecture |
| corr. | correction |
| Ed. | edition |
| f. | folio |
| fol. | followed by |
| interl.s. | interlinear space |
| l.m. | left margin |
| m. | margin |
| m.t. | main text |
| ms. | manuscript |
| mss. | manuscripts |
| p.c. | post correctionem |
| pre. | preceded by |
| r.m. | right margin |
| t.m. | top margin |
| * | dot or dash marking a lacuna or an illegible character in a manuscript source |
| (***) | lacuna not indicated in any manuscript source (number of missing characters unknown) |
| ? | illegible character |
| / | line-filling *daṇḍa* |

### VIVṚTI

*tad evaṃ tāvat prakāśasya svasaṃvedanāntaḥ* ***sarvatra****ikyasamarthanayā jñānaśaktiś coditāśrayasadbhāvā vicārayitum adhikṛtaṃ pūrvāparasarvapramātṛgatatvena pratipāditā. idānīṃ kriyāśaktisamarthanāyāhāta eveti.*

### ĪPK 2.1.1

*ata eva yad apy uktaṃ kriyā naikasya sakramā* |
*eketyādi pratikṣiptaṃ tad ekasya samarthanāt* ||

### VṚTTI

*ekacittattvasamarthanād ekasambandhī vyāpāra eka eveti kriyāpy apākṛtadūṣaṇā.*

---

2 *tad*...4 *eveti*] S12 (f. 202a, r.m.), J11 (f. 203b, r.m.), S15 (f. 88a, t.m.). 9 *ekacittattvasamarthanād*...*apākṛtadūṣaṇā*] S12 (f. 202a, l.m.), J11 (f. 203b, r.m.), S10 (f. 88b, b.m., fol. *vṛttiḥ*), S15 (f. 88a, t.m.), S15 (f. 88a, b.m., pre. *oṃ*), S19 (f. 26b, m.t.), D2 (f. 207a, l.m., fol. *iti vṛttiḥ*), SOAS (f. 195b, r.m., fol. *iti vṛttiḥ*), *Vṛtti* Ed. (p. 42).

---

2 *svasaṃvedanāntaḥ*] S12, J11; *svasaṃvedanā* * * * *s* S15. 3 *coditāśrayasadbhāvā*] S12, J11; *coditāśrayasadbhāvyā* S15. | *pūrvāparasarvapramātṛgatatvena*] S12, J11; *pūrvāpara* * * *vaṣṭhamātṛgatatvena* S15. 9 *eka eveti*] S12, J11, S10, S15 (b.m.), S19, D2, SOAS, *Vṛtti* Ed.; *eva eveti* S15 (t.m.). | *apākṛtadūṣaṇā*] S12, J11, S10, S15 (t.m.), S15 (b.m.), S19, D2, SOAS; *apakṛtadūṣaṇā* *Vṛtti* Ed.

## VIVṚTI

*kriyāyāḥ sakramāyā ekatvam ekasambandhitvaṃ ca nopapannam ity uktam. tatra jñānasamarthanaprasaṅgena svasaṃvedanasaṃjñasyātmanaḥ prakāśātmanaḥ prakāśalakṣaṇo vyāpāro vimarśāparaparyāyasvabhāvabhūto yāvad uktas tāvad ekatvam ekasambandhitvaṃ ca kriyāyāḥ sam-*

---

**12** *kriyāyāḥ*… 13 *uktam*] S12 (f. 202a, l.m.), J11 (f. 203b, r.m.), S15 (f. 88a, t.m.). **13** *tatra*… 16 *āhaikacittattveti*] S12 (f. 202a, l.m.), J11 (f. 203b, r.m.), S10 (f. 88b, b.m.), S15 (f. 88a, t.m.), S19 (f. 26b, interl.s.), KAWAJIRI 2016b (p. 21).

---

**12** *sakramāyā*] S15; *sakramāyā* / S12[later addition?], J11. | *ekatvam ekasambandhitvaṃ*] conj.; *eva tva* * * * * * *sambandhitvaṃ* S12, J11; *eva tva* * * * * *sambandhitvaṃ* S15. **13** *jñānasamarthanaprasaṅgena*] S12, J11, S10, S19, KAWAJIRI 2016b; *jñānasamarthanaprasaṅga na* S15. | *svasaṃvedanasaṃjñasyātmanaḥ*] S12, J11, S10, S15, KAWAJIRI 2016b; *svasaṃvedanasaṃjñakasyātmanaḥ* S19. **14** *prakāśātmanaḥ*] S12, J11; *prakāśatmana* S15; om. S10, S19, KAWAJIRI 2016b. | *vimarśāparaparyāyasvabhāvabhūto*] S12, J11; *vimarśāparaparyāyaḥ svabhāvabhūto* S10, S19, KAWAJIRI 2016b; *vimarśāparaparyāḥ svabhāvabhūto* S15. **15** *uktas*] S12, J11, S15, S19 (p.c.); *ukta* S19 (a.c.); *uktaṃ* KAWAJIRI 2016b.

---

**12** *ekatvam ekasambandhitvaṃ*] Cf. the sequel of the *Vivṛti* on this verse, which uses twice the compound *ekasambandhitvam*. Note, however, that the three mss. in which the passage is preserved indicate a greater number of missing *akṣaras* than is assumed in this conjecture. Given the formulation (under ĪPK 1.2.9) of the Buddhist argument to which this passage responds, and Abhinavagupta's commentaries on ĪPK 1.2.9 and the present verse, which all discuss the possibility for action of having a single (*eka*) substratum (*āśraya*), one could rather conjecture *ekāśrayasambandhitvam*; but the assessment of the number of missing characters in the lacunae indicated by S12 and J11 turns out to be often slightly pessimistic (they indicate e.g. six *akṣaras* for the missing *saṃsāriṇa* in the introduction on ĪPK 2.1.6, or five *akṣaras* for the missing °*lakrama* in the *Vivṛti* on ĪPK 2.1.4). **14** *prakāśātmanaḥ*] Since the compound is omitted in several sources one could suspect that this is a gloss of *ātmanaḥ* that has crept into the text. It seems to me, however, that some scribes omitted it because they were puzzled by the alternation of the words *ātman* and *prakāśa* in *ātmanaḥ prakāśātmanaḥ prakāśalakṣaṇo vyāpāraḥ*, which in fact makes sense if Utpaladeva is playfully highlighting his main point here (namely, that the self's activity of manifestation is in fact its very essence).

*arthitam eva, tad āhaikacittattveti. ekasya hi svabhāva eka eva, kriyāṃ ca vyāpārarūpām api samavāyabalād avibhāgena pratīyamānāṃ svabhāvakalpām* ***icchanti*** *kriyābhedavādino 'pi,* ***iha tv*** *abhedapratīter yad etad ekopaśleṣarūpam ekasambandhitvaṃ kriyāyās tad ekatayaiva yuktam, tad āha kriyāpīti.*

*sakramatvam idānīṃ viruddham iva lakṣyamāṇaṃ paryālocayitum āha sakramatvam iti.*

## ĪPK 2.1.2

*sakramatvaṃ ca laukikyāḥ kriyāyāḥ kālaśaktitaḥ |*
*ghaṭate na tu śāśvatyāḥ prābhavyāḥ syāt prabhor iva ||*

---

**16** *ekasya*... 19 *yuktam*] S12 (f. 202a, l.m.), J11 (f. 203b, r.m.), S15 (f. 88a, t.m.), D2 (f. 208a, b.m.; pre. *ayam arthaḥ*, fol. ĪPVV sentence), SOAS (f. 196b, b.m.; pre. *ayam arthaḥ*, fol. same ĪPVV sentence), ĪPV, vol. II, p. 4, fn. 20 (pre. *ayam arthaḥ*, fol. same ĪPVV sentence). **19** *tad āha kriyāpīti*] S12 (f. 202a, l.m.), J11 (f. 203b, r.m.), S15 (f. 88a, t.m.). **21** *sakramatvam*[1]... 22 *iti*] S12 (f. 202b, r.m.), J11 (f. 204a, l.m.), S10 (f. 89b, l.m.), S15 (f. 88b, r.m.), KAWAJIRI 2016b (p. 22).

---

**16** *eva*[1]] S12, J11, S19, KAWAJIRI 2016b; *evaṃ* S15. | *svabhāva*] S12, J11, S15 (p. c.); *svabhāvasya* S15 (a.c.). | *kriyāṃ*] S12, J11; *kriyā* S15. **17** *avibhāgena*] S12, S15, D2, SOAS, ĪPV (fn. 20); *evibhāgena* J11. | *pratīyamānāṃ*] S12, J11, D2, SOAS, ĪPV (fn. 20); *pratīyāmānāṃ* S15. **18** *kriyābhedavādino 'pi*] S12, J11, D2, SOAS, ĪPV (fn. 20); *bhedavādino 'pi* S15. | ***iha tv*** *abhedapratīter*] S12, J11, S15; *iha punar ābhāsasāravastuvāde 'bhedapratīter* D2, SOAS, ĪPV (fn. 20). | *ekopaśleṣarūpam*] S12 (p.c.), J11, S15, D2, SOAS, ĪPV (fn. 20); *ekośle?rūpam* S12 (a. c.). **19** *kriyāyās*] S12, J11, D2, SOAS, ĪPV (fn. 20); *krayāyās* S15. **20** *kriyāpīti*] corr.; *kim iheti* S12; *kimi//heti* J11; *ki iveti* S15. **21** *viruddham iva*] S12 (p.c.), S10, S15, KAWAJIRI 2016b; *viruddhām iva* S12 (a.c.)[?], J11. | *lakṣyamāṇaṃ*] S12, J11, S10, S15, KAWAJIRI 2016b (em.); *lakṣamāṇaṃ* KAWAJIRI 2016b (ms). | *paryālocayitum*] S12, S10, S15, KAWAJIRI 2016b; *paryalocayitum* J11. | *sakramatvam*[2]... 22 *iti*] S12, J11; *sakramatvam* [fol. entire verse] *iti* S15; *sakrameti* S10; *sakrametyādi* KAWAJIRI 2016b.

---

**18** ***iha tv*** *abhedapratīter*] Cf. ĪPVV, vol. II, p. 2: ***iha tv*** *ity ābhāsasāravastuvāde*; in D2, SOAS and ĪPV (fn. 20), Abhinavagupta's gloss of *iha tu* has obviously crept in; the text given in ĪPV, fn. 20 should be corrected with the missing *avagraha* before *bhedapratīter*.

## VṚTTI

*māyāśakter bhinnāvabhāsānāṃ kriyā kālaśaktivaśāt sakramā na tv ātmavimarśarūpānādinidhanā prabhoḥ svabhāvabhūtā.*

## VIVṚTI

*iha māyāśaktyā vicchinnāvabhāsiny eva saṃvedyabhāge grāhyagrāhakabhāvaprakāśanena saṃsārasthitir nirvartyate. tatra saṃvedyabhāge vakṣyamāṇanyāyena kālaśaktyavacchedāt kriyā kālāvacchinnā sakramatvenopapādayiṣyamāṇarūpā syāt, tad āha māyāśakter iti. yā punaḥ prabhoḥ prakāśātmano 'haṃvimarśākhyasvabhāvabhūtā sā kālāvaruddhasaṃve-*

---

27 *māyāśakter*...28 *svabhāvabhūtā*] S12 (f. 202b, r.m.), J11 (f. 204a, l.m.), S10 (f. 89b, l.m., fol. *vṛttiḥ*), S15 (88b, t.m.), S15 (88b, r.m.), S19 (f. 26b, m.t.), D2 (f. 208b, b.m., pre. *atra vṛttiḥ*), SOAS (f. 197b, r.m., pre. *atra vṛttiḥ*), *Vṛtti* Ed. (p. 42). **30** *iha*...35 *akramaiva*] S12 (f. 202b, r.m.), J11 (f. 204a, l.m.), S10 (f. 89b, l.m. and b.m.), S15 (f. 88b, b.m.), S19 (f. 26b, r.m. and interl.s.), KAWAJIRI 2016b (p. 21), D2 (f. 209b, t.m., pre. *madhyāyām*), SOAS (f. 198a, l.m., pre. *madhyāyām*), ĪPV, vol. II, p. 7, fn. 34 (pre. *ayaṃ bhāvaḥ*, fol. *iti madhyāyām*).

---

27 *ātmavimarśarūpānādinidhanā*] S12 (p.c.), J11, S10, S15 (t.m.), S15 (r.m.), S19, D2, SOAS, *Vṛtti* Ed.; *ātmavimarśarūpānā?nidhanā* S12 (a.c.). **30** *eva*] S12, J11, S10, D2, SOAS, S19, KAWAJIRI 2016b, ĪPV (fn. 34); *ava* S15. | *grāhyagrāhakabhāvaprakāśanena*] S12, S10, S15, D2, SOAS, S19, ĪPV (fn. 34); *grāhyagrāhakabhāvapra/kāśanena* J11; *grāhyagrāhakaprakāśanena* KAWAJIRI 2016b. **31** *nirvartyate*] S12, J11, D2, SOAS, KAWAJIRI 2016b, ĪPV (fn. 34); *nivartyeta* S10; *nivartyete* S15; *nivartye* S19. **32** *kālaśaktyavacchedāt*] S12, J11, S10, S15, D2, SOAS, ĪPV (fn. 34); *kālaśaktyāvacchedāt* S19, KAWAJIRI 2016b. | *kālāvacchinnā*] S12, S10, S15, S19, D2, SOAS, KAWAJIRI 2016b, ĪPV (fn. 34); *kālāva/cchinnā* J11. | *sakramatveno°*] S12, J11, S10, S15, D2, SOAS, KAWAJIRI 2016b, ĪPV (fn. 34); *samatveno°* S19. **33** *tad āha māyāśakter iti*] S12, J11, S10, S15, S19, KAWAJIRI 2016; om. D2, SOAS, ĪPV (fn. 34). | *punaḥ*] S12, J11, S10, S15, D2, SOAS, KAWAJIRI 2016b, ĪPV (fn. 34); om. S19. **34** *'haṃvimarśākhyasvabhāvabhūtā*] S10, S15, D2, SOAS, S19, KAWAJIRI 2016b, ĪPV (fn. 34); *'haṃvimarśākhyabhūtā* S12, J11. | *sā kālāvaruddha°*] D2, SOAS, KAWAJIRI 2016b (conj.); *sā kalāvaruddha°* S12, J11, S15; *sakālāvaruddha°* S10, ĪPV (fn. 34); *sakalāvaruddha°* S19; *sā valāvaruddha°* KAWAJIRI 2016b (ms.). | *°kulakavalīkaraṇena*] S12, J11, S10, S19, D2, SOAS, KAWAJIRI 2016b (conj.), ĪPV (fn. 34); *°kulaka*[??]*līkaraṇena* KAWAJIRI 2016b (ms.); *°kulākavalīkaraṇena* S15.

---

30 *iha*...35 *akramaiva*] The passage is quoted in several marginal annotations as belonging to the *Madhyā*: the *Vivṛti* is often called thus, or *Madhyavimarśinī*, or *Madhyapratyabhijñā* (see TORELLA 1988, p. 138, quoting Bhāskarakaṇṭha's testimony; cf. e.g. ĪPV, vol. I, p. 124, fn. 62: *yathoktaṃ madhyapratyabhijñāyām*, etc.).

*dyakulakavalīkaraṇena* ***kālagrāsād apy*** *akramaiva, tad āha na tv ātmavimarśeti. sā paraṃ śuddhasvātantryamayā kṛtrimakartṛtāparyavasānā.*

*kriyāsakramatvavicāraprasaṅgād īśvarapratyabhijñopayogād api ca* ***vakṣyamāṇāt*** *kālasvarūpaṃ nirūpayitum āha:*

ĪPK 2.1.3

*kālaḥ sūryādisaṃcāras tat tat puṣpādijanma vā* ||
*śītoṣṇe vātha tallakṣyaḥ krama eva sa tattvataḥ* ||

---

**35** *tad*...36 *kṛtrimakartṛtāparyavasānā*] S12 (f. 202b, r.m.), J11 (f. 204a, l.m.), S10 (f. 89b, b.m.), S15 (f. 88b, b.m.), S19 (f. 26b, interl.s.), KAWAJIRI 2016b (p. 21). **37** *kriyāsakramatvavicāraprasaṅgād*...38 *āha*] S12 (f. 202b, b.m.), J11 (f. 204b, t.m.), S15 (f. 89a, l.m.).

---

**35** ***kālagrāsād api***] conj.; *kālagrāsād* S12, S10, S15, D2, SOAS, S19, KAWAJIRI 2016b, ĪPV (fn. 34); *kālāgrāsād* J11. | *akramaiva*] S12, S10, S15, D2, SOAS, S19, KAWAJIRI 2016b (em.); *akra[me]va* KAWAJIRI 2016b (ms.). **36** *paraṃ*] S12, J11, S10, S15, S19, KAWAJIRI 2016b (ms.); *para°* KAWAJIRI 2016b (em.). | *śuddhasvātantryamayā*] S12, J11, S10; *śuddhasvātantryamayā°* KAWAJIRI 2016b; *śuddhasvātantryamāyā* S19; *śuddhasvā * ntryamayā* S15. **38** *nirūpayitum*] S12 (a.c.)?, S15, J11; *nirūpayatum* S12 (p.c.).

---

**35** *kālagrāsād apy*] Cf. ĪPVV, vol. III, p. 3: ***kālagrāsād apīti***; S12 (m.t.) and J11 (m.t.) have the same reading, even though none of them (and in fact no available marginal source at all) has *api* in the corresponding *Vivṛti* quotation. At any rate Abhinavagupta evidently commented on a text that included *api* (see *ibid.*: *yāvad eva bāhyāntararūpaṃ vedyakulaṃ svātmani... grasate viśrāmyati tāvat tanniṣṭho 'vabhāsanakramo 'pi grasta eva...*), hence the choice made here against the marginalia's readings. **36** *śuddhasvātantryamayā*] S15 does not use a dot but a blank space to indicate the missing character marked here with *. **38** *nirūpayitum*] It seems that originally S12 had written the *i* after the *y* instead of rightly placing it before, and there was an attempt to correct this by deleting it with yellowish paste, but without writing it again where it belongs. **40** *tat tat puṣpādijanma*] It might seem more natural to read *tattatpuṣpādijanma*; however, Utpaladeva himself specifies from the very beginning of the *Vṛtti* (*sā sā prasiddhā kriyā...*) that the repetition of the article concerns the action itself (i.e., in the verse, *janman*).

## VṚTTI

*sā sā prasiddhā kriyā kālaḥ śītādi vā; tadupalakṣitaḥ sarvabhinnāvabhāsamānabhāvopādhibhūtaḥ krama evāsau tasyaivopayogāt.*

## VIVṚTI

*padārthasvarūpaviśeṣaparicchedahetur vyavahārāya kālapadārtho 'bhyupagato 'vacchedakaś ca prasiddha eva bhavatīti bahutarapratipādyapratipādakaprasiddho* ***nālikādi****vyapadeśyasūryādisaṃcāraviśeṣo nirdiṣṭaḥ prasiddhakriyopalakṣaṇārthaḥ, tad āha sā sā prasiddheti.* ***viśiṣṭā****nyā kramanirvartyatayā prasiddhatvāt tasyāḥ saiva* ***kālaḥ****. tena* ***godohādīnām*** *api*

---

**43** *sā*[1]...44 *tasyaivopayogāt*] S12 (f. 202b, b.m.), J11 (f. 204b, t.m.), S10 (f. 90a, l.m., fol. *vṛttiḥ*), S15 (f. 89a, l.m. and b.m.), S15 (f. 89b, r.m.), S19 (f. 27a, m.t.), D2 (f. 209b, b.m., pre. *atra vṛttiḥ*), SOAS (f. 198b, r.m., pre. *atra vṛttiḥ*), *Vṛtti* Ed. (pp. 42–43). **46** *padārthasvarūpaviśeṣaparicchedahetur*...49 *prasiddheti*] S12 (f. 203a, t.m.), J11 (f. 204b, r.m.), S15 (f. 89a, b.m.), KAWAJIRI 2016b (p. 23). **49** *viśiṣṭānyā*...51 *grahaṇam*] S12 (f. 203a, t.m.), J11 (f. 204b, r.m.), S15 (f. 89a, b.m.).

---

**43** *sarvabhinnāvabhāsamāna°*] S10, S15 (f. 89b), S19, *Vṛtti* Ed.; *sarvabhinnābhāsamāna°* S12, J11, S15 (f. 89a), D2, SOAS. **44** *evāsau*] S12, J11, S10, S15 (f. 89a), S15 (f. 89b), S19, D2, SOAS; *eva vāsau Vṛtti* Ed. **46** *°viśeṣaparicchedahetur vyavahārāya*] KAWAJIRI 2016b; *°viśeṣaparicchedahetuvyavahārāya* S12, J11; *°viśeṣaṃ paricchedahetur vyavahārāya* S15. **47** *'vacchedakaś*] S15, KAWAJIRI 2016b; *'vabodakaś* S12, J11. **48** ***nālikādi****vyapadeśyasūryādisaṃcāraviśeṣo*] S12, S15; ***nālikādi****vyapadeśasūryādisaṃcāraviśeṣo* J11; [*ā?si?krā*]*divyapadeśyaḥ sūryādisaṃcāraviśeṣo* KAWAJIRI 2016b. **49** *sā sā prasiddheti*] S15, KAWAJIRI 2016b; *sā prasiddheti* S12, J11. | ***viśiṣṭā****nyā*] conj.; ***viśiṣṭā****sya* J11; *viśiṣṭasya* S12; *viśiṣṭakriyā* S15. | *kramanirvartyatayā*] S12, S15; *kramanivartyatayā* J11. **50** ***kālaḥ***] S12, J11; *kātraḥ* S15.

---

**49** *viśiṣṭānyā*] In J11 the scribe apparently tried to cancel the *ā* in *viśiṣṭāsya*. Given Abhinavagupta's commentary (ĪPVV, vol. III, p. 5, has ***viśiṣṭa*** *iti*, to be corrected into ***viśiṣṭeti*** according to the m.t. in S12 and J11), it seems probable that the original text had *viśiṣṭā*, and I do not see what the word *asya* might refer to here, nor how, if we postulate *viśiṣṭā kriyā* as the original text on the basis of S15's reading (*viśiṣṭakriyā*), *kriyā* could have been corrupted into *°sya*; hence the conjecture. **50** *tena*] The words *cinmaya eveti* were marked in the ĪPVV Ed. as a *pratīka*, but they probably belong to Abhinavagupta's commentary; cf. S12 and J11 (m.t.) which both omit *iti* after *cinmaya eva* (so does ms. *kha* according to ĪPVV, vol. III, p. 6, fn. 2).

*grahaṇam; sūryādīty ādigrahaṇād **anyagraha**parigrahaḥ. puṣpādijanma sūryādisaṃcārāvyutpannānāṃ hālikādīnāṃ prasiddham, tena te sūryādisaṃcāraṃ vasantādisaṃjñam apy upalakṣayanti. atrāpy ādigrahaṇāc chālyādijanma kārṣikāṇāṃ prasiddhaṃ gṛhītam, tato 'py anabhijñānāṃ tat tad iti vīpsayā pakṣiviśeṣāgamanāder grahaṇam, hālikāprasiddhasyopalakṣaṇaṃ caitat. **tat sarvaṃ** sā seti vīpsayā vivṛtam.*

---

**51** *sūryādīty…anyagrahaparigrahaḥ*] S12 (f. 203a, t.m.), J11 (f. 204b, r.m.), S15 (f. 89a, b.m.), S19 (f. 27a, interl.s.), KAWAJIRI 2016b (p. 22). | *puṣpādijanma…*52 *prasiddham*] S12 (f. 203a, t.m.), J11 (f. 204b, r.m.), S15 (f. 89a, b.m.), D2 (f. 210a, interl.s. and l.m.), SOAS (f. 199a, t.m.), S19 (f. 27a, interl.s.), KAWAJIRI 2016b (p. 22), ĪPV (vol. II, p. 9, fn. 38). **52** *tena…*53 *upalakṣayanti*] S12 (f. 203a, t.m.), J11 (f. 204b, r.m.), S15 (f. 89a, b.m.), D2 (f. 210a, interl.s. and l.m.), SOAS (f. 199a, t.m.), ĪPV (vol. II, p. 9, fn. 38). **53** *atrāpy…*54 *gṛhītam*] S12 (f. 203a, t.m. and l.m.), J11 (f. 204b, r.m.), S15 (f. 89a, b.m.), D2 (f. 210a, interl.s. and l.m.), SOAS (f. 199a, t.m.), KAWAJIRI 2016b (p. 22), ĪPV (vol. II, p. 9, fn. 38). **54** *tato…*55 *grahaṇam*] S12 (f. 203a, t.m.), J11 (f. 204b, r.m.), S15 (f. 89a, b.m.), D2 (f. 210a, interl.s. and l.m.), SOAS (f. 199a, t.m.), ĪPV (vol. II, p. 9, fn. 38). **55** *hālikāprasiddhasyopalakṣaṇaṃ…*56 *vivṛtam*] S12 (f. 203a, l.m.), J11 (f. 204b, r.m.), S15 (f. 89a, b.m.).

---

**51** *sūryādīty ādigrahaṇād **anyagraha**parigrahaḥ*] conj.; *sūryādīti puṣpādigrahaṇād **anyagraha**parigrahaḥ* S12, J11, S15; *ādigrahaṇād **anyagraha**parigrahaḥ* KAWAJIRI 2016b; *puṣpādijanmādigrahaṇād **anyagraha**parigrahaḥ* S19. | *puṣpādijanma*] S12, J11, S15, D2, SOAS, ĪPV (fn. 38); om. S19, KAWAJIRI 2016b. **52** *sūryādisaṃcārāvyutpannānāṃ*] S12, J11, S15, KAWAJIRI 2016b, D2, SOAS, ĪPV (fn. 38); *sūryādisaṃcāravyutpannānāṃ* S19. | *hālikādīnāṃ prasiddham*] S12, J11, S15, D2, SOAS, S19, ĪPV (fn. 38); *hālikādīnāṃ puṣpādijanma* KAWAJIRI 2016b. **53** *vasantādisaṃjñam*] S12, J11, S15; *vasantādikasaṃjñam* D2, SOAS, ĪPV (fn. 38). | *atrāpy ādigrahaṇāc*] S12, J11, S15; *atrādigrahaṇāc* D2, SOAS, ĪPV (fn. 38); *ādigrahaṇād* KAWAJIRI 2016b. **54** *kārṣikāṇāṃ…gṛhītam*] D2, SOAS, ĪPV (fn. 38); *gṛhītam* S12, J11, S15, KAWAJIRI 2016b. | *tato…*55 *grahaṇam*] D2, SOAS, ĪPV (fn. 38); *pakṣiviśeṣāgamanāder* S12, J11; *pakṣiviśeṣāgamanādi* S15.

---

**51** *puṣpādijanma*] The compound is in fact present but misplaced in both S19 (where it appears in the previous sentence) and KAWAJIRI 2016b (where it has replaced *prasiddham* in this sentence). **53** *chālyādijanma*] KAWAJIRI 2016b takes *chālyādijanma* and *gṛhītaṃ* as forming a compound, and believes that *sūryādisaṃcārāvyutpannāṃ hālikādīnāṃ puṣpādijanma* and *ādigrahaṇāc chālyādijanma gṛhītaṃ* constitute a single fragment. | *chālyādijanma…*55 *grahaṇam*] I assume (perhaps wrongly) that here the text in the ĪPVV mss. is incomplete and that the passage is better preserved in some of the ĪPV sources.

***na kevalaṃ*** *pratītyavacchedāyaivopayogī kālo yāvat* ***siddharūpaḥ*** *sahakārikāraṇat**ādy**upayogy apy uṣṇādiḥ prasiddhaḥ, tad āha śītādīti.* ***etad*** *anyadarśanasiddhāntopadarśanamātram, nātra kvacid abhiniveśaḥ svecchāmātreṇāvacchedakānām upakalpitatvāt* ***prasiddheś*** ***cā****navasthitatvāt.* ***śītādīnāṃ*** *kāryajananopayoge ca kāraṇataiva na kālatvam, kālatvaṃ punar avacchedakatvād eva, e**tac cā**navasthitam ity uktam.*

*tad evam etatsarvopalakṣyamāṇaṃ* ***yat kiñcit*** *tad eva* ***sthirarūpaṃ padārtha****pratītyavacchedopayogi kālo 'stu. sa ca pratītiparyālocanayā* ***krama***

---

57 *na*...58 *śītādīti*] S12 (f. 203a, l.m.), J11 (f. 204b, r.m.), S15 (f. 89a, b.m.), D2 (f. 210a, l.m.), SOAS (f. 199a, l.m.), KAWAJIRI 2016b (p. 23). **58** *etad anyadarśanasiddhāntopadarśanamātram*] S12 (f. 203a, l.m.), J11 (f. 204b, r.m.), S15 (f. 89a, b.m.), KAWAJIRI 2016b (p. 23). **59** *nātra*...60 *cānavasthitatvāt*] S12 (f. 203a, l.m.), J11 (f. 204b, r.m.), S15 (f. 89a, b.m.). **60** *śītādīnāṃ*...62 *eva*] S12 (f. 203a, l.m.), J11 (f. 204b, r.m. and b.m.), S15 (f. 89a, b.m. and r.m.), S3 (f. 80b, b.m.), D2 (f. 210a, l.m.), SOAS (f. 199a, l.m.), KAWAJIRI 2016b (p. 23). **62** *etac cānavasthitam ity uktam*] S12 (f. 203a, l.m.), J11 (f. 204b, b.m.), S15 (f. 89a, r.m.), S3 (f. 80b, b.m., fol. *iti ṭīkā*), D2 (f. 210a, l.m.), SOAS (f. 199a, l.m.). **63** *tad*[1]...65 *evopapannaḥ*] S12 (f. 203a, l.m.), J11 (f. 204b, b.m.), S15 (f. 89a, r.m.), S3 (f. 80b, b.m., fol. *ity ayam arthaḥ*), D2 (f. 210a, b.m., fol. *ity ayam arthaḥ*), SOAS (f. 199a, l.m., fol. *ity ayam arthaḥ*).

---

57 *pratītyavacchedāyaivopayogī*] D2, KAWAJIRI 2016b; *pratītyāvacchedāyaivopayogī* SOAS; *pratītyavacchedāyaivopabhogī* S12, J11, S15. | ***siddharūpaḥ***] S12, J11 (p.c.), S15, KAWAJIRI 2016b, SOAS; *siddho rūpaḥ* J11 (a.c.); *siddharūpoḥ* D2. | *sahakārikāraṇat**ādy**upayogy apy uṣṇādiḥ*] S12, J11, S15, KAWAJIRI 2016b; *sahakārikāraṇat**ādy**upayogī coṣṇatādiḥ* D2, SOAS (with an attempt to delete the *ḥ*). **58** *tad āha śītādīti*] S12, J11, S15, KAWAJIRI 2016b; *iti* D2, SOAS. **62** ***etac cā****navasthitam*] S12, S15; *etaś cānavasthitam* J11; ***etac cā****vacchedakatvam anavasthitam* S3, D2, SOAS.

---

59 *nātra*...60 *cānavasthitatvāt*] KAWAJIRI 2016b (p. 23) assumes a continuity in the marginal annotation between °*upadarśanamātram* and *śītādīnām* despite evidence to the contrary in Abhinavagupta's commentary (ĪPVV, vol. III, p. 7: *ity āha* ***prasiddheś ce****ti*..., etc.). | *kvacid*] This could be a corruption for *kaścid* (on this common confusion see e.g. the *Vivṛti* fragment on ĪPK 1.7.11 edited in RATIÉ forthcoming b, where the erroneous reading *kaścit* for *kvacit* is found in both S12 and J11). However, here *kvacid* seems to refer to the two different aspects of the view just presented and about to be criticized, so that I have kept it. **62** *etac cānavasthitam*] Abhinavagupta's gloss (ĪPVV, vol. III, p. 7: ***etac ce****ty avacchedakatvam*) has obviously crept into the annotations in S3, D2 and SOAS. **63** ***sthirarūpaṃ padārtha***°] Abhinavagupta is aware of a variant reading *sthirarūpapadārtha*° (see ĪPVV, vol. III, p. 7: *sthirarūpapadārtheti vā samastam padam*). I have

***evo**papannaḥ, tad āha tadupalakṣita iti.* ***tathā hi*** *tasya vasantāder ādityādyudayakramarūpasyaivādityādyupādhibhūtasyānubhavaḥ.* ***tenaiva*** *sūryādisaṃcārādinā bhāvānām abhūtānāṃ bhāvopalakṣaṇāt krama evopalakṣitaḥ, yenopādhinā kramiko 'rthaḥ puṣpādir devadattādir api vāvabhāsyate, tad āha bhinnāvabhāsamāneti.*

***vasantādi**śabdo bhūtabhaviṣyadādiśabdaś ca na sākṣāt kālātmānam āha yathā kriyāśabdaḥ kriyām, api tu yugapadvyavasthitasiddhārthapratipādanadvāreṇa, āsīd bhavati bhavitetyādayas tu śabdāḥ kālānubhavocitaprati-*

---

**65** *tad āha tadupalakṣita iti*] S12 (f. 203a, l.m.), J11 (f. 204b, b.m.), S15 (f. 89a, r.m.). | *tathā…ādityādyudayakramarūpasyaivādityādyupādhibhūtasyānubhavaḥ*] S12 (f. 203b, b.m.), J11 (f. 204b, b.m.), S10 (f. 90a, t.m.), S15 (f. 89a, r.m.), S3 (f. 80b, b.m. and r.m.), D2 (f. 210b, b.m., fol. ĪPVV quotation), SOAS (f. 199b, r.m., fol. same ĪPVV quotation), ĪPV (vol. II, p. 10, fn. 45; fol. same ĪPVV quotation). **66** *tenaiva…69 bhinnāvabhāsamāneti*] S12 (f. 203b, b.m.), S3 (f. 80b, r.m., pre. an ĪPVV quotation and *ity āśaṅkya brūte ṭīkākāraḥ*), S10 (f. 90a, t.m., fol. *iti ṭīkāyām*), D2 (f. 210b, b.m.), SOAS (f. 199b, t.m.), ĪPV (vol. II, p. 10, fn. 45). **70** *vasantādiśabdo…76 vivṛtam*] S12 (f. 203b, b.m.).

---

**65** *tadupalakṣita iti*] corr.; *tadupalakṣiteti* S12, J11, S15. | ***tathā hi*** *tasya vasantāder*] S12, J11, S3, S10, S15; *vasantāder hi kālasya* D2, SOAS, ĪPV (fn. 45). **66** ***tenaiva***] conj.; *tena vā* S12, S3, S10; *yataḥ* D2, SOAS, ĪPV (fn. 45). | *sūryādisaṃcārādinā*] S12, S3; *sūryasaṃcārādinā* S10, D2, SOAS, ĪPV (fn. 45). **67** *bhāvānām*] S3, S10, D2, SOAS, ĪPV (fn. 45); *bhāvanām* S12. **68** *yenopādhinā*] S12, S3, S10; *tenopādhinā* D2, SOAS, ĪPV (fn. 45). | *puṣpādir*] S3, S10, D2, SOAS, ĪPV (fn. 45); *puṣpādi* S12. **69** *tad āha bhinnāvabhāsamāneti*] conj.; *tad āha vṛttau bhinnāvabhāsamāneti* S10; *tad āha bhinnabhāsamāneti* S12; *tad āha bhinnābhāsa* S3; *ity arthaḥ* D2, SOAS, ĪPV (fn. 45).

---

kept *sthirarūpaṃ padārtha°*, however, because all available witnesses bear this reading, Abhinavagupta favours it, and the context seems to require it. **65** ***tathā hi*** *tasya vasantāder*] Cf. ĪPVV, vol. III, p. 8: ***tathā hīti***. **66** ***tenaiva***] Cf. ĪPVV, vol. III, p. 8: ***tenaiveti*** (also found in the m.t. of S12 and J11). Note, however, Abhinavagupta's next sentence (also found in the m.t. of S12 and J11): ***vāśabde**nāsyaiva pakṣasya dārḍhyaṃ dyotayati*. Nevertheless I do not see how the word *vā* might "indicate the strength of Utpaladeva's own thesis," whereas the word of emphasis *eva* here would help point out that according to Utpaladeva, the *same* action can be an *upādhi* of different objects by marking the same sequence in them. I therefore assume (without certainty) that the first ĪPVV quotation (***tenaiva***) is correct, whereas ***vāśabdena***... should be corrected into ***eva**śabdena*. **69** *tad āha bhinnāvabhāsamāneti*] In S3 a word underneath *tad āha bhinnābhāsamāneti* is no longer legible (the m. seems to have been cut).

*kāriṇaḥ.* ***tad evaṃ*** *janmasattāvipariṇāmādikramātmaiva sa vyavatiṣṭhamānaḥ kālalakṣaṇo 'rthas tathaiva vicāryaḥ, tad āha tasyaivopayogād iti. krama eva hi tāvadbhedāvacchedāyopayujyamāno 'vasīyata ity arthaḥ. anena tattvata iti vivṛtam.*

***kramas****varūpa****paryālocanayā*** *tadavabhāsakārī maheśvara eva kālaśaktimān upakalpyata ity āha krama ityādi.*

## ĪPK 2.1.4

*kramo bhedāśrayo bhedo 'py ābhāsasadasattvataḥ* |
*ābhāsasadasattve tu citrābhāsakṛtaḥ prabhoḥ* ||

## VṚTTI

*anyonyābhāsaśūnyabhinnabhāvāvabhāsavaicitryakriyaiva prabhor bhāveṣu kramahetuḥ.*

---

77 *kramasvarūpaparyālocanayā*...78 *ityādi*] S12 (f. 204a, l.m.), D2 (f. 211a, interl.s.), SOAS (f. 199b, b.m.), ĪPV (vol. II, p. 11, fn. 47, last two ll.), KAWAJIRI 2016b (p. 23). **83** *anyonyābhāsaśūnyabhinnabhāvāvabhāsavaicitryakriyaiva*...84 *kramahetuḥ*] S12 (f. 204a, l.m., pre. *vṛttiḥ*), S10 (f. 90b, r.m., fol. *vṛttiḥ*), S15 (f. 90a, l.m.), S19 (f. 27a, m.t.), D2 (f. 211a, l.m., pre. *atra vṛttiḥ*), SOAS (f. 199b, r. m., pre. *atra vṛttiḥ*), *Vṛtti* Ed. (p. 43).

---

73 *janmasattāvipariṇāmādikramātmaiva*] corr.; *janmasattādipariṇāmādikramātmaiva* S12. **75** *tāvad°* corr.; *tāva* S12. **76** *tattvata*] corr.; *tattva* S12. **77** ***kramas****varūpa****paryālocanayā***] S12 (p.c.), KAWAJIRI 2016b; ***kramas****varū****paryālocanayā*** S12 (a.c.); *tataś ca* ***kramas****varūpa****paryālocanayā*** D2, SOAS, ĪPV (fn. 47). | *tadavabhāsakārī*] S12, D2, KAWAJIRI 2016b; *tadabhāvasahakārī* SOAS, ĪPV (fn. 47). | *kālaśaktimān upakalpyata ity āha krama ityādi*] corr.; *kālaśaktiman upakalpyata ity āha krametyādi* S12; *kālaśaktimān iti prabhor ity asyāśayaḥ* D2, SOAS, ĪPV (fn. 47); *kālaśaktim upakalpyate ity āha krama iti* KAWAJIRI 2016b (em.); *kālaśaktim upakalpyate ity āha kramam iti* KAWAJIRI 2016b (ms.). **83** *°bhāvāvabhāsavaicitryakriyaiva*] S12, S10, S15, S19, D2, SOAS (p.c.), *Vṛtti* Ed.: *°?vā?vasavaicitryakriyaiva* SOAS (a.c.). **84** *kramahetuḥ*] S12, S10, S15, S19, D2, *Vṛtti* Ed.; *krame hetuḥ* SOAS.

---

73 *janmasattāvipariṇāmādikramātmaiva*] Not to mention that two *ādi*s in this compound do not make sense since it is obviously a single list that is given before the word *°krama°*, see above, Chapter 8, §7, on the enumeration of *bhāvavikāra*s given by Vārṣyāyaṇi according to Yāska and Patañjali, which includes the verb *vipariṇam-*. **77** ***kramas****varūpa****paryālocanayā***] Cf. ĪPVV, vol. III, p. 10: *enam avatārayati* ***krame****ti...*

VIVṚTI

***vicitra**ghaṭapaṭādy**avabhāsa**kāritvam eveśvarasya **kalanakriyā** bhāvopādhikramalakṣaṇakālāviṣkaraṇaśaktiḥ, **tad āhā**nyonyābhās**etyādāv** avabhāsavaicitryakriyaiveti. ghaṭādyābhāsānāṃ vaicitryeṇa hy anyonyābhāvaḥ, tad āhābhāsasadasattve tv ity **asya** vivaraṇam anyonyābhāseti. ābhāsasadasattvayor **ekāśrayatvāyogād bhedahetutvena copādānād** anyonyaśabdārthalābhaḥ, anyonyāsadbhāvaś ca ghaṭādyavabhāsānāṃ bhedo bhavati kramabuddher āśrayaḥ, tad āha śūnyabhinneti.*

*anyonyābhāsaśūnyatvād **bhinnatvam** uktaṃ bhāvānām. **ata evā**vabhāsacitratvaṃ bhedaś ca bheden**opātte**. **citratvam** ekatve 'pi **bodhātmano** bhava-*

---

**86** *vicitraghaṭapaṭādyavabhāsakāritvam*…87 *āhānyonyābhāsetyādāv*] S12 (f. 204a, b.m.), KAWAJIRI 2016b (p. 24). **87** *avabhāsavaicitryakriyaiveti*…89 *anyonyābhāvaḥ*] S12 (f. 204a, b.m.). **89** *tad*…93 *bhāvānām*] S12 (f. 204a, b.m.), KAWAJIRI 2016b (p. 24). **93** *ata*…94 *bhedenopātte*] S12 (f. 204b, t.m.), J11 (f.

---

**86** *kalanakriyā*] S12; *kālanakriyā* KAWAJIRI 2016b (ms.); *kalanakriyā°* KAWAJIRI 2016b (em.). | *bhāvopādhikrama°*] S12; *bhāvopādhibhūtakrama°* KAWAJIRI 2016b. **87** ***āhā**nyonyābhās**etyādāv***] S12; ***āhā**nyonyābhāseti* KAWAJIRI 2016b (em.); ***āhā**nyonyabhāseti* KAWAJIRI 2016b (ms.). **88** *vaicitryeṇa hy*] conj.; *vaicitrye na hy* S12. **89** *tad āhābhāsasadasattve tv ity*] corr.; *tad āhābhāsasadasattve cety* S12; *sadasattve ceti* KAWAJIRI 2016b (ms.); *sadasattve iti ca* KAWAJIRI 2016b (em.). | *anyonyābhāseti*] S12, KAWAJIRI 2016b (em.); *anyonyābhāveti* KAWAJIRI 2016b (ms.). **91** *anyonyāsadbhāvaś*] corr.; *anyonyasadbhāvāś* S12, KAWAJIRI 2016b (ms.); *anyonyasadbhāvaś* (!) KAWAJIRI 2016b (em.). **93** ***ata evā**vabhāsacitratvaṃ*] S12; ***ata evā**vattāmasacitratvaṃ* J11 (the *i*'s curl being misplaced).

---

**86** *bhāvopādhikrama°*] I assume that a part of Abhinavagupta's gloss (ĪPVV, vol. III, p. 10: *bhāvopādhibhūtasya kramātmanaḥ...*) has crept into the ms. studied in KAWAJIRI 2016b. **87** ***āhā**nyonyābhāsety°*] Contrary to what is assumed in KAWAJIRI 2016b, from this point onwards the sentence found in the *Vṛtti* ms. studied in that article is lacunary, as shown by the absence of the *pratīka* ***ity ādāv*** *iti* quoted in ĪPVV, vol. III, p. 10. **88** *vaicitryeṇa hy*] The conj. seems required by Abhinavagupta's commentaries on the passage (on which see above, Chapter 7, §2), since they both explain that objective entities are mutually exclusive due to the variety (*citratayā*) of ways in which the Lord manifests their phenomena. **93** *ata* …101 *citratocyate*] The marginal annotation quoted in KAWAJIRI 2016b, p. 24 (*tau cābhāsānāṃ bhāvābhāvau* etc.) as a "fragment" that "seems to be" from the *Vivṛti* on ĪPK 2.1.4 is of course a quotation from Abhinavagupta's ĪPV, vol. II, p. 12. **94** **bodhātmano**] Cf. ĪPVV, vol. III, p. 11: **bodhātmana** *iti citrajñānasya*; I assume that Abhinavagupta's gloss, *citrajñānasya*, ended up replacing the words that it was meant to explain. In S12, the original reading *bodhātmano* was corrected into *citrajñānasya*—unless it was only provided as a gloss or an alternative

*ti, bhedas tu parasparaparihārād ekatvena virudhyate.* ***tathā cārya****dharmakīrtiḥ*

> *nīlādiś citravijñāne jñānopādhir ananyabhāk |*
> *aśakyadarśanas taṃ hi pataty arthe vivecayan || iti*

***nīlādīnāṃ*** *hi vibhāgenānyonyabhinnatayā vyavasthāpane saty arthatvena deśakrama ekatvābhāvaś ca, bodharūpatayā tv aikyād* ***anyonyāparityāgena paricchedāt tair eva*** *brahmatattvasya citratocyate.*

---

206a, l.m.). **94** *citratvam*... 101 *citratocyate*] S12 (f. 204b, t.m.), J11 (f. 206a, l. m.).

---

**94** ***bodhātmano***] S12 (a.c.), J11 (p.c.[1]); *citrajñānasya* S12 (p.c.), J11 (a.c.); *tmano* J11 (p.c.[2]). **95** *parasparaparihārād*] S12; *parasparaparihārad* J11. **97** *jñānopādhir*] corr.; *jñānopadhir* S12, J11. **101** ***tair eva***] S12 (a.c.); *tair eva* ????????????? ????? S12 (p.c.); *tair etaivoktarūpair nīlādibhir brahmādibhir vāva* J11.

---

reading? The latter compound is given there with the correction marks listed in EINICKE 2009 as Sar17(1895)_16, i.e. without crossing out or deleting the words to be corrected. There is a similar instance of these marks in S12, f. 189a, m.t., where *darśane 'pi na ka*° was corrected into *samate tu na ka*° (for *svamate...*?), but there too, one wonders if it was indeed meant as a correction or just as an alternative reading. Perhaps the scribe who wrote down the annotations in S12 copied them from an antigraph that gave *citrajñānasya* above *bodhātmano* as a gloss for the latter; and he may or may not have mistaken the gloss for a correction or an alternative reading. In any case J11 first gives the reading *citrajñānasya*, but °*tmano* was added in Śāradā script after *citrajñānasya* (in the l.m. of the m., so to speak), and above the fragment, the compound *bodhātmano* is written in Grantha script (on such annotations in Grantha and Telugu scripts, see above, Chapter 2, §§1 and 8, under J11). I am not sure which of the two corrections preceded the other, but the Śāradā annotation °*tmano* may have been added after the Grantha one, perhaps simply to clarify the end of the latter (the character °*tma*° is difficult to read). **97** *nīlādiś citravijñāne... vivecayan || iti*] PV, *Pratyakṣapariccheda* 220. **101** ***tair eva***] In S12, words are written above the marginal annotation and marked as an addition to be inserted after ***tair eva*** (with two circles, one below and one above *tair eva*, indicating the correction, the beginning of the additional text being marked with similar circles). They are illegible on the scan at my disposal, but could probably still be read in the ms. itself; the reading in J11 was in all probability taken from this addition in S12. Given the corresponding passage in ĪPVV, vol. III, p. 11 and the absence of an *iti* indicating a quotation there, I assume that a corrupted form of Abhinavagupta's gloss has crept into the *mūla*-text (the gloss was printed in a corrupted form in the ĪPVV edition: as explained above, Chapter 7, §5, the words *uktarūpair nīlādibhir brahmavādibhir vaivaṃ* in ĪPVV, vol. III, p. 11, also found in the m.t. of S12 and J11, must be a corruption for *uktarūpanīlavādibhir brahmavādibhir vaivaṃ*; cf. the additional corruption *brahmādibhir* for

*tad evaṃ vicitraviśvātmabhāvasthitiḥ parameśvarasya kālaprathābījam, tad āha bhāveṣu kramahetur iti.* ***māyā****śaktyāvabhāseṣv eva vicitreṣu bhinnabhāvarūpatayābhimānād anyonyaparihārād eṣām* ***ubhayarūpāpi*** *deśakālābhyāṃ kramāvabhāsasthitiḥ.*

*tad vicitratvaṃ mūrtīnāṃ kriyāṇāṃ ca bhavad yathākramaṃ deśakālābhyām ubhayātmakam api kramam upakalpayatīty āha mūrtītyādi.*

ĪPK 2.1.5

*mūrtivaicitryato deśakramam ābhāsayaty asau |*
*kriyāvaicitryanirbhāsāt kālakramam apīśvaraḥ ||*

---

**102** *tad*... 103 *iti*] S12 (f. 204b, t.m.), J11 (f. 206a, l.m.), S19 (f. 27a, interl.s.), KAWAJIRI 2016b (p. 24). **103** *māyāśaktyāvabhāseṣv*... 105 *kramāvabhāsasthitiḥ*] S12 (f. 204b, t.m. and r.m.), J11 (f. 206a, l.m.). **106** *tad*... 107 *mūrtītyādi*] S12 (f. 204b, r.m.), J11 (f. 206b, t.m.), S19 (f. 27a, interl.s.), KAWAJIRI 2016b (p. 25), D2 (f. 212b, r.m.) SOAS (f. 201a, l.m.), ĪPV (vol. II, p. 13, fn. 55).

---

**102** *evaṃ*] S12, J11, KAWAJIRI 2016b; *eva* S19. | *kālaprathābījam*] S12, J11, S19; *kālapra*[*thā*?*ītaṃ*] KAWAJIRI 2016b (ms.); *kālaprathānimittam* KAWAJIRI 2016b (conj.). **103** *bhāveṣu*] S12, J11, KAWAJIRI 2016b; *bhāveṣu bhāveṣu* S19. **106** *tad vicitratvaṃ mūrtīnāṃ*] S12, J11, S19; [??*vicitratvaṃ mūrtīnāṃ*] KAWAJIRI 2016b (ms.); *tadvicitratvaṃ mūrtīnāṃ* KAWAJIRI 2016b (em.). | *bhavad*] S12, J11, S19, KAWAJIRI 2016b, D2, ĪPV (fn. 55); *bhaved* SOAS. **107** *ubhayātmakam*] S19, KAWAJIRI 2016b; *ubhayārmakam* S12, J11; *ubhayathātmakam* D2, SOAS, ĪPV (fn. 55). | *upakalpayatīty āha*] S12, J11, S19, KAWAJIRI 2016b (em.); *upakalpayīty āha* KAWAJIRI 2016b (ms.); *upakalpayatīty arthaḥ* D2, SOAS, ĪPV (fn. 55). | *mūrtītyādi*] KAWAJIRI 2016b; *mūrtītyādiḥ* S12, J11; om. S19, D2, SOAS, ĪPV (fn. 55).

---

*brahmavādibhir* in ms. Ga, reccorded by the editors, which is also found in J11's addition). Perhaps this was given as a mere gloss in S12's exemplar and was confused with a correction by the scribe who copied S12. **105** *kramāvabhāsasthitiḥ*] Number 92 (corresponding to ĪPK 2.1.4 when verses are numbered continuously from the beginning of the treatise) is given in S12 and J11 at the end of the commentary on ĪPK 2.1.4.

## VṚTTI

*anekasyānyonyabhedābhāsād deśakramaḥ kriyāmukhena kālakramo 'pi. ekasya tu bhāvasya tattajjanmasattāvipariṇāmādikriyābhedāt kālakrama eva.*

## VIVṚTI

***svarūpamātram*** *anyonyabhedenāvabhāsamānam arthānāṃ mūrtiḥ. bodhasya smṛtyanubhavādyātmanaḥ svasaṃvedanaikyena bhedāvabhāsanābhāvān na mūrtatvam. śabdasy**ākāśīyasyā**ntarasya vācakarūpasya grāhakātmano grahaṇātmano vā svasaṃvidaikyād eva* ***bhedābhāvān*** *na mūrtiḥ,* ***vāyavīyādes*** *tu bhedaprathāto bhavati.*

---

112 *anekasyānyonyabhedābhāsād*... 114 *eva*] S12 (f. 204b, r.m., pre. *vṛttiḥ*), J11 (f. 206b, t.m., pre. *vṛttiḥ*), S10 (f. 91a, b.m., fol. *vṛttiḥ*), S15 (f. 90b, t.m.), S19 (f. 27b, m.t.), D2 (f. 212b, t.m., pre. *atra vṛttiḥ*), SOAS (f. 201a, l.m., pre. *atra vṛttiḥ*), *Vṛtti* Ed. (p. 43). **116** *svarūpamātram*... *mūrtiḥ*] S12 (f. 204b, b.m., pre. *ṭīkā*), J11 (f. 206b, r.m.), S15 (f. 90b, r.m., fol. *iti ṭīkā*), S2 (f. 44a, r.m., fol. *iti ṭīkā*), KAWAJIRI 2016b (p. 25), S5 (f. 123a, l.m., fol. *iti ṭīkā*), S9 (f. 92a, r.m., fol. *iti ṭīkā*), L (f. 93b, b.m., fol. *iti ṭīkā*), S1 (f. 122a, l.m., fol. *iti ṭīkā*), D2 (f. 212b, interl.s.), SOAS (f. 201a, interl.s.), ĪPV (vol. II, p. 13, fn. 56, fol. *iti ṭīkāyām*). | *bodhasya*... 136 *tena*] S12 (f. 204b, b.m., and f. 205a, t.m.), J11 (f. 206b, r.m.).

---

**112** *anekasyānyonya°*] S12, J11, S10, S15, S19, D2 (a.c.), *Vṛtti* Ed.; *anyonyasyānyonya°* D2 (p.c.), SOAS. **113** *°vipariṇāmādikriyābhedāt*] S12, J11 (p.c.), *Vṛtti* Ed.; *°viparīṇāmādikriyābhedāt* J11 (a.c.); *°pariṇāmādikriyābhedāt* S10, S15, S19; *°vipariṇāmādibhedāt* D2, SOAS. | *kālakrama eva*] S15, S19, *Vṛtti* Ed.; *kālakramam iva* S10; *kālabheda eva* S12, J11, D2, SOAS. **116** ***svarūpamātram*** *anyonyabhedenāvabhāsamānam*] S12, J11, S15, S2, KAWAJIRI 2016b (em.), S5, S1, D2, SOAS, ĪPV (fn. 56); ***svarūpamātram*** *anyonyabhe?nāvabhāsamānam* S9; [***svarūpa***??????????*bhedenāva*]*bhāsamānam* KAWAJIRI 2016b (ms.); ***svarūpamātram*** *anyonyabhedenāvabhāsanam* L. | *arthānāṃ*] S12, J11, S15, S2, KAWAJIRI 2016b, S5, L, S1, D2, SOAS, ĪPV (fn. 56); *artha??* S9. **118** *grāhakātmano*] S12; *grāhakārmane* J11. **119** *svasaṃvidaikyād*] S12; *svasaṃvidaikyad* J11. | ***bhedābhāvān*** *na*] S12; *bhedābhāvāna* J11.

---

**116** ***svarūpamātram***... *mūrtiḥ*] In J11 the edge of the r.m. is somewhat damaged and this renders the last *akṣara* at every end of the line difficult to read; but in most cases the scribe (or another hand?) copied the missing *akṣara*s at the beginning of the next lines (one can see that they are a later addition as they are smaller to fit the scant space left).

*mūrtatayā deśakramaḥ, tad āhānekasyānyonyeti. anekasyeti mūrtir* ***vivṛtā*** *mūrtimatām anyonyabhedābhāsād anekatvād deśapaurvāparyaṃ vaitatyaṃ cābhāti.*

***nanu*** *vāyavīyo 'pi śabdo yadi vāyoḥ kevalaṃ* ***kāryo*** *vā* ***kāraṇaṃ*** *vā, na tu vāyusvarūpam* ***āviśati, āviśann api vā*** *na tarhy asyaikyam eti virodhāt* ***tasyānyasya*** *ca śabdasyātyantabhedataḥ, tasya śabdasya mahābhūtāntaraguṇasyāpi cāmūrtatvam eva pratipannam. tat katham amūrtasyāpy asya mūrtivaicitryanibandhano deśakramaḥ syāt.* ***yugapad eva ca*** *bhinnadeśāḥ śabdāḥ pratibhāsanta eva, tan na deśabhedo mūrtānām eveti.*

***astv evam, iha tu*** *mūrtir iti vastusvarūpam eva* ***kriyārahitaṃ*** *nirdiṣṭam, na tu śāstrāntaraparibhāṣitāsau. ata eva vṛttau vastusvarūpatvamātratvenān-*

---

121 *anekasyeti mūrtir*] conj.; *anekamūrtir* S12, J11. 122 *vaitatyaṃ*] S12; *caitanyaṃ* J11. 124 ***kāraṇaṃ***] corr.; *karaṇaṃ* S12, J11. 125 *vāyusvarūpam* ***āviśati***] conj.; *vāyu* * * * * * *sāviṣatv* S12, J11. | *na tarhy asyaikyam eti*] conj.; *na tarhy aśaikyam eti* S12, J11. | *virodhāt* ***tasyānyasya*** *ca śabdasyātyantabhedataḥ*] conj.; *virodhā* * * * * * * * * * * * *ntarameyataḥ* S12; *vivodhā* * * * * * * * * * * * *ntarameyataḥ* J11. 126 *mahābhūtāntaraguṇasyāpi*] conj.; *mahābhūtāntānuguṇasyāpi* S12, J11. 127 *pratipannam*] corr.; *pratipannās* S12, J11. | *amūrtasyāpy*] S12, J11 (p.c.)?; *amūrtasyapy* J11 (a.c.). 128 *syāt.* ***yugapad***] conj.; *syād yad* ***yugapad*** S12; *syād ya* ***yugapad*** J11. 130 ***astv***] corr.; *asty* S12, J11. 131 *vastu°*] S12; *vastva°* J11.

---

124 ***kāraṇaṃ***] Cf. ĪPVV, vol. III, p. 13: ***nanv*** *iti.* ***kārya*** *iti śukaśukādi,* ***kāraṇam*** *iti śabdatanmātram api hi vāyoḥ kāraṇam.* 125 *vāyusvarūpam āviśati*] The corresponding passage in ĪPVV, vol. III, p. 13 reads as follows in the Ed.: *śabdasparśajo hi vāyur āviśatīti na vāyur evāsau yena mūrtaḥ syād ity arthaḥ.* This is misleading, since up to *hi vāyuḥ,* Abhinavagupta is explaining the word *kāraṇam,* whereas *āviśatīti* is a new *pratīka* (as is confirmed by S12 and J11, which both refrain from applying the *sandhi* rule between *vāyuḥ* and *āviśatīti*). The text of the Ed. should therefore be corrected into *śabdasparśajo hi vāyuḥ.* ***āviśatīti*** *na vāyur...* | *virodhāt*... 126 *śabdasyātyantabhedataḥ*] This is of course tentative; see, however, ĪPVV, vol. III, p. 13: ***tasyeti*** *vāyavīyasya,* ***anyasyeti*** *taijasādeḥ*; and I cannot make sense of *antarameyataḥ* in the context, so that I assume a corruption. One could suspect that the original text was longer given the extent of the lacuna indicated in S12 and J11; it is possible, however, that here as elsewhere, the scribes who annotated both mss. where slightly too pessimistic in their assessment of the number of missing characters (cf. above, n. on l. 12). 126 *mahābhūtāntaraguṇasyāpi*] Here too I assume a corruption, the point here being that even if *śabda* belongs to another material element (*mahābhūtāntara*), i.e. one that is not *ākāśa,* it must be *amūrta* anyway. 130 ***astv***] Cf. ĪPVV, vol. III, p. 13: ***astv evam*** *iti loke bhavatu...* (The reading ***astv*** in the ĪPVV's *pratīka* is also found in the m.t. of both S12 and J11).

***ekasyeti*** *mūrtir vivṛtā.* ***tatrabhavad****bhartṛharir api vastusvarūpamātram eva mūrtim* ***icchann*** *uktavān*

> *apūrvāparaṃ hīdaṃ mūrtitaḥ kriyātaś ca sarvaṃ sarvataḥ paripūrṇam iti.*

*tathā vadatā hi tena mūrtikriyākṛtaṃ deśakālapaurvāparyam eva bhāvānāṃ nirdiṣṭam,* ***jñānā****kāśīyaśabdayos tu deśabhedaparyavasāyi mūrtatvaṃ nāstīty amūrtatvam uktam.*

***athavā*** *guṇānāṃ guṇy eva deśaḥ sa eva ca tair viśeṣyate, na tu pṛthak svātantryeṇa sthīyate guṇino vāyvāder mūrtir guṇyantarāpekṣayā cāsya vaicitryapaurvāparyādibhedo 'pi syāt.*

---

**136** *mūrtikriyākṛtaṃ*... 141 *syāt*] S12 (f. 205a, l.m.), J11 (f. 207a, t.m.).

---

**135** *paripūrṇam*] J11; *pa paripūrṇam* S12. **136** *tena mūrtikriyākṛtaṃ*] conj.; *tena na mūrtikriyākṛtam* S12, J11. **137** *mūrtatvaṃ nāstīty*] S12; *mūrtatvaṃ stīty* J11. **139** *tair viśeṣyate*] S12; *tai viśeṣyate* J11.

---

**132** *mūrtir vivṛtā.* ***tatrabhavad****bhartṛharir*] If one follows the ĪPVV Ed., there should be a lacuna here, since after explaining *mūrtir vivṛtā* and before commenting on ***tatrabhavad***°..., Abhinavagupta quotes a word that does not appear in the *Vivṛti* fragment preserved in S12 and J11. See ĪPVV, vol. III, p. 14: ***lakṣaṇa*** *itītthaṃbhūtalakṣaṇe tṛtīyā*. Not to mention, however, that the text of the *Vivṛti* does not seem to lack anything at this point, S12 and J11 both give a different reading, *lakṣaṇenetthaṃbhūtalakṣaṇena tṛtīyā*, which does not include the particle *iti* (nor is *lakṣaṇena* rubricated). It seems to me that here, Abhinavagupta is simply explaining the meaning of the instrumental case in the *Vivṛti* compound *vastusvarūpatvamātratvena* according to Pāṇinian *sūtra* 2.3.21 (*itthaṃbhūtalakṣaṇe*); I therefore assume that both readings are corrupted, and that the original text only read *lakṣaṇe tṛtīyā*, "the instrumental is in the sense of a characteristic" (cf. ĪPVV, vol. II, p. 233, where Abhinavagupta uses the same shortened expression). A marginal gloss clarifying it by specifying *itītthaṃbhūtalakṣaṇe* could then have crept into the main text as recorded in the Ed. (the reading in S12 and J11 could reflect a failed attempt to correct it by someone who was aware that *lakṣaṇa iti* could not be a quotation from the *Vivṛti*?). **134** *apūrvāparaṃ... paripūrṇam iti*] Quotation untraced; see above, Chapter 8, §1, on other occurrences of it and Abhinavagupta's comments in ĪPVV, vol. III, p. 14.

***saṃvedanātmana eva*** *kartṛtvāt kartraikāśrayatvāc ca kriyā* ***mūrtimatām*** *api* ***kartṛtopacārād*** *gauṇī.* ***yathāpratīti mukhyāṃ vā*** *kriyām āśritya tadvaicitryāt* ***kālabhedo 'pi*** *syāt.*

***tathā ca yasya pramātuḥ*** *svakāle* ***yasya*** *sattāvabhāti* ***tasya sa vartamāno bhāti***, * * *puna* * * * * *ca kriyāvabhāsa* * * * * * *syātīto* ***yasya*** *punar avartamānasyaiva puro 'vasthi* * * * * * *si kāraṇādyarthāvabhāsavināśābhāsasahitavartamānāvabhāsatāparikalpanā kāraṇasattāvabhāsanena jāyate.*

---

142 *saṃvedanātmana*... 151 *kriyāmukheneti*] S12 (f. 205b, t.m.), J11 (f. 207a, r.m.).

---

142 *kartṛtvāt kartraikāśrayatvāc ca*] corr.; *kartṛtvāt kartraikāśrayatvāś ca* S12; *kartṛtvākartraikāsrayatvāś ca* J11. | *kriyā*] conj.; *kriyāyā* S12, J11. **143 *yathāpratīti mukhyāṃ vā*]** conj.; *yathāpratīti vā mukhyām eva* S12, J11. **144 *kālabhedo 'pi*]** corr.; *kālabhedaḥ* S12, J11. **145 *vartamāno bhāti*, * *]** conj.; *varta* * * * * * * S12; *varta* * * * * * * * * * * * J11. **146** *puna* * * * *] S12; *pu* * * * * J11. | *kriyāvabhāsa* * * * * *] S12; *kriyāvabhāsa* * * * * * * J11. **147** *puro 'vasthi* * * * * *] S12; *purīvāsthi* * * * * * J11.

---

**142** *kriyā*] I assume that the reading *kriyāyā* is the result of a dittography, as the sentence needs a subject that is said to be *gauṇī*. One could suppose that the latter is *kartṛtā* in light of ĪPVV, vol. III, p. 14: ***gauṇī*** *kartṛtety atra hetuḥ* ***kartṛtopacārād*** *iti*. It seems, however, that the first *kartṛtā* in this sentence of the commentary is a corruption, because Abhinavagupta immediately goes on to explain that the reason for this assertion is provided with the words ***kartṛtopacārād***, which he evidently takes to constitute a compound (cf. e.g.. his quotation of the same compound from the *Vivṛti* on ĪPK 2.4.20 in ĪPVV, vol. III, p. 252: *āha* ***kartṛtopacāras tv*** *iti*...). Most of all, in the next sentence, the *Vivṛti* makes clear that in the current one it is *kriyā* that is *gauṇī*, since it further explains that *kriyā* can also be taken to be *mukhyā*. **143 *yathāpratīti mukhyāṃ vā*]** Cf. ĪPVV, vol. III, p. 15: *evaṃ paramārthasthityā gauṇatvaṃ nirūpya prasiddhyanusāreṇāha* ***yathāpratīti mukhyāṃ veti.*** **144 *kālabhedo 'pi*]** Cf. ĪPVV, vol. III, p. 15: ***kālabhedo 'pīty*** *anekasya na paraṃ deśabhedaḥ, yāvad ayam apīty* ***api****r anekatām ākṣipati.* **145 *yasya*... *bhāti*]** Cf. ĪPVV, vol. III, p. 15: ***yasye****ti pramātuḥ,* ***yasye****ty arthasya,* ***tasye****ti pramātuḥ,* ***sa*** *ity arthaḥ,* ***vartamāno bhātī****ti sambandhaḥ*. From this one might wonder whether ***pramātuḥ*** is not in fact Abhinavagupta's gloss having crept into the *mūla*-text, but see ibid., later in the explanation of the sentence, l. 22: *kimarthaṃ* ***pramātur*** *iti* ***bhātī****ti ca vivṛtau darśitam.* **147** °*vartamānāvabhāsatāparikalpanā*] It is tempting to emend into °*vartamānāvabhāsasattāparikalpanā*, but evidently Abhinavagupta already had the reading found in S12 and J11 (see the gloss *vartamānāvabhāsatvaṃ kalpyate* in ĪPVV, vol. III, p. 15).

*pramātuḥ sa bhāvī* ***yathā****tītābhāsakāle vartamānābhāso bhāvīti sattāvināśadvikriyāpekṣayaiva mūrtānām anyonyāpekṣayā kālavibhāgo 'pi, tad āha kriyāmukheneti.* ***askhalita****pratītāpi jaḍānāṃ sattādikriyā tathecchābhāvāc citsambandhakṛ****taive****ti ca* ***vakṣyate****.*

***ekasya punar*** *arthasya caitrāder gṛhaprāsādāṅganādāv ābhāsabhede 'pi yugapadātmabhedābhāvād vaitatyānavabhāse sati svarūpatvena deśatvālābhān na deśakramaḥ.*

*janmasattāvipariṇāmādisamāśrayāt tu bālo 'yam abhavat sthaviro bhaviteti kriyāmātraṃ yadā bhidyate tadā tathātathākriyāvabhāsasadasattvā-*

---

**151** *askhalitapratītāpi* ... 155 *deśakramaḥ*] S12 (f. 205b, b.m.), J11 (f. 207b, r.m.). **156** *janmasattāvipariṇāmādisamāśrayāt* ... 157 *bhidyate*] S12 (f. 205b, b.m.), J11 (f. 207b, r.m.), S19 (f. 27b, r.m.), KAWAJIRI 2016b (p. 25). **157** *tadā* ... 159 *paurvāparyam*] S12 (f. 205b, b.m.), J11 (f. 207b, r.m.), S19 (f. 27b, r.m.), KAWAJIRI 2016b (p. 25), D2 (f. 213a, l.m., fol. *ity arthaḥ*), SOAS (f. 201b, r.m., fol. *ity arthaḥ*).

---

**149** *sattāvināśadvikriyāpekṣayaiva*] corr.; *sattāvināśādikriyāpekṣayaiva* S12, J11. **151** *tathecchābhāvāc*] corr.; *tathecchābhāvāś* S12, J11. **154** *yugapadātma°*] S12; *yugapadārma°* J11. | *vaitatyānavabhāse*] S12; *vaitakyānavabhāse* J11. **156** *janmasattāvipariṇāmādisamāśrayāt*] conj.; *janmasattāpariṇāmādisamāśrayāt* S19; *janmapariṇāmādisamāśrayāt* S12; *janmapariṇāmādisamāśrayārt* J11; *janmapariṇāmādipariśrayāt* KAWAJIRI 2016b. | *sthaviro bhaviteti*] S12, J11, S19; *sthaviro yaṃ bhava{ti}tīti* KAWAJIRI 2016b. **157** *tadā tathātathākriyāvabhāsasadasattvābhyāṃ*] S19; *tadā tathā tathā kriy[a?]vabhāsasadasatvābhyāṃ* KAWAJIRI 2016b (sic); *tadā tathātathāvabhāsasadasattvābhyāṃ* S12, J11; *tattadābhāsasadasattvābhyāṃ* D2, SOAS.

---

**149** *sattāvināśadvikriyāpekṣayaiva*] The reading in S12 and J11 shows that this was taken to refer to the six *bhāvavikāra*s rather than just *sattā* and *vināśa*. Here, however, Utpaladeva is specifically referring to these two, as is made clear in ĪPVV, vol. III, p. 15: *sattāvināśau dvāv iti bhāvavikārau dvābhyām evāvabhāsabhāvābhāvābhyāṃ saṃgṛhītāv iti darśayati.*

*bhyāṃ bhede sati* ***vimarśaikyenātirohitābhinnadravyātmanaḥ*** *kāla****mātre-ṇaiva*** *paurvāparyam, tad āhaikasya tv iti.*

*sarvasyaiva kāryātmano vastunaḥ ṣaṇṇāṃ bhāvavikārāṇāṃ tāvat kramaḥ sthitaḥ, tathā cāsau jāyata iti janmakriyāvabhāsaḥ, tathāsti vipariṇamate vivardhate 'pakṣīyate vinaśyatīti sattādikriyāṇāṃ prakāśaḥ.* ***teṣām eva ca***

---

**159** *tad āhaikasya tv iti*] S12 (f. 205b, b.m.), J11 (f. 207b, r.m.), S19 (f. 27b, r.m.), KAWAJIRI 2016b (p. 25). **160** *sarvasyaiva*. . . 161 *sthitaḥ*] S12 (f. 205b, b.m.), J11 (f. 207b, r.m.), S19 (f. 27b, r.m.), KAWAJIRI 2016b (p. 25), D2 (f. 214b, b.m., pre. *tathā hi*), SOAS (f. 203a, b.m., pre. *tathā hi*), ĪPV (vol. II, p. 18, fn. 77, pre. *tathā hi*). **161** *tathā*. . .*janmakriyāvabhāsaḥ*] S12 (f. 205b, b.m.), J11 (f. 207b, r.m.), S19 (f. 27b, r.m.), KAWAJIRI 2016b (p. 25), D2 (f. 213b, t.m.), D2 (f. 214b, b.m.), SOAS (f. 202a, t.m.), SOAS (f. 203a, b.m.), ĪPV (vol. II, p. 18, fn. 77). | *tathā-sti*. . . 162 *prakāśaḥ*] S12 (f. 205b, b.m.), J11 (f. 207b, r.m.), S19 (f. 27b, interl.s.), KAWAJIRI 2016b (p. 26), D2 (f. 213b, t.m.), D2 (f. 214b, b.m.), SOAS (f. 202a, t.m.), SOAS (f. 203a, b.m.), ĪPV (vol. II, p. 18, fn. 77). **162** *teṣām*. . . 163 *bhāgāvabhāsa*] S12 (f. 206a, t.m.), J11 (f. 207b, r.m.), D2 (f. 213b, t.m.), D2 (f. 214b, b.m.), SOAS (f. 202a, t.m.), SOAS (f. 203a, b.m.), ĪPV (vol. II, p. 18, fn. 77).

---

**158** ***vimarśaikyenātirohitābhinnadravyātmanaḥ***] corr.; *vimarśaikyenātirohitādra-vyātmanaḥ* S12; *vimarśaikenātirohitādravyātmanaḥ* J11; *vimarśaikyenātirohitatā-dravyātmanaḥ* D2, SOAS; om. S19, KAWAJIRI 2016b. | *kāla****mātreṇaiva***] S12, J11, S19, KAWAJIRI 2016b; *kālātmanaiva* D2, SOAS. **159** *paurvāparyam*] D2, SOAS, S19, KAWAJIRI 2016b; *paurvaparyaṃ* S12, J11. | *āhaikasya*] S12, J11, S19; *āh*[??]*kasya* KAWAJIRI 2016b. **160** *bhāvavikārāṇāṃ*] S12, J11, D2, SOAS, S19, ĪPV (fn. 77); *bhāvavikārāṇaṃ* KAWAJIRI 2016b (sic). | *kramaḥ sthitaḥ*] S19, KAWAJIRI 2016b, D2, SOAS, ĪPV (fn. 77); *kramasthitaḥ* S12, J11. **161** *tathāsti*] S12, J11, D2 (213b, 214b), SOAS (202a, 203a), ĪPV (fn. 77); *jāyate 'sti* S19, KAWAJIRI 2016b. | *vipariṇamate*] D2 (213b, 214b), SOAS (202a, 203a), ĪPV (fn. 77); *vipariṇamater* S12, J11. **162** *vinaśyatīti*] S12, J11, D2 (213b, 214b), SOAS (202a, 203a), ĪPV (fn. 77); *vinaśyatītyādiṣu* S19, KAWAJIRI 2016b. | *sattādikriyā-ṇāṃ*] S12, J11, D2 (213b, 214b), SOAS (202a, 203a), ĪPV (fn. 77); *janmādikriyā-ṇāṃ* S19, KAWAJIRI 2016b. | ***teṣām eva ca***] S12, J11, D2 (f. 214b), SOAS (f. 203a), ĪPV (fn. 77); *teṣām api ca* D2 (f. 213b), SOAS (f. 202a).

---

**158** ***vimarśaikyenātirohitābhinnadravyātmanaḥ***] Cf. ĪPVV, vol. III, p. 12: *yad va-kṣyati* ***vimarśaikyenātirohitābhinnadravyātmana*** *iti.* | *kālamātreṇaiva*] Cf. ĪPVV, vol. III, p. 16: ***mātra****padena deśakramam* ***eva****kāreṇa svarūpabhedaṃ nirasyati.* **161** *tathāsti... sattādikriyāṇāṃ prakāśaḥ*] KAWAJIRI 2016b, p. 26, states that this passage does "not seem to be from the *Vivṛti*." Admittedly, the ĪPVV does not quote directly from it; yet the latter repeatedly mentions the six *bhāvavikāra*s while explaining the *Vivṛti* on this verse, and the passage, which appears in several marginal sources, certainly belongs to the *Vivṛti*, since it is found in S12 and J11, whose margins exclusively quote from the *Vṛtti* and *Vivṛti*.

*pratyekaṃ janmasattāvipariṇāmādīnāṃ svātmany api bhāgāvabhāsa ity eṣa kālakrama ekasyāpi kriyāśritaḥ anyonyaparihāreṇa viruddhāvayavābhāsānām, ekatrāśraye sahāprathane 'pi yathā bhedena sa eva kālakramo bhavati bhāvavikāraṣaṭkena, anena ca sarvakriyāṇāṃ vyāpteḥ. snātvā bhuktvā vrajatīty atrāpi snānādipariṇāmādikriyāviśeṣābhāsabheda ekatra kālakramaḥ, snānabhojanādeḥ svātmany api svāvayavābhāsabhedaḥ. tathā bhavati* ***dāḍimādiphale*** *śyāmatāraktatādyābhāsabhedaḥ* ***pariṇāma****kriyābhāsabheda eva. rūpaviśeṣa eva hi viruddhāvayavabhāsamāna ekārthāśrayaḥ kriyā kathyate. viruddhatvād eva hi tasyaikatra prathānupapannāpy* ***udbhavantī*** *kramaṃ prakāśayati sa c****aikāśrayatvena*** *deśakramād bhidyate.*

---

**163** *ity*... 164 *kriyāśritaḥ*] S12 (f. 206a, t.m.), J11 (f. 207b, r.m.), D2 (f. 213b, t.m.), SOAS (f. 202a, t.m.). **164** *anyonyaparihāreṇa*... 166 *vyāpteḥ*] S12 (f. 206a, t.m.), J11 (f. 207b, r.m. and b.m.). **166** *snātvā*... 171 *kathyate*] S12 (f. 206a, t.m.), J11 (f. 207b, b.m.), D2 (f. 213b, r.m.), SOAS (f. 202a, t.m. and l.m.). **171** *viruddhatvād*... 175 *anyonyābhāvābhāsāvyavadhānād*] S12 (f. 206a, t. m. and l.m.), J11 (f. 207b, b.m.).

---

**163** *janmasattāvipariṇāmādīnāṃ*] conj.; *janmapariṇāmādīnāṃ* S12, J11, D2 (ff. 213b, 214b), SOAS (ff. 202a, 203a), ĪPV (fn. 77). | *svātmany api*] S12, J11, D2 (f. 213a), SOAS (f. 202a); om. D2 (f. 214b), SOAS (f. 203a), ĪPV (fn. 77). **164** *kālakrama*] D2, SOAS; *kā* * * * * * S12, J11. | *viruddhāvayavābhāsānām*] conj.; *viruddhā* * * * * * *bhāsānām* S12, J11. **165** *ekatrāśraye*] S12; *ekatrāśraye/* J11. **166** *bhāvavikāraṣaṭkena*] S12; *bhāvavikāraṣaṃkena* J11. **167** *atrāpi*] S12, J11; om. D2, SOAS. **168** *snānabhojanādeḥ*] conj.; *snānagamanādeḥ* S12, J11, D2, SOAS. | *svāvayavābhāsabhedaḥ*] D2, SOAS; *svavayavābhāsabhedaḥ* S12, J11. **169** ***dāḍimādiphale***] corr.; *dāḍimaphale* S12, J11; *dāḍimaphale 'pi* D2, SOAS.

---

**163** *janmasattāvipariṇāmādīnāṃ*] All the witnesses give *janmapariṇāmādīnāṃ*, which does not seem to make sense in this context (Utpaladeva should be quoting the list of *bhāvavikāra*s in the correct order). I therefore assume that *janmasattāvipariṇāmādīnāṃ* first got corrupted into *janmasattādipariṇāmādīnāṃ* (as has occurred above as well) and that the presence of the compound *sattādikriyāṇāṃ* (which appears shortly before this one) then led someone to think that the next compound in the genitive plural should be corrected so as to exclude *sattādi*; in fact *sattādikriyāṇāṃ* was used in the previous sentence (while excluding the first member of the *bhāvavikāras*, *janman*) only because Utpaladeva had already mentioned *janmakriyāvabhāsaḥ* in that same sentence. **164** *viruddhāvayavābhāsānām*] Cf. below: *rūpaviśeṣa eva hi viruddhāvayavabhāsamāna ekārthāśrayaḥ kriyā kathyate.* **169** ***dāḍimādiphale***] Cf. ĪPVV, vol. III, p. 17: *acetanagatam api pariṇāmaṃ bhedena vyācaṣṭe* ***dāḍimādiphala*** *iti.*

***snāna**bhojanādyābhāsānāṃ caikatra bhāva eva yāvat kramatvam eti tāvad vakṣyamāṇanyāyen**āntar** anyonyābhāvābhāsāvyavadhānād grāhakāvabhāsena saha yasya prathā sa eva tathā **sphuṭo** 'bhinavo 'vabhāso vartamāna ucyate. sphuṭābhāsasya sattvam eva vartamānatā, sattvāsattve bhūtatā, **asattvam eva** tu bhaviṣyattā; **bālo** 'bhūd iti hi bālyāvabhāso **bhavanadharmāpi** nāsti bahiḥ, sthaviro bhaviṣyatīti punaḥ sarvath**āvabhāsasyā**sattaiva. kalpanāmātraviṣaya eva saḥ.*

***ata eva** vastuta * * * * * sya sattāsatte yathā viruddhe **tathā** kālakramo 'pi tathā sa * * * * vināśo nirākariṣyate, jñānāvabhāsasāratvena tv īśvaraśakti * * * * * * * * * * bhāsavartamāna * * * * * * .* (* * *)

---

**175** *grāhakāvabhāsena* ... 178 *bhaviṣyattā*] S12 (f. 206a, l.m.), J11 (f. 207b, b.m., and f. 208a, r.m.), D2 (f. 213b, r.m.), D2 (f. 215a, b.m.), SOAS (f. 202a, l.m.), SOAS (f. 203b, b.m.), ĪPV (fn. 83, p. 19). **178** *bālo* ... 183 *[19]] S12 (f. 206a, l.m.), J11 (f. 208a, l.m.).

---

**174** ***snāna**bhojanādyābhāsānāṃ*] corr.; ***snāna**bhojanādyabhāsānāṃ* S12, J11. **175** *°nyāyenāntar*] S12 (p.c.), J11; *°nyāyenantar* S12 (a.c.). **176** *yasya prathā*] S12, J11, D2 (ff. 213b, 215a), SOAS (f. 203b), ĪPV (fn. 83); *yady aprathā* SOAS (f. 202a). | ***sphuṭo***] S12, J11, D2 (f. 215a), SOAS (f. 203b), ĪPV (fn. 83); *bhūto* D2 (f. 213b); *bhūte* SOAS (f. 202a). | *'bhinavo 'vabhāso vartamāna ucyate*] S12, J11, D2 (f. 213b); *'bhinavo 'vabhāso vartamāna ucyeta* SOAS (f. 202a); *'bhinavo vartamāna ity ucyate* D2 (f. 215a), SOAS (f. 203b), ĪPV (fn. 83). **177** *sphuṭābhāsasya*] S12, J11; *sphuṭāvabhāsasya* D2 (ff. 213b, 215a), SOAS (ff. 202a, 203b), ĪPV (fn. 83). | *bhūtatā, **asattvam***] S12, J11, D2 (ff. 213b, 215a), SOAS (f. 203b), ĪPV (fn. 83); *bhūtā, **asattvam*** SOAS (f. 202a). **178** *tu bhaviṣyattā*] S12, J11; *bhaviṣyattā* D2 (f. 215a), SOAS (f. 203b), ĪPV (fn. 83); *bhūtatā* D2 (f. 213b), SOAS[?] (f. 202a, p.c.). **181** *vastuta * * * * **] S12; *vastuta * * * * * ** J11. | *viruddhe*] S12; *vinaddhe* J11. **182** *sa * * * **] S12; *sa * * ** J11. | *nirākariṣyate*] S12; *nirākariṣyate /* J11. | *īśvaraśakti*] conj.; *īśvaraśa * i* S12, J11.

---

**176** *'bhinavo 'vabhāso vartamāna ucyate*] The reading that includes *ity ucyate* might be deemed preferable, but the sources that record it are obviously corrupted here (they omit the necessary *avabhāso*), and Utpaladeva often omits *iti* in similar instances (see e.g. *Vṛtti*, p. 67: *tanmalatrayanirmāṇe prabhor icchā māyāśaktir ucyate*; cf. the *Vivṛti* fragment edited in TORELLA 1988, p. 148: *yat prakāśyaṃ taj jaḍam ucyate*, etc.). **183** * * *[13]] (* * *)] The end of the commentary on ĪPK 2.1.5 is missing, as is obvious from ĪPVV, vol. III, pp. 18–19, which mentions several *pratīka*s absent in the mm. of S12 and J11: ***sataḥ**, **yogināṃ tu**, **anyonya°***.

*ābhāsasadbhāvāsadbhāvakramo 'pi saṃsāriṇa eva pramātur ātmīyakālāpekṣayā bhāveṣv avabhāti na tv īśvarasyety āha sarvatreti.*

## ĪPK 2.1.6

*sarvatrābhāsabhedo 'pi bhavet kālakramākaraḥ |*
*vicchinnabhāsaḥ śūnyāder mātur bhātasya no sakṛt ||*

## VṚTTI

*sarvatrārthe vicitro 'vabhāsaḥ śūnyadehāder eva pramātuḥ kālakramābhāsahetuḥ, sa hi prākkālo na tathā tadānīṃ bhāsate smṛtiṃ vihāya svavartamānāpekṣayā cāsau bhūtabhaviṣyatte vyavaharati. sakṛdvibhātasya tu*

---

**184** *ābhāsasadbhāvāsadbhāvakramo*... 185 *sarvatreti*] S12 (f. 206a, l.m. and f. 206b, r.m.), J11 (f. 208a, l.m. and f. 208b, r.m.), S19 (f. 27b, l.m.), KAWAJIRI 2016b (p. 26). **190** *sarvatrārthe*... 194 *kālabhedaḥ*] S12 (f. 206b, r.m., pre. *vṛttiḥ*), J11 (f. 208b, r.m., pre. *vṛttiḥ*), S10 (f. 92a, b.m.), S15 (f. 91a, b.m.), S19 (ff. 27b–28a, m.t.), D2 (f. 214b, r.m., pre. *atra ślokadvaye vṛttiḥ*), SOAS (f. 203a, t.m., pre. *atra ślokadvaye vṛttiḥ*), *Vṛtti* Ed. (pp. 43–44).

---

**184** *ābhāsasadbhāvāsadbhāvakramo 'pi*] S12, J11; *ābhāsasadasadbhāvakramo 'pi* S19, KAWAJIRI 2016b. | *saṃsāriṇa eva*] S19, KAWAJIRI 2016b; * * * * * * *eva* S12, J11. **190** *'vabhāsaḥ*] S12, S10, S15, S19, D2, SOAS, *Vṛtti* Ed.; *'vatāsaḥ* J11. | *śūnyadehāder*] S12, J11, S15, S19, D2, SOAS, *Vṛtti* Ed.; *śūnyadehādir* S10. **191** *tadānīṃ*] S12, J11, S10, S15, *Vṛtti* Ed.; *tadāṃnī* S19, D2, SOAS. | *svavartamānāpekṣayā*] S10, S15, S19, D2, SOAS, *Vṛtti* Ed.; *svavartamā?pekṣayā* S12; *svavartamāṇapekṣayā* J11. **192** *sakṛdvibhātasya*] S12, J11, S10, S15, D2, SOAS, *Vṛtti* Ed.; *sadvibhātasya* S19.

---

**184** *ābhāsasadbhāvāsadbhāvakramo 'pi*] Cf. e.g. ĪPVV, vol. III, p. 9: *ābhāsasadbhāvāsadbhāvau*; p. 23: *ābhāsasya... sadbhāvāsadbhāvau*, etc. In S12 and J11, this is presented as belonging to the commentary on 2.1.5, but as confirmed by the other witnesses, it is obviously the subject of the sentence introducing ĪPK 2.1.6. **190** *sarvatrārthe*... 194 *kālabhedaḥ*] In J11 the *Vṛtti* quotation is not written in Nāgarī (as the m.t. and most marginal annotations) but in Śāradā. **191** *svavartamānāpekṣayā*] There appears to have been an attempt at correcting S12, but the result is not legible.

*bhāsanakriyāvicchedād abhyāvṛttigaṇanābhāvād ātmanīvārtheṣv api na kālabhedaḥ.*

## Vivṛti

*kālo nāma saṃvedakāśrayaḥ saṃvedyadharmo na tu nīlapītatādir ivānyanirapekṣa evāvicalitasvarūpaḥ.* ***tathā hi*** *sa evārtho vartamānasya pramātuḥ svasattākāle 'vabhāsamānasattākatvād vartamāno* ***'tītānāṃ*** *tu pramātṝṇāṃ bhaviṣyann* ***āgāminām*** *pramātṝṇāṃ cātīta ity evaṃ saṃvedakasya svakālāpekṣayaivārthakālavyavasthāpane saṃvedakaḥ svakriyābhāsasadasattvābhyām uktanītyā kālapaurvāparyavān saṃsāry eva śūnyaprāṇabuddhidehānyatamaḥ pramātā vyavahārapatito 'rtheṣu teṣu teṣu vināśādikri-*

---

**196** *kālo*...205 *[7]] S12 (f. 206b, b.m., pre. *ṭī*), J11 (f. 208b, b.m.).

---

**193** *bhāsanakriyāvicchedād*] S12, J11, D2, SOAS, *Vṛtti* Ed.; *bhāsamānakriyāvicchedād* S10, S15 (p.c.), S19; *bhāsamānasya kriyāvicchedād* S15 (a.c.). | *abhyāvṛttigaṇanābhāvād*] S15, S19, D2; *abhyāvṛttigaṇanābhāv°* SOAS; *avyāvṛttigaṇanābhāvād* S12, J11; *avyāvarttigaṇanābhāvād* S10; *āvṛttigaṇanābhāvād Vṛtti* Ed. *ātmanīvārtheṣv api na*] S12, J11, S10, S15, S19, D2, SOAS; *nātmanīvārtheṣv api Vṛtti* Ed. **196** *nīlapītatādir*] conj.; *nīlapītādir* S12, J11. **198** *'vabhāsamānasattākatvād*] conj.; *'vabhāsamāna ma* * * * *katvād* S12, J11. **199** *pramātṝṇāṃ cātīta*] conj.; *pa* * * * * * * * * * * *ta* S12; *pa* * * * * * * * * *ta* J11. **201** *kālapaurvāparyavān*] conj.; * * * * *paurvāparyavān* S12; * * * * *paurvāparyavān* J11. **202** *pramātā*] conj.; *pra* * * * * S12; *pra* * * * * * J11. | *teṣu teṣu vināśādikriyābhāsānurodhena*] conj.; *teṣu teṣv avināśādikriyāmānurodhena* S12, J11.

---

**193** *abhyāvṛttigaṇanābhāvād*] The *Vṛtti* Ed. specifies (p. 44, fn. 22) that four of the *Vṛtti* mss. consulted by R. Torella have *abhyāvṛtti°*; the others read *avyāvartti°*, *abhyavartti°*, *avyāvṛtti°* or *āvṛtti°*. I take all of these variant readings to be corruptions of *abhyāvṛtti°*, as this is in fact a reference to Pāṇini (A 5.4.17): *saṃkhyāyāḥ kriyābhyāvṛttigaṇane kṛtvasuc* (see above, Chapter 9, §2). | *ātmanīvārtheṣv api na*] I could not find the reading provided in the *Vṛtti* Ed. (which mentions no variant here) in any of the mss. consulted, including S19 (=Ṅ in the *Vṛtti* Ed.). **196** *kālo*] In S12 the *°kā* that should have completed the word *ṭī*[*kā*] introducing the quotation of the *Vivṛti* on this verse ended up as the first syllable of the *Vivṛti*'s first word. | *nīlapītatādir*] Cf. ĪPVV, vol. III, p. 20: *yad avicalaṃ bhāvasya, tan nānyāpekṣaṃ nīlatvam iva.* **198** *'vabhāsamānasattākatvād*] Or perhaps, given the indicated number of missing *akṣaras*, *'vabhāsamānasattākriyākatvād*; but on the whole S12 and J11 seem to be slightly too pessimistic about the length of the lacunae that they report, as mentioned above. Both mss. also present *'vabhāsamāna* as not being the initial member of a compound, which cannot be right. **201** *kālapaurvāparyavān*] This tentative conj. is not redundant, since *paurvāparya*, just as *krama*, concerns both *kāla* and *deśa/diś* (see e.g. $TS_Ś$ 628–629/$TS_K$ 629–630).

*yābhāsānurodhena kālavibhāgaṃ kuryāt, tad āha sarvatrārtha iti. saṃvedakaś ca saṃsārī saṃvedyān* ***yadā*** *svato bhinnān adhyavasyati* ***tadā*** *teṣu* * * * * * * * (* * *)

## ĪPK 2.1.7

*deśakramo 'pi bhāveṣu bhāti mātur mitātmanaḥ |*
*svātmeva svātmanā pūrṇā bhāvā bhānty amitasya tu ||*

## VṚTTI

*parimitaṃ pramātāram apekṣya bhāvās tato 'nyonyaṃ ca bhinnā dūrādivyapadeśabhājaś ca, prakāśaikarūpatvena tv īśvarasya na kvāpy aprakāśasambhavāt paramāṇāv api prakāśaghanasya nātmano bhinnaṃ dūraṃ vānyonyato vā kiṃcid ābhāti.*

(* * *)

---

**210** *parimitaṃ*…213 *ābhāti*] S10 (f. 92a, b.m., pre. text of *Vṛtti* on ĪPK 2.1.6, fol. *sūtradvayasya vṛttiḥ*), S15 (f. 91a, b.m., pre. text of *Vṛtti* on ĪPK 2.1.6), S19 (f. 28a, m.t.), D2 (f. 214b, r.m., pre. text of *Vṛtti* on ĪPK 2.1.6), SOAS (f. 203a, t.m., pre. text of *Vṛtti* on ĪPK 2.1.6), *Vṛtti* Ed. (p. 44).

---

**204** *adhyavasyati*] conj.; *a * * syati* S12, J11. **210** *ca bhinnā*] S10, S19, D2, SOAS, *Vṛtti* Ed.; om. S15. **211** *na kvāpy*] S15, S19 (p.c.), D2, SOAS, *Vṛtti* Ed.; *nākvāpy* S10, S19 (a.c.).? | *aprakāśasambhavāt*] S10, S19 (a.c.), D2, SOAS, *Vṛtti* Ed.; *aprasambhavaḥ* S15, S19 (p.c.).

---

**205** (* * *)] The rest of the commentary on this verse and the entire commentary on the next verse are not found in any of the mss. consulted here. In J11, f. 208b, at the bottom of the page where the break occurs, next to the edge of the m., the words *itaḥ patitaṃ* are written (pre. * * *, fol. * * * *, with *itaḥ pati°* written in Śāradā and *°taṃ* is in Nāgarī!). No fragment is recorded in KAWAJIRI 2016b from verse 2.1.6 to the end of this chapter. **211** *na kvāpy aprakāśasambhavāt*] Abhinavagupta makes clear that this is a reference to a scriptural source that he quotes (ĪPVV, vol. II, p. 23): *na kvāpy aprakāśeti vṛttivākyasyeyaṃ yojanā sakṛdvibhāto 'yam ātmā pūrṇasyāsya na kvāpy aprakāśanasambhava iti sārasvatasaṃgrahasūtraikadeśārtho*... On this quotation and its source see above, Chapter 9, §2. As al ready noted in *Vṛtti* Ed., p. 44, the reading *aprakāśasambhavāt* must be correct since Abhinavagupta specifies that Utpaladeva uses the compound in the ablative (instead of the nominative found in the quotation) so as to indicate that this is the reason justifying the statement in the sentence's sequel (ibid.: ... *pañcamīṃ vidhāya hetutayā vṛttāv uktaḥ*).

## ĪPK 2.1.8

*kiṃtu nirmāṇaśaktiḥ sāpy evaṃ viduṣa īśituḥ |*
*tathā vijñātṛvijñeyabhedo yad avabhāsyate ||*

### VṚTTI

*evaṃ pūrṇatayā prakāśamānasyāpi parameśvarasya saiṣā sṛṣṭiśaktir yaj jñātṛjñeyasvabhāvā bhāvāḥ svato 'nyonyaṃ ca vibhāgenāvasīyante, na ca tathāvasāyena tasya svarūpasthitis tirodhīyate.*

### VIVṚTI

(* * *) ***parameśvarato**ktā sāmānyarūp**aiṣā** tāvan**mahāsṛṣṭiśaktir yatrā**ntaḥ saṃhāro **'pi** praviṣṭaḥ. **saṃhāre 'pi hi bījātmanā**vasthitānāṃ bhāvānāṃ tāvatīdantāsty eva. **kevalaṃ** bāhyāntaratābhedena viśiṣṭau sṛṣṭisaṃhārau*

---

**219** *evaṃ*...221 *tirodhīyate*] S12 (f. 207b, r.m., pre. *vṛttiḥ*), J11 (f. 209b, r.m., pre. *vṛttiḥ*), S10 (f. 93b, t.m., fol. *vṛttiḥ*), S15 (f. 92a, b.m.), S19 (ff. 28ab, m.t.), D2 (f. 217a, l.m., pre. *atra vṛttiḥ*), SOAS (f. 205b, r.m., pre. *atra vṛttiḥ*), *Vṛtti* Ed. (pp. 44–45). **223** *parameśvaratoktā*...234 *prathante*] S12 (f. 208a, l.m.), J11 (f. 210a, l.m.).

---

**219** *evaṃ pūrṇatayā*] S12, J11, S10, S19, *Vṛtti* Ed.; *evaṃ paripūrṇatayā* S15; *evaṃrūpatayā* D2, SOAS. | *prakāśamānasyāpi*] S12, J11, S10, S15, S19, *Vṛtti* Ed.; *prakāśamānasya* D2, SOAS. **220** *jñātṛjñeyasvabhāvā*] S12, S10, S19, D2, SOAS, *Vṛtti* Ed.; *jñātyajñeyasvabhāvā* J11. | *bhāvāḥ*] S12, J11, S10, D2, *Vṛtti* Ed.; *bhāvaḥ* SOAS; om. S19. **221** *tasya*] *Vṛtti* Ed.; om. S12, J11, S10, S15, S19, D2, SOAS. **224** ***bījātmanā***°] S12; *bījārmanā* J11. **225** *viśiṣṭau*] S12; *viṣiṣṭau* J11.

---

**223** (* * *)] From ĪPVV, vol. III, p. 25, it seems that a few sentences are missing in S12 and J11, where the *pratīka*s ***tad atra, sthitaiva*** and ***tatra tu*** are not found. ***parameśvarato**ktā... praviṣṭaḥ*] This sentence is probably incomplete and may have originally started with the words ***tatra tu*** recorded in ĪPVV, vol. III, p. 25, since the words ***parameśvarataiṣā śaktir** iti* used by Abhinavagupta at that point can be seen as a series of words selectively quoted from it so as to emphasize its overall structure. The words immediately preceding this series in the commentary, *nirbharatayā camatkṛtimato yā*, could well be an actual (albeit it selective) quotation as well. | *tāvan**mahā**sṛṣṭi**śaktir***] This could also be *tāvan mahāsṛṣṭiśaktir*; but as mentioned above, the beginning of the *Vivṛti* is missing for this verse, so that *tāvat* in the sense of "to begin with" is rather unlikely, and I tentatively take it as part of the following compound and as the correlative of *yatra* (cf. ĪPVV, vol. III, p. 25, although admittedly it makes no mention of *tāvat*: ***mahac**chabdaṃ vyācaṣṭe **yatre**ti*).

*vakṣyete. ayaṃ* ***cāsyā*** *viśeṣo māyāśaktyā kṛto yā brahmaviṣṇurudrarūpatayā sṛṣṭir jñātṝṇām aparyantabhedānāṃ jñeyānāṃ ca guṇānām.* ***tatra hi*** *brahmādirūpād īśvarād vibhāgaḥ sarveṣāṃ jñātṝṇāṃ jñeyānāṃ cāvasīyate, tad āha saiṣā sṛṣṭiśaktir yaj jñātṛjñeyeti. sarvadā brahmāditrayātman****ā-pi*** *parameśvarasyāntaḥsthitānām uktavibhāgāvasānaiva sṛṣṭiḥ.* ***tādṛśāṃ ca*** *teṣāṃ kaṃcit kālam anuvṛttiḥ sthitiḥ. punar bījātmatayaiva jñātrādīnām uktavibhāgenāvasthāpanaṃ saṃhāraḥ. saiṣā mahāsṛṣṭir eveśvarasy****aivaṃ trairūpyeṇa*** *kalpitā.* ***tatra ca*** *bhagavato rudrasya saṃhārakāritvād bahirvibhāgavigalane 'pi brahmaviṣṇvor vibhāgenaiva bhāvāḥ prathante.*

***maheśvarasya tu*** *tathākāriṇo 'pīdantānirdiṣṭā apy ahantāvacchāditā eva bhāsante kartṛtodrekāt, tad āha na ca tathāvasāyeneti.* ***etena*** *pūrṇatayā prakāśamānasyāpīty apiśabdena jñātṛjñeyavibhāgāvasāyasya prakāśaikaghanatāyāś ca virodha āśaṅkito yaḥ sa parihṛtaḥ. atrāpi mahāsṛṣṭau chāyāmātreṇa bhāvānām ahaṃvibhāgāvibhāgena prathārūpa****sadāśiva****tāyāṃ saṃhār****oktir*** *api syāt,* ***na tu*** *tatra kālavibhāgaḥ.*

---

**235** *maheśvarasya*...240 *kālavibhāgaḥ*] S12 (f. 208a, l.m. and b.m.), J11 (f. 210a, l.m. and b.m.).

---

**226** *ayaṃ* ***cāsyā*** *viśeṣo māyāśaktyā kṛto*] conj.; *ayaṃ cāsyā māyāśaktyā viśeṣaḥ sṛṣṭiśakteḥ kṛto* S12, J11. | *brahmaviṣṇurudrarūpatayā*] S12; *brahmavisnurudrarūpatayā* J11. **228** *jñātṝṇāṃ jñeyānāṃ cāvasīyate*] conj.; *jñātṛjñeyānāṃ cāvasīyate* S12, J11. **229** *sarvadā*] corr.; *sa yadā* S12, J11. **230** *parameśvarasyāntaḥsthitānām*] corr.; *parameśvarasyāntasthitānām* S12, J11. **231** *anuvṛttiḥ sthitiḥ*] S12; *anuvṛttisthitiḥ* J11. **233** *kalpitā*] corr.; *kalpite* S12, J11. **234** *brahmaviṣṇvor*] S12; *brahmavisnvo* J11. **235** *ahantāvacchāditā*] S12 (p.c.); *ahantāvacchādita* S12 (a.c.), J11.

---

**226** *ayaṃ* ***cāsyā*** *viśeṣo māyāśaktyā kṛto*] In the mss.' reading, *māyāśaktyā* and *sṛṣṭiśakteḥ* obviously occupy each other's natural place in the sentence; besides, given ĪPVV, vol. III, p. 25 (***asyā*** *iti mahatyāḥ sṛṣṭiśakteḥ*), it seems that a part of Abhinavagupta's gloss, *sṛṣṭiśakteḥ*, has crept into Utpaladeva's text. **229** *sarvadā*] Cf. ĪPVV, vol. III, p. 26: *sarvadā brahmarūpeṇa viṣṇurūpeṇa rudrarūpeṇa īśvararūpeṇa ca...* **240** *kālavibhāgaḥ*] At this point in the annotations in S12 and J11, the number 96 is given (corresponding to the number of verse 2.1.8 from the beginning of the treatise).

# Bibliography


## 1. Primary sources: manuscripts

[A1] Photocopy ("photo print") of an *Īśvarapratyabhijñāvimarśinī* from Srinagar [=S5], Allahabad: Ganganatha Jha Kendriya Sanskrit Vidyapeetha, no. 1212 [Śāradā script]. See above, chapter 2, §9 (under S5).

[D] *Īśvarapratyabhijñāvivṛti*, Delhi: National Archives of India (Manuscripts belonging to the Acheology and Research Department, Jammu and Kashmir Government, Srinagar, in "List of Gilgit Manuscripts and Sanskrit Mss"), no. 30, vol. IX [paper, Śāradā script].

[D2] *Īśvarapratyabhijñāvimarśinī*, Delhi: National Archives of India (Manuscripts belonging to the Acheology and Research Department, Jammu and Kashmir Government, Srinagar, in "List of Gilgit Manuscripts and Sanskrit Mss"), no. 5, vol. II [paper, Śāradā script]. See above, chapter 2, §9.

[D3] *Śivadṛṣṭivṛtti*, Delhi: National Archives of India (Manuscripts belonging to the Acheology and Research Department, Jammu and Kashmir Government, Srinagar, in "List of Gilgit Manuscripts and Sanskrit Mss"), no. 7, vol. II [paper, Śāradā script].

[D4] *Īśvarapratyabhijñāvivṛtivimarśinī*, Delhi: National Archives of India (Manuscripts belonging to the Acheology and Research Department, Jammu and Kashmir Government, Srinagar, in "List of Gilgit Manuscripts and Sanskrit Mss"), no. 62, vols. XXXVII–XXXIX [paper, Śāradā script].

[D5] *Śivadṛṣṭi*, Delhi: National Archives of India (Manuscripts belonging to the Acheology and Research Department, Jammu and Kashmir Government, Srinagar, in "List of Gilgit Manuscripts and Sanskrit Mss"), no. 83, vol. LXVI [paper, Nāgarī script].

[J] *Īśvarapratyabhijñāvimarśinī*, Jammu: Sri Ranbir Institute, Raghunath mandir, no. 19 [birch bark, Śāradā script].

[J11] *Īśvarapratyabhijñāvivṛtivimarśinī* ("*Pratyabhijñāvṛttī īśvarapratyabhijñāvivṛti*"), Jammu: Sri Ranbir Institute, Raghunath Mandir Library, no. 5077 [paper, Nāgarī script]. See above, chapter 2, §8.

[J[R]] *Īśvarapratyabhijñāvimarśinī*, Jammu: Rashtriya Sanskrit Sansthan, no. 47 & 70 (formerly no. 52A & 52B) [paper, Śāradā script].

[L] *Īśvarapratyabhijñāvimarśinī* ("*Pratyabhijñāsūtravimarśinī laghvī*"), Lucknow: Akhila Bhāratīya Saṃskṛta Pariṣad, no. 3366 [paper, Śāradā script]. See above, chapter 2, §9.

[L2] *Īśvarapratyabhijñāvṛtti*, Lucknow: Akhila Bharatiya Sanskrit Parishad, no. 4408 [paper, Nāgarī script]. See above, chapter 2, §10.

[P] *Īśvarapratyabhijñāvimarśinī* ("*Īśvarapratyabhijñāsūtravimarśinī*"), Poona: Bhandarkar Oriental Institute, no. 466 of 1875–76 [birch bark, Śāradā script].

[S1] *Īśvarapratyabhijñāvimarśinī*, Srinagar: Oriental Research Library, no. 816 [paper, Śāradā script]. See above, chapter 2, §9.

[S2] *Īśvarapratyabhijñāvimarśinī*, Srinagar: Oriental Research Library, no. 1035 [paper, Śāradā script]. See above, chapter 2, §9.

[S3] *Īśvarapratyabhijñāvimarśinī*, Srinagar: Oriental Research Library, no. 838 ("*Īśvarapratyabhijñākaumudī*") [paper, Śāradā script]. See above, chapter 2, §9.

[S5] [*Īśvarapratyabhijñāvimarśinī*, Srinagar: Oriental Research Library, no. 1212 [paper, Śāradā script]. See above, chapter 2, §9.

[S7] *Īśvarapratyabhijñāvimarśinī*, Srinagar: Oriental Research Library, no. 2250 [paper, Nāgarī script].

[S8] *Īśvarapratyabhijñāvimarśinī*, Srinagar: Oriental Research Library, no. 1037 [paper, Śāradā script].

[S9] *Īśvarapratyabhijñāvimarśinī*, Srinagar: Oriental Research Library, no. 1161 [paper, Śarada script]. See above, chapter 2, §9.

[S10] *Īśvarapratyabhijñāvimarśinī*, Srinagar: Oriental Research Library, no. 1477 [paper, Śāradā script]. See above, chapter 2, §9.

[S12] *Īśvarapratyabhijñāvivṛtivimarśinī* ("*Īśvarapratyabhijñā(vimarśinī)*"), Srinagar: Oriental Research Library, no. 2403 [paper, Śāradā script]. See above, chapter 2, §8.

[S15] *Īśvarapratyabhijñāvimarśinī*, Srinagar: Oriental Research Library, no. 787 [paper, Śāradā script]. See above, chapter 2, §9.

[S17] *Īśvarapratyabhijñāvṛtti*, Srinagar: Oriental Research Library, no. 860 [paper, Śāradā script].

[S18] *Īśvarapratyabhijñākaumudī*, Srinagar: Oriental Research Library, no. 1089 [paper, Śāradā script].

[S19] *Īśvarapratyabhijñāvṛtti*, Srinagar: Oriental Research Library, no. 824 [paper, Śāradā script]. See above, chapter 2, §10.

[SOAS] *Īśvarapratyabhijñāvimarśinī*, London: School of Oriental and African Studies Library, no. 207 in DOGRA 1978/no. 44255 [paper, Śāradā script]. See above, chapter 2, §9.

## 2. Primary sources: editions

[A = *Aṣṭādhyāyī*]—see RENOU 1966.

[ABh = *Abhinavabhāratī*] *Nāṭyaśāstra of Bharatamuni, with the Commentary Abhinavabhāratī by Abhinavaguptācārya*, ed. M. Ramakrishna Kavi, Baroda: Oriental Institute, Gaekwad's Oriental Series 36, 68, 124, & 145, 1934–1964.

[*Āgamaśāstra*] *Gauḍapāda-Kārikā*, ed. and transl. Raghunath Damodar Karmakar, Poona: Bhandarkar Oriental Research Institute, 1953.

[*Āgamaśāstravivaraṇa*, in] *Complete Works of Sri Sankaracharya in the Original Sanskrit*, vol. VIII: *Commentaries on the Upanishads*, [Srirangam: Sri Vani Vilas Press, 1910] Madras: Samata Books, 1983, pp. 391–540.

[AKBh, chapter 9] *Abhidharmakośabhāṣya of Vasubandhu. Chapter IX: Ātmavādapratiṣedha*, ed. Jong Cheol Lee, Tokyo: The Sankibo Press, 2005.

[APS = *Ajaḍapramātṛsiddhi*, in] *The Siddhitrayī and the Pratyabhijñākārikā-vṛtti of Rājānaka Utpala Deva*, ed. Madhusudan Kaul Shastri, Srinagar: Kashmir Series of Texts and Studies 34, 1921.

[*Arthaśāstra*] *The Kauṭilīya Arthaśāstra*, Part I: *Sanskrit Text with a Glossary*, ed. R.P. Kangle, 2nd ed., repr., Delhi: Motilal Banarsidass, 2000.

*Āryabhaṭīya of Āryabhaṭa with the Commentary of Bhāskara I and Someśvara*, ed. Kripa Shankar Shukla, New Delhi: Indian National Science Academy, 1976.

*Āryabhaṭīyabhāṣya*—see *Āryabhaṭīya*.

[AS = *Ambāstava*, in *Pañcastavī*, in] *Kāvyamālā*, Part 3, ed. Paṇḍit Durgāprasāda & Kavināth Pāṇḍurang Parab, Bombay: Nirnaya Sagar Press, 1887.

[BĀU = *Bṛhadāraṇyakopaniṣad*]—see OLIVELLE 1998.

[*Bhāmatī*]—see *Brahmasūtrabhāṣya*.

[*Bhāskarī*] *Īśvarapratyabhijñāvimarśinī of Abhinavagupta, Doctrine of Divine Recognition*, vols. I–II: *Sanskrit Text with the Commentary Bhāskarī*, ed. K.A. Subramania Iyer & K.C. Pandey, [Allahabad: The Princess of Wales Saraswati Bhavana Texts, 1938] Delhi: Motilal Banarsidass, 1986.

[BhG = *Bhagavadgītā*] *Śrīmadbhagavadgītā with Gītārthasaṅgraha of Abhinavagupta*, Part I: Text, ed. S. Sankaranarayanan, Tirupati: Sri Venkateswara University Oriental Research Institute, 1985.

[*Bhogakārikā*, in] *Aṣṭaprakaraṇam*, ed. Vrajavallabha Dvivedī, Varanasi: Sampūrṇānandasaṃskṛtaviśvavidyālaya, 1988.

[*Bhogakārikāvṛtti*]—see *Bhogakārikā*.

[*Brahmasūtrabhāṣya*] *The Brahmasūtra Śāṅkara Bhāṣya, with the Commentaries Bhāmatī, Kalpataru and Parimala*, ed. Anantkṛṣṇa Śāstrī, 2nd ed., revised by Bhārgav Śāstrī, Bombay: Pandurang Jawaji, 1938.

[ChU = *Chāndogyopaniṣad*, in] OLIVELLE 1998.

[ChUBh = *Chāndogyopaniṣadbhāṣya*] *Chāndogyopaniṣat, ānandagirikṛtaṭīkāsaṃvalitaśāṃkarabhāṣyasametā*, ed. Hari Nārāyaṇa Āpaṭe, Puṇyākhyapattana: Ānandāśramamudraṇālaya, 1913.

[*Devīśatakam*, ed. in] *Kāvyamālā*, Part 9, ed. Paṇḍit Shivadatta & V.L. Sāstrī Paṇaśikar, Bombay: Nirnaya Sagar Press, 1916.

[DhĀ] *The Dhvanyāloka of Śrī Ānandavardhanāchārya with the Lochana & Bālapriyā Commentaries*, ed. Pattābhirāma Sāstri, Benares: Chowkhambā Sanskrit Series Office, 1940.

[DhĀL = *Dhvanyālokalocana*]—see DhĀ.

[ĪPK] *Īśvarapratyabhijñākārikā*—see TORELLA 2002.

[ĪPV] *Īśvarapratyabhijñāvimarśinī*, ed. Mukund Rām Shāstrī/Madhusudan Kaul Shāstrī, 2 vols., Srinagar: Kashmir Series of Texts and Studies 22 & 33, 1918–1921.

[ĪPVV] *Īśvarapratyabhijñāvivṛtivimarśinī by Abhinavagupta*, 3 vols., ed. Madhusudan Kaul Shāstrī, Srinagar: Kashmir Series of Texts and Studies 60, 62 & 65, 1938–1943.

[KV = *Kāśikāvṛtti*] *Kāsikā—a commentary on Pāṇini's grammar by Vāmana and Jayāditya*, ed. Aryendra Sharma, Khanderao Deshpande & D.G. Padhye, 2 vols., Hyderabad: Osmania University, Sanskrit Academy, 1969–1985.

[*Mahānayaprakāśa*] *The Mahānaya-prakāśa of Rājānaka Śiti Kaṇṭha*, ed. Mukunda Rāma Shāstrī, Bombay: Kashmir Series of Texts and Studies 21, 1918.

[MBh] The *Vyākaraṇa-Mahābhāṣya* of Patañjali, ed. Franz Kielhorn, 3 vols., Bombay: Government Central Book Depot, 1880–1884.

[MŚV 1 = *Mālinīślokavārttika* 1]—see HANNEDER 1998.

[MT = *Mṛgendratantra*]—see MTV.

[MTV = *Mṛgendratantravṛtti*] *The Śrī Mṛgendra Tantram (Vidyāpāda and Yogapāda) with the Commentary of Nārāyaṇakaṇṭha*, ed. Madhusudan Kaul Shastri, Bombay: Kashmir Series of Texts and Studies 50, 1930.

[NBh = *Nyāyasūtrabhāṣya*] *Gautamīyanyāyadarśana with Bhāṣya of Vātsyāyana*, ed. Anantalal Thakur, New Delhi: Indian Council of Philosophical Research, Nyāyacaturgranthikā 1, 1997.

[*Nirukta*, in] *The Nighaṇṭu and the Nirukta*, ed. Lakshman Sarup, [Oxford: 1927] Delhi: Motilal Banarsidass, 1967.

[NK] *Nyāyakandalī, Being a Commentary on Praśastapādabhāṣya, with Three Sub-commentaries*, ed. J.S. Jetly & Vasant G. Parikh, Baroda: Oriental Institute, 1991.

[NM$_M$ = *Nyāyamañjarī*, Mysore edition] *Nyāyamañjarī of Jayanta Bhaṭṭa, with Ṭippaṇī—Nyāyasaurabha by the Editor*, ed. K.S. Varadacharya, 2 vols., Mysore: Oriental Research Institute Series 116 & 139, 1969–1983.

[NM$_V$ = *Nyāyamañjarī*, Varanasi edition] *Nyāyamañjarī of Jayanta Bhaṭṭa, with the Commentary of Granthibhaṅga by Cakradhara*, ed. Gaurinath Sastri, 3 vols., Varanasi: Sampurnanand Sanskrit Vishvavidyalaya, 1982.

[NS = *Nyāyasūtra*]—see NBh.

[NTU = *Netratantroddyota*] *The Netra Tantram with Commentary by Kshemarāja*, ed. Madhusudan Kaul Shāstrī, 2 vols., Srinagar: Kashmir Series of Texts and Studies 46 & 61.

[NV] *Nyāyabhāṣyavārttika of Bhāradvāja Uddyotakara*, ed. Anantalal Thakur, New Delhi: Indian Council of Philosophical Research: Nyāyacaturgranthikā 2, 1997.

[NVTṬ] *Nyāyavārttikatātparyaṭīkā of Vācaspatimiśra*, ed. Anantalal Thakur, New Delhi: Indian Council of Philosophical Research, Nyāyacaturgranthikā 3, 1996.

[*Nyāyakośa*] *Nyāyakośa or Dictionary of Technical Terms of Indian Philosophy* by Bhīmācārya Jhalakīkar, [1874,] revised and re-edited by Vāsudev Shāstri Abhyankar, Poona: Bhandarkar Oriental Research Institute, 1928.

[*Nyāyakusumāñjali*] *The Kusumāñjali or Hindu Proof of the Existence of a Supreme Being by Udayana Āchārya, with the Commentary of Hari Dāsa Bhaṭṭāchārya*, ed. and transl. E.B. Cowell, assisted by Maheśa Chandra, Calcutta: Baptist Mission Press, 1864.

[PDhS = *Padārthadharmasaṅgraha*]—see NK.

[PH] *The Pratyabhijñā Hṛdaya Being a Summary of the Doctrines of the Advaita Shaiva Philosophy of Kashmir by Kṣemarāja*, ed. J.C. Chatterji, Srinagar: Kashmir Series of Texts and Studies 3, 1911.

[*Parāśaropapurāṇa*] *Parāśaropapurāṇaṃ (samīkṣātmakaṃ saṃpādanaṃ)*, ed. Kapiladeva Tripāṭhī, Varanasi: Sampurnand Sanskrit University, 1990.

[PP] *Prakīrṇaprakāśa*—see VP 3.1 and 3.2.

[PraP = *Prakaraṇapañcikā*] *Prakarṇa Panchikâ, A Treatise on Mimânsâ Philosophy by Mahopâdhyâya Shrî Shâliknâth Misra*, ed. Mukunda Shâstri, Benares: Chowkhamba Sanskrit Series, 1903.

[PSam] *Pramāṇasamuccaya, Chapter 1. A Hypothetical Reconstruction of the Sanskrit Text*, ed. Ernst Steinkellner, unpublished (2005), available at: www.oeaw.ac.at/ias/Mat/dignaga_PS_1.pdf.

[PSV = *Paramārthasāravivṛti*] *The Paramārthasāra by Abhinavagupta with the Commentary of Yogarāja*, ed. J.C. Chatterji, Srinagar: Kashmir Series of Texts and Studies 7, 1916.

[PTV = *Parātrīśikāvivaraṇa*] *The Parā-Trimshikā with Commentary, the Latter by Abhinava Gupta*, ed. Mukunda Rāma Shāstrī, Srinagar: Kashmir Series of Texts and Studies 18, 1918.

[PV] *Pramāṇavārttika-kārikā (Sanskrit and Tibetan)*, ed. Yūsho Miyasaka, *Acta Indologica* 2, 1971–1972, pp. 1–206.

[PV 1 = *Pramāṇavārttika* 1] —see GNOLI 1960.

[PVA = *Pramāṇavārttikālaṅkāra*] *Pramāṇavārtikabhāshyam or Vārtikālaṅkāraḥ of Prajñākaragupta (Being a Commentary on Dharmakīrti's Pramāṇavārtikam)*, ed. Rāhula Sāṅkṛityāyana, Patna: Kashi Prasad Jayaswal Research Institute, 1953.

[PVin 1] *Dharmakīrti's Pramāṇaviniścaya, Chapters 1 and 2*, ed. Ernst Steinkellner, Beijing/Vienna: China Tibetology Publishing House/Austrian Academy of Sciences Press, 2007.

[PVV = *Pramāṇavārttikavṛtti*] *Dharmakīrti's Pramāṇavārttika with Commentary by Manorathanandin*, ed. Rāhula Sāṅkṛtyāyana, *Journal of the Bihar and Orissa Research Society* 24–26, 1938–1940, Appendix.

[PYV= *Pātañjalayogaśāstravivaraṇa*] *Patnjala-Yogasūtra-Bhāṣya Vivaraṇam of Śaṅkara-Bhagavatpāda*, ed. Polakam Sri Rama Sastri & S.R. Krishnamurthi Sastri, Madras: Government Oriental Manuscripts Library, 1952.

[RT] *Kalhaṇa's Rājataraṅginī or Chronicle of the Kings of Kashmir*, ed. Marc Aurel Stein, Vol. I: Sanskrit Text with Critical Notes [Bombay: Education Society's Press, 1892], Delhi: Motilal Banarsidass, [1988] 2003 (repr. as vol. III of STEIN 1900).

[ŚD] *Śivadṛṣṭi of Śrīsomānandanātha with the Vṛtti by Utpaladeva*, ed. Madhusudan Kaul Shastri, Srinagar: Kashmir Series of Texts and Studies 54, 1934.

[ŚDī = *Śāstradīpikā*] *The Shāstradīpikā with the Commentary Mayūkhamālikā... by Somanātha and with the Commentary Yuktisnehaprapūraṇi with Gūḍhārthavivaraṇa... by Rāmakrishṇa*, ed. Srī Dharmadattasūrī, Bombay: Tukārām Jāvajī, Niryaya-Sagar Press, 1915.

[SDS = *Sarvadarśanasaṅgraha*] *Śrīmatsāyaṇamādhavācāryapraṇītaḥ Sarvadarśanasaṃgraha*, ed. Vasudev Shastri Abhyankar, Poona: Bhandarkar Oriental Research Institute, 1924.

[ŚDV = *Śivadṛṣṭivṛtti*]—see ŚD.

[SK = *Sāṃkhyakārikā*] see *Tattvakaumudī*.

[*Spandasandoha*] *The Spanda Sandoha of Kshemarāja*, ed. Mukunda Rāma Shāstri, Bombay: Kashmir Series of Texts and Studies 16, 1917.

[ŚSĀ] *The Śivastotrāvalī of Utpaladevāchārya, with the Sanskrit Commentary of Kṣemarāja*, ed. Rājānaka Lakṣmaṇa [Joo], Varanasi: Chowkhamba Sanskrit Series 15, 1964.

[ŚSĀ, Chowkhamba Ed.] *Śivastotrāvalī by Utpala Devāchārya, with the Commentary of Kshemarāja*, ed. Rai Pramadādāsa Mittra Bahādur, Benares: Chowkhamba Sanskrit Series, 1903.

[STU = *Svacchandatantroddyota*]—see *Svacchandatantra*.

[*Svacchandatantra*] *The Svacchanda Tantram with commentary by Kshemarāja*, ed. Madhusudan Kaul Shāstrī, 6 vols., Srinagar: Kashmir Series of Texts and Studies 31, 38, 44, 48, 53 & 56, 1921–1935.

[TĀ] *Tantrāloka of Abhinavagupta with Commentary by Rājānaka Jayaratha*, ed. Madhusudan Kaul Shāstrī, 12 vols., Srinagar: Kashmir Series of Texts and Studies 23, 28, 29, 30, 35, 36, 41, 47, 52, 57, 58 & 59, 1918–1938.

[*Taittirīyopaniṣad*]—see OLIVELLE 1998.

[*Tattvasaṅgraha* by Sadyojyotis, in] *Aṣṭaprakaraṇam*, ed. Vrajavallabha Dvivedī, Varanasi: Saṃpūrṇānanda University, 1988.

[*Tattvasaṅgraha* by Śāntarakṣita]—see $TS_K$ and $TS_Ś$.

[*Tattvasaṅgrahaṭīkā*]—see *Tattvasaṅgraha* by Sadyojyotis.

[TĀV = *Tantrālokaviveka*]—see TĀ.

[TK = *Tattvakaumudī*] *Vācaspatimiśras Tattvakaumudī. Ein Beitrag zur Textkritik bei kontaminierter Überlieferung*, ed. Srinivasa Ayya Srinivasan, Hamburg: Cram, De Gruyter & Co., 1967.

[$TS_K$] *Tattvasaṅgraha of Śāntarakṣita with the Commentary of Kamalaśīla*, ed. Embar Krishnamacharya, 2 vols., Baroda: Gaekwad's Oriental Series 30 & 31, Oriental Institute, 1926.

[$TS_Ś$] *Tattvasaṅgraha of Ācārya Shāntarakṣita with the Commentary "Pañjikā" of Shri Kamalshīla*, ed. Dwarikadas Śastri, 2 vols., Varanasi: Bauddha Bharati Series 1, 1968.

[TSā] *The Tantrasāra of Abhinavagupta*, ed. Mukund Rām Shāstrī, Bombay: Kashmir Series of Texts and Studies 17, 1918.

[$TSP_K$/$TSP_Ś$ = *Tattvasaṅgrahapañjikā*]—see $TS_K$ and $TS_Ś$.

[*Upadeśasāhasrī*, in] *Śrīśaṅkarabhagavatpādācāryaviracitā Prakaraṇadvādaśī, Śrīmatpadmapāda-śrīmadvidyāraṇya-śrīmadānandagiryādiprācīnācāryaviracitaṭīkābhiḥ Samalaṅkṛtā*, ed. S. Subrahmanya Shastri, Mount Abu/Varanasi: Mahesh Research Institute, 1981.

[*Vijñānabhairavavivṛti*] *The Vijñāna-Bhairava with Commentary Partly by Kṣhemarāja and Partly by Shivopādhyāya*, ed. Munkunda Rāma Shāstrī, Bombay: Kashmir Series of Texts and Studies 8, 1918.

[VP 1] *Vākyapadīya of Bhartṛhari with the Commentaries Vṛtti and Paddhati of Vṛṣabhadeva, Kāṇḍa I*, ed. K.A. Subramania Iyer, Poona: Deccan College, [1966] 1995.

[VP 3.1] *Vākyapadīya of Bhartṛhari with the commentary of Helārāja, Kāṇḍa III, Part 1*, ed. K.A. Subramania Iyer, Poona: Deccan College, 1963.

[VP 3.2] *Vākyapadīya of Bhartṛhari with the commentary of Helārāja, Kāṇḍa III, Part 2*, ed. K.A. Subramania Iyer, Poona: Deccan College, 1973.

[VP (Rau)] *Bhartṛhari's Vākyapadīya. Die Mūlakārikās nach den Handschriften herausgegeben und mit einem Pāda-Index versehen*, ed. Wilhelm Rau, Wiesbaden: Deutsche Morgenländische Gesellschaft, 1977.

[VPP = *Vākyapadīyapaddhati*]—see VP 1.

[VPV = *Vākyapadīyavṛtti*]—see VP 1.

[*Vṛtti* = *Īśvarapratyabhijñāvṛtti*]—see TORELLA 2002.

[VS] *Vaiśeṣikasūtra of Kaṇāda, with the Commentary of Candrānanda*, ed. Muni Śrī Jambuvijayaji, Baroda: Gaekwad Oriental Series 136, Oriental Institute, 1961.

[VSV] *Vaiśeṣikasūtravṛtti*—see VS.

[*Vyomavatī*] *Vyomavatī of Vyomaśivācārya*, ed. Gaurinath Sastri, 2 vols., Varanasi: Sampurnand Sanskrit Vishvavidyalaya, 1983–1984.

[YD] *Yuktidīpikā. The Most Significant Commentary on the Sāṃkhyakārikā*, ed. Albrecht Wezler & Shujun Motegi, vol. I, Stuttgart: Franz Steiner Verlag, 1998.

[YS 1] *Samādhipāda. Das erste Kapitel des Pātañjalayogaśāstra zum ersten Mal kritisch ediert*, ed. Philipp André Maas, Aachen: Shaker Verlag, 2006.

### 3. Translations, studies, catalogues, dictionaries

Daud ALI (2016), "Bhoja's mechanical garden: Translating wonder across the Indian ocean, circa 800–1100 CE," *History of Religions* 55(4), pp. 460–493.

Harvey ALPER (1987), "*svabhāvam avabhāsasya vimarśam*: Judgment as a transcendental category in Utpaladeva's Śaiva theology," *The Adyar Library Bulletin* 51, pp. 176–241.

Dan ARNOLD (2005), "Is *Svasaṃvitti* transcendental? A tentative reconstruction following Śāntarakṣita," *Asian Philosophy* 15(1), pp. 77–111.

Dan ARNOLD (2008), "Buddhist idealism, epistemic and otherwise: Thoughts on the alternating perspectives of Dharmakīrti," *Sophia* 47, pp. 3–28.

Dan ARNOLD (2010), "Self-awareness (*svasaṃvitti*) and related doctrines of Buddhists following Dignāga: philosophical characterizations of some of the main issues," *Journal of Indian Philosophy* 38, pp. 323–378.

Anindita Niyogi BALSLEV (1983), *A Study of Time in Indian Philosophy*, Wiesbaden: Otto Harrassowitz.

Lyne BANSAT-BOUDON & Kamaleshadatta TRIPATHI (2011), *An Introduction to Tantric Philosophy. The Paramārthasāra of Abhinavagupta with the Commentary of Yogarāja*, London/New York: Routledge.

Sadananda BHADURI (1947), *Studies in Nyāya-Vaiśeṣika Metaphysics*, Poona: Bhandarkar Oriental Research Institute.

Govardhan P. BHATT (1989), *The Basic Ways of Knowing. An In-depth Study of Kumārila's Contribution to Indian Epistemology*, revised ed., Delhi: Motilal Banarsidass.

Madeleine BIARDEAU (1968), "L'*Ātman* dans le commentaire de Śabarasvāmin," in *Mélanges d'indianisme à la mémoire de Louis Renou*, Paris: De Boccard, pp. 109–125.

Johannes BRONKHORST (1994), "The qualities of Sāṃkhya," *Wiener Zeitschrift für die Kunde Südasiens* 38 (*Orbis Indicus, Festschrift G. Oberhammer*), pp. 309–322.

Georg BÜHLER (1877), *Detailed Report of a Tour in Search of Sanskrit MSS. Made in Kaśmīr, Rajputana, and Central India*, Extra Number of the *Journal of the Bombay Branch of the Royal Asiatic Society*.

José Ignacio CABEZÓN (1992), "Vasubandhu's *Vyākhyāyukti* on the authenticity of the Mahāyāna *sūtra*s," in Jeffrey R. Timm (ed.), *Texts in Context. Traditional Hermeneutics in South Asia*, Albany: State University of New York Press, pp. 221–243.

George CARDONA (1974), "Pāṇini's *kāraka*s: agency, animation and identity," *Journal of Indian Philosophy* 2, pp. 231–306.

George CARDONA (1991), "A path still taken: some early Indian arguments concerning time," *Journal of the American Oriental Society* 111(3), pp. 445–464.

Arindam CHAKRABARTI (1982), "The Nyāya proofs for the existence of the soul," *Journal of Indian Philosophy* 10, pp. 211–238.

Arindam CHAKRABARTI (1992), "I touch what I saw," *Phenomenological Research* 52(1), pp. 103–116.

J.C. CHATTERJI (1914), *Kashmir Shaivism (Being a Brief Introduction to the History, Literature and Doctrines of the Advaita Shaiva Philosophy of*

*Kashmir, Specifically Called the Trika System)*, Srinagar: Kashmir Series of Texts and Studies 2(1).

George CHEMPARATHY (1972), *An Indian Rational Theology. Introduction to Udayana's Nyāyakusumāñjali*, Vienna: de Nobili Research Library.

Whitney COX (forthcoming), "The *Tantrāloka*, the Rājarājeśvaram, and the study of Śaiva civilization," paper for the Symposium *After the Śaiva Age: Transformation and Continuity in the Regional Śaivisms of South India* (47th Annual Conference on South Asia, Madison, WI, 2018).

Daniele CUNEO (2016), "Detonating or defusing desire. From Utpaladeva's ecstatic aesthetics to Abhinavagupta's ecumenical art theory," in Raffaele Torella & Bettina Bäumer (eds.), *Utpaladeva, Philosopher of Recognition*, Delhi: DK Printworld, pp. 28–73.

DEPARTMENT OF LIBRARIES AND RESEARCH, JAMMU & KASHMIR, SRINAGAR (2011), *Catalogue of Manuscripts*, Srinagar: Department of Libraries and Research, Jammu & Kashmir.

Silvia D'INTINO & Sheldon POLLOCK (eds. 2018), *L'Espace du sens. Approches de la philologie indienne/The Space of Meaning. Approaches to Indian Philology*, Paris: De Boccard, Publications de l'Institut de Civilisation Indienne du Collège de France 84, pp. 305–354.

R.C. DOGRA (1978), *A Handlist of the Manuscripts in South Asian Languages in the* [*SOAS*] *Library*, London: School of Oriental and African Studies.

Wendy DONIGER O'FLAHERTY (1984), *Dreams, Illusions and Other Realities*, Chicago: The University of Chicago Press.

James DUERLINGER (2003), *Indian Buddhist Theories of Persons. Vasubandhu's 'Refutation of the Theory of a Self'*, London/New York: Routledge.

John DUNNE (2004), *Foundations of Dharmakīrti's Philosophy*, Somerville (MA): Wisdom Publications.

Katrin EINICKE (2009), *Korrektur, Differenzierung und Abkürzung in indischen Inschriften und Handschriften*, Wiesbaden: Harrasowitz Verlag.

Vincent ELTSCHINGER, Helmut KRASSER & John TABER (2012), *Can the Veda Speak? Dharmakīrti Against Mīmāṃsā Exegetics and Vedic Authority.*

*An Annotated Translation of PVSV 164,24–176,16*, Wien: Verlag der Österreichischen Akademie der Wissenschaften.

Vincent ELTSCHINGER & Isabelle RATIÉ (2013), *Self, No-Self, and Salvation. Dharmakīrti's Critique of the Notions of Self and Person*, Vienna: Verlag der Österreichischen Akademie der Wissenschaften.

Pierre-Sylvain FILLIOZAT (2009), "Time as a power of word according to Bhartṛhari," in Mithilesh Chaturvedi (ed.), *Bhartṛhari. Language, Thought and Reality*, Delhi: Motilal Banarsidass, pp. 215–224.

Camillo FORMIGATTI (2011), *Sanskrit Annotated Manuscripts from Northern India and Nepal*, unpublished doctoral dissertation (supervised by Harunaga Isaacson), University of Hamburg [revised version, 2015].

Eli FRANCO (2011), "Perception of yogis—Some epistemological and metaphysical considerations," in Helmut Krasser, Horst Lasic, Eli Franco & Birgit Kellner (eds.), *Religion and Logic in Buddhist Philosophical Analysis. Proceedings of the Fourth International Dharmakīrti Conference, Vienna, August 23–27, 2005*, Wien: Verlag der Österreichischen Akademie der Wissenschaften, pp. 81–98.

Erich FRAUWALLNER (1956), *Geschichte der indischen Philosophie, II. Band*, Salzburg: Otto Müller Verlag.

Jonardon GANERI (1999), "Self-intimation, memory and personal identity," *Journal of Indian Philosophy* 27, pp. 469–483.

Jonardon GANERI (2000), "Cross-modality and the self," *Philosophy and Phenomenological Research* 61(3), pp. 639–657.

Jonardon GANERI (2010), "Sanskrit philosophical commentary," *Journal of the Indian Council of Philosophical Research* 25(1), pp. 187–207.

Raniero GNOLI (1960), *The Pramāṇavārttikam of Dharmakīrti. The First Chapter with the Autocommentary. Text and Critical Notes*, Roma: Istituto Italiano per il Medio ed Estremo Oriente.

Raniero GNOLI (1985), *The Aesthetic Experience According to Abhinavagupta*, Varanasi: Chowkhamba Sanskrit Studies.

Raniero GNOLI (1985b), *Il Commento di Abhinavagupta alla Parātriṃśikā (Parātriṃśikāvivaraṇa). Traduzione e Testo*, Rome: Istituto Italiano per il Medio ed Estremo Oriente, Serie Orientale Roma 58.

Raniero GNOLI (1999), *Abhinavagupta. Luce dei Tantra. Tantrāloka*, Milano: Adelphi Edizioni.

Dominic GOODALL & Harunaga ISAACSON (2003), *The Raghupañcikā of Vallabhadeva, Being the Earliest Commentary on the Raghuvaṃśa of Kālidāsa*, vol. I, Groningen: Egbert Forsten.

Dominic GOODALL & Marion RASTELLI (2013, eds.), *Tāntrikābhidhānakośa. A Dictionary of Technical Terms from Hindu Tantric Literature*, vol. III (Ṭ–Ph), Wien: Verlag der Österreichischen Akademie der Wissenschaften.

François GRIMAL (2000), "Pour décrire un commentaire traditionnel sur une œuvre littéraire sanskrite," *Bulletin de l'École Française d'Extrême-Orient* 87(2), pp. 765–785.

Paul HACKER (1953), *Vivarta. Studien zur Geschichte der illusionistischen Kosmologie und Erkenntnistheorie der Inder*, Wiesbaden: Verlag der Akademie der Wissenschaften und der Literatur in Mainz, in Komission bei Franz Steiner Verlag Gmbh.

Wilhelm HALBFASS (1992), *On Being and What There Is. Classical Vaiśeṣika and the History of Indian Ontology*, New York: State University of New York Press.

Jürgen HANNEDER (1998), *Abhinavagupta's Philosophy of Revelation. Mālinīślokavārttika I,1–399*, Groningen: Egbert Forsten.

Jürgen HANNEDER (2017), *To Edit or Not to Edit. On Textual Criticism of Sanskrit Works*, Pune: Pune Indological Series.

Jürgen HANNEDER, Stanislav JAGER & Alexis SANDERSON (2013), *Ratnakaṇṭhas Stotras—Sūryastutirahasya, Ratnaśataka und Śambhukṛpāmanoharastava*, München: P. Kirchheim Verlag.

Masaaki HATTORI (1968), *Dignāga, On Perception, Being the Pratyakṣapariccheda of Dignāga's Pramāṇasamuccaya*, Cambridge: Harvard University Press.

Yoshichika HONDA (2011), "Bhoja and Dharmakīrti," in Helmut Krasser, Horst Lasic, Eli Franco & Birgit Kellner (eds.), *Religion and Logic in Buddhist Philosophical Analysis. Proceedings of the Fourth International Dharmakīrti Conference, Vienna, August 23–27, 2005*, Wien: Verlag der Österreichischen Akademie der Wissenschaften, pp. 151-158.

Jan E.M. HOUBEN (1995), *The Saṃbandha-samuddeśa (Chapter on Relation) and Bhartṛhari's Philosophy of Language. A Study of Bhartṛhari's Saṃbandha-samuddeśa in the Context of the Vākyapadīya with a Translation of Helārāja's Commentary Prakīrṇa-prakāśa*, Groningen: Egbert Forsten, Gonda Indological Studies 2.

Masahiro INAMI (2011), "Nondual cognition," in Helmut Krasser, Horst Lasic, Eli Franco & Birgit Kellner (eds.), *Religion and Logic in Buddhist Philosophical Analysis. Proceedings of the Fourth International Dharmakīrti Conference, Vienna, August 23–27, 2005*, Wien: Verlag der Österreichischen Akademie der Wissenschaften, pp. 177–196.

Daniel H.H. INGALLS, Jeffrey Moussaieff MASSON & M.V. PATWARDHAN (1990), *The Dhvanyāloka of Ānandavardhana with the Locana of Abhinavagupta*, Cambridge (Mass.): Harvard University Press.

Stanislav JAGER (2018), *Bhāskarakaṇṭhas Cittānubodhaśāstra. Kritische Edition der ersten drei Kapitel nebst Erstedition des Autokommentars*, Marburg: Indica et Tibetica Verlag.

Ganganatha JHA (1911), *The Prābhākara School of Pūrva Mīmāṃsā*, [Allahabad: 1911,] Delhi: Motilal Banarsidass, 1978.

Ganganatha JHA (1916), *The Padārthadharmasaṅgraha of Praçastapāda with the Nyāyakandalī of Çrīdhara, Translated into English*, [repr. from *The Pandit*,] Allahabad: E.J. Lazarus & Co.

Shivaram Dattatray JOSHI (1993), "Kauṇḍa Bhaṭṭa on the meaning of Sanskrit verbs (1). An English translation and annotation of the *Vaiyākaraṇabhūṣaṇasāra*, chapter 1 with the introduction," *Sambhāṣā* 14, pp. 1–40.

Mari JYVÄSJÄRVI (2010), "Retrieving the hidden meaning: Jain commentarial techniques and the art of memory," *Journal of Indian Philosophy* 38, pp. 133–162.

Eivind KAHRS (2013), "Action, being and *brahman*," *The Journal of Hindu Studies*, pp. 1–16.

Yuichi KAJIYAMA (1966), *An Introduction to Buddhist Philosophy. An Annotated Translation of the Tarkabhāṣā of Mokṣākaragupta*, [Kyoto: Kyoto

University, 1966] repr. with corrections in the author's hand, Wien: Arbeitskreis für Tibetische und Buddhistische Studien Universität Wien, 1998.

Ramchandra KAK & Harabhatta SHASTRI (1927), *A Descriptive Catalogue of Sanskrit Manuscripts in the Private Library of His Highness Shri Rajarajeshwar Maharajadhiraj Maharaja Shri Harisinghji Bahadur of Jammu and Kashmir*, Poona: Aryabhushan Press.

R.P. KANGLE (1963), *The Kauṭilīya Arthaśāstra,* Part II: *An English Translation with Critical and Explanatory Notes*, 2nd ed., repr., Delhi: Motilal Banarsidass, 2003.

Yohei KAWAJIRI (2016a), "New fragments of the *Īśvarapratyabhijñā-vivṛti*," in Raffaele Torella & Bettina Bäumer (eds.), *Utpaladeva, Philosopher of Recognition*, Delhi: DK Printworld, pp. 77–101.

Yohei KAWAJIRI (2016b), "New fragments of the *Īśvarapratyabhijñā-vivṛti* (3)," *Nagoya Studies in Indian Culture and Buddhism: Saṃbhāṣā* 33, pp. 17–46.

Yohei KAWAJIRI (forthcoming), "New fragments of the *Īśvarapratyabhijñā-vivṛti* (2)," in Ernst Prets & Hiroshi Marui (eds.), *Proceedings of the Japan-Austria Symposium on Transmission and Tradition.*

Arthur Berriedale KEITH (1921), *Indian Logic and Atomism. An Exposition of the Nyāya and Vaiçeṣika Systems*, Oxford: Clarendon Press.

Birgit KELLNER (2010), "Self-awareness (*svasaṃvedana*) in Dignāga's *Pramāṇasamuccaya* and *-vṛtti*: a close reading," *Journal of Indian Philosophy* 38, pp. 203–231.

Birgit KELLNER (2011), "Dharmakīrti's criticism of external realism and the sliding scale of analysis," in Helmut Krasser, Horst Lasic, Eli Franco & Birgit Kellner (eds.), *Religion and Logic in Buddhist Philosophical Analysis. Proceedings of the Fourth International Dharmakīrti Conference, Vienna, August 23–27, 2005*, Wien: Verlag der Österreichischen Akademie der Wissenschaften, pp. 291–298.

Birgit KELLNER (2011b), "Self-awareness (*svasaṃvedana*) and infinite regresses: a comparison of arguments by Dignāga and Dharmakīrti," *Journal of Indian Philosophy* 39, pp. 411–426.

Birgit KELLNER (2017), "Proofs of idealism in Buddhist epistemology," in Joerg Tuske (ed.), *Indian Epistemology and Metaphysics*, London: Bloomsbury, pp. 103–128.

Birgit KELLNER & John TABER (2014), "Studies in Yogācāra-Vijñānavāda idealism I: The interpretation of Vasubandhu's *Viṃśikā*," *Études Asiatiques /Asiatische Studien* 68(3), pp. 709–756.

Helmut KRASSER (1999), "Dharmakīrti's and Kumārila's refutations of the existence of God: A consideration of their chronological order," in Shōryū Katsura (ed.), *Dharmakīrti's Thought and Its Impact on Indian and Tibetan Philosophy*, Vienna: Verlag der Österreichischen Akademie der Wissenschaften, pp. 215–224.

Helmut KRASSER (2002), *Śaṅkaranandanas Īśvarāpākaraṇasaṅkṣepa*, 2 vols., Vienna: Verlag der Österreichischen Akademie der Wissenschaften.

K. KUNJUNNI RAJA (1969), *Indian Theories of Meaning*, Madras: The Adyar Library and Research Centre [1963], 2nd ed., repr. 1977.

Étienne LAMOTTE (1949), *Le Traité de la grande vertu de sagesse de Nāgārjuna (Mahāprajñāpāramitāśāstra)*, Tome I: *Chapitres I–XV*, Louvain: Université de Louvain, Institut Orientaliste, Bibliothèque du Muséon 18.

David Peter LAWRENCE (2005), "Remarks on Abhinavagupta's use of the analogy of reflection," *Journal of Indian Philosophy* 33, pp. 583–599.

Charles Cheuk Him LI (2018), *Limits of the Real. A Hypertext Critical Edition and Translation of Bhartṛhari's Dravyasamuddeśa, with the Commentary of Helārāja*, unpublished doctoral dissertation (supervised by Vincenzo Vergiani), University of Cambridge.

Jeremiah P. LOSTY (1982), *The Art of the Book in India*, London: The British Library.

Lawrence MCCREA (2008), *The Teleology of Poetics in Medieval Kashmir*, Cambridge (Mass.): Harvard University, Harvard Oriental Series 71.

Lawrence MCCREA (2016), "Abhinavagupta as intellectual historian of Buddhism," in Eli Franco & Isabelle Ratié (eds.), *Around Abhinavagupta. Aspects of the Intellectual History of Kashmir from the Ninth to the Eleventh Century*, Berlin: Lit Verlag, pp. 263–286.

Lawrence MCCREA & Parimal PATIL (2010), *Buddhist Philosophy of Language in India—Jñānaśrīmitra on Exclusion*, New York: Columbia University Press.

John Ellis MCTAGGART (1908), "The unreality of time," *Mind* 17(68), pp. 457–474.

Roque MESQUITA (1994), "Die Idee der Erlösung bei Kumārilabhaṭṭa," *Wiener Zeitschrift für die Kunde Südasiens* 38, pp. 451–484.

Katsumi MIMAKI (1976), *La Réfutation bouddhique de la permanence des choses (Sthirasiddhidūṣaṇa) et la preuve de la momentanéité des choses (Kṣaṇabhaṅgasiddhi)*, Paris: de Boccard, Institut de Civilisation Indienne.

Monier MONIER-WILLIAMS (1899), *A Sanskrit-English Dictionary, Etymologically and Philologically Arranged, with Special Reference to Cognate Indo-European Languages*, new ed. by Ernst Leumann & Carl Capeller, [Oxford: 1899] New Delhi: Asian Educational Services, 2001.

Mamoru NAMAI (1976), "Kōki Bukkyōto ni yoru Bārhaspatya Hihan (I)," *Indological Review* 2, pp. 33–74.

John NEMEC (2011), *The Ubiquitous Śiva. Somānanda's Śivadṛṣṭi and His Tantric Interlocutors*, Oxford/New York: Oxford University Press.

John NEMEC (2016), "Influences on and legacies of Somānanda's conception of Materiality," in Eli Franco & Isabelle Ratié (eds.), *Around Abhinavagupta. Aspects of the Intellectual History of Kashmir from the Ninth to the Eleventh Century*, Berlin: Lit Verlag, pp. 341–373.

Claus OETKE (1988), *'Ich' und das Ich. Analytische Untersuchungen zur buddhistisch-brahmanischen Ātmankontroverse*, Stuttgart: Franz Steiner Verlag, 1988.

Hideyo OGAWA (1995), "An action (*kriyā*) and its cognition: grammarians' approach," *Journal of Indian and Buddhist Studies* 44(1), pp. 490–485 (5–10).

Hideyo OGAWA (2019), "Two truths theory: what is *vyavahāra*? Language as a pointer to the truth," *Journal of Indian Philosophy* 47, pp. 613-633.

Patrick OLIVELLE (1998), *The Early Upaniṣads. Annotated Text and Translation*, Oxford: Oxford University Press.

André PADOUX (1990), *Vāc. The Concept of the Word in Selected Hindu Tantras*, transl. Jacques Gontier, Albany: State University of New York Press.

Ganesh Prasad PANDA (1997), "The concept of time in Indian grammatical tradition (1)," *Nagoya Studies in Indian Culture and Buddhism: Saṃbhāṣā* 18, pp. 97–124.

Ganesh Prasad PANDA (1998), "The concept of time in Indian grammatical tradition (2)," *Nagoya Studies in Indian Culture and Buddhism: Saṃbhāṣā* 18, pp. 21–62.

Ganesh Prasad PANDA (2003), "The concept of time in Indian grammatical tradition (3)," *Nagoya Studies in Indian Culture and Buddhism: Saṃbhāṣā* 23, pp. 79–105.

Kanti Chandra PANDEY (1935/1963), *Abhinavagupta. An Historical and Philosophical Study*, Varanasi: Chowkhamba, [1935] enlarged ed. 1963.

Kanti Chandra PANDEY (1954), *Īśvarapratyabhijñā-vimarśinī of Abhinavagupta. Doctrine of Divine Recognition*, vol. III: English Translation, Delhi: [The Princess of Whales Saraswati Bhavana, 1954] Motilal Banarsidass, 1986.

Hari Shankar PRASAD (1984), "Time as a substantive reality in Nyāya-Vaiśeṣika," *East and West* 34, pp. 233–266.

Karin PREISENDANZ (1994), *Studien zu Nyāyasūtra III.1 mit dem Nyāyatattvāloka Vācaspati Miśras II*, 2 vols., Stuttgart: Franz Steiner Verlag.

Navjivan RASTOGI (1979), *The Krama Tantricism of Kashmir. Historical and General Sources*, Delhi: Motilal Banarsidass.

Navjivan RASTOGI (1984), "Some more *nyāya*s as employed by Abhinavagupta," *Annals of the Bhandarkar Oriental Research Institute* 65(1), pp. 27–42.

Isabelle RATIÉ (2006), "La Mémoire et le Soi dans l'*Īśvarapratyabhijñāvimarśinī* d'Abhinavagupta," *Indo-Iranian Journal* 49, pp. 39–103.

Isabelle RATIÉ (2009), "Remarks on compassion and altruism in the Pratyabhijñā philosophy," *Journal of Indian Philosophy* 37, pp. 349–366.

Isabelle RATIÉ (2010a), "The dreamer and the yogin: on the relationship between Buddhist and Śaiva idealisms," *Bulletin of the School of Oriental and African Studies* 73(3), pp. 437–478.

Isabelle RATIÉ (2010b), "'A five-trunked, four-tusked elephant is running in the sky': How free is imagination according to Utpaladeva and Abhinavagupta?," *Études Asiatiques/Asiatische Studien* 64(2), pp. 341–385.

Isabelle RATIÉ (2010c), "Le non-être, une preuve de l'existence du Soi? La notion d'*abhāva* dans la philosophie de la Pratyabhijñā," *Journal Asiatique* 298(2), pp. 421–493.

Isabelle RATIÉ (2011a), *Le Soi et l'Autre. Identité, différence et altérité dans la philosophie de la Pratyabhijñā*, Leiden/Boston: Brill.

Isabelle RATIÉ (2011b), "Can one prove that something exists beyond consciousness? A Śaiva criticism of the Sautrāntika inference of external objects," *Journal of Indian Philosophy* 39, pp. 479–501.

Isabelle RATIÉ (2013), "*Pāramārthika* or *apāramārthika*? On the ontological status of separation according to Abhinavagupta," in Nina Mirnig, Péter-Dániel Szántó & Michael Williams (eds.), *Puṣpikā: Tracing Ancient India Through Texts and Traditions. Contributions to Current Research in Indology*, vol. I, Oxford: Oxbow Books, pp. 381–406.

Isabelle RATIÉ (2014a), *Une Critique bouddhique du Soi selon la Mīmāṃsā. Présentation, édition critique et traduction de la Mīmāṃsakaparikalpitātmaparīkṣā de Śāntarakṣita (Tattvasaṅgraha 222–284 et Pañjikā)*, Wien: Verlag der Österreichischen Akademie der Wissenschaften.

Isabelle RATIÉ (2014b), "A Śaiva interpretation of the *satkāryavāda*: the Sāṃkhya notion of *abhivyakti* and its transformation in the Pratyabhijñā treatise," *Journal of Indian Philosophy* 42, pp. 127–172.

Isabelle RATIÉ (2014c), "On the distinction between epistemic and metaphysical Buddhist idealisms: a Śaiva perspective," *Journal of Indian Philosophy* 42, pp. 353–375.

Isabelle RATIÉ (2016a), "Some hitherto unknown fragments of Utpaladeva's *Vivṛti* (I): on the Buddhist controversy over the existence of other conscious streams," in Raffaele Torella & Bettina Bäumer (eds.), *Utpaladeva, Philosopher of Recognition*, Delhi: DK Printworld, pp. 224–256.

Isabelle RATIÉ (2016b), "Some hitherto unknown fragments of Utpaladeva's *Vivṛti* (III): on memory and error," in Eli Franco & Isabelle Ratié (eds.), *Around Abhinavagupta. Aspects of the Intellectual History of Kashmir from the Ninth to the Eleventh Century*, Berlin: Lit Verlag, pp. 375–400.

Isabelle RATIÉ (2016c), "Utpaladeva's proof of God: on the purpose of the *Īśvarasiddhi*," in Raffaele Torella & Bettina Bäumer (eds.), *Utpaladeva, Philosopher of Recognition*, Delhi: DK Printworld, pp. 257–340.

Isabelle RATIÉ (2017a), "In search of Utpaladeva's lost *Vivṛti* on the Pratyabhijñā treatise: A report on the latest discoveries (with the *Vivṛti* on the end of chapter 1.8)," *Journal of Indian Philosophy* 45, pp. 163–189.

Isabelle RATIÉ (2017b), "An Indian debate on optical reflections and its metaphysical implications: Śaiva nondualism and the mirror of consciousness," in Joerg Tuske (ed.), *Indian Epistemology and Metaphysics*, London: Bloomsbury, pp. 207–240.

Isabelle RATIÉ (2017c), "Utpaladeva and Abhinavagupta on the freedom of consciousness," in Jonardon Ganeri (ed.), *Oxford Handbook of Indian Philosophy*, Oxford: Oxford University Press, pp. 437–468.

Isabelle RATIÉ (2018a), "On the *Ṣaḍdhātusamīkṣā*, a lost work attributed to Bhartṛhari: an examination of testimonies and a list of fragments," *Journal of the American Oriental Society* 138(4), pp. 709–741.

Isabelle RATIÉ (2018b), "For an Indian philology of margins: the case of Kashmirian Sanskrit manuscripts," in Silvia D'Intino & Sheldon Pollock (eds.), *L'Espace du sens. Approches de la philologie indienne/The Space of Meaning. Approaches to Indian Philology*, Paris: De Boccard, Publications de l'Institut de Civilisation Indienne du Collège de France 84, pp. 305–354.

Isabelle RATIÉ (2020), "Some hitherto unknown fragments of Utpaladeva's *Vivṛti* (II): against the existence of external objects," in Dominic Goodall, Shaman Hatley, Harunaga Isaacson & Srilata Raman (eds.), *Śaivism and the Tantric Traditions. Essays in Honour of Alexis G.J.S. Sanderson*, Leiden-Boston: Brill, pp. 106–143.

Isabelle RATIÉ (2020b), "A note on Śaṅkaranandana's 'intuition' according to Abhinavagupta," in Vincent Eltschinger, Marta Sernesi & Vincent Tournier (eds.), *Archaeologies of the Written: Indian, Tibetan, and Buddhist*

*Studies in Honour of Cristina Scherrer-Schaub*, Napoli: Università degli Studi di Napoli "L'Orientale," pp. 493–516.

Isabelle RATIÉ (forthcoming a), "Some hitherto unknown fragments of Utpaladeva's *Vivṛti* (IV): on non-being (*abhāva*) and imperceptible demons," forthcoming in Francesco Sferra et Vincenzo Vergiani (eds.), [Festschrift], Napoli: Università di Napoli "L'Orientale," Dipartimento Asia Africa e Mediterraneo.

Isabelle RATIÉ (forthcoming b), "A History of time in the Sāṃkhya tradition," in Vincent Eltschinger et al. (eds.), [Festschrift], Wien: Wiener Studien zur Tibetologie und Buddhismuskunde, Arbeitskreis für Tibetische und Buddhistische Studien.

Isabelle RATIÉ (forthcoming c), "A path for whom? On the intended readership of the Pratyabhijñā treatise."

Louis RENOU (1957), *Terminologie grammaticale du sanskrit*, Paris: [Bibliothèque de l'École des Hautes Études, 3 fasc., 1942] Librairie Ancienne Honoré Champion.

Louis RENOU (1966), *La Grammaire de Pāṇini. Texte sanskrit, traduction française avec extraits des commentaires*, 2 vols., Paris: École Française d'Extrême-Orient.

Louis RENOU (1977), *Prolégomènes au Vedānta*, Paris: IPEC.

T.S. RUKMANI (2001), *Yogasūtrabhāṣyavivaraṇa of Śaṅkara. Vivaraṇa Text with English Translation, and Critical Notes along with Text and English translation of Patañjali's Yogasūtras and Vyāsabhāṣya*, 2 vols., New Delhi: Munshiram Manoharlal.

Alexis SANDERSON (1985), "Purity and power among the Brahmans of Kashmir," in Michael Carrithers, Steven Collins & Steven Lukes (eds.), *The Category of the Person: Anthropology, Philosophy, History*, Cambridge: Cambridge University Press, pp. 190–216.

Alexis SANDERSON (1992), "The Doctrine of the *Mālinīvijayottaratantra*," in Teun Goudriaan (ed.), *Ritual and Speculation in Early Tantrism. Studies in Honor of André Padoux*, Albany: State University of New York Press, pp. 281–312.

Alexis SANDERSON (1995), "Meaning in Tantric ritual," in Anne-Marie Blondeau & Kristofer Schipper (eds.), *Essais sur le rituel III. Colloque du centenaire de la section des Sciences religieuses de l'École Pratique des Hautes Études*, Louvain/Paris: Peeters, pp. 15–96.

Alexis SANDERSON (2005), "A commentary on the opening verses of the *Tantrasāra* of Abhinavagupta," in Sadananda Das & Ernst Fürlinger (eds.), *Sāmarasya. Studies in Indian Arts, Philosophy and Interreligious Dialogue in Honour of Bettina Bäumer*, New Delhi: D.K. Printworld, pp. 79–138.

Alexis SANDERSON (2007a), "The Śaiva exegesis of Kashmir," in Dominic Goodall & André Padoux (eds.), *Mélanges tantriques à la mémoire d'Hélène Brunner*, Pondicherry: Institut Français de Pondichéry/École Française d'Extrême-Orient, pp. 231–442.

Alexis SANDERSON (2007b), "Atharvavedins in Tantric territory. The *Āṅgirasakalpa* texts of the Oriya Paippalādins and their connection with the Trika and the Kālīkula, with critical editions of the *Parājapavidhi*, the *Parāmantravidhi*, and the **Bhadrakālīmantravidhiprakaraṇa*," in Arlo Griffiths & Annette Schmiedchen (eds.), *The Atharvaveda and its Paippalāda Śākhā: Historical and Philological Papers on a Vedic Tradition*, Aachen: Shaker Verlag, pp. 195–311.

Alexis SANDERSON (forthcoming), *The Tantrāloka of Abhinavagupta. Āhnika One: The Modes of Enlightenment. A Critical Edition of the Sanskrit Text with a Translation and Commentary* (07/05/2018).

Prabal Kumar SEN (2003), *Nyāyasūtras with Nyāyarahasya of Rāmabhadra Sārvabhauma and Ānvīkṣikītattvavivaraṇa of Jānakīnātha Cūḍāmaṇi*, vol. I, Kolkata: The Asiatic Society, Bibliotheca Indica Series 324.

David SEYFORT RUEGG (1959), *Contributions à l'histoire de la philosophie linguistique indienne*, Paris: de Boccard, Institut de Civilisation Indienne.

Nagin J. SHAH (1998), "Nature of time," in *Essays in Indian Philosophy*, Ahmedabad: Sanskrit-Sanskriti Granthamala, pp. 1–28.

Peri Sareswara SHARMA (1972), *The Kālasamuddeśa of Bhartṛhari's Vākyapadīya (together with Helārāja's commentary translated from the Sanskrit for the first time)*, Delhi: Motilal Banarsidass.

D.C. SIRCAR (1965), *Indian Epigraphy*, Delhi: Motilal Banarsidass.

Peter SKILLING (2000), "Vasubandhu and the *Vyākhyāyukti* literature," *Journal of the International Association of Buddhist Studies* 23(2), pp. 297–350.

Walter SLAJE (2005), "The *Mokṣopāya* project (III). Manuscripts from the Delhi and Śrīnagar collections," in Jürgen Hanneder (ed.), *The Mokṣopāya, Yogavāsiṣṭha and Related Texts*, Aachen: Shaker Verlag, pp. 37–54.

Marc Aurel STEIN (1894), *Catalogue of the Sanskrit Manuscripts in the Raghunatha Temple Library of His Highness the Mahārāja of Jammu and Kashmir*, Bombay: Nirnaya-Sagara Press.

Marc Aurel STEIN (1900), *Kalhaṇa's Rājataraṅgiṇī, A Chronicle of the Kings of Kaśmīr, Translated, with an Introduction, Commentary, and Appendices*, 2 vols., Westminster: Archibald Constable and Company.

Elliot M. STERN (1991), "Additional fragments of *Pramāṇa-viniścaya* I–II," *Wiener Zeitschrift für die Kunde Südasiens* 35, pp. 151–168.

K.A. SUBRAMANIA IYER (1969), *Bhartṛhari. A Study of the Vākyapadīya in the Light of the Ancient Commentaries*, Poona: Deccan College.

John TABER (1986), "Utpaladeva's *Īśvarasiddhi*", *The Adyar Library Bulletin* 52, pp. 106–137.

John TABER (1990), "The Mīmāṃsā theory of self-recognition," *Philosophy East and West* 40(1), pp. 35–57.

John TABER (1994), "Kumārila's refutation of the dreaming argument: The *Nirālambanavāda-adhikaraṇa*," in R.C. Dwivedi (ed.), *Studies in Mīmāṃsā. Dr. Mandan Mishra Felicitation Volume*, Delhi: Motilal Banarsidass, pp. 27–52.

John TABER (2005), *A Hindu Critique of Buddhist Epistemology. Kumārila on Perception. The "Determination of Perception" Chapter of Kumārila Bhaṭṭa's Ślokavārttika, Translation and Commentary*, London/New York: RoutledgeCurzon.

John TABER (2007), "Kumārila the Vedāntin?," in Johannes Bronkhorst (ed.), *Mīmāṃsā and Vedānta. Interaction and Continuity*, Delhi: Motilal Banarsidass, pp. 159–184.

Raffaele TORELLA (1988), "A fragment of Utpaladeva's *Īśvarapratyabhijñā-vivṛti*," *East and West* 38, pp. 137–174.

Raffaele TORELLA (1992), "The Pratyabhijñā and the logical-epistemological school of Buddhism," in Teun Goudriaan (ed.), *Ritual and Speculation in Early Tantrism, Studies in Honor of André Padoux*, Albany: State University of New York Press, pp. 327–345.

Raffaele TORELLA (1998), "The *kañcuka*s in the Śaiva and Vaiṣṇava Tantric tradition: Some considerations between theology and grammar," in Gerhard Oberhammer (ed.), *Studies in Hinduism II. Miscellanea to the Phenomenon of Tantras*, Vienna: Verlag der Österreichischen Akademie der Wissenschaften, pp. 55–86.

Raffaele TORELLA (1999), *Vasugupta. Gli Aforismi di Śiva con il Commento di Kṣemarāja (Śivasūtravimarśinī), Traduzione dal sanscrito, introduzione e note*, Milano: Mimesis.

Raffaele TORELLA (2002), *Īśvarapratyabhijñākārikā of Utpaladeva with the Author's Vṛtti, Critical Edition and Annotated Translation*, [Roma: 1994], Corrected Edition, Delhi: Motilal Banarsidass.

Raffaele TORELLA (2007a), "Studies on Utpaladeva's *Īśvarapratyabhijñā-vivṛti*. Part I: *anupalabdhi* and *apoha* in a Śaiva garb," in Karin Preisendanz (ed.), *Expanding and Merging Horizons. Contributions to South Asian and Cross-Cultural Studies in Commemoration of Wilhelm Halbfass*, Wien: Verlag der Österreichischen Akademie der Wissenschaften, pp. 473–490.

Raffaele TORELLA (2007b), "Studies on Utpaladeva's *Īśvarapratyabhijñā-vivṛti*. Part II: What is memory?", in Konrad Klaus & Jens-Uwe Hartmann (eds.), *Indica et Tibetica. Festschrift für Michael Hahn zum 65. Geburtstag von Freunden und Schülern überreicht*, Wien: Wiener Studien zur Tibetologie und Buddhismuskunde 66, pp. 539–563.

Raffaele TORELLA (2007c), "Studies on Utpaladeva's *Īśvarapratyabhijñā-vivṛti*. Part III. Can a cognition become the object of another cognition?", in Dominic Goodall & André Padoux (eds.), *Mélanges tantriques à la mémoire d'Hélène Brunner*, Pondicherry: Institut Français de Pondichéry/ École Française d'Extrême Orient, pp. 475–484.

Raffaele TORELLA (2007d), "Studies on Utpaladeva's *Īśvarapratyabhijñā-vivṛti*. Part IV. Light of the subject, light of the object", in Birgit Kellner,

Helmut Krasser & Helmut Tauscher (eds.), *Pramāṇakīrtiḥ. Papers dedicated to Ernst Steinkellner on the Occasion of his 70th Birthday*, Wien: Wiener Studien zur Tibetologie und Buddhismuskunde 70(2), pp. 925–940.

Raffaele TORELLA (2008), "From an adversary to the main ally: The place of Bhartṛhari in the Kashmirian Śaiva Advaita," in Mrinal Kaul & Ashok Aklujkar (eds.), *The Linguistic Traditions of Kashmir: Essays in Memory of Pandit Dinanath Yaksh,* Delhi: DK Printworld, pp. 508–524.

Raffaele TORELLA (2012), "Studies in Utpaladeva's *Īśvarapratyabhijñā-vivṛti.* Part V: Self-awareness and yogic perception," in François Voegeli et al. (eds.), *Devadattīyam. Johannes Bronkhorst Felicitation Volume*, Bern: Peter Lang, pp. 275–300.

Raffaele TORELLA (2014), "Utpaladeva's lost *Vivṛti* on the *Īśvarapratyabhijñā-kārikā*," *Journal of Indian Philosophy* 42, pp. 115-126.

Gary A. TUBB & Emery R. BOOSE (2007), *Scholastic Sanskrit. A Manual for Students*, New York: Columbia University Press.

Giuseppe TUCCI (1929), *Pre-Diṅnāga Buddhist Texts on Logic from Chinese Sources*, Baroda: Oriental Institute.

H. UI (1917), *The Vaiśeṣika Philosophy according to the Daśapadārthaśāstra: Chinese Text with Introduction, Translation, and Notes*, London: Royal Asiatic Society.

Somdev VASUDEVA (2004), *The Yoga of the Mālinīvijayottaratantra. Chapters 1–4, 7, 12–17*, Pondicherry: Institut Français de Pondichéry/École Française d'Extrême-Orient.

Vincenzo VERGIANI (2004), "Spazio fisico, categorie concettuali e realtà ultima nel pensiero di Bhartṛhari," in *Atti del seminario "La natura nel pensiero, nella letteratura e nelle arti dell'India," in occasione dell'XI Convegno nazionale di Studi Sanscriti*, Turin: Associazione Italiana di Studi Sanscriti, pp. 147–57.

Peter C. VERHAGEN (2008), "Studies in Indo-Tibetan Buddhist hermeneutics (6): Validity and valid interpretation of scripture according to Vasubandhu's *Vyākhyāyukti*," in Richard Gombrich & Cristina Scherrer-Schaub (eds.), *Buddhist studies: Papers of the 12th World Sanskrit Conference*, vol. VIII, Delhi: Motilal Banarsidass, pp. 233–258.

Toshihiro WADA (2007), "Gaṅgeśa on the meaning of verbal suffixes (1)," in Karin Preisendanz (ed.), *Expanding and Merging Horizons. Contributions to South Asian and Cross-Cultural Studies in Commemoration of Wilhelm Halbfass*, Wien: Österreichische Akademie der Wissenschaften, pp. 415–429.

Martin L. WEST (1973), *Textual Criticism and Editorial Technique*, Stuttgart: B.G. Teubner.

Paul WILLIAMS (1998), *The Reflexive Nature of Awareness. A Tibetan Madhyamaka Defense*, Richmond: Curzon Press.

Michael WITZEL (1985), "Die Atharvaveda-Tradition und die Paippalāda-Saṃhitā," *Zeitschrift der Deutschen Morgenländischen Gesellschaft*, Supplement 6, pp. 256–271.

Michael WITZEL (1994), "Kashmiri manuscripts and pronunciation," in Yasuke Ikari (ed.), *A Study of the Nīlamata: Aspects of Hinduism in Ancient Kashmir*, Kyoto: Institute for Research in Humanities, Kyoto University, pp. 1–53.

Zhihua YAO, *The Buddhist Theory of Self-Cognition*, London/New York: Routledge, 2005.

Kiyotaka YOSHIMIZU (2007), "Kumārila's reevalutation of the sacrifice and the Veda from a Vedānta perspective," in Johannes Bronkhorst (ed.), *Mīmāṃsā and Vedānta. Interaction and continuity*, Delhi: Motilal Banarsidass, pp. 201–253.